307
c

AThomas
Manchester
Mar. 3 . 1922

JOHN WYCLIFFE.

FROM A MEZZOTINT BY G. WHITE IN THE PRINT ROOM OF THE BRITISH MUSEUM; AFTER THE KNOLE PORTRAIT. ENGRAVED BY E. WHYMPER.

NOTE ON WYCLIFFE'S PORTRAITS.—The *Life* by Lewis (ed. 1820) has an engraving of the well-known portrait with the pastoral staff, in the possession of the Earl of Denbigh. There is a copy of the picture in the Lutterworth vestry. Dr. Vaughan's *Monograph* (1853) has a frontispiece from a painting by Sir Antonio More (Henry VIII.'s time), preserved as an heirloom in the rectory at Wycliffe, Yorkshire. These two, with that engraved above, are the best existing portraits, and well correspond with the descriptive hints of the Reformer's personal appearance that have come down to us.

JOHN WYCLIFFE

AND HIS

ENGLISH PRECURSORS.

BY

PROFESSOR LECHLER, D.D.,

OF THE UNIVERSITY OF LEIPZIG.

Translated from the German,

WITH ADDITIONAL NOTES,

BY THE LATE

PROFESSOR LORIMER, D.D.

A NEW EDITION, REVISED;
WITH CHAPTER ON THE EVENTS AFTER WYCLIFFE'S DEATH.

London:

THE RELIGIOUS TRACT SOCIETY,
56, PATERNOSTER ROW; 65, ST. PAUL'S CHURCHYARD;
AND 164, PICCADILLY.

AUTHOR'S PREFACE.

SCIENCE is an international good. It is not confined by territorial boundaries, nor restricted by the ties of nationality. Nowhere does it stand written that only an Englishman can suitably write the history of England, or a portion of it. It may easily happen that a German may have access to sources of English history from which the Englishman may have less opportunity to draw. It is from such sources that I believe myself able to offer not a little which may serve to supplement and enrich, and even to correct, the knowledge which has hitherto been current respecting the history and the characteristic genius of Wycliffe.

All the men whose Wycliffe-researches have hitherto acquired importance and authority have in every instance been able to bring to light, and make use of for the first time, fresh documentary materials. It was so with John Lewis in the last century, who wrote the first independent biography of Wycliffe. The chief value of that book—a value still fully recognised at the present day—lies not in its style of execution, but purely in the mass of materials which it brought together and published. In the present century, Dr. Robert Vaughan, by his works upon the same subject, increased our historical knowledge of Wycliffe to such a degree, that these works have been everywhere recognised as authorities, and used as a storehouse of information. The chief distinction of these writings was the extensive use made in them, by quotation and otherwise, of Wycliffe's manuscript Tracts and Sermons. More recently, at the suggestion of the late Professor Shirley, these English writings of the Reformer have been published by the Clarendon Press, which had already, in 1850, given to the world a model edition of the Wycliffe Translation of the Bible. The *Select English Works of John Wiclif,* edited in excellent style by Thomas Arnold, M.A., of University College, Oxford, contains a complete collection of the Reformer's English sermons, and a selection of his English tracts, popular pieces, and fly-leaves—a service to literature and religious history which calls for the warmest acknowledgments.

It was as an integral part of the same projected collection of *Select Works of Wiclif,* that the author of the present work brought out in 1869 a critical edition of the *Trialogus,* upon the authority of a collation of *four* Vienna MSS. of the work, accompanied by the *Supplementum Trialogi,* which had never been in print. It was the treasures of the

Imperial Library of Vienna which put him in a position to execute that critical task. When, at the beginning of the fifteenth century, the Wycliffe spirit took so strong a hold of Bohemia and Moravia, Bohemian hands were busily employed through several decades of years in multiplying copies of the books, sermons, and tracts of the *Evangelical Doctor*. Hence there are still to be found at the present day, not only in Prague itself, but also in Vienna and Paris, and even in Stockholm, MSS. of Wycliffe's works, of which little use has hitherto been made. In particular, the Imperial Library of Vienna, owing to the secularisation of the Bohemian monasteries under Joseph II., is in possession of nearly forty volumes, which consist either entirely or chiefly of unprinted Latin works of Wycliffe, of which, in some instances, not a single copy is to be found in England. By the kind mediation of the Saxon Government with the Imperial Government of Austria, I obtained from the latter the leisurely and unrestricted use of all those volumes of the collection which I required, and which were sent to me from Vienna as I needed them with the utmost liberality—a gracious furtherance of literary labours, for which, I trust, I may be allowed in this place to express my most respectful and most sincere thanks.

When I compare the two groups of *Sources* which serve to elucidate the personality and the entire historical position of Wycliffe, I come in sight of the fact that the English sermons and tracts most recently printed belong, almost without exception, to the last four years of his life (1381-1384). They serve, therefore, to throw upon his latest convictions and efforts—however comparatively well known these were before—a still clearer and fuller documentary light. The Latin works, on the other hand, so far as they only exist in MS., were for the most part written at earlier dates; some of them, indeed, going back as far as the year 1370. These latter, therefore, have a specially high value, because we learn from them the thoughts and doings of Wycliffe during an earlier stage of his life; and, what is most important of all, they open up to us a view of his gradual development—of the progress of his mind in insight and enlightenment.

I cannot allow the present opportunity to pass of expressing my conviction how much it is to be wished that several of these earlier Latin writings of Wycliffe were printed and published. Not only would they be made thereby more accessible to learned investigators; they would also be secured against the possibility of destruction, in view of the fact that some of them continue to exist only in a single copy. It is alarming to think what an irreparable loss might be caused by fire in a library rich in manuscripts. Should the Clarendon Press determine to include in the series of the *Select Works* an additional number of Wycliffe's Latin writings, I would, with all submission, advise that works of an earlier date than 1381 should be the first to be selected. Most of all, the publication of the *De Veritate Sanctae Scripturae* is to be recommended; and next to this a collection of forty Latin sermons, preserved in the Vienna MS. 3928, and which reflect an earlier stage of Wycliffe's opinions. The book *De Ecclesia*—the best MS. of which is the Vienna MS. 1294—and the *De Dominio Civili*, would also be worthy of being sent to press.[1]

In the summer of 1840, I studied in the University Library of Cambridge the MS. of *Repressor*—the interesting polemical treatise of the rationalising Bishop Pecock, directed against the Wycliffite 'Biblemen' about the middle of the fifteenth century. Twenty years after I had made acquaintance with it, it was published by Babington. By that perusal I was conducted into the history of the Lollards; and from them I saw myself thrown back upon Wycliffe himself. It was thus by a retrogressive movement that the present work gradually took shape, the main impulse to undertake it having come from my good fortune in obtaining access to the Vienna MSS. As I continued to be thus occupied with Wycliffe's life and writings, my respect and love for the venerable man—'the evangelical doctor,' as his contemporaries were wont to call him—went on ever growing. He is truly, in more than one respect, a character of the genuine Protestant type, whose portraiture it may not be without use to freshen up again in true and vivid colours in the eyes of the present generation.

In the present English edition, several portions of the original work have been omitted which did not appear likely to interest English readers so much as what relates directly to England and Wycliffe himself.

The Author can only congratulate himself that he has found in Professor Lorimer a translator who, along with a perfect acquaintance with German, combines so rich a knowledge of the subject, and, what is not the smallest requisite for the task, so enthusiastic a love for the personality of Wycliffe. He has given a special proof of his love to the subject of this book, and of his learned knowledge of it, in a number of 'Additional Notes.' In these, with the help of mediæval records and chronicles which have appeared since the publication of the German original (1873), he has been able sometimes to confirm, and sometimes to correct, the investigations of the Author. And as, in my esteem, the truth is above all else, I am able, without jealousy, to rejoice in every rectification which the views I set forth may receive from later researches among documents which were not accessible to me at the time of my own investigations.

May the Father of Lights, from whom cometh down every good and perfect gift, be pleased to make His blessing rest upon this English edition of my work, to His own glory, to the furtherance of evangelical truth, and to the well-being of the Church of Jesus Christ.

GOTTHARD LECHLER.

LEIPZIG, 1878.

---

[1] Since the above was written, the first steps have been taken by the Wyclif Society towards the publication of the Reformer's Latin works. His Polemical Treatises have already appeared, under the masterly editorship of Dr. Rudolf Buddensieg, and other works are in progress, 1884.

WYCLIFFE! strong soul nursed as in eagles' nest
In upper air, it needed breath of Alps,
The keen invigorative air which girds
The Maiden, Monk, and Eiger, with their zones
Of thick-ribbed ice, to give me strength to cope
With the new history of thy mighty thoughts,
And deeds and giant strife with Papal Rome—
From fountains fresh deduced, in Teuton speech
Of Lechler's learned page, and to give back
Thy thoughts, full rendered, to thine own dear land.
Sire of our English tongue! Translator once
Thyself of God's own Word.—Immortal work!
A well of truth and English undefiled!
Accept, Great Shade! my toil, humble itself,
Yet noble made by thee—to whom 'twas given
In love and laud, unbought, spontaneous.

                                          P. L.

LAUTERBRUNNEN,
    August 22, 1876.

TRANSLATOR'S PREFACE.

PROFESSOR LECHLER'S work is not only a Biography of Wycliffe, but also a preliminary history of the Reformation ; beginning far back in the mediæval centuries, and carried down along the parallel lines of the Lollards and the Hussites, to the first decades of the sixteenth century. The two volumes extend to 1400 closely printed pages ; and it was found impracticable to carry out the original idea of publishing a translation of the whole work.

My design was then reduced to the reproduction of the Biography, and of so much of the preliminary history as concerned Wycliffe's English Precursors. From the English point of view, it seemed perfectly fitting that the life and teaching of Wycliffe should be presented as a subject complete in itself, without implication with the general history of the Church, either earlier or later ; and it was found that a single preliminary chapter would suffice to communicate all that the Author had written respecting Grossetête, Occam, and the rest of Wycliffe's forerunners upon English soil. Professor Lechler at once acceded to this reduced programme of the translation, and not only prepared for my use a new arrangement of the original text, so far as this was called for, but also made a careful revision both of text and notes for the present edition.

The whole original work is of much value and well worth translation, but its chief importance lies in the Biography of Wycliffe himself. In the execution of this kernel portion of his work, the Author had the immense advantage of free and leisurely access to the Wycliffe MSS. of the Imperial Library of Vienna ; and he has used this advantage to the utmost, and with the best effect. Never before has the whole teaching of the Reformer —philosophical, theological, ethical, and ecclesiastical, been so copiously and accurately set forth ; and never before has so large a mass of classified quotations from all his chief scientific writings been placed under the eyes of scholars.

It is a singular fact that five hundred years should have passed away before it became possible to do this service of justice to the memory of so great a man—the very 'Morning Star of the Reformation ;' and it is much to be wished that the University of Oxford, Wycliffe's *Alma Mater*, should complete the service, by carrying out to the full her own noble design, already considerably advanced, of a collection of the 'Select Works' of Wycliffe—in the direction of the suggestions offered by Professor Lechler in the foregoing Preface.

PETER LORIMER.

English Presbyterian College,
   London, *March*, 1878.

_{*} The present Edition is a complete reprint of Dr. Lorimer's translation, with such close revision as he himself might have given to it had his life been spared. The numerous and valuable notes have been printed in a form more convenient for reference: marginal summaries of the paragraphs have been introduced, and a copious index has been added. The long quotations from Wycliffe's Latin works, which formed a large part of Dr. Lechler's Appendix, have been omitted as hardly necessary, in view of the probable publication of the Reformer's whole works. A chapter has, however, been added, containing a compendious summary of parts of Dr. Lechler's second volume, *Die Nachwirkungen Wiclif's*, with other matters bearing on the diffusion of his doctrines.—S. G. G.

56, Paternoster Row,
   October, 1884.

LIST OF ILLUSTRATIONS.

Portrait of Wycliffe	*Frontispiece*
Ludgarshall Church	*p.* xxiv
Lutterworth Church	*ib.*
Facsimile of Wycliffe Bible MS.	220
Chair in Lutterworth Chancel	438
The River Swift at Lutterworth	467
Wycliffe Church, Yorkshire	500

CONTENTS.

INTRODUCTION.

	PAGE
Writers on Pre-Reformation History	1
In the Sixteenth Century	2
In the Seventeenth Century	6
In the Eighteenth Century	6
In the Present Century	8
The Wycliffite Versions of the Bible	10

CHAPTER I.

ENGLISH PRECURSORS OF WYCLIFFE.

1.—**Mixture and Consolidation of Races in the English People** 13

    Mixture of races in the English people; the German element. Changes in religion. Height of Rome's power over England under John Lackland. Revolt of public opinion as expressed by Magna Charta; consolidation of the nation on the basis of the Saxon element; steps towards establishing the independence of the Anglican Church.

2.—**Robert Grossetête, Bishop of Lincoln** . . . 20

    His mental endowments. His course of life and development. Appointed Bishop of Lincoln; his labours and aims. Estimate of his character. The kernel of his work : care for souls. Memorial on the abuses of the Church. Protest against the nomination of a relative of Innocent IV. Grossetête's death, 1253. Veneration of his memory.

3.—Henry Bracton and William Occam . . . 40

The State in opposition to the Church. National feeling of the monarch and the people; opposed to the claims of Boniface VIII. Influence of Occam: controversy on apostolic poverty: protest against papal absolutism.

4.—English Church Politics in the Fourteenth Century 49

Growth of English patriotic feeling. Papal nominations and provisions. Statutes of Provisors and Præmunire. Early awakenings of the Reformation spirit in England and abroad.

5.—Richard of Armagh and the Mendicant Orders . 54

His career and writings. He takes a stand against the Mendicant Monks, and especially against their encroachments on the pastoral office. Comparison of Richard of Armagh with Robert Grossetête and Wycliffe. Polemic treatise of the Franciscan, Roger Conway, against Richard of Armagh. The treatise, *Of the Last Age of the Church.*

6.—Thomas Bradwardine, his Teaching and Spirit . 64

His doctrine of grace. *Doctor Profundus.* His early life and conversion. His work, *Of the Cause of God.* Its leading thought developed and criticised. His moral and religious spirit.

7.—'The Vision of Piers Plowman' 70

The feeling of the English people in the middle of the fourteenth century finds its expression in this poem. Its author and spirit. Its language and form; time of its appearance. Sketch of its contents. Tendency of the poem. Predictions of reform.

CHAPTER II.

WYCLIFFE'S YOUTH AND STUDENT LIFE.

1.—Birthplace and Family 79

Spreswell, near Old Richmond, his birthplace. Character of the population of that district. The Wycliffe family. Date of Wycliffe's birth.

2.—Wycliffe's Course of Study 84

His childhood and early youth in Yorkshire. As scholar at Oxford. Colleges and 'Nations' in the University. Wycliffe's studies; general course of study in the Universities of the Middle Ages. The *artes liberales*. Wycliffe's theological studies. Length of time covered by his student life.

CHAPTER III.

QUIET WORK IN OXFORD—1345–1366.

1.—Wycliffe as a Member of Balliol and of Merton 97

Wycliffe as Fellow of a College in Oxford: which College was this? Probably Balliol. Wycliffe becomes Master of this College, 1360; having already been Fellow of Merton; 1361 he was appointed by Balliol to the parish of Fillingham, and gave up his Mastership. His earnest work.

2.—Wycliffe as Head of Canterbury Hall and Doctor of Theology 102

Archbishop Islip appoints Wycliffe in 1365 to the Wardenship of Canterbury Hall, founded by himself; his successor, Archbishop Langham, replaces Wycliffe by the former Warden, Woodhall; proceedings in consequence end in the rejection of Wycliffe and his friends. Critical examination of the question whether the Warden of Canterbury Hall was really John Wycliffe or some other member of the family. Decision in favour of the former. Discussion as to whether the deposition of Wycliffe from the Wardenship was contrary to the laws of foundation, or not. Wycliffe's promotion as Doctor of Theology.

CHAPTER IV.

WYCLIFFE'S FIRST PUBLIC APPEARANCE IN THE ECCLESIASTICO-POLITICAL AFFAIRS OF ENGLAND.

1.—Wycliffe as a Patriot 118

The quiet student steps out into public life; declares himself as a patriot. That his first appearance in public was in a controversy with the Mendicant Orders has no historical foundation.

2.—**Wycliffe's Concern in the Rejection of the Papal Claim to Feudatory Tribute** . . . 122

    Pope Urban V. claims anew in 1365 the feudal tribute. Edward III. lays the matter before the Parliament, and the Pope is defied. Wycliffe's participation in this affair; his account of the speeches of seven lords. Supposition that Wycliffe himself had a seat and voice in the Parliament then assembled.

3.—**Events after 1366** 134

    Political events of 1367. Parliament of 1371. Prelates in State Offices. Resistance to Papal exactions. Wycliffe's criticism on the oath taken by the Papal commissioner, Garnier.

4.—**Wycliffe as a Royal Commissary in Bruges, 1374, and his Influence in the 'Good Parliament' of 1376** 141

    Topics of the conference. Wycliffe's relations with the Duke of Lancaster. Result of negotiations. Fresh complaints against Rome from the 'Good Parliament,' 1376. Memorial to the King. Evidence of Wycliffe's influence. Court intrigues; court politics. Wycliffe's attitude.

CHAPTER V.

PROCEEDINGS OF THE HIERARCHY AGAINST WYCLIFFE IN 1377 AND 1378.

1.—**Wycliffe summoned before the Convocation** . 156

    His influence at its height. Successive preferments. Rector of Lutterworth, 1374. Attack of the hierarchy, 1377. Political motives prompting his summons. The Duke of Lancaster protects him; scene in St. Paul's. Excitement of the citizens against the Duke. Results of the citation.

2.—**Papal Bulls against Wycliffe** 162

    Accusations brought against Wycliffe by English bishops in Rome. Five bulls in consequence issued against him. The doctrines of Wycliffe condemned in them. Nineteen articles of accusation.

3.—First Effects of the Five Bulls in England . 167

Delay in publishing them. Death of Edward III. Proceedings of the Papal commissaries. Wycliffe cited to London. Attitude of the University of Oxford.

4.—The Process against Wycliffe. 171

He appears before the commissaries at Lambeth. Interference of the Princess of Wales and the citizens on his behalf. A glance over the two plans of attack on Wycliffe by the hierarchy. Death of Pope Gregory XI. and the Papal Schism.

CHAPTER VI.

WYCLIFFE AS A PREACHER. HIS EFFORTS FOR REFORM IN PREACHING AND FOR THE ELEVATION OF THE PASTORAL OFFICE.

1.—Wycliffe as a Preacher; his Homiletical Principles 176

He considers the pulpit a means of reform; his English and Latin sermons. His views of the sermon and its mission; his opinion of the manner of preaching in his time. Principles laid down by him on the subject of *what* and *how* a man should preach. Wycliffe himself in the pulpit; *what* he preached, and *how* he preached it. Chaucer's 'country priest,' a portrait of Wycliffe.

2.—Wycliffe's Itinerant Preachers . . . 189

Wycliffe as Rector of Lutterworth. Sends out itinerant preachers. In 1382 itinerant preaching is in full activity. Reasons for believing that Wycliffe began to send out itinerant preachers while still in Oxford (and at Ludgarshall). Purpose and spirit of the institution. The itinerant preachers themselves; at first only priests, afterwards laymen as well. Oxford the first, Leicester the second starting-point. Subject and form of their sermons. Wycliffe's writings relating to the itinerant preachers.

CHAPTER VII.

WYCLIFFE AS BIBLE TRANSLATOR; AND HIS SERVICE DONE TO THE ENGLISH LANGUAGE.

PAGE

1.—The Novelty of the Idea of an English Translation of the whole Bible 202

Wycliffe, convinced that the Holy Scriptures should be accessible to all alike, translates the whole Bible into English: he is the first to undertake the work. Older translations of separate books in Anglo-Saxon, in Anglo-Norman, and in Old English.

2.—How Wycliffe came to engage in this Undertaking 208

Certain that Wycliffe was the originator of the idea, and the first to carry it into effect. Early steps towards the work. Translations of single books of the New Testament in particular.

3.—The Wycliffe Translation 215

Made from the Latin Vulgate. The New Testament translated first. Prefaces to the several Books. Wycliffe's fellow-labourers; Hereford and Purvey. Completion of the work. Its revision after Wycliffe's death. The Wycliffe Bible and the English language.

CHAPTER VIII.

WYCLIFFE AS A THINKER AND WRITER; HIS PHILOSOPHICAL AND THEOLOGICAL SYSTEM.

1.—His Gradual Development as a Thinker and Reformer 223

2.—Wycliffe as a Philosophical Thinker and Writer 225

Lack of extant printed writings. Wycliffe's logic. Metaphysics: his realism and its meaning; its basis on Scripture. Idea of the Logos. Ethical aspect of his philosophy.

3.—Wycliffe's Theological System . . . 232

Reason and Revelation, the sources of Christian Truth. Decisive authority of the Bible. Application of the principle. Wycliffe the *Doctor Evangelicus*. His independence in asserting his Scriptural principle. His opinions on the interpretation of Scripture. Relation between the Old and New Testaments. The right of all Christians to the Bible.

CONTENTS.

4.—Doctrine of God and the Divine Trinity . . 250
Proofs of the existence of God. The Divine Attributes. Doctrine of the Trinity.

5.—Doctrine of the World, of the Creation, and of the Divine Dominion 254
The creation of the world in itself a necessary act of God. Finiteness and mutability of the world. The Divine dominion. Wycliffe's central thought. His writings on the subject. Fundamental principles. Acts resulting from dominion, *e.g.*, giving and granting. Idea of merit. Doctrine of good and evil angels.

6.—Doctrine of Man and of Sin 261
Wycliffe's anthropology generally. Doctrine of the human will; of the evil in man. Wycliffe's view of sin as a free act. The negativity of evil. State of innocence, and the Fall.

7.—Doctrine of the Person of Christ and the Work of Redemption 267
The Person of Christ, the God-man. Christ the centre of humanity; the only Head of the redeemed. Work of Christ. (1) As Prophet (Lawgiver) in His doctrine and example. (2) As everlasting Priest, in His work of reconciliation; (3) As King of kings. Wycliffe's views respecting the Virgin Mary.

8.—Doctrine of the Order of Personal Salvation . 275
(1) Conversion, consisting of repentance and faith. Faith, partly a knowledge and recognition of truth, partly moral feeling and action. Wycliffe seized neither the evangelical idea of faith nor that of justification by faith alone. (2) Sanctification. Wycliffe's doctrine of good; and of virtue. Humility the principal virtue. Love of God and one's neighbour the kernel of Christianity. Christ's example. The difference between command and counsel. Wycliffe's views respecting merit; his reasons for them. Melancthon's judgment upon Wycliffe's doctrine of the way of salvation.

9.—Doctrine of the Church as the Communion of the Saved 287
Three divisions of the Church. Idea of the Church; her eternal basis; Divine election. Wycliffe repudiates the identification of the Church with the clergy and hierarchy. His idea of the Church as 'the whole body of the elect' draws a line of distinction through the mass of mankind, which does not keep without the

1a

so-called Church, but penetrates within it, separating the elect from the members of Antichrist. Uncertainty appertaining to the condition of grace; moral standard.

10.—The Worship of the Church 296

The sermon. Images and pictures. Worship of saints. Canonisation. Moral benefit or uselessness of devotions and feasts in memory of saints. Relics and pilgrimages. Masses for the dead. Wycliffe's conviction of the low and sinking condition of Christendom; corruption of the clergy.

11.—Constitution of the Church 305

Wycliffe rejects the Roman Catholic division of the Church into clergy and laity. Rights of the latter. The universal priesthood of believers. The pastoral office: what it is, and what it should be. Celibacy of the clergy. The higher grades of the hierarchy. Primitive identity of presbyter and bishop. The manner in which the bishops became superior. The Papacy; stages of development in Wycliffe's ideas. First stage, to 1378: conditional recognition of the Pope. Second stage, to 1381: emancipation in principle from the Pope. Third stage, from 1381 onwards: decisive conflict with the Pope as Antichrist. Wycliffe's opinions on the monastic orders: mistake in the supposition that he combated the Mendicant Orders from the first: on the contrary, he was against the Endowed Orders, and praised the Mendicant Friars in his earlier years. Not till 1381 did he begin to attack them. Once he thought it possible that the Mendicant Orders would reform the Church. Wycliffe's thoughts on the reform of the Church. Necessity for reform. Advance of corruption in the Church. Means of reform. Who shall begin the reform? The State; true Christians; the Spirit of God.

12.—Doctrine of the Sacraments 332

(1) *Of the Sacraments generally;* their fundamental idea; their number; their efficacy. Does Wycliffe make the efficacy of the Sacraments dependent upon the moral worthiness of the ministrant? (2) *Of the Lord's Supper.* Why did Wycliffe especially attack the doctrine of Transubstantiation? His reasons against it. His positive views concerning the presence of the Body and Blood of Christ in the Supper. There is present in the sacrament of the altar real bread and wine, but also the Body and Blood of Christ; not, indeed, visibly and corporeally, but sacramentally. Only spiritual enjoyment of these is possible; therefore only believing communicants can partake of Christ's Body and Blood. Survey of Wycliffe's doctrine of the Lord's Supper and his controversy on Transubstantiation.

CHAPTER IX.

THE EVENTS OF THE LAST YEARS OF WYCLIFFE'S LIFE, 1378–1384.

                                          PAGE

1.—**The Papal Schism, and its Effect upon Wycliffe** 362

    Urban VI. and the great schism in the Papacy. Impression made upon Wycliffe. For some time he remains neutral towards both Popes; afterwards opposes the Papacy entirely. Meanwhile he continues his Bible translation, and sends out itinerant preachers.

2.—**Wycliffe's Attack upon the Doctrine of Transubstantiation** 367

    Wycliffe's twelve theses against the doctrine. Proceedings of the University against him.

3.—**The Peasants' Revolt in 1381** 371

    Are there any reasons for blaming Wycliffe as the cause of this revolt? Course of the insurrection. Confessions of John Ball. Facts which are opposed to any connection between Wycliffe and the rising.

4.—**Preparations for Persecution on the part both of the Church and the State** 378

    The new Archbishop, Courtenay: he begins proceedings against Wycliffe; condemns his doctrines, and attempts to attack his followers. Synod at Blackfriars, sometimes called the 'Earthquake Council.' The doctrines condemned. The Archbishop's appeal to Parliament. Its failure. The royal ordinance.

5.—**The Wycliffe Party intimidated by the Measures of the Archbishop** 388

    The state of parties in Oxford; their action. Hereford's sermon on Ascension Day, 1382. Repyngdon's Corpus Christi sermon. Menacing measures and continued disputations. Measures of the Archbishop. Submission of the Chancellor. Excommunications. Aston, Hereford, and Repyngdon. Further action against Wycliffe's party. Persecution of the itinerant preachers. Repyngdon and Aston recant. Nicholas Hereford appeals to the Pope and goes to Rome.

6.—**The Cautious Proceedings of the Hierarchy against Wycliffe himself** 401

Wycliffe remains for a time free from personal attack. Summoned before the Council at Oxford, November, 1382, but permitted to retire unmolested, and without having recanted. Motives of such mildness.

7.—**The Last Two Years of Wycliffe, and his Death** 406

Wycliffe at Lutterworth. Pastoral labours and literary activity during the last two years of his life. Crusade in Flanders against the adherents of Clement VII., under the conduct of Bishop Spencer, of Norwich. Preparations. Wycliffe's opinion; his tract, *Cruciata*. The crusade itself and its ignominious end. Supposed citation of Wycliffe to Rome, and his letter to Urban VI. Unhistorical story of Wycliffe's exile and stay in Bohemia. He spent his last years at Lutterworth, retaining his position in the Church, honoured by many. Year and day of his death determined (December 31, 1384). Circumstances of his death.

8.—**Character of Wycliffe, and his important place in History** 423

His scholastic attainments; the many sides of his character; his critical spirit. The strong point in his character was not, however, his knowledge, nor his literary power, but his will and moral earnestness, with which was blended a certain humour. In spite of his marked individuality, he does not assert himself, but always aims to serve Christ. Character of his efforts for reform. Wycliffe the first to devote himself to such endeavours.

CHAPTER X.

THE SUCCESSORS OF WYCLIFFE; AND SURVIVAL OF HIS INFLUENCE.

1.—**The Lollards** 439

Origin of the designation. Two sections of the Lollard party in England; an outer and an inner circle. Hereford, Aston, and Purvey, the 'first three.' Other noteworthy names. Extent of the movement. Life and work of the Lollards. Results.

CONTENTS.

2.—Controversies between the Lollards and their Opponents before 1399 445

The defensive attitude of the Lollards changed for an aggressive course. Appeal to Parliament. The 'Fifteen Conclusions' of 1395. This date marks the culmination of the Lollards' power. 'Piers Plowman's Creed' and 'The Plowman's Tale.'

3.—Position of the Lollards at the close of the Century 450

Archbishop Arundel, a more determined opponent of Wycliffe's doctrines than Courtenay himself. The *Trialogus* synodically condemned. Woodford's treatise. Deposition and assassination of Richard II.

4.—Persecution of the Lollards 451

Accession of the House of Lancaster, and beginnings of persecution. The Act *de haeretico comburendo*. Sawtree the first martyr. Purvey recants. Badby the martyr, Thorpe the confessor. Other sufferers.

5.—Proceedings at Oxford, 1406-1414 455

A declaration in favour of Wycliffe, under the University seal. Question as to its genuineness. A change in the spirit of Oxford, and decadence of the University.

6.—The Lollards in the Reign of Henry V.; Lord Cobham 457

Another King, and another Primate. The persecution becomes more bitter, being complicated with political animosities. The Lollard party accused of disaffection to the Government. Gathering in St. Giles's Fields. The 'Good Lord Cobham,' an illustrious martyr. Accession of Henry VI. and relaxation of persecuting measures, only to break out with new fury. The conflict gradually exhausts itself, but the Lollard testimony continues.

7.—Wycliffe, Huss, and the Council of Constance . 460

Anne of Bohemia, consort of Richard II. Intercourse of England and Bohemia. Wycliffism spreads from Oxford. John Huss in the University of Prague. Eager and bitter controversies ensue, in all of which Wycliffe's name is mixed up. A council summoned at Constance; Huss condemned and burned, in spite of the safe-conduct given. Posthumous condemnation of Wycliffe; carried out after long delay. 'The Swift, the Avon, and the Sea.' Wycliffe, Huss, Luther, and THE REFORMATION.

APPENDIX.

NOTE on *The Last Age of the Church* and *The Poor Caitiff* . . 468

1.—Richard Fitzralph, Archbishop of Armagh . . 469

2.—The Vision of Piers Plowman 470

3.—Balliol College in Wycliffe's Time . . . 472

    1. Illustrations of its Educational Discipline. 2. Provisions of the Statutes of Sir Philip de Somerville for the Study of Theology. 3. Disputes among Philosophical University Sects. 4. Wycliffe's College contemporaries.

4.—Identity of John Wycliffe the Reformer with John Wycliffe the Warden of Canterbury Hall . . 475

5.—On the Late Date at which Wycliffe began his Attacks upon the Mendicant Orders . . . 476

6.—The Popularity of Wycliffe and his earliest Disciples as Preachers in London 478

    ⁎ These six chapters are by Dr. Lorimer, the next is by Dr. Lechler.

7.—Wycliffe's Writings 480

    1. The chief Wycliffe catalogues: Bale, Lewis, Baber, Vaughan, Shirley, Arnold. 2. Language of Wycliffe's writings. 3. Classified list. Note (*by Dr. Lorimer*) on the Vienna MSS. of Wycliffe's Works. Comparison between Lechler's Catalogue and Shirley's.

LUDGARSHALL CHURCH.
THE SCENE OF WYCLIFFE'S MINISTRATIONS, 1368–1374.

LUTTERWORTH CHURCH.
THE SCENE OF WYCLIFFE'S MINISTRATIONS, 1374–1384.

INTRODUCTION.

THERE lies between the commencement of the Reformation and our own day an interval of more than three hundred and sixty years,[1] a period of time considerable enough to allow of our taking a tolerably free and comprehensive survey. We are thus placed in a position to embrace in one view the whole effects of the Reformation, in so far as these have as yet developed themselves. It has also become possible for us to attain a right understanding of the conditions under which the movement took its rise, and of the manner in which its way was prepared in the preceding centuries.

Our power of insight, indeed, in this matter as in others, must have its limits. Beyond all doubt, a later time will command a wider horizon and gain deeper reaches of insight. For what the poet says of the past is not true of it in every respect—

'Still stands the past for evermore.'

On the contrary, the image of the past is for ever shifting and changing with the conditions of the present in which it is reflected. 'The living man, too, has his right:' he has a right to the inheritance of the generations which have gone before; he has also the right to put the history of the past in relations to the present—to study it in connection with the events and the needs and the questions of his own time—and thereby to arrive at a clear vision and comprehension of it for himself. Nothing but our own experience can give us the interpretation of history. As a general truth, the actual knowledge which we are able to acquire is commensurate with our experience; and the more thorough and comprehensive the experience which any man has acquired, the deeper and more correct is the understanding of the past which he is in a condition to attain.

On this ground, the period of more than three centuries and a half

---

[1] [Luther affixed his Theses to the church door at Wittenberg, October 17, 1517. He burned the Pope's bull, December 10, 1520.]

which has elapsed since the commencement of the Reformation, both enables and calls us, in a much higher degree than the generations which have preceded us, to attain to a thorough understanding of its preliminary history, or the long series of events and transactions by which its advent was prepared. A beginning of such studies, indeed, was made as early as the sixteenth century; and even while the Reformation itself was still in progress, there were historical inquirers who cast back their eyes to men and religious brotherhoods of the past who appeared to bear some resemblance to the Reformers and Reformed Churches of their own generation. These researches into comparative pre-Reformation history were of course of very different kinds, and issued in the most opposite results, according as they were undertaken by friends or foes of the Reformation itself.

Reformers before the Reformation.

When Luther received from the Utraquists of Bohemia one of Huss's writings, and studied it, he was lost in astonishment, for all at once the light dawned upon him that he and Staupitz and the rest had been Hussites all the time, without being aware of the fact.[1] A few years later, he became acquainted with the writings of John Wessel, which filled him with sincere admiration of the man, and with a wondering joy; so much so that he felt himself strengthened as Elijah was when it was revealed to him that he was not left alone, for there were seven thousand men still living who had not bowed their knees to Baal. 'If I had read Wessel before now, my enemies might have thought that Luther had taken all his ideas from Wessel, so much are we of one mind.'[2] At a later date the Reformer gave his judgment on the subject in a quieter tone, but not more correctly, when he remarked that Wycliffe and Huss had attacked the life of the Church under the Papacy, whereas he fought not so much against the life as the doctrine.'[3] Still he saw in these men his fellow-combatants of an earlier time, and men of kindred spirit and principles to his own. When Luther, in 1522, wrote an Anthology from John Wessel, and in 1523 prefixed an appreciative preface to Savonarola's commentaries on the 31st and 37th Psalms; and when again, in 1525, the *Trialogus* of Wycliffe was published in Basel, the meaning of all these incidents was to justify the Reformers

Luther on his predecessors.

---

[1] See Letter to Spalatin (Feb. 1520), in Luther's *Letters*, by De Wette (Berlin, 1826). Vol. I., No. 208, p. 425. Comp. No. 162, to Staupitz (Oct. 3, 1519), p. 341.

[2] Luther's *Works*, by Walch, Vol. XIV., p. 220. In the preface to one of the earliest editions of Wessel's *Farrago Rerum Theologicarum* (Basel, 1522), Melancthon speaks of Wessel in the same way. He mentions him at considerable length in his *Postils*, in the following terms, among others: 'De plerisque capitibus religionis evangelicæ sensit idem quod a nobis nunc traditur, postquam nostra ætate repurgatio ecclesiæ facta est.'

[3] Luther's *Table Talk*. By Foerstemann. 1845. II., 441; IV., 391.

of the sixteenth century by the testimony of men of earlier ages who had fought the same battle.

The case is altered, of course, when writers opposed to the Reformation direct their inquiries to the same class of facts, the results at which they arrive being always unfavourable to the Reformers. In comparing the latter with their precursors, the uniform aim of these writers is to throw them and their doctrines into shadow, either by identifying Luther's principles with those of earlier heretics, so as to place them under a like condemnation, or by attempting to prove that Luther was even worse than his precursors of like spirit. The former was what was aimed at, when the Theological Faculty of Paris, in 1523, decided that the great work against Wycliffe, of the English Carmelite, Thomas of Walden (died 1431), *The Antiquities of the Catholic Faith*, was worthy to be printed and published, 'because the same is of great use for the refutation of the destructive Lutheran errors;' for herein the Parisian doctors declared the doctrines of the Reformers to be essentially the same as those of Wycliffe and the Lollards. John Faber, on the other hand, the South German polemic, who died Bishop of Vienna in 1541, drew a comparison in a controversial work of 1528, between Luther on the one hand, and John Huss and the Bohemian Brethren and John Wessel on the other, in which he reached the conclusion that the latter were all more Christian and less offensive than Luther. He even went so far at the close of his treatise as to say that if it were possible for all the heretics who lived in the Apostles' days and afterwards, to rise from the dead and to come together face to face with Luther in a general council or otherwise, they would no doubt damn him as a godless arch-heretic, and refuse to have any fellowship with him; so unheard-of, dreadful, and abominable was the false doctrine which Luther had put forward.[1]

Testimony of enemies.

These first attempts to bring into view the historical parallels of earlier times, whether proceeding from the Reformers or their adversaries, were all partial and incomplete, and possessed no value beyond that of occasional pieces. A more comprehensive treatment of the Reformers before the Reformation, their doctrines and their lives—a treatment under which the different

Later researches.

---

[1] This rare tract has the title, *Wie sich Johannis Huss, der Pickarder, und Johannis von Wessalia Leren und Bücher mit Martino Luther vergleichen.* Beschrieben durch Doctor Johann Fabri. Preface dated, 'Prag, 1 Sep., 1528.' There is a copy in the Royal Library at Dresden. Under the name 'Pickards,' the author no doubt refers to the Waldenses; but, in fact, he treats in this part of his tract, without knowing it, of the Bohemian Brethren, for he founds his remarks upon the Confession presented by the latter to King Wladislaus.

individualities were exhibited in the light of their unity of principle and spirit—became possible only after the Reformation had, in some measure at least, been brought to a close, and admitted of being taken into one view as a completed work. And this point was not reached till the middle of the sixteenth century.

From that date important works of such a character began to appear on the evangelical side. On the side of Rome only one work has a claim to be mentioned in this connection, viz., the *Collection of Documents, Controversial Tracts, and the like, relating to Pre-Reformation Persons and Parties*, published by Ortuin Gratius of Cologne in 1535, in prospect of the general council which had then been announced. He was himself one of the Cologne '*Obscuri Viri*,' but was favourable to Church Reform in the Catholic sense; and it was with this view that he selected and published these pieces in the well-known *Fasciculus*.[1]

The Romish view: Gratius.

The corresponding works on the evangelical side divide themselves into two groups, according to the point of view from which they regard the particular facts which they embrace. The first group—and this is by far the most numerous—views its subject as a history of persecution, or of evangelical martyrs. The second group deals with the personalities whom it introduces as witnesses of the truth, who in earlier times opposed themselves to the Papacy and its 'superstition.' The first group may be correctly described as more or less belonging to the sphere of the history of the Church, and the second as belonging to the history of doctrine.

Protestant views.

The most important, and indeed almost the only representative of the latter group, is Matthias Flacius of Illyricum, properly called Matthias Vlatzich Frankowitsch. This greatest of the historians belonging to the Lutheran Church of the sixteenth century, the founder of *The Magdeburg Centuries*, published in 1556 his *Catalogue of Witnesses to the Truth who opposed themselves to the Pope before our Age*, as a work preliminary to the *Centuries*, which appeared in repeated editions, and continued to receive considerable enrichments even in the seventeenth century.[2]

Flacius.

The lead of the first group is taken by an Englishman, the venerable John Foxe. The experiences of his own life and of the Church of his native country suggested to him the plan of a Church History, arranged under the leading idea of the persecu-

Foxe.

---

[1] *Fasciculus rerum expetendarum ac fugiendarum.* Colon, 1535, fol. It was not difficult for the English theologian, Edward Brown, to revise, with additions, this collection in the interests of Protestantism. London, 1690, fol. 2 vols.

[2] *Catalogus testium Veritatis qui ante nostram aetatem reclamarunt Papae.* Basel, 1556, 8vo. 1562, fol. Geneva, 1608, fol. Frankf., 1666, 4to., with a supplement, printed in Cassel, 1667.

tions directed in successive ages against the friends of evangelical truth. During the bloody persecutions which took place under Queen Mary, many faithful men fled to the Continent and found an asylum in the Rhinelands and Switzerland—*e.g.*, in Frankfort and Strasburg, in Basel, Zurich, Geneva, and elsewhere. Among others John Foxe repaired to Strasburg, and here appeared in 1554 the first edition of the first book of his *History of the Church and its Chief Persecutions in all Europe from the times of Wycliffe down to the Present Age*, a work which he had proceeded with thus far before he left England, and which he dedicated to Duke Christopher of Würtemberg.[1] He commenced the history with Wycliffe, partly, no doubt, from patriotic feeling, but partly also because he regarded the measures adopted against Wycliffe as the beginning of the storm of persecution which had continued to rage in England, Bohemia, and Scotland down to his own day. Nor must we omit to mention here that at the end of the sixteenth century and in the first half of the seventeenth, *Foxe's Book of Martyrs* was a favourite family book in many godly English households. Ladies were wont to read it aloud to their children, and to their maidens while at work; and boys as soon as they could read took to the much-loved book. It helped in no small degree to steel the Protestant character of the English people in the seventeenth century.

Foxe's work gave the key-note, and became a model for many similar works in the German, French, and Bohemian tongues; and in most cases these writings, under the title of *Martyrologies*, did not confine themselves, any more than Foxe had done, to the domestic persecutions of the countries of their several authors, but included Germany, France, and England, and went back also to the centuries which preceded the Reformation. When a new edition of Foxe was in preparation in 1632, the Bohemian exiles then living in the Netherlands were requested to draw up an account of the persecutions which had fallen upon their native church, with a view to its being incorporated with the English *Book of Martyrs*. But the new edition was finished at press before the narrative was ready, and the Bohemian work remained in manuscript till it appeared

---

[1] *Commentarii rerum in Ecclesia gestarum, maximarumque per totam Europam persecutionum a Wiclivi temporibus ad hanc usque aetatem Descriptio.* Liber I. Autore Joanne Foxo, Anglo. Argentorati, MDLIV. Small 8vo. 221 pp. The second Latin edition, considerably enlarged, appeared at Basel, in folio, in 1559. After his return to England Foxe published his work in English in 1563; and, after his death, in 1587, a second English edition came out in 1610. But the completest edition was that of 1684, in three large folios, with the title, *Acts and Monuments of these latter and perilous days*, etc. Several editions have also appeared in our own time, the best being that edited, with copious and valuable notes, by the Rev. Josiah Pratt and the Rev. Dr. Stoughton.

in 1648 at Amsterdam or Leyden, under the title, *Historia Persecutionum Ecclesiæ Bohemicæ*, which was subsequently translated into German and Bohemian.

During the polemical period which reached from the last quarter of the sixteenth to nearly the close of the seventeenth century, all
<small>Seventeenth Century—Thomas James.</small> that was done in the field of pre-Reformation history and research was deeply tinged with a controversial character—a remark which applies equally to Germany, France, and England. The first Bodley librarian at Oxford, Thomas James, was an instance in point. This indefatigable scholar, one of the most learned and acute controversialists against Rome, published in 1608 *An Apology for John Wyclif*.[1] It was written with a polemical view—but at that date it needed a learned and historical interest to be uppermost in the mind even of a polemical writer to induce him to take up the subject of a precursor of the Reformation. Most men were so completely engrossed by the controversies of their own time, that they had neither inclination nor leisure to make researches into the history of the past.

It was not till the storm-waves of controversial excitement subsided that the early Reformers began to awaken a purer and more unprejudiced historical interest. From that time, about the beginning of the last century, two classes of works claim attention. Some writers occupied themselves with the lives and labours of individual men of pre-Reformation times, and generally in the way of collecting and publishing materials which might serve the purpose of making our knowledge of them more assured and complete; while others dealt with the different ways and means in and by which the pre-Reformation movement had been carried on as a whole.

The first of these functions was undertaken by men such as the industrious collector, John Lewis, a clergyman of the Church of
<small>Eighteenth Century—John Lewis.</small> England, who published in 1720 the earliest complete biography of Wycliffe,[2] a work full of material, which he had brought together from public archives and manuscript sources. His subsequent monograph on Bishop Pecock was designed to be a sequel to the biography of Wycliffe, and had the same general character.[3] Both works leave much to be desired in

---

[1] *An Apology for John Wikliffe, showing his conformity with the now Church of England. Collected chiefly out of diverse works of his in written hand, by God's especiall providence remaining in the Publike Library at Oxford, of the Honorable Foundation of Sir Thomas Bodley, Knight*. Oxford, 1608. 4to.

[2] *The History of the Life and Sufferings of the Rev. and Learned John Wiclif, D.D.* London, 1720. New Edition, Oxford, 1820.

[3] *The Life of the Learned and Right Rev. Reynold Pecock, faithfully collected from records and MSS.* London, 1725 and 1742. New Edition, Oxford, 1820.

point of literary execution; but for their wealth of original documents they are still of no little value.

Among German scholars, the man who rendered the most meritorious services in the collection and publication of pre-Reformation documents was Professor Hermann Von der Hardt of Helmstadt. His vast and masterly collection of monuments, in illustration of the history of the Council of Constance,[1] had for its chief object to establish by documentary proof the necessity for Reformation which existed at the time of that reforming council. The excellent example set by Von der Hardt served as a spur to others, and stimulated, in particular, the younger Walch to publish his *Monuments of the Middle Age*, which began to appear in Göttingen in 1757.[2] The work consists entirely of documents relating to Church reform, and all belonging to the fifteenth century, being in part speeches which were delivered in the Council of Constance, and partly treatises and tractates of John of Goch, John of Wesel, and others.

<small>Von der Hardt: Walch.</small>

On the other hand, we find that since the commencement of the eighteenth century, works began to appear conceived in a purely historical and unprejudiced spirit, containing studies or reflections on the Reformation movements viewed together as a whole; on the various means and ways which were chosen to promote them; and on the different groups of the Reformers. Walch calls attention in one place to the fact, that there are two classes of witnesses to the truth—those who complain of the vices of the clergy of all degrees, and those who complain of the errors of the teachers. It is well known that the number of writers belonging to the second class is a small one; but all the more highly must the few works be valued in which Roman doctrines are confuted. Among writings of this category Walch rightly reckons John of Goch's tractate on *Errors in reference to the Evangelical law*.

<small>John of Goch.</small>

This distinction among the Reformers was not new; it rests, at all events, upon the saying of Luther before mentioned, that Wycliffe and Huss mainly attacked the life of the Popish Church, while he, on the contrary, attacked chiefly its doctrine. But, though not new, this reflection, together with others of a similar kind occurring in different writers of that period, indicates a mode of regarding the subject from a purely historical point of view, far removed from the bitterness of polemical feeling.

In the second and third decades of the present century, when

---

[1] *Rerum Concilii Constantiensis Tomi* I.–VI. Fol. 1696–1700.

[2] *Monimenta medii aevi*. Vol. I., fasc. 1–4 (1757–1760). Vol. II., fasc. 1, 2 (1761–1764).

Protestant writers applied themselves to the production of historical monographs with so much interest, and in such a masterly style both of research and composition, it is at first sight surprising that no one, for a long time, took for a subject of portraiture any of the Reformation figures of the middle age. Chrysostom and Tertullian, Bernard of Clairvaux, and even Gregory VII. and Innocent III., all found at that time enthusiastic biographers; but no one had an eye for Huss, for John of Wesel, and least of all, for Wycliffe. This is explained in some measure by the circumstance that the historical branch of theology had to take a share in the general aim of those years, and was called upon, before everything else, to contribute to the regeneration of Christian feeling, and the new upbuilding of the kingdom of God, after a long period of negation and deadness. This situation determined the choice which was made of subjects for fresh historical portraiture. Both writers and readers felt an inferior degree of sympathy for men in whom the critical spirit had prevailed, and who had taken up a position of antagonism to the Church-institutions and teaching of their age; and perhaps, too, both writers and readers were less capable of understanding them.

Modern historical tendencies.

It was not till the commencement of the second quarter of our century that due attention began again to be directed to 'the Reformers before the Reformation;' and as, once before, in the middle age itself, England was the country where the first important precursor of the Reformation arose, so also, in our century, England led the way in recalling the memory of her own great son by the appliances of historical science, and thereby setting an example which other countries followed. Dr. Robert Vaughan published, in 1820, his *Life of Wycliffe*, a work founded upon a laborious study of the manuscript writings of Wycliffe, especially of his English sermons and tracts.[1] The way was now opened up, and other explorers soon

Revived interest in Wycliffe: Dr. Vaughan.

---

[1] *Life and Opinions of John de Wycliffe, D.D., illustrated principally from his unpublished Manuscripts.* 2 vols. London, 1828. The second improved edition appeared in 1831, and in 1853 Dr. Vaughan published a new work in one volume, entitled, *John de Wycliffe: A Monograph.* The merits of Vaughan's labours on Wycliffe consist of two things: (1) In the copious information touching Wycliffe obtained from manuscript sources. Vaughan was, in particular, the first who communicated a fuller knowledge of Wycliffe's English sermons. (2) In a certain degree of chronological order, which he introduced into the series of Wycliffe's writings—a circumstance of much importance, because thereby it became possible to follow, in some degree, the gradual progress of the Reformer's opinions; and a comparison of the dates of his numerous writings served to exhibit his character for consistency and firmness in a more honourable light. The chief defects of Vaughan's work were that he manifested less interest in the speculative and strictly theological element of Wycliffe's writings than in their practical and religious bearing, and that he left almost entirely out of consideration his Latin works, being of opinion that they were scholastic treatises of comparatively

followed, partly at first under the influence of national and provincial interest; for the first writers, so far as I can find, who followed Vaughan's example, as early as 1829 and 1830, were Netherlanders, who chose for their subject the history of their countrymen, Gerhard Groot and the Brethren of the Common Life.

But now German historical research appeared upon the field, and without confining itself to its own nationality, devoted to the precursors of the Reformation a series of investigations which were equally conspicuous for thoroughness and success. *Works on early Reformers.* First in time, and most distinguished in merit as a labourer in the field, was Carl Ullmann, with his monograph on John Wessel, which appeared in 1834, a work which he expanded so much in the second edition by the addition of accounts of John of Goch, John of Wesel, the German Mystics, and the Brethren of the Common Life, that he could give to the whole the title of *Reformers before the Reformation.*[1] The first edition of Ullmann's work was speedily followed by two works on Savonarola, by German scholars, Rudelbach and Meier.[2] And here I may be allowed to add the remark, that in 1860 a third work on Savonarola was published by an Italian, Pasquale Villari, a Roman Catholic, which discovers able research, earnest feeling, and deep veneration for his great and noble countryman.[3] This instance of improvement in the manner of treating such subjects, on the side of the Roman Catholic Church, does not stand alone. It is a gratifying fact, which we are here very happy to acknowledge, that much has been done in our own time by writers of that Church to put the Reformation efforts of the fourteenth and fifteenth centuries in their true light. As instances, we may mention the work on the *Reforming Councils*, by Herr Von Wessenberg,[4] and the monograph of Dr. Schwab of Würzburg, on John Gerson, a work of solid merit.[5] It cannot of

---

little worth. But, notwithstanding these defects, Vaughan's work must always take a foremost place as the basis of all accurate knowledge of Wycliffe, and it has, in fact, been drawn upon by many later writers, *e.g.*, in England, by Le Bas, in his *Life of Wycliffe*, 1853; in the Netherlands, by De Ruever-Gronemann, *Diatribe in Johannis Wicliffi Vitam, Ingenium, Scripta*, Utrecht, 1837; in Germany, by Engelhard, *Wycliffe als Prediger*, Erlangen, 1834; by Neander and Gieseler, in their histories of the Church, published in English by T. and T. Clark, of Edinburgh; and, further, in my *Essay on Wiclif and the Lollards*, 1853.

[1] *Johann Wessel, ein Vorgänger Luther's.* Gotha. 1834. The second edition, in two volumes, appeared in 1841, under the title *Reformatoren vor der Reformation, vornähmlich in Deutschland und den Niederlanden.* English translation by Rev. Robert Menzies. Clark, Edinburgh, 1855.

[2] Rudelbach, *Savonarola und Seine Zeit.* 1835. Fredr. Karl Meier, *Girolamo Savonarola, aus zum grossen Theile handschriftlichen Quellen dargestellt.* 1836.

[3] Paschalis Villari, *Geschichte Girolamo Savonarola's und seiner Zeit. Nach neuen Quellen dargestellt.* Two volumes. 1860 and 1861.

[4] *Die grossen Kirchenversammlungen des fünfzehnten und sechzehnten Jahrhunderts, in Beziehung auf Kirchenverbesserung, geschichtlich und kritisch dargestellt.* In four volumes. Constanz, 1840.

[5] *Johannes Gerson, Eine Monographie.* Würzburg, 1858.

course astonish any one that there should be other writers of that Church who still treat all Reformers with undisguised aversion, as in the case of John Huss.[1]

Returning to Protestant Church historians, the example of Ullmann has stimulated many to similar researches in the same field. On the subject in particular of the German mystics of the thirteenth, fourteenth, and fifteenth centuries, the labour of investigation during the last thirty years has been so widely extended, that in order not to lose ourselves in a useless enumeration of names and writings, we must content ourselves with mentioning one man instead of many, namely, Charles Schmidt, of Strasburg.[2] Nor would it be just to pass over here in silence the services of Dr. Palacky of Prague, in elucidating the history, not only of Huss, but his precursors and successors. Not only as a historian, but also as a collector and editor of original documents of history, Palacky has undeniable merits.[3] His collection of documents for the history of John Huss, in point of completeness, criticism, and orderly arrangement, is a veritable model.[4]

It is a fact which applies generally to the third quarter of our century, that the labours of research among the original sources of history, have been such as to result in the discovery and publication of a multitude of hitherto concealed or scarcely accessible original documents, and in the re-issue of several others which were known before, in a more critical and trustworthy form. To these belong, for example, the writings of Eckart, the speculative mystic, edited by Franz Pfeiffer, the edition of the works of John Staupitz, commenced by Knaake, and the publication of the collected Bohemian sermons and tracts of Huss, by Karl Jaromir Erben.[5] In addition, Constantin Höfler, in Prague, has published a series of *The Historians of the Hussite Movement in Bohemia.*[6]

Nor has England remained behind. Her most important achievement in this field, and the fruit of the industry and critical labour of many years, is the complete critical edition of the Wycliffite versions of the Bible, edited by the Rev. Josiah Forshall and Sir Frederick Madden.[7] Among the numerous chronicles and documents bearing upon the mediæval history of England, which for a series of years back have been published at

Publication of the Wycliffite Bible.

---

[1] Von Helfert, *Hus und Hieronymus*, 1853. Höfler, *Magister Johannes Hus*. Prague, 1864.
[2] *Johann Tauler von Strassburg.* Hamburg, 1841. *Nicolaus von Basel.* Vienna, 1866.
[3] *Geschichte von Böhmen.* In five parts. Prague, 1836-1867.
[4] *Documenta Joannis Hus vitam doctrinamque illustrantia.* Prague, 1869.
[5] Published in Prague in three volumes, 1865-8.
[6] Published in Vienna, 1856, in 3 vols. (*Fontes rerum Austriacarum*, div. 1. vol. 2).
[7] *The Wycliffite Versions of the Holy Bible.* In four volumes, 4to. Oxford, 1850.

the cost of the State, some of them never before in print, and others in improved critical editions, there are found many writings in the department of ecclesiastical history, and especially such as have a bearing upon pre-Reformation subjects.

To mention only some of these, the *Political Poems*, edited by Thomas Wright, contain a whole series of polemical and satirical poems, which appeared for and against the Wycliffe movement in the fourteenth and fifteenth centuries.[1] Further, of important interest in connection with our subject is the correspondence of Grossetête, the celebrated Bishop of Lincoln, edited by the Rev. H. R. Luard, of Cambridge.[2] A highly rich and acceptable new source for the history of Wycliffe and his followers, has been opened up in the *Fasciculi Zizaniorum Magistri Johannis Wyclif*, collected without doubt by the controversialist, Thomas Netter, of Walden, and published for the first time in 1858, by Professor Walter Waddington Shirley, of Oxford, with an Introduction and Notes full of very valuable matter.[3] At Shirley's suggestion, recommended on the strongest grounds, the curators of the Clarendon and University Press resolved to publish a selection of Wycliffe's works. Of this collection first appeared the *Trialogus*, with a text critically amended from four Vienna MSS. of the work;[4] and next followed Wycliffe's English sermons, with a large number of his short English tracts, edited by Mr. Thomas Arnold,[5] son and namesake of the illustrious 'Arnold of Rugby.'

Works in the 'Rolls Series.'

Wycliffe's English Works.

[More recently still, the publication of Wycliffe's English works has been completed by the issue of a volume, edited by Mr. F. D. Matthew, in the series of the 'Early English Text Society.' The 'Wyclif Society' has made a beginning with the Latin works by the publication of the Polemical Tracts, in two volumes, edited by Dr. Rudolf Buddensieg, of Leipsic, other works being promised to follow. A remarkable monograph on *Wiclif and Hus*, showing in a way hitherto unattempted the connection between the later and the earlier Reformers, has been published in German by Dr. Johann Loserth, Professor of History in the University of Czernowitz. An

---

[1] *Political Poems and Songs relating to English History. Composed during the period from the accession of Edward III. to that of Richard III.* Edited by Thomas Wright. London, 1859. 2 vols. (Rolls Series.)

[2] *Roberti Grosseteste Episcopi quondam Lincolniensis Epistolæ.* Edited by H. R. Luard. London, 1861. (Rolls Series.)

[3] *Fasciculi Zizaniorum Magistri Johannis Wyclif, cum Tritico.* Ascribed to Thomas Netter of Walden. Edited by the Rev. Walter Waddington Shirley, M.A. London, 1858. (Rolls Series.)

[4] *Joannis Wiclif Trialogus, cum Supplemento Trialogi.* Edidit Gotthardus Lechler. Oxonii, 1869.

[5] *Select English Works of John Wycliffe.* Edited by Thomas Arnold, M.A., Oxford. Vol. I. (1869) Sermons on the Gospels for Sundays and Festivals. Vol. II. (1871) Sermons on the Ferial Gospels and Sunday Epistles. Treatises. Vol. III. (1871) Miscellaneous Works.

English translation has appeared (1884) by the Rev. M. J. Evans. References will be made to this important work in another part of the present volume.]

Thus much has been done since the middle of the present century to elucidate Reformation history, partly by the opening up of new historical sources and the publication of original documents, and partly by the monographic elucidation of single parts of the subject. We venture to come forward as fellow-labourers in the same field, in undertaking to set forth anew the life and teaching of Wycliffe, *Importance of Wycliffe's life.* according to the original sources. John Wycliffe appears to us to be the centre of the whole pre-Reformation history. In him meet a multitude of converging lines from the centuries which preceded him; and from him again go forth manifold influences, like wave-pulses, which spread themselves widely on every side, and with a force so persistent that we are able to follow the traces of their presence to a later date than the commencement of the German Reformation. Such a man deserves to have an historical portraiture which shall aim to do justice to the greatness of his personality, and to the epochal importance of his work.

CHAPTER I.

ENGLISH PRECURSORS OF WYCLIFFE.

1.—Mixture and Consolidation of Races in the English People.

IT is impossible to take a rapid survey of the course of English history during the middle ages, without being struck with the observation how many foreign elements mingled with it in ever varying succession, and how violent were the collisions and deep-reaching the contests which sprang from this cause.

We leave out of view, of course, the Romans who had quitted the soil of Britain before the close of ancient history, and had left the country to itself. In the middle of the fifth century, the Angles, Jutes, and Saxons, all sea-going tribes of Lower Germany, effected a conquest of the land, and drove back the Celtic inhabitants to its western borders. That was an immigration of pure German races. Five centuries later the predatory and devastating expeditions of the Danes broke over the country. That was the Scandinavian invasion, which in the end took the form of a personal union between England and Denmark. But when, after two more centuries, the long-settled Saxon population stirred itself again and bestowed the crown upon one of its own race, Duke William of Normandy intervened with a strong hand: with the Conquest the Franco-Norman nationality gained the ascendency in England; and it was not till two more centuries had passed away that the Saxon element wrought itself again into prominence and power. *Successive Immigrations.*

What a piebald mixture of peoples! What changes of fortune among the different nationalities! And yet the result of all was not a mere medley of peoples, without colour and character, but, on the contrary, a nation and a national character of remarkable vigour, and extremely well defined. For the numerous collisions and hard conflicts which occurred among the different races served only to strengthen and steel the kernel of the Saxon element of the population. This effect can be clearly seen and measured in the language and literature of the country, which are the first things upon which every people stamps its own impress.

It is a fact that after the first and earliest efflorescence of the Anglo-Saxon language, in the age immediately succeeding the conversion of the people to Christianity, a second took place in the days of Alfred the Great—not without a deep connection with the elastic reaction of the Saxon nationality against Danish despotism. And it is a circumstance of the same kind that the new Anglo-Saxon dialect developed itself from about the year 1100—a fact unquestionably owing to the Conquest which had taken place not long before, and an indication that the old Saxon stock was once more gathering up its strength in reaction against the new Norman-French element. On the other hand, the first development of the language which is called 'English,' in distinction from Anglo-Saxon—old English, we mean—belongs to the period in which a fusion began to take place between the Norman families and the Saxon stock, and that in the direction of an approximation of the Norman nobility to the Saxons—not the converse. The former ceased to feel as Frenchmen, and learned to think and speak as Englishmen.

Successive developments of the language.

We shall soon have an opportunity of convincing ourselves what an important share the religious interest had in producing this change. Meanwhile so much as this is clear, that the introduction of the Norman-French element, like the Danish invasion of an earlier time, did not in the least hinder, but on the contrary gave a stimulus to, the development of a compact and independent Saxon nationality. It was in conflict with foreign elements and their usurped power that the Saxon nation first of all maintained its own individuality, and next developed itself into the English people.

When we turn our attention to the faith of the nation and the religious side of their life, the antagonisms and the successive changes which they present to view are scarcely less abrupt. The British inhabitants of the country had received the Gospel during the Roman occupation, but apparently not from Rome, but rather, in the first instance, from the shores of the Levant. When the Roman domination of the island came to an end, the Britons had already for the most part been converted to Christianity. On the other hand, the Saxons and Angles, the Frisians and Jutes, when they established themselves in the country, were entirely ignorant of the Gospel. They brought with them the old German Paganism, they drove back the British population and Christianity along with it,

Religious development.

and they stamped again upon the land, as far as they might, a heathen impress.

Then arrived, at the end of the sixth century, at the instance of Gregory the Great, a completely organised Christian mission; and within the comparatively brief period of less than a hundred years this mission accomplished the result of carrying over to Christianity the whole of the related kingdoms of the Saxon Heptarchy. And now the old inhabitants of Celto-British descent and the Saxons (as the Britons called the others) might have joined hands as Christians, had it not been for an obstacle which could not be taken out of the way. *Conversion of the Saxons.*

The social and liturgical form in which Christianity was planted among the Saxons in England was essentially different from the ecclesiastical order and usage of the old British Christians. Among the latter, to say nothing of smaller liturgical differences, the ecclesiastical centre of gravity was in the monasteries, not in the episcopate, in addition to which they were under no subjection to the Bishops of Rome—their church life was entirely autonomous and national. The missionaries to the Saxons had been sent forth from Rome, and the Anglo-Saxon Church was, so to speak, a Roman colony; its whole church order received, as was to be expected, the impress of the Church of the West: in particular, the government of the church was placed in the hands of the bishops, who in their turn were dependent upon the See of Rome. The difference, or rather the opposition, was felt on both sides vividly enough, and led to severe collisions—to a struggle for victory, the prize of which on the one side was exclusive domination by the Roman Church, on the other, if not the dominancy, at least the continued existence of the old British ecclesiastical constitution. On which side lay the better hope of victory it is not difficult to estimate. A like contest repeated itself somewhat later upon the German soil, where a missionary who went forth from the young Anglo-Saxon Church opened fight against the church which had been planted among the Germans in part by old British missionaries, and at last bound the German Church so closely and tightly to Rome, that it too was converted by Boniface very much into a Roman colony. *The Saxon Church Roman.*

It would be an error, nevertheless, to believe that Rome obtained in England an absolute victory, or that the old British Church, with its peculiar independent character, disappeared in the Romish Anglo-Saxon Church without a trace. It is nearer the truth to say, that the British Church made its influence felt in the Anglo-Saxon, at least in single provinces, especially in the north of *Moderating Influences.*

England; and perhaps it was due in part to this influence that a certain spirit of church autonomy developed itself at an early period among the Anglo-Saxon people. It was not long after this development began to manifest itself that the Danes invaded the country, and transplanted into England the heathenism of Scandinavia. The threatening danger woke up the Saxon elasticity to a vigorous resistance. The wars of freedom under King Alfred were animated by a Christian inspiration, and by the feeling that not only the existence of the nation, but also of the Church of Christ in the land was at stake.

But what a new spirit prevailed in church affairs after the Norman Conquest! It was a genuine adventure of the Norman type—an enterprise of bold, romantic daring, when Duke William, **The Norman Conquest and the Papacy.** with a show of right, and availing himself of favouring circumstances, seized upon the English crown. But he took the step not without the previous knowledge and approval of the Pope. Alexander II. sent him, for use in the enterprise, a consecrated banner of St. Peter. The Duke was to carry it on board his own ship. With the conquest of England by the Normans, Rome hoped to make a conquest for herself, and not without reason. In the noble families of Normandy the knightly lust of battle and conquest was most intimately blended with knightly devotion to the Church and the Pope. In point of fact, from the moment of the conquest, the bond between Rome and the English Church was drawn incomparably closer than it had ever been under the Saxon dynasty.

The clergy, partly of Norman-French, partly of pure Roman descent, to whom the English sees were now transferred, could have no national sympathies with Anglo-Saxon Christianity. Strangers, they passed into the midst of a strange church. It was natural that they should take up the position of abstract ecclesiastical right. We may recall the instance of Lanfranc, an Italian, who, in 1070, four years after the battle of Hastings, from being Prior of Bec, was promoted to be Archbishop of Canterbury. At the same date a Norman became Archbishop of York. As a general rule, the highest dignities of the English Church fell to Normans; and these priests of the Continent were all supporters of the new hierarchical movement, which began in the middle of the same century—of those ideas touching the supremacy of the Pope over the Church, and of the Church over the State, of which Hildebrand himself had been the deliberate and most emphatic champion. William the Conqueror, indeed, was not the man to suffer in silence any encroachments of the Pope upon the rights of his crown, to say nothing of the pretensions of any ecclesiastical dignitary in his own kingdom. A serious discord, which took place between the crown and the Primate, now Anselm of Canterbury, arising out of the investiture controversy, was only composed by the prudent concessions of Paschal II. to Henry I. in 1106.

All the more formidable was the conflict between the royal and ecclesiastical powers under Henry II., exactly a hundred years after the conquest. The quarrel in the main concerned the limits of the civil and ecclesiastical jurisdictions—the right of exemption, *e.g.*, from the jurisdiction of the municipal courts, which was claimed for the clergy by Archbishop Thomas Becket; and it may suffice to remind the reader in passing how in the end the Archbishop was assassinated (1170) by several knights, not without the indirect complicity of the king, and how, in consequence of that evil deed, Henry had to bow himself down in most humiliating penance (July 12, 1174) at the grave of the now canonised champion of the Church's rights and liberties—a penance far more ignominious even than that of Canossa. The hierarchy obtained a great victory, which indeed had been in prospect ever since the Norman Conquest. *[Henry II. and Becket.]*

And yet this was not the culminating point to which the power of the Church attained in England. It did not reach that till forty years later. Innocent III. accomplished what Gregory VII. had striven for in the Conqueror's day in vain. *[Innocent III. and John.]* King John, son of Henry II., finding himself in the greatest danger, both from without and within the realm, had recourse to a desperate step. On May 15, 1213, he surrendered his kingdom, in favour of the apostles Peter and Paul and the Church of Rome, into the hands of Innocent III. and his successors. He received it, indeed, immediately back again from the Pope in fief, but not before taking for himself and his successors, in all due form, the oath of fealty to the Pope as his liege lord, and binding himself to pay an annual tribute of one thousand marks sterling, in addition to the usual Peter's pence. Thereby England became literally a portion of the 'Estates of the Church,' the King a vassal of the Pope, and the Pope liege lord and sovereign of England. England entered into and became a member of the Papal state system, which already included Portugal, Arragon, the kingdom of Sicily, Hungary, Bulgaria, and other States—a relation to the Papacy which was turned to practical account to the utmost of the Church's power, by the levying of imposts from the kingdom, as well as by the accumulation of English Church offices and dignities in the hands of Italians.

But from the moment when King John made over to the Papal

See a feudal supremacy in England, the moral influence of the Papacy in the country began to stoop towards its overthrow. The English nobility were the first to feel the humiliation most deeply, and complained indignantly to the king that he had brought what he had found a free kingdom into bondage.[1] Within two years the condition of things for a considerable time was such that the revolted barons held the chief power of the State in their hands. And then it was that *Magna Charta*, the fundamental charter of the nation's liberties, was negotiated between John and his subjects (June 15, 1215). In this document, the importance of which was even then universally felt, not a word was said of the liege-lordship of the Pope, although only two years had passed since this relation had been entered into. No doubt this omission was intentional on the part of the barons.

Still the whole movement which had been called forth in ever-growing force against the despotic rule of the distrusted prince, was also aimed, in the second instance, against Rome. The King himself, in a letter to Innocent III. (September 13, 1215), assures him that the earls and barons of the kingdom publicly alleged as the chief cause of their revolt, his own act of submission to the Pope;[2] and the Pope, on his side, considered the insurrection as directed in part against himself. An important reaction in the spirit of the Anglican Church,[3] and in its attitude towards the Roman See, could not fail to be produced by the fact, that in that celebrated state-treaty there was a guarantee given for all the liberties and rights of the national church, as well as for all those of all other classes and corporations in the kingdom. While, in the first instance, the great nobles and hierarchy, the lower nobility and the municipalities, all learned to feel their oneness as a nation, and to be sensible of their interests in common, there was no less a development in the ecclesiastical body of a national spirit. The spirit of insular independence began to make itself felt also in the religious sphere.

Reaction against Rome.

It had a powerful influence in the same religious direction, that from the beginning of the thirteenth century the Saxon element of the nation was again steadily coming to the front, and pressing the Norman element more and more into the background. Already, in 1204, Normandy had fallen to the crown

Growth of the Saxon element.

---

[1] The complaint against King John, made by the barons, 'quod suo tempore ancillavit regnum quod invenit liberum,' is given by Abbot William in his *Chronicle of the Monastery of St. Andrew*, in D'Achery's *Spicilegium*, Vol. II., p. 853.

[2] Rymer, *Foedera*. Vol. I., Part I, p. 138.

[3] So the Church was called even thus early—*e.g.*, in Magna Charta itself—Rymer, I, 132. Comp. Pauli, *Geschichte von England*, Vol. III., pp. 898, 909.

of France. This loss had naturally the effect of first diminishing the immigration from Normandy, and then, in time, of stopping it altogether. On the other hand, the families which had previously immigrated—to say nothing of the decimation which they had suffered in consequence of the political movements under King John and his successor, Henry III.—had in process of time drawn closer in many ways to the Saxon population. The arbitrary oppression which the nobles suffered at the hand of the kings brought up the memory of the earlier rights and privileges of the nobility under the Saxon kings. The barons began to claim the like for themselves, and appealed to them in support of their claim in their struggle with King John. The nobles no longer felt themselves to be Normans, but Englishmen; and all the more so, the more clearly men became conscious how much in questions of freedom and popular right was owing to the support of the lower nobility, and even to the municipalities, especially to the citizens of London.

This consolidation of the nation, in which the Saxon population constituted the kernel, could not remain without influence upon the self-consciousness and the hereditary independent genius of the Anglican Church. A symptom of this appeared in the secret combination of noblemen and priests, which, in 1231 addressed threatening letters to the capitular bodies and the abbacies, demanding of them to refuse payment to the agents of Rome of all imposts in money and kind. Not only so; but things, in fact, went so far that a Roman cleric, who was in possession of an English prelacy, was captured by the conspirators, and not set at liberty again for five weeks, after the loss of all his goods; while in country districts the full corn lofts of Roman parish priests were plundered and emptied.[1] In 1240 the cardinal legate Otho himself was menaced most seriously by an insurrection of students in Oxford. Such tumultuous proceedings were of course not suffered by the government. But neither were there wanting lawful measures directed against the Roman usurpations. The nobles, in a letter to Gregory IX., put in a protest in support of their violated rights of church patronage; and even bishops and prelates submitted complaints, sometimes to the papal legates, and sometimes to the Pope himself.

Anti-Roman Proceedings.

---

[1] Roger of Wendover, *Flores Historiarum;* in Matthew of Paris, *Historia Major.* London, 1686, p. 313. Compare Roberti Grosseteste *Epistolæ,* by Henry R. Luard. (Rolls Series.) Lond., 1862, 3, p. 22.

2.—Robert Grossetête, Bishop of Lincoln.

OF this state of feeling the most important and venerable representative was indisputably the learned and courageous Bishop of Lincoln, Robert Grossetête—a man who was held in exceptionally high admiration by his contemporaries, to whom England in the following centuries also deferred as a high authority, and who was ever regarded by Wycliffe in particular (who refers to him on innumerable occasions) with the highest respect. To such a man it is due that we should here present at least in outline a sketch of his character and career.

Robert Grossetête (in Latin *Capito*, in English *Greathead*) was one of those rare men who so harmoniously combine mastery in science with mastery in practical life, that they may be termed princes in the domain of mind. As to science, he united in himself the whole knowledge of his age to such an extent that a man so eminent in genius as Roger Bacon, his junior contemporary and grateful friend, said of him that 'The Bishop of Lincoln was the only man living who was in possession of all the sciences.'[1] But, however comprehensive and independent his knowledge was, it would be a great error to think of him as a man who was more than everything else a man of learning. On the contrary, with all his scientific greatness, Grossetête was still predominantly a man of action—a man full of character in the highest sense, a churchman such as few have ever equalled; and, from the day of his elevation to the episcopate, every inch a bishop.

Character of Grossetête.

But when I ask myself what was the moving-spring, the innermost kernel of his aims and actions, I am able to name nothing but his godly solicitude and care for souls. When he carries on for years a law-suit with his chapter for the right of episcopal visitation; when he contends for 'the freedom of the church,' apparently in a hierarchical spirit; when he repels with decision the encroachments of the Pope and his legates; when he brings sharp discipline to bear upon careless and worldly monks and priests, and labours to put a stop to the desecration of churches and churchyards; when he forms and draws out the young Orders of the Franciscans and Dominicans—in all this he has nothing else in view but the good of souls. That is his last and highest aim, in the pursuit of which the consciousness of his heavy responsibility attends him at every step, while a sincere fear of God imparts such strength to his mind as to give him victory over all the fear of man.

How did Grossetête become the man he was? Let us glance at

[1] *Opus tertium*, Ed., Brewer, 1869, pp. 31, 91.

the course of his outer and inner life. There are at least some original materials from which we can attempt to obtain an answer to this inquiry.[1]

It is an accepted date that Grossetête was born in 1175, or one or two years earlier. For it is certain that at his death, in 1253, he was a man of great age; and when the learned Giraldus Cambrensis recommended him to the Bishop of Hereford, William de Vere, which took place at latest in 1199 (for in this year the bishop just named died), he gave him the title of *Magister*, so that he was already a Master of Arts, and must have been a young man of from twenty to twenty-five years; and this takes us back for his birth to nearly the same date as before. He was a native of Stradbrooke, in the county of Suffolk, and according to some chronicles, of humble extraction. The chronicle of Lanercost has a notice, which is credible enough in itself, and significant of his character,[2] that on one occasion Grossetête replied to an earl, who had expressed some astonishment at his noble bearing and manners, that it was true he was sprung of parents in humble station, but from his earliest years he had made a study of the characters of the best men in the Bible, and that he had formed himself upon their model.

Of his student and travelling years we know little. Only so much is certain, that he studied in Oxford. It is less clearly established,

---

[1] Of Grossetête's numerous works nothing more than a few pieces have as yet been published. At the beginning of the sixteenth century his *Commentaries on Aristotle*, and on the *Mystical Theology of the Pseudo Dionysius*, were printed, the latter in Strasburg in 1502; but these subjects have very little interest for the present age. In the seventeenth century one of his successors in the See of Lincoln, John Williams (1612–1641), who died Archbishop of York in 1649, conceived the design of publishing his collected works in three folios, and he had already made collections and preparations with that view; but the outbreak of the civil war prevented the execution of the design. Towards the end of the same century, Edward Brown published in his *Appendix* to the *Fasciculus Rerum Expetendarum*, etc., several pieces of Grossetête, especially several of his sermons, theological thoughts, and a portion of his correspondence. This correspondence has recently been edited more critically and in a complete form by the Rev. H. R. Luard, M.A., of Cambridge, in the collection of *Rerum Britannicarum Medii aevi Scriptores*, published at the cost of the English Government, under the title, '*Roberti Grosseteste, Episcopi quondam Lincolniensis, Epistolæ.* London, 1862.' This valuable correspondence is the most trustworthy source for learning the development of the man and his character. Repeated attempts have been made to furnish a Biography of Grossetête, but several of these never got beyond the stage of the collection of materials. So it befell Bishop Barlow of Lincoln, Samuel Knight, Anthony Wood, and Edward Brown. It was not till the end of last century that a biography of the venerable man was prepared and sent to the press—Samuel Pegge's *Life of Grosseteste*. Lond., 1793. But the book was an ill-starred one; most of the copies are said to have perished in a fire which broke out in the printing office. The fact is certain, that the book is a very rare one even in England, and that there is hardly a single copy of it to be found in all the libraries of Germany. Luard, in his preface, has thrown some fresh light upon the life of Grosseteste. See preface, pp. ix.–xciv.

[2] In Luard's Roberti Grosseteste's *Epistolæ*. Preface, p. xxxii.

but not in itself improbable, that he completed his studies in Paris. Later, as already stated, he was introduced by Giraldus to the Bishop of Hereford as a young man who would be of service to him, not only in his manifold public employments and judicial decisions, but also in the care of his health. In addition to theology, therefore, Grossetête must have prosecuted successfully the study of medicine and canon law. But Bishop de Vere died in 1199, and Grossetête betook himself again to Oxford, where he remained for the next thirty-five years, in the course of which he became Doctor of Theology and *Rector scholarum*. Several of his writings, including his Commentaries on Aristotle and Boethius, besides several theological works, no doubt had their origin in lectures which he delivered in the University. Several church preferments were also conferred upon him, such as a stall in the Cathedral of Lincoln, the Archdeaconry of Leicester, etc.

Towards the close of his residence in Oxford, he seems to have experienced a religious awakening. In the end of October, 1231 or 1232, he had a dangerous illness. On his sick-bed and during his recovery his heart appears to have been deeply moved. He took counsel with his conscience, particularly on the question whether it was right before God for him to hold several livings at the same time.[1] It was, without doubt, at this time that, by the medium of a pious man whose name has not come down to us, he submitted to the Pope the question whether he could, with a good conscience, retain the parochial charge which he held, along with his sinecure prebends. The answer which was orally communicated to him was thoroughly Roman—by no means could he retain such a plurality *without a dispensation*. But this was a mode of arrangement which his awakened conscience forbade him to make use of, and without more ado he resigned the whole of the benefices which he possessed, with the sole exception of his stall at Lincoln. We learn this from a letter of the year 1232 to his sister Inetta—a nun.[2] The sister by no means approved of her brother's self-denying step. She feared that by his act of renunciation of income he had reduced himself to penury. But his only feeling was one of relief from a burden on his conscience, and he endeavours to remove her anxiety on that score, and to reconcile her to the resolution to which he had already given effect. The conscientiousness and the concern for his own soul, of which we have here a

His conscientiousness.

---

[1] Grossetête alludes to this question having been put by him in a letter to the Cardinal-Legate Otho, written in 1239,—Ep. 74 of Luard's Coll., p. 242; and I know of no incident in his life with which I can more suitably connect it than with that given in the text.

[2] *Epistolæ*, by Luard, 8, p. 43.

glimpse, awakened in Grossetête an earnest concern for the cure of souls at large, of which from that time forward he gave ever stronger proofs.

After the death of the Bishop of Lincoln, Hugh of Wells, with whom he was on terms of personal friendship, Grossetête, in the spring of 1235, was elected by the chapter to the bishopric. As Chancellor of the University of Oxford, as Archdeacon of Leicester, and in other positions, he had already been successful in carrying out many measures of a practical kind; and now he was advanced to a post in which his action as an ecclesiastical ruler shone out conspicuously far and wide.

Bishop of Lincoln.

This was in part owing to the importance of this particular see. The diocese of Lincoln was then, and for some centuries afterwards, by far the largest and most populous in the whole of England. More than once in his letters Grossetête refers to its immense extent and numerous inhabitants.[1] It included at that day eight archdeaconries, of which only two may here be mentioned, Oxford and Leicester—the former, because the University was subject to the Bishop of Lincoln as its ordinary, and the latter, because to the archdeaconry, a century later, Wycliffe, as parish priest of Lutterworth, belonged. The cathedral, built at the commencement of the Norman period, stands, with the older portion of the city, upon a height, while the newer portion of the city descends the hill to the plain watered by the river Witham. None of the English cathedrals has so splendid a site as that of Lincoln; with its three towers it is seen at a distance of fifty miles to the north and thirty to the south, and is considered one of the most beautiful cathedrals in the kingdom.[2]

As soon as he was installed, Grossetête grasped the helm with a firm hand, and took immediate steps for the removal of abuses which had found their way into the diocese. His first act was to address a circular letter to all his archdeacons, in which he instructed them to admonish the parishes of various evil customs which were on the increase, by which Sundays, festivals, or holy names were desecrated. This missive goes right into matters of practical life, and is inspired by a high moral earnestness, by a conscientious solicitude for the good of souls, and by a burning zeal for the House of God.[3] Nor was it only in writing or by intermediaries, but also directly and personally, that the new bishop intervened. In the very first year after his admis-

Reforming measures.

---

[1] *Epistolæ*, 40, p. 132; 41, p. 134; 50, p. 146; 88, p. 275.
[2] See Dugdale, *Monast. Anglicanum*.
[3] *Ib.* 22, p. 72.

sion to office he commenced a personal visitation of the monasteries of the diocese, which resulted in not fewer than seven abbots and three priors being immediately deprived.

Nor was it Grossetête's intention only to interfere in cases at a distance, and to shut his eyes to disorders which lay nearer home. He took steps to visit and reform the chapter of his own cathedral. But now his troubles began. The chapter, consisting of not fewer than twenty-one canons, took a protest against his proceedings, alleging that the bishop was allowing himself in unexampled encroachments of authority, and was touching their immemorial rights. The chapter had an autonomy of its own, and was subject only to its own dean; only if the dean neglected his duty, or himself appealed to the bishop, had the latter a right to say a single word.[1] In 1239 the matter grew to a quarrel between bishop and chapter. The dispute became known all over the kingdom, and could not be healed either by the Archbishop of Canterbury or by Otho, the Pope's legate. Bishop Robert made a journey in November, 1244, to Lyons, where Innocent IV. was then residing. A commissioner of the chapter was already there before him. The Pope's decision on the main point—the right of visitation—was soon obtained, and was entirely in favour of the bishop; and, this gained, Grossetête lost no time in making use of his right now finally established, although he had still to encounter difficulties in carrying it into effect.

Along with this business he carried forward with zeal his visitation of parishes and cloisters. As the effect of this, several unworthy parish priests were removed, and many priors who had been guilty of acts of violence resigned their offices. Other bishops also were stimulated to do the like by the persistency and emphasis with which Grossetête prosecuted this visitorial work. It even appears as though the estimation and influence of the vigorous bishop rose higher and higher in proportion to the amount of conflict which it cost him to carry through his plans for the well-being of the Church. In fact, his episcopal career was an almost unbroken succession of collisions and conflicts. Long before the affair with his own chapter had been brought to a settlement, he became involved in differences with powerful spiritual corporations—with the Abbot of Westminster, and with the convent of Christ Church in Canterbury. Nay, the heroic opposition to wrong which he was compelled from time to time to undertake, rose higher still. In repeated instances, sometimes single-handed, sometimes along with other bishops, he stood forward in

[1] *Epistolæ*, 73, p. 235.

resistance to King Henry III. himself; and what for a man in his position, and in view of the spirit of his age, will be seen to amount to a vast deal more—he remained true to his own convictions of duty and to his own resolves, even against the Pope himself, and that Pope a man like Innocent IV. But of this more in the sequel.

In view of this multitude of spiritual conflicts we can easily understand that his opponents accused him of a want of heart and a love of strife. Even at this distance of time, after the lapse of six centuries, upon a superficial consideration of a life so full of contention, one might easily receive the impression that this energetic man was all too fond of strife, if not even a hierarch of haughty and imperious temper. But on a closer inspection the case stands quite otherwise. A careful examination of his correspondence has forced upon me the conviction that in entering into these numerous contentions Grossetête was influenced, not by a violent temperament, but by the dictates of conscience. On one occasion he writes as follows to the Abbot of Leicester :—'You accuse us of iron-heartedness and want of pity. Alas! would that we had an iron heart, steeled against the flatteries of tempters, a strong heart, proof against the terrors of the wicked, a sharp heart, cutting off sins and hewing in pieces the bad when they oppose themselves.'[1]

His ruling motive.

From this single utterance we may perceive that what he did could not have been the outflow of mere natural temperament, but must have been the result of principle and conviction. It was in this sense he replied to the dean and chapter of Sarum, who admonished him to live in peace with his own chapter. That peace, he said, was what he aimed at beyond everything else, but the true peace, not the false; for the latter is only a perversion of the true God-appointed order.[2] But that he was not led by a determination to have everything his own way is plain, from the circumstance that what he laid the whole stress upon in his conflicts was not to have success in them, but to preserve in all of them a good conscience. While he was still Archdeacon of Leicester he had a difference with the Benedictine Convent of Reading—but he was prepared to submit himself unreservedly to the decision of an umpire whom both parties might be able to agree upon.[3] And on a later occasion when he had expressed himself at full length against an appointment which Cardinal Otho had desired for a favourite of his, he contented himself with having thus referred the matter to the Cardinal's own conscience, and left it in quiet to his own decision.[4] It is his

---

[1] *Epistolæ*, 55, p. 170.
[2] *Ib.* 93, p. 290.
[3] *Ib.* 4, p. 32.
[4] *Ib.* 74, p. 241.

abiding sense of responsibility, and his fear of 'Him who is able to destroy body and soul in hell,' which moves him in all cases when he is compelled to place himself in opposition to personages of high influence and place.

But does not, at least, the suspicion of hierarchical pride still remain attached to him? The answer to this is, that however little Grossetête was inclined at any time to abate aught of his episcopal right, whether in dealing with his subordinates or his superiors, with the great men of the realm, or with the supreme Head of the Church himself, in every case the episcopal dignity and power was looked upon by him not as an end but a means. The last end to him was the good of souls. To that end, and to that alone, behoved to be subservient both priestdom and patrondom, bishopdom and popedom, the Church's liberties and the Church's wealth, each in its own measure and after its own manner. When in his official journeys he gathered around him the parochial clergy of a rural deanery, and preached before them, he had in his thoughts the whole of the congregations of these parish priests, and used to say that 'it was his duty to preach the Word of God to all the souls in his diocese; but it was impossible for him to do so personally, considering the multitude of parish churches and the immense population of the diocese; and he could think of no other way of helping himself than to preach God's Word to the priests and vicars and curates of each deanery, assembled around him in the course of his visitations, in order to do through them, at least to some extent, what he found himself entirely unable to do for the people in person.'[1]

It is surprising, indeed, to hear a man of such sentiments as these laying down, at an earlier period of his life, to an officer of State, the principle that civil legislation behoves to conform itself to the laws of the Church, because temporal princes receive from the Church all the power and dignity which they possess; that both swords, material and spiritual, belong to St. Peter, with only this difference, that the princes of the Church handle only the spiritual sword, while they wield the material sword through the hands of temporal princes, who, however, are bound to draw it and sheathe it under their direction.[2] That is quite the language of an Innocent III.

Grossetête on Church authority.

It looks as if Grossetête, in his later life, must have passed over to

---

[1] *Epistolæ*, 50, p. 146. The *Sermones ad Clerum*, published by Edward Brown in 1690, were no doubt made use of by the bishop in his visitations in addressing the clergy of the different rural deaneries. See note, p. 21.

[2] *Ib.* 23, p. 90. Comp. his Letter to King Henry III. No. 124, p. 348.

the other camp. But that is not the true state of the case.[1] Even in his earlier life it was not the deepest meaning of his thoughts to surrender up all unconditionally to St. Peter's successor, or to claim plenary powers for the episcopate for its own sake. It is true that he puts the law of the Church on a footing of full equality with the commandments of God. It is true also that he puts the State decidedly under the Church, and denies its autonomy. But he sees these things through the spectacles of his own century, and is unable to set himself loose from its ideas. Still, neither the episcopate nor the papacy exists in his view for itself; both exist for the glory of God and for the good of God's kingdom. The whole conduct and action of the man, not only in later but also in earlier life, justifies us in so interpreting his innermost thoughts. We can see from the rejoinder which he made to the statesman's reply, which would appear to have been couched in a tone of cutting irony, that our bishop had had no intention in his first letter to mount the high horse of hierarchical pride.[2]

If we look for the innermost kernel of all the thought and effort of this man who had an incredible amount of business to get through, we can find it in nothing else than in his earnest solicitude for souls. To this end he laboured with special zeal for the moral and religious elevation of the pastoral office. A doctor of theology, William of Cerda, having been appointed to a pastoral charge, found much more pleasure in carrying on his lectures in the University of Paris than in taking personal charge of his parishioners in England. But Grossetête reminds him with equal tenderness and warmth that he should choose rather to be himself a pastor, and to feed the sheep of Christ in his own parish, than to read lectures to other pastors from the chair.[3] We see here how high a place he assigned to the pastoral office, and that though at the summit of the science of his time, he did not look upon science as the highest thing, but upon life, and especially the devoted cure of souls. What else but the reform of the pastoral office was the drift of all the visitation work which Grossetête undertook and carried through with such peculiar zeal? And the sermons which he was accustomed to preach in his visitation tours—at ordinations and consecrations of churches before the assembled pastors of one or other of his seventy-two rural deaneries, were nothing else but appeals of the chief pastor of the flock to the under shepherds, designed to quicken their consciences and to press the duties of their office close upon their hearts.

His solicitude for souls.

---

[1] Comp. Brown's *Appendix ad Fasciculum*, p. 322.
[2] *Epistolæ*, 24, p. 95.
[3] *Ib.* 13, p. 57. Comp. 51, p. 147.

Some of these addresses which have come down to us, form in fact a pastoral theology *in nuce*.[1] When, in the course of his visitations, he made use of his disciplinary powers to depose unworthy priests upon the spot, and when he used his patronage to fill vacant benefices with active, well-educated men, accustomed to preach, he did his utmost to raise the character of the pastorate. Add to this the watchful eye which he kept upon the appointments made to parishes in his diocese by private patrons and corporations, and even by the crown and the papal court. In how many instances did he put off the canonical admission of a presentee! and what a multitude of unpleasant conflicts were brought upon him by his conscientious vigilance in this respect! A considerable portion of his correspondence is taken up exclusively with this subject.

Grossetête had scarcely taken possession of his see when an officer of State, William of Raleyer (Raleigh), presented to a parish a youth called William of Grana. The bishop refused to confirm the appointment, partly on account of his being under age, and partly on account of his inadequate attainments; and the refusal was highly resented by the patron. We have still the letter in which the bishop stated his reasons for the act, and he does so in a way which fills us with high appreciation of his conscientiousness and piety.[2] And there were numerous other instances of a similar kind, in which he withheld his consent to appointments on account either of deficient age or inadequate scholarship, or both together, or on the ground of conduct and deportment wholly unbecoming the priestly office.[3]

Episcopal discipline.

With no less vigilance did this faithful and watchful chief pastor take heed to the manner in which parish priests after their appointment fulfilled the duties of their office. As may be easily conceived, he looked with no friendly eye upon the accumulation of livings in the same hands—a practice in which personal revenue was the only thing considered, and the interests of parishioners were treated as quite a secondary affair. More than once he opposed himself to this *pluralitas beneficiorum*.[4]

At the time of his awakening, about 1232, he had been strict with himself in this respect, and now he was also strict with others. In repeated instances he insisted that every one who was entrusted with

---

[1] *E.g. Sermo ad Clerum*, in Brown. *Monitio et persuasio pastorum*, on the text, 'I am the Good Shepherd,' p. 260 f.

[2] *Epistolæ*, 17, p. 63 f. Comp. 11, p. 50 f., where his feeling of responsibility for the salvation of the souls committed to his episcopal charge is strikingly expressed.

[3] *Ib.* 26, p. 102. Epp. 19 and 71, pp. 68 and 204.

[4] *Epistolæ*, 74, p. 241 f. With special earnestness he appeals in this matter to the conscience of a certain Hugo of Pateshull (Ep. 25, p. 97 f.), who died in 1241, Bishop of Lichfield.

the care of souls should be resident in his parish. One of these was the case of a Magister Richard of Cornwall, to whom he had given a living on the recommendation of the Cardinal Egidius, and who had manifested a preference for Rome as a residence, to the neglect of his cure. The bishop sent to him, through the Cardinal, a very peremptory injunction to reside in his parish, begging him sarcastically not to refuse 'to let himself down from the height of Rome to the level of England, in order to feed the sheep, as the Son of God had descended from the throne of His majesty to the ignominy of the cross in order to redeem them.'[1]

Another matter which from time to time gave the bishop much trouble, had a like bearing upon the elevation of the spiritual offices of the Church, viz., the resistance which he offered to the appointment of abbots and clerics to judicial functions, and his efforts to bring back all offices ordained for the good of souls to their purely ecclesiastical and religious destination and use. In the year 1236 the King appointed the Benedictine Abbot of Ramsey to be a Judge in Council, an appointment which gave great distress to the conscientious chief pastor. That an abbot should undertake such a function appeared to him to be irreconcilable with the vows of his order, and with the clerical office in general; and this all the more that a judge might easily find himself in the position of having to pronounce sentences of death. He therefore addressed himself to the Archbishop of Canterbury to request him to use his influence with the King to obtain, if possible, a recall of the appointment. The archbishop was of opinion that the question of principle involved in the case ought to be referred for decision to the next general council. But for the bishop it became more and more urgently a question of conscience, whether it was not sin in a monk to undertake the office of judge. It seemed to him clear that the question could only be answered in the affirmative. But, if so, then it was also certain that the bishop, who allowed this to be done, was likewise in sin. In a second letter, therefore, he begs and conjures the Archbishop to give a plain and clear answer to the question—whether, yea or nay, it is sin in a monk or cleric to accept a judge's commission, and whether, yea or nay, it is a sin in a bishop to allow this to be done.[2] What the issue of the matter was cannot be learnt from the correspondence, and is of less interest to us than the fact that Grossetête laboured in this direction as well as in others for the restoration of good order in all the spiritual offices of the Church.

Ecclesiastics in secular employments.

---

[1] *Epistolæ*, 46, p. 138.   [2] *Ib.*, 27 and 28, pp. 105 and 108, and still more fully in Ep. 72, pp. 205-213.

But that both church and church-office did not appear to him to be their own end and object, that in his eyes the cure and the salvation of souls held a higher place than the pastoral office taken by itself, is manifest beyond all doubt, from the circumstance that Grossetête brought forward the new Mendicant orders to the work of preaching and cure of souls. Already, in his earlier days while he still worked in Oxford, he had entered into close relations with the Franciscans, and had done his best to bring them forward in the University.[1] When he became bishop he associated with himself both Franciscans and Dominicans as his coadjutors in his episcopal office.[2] And not only so—he gladly welcomed, protected, and promoted their activity throughout his diocese at large, and did not shrink from openly expressing his opinion, that by preaching and the confessional, by their example and their prayers, they were doing an inestimable amount of good in England, and compensating for the shortcomings and mischievous influence of the secular clergy.[3] In this matter Grossetête differed widely in judgment from many of his clergy, who looked upon it as an encroachment upon the pastoral office when a Dominican or Franciscan preached or heard confession in their parishes,[4] and did their utmost to keep back their flocks from listening to such sermons, or confessing to a begging friar. Bishop Grossetête, on the contrary, wrote on one occasion to Pope Gregory IX. as follows:—'O, if your Holiness could only see with what devotion and humility the people flock together to hear from them (the Mendicant monks) the word of life, and to make confession of their sins, and how much advantage the clergy and religion have derived from the imitation of their example, your Holiness would certainly say the people who walked in darkness have seen a great light.'[5] Accordingly he sought to induce the parochial clergy of his diocese to stir up their parishioners to frequent the sermons and the confessionals of the friars[6]—a proceeding which shows clearly enough that however highly he valued the pastoral office, and however zealously he laboured to further and to elevate it, he was still far from exalting it only for its own sake. In his view, the fear of God and the salvation of souls, as the ultimate ends which the spiritual office was designed to subserve, were of immeasurably higher account.

---

[1] Comp. Pauli's *Programm on Grossteste and Adam of Marsh.* Tübingen, 1864.
[2] *Epp.* 40 and 41, pp. 131, 133—the former addressed to the Dominican General, the latter to the Franciscan, both in very similar terms.
[3] *Epistolæ*, 34, p. 121.
[4] *Ib.* 107, p. 317.
[5] *Ib.* 58, p. 180.
[6] In the 'Circulars' to the Archdeacons above referred to. Ep. 107, p. 317.

Grossetête's whole views, religious and ecclesiastical, are to be seen in their purest and truest expression in a Memorial, in which he set down all his complaints concerning the disorders of the Church of his time, and which he submitted in a personal audience to the Pope. The occasion of the Memorial was this. The practice of what was called 'appropriation' was becoming increasingly common, *i.e.*, the practice of transferring church tenures, tithe-rights, and glebe-lands, into the possession of monasteries, knightly orders, &c. This was a loss to local church property—an impoverishment of the parochial churches concerned. The parish lands were no longer in a condition to secure a living to the parish priest. The consequence was that a priest could no longer reside on the spot. The charge was only supplied from without, either from a cloister or at the cost of a knight commander, sometimes by one, sometimes by another priest or monk. In short, the office was neglected—the parish was spiritually orphanised. In his later years, Bishop Grossetête observed in his visitations that this evil was always on the increase. He saw in it an injury, not only to the pastoral office, but to the souls entrusted to it, which called for the most serious attention. The first step he took to remedy the mischief was to obtain a Papal authorisation, enabling him to declare all transferences and compacts of this kind to be null and void.

Appropriations.

As soon as these full powers reached his hands, he called before him all the monks of his diocese who had been provided with these livings, and produced and read to them the Papal rescript. He was resolved, he said, to take over immediately into his own administration all those parish church-lands, the acquisition of which, with the consent of the cathedral chapter, the monasteries might not be able to establish by written documents. But experience proved that the Papal authorisation was of little avail. It was only too easy to obtain exemptions by means of corruption at the Papal Court, and the well-meant intentions of the Bishop were frustrated. But Grossetête was not the man to give way before such an obstacle. Regardless of his advanced age, he determined to make a second journey to Lyons, where Pope Innocent IV. was still residing, as he had been six years before. In the year 1250 he crossed the Channel with a numerous spiritual train. Arriving in Lyons, he experienced from the Curia a much cooler reception than he had done on the previous occasion and in the main business which brought him he accomplished as good as nothing. He remained, however, the whole summer in Lyons, occupied with various affairs.

In an audience obtained by him, 13th May, he handed to the Pope

himself, and to three of the Cardinals in attendance, copies of the
<small>Memorial to the Pope.</small> Memorial referred to, in which he gave utterance to all that was in his heart. It was immediately read in the Pope's presence by Cardinal Otho, who had lived in England for some time as legate, and had come much into contact with Grossetête.

This Memorial has come down to us under the incorrect title of a sermon.[1] It is full of earnest moral zeal, and of fearless frankness of speech. We confine ourselves to the simplest outlines of the course of thought. The way in which he gives expression to his thoughts, while making use of the most powerful rebukes of the inspired prophets, is sometimes such as must have made the hearers tremble.

Grossetête begins with the observation that zeal for the salvation of souls—the sacrifice most well-pleasing to God—had brought down to earth and humiliation the eternal Son of God, the Lord of glory. By the ministry of His Apostles and the pastors appointed by them, among whom, above all others, the Pope bears the image of Christ, and acts as His representative, the kingdom of God came, and the house of God was made full. But at the present day, alas! the Church of Christ is sorely diminished and narrowed; unbelief prevails in the greatest part of the world; in Christendom itself a considerable portion of it has been separated from Christ by division,[2] and in the small remainder heresy goes on increasing in some quarters, and the seven deadly sins prevail in others; so that Christ has had for ages to complain, 'Woe is me, for I am as when they have gathered the summer fruits, as the grape-gleanings of the vintage. There is no cluster to eat, my soul desireth the first ripe fruit. The good man is perished out of the earth, and there is none upright among men.'

'But what is the cause of this hopeless fall of the Church? Unquestionably the diminution in the number of good shepherds of souls, the increase of wicked shepherds, and the circumscription of the pastoral authority and power. Bad pastors are everywhere the cause of unbelief, division, heresy, and vice. It is they who scatter the flock of Christ, who lay waste the vineyard of the Lord, and desecrate the earth. No wonder, for they preach not the Gospel of Christ with that living word which comes forth from living zeal for the salvation of souls, and is confirmed by an example worthy of Jesus Christ; and to this they add every possible form of transgression—their pride is ever on the increase, and so are their avarice,

---

[1] *Sermo Roberti Lincolniensis Episcopi*, etc., in Brown, *Appendix*, pp. 250, 257. The state of the text of this memorial leaves much to be desired.
[2] An allusion to the Greek Church.

luxury and extravagance; and because the life of the shepherds is a lesson to the laity, they become thus the teachers of all error and all evil. Instead of being a light of the world, they spread around, by their godless example, the thickest darkness and the icy coldness of death.

'But what, again, is the cause of this evil? I tremble to speak of it, and yet I dare not keep silence. The cause and source of it is the *Curia* itself! Not only because it fails to put a stop to these evils as it can and should, but still more, because, by its dispensations, provisions, and collations, it appoints evil shepherds, thinking therein only of the living which it is able to provide for a man, and, for the sake of that, handing over many thousands of souls to eternal death. He who commits the care of a flock to a man in order that the latter may get the milk and the wool, while he is unable or unwilling to guide, to feed, and protect the flock, such an one gives over the flock itself to death as a prey. That be far from him who is the representative of Christ! He who so sacrifices the pastoral office is a persecutor of Christ in His members. And since the doings of the Curia are a lesson to the world, such a manner of appointment to the cure of souls, on its part, teaches and encourages all who have patrons rights to make pastoral appointments of a like kind, as a return for services rendered to themselves, or to please men in power, and in this way to destroy the sheep of Christ. And let no one say that such pastors can still save the flock by the ministry of middlemen. For among these middlemen many are themselves hirelings who flee when the wolf cometh.

'Besides, the cure of souls consists not only in the dispensation of the sacraments, in singing of "hours," and reading of masses, but in the true teaching of the word of life, in rebuking and correcting vice; and, besides all this, in feeding the hungry, giving drink to the thirsty, clothing the naked, lodging the strangers, visiting the sick and the prisoners—especially among the parish priest's own parishioners—in order, by such deeds of charity, to instruct the people in the holy exercises of active life; and to do such deeds is not at all in the power of these middlemen, for they get so small a portion of the church's goods that they have scarcely enough to live upon.[1] In the midst of such evils men might still have the consolation of hoping that possibly successors might follow who would better fulfil the pastor's calling. But when parish churches are made over to monasteries these evils are made perpetual. All such things end not in the

---

[1] Here he comes to speak of the evil state of matters which was the occasion of his undertaking the journey to Lyons.

upbuilding, but the destruction of the Church. God forbid that even the Holy See and its possessor should act against Christ, and thereby incur the guilt of apostasy and division! Further, the pastoral office, especially of the bishops, is at the present time circumscribed and restrained, particularly in England, and this in three ways. First, by the exemptions and privileges of monasteries, for when the inmates of these addict themselves outside their walls to the worst vices, the bishops can take no action against them—their hands are tied by the privileges of the convents. Secondly, the secular power puts obstacles in the way, in cases where investigations are made into the sins of laymen, in order to prevent other laymen from being sworn as witnesses. To which are to be added, thirdly, appeals to the Pope or Archbishop; for if the bishop takes steps according to his duty to punish vice and depose unworthy pastors, protest is taken, the "liberty" of the Church is appealed to, and so the matter is delayed and the action of the bishop lamed.'

In conclusion, Grossetête invokes the Holy See to put a stop to all disorders of this character, and especially to put a check upon the excesses of its own courtiers, of which there were loud complaints, to leave off the unevangelical practice of using the interposition of the sword, and to root out the notorious corruption of the Papal Court. It was to be feared that the Holy See, unless it reformed itself without delay, would draw upon itself the heaviest judgments—yea, destruction itself. The Holy Father would not interpret as presumption what the author of this Memorial had ventured to lay before him in all devotion and humility, under many misgivings and tears, and purely at the bidding of dread of the prophet's 'Woe,' and of a longing desire to see a better state of things.

This utterance can only call forth the deepest respect for the godly-mindedness of the author and for his burning zeal for God's house, for the salvation of souls, and the reformation of the Church. But, on the other hand, it can easily be understood that such unheard-of freedom of speech was not likely to obtain for the strong man who uttered it any favour or influence at the Papal Court. When Grossetête left Lyons in September, and arrived again at home at Michaelmas, 1250, he was for some time so much out of heart that he had some thoughts of resigning his episcopal office. However, matters did not go that length. He gathered up his strength again, and from that day forward acted only with all the more emphasis, and with all the less reference to the Pope and the Crown. His visitation of convents and parish churches was taken up again with, if possible, still greater strictness than before. Unworthy pastors were set aside, and in all places where there was need for it he appointed vicars in their room, who were supported out of the revenues, in virtue of an authorisation to that effect, which he at last obtained from the Pope.

In Parliament his voice carried with it decisive weight In a letter of 1252 which he addressed to the nobles of the realm, to the citizens of London, and to the 'Community' of England, he expressed himself strongly on the subject of the illegal encroachments of the Apostolic See, by which the country was drained.

But in the year of his death there occurred an incident which raised the name of the Bishop of Lincoln to the highest celebrity. Innocent IV. had conferred upon one of his grandsons, Frederick of Lavagna (the Pope was himself a Count of Lavagna), a canonry in the Cathedral of Lincoln, and taken steps to have him immediately invested with it by a cardinal. From Perugia, on January 26, 1253, an apostolic brief was addressed, not to the Bishop, but to an archdeacon of Canterbury, and to Magister Innocent, a Papal agent in England, with the distinct injunction to put the young man before named, in the person of his proxy, into actual possession of that dignity and living. And, that there might be no delay, much less any obstacle put in the way, the Papal brief expressly set aside, for this occasion, all and sundry opposing rights and statutes, even such as had received apostolic confirmation, nay, even all direct apostolic concessions to whomsoever given, and howsoever worded.[1] Nor was this enough. In case any one should oppose himself to the carrying out of this injunction, either by word or deed, the Pope authorised his agents immediately to summon any such person within two months to appear in person before the Pope and answer for himself to the challenge of Frederick of Lavagna. This, it was thought, had made failure impossible; every imaginable means of escape was cut off, every bolt was made sure; and yet the measure issued in failure after all.[2]

Controversy with the Pope.

The Bishop of Lincoln, though now eighty years old, was not accustomed to allow himself to be frightened. With all the energy which a sense of right, springing from the holy feeling of duty, inspires, he stood forward to object to the proceeding, and to withstand it; and the document in which he couched his opposition had not only an electric effect upon the English nation at the time, but its in-

---

[1] *Non obstantibus privilegiis,* etc.—the clause so often made use of when the Pope of the day evaded, or rather set aside, *ad hoc,* the ordinances of his predecessors or even his own, still in legal force, in favour of a special case, or in behalf of some favoured individual.

[2] The Papal Brief has been printed in full by Brown in his Appendix, p. 399, and in Luard, p. 432, note.

fluence continued to be felt for centuries afterwards; and, more than all his learning, more than all the services of his long, active, and fruitful life, it made the name of the God-fearing, upright, and inflexible man popular and illustrious.

Grossetête had no thoughts of writing direct to the Pope himself;[1] and this was not prudent merely, it was also due to his own dignity. Innocent had intentionally passed by the Bishop, though the question related to a canonry in his own cathedral; and it was therefore in every way suitable and well considered, that the Bishop on his side should leave the Pope entirely out of the game. He addressed himself exclusively to the Archdeacon of Canterbury and to Magister Innocent.[2]

[1] This is indeed the view commonly taken. Even Luard in his Preface, p. lxxix., and Pauli in his *Programm* on Grossetête, and Adam von Marsh, p. 24, assume that the letter was addressed to the Pope. The superscription, also, which Luard has given to the letter, no doubt on MS. authority, indicates the same. Nevertheless, this superscription is, in my judgment, erroneous and ungenuine. For, in the first place, the address, *Discretio vestra*, is quite unsuitable to the Pope. Grossetête himself makes use of *Sanctitas vestra* in the two Epp. 110 and 117, pp. 328 and 338, which were certainly addressed to the Pope—a circumstance which was not unnoticed by Brown. But next, the fact is a decisive one that toward the end of the letter, the address, *reverendi domini* occurs, which undeniably presupposes a plurality of persons addressed. Besides, the tone of the letter, on the supposition that it was addressed to the Pope, would have been quite unaccountable. The fact is not ignored by Luard, that the style of this letter differs greatly from that of the two which were, without doubt, intended for the Pope, Preface lxxix. But what he brings forward to account for this difference is not quite satisfactory. Still Brown is right in maintaining that the letter was intended for the eye of the Pope, whether it came to his hands directly or indirectly. Undoubtedly so, and for this reason it required no little courage and good conscience to write to both the Pope's commissaries in such a strain; whereas we should be compelled to think far otherwise of the tact and good taste of the writer, if it were certain that he had meant his words directly for the eye of the Pope himself. The mistake, however, is explained in some measure by the circumstance that the Pope's agent, Innocent, bore the same name as the Pope himself.

[2] This celebrated letter is to be found in Brown, p. 400; in Oudin's *Commentaria de Scriptoribus Eccles. Antiquae*, Vol. III., p. 142; and in Luard, *Ep.* 128, pp. 432. Luard tells us that it occurs times without number in the MSS. Among those who have referred to it, I have to name Wycliffe himself. He was not only well acquainted with its contents, but he has also in one place reproduced it almost entire—I mean in his still unprinted work, *De Civili Dominio*, Lib. I., c. 43, MS. 1341, of the Imperial Library of Vienna, side by side with the Pope's two letters. And Wycliffe not only incorporated the letter with his own work, but also added to it a kind of commentary in the way of justifying its contents, in which he states precisely its principal thoughts, and adopts them as his own. Huss also knew the Bishop's Epistle, and cited it in part in his work, *De Ecclesia*, c. 18 (Opera, 1558, v. I., p. 235.) As to the state of its text, it is by no means free from errors in the Wycliffe MS. just named; but still in some places this MS. supplies readings materially superior to those of Brown and Luard. May I add in this place one more remark in conclusion? Luard has observed, p. xli., that it is not known when or by whom the collection of Grossetête's letters was made. Now, as the MSS. used by Luard, which comprise the whole collection or the greater part of it, are of no higher age than the fifteenth century, and as only single letters were found in copies dating from the fourteenth century, I do not think it superfluous to mention that I find in Wycliffe—who more than once gives accurate citations from other letters of Grossetête besides the one mentioned above—exactly the same ordering or numbering of the letters which Brown gives, and which is retained also by Luard. Now as those writings of Wycliffe, which

In this celebrated paper he takes up the position, that in opposing himself to the demand in question, he is giving proof of his veneration and obedience to apostolic mandates, and of his zeal for the honour of the Roman Mother Church. For this demand is not an apostolical one, inasmuch as it is in contradiction to the teaching of the apostles and of Christ Himself. It is also totally irreconcilable with apostolic holiness, and this upon a double ground—first, because the 'notwithstanding' (*non obstante*) of the brief, carries along with it a whole flood of inconsistency, recklessness, and deception, undermines truth and faith, and shakes to the centre all Christian piety, as well as all intercourse of confidence between man and man. In the second place, it is a thing entirely unapostolic and unevangelical, abhorred by Christ Himself, and in the eyes of men nothing less than a sin of murder, when men's souls, which should be brought unto life and salvation by means of the pastoral office, are destroyed by being deceived and defrauded in the matter of that very office. And this is what is done, when those who are appointed to a pastoral charge only use the milk and the wool of the sheep to satisfy their own bodily necessities, but have no wish or purpose to fulfil the ministry of their office for the eternal salvation of the sheep of Christ. The most holy Apostolic See, to which Christ has given all power, 'for edification, not for destruction' (2 Cor. x. 8), can command nothing which has such a sin for its issue. And a truly devoted subject of the Holy See can in no wise give heed to such a command, but must rather resist it with all his might. Such thoughts as this contemplated appointment are in fact inspired by 'flesh and blood, and not by the Father which is in heaven.'

Grossetête's letter and its result.

Such was the substance of this memorable writing. The installation of the Pope's grandson into the canonry and prebend of Lincoln came to nothing, and the resolute Bishop remained unmolested. So much we know for certain; and it may well be supposed that the men who were entrusted with the execution of the Pope's mandate, in the fatal difficulty into which they were thrown by the redoubtable protest of Grossetête, knew of no better plan than to forward it to Italy for the consideration of the Pope, without a moment's delay. Matthew Paris, the Benedictine Abbot of St. Albans, who cannot, it is true, be accepted as an unprejudiced authority, says in his chronicle

contain accurate quotations from the letters of Grossetête belong to the years 1370–78, the fact becomes certain that even as early as that date the collection existed the same in extent and order as we now know it. And as Wycliffe quotes the letters by their numbers, and assumes this order to be already known, we may very well infer that the collection is at least fifty years older, and may even be carried back in date to the thirteenth century.

that Innocent IV. was almost beside himself with rage when he saw the letter. 'Who,' he exclaimed, 'is that crazy, foolish, and silly old man who has the effrontery to sit in judgment thus upon my doings? Is not the King of England our vassal, yea, slave, who at a wink from us can shut him up in prison and send him to ruin?' But the cardinals, and especially the cardinal deacon, Aegidius, a personal friend of the bishop, are said to have quieted the Pope by representing to him 'that it was of no avail to take severe measures against Grossetête, for, to speak candidly, he was in the right, and no man could condemn him. The bishop was orthodox, and a very holy man; he was a more conscientious and holy man than they, the cardinals, were themselves. Among all the prelates he had not his match.'[1]

Whatever may be the truth of this account, it is certain that the bold answer of the bishop was ignored, and he was left in peace.

Death of Grossetête. Perhaps it was also remembered that he was now an old man, and that he could not much longer give any trouble. And so, in fact, it befell. In October of the same year, 1253, Grossetête had a serious seizure at Buckden, and on the 9th of the same month he died. On the 13th he was buried in the Cathedral of Lincoln.

Soon after his decease, it began to be reported that on the night of his death, sounds of bells, indescribably beautiful, had been heard high in the air, and ere long men heard of miracles taking place at his tomb. Fifty years later it was proposed that he should be canonised, and the proposal came at one and the same time from the king, from the University of Oxford, and from the Chapter of St. Paul's. It was Edward I., in the last year of his reign, 1307, who made the suggestion,[2] and, in so doing, gave utterance to what was in the heart of the whole kingdom. But, as may easily be supposed, the proposal did not meet with the most favourable acceptance at the Papal Court. The nation's wish was never complied with by the Curia; but none the less did the venerable bishop remain unforgotten in England, and his memory continue to be blessed through long centuries. His image was universally revered by the nation as an ideal—as the most perfect model of an honest Churchman. 'Never from the fear of any man had he forborne to do any good action which belonged to his office and duty. If the sword had been unsheathed against him, he stood prepared to die the death of a martyr.' Such

---

[1] Matth. Paris, *Hist. Maj. Angliae.* Edit., W. Watts, p. 872.
[2] The letter of Edward I. to Clement V., of May 6, 1307, is to be found in Rymer, *Foedera,* II., p. 1016, and in Wood, *Hist. Univ. Oxon.,* Vol. I., p. 105.

was the solemn testimony borne to him by his own University of Oxford, when it pleaded for his canonisation.[1]

In the public estimation of England, Grossetête was, in point of fact, a saint. In the following century he appears to have been so regarded by Wycliffe, who in numberless passages refers to him under the name of *Lincolniensis*.[2] And there is reason to think that this estimate was one not at all personal to Wycliffe himself, but in harmony with the feeling of his countrymen at large. We have the testimony of Thomas Gascoigne, who died in 1457, that Grossetête was commonly spoken of by the people as St. Robert.[3] It was natural, too, that when, at a later period, the whole of Western Christendom came to be strongly convinced of the necessity of a 'Reformation in Head and Members,' the memory of the bold and outspoken Bishop of Lincoln should have flamed up again brightly among the English friends of Church Reform.

His memory cherished.

At that period an Anglican member of the Council of Constance, the Oxford divine, Henry Abendon, in a speech which he delivered before the Council, October 27, 1415, repeatedly referred as an authority to *dominus Lincolniensis* ;[4] and on one occasion made express mention of the Memorial to the Pope which is mentioned above. As late as the year 1503, an English monk, Richard of Bardney, sung of Grossetête's life in some indifferent Latin distichs, which conclude with an invocation of him in form as a canonised saint.[5] A fact like this—that Grossetête, in spite of the Papal refusal of his canonisation, continued to live for centuries in the mouth and the heart of the English people as 'St. Robert,' is a speaking proof of the change which had already come over the spirit of the age; that the absolute authority of Papal decrees was already shaken; that the nimbus which surrounded the Holy See itself was paling.[6]

---

[1] Wood, *Hist. et Antiquit. Univ. Oxon.*, Vol. I., p. 105, from a MS. of Gascoigne. The Oxford Declaration does not belong to the year 1254, as Luard seems to suppose, p. lxxxiv., but was first made in 1307, in connection with the proposal for the canonisation of the Bishop. Wood introduced this subject under the year 1254, merely because Grossetête's death had occurred immediately before.

[2] Especially in the passage quoted above from *De Civili Dominio*, Wycliffe calls the Bishop of Lincoln a Saint, *ex istis . . . istius sancti. . . . primo sequitur*, etc.

[3] Wood, Vol. I., p. 106, as cited above.

[4] Printed in Walch, *Monimenta medii aevi*, Vol. I., Fasc. 2, p. 181 f. Comp. especially pp. 190, 192.

[5] *Precor, O pater alme, Roberte*, etc. The whole is printed, with a few omissions, in Henry Wharton's *Anglia Sacra*. Lond., 1691. Vol. II., pp. 325-341.

[6] During the period when the Papal power was at its zenith, we can as little imagine the case of a man being venerated as a saint in a considerable portion of Western Christendom, where canonisation had been positively refused by the Curia, as the converse case of a design on the part of Rome to canonise a churchman being upset by the opposition of a portion of the Catholic Church—an event which actually occurred when, in 1729, Benedict XIII. proposed to canonise Gregory VII., but was compelled to give up the idea out of regard to the decided declarations of France and Austria.

As Protestants, we have both a right and a duty to hold in honour the memory of a man like Grossetête. His creed, indeed, was not the pure confession of the Evangelical Churches; but his fear of God was so earnest and upright; his zeal for the glory of God was so glowing; his care for the salvation of his own soul and of the souls committed to him by virtue of his office was so conscientious; his faithfulness so approved; his will so energetic; his mind so free from man-fearing and man-pleasing; his bearing so inflexible and beyond the power of corruption,—that his whole character constrains us to the sincerest and deepest veneration. When, in addition, we take into view how high a place he assigned to the Holy Scriptures, to the study of which, in the University of Oxford, he assigned the first place as the most fundamental of all studies,[1] and which he recognises as the only infallible guiding star of the Church;[2] when we remember with what power and persistency, and without any respect of persons, he stood forward against so many abuses in the Church, and against every defection from the true ideal of church-life; when we reflect that he finds the highest wisdom to stand in this—'To know Jesus Christ and Him crucified'[3]—it is certainly not saying too much when we signalise him as a venerable witness to the truth, as a churchman who fulfilled the duty which he owed to his own age, and in so doing lived for all ages; and who, through his whole career, gave proofs of his zeal for a sound reformation of the Church's life.

His high character.

3.—Henry Bracton and William Occam.

A MAN of kindred spirit to Grossetête, though differing from him in important points, was Henry of Bracton, a younger contemporary of the celebrated Bishop of Lincoln.

Bracton, the greatest lawyer of England in the Middle Ages, was a practical jurist, but also a learned writer upon English Common Law.[4] Both as a municipal judge and scientific jurist, he maintained the rights of the State in opposition to the Church, and sought to define as accurately as possible the limits of the secular and the spiritual jurisdictions. In particular, he treated as encroachments of the

---

[1] *Epistolæ*, 123, p. 346.
[2] *Hac sola ad portum salutis dirigitur Petri navicula.* Ep. 115, p. 336. The *hac sola* answers completely to the Reformation principle—*verbo solo*—which constitutes the *formal* principle of Protestantism.
[3] *Epistolæ*, 85, p. 269.

[4] His work in five books, *De Legibus et Consuetudinibus Angliæ*, written in the years 1256–59, ranks among jurists, not only as the earliest, but also as the foremost scientific treatment of English law in the middle ages.

spiritual jurisdiction its claims of right in questions of patronage. On this point, it is true, Bracton and Grossetête would hardly have been of one mind; but none the less they both stood upon common ground, in being decidedly national in their spirit and views, and in offering strenuous opposition to the aggressions of the Court of Rome.

Only a few years after Grossetête's death, contests arose on constitutional questions, in which the opposition of the barons was for some time in the ascendant. At the head of this party *The Barons and* stood Simon of Montfort, Earl of Leicester, who had *the Church.* been a friend of Grossetête. In the year 1258, the Parliament of Oxford appointed an administration, which, while Henry III. continued nominally to reign, was to wield all the real power of the State; and it was by no means only the great barons of the kingdom who had a voice in this government. Earl Simon was the champion and hero of the lower clergy and the Commons, who stood behind him and his allied barons. The object in view was to put an end to arbitrary and absolute government, and to put in its place the rule of the Constitution, of Law, and of Right. The movement found its most powerful support in the Saxon population of the country. It was directed not least against the undue influence of foreigners upon public affairs. Under the powerful Edward I. (1272–1307) the kingdom again recovered its strength; and after the feeble, unfortunate reign of Edward II., national feeling was again roused by the French war of succession in the reign of Edward III. (1327–1377), when the nation gathered up its strength for the long wars with France—a struggle which had a powerful effect in developing both the national character and language.

What the kingdom had chiefly stood in need of was a higher authority and a more concentrated strength than had prevailed under Henry III., and Edward I. was exactly the man to remedy that defect. He had made many concessions, it is true, to the estates of his kingdom in the matter of Parliamentary rights, under the repeated pressure of his undertakings against Wales, Scotland, and the Continent; but he had done this without any loss to the Crown. On the contrary, the Crown had only been a gainer by the freedom and rights which had been guaranteed to the nation. It was now, for the first time, that the Crown entered into a compact unity with the nation, acquired a full national character, and became itself all the stronger thereby.

This immediately showed itself when Boniface VIII. attempted to interfere with the measures of the King against Scotland, as he had done a few years before in the transactions between England and

France. In a bull, dated June 27, 1299, Boniface not only asserted his direct supremacy over the Scottish Church as a church independent of England, but also put himself forward, without ceremony, as arbiter of the claims which Edward I. was then advancing to the Scottish Crown. 'If Edward asserted any right whatever to the kingdom of Scotland, or any part thereof, let him send his plenipotentiaries with the necessary documents to the Apostolic See; the matter will be decided there in a manner agreeable to right.'[1]

Rival claims on Scotland.

In resisting such assumptions the King found the most determined assistance in the spirit of the country itself. He laid the matter, with the necessary papers, before his Parliament, which met at Lincoln on January 20, 1301; and the representatives of the kingdom took the side of their King without reserve. The nobles of the realm sent, February 12, 1301, a reply to that demand of Boniface VIII., in which they repelled, in the most emphatic manner, the attempted encroachment. No fewer than 104 earls and barons, who all gave their names at the beginning of the document, and sealed it with their seals at the end, declared in it, not only in their own name, but also for the whole community of England, 'that they could feel nothing but astonishment at the unheard-of pretensions contained in the Papal brief. The kingdom of Scotland had never been a fief of the Pope, but, from time immemorial, of the English Crown; they had therefore, after mature consideration, with one voice resolved that the King should in no way acknowledge the Papal jurisdiction in this affair; yea, they would not even allow the King to acknowledge it, if he were himself disposed to do so. In conclusion, they implored his Holiness, in the most respectful manner, to leave untouched the rights of their King, a monarch who was entirely devoted to the interest of the Church.'[2]

It was not till later that Edward himself addressed a letter of great length to Boniface, in which he confined himself to a historical proof of his alleged rights to the Scottish Crown, and referred to the Pope's claim of jurisdiction in the matter only in the briefest way, and only to decline and protest against it; and, in point of fact, the King went forward in his measures affecting Scotland without troubling himself further in any way about the claims of the Papal Court.

Papal pretensions repelled.

It was thus that the English Crown, by an appeal to the nation, successfully repelled the unrighteous aggression of the Roman Curia;

[1] Rymer, *Foedera*, Vol. I., p. 907. Dated Anagni, June 27, 1299.   [2] Rymer, *Foedera*, Vol. I., p. 928.

and I know not if the fact has hitherto been sufficiently recognised by historians that England set an example in this business, which Philip the Fair of France only imitated a year later in his dispute with Boniface VIII., when, in April, 1302, he assembled a national Parliament. It was also in imitation of the example of the English barons that the French nobles and the Third Estate protested, in a letter to the cardinals, against the Papal pretensions. If in this case the leaning of the King upon the nation issued in benefit to the Crown, no less, on the other side, did the national attitude of the Government lend strength and emphasis to the patriotic spirit of the people. When Edward I., in the last year of his reign, proposed the canonisation of the universally venerated Bishop of Lincoln, he was only giving utterance to what was in the heart of the whole country; and the effect of the movement could only be to heighten and strengthen the interest of the nation in ecclesiastical affairs.

The ablest and most strongly-marked representative of this state of feeling in the first half of the fourteenth century was a man who was born in England, and trained under the influence of the English spirit, but who spent the later portion of his life on the Continent, partly in the University of Paris, and partly at the Court of the Emperor Louis of Bavaria. We refer to William of Occam, a man who, as a scholar, as a copious writer, as a dignitary of the Franciscan Order, and finally, as a strenuous leader of the opposition against the absolutism of the Papacy, took a position of great prominence in his day. His philosophical nominalism had a prophetic and national significance, inasmuch as it prepared the way for that inductive method of philosophising which was put forward several centuries later by able countrymen of his own, such as Francis Bacon, Thomas Hobbes, and John Locke. *William of Occam, Franciscan friar.*

But what chiefly concerns us here in Occam was his character as a keen and independent thinker on ecclesiastical matters. It is not a little remarkable that along with several other men, his personal friends of Italian birth, he was brought into a position of bold opposition to the Papacy, and came in sight of many great and free ideas, entirely through his standing as a member and provincial of the Franciscan order. It was a trifling question of the Order, but out of it was developed a grand world of thoughts.

In the year 1321 it came to the knowledge of a Dominican Inquisitor in Narbonne, in the south of France, that it was an opinion held by some that neither Christ nor His apostles had

ever, either as individuals or as a society, been in possession of
property. This proposition appeared to the Dominican
to be heretical; but a learned Franciscan in that
city, Berengar Taloni, maintained it to be perfectly
orthodox, and, ere long, the whole Franciscan order, at a general
chapter held in Perugia in June and July, 1322, declared for the
same view. Thus the point became a question of controversy
between the two great Mendicant orders.

Controversy respecting apostolic poverty.

On an appeal being carried to the Papal See in Avignon, a decision
was given on the side of the Dominicans. John XXII. (1316–1334)
in truth was as far removed from apostolic poverty as the east is from
the west. He kept his eye so steadily upon the interest of the
Papal treasury, that twenty-five millions of gold crowns in coin and
jewels were found in it after his death. Of course such a chief of
the Church could not be suspected to look upon absolute poverty as
a requirement of Christian perfection. He would have preferred,
indeed, to avoid giving a decision on the question which was at issue
between the two orders. But that was impossible. The controversy
would admit neither of silence nor delay. A decision clear and
round—yea or nay—was unavoidable.

In the years 1322–1324, the Pope pronounced against the Franciscans in a series of bulls. The two first (*Quia nonnunquam*, and *Ad Conditorem Canonum*), published in 1322, were only of a preparatory character. The third constitution of 1323 (*Cum inter nonnullos*) contained the decision upon the principle involved, declaring the proposition that Christ and His apostles were never, either singly or collectively, holders of property to be contrary to Scripture and erroneous. And, last of all, in 1324 followed two more bulls; in the constitution, *Quia quorundam*, the Pope pronounced sentence of excommunication upon the opposers of his determination; and in the bull, *Quia vir reprobus*, he rejected the appeal of Michael of Cesena, the General of the Order of Franciscans.

Papal decision against the Franciscans.

The majority of the Franciscan order now bowed to the decision, and after some years elected another general. But those who had stood forth as the firmest defenders of the doctrine of apostolic poverty withheld their submission. They left Avignon; and William of Occam, Michael of Cesena, and Bonagratia of Bergamo attached themselves, in 1328, to the service of the Emperor Louis of Bavaria.

Occam banished.

Out of this conflict between the Papal Court and the Minorites ideas developed themselves which were of the greatest importance, and which made their influence felt in succeeding centuries; and of all the polemical writings produced by the repulsed and banished Franciscans, those of Occam were by far the richest in substance. While Michael of Cesena confined himself chiefly to personal polemics of defence and attack, Occam's writings, published several years later, though not altogether silent on topics of this nature, are in the main occupied with the substance of the great objective questions in dispute; and his investigations possess, in this way, a value and width of bearing which far transcend what was of mere ephemeral interest.

This discussion, indeed, makes a highly mixed impression upon an evangelical reader who follows it after the lapse of more than 500 years. Who can miss seeing that the Franciscan, in his deep contemplation of the life of Jesus and the apostolic age, unconsciously looks at the Redeemer and His apostles from the standpoint of the begging friar, and conceives of them in a thoroughly monkish and ascetic manner? In opposing such a view, John XXII. was not without good ground to stand upon. But unquestionably the Pope fell into an error very much greater himself. Not so unconsciously, perhaps, as his opponent, he carried over to primitive Christianity the conditions of his own age; and, influenced by his own interests, he allowed himself to justify, by the example of the Redeemer and the precedent of the apostles, the whole hierarchical system of his own time, richly endowed and secularised in spirit as it was, including even the territorial possessions of the Holy See, and its well-filled treasury. And therein, no doubt, the Pope was in the wrong, and Occam, his adversary, in the right.

Occam's principles.

The deepest ground, however, of the unsparing antagonism of the Roman Court to the stringent principles of the Franciscans was, in truth, no other than this—that the Popes felt that the spirit of world-abnegation which animated these men was a tacit censure of their own spirit and habit of life; from which again sprang 'the hatred of the evil conscience.' But it was the very persecutions which this hatred prompted which served, in the course of time, to bring to full light and ripeness all the principles touching the spirituality of Christ's kingdom, which at first still lay in a deep slumber, and had only revealed themselves from afar to the prophetic sense of a few men of a larger mind than their contemporaries. Occam's whole exposition on the subject of the kingdom of Christ being not an earthly, but a heavenly and eternal kingdom—that Christ is indeed, as to His Godhead, King and Lord over all, but, as God-man, only King of His believing people, and in no respect the administrator of a worldly government—is an indirect but Scriptural criticism of the mediæval hierarchy—an unconscious evangelical protest against the Papacy in that form which it had assumed since the days of Gregory VII.

But, on the other hand, Occam's protest against Papal absolutism —against the assertion of an unlimited *plenitudo potestatis* of the Pope—is the result of clear, self-conscious, profound reflection. He declares it to be totally erroneous, heretical, and dangerous to souls, to maintain that the Pope, by the ordinance of Christ, possesses unlimited power, both spiritual and temporal. For if this were so, he might depose princes at his pleasure—might at his pleasure dispose of the possessions and goods of all men. We should all be the Pope's slaves; and in spiritual things the position would be the same. In that case the law of Christ would bring with it an intolerable slavery, much worse than the Old Testament ever knew; whereas the Gospel of Christ, in comparison with the old covenant, is a law of liberty. In this connection Occam opposes, in the most emphatic manner, the assertion of some flatterers of the Roman Court, that the Pope has power to make new articles of faith; that he is infallible; that into no error, no sin of simony, can he possibly fall. He starts from the general principle, that the whole hierarchy, including the Papal Primacy, is not an immediately Divine, but only a human order. In one place he even gives expression to the bold thought, that it would, to the general body of believers, be of more advantage to have several primates or chief priests (*summi pontifices*), than to have one only; the unity of the Church does not depend upon there being only one *summus pontifex;* the danger of moral corruption of the whole body is much greater with only one head than with several.

Protest against Papal Absolutism.

In the event of a Pope becoming heretical, every man must have the competency to be his judge, but his ordinary judge is the Emperor. But the Church at large also has jurisdiction over the Pope in such an event, and hence also a General Council, as the representative of the whole Church; the bishops, in case of need, may even depose him. Here we have a practical question anticipated, which some sixty years later became a burning question in Christendom, and not only raised but determined precisely as it was one day to be solved in actual fact.

Further, in solving the doubt, whether a Council, in case of necessity, could assemble without Papal sanction, Occam came upon thoughts entirely his own. Every society (*communitas*) and corporation can enact laws for itself, and elect individuals to act for the whole body (*vice gerant*). Now, all believers

Pope and Council.

are one body and one society (Rom. xii. 5); it is competent for them, therefore, to choose representatives of the whole body. When those thus elected meet together, they form a General Council of the whole of Christendom. He conceives of the carrying out of such a Council in this manner—that from every parish one or more should be sent to the synod of the diocese, or to the Parliament of the prince. This assembly proceeds to another election, and the meeting of all those chosen by the Diocesan Synods, or the Parliaments, constitutes the General Council. That is not a Papal Curial Synod, neither is it a church assembly constituted upon hierarchical principles; it is a Synod framed upon the parochial principle.

And yet it is not Occam's meaning to advise a leap from the ground of the absolute and sole domination of the Papacy to that of an unconditioned parochial principle, as if this latter contained in it all the safeguards of truth and weal. No; only to the Church itself as a whole, but not to any part of it (and every council is only a part of it), is the promise given that it can never fall into any error contradictory to the faith. Although all the members of a General Council should fall into error, the hope would not need on that account to be surrendered, that God would reveal His truth unto babes (Matt. xi. 25), or would inspire men who already knew the truth to stand forth in its defence. And such an occurrence must issue in glory to God, for thereby He would show that our faith does not rest upon the wisdom of men, such as are called to a General Council, but upon the Power who has sometimes chosen 'the foolish things of the world to confound the wise' (1 Cor. i. 27). In another place Occam expresses the thought that it is even possible that on some occasion the whole male sex, clergy as well as laity, might err from the faith, and that the true faith might maintain itself only among pious women. We see where all this is tending to. High above the Pope, and high above the Church itself, in Occam's view, stands Christ the Lord. 'The Head of the Church and its foundation is one—Christ alone.' Occam is conscious that his contention is for Christ and for the defence of the Christian faith.

It makes a touching and deeply mournful impression, to look into Occam's heart, as he opens it in the following confession:—

'The prophecy of the Apostle, 2 Tim. iv. 3, is now being fulfilled. Chief Priests and Elders, Scribes and Pharisees, are acting now-a-days exactly as they did then when they put Jesus on the cross. They have banished me and other honourers of Christ to Patmos. Yet we are not without hope. The hand of the Lord is not shortened yet. We live in trust in the Most

Occam's confidence and hope.

High that we shall yet one day return with honour to Ephesus. But should the will of God be otherwise, still I am sure that neither death nor life nor any other creature shall be able to separate us from the love of God, or draw us away from the defence of the Christian faith.'

By the side of this testimony of pious, joyful trust in God, we place a passage where Occam speaks of the value of his own writings and their importance for the future. This occurs in his *Dialogue*, at the point where he passes on to a discussion which we may describe as a piece of political philosophy. Here he puts into the mouth of the scholar in the *Dialogue* the following words addressed to his master:—'Although we are unable at present to produce a complete work on the subject, as no treatise upon it, to my knowledge, has ever hitherto been attempted by any other writer, still it was useful not to be altogether silent upon a subject of so much importance, that we may stir up others who have the command of books, to produce complete works upon it. My meaning is this, that by means of our essay men of future times who are zealous for truth, righteousness, and the common weal, may have their attention drawn to many truths upon these matters which, at the present day, remain concealed from rulers, councillors, and teachers, to the loss of the common weal.'

Nor, in point of fact, was this saying too much. For Occam, along with the small group of like-minded independent thinkers with whom he was associated, represents a high flight of human thought which did not pass uselessly overhead, like a transient meteor, but worked upon the minds of men with a kindling power. Out of a mere question affecting a religious order developed itself an unimagined life-force, an antagonism to the Papacy as a centralising world-power, still blended, it is true, with ascetic convictions, and even deriving its moral strength from these, and still only half conscious of the extent of its own bearings, but none the less an antagonism to the Papacy, which in its positive kernel was a contention for Christ as the alone Head of the Church. In this conflict of minds by thrust and counter-thrust there were kindled sparks of evangelical thought and feeling, and there were struck out new lights of political truth, which proved of use and advantage to succeeding generations, and rendered essential service to progress in the direction of an evangelical renovation of the Church.

His influence against the Papacy.

4.—English Church Politics in the Fourteenth Century.

It will be easily understood that ideas and sentiments like these, so far outrunning the current century, could not pass at once into the blood of the existing generation. In the first instance, only what concerned the autonomy of the State, in opposition to the Curia, was grasped and realised by the English nation during the fifty years' reign of Edward III. (1327–1377). Even the foreign wars, which fill up so large a portion of this period, were constrained to help to this end:—not, indeed, so much the expeditions against Scotland, which followed one after another during the first seven years, but mainly the French wars of succession which Edward III. commenced in 1339. These foreign relations had a reaction upon the domestic: the wars rendered increased subsidies necessary, and these were voted by the estates of the realm represented in Parliament, only at the price of guaranteed political rights and franchises, as, *e.g.*, in the Parliament of 1341. But the more closely Crown and Parliament held together, the more resolutely they opposed themselves to all foreign attempts. This the Papal Court was compelled to feel acutely, and all the more that the Court at Avignon was seen to be dependent upon the same France with which England was at war.

Growth of English patriotic feeling.

When Clement VI., immediately after his accession to the Holy See, endeavoured to make peace between Edward III. of England and Philip VI. of France, he succeeded, indeed, so far as to bring about a truce for a time; but as early as Easter, 1343, with the full assent of his Parliament, Edward roundly declined all official intervention of the Pope as head of the Church; only as a private individual and personal friend should Clement attempt a mediation.

But still more deeply felt than this refusal was the determination with which King and Parliament repudiated the Pope's nominations to English livings in favour of foreign prelates and priests. It is well known that the Popes of Avignon went far beyond the earlier Popes in draining the finances of the national churches. But, on the other side, there had also been no small growth of courage and resolution in opposing such abuses. In England, at least, the *Provisions* granted by the Pope to foreign clergy were barred in the most effectual manner. When Clement VI. had granted to two newly-made cardinals—one of them his own grandson—provisions to English dignities and incomes worth in all two thousand marks yearly, the barons, knights, and

Papal nominations and provisions.

burgesses of the realm, in Parliament assembled at Westminster, May 18, 1343, joined in an open letter to the Pope, in which they respectfully, but in a firm tone, begged for the removal of the scandal which was given by reservations, provisions, and nominations to English dignities and livings, and which had become greater under Clement than ever before. They urged that the numerous rich endowments of their country had been designed for the maintenance of God's service, for the furtherance of the Christian faith, and for the benefit of the poor parishioners, and were intended only for men who had been thoroughly instructed for their office, and who were able, in particular, to hear confessions in the mother tongue. On the other hand, by the appointment of strangers and foreigners, in some cases even of enemies of the kingdom, ignorant of the language of the country, and of the conditions of those among whom it was their duty to exercise the pastoral care, the souls of the parishioners were put in jeopardy; the spiritual cure was neglected; the religious feelings of the people impaired; the worship of God abridged; the work of charity diminished; the means of bringing forward young men of merit crippled; the wealth of the kingdom carried off to foreign parts; and all this in opposition to the design of the founders.[1]

Nor did men stop at mere representations of the case. When the cardinals referred to sent their agents to England to exercise their new rights and collect the revenues, these men fared badly enough. The population laid violent hands upon them; the king's officers put hindrances in the way of their proceedings; they were thrown into prison; and in the end were driven out of the country with insult and shame. The Pope with his own hand wrote to King Edward from Villeneuve, near Avignon, August 28, 1343, complaining of these proceedings, and requiring the King to interfere to put a stop to what was so 'unreasonable.'[2]

But Clement had ill success in this step. The King sent a reply which was by no means conciliatory, but called upon the Pope with great emphasis to do away with the practice of 'Provisions.' He referred to an urgent petition which he had received from the last Parliament, praying that a speedy stop might be put to 'impositions' of that kind, which were intolerable to the country; it was no more than the fact, he remarked, that these measures were fitted to inflict injury upon the kingdom in more ways than one, which he pointed out in terms partly borrowed

Clement VI. and Edward III.

---

[1] John Foxe, *Acts and Monuments.* Vol. II., 689.

[2] The Brief is printed in Walsingham's *Historia Anglicana.* Ed., Ridley, 1863, I., 259.

from the Parliament's petition. In addition, he brings into view the violation of right which was involved in these provisions and reservations of the Curia: the right of patronage and collation belonging to the Crown and its vassals is thereby infringed; the jurisdiction of the Crown in questions of patronate right is ignored; by the export of money, as well as by the deterioration of the priesthood, the kingdom is weakened;—on all which accounts he turns himself to the successor of the Prince of the Apostles, who received from Christ the command to feed the Lord's sheep, and not to fleece them, to strengthen his brethren, and not to oppress them, with the urgent entreaty that this burden of provisions may be taken away; that the patrons may have the use of their patronate rights; that the chapters may exercise, without hindrance, the right of election; that the rights of the Crown may remain without injury; and that the former long-descended devotion of England to the holy Roman Church may again revive.[1]

But in Avignon men did not readily give ear to representations of this sort, let them be ever so well grounded. The abuse went on as before, as far as was practicable, and the nation was at last convinced that the Papal Court was not in the least disposed to abandon a practice which was so profitable to itself. A resolution was come to to take the matter into their own hand, and to put a stop to these usurpations by the legislature of the kingdom. In 1350, the King, with consent of his Parliament, enacted a severe penal law against all who in any way should take part in the filling up of church-offices, injuriously to the rights of the King, or of the chapters or private patrons concerned. Every act of this kind was declared null and void; all offenders in this sort were threatened with fines and imprisonment; and all appeals against the same to foreign tribunals prohibited. This was the 'Statute of Provisors;'[2] which was followed three years later by another penal act, which is commonly called simply the 'Præmunire;'[3] which among other things was directed against the abuse of carrying appeals to the Pope from the English courts on questions of personal property. The law threatened offenders in this kind for the future with fine and imprisonment.

Statutes of Provisors and Præmunire.

In connection with this legislation against 'Provisions,' we naturally recall again to mind the form of the venerable Bishop of Lincoln, who, exactly one century earlier, had manfully resisted the like encroach-

---

[1] The King's reply is also in Walsingham, I., 255.
[2] *A Statute of Provisors of Benefices,* in Ruffhead, 'The Statutes,' 1786, 4to, pp. 260-64.

[3] The word *præmunire* (instead of *præmonere*) does not stand in the text of the law itself, but used to be employed in the writ of the sheriffs appointed by the law to issue.

ments, and whose spirit seemed now to inspire the whole nation. It was the same spirit, in fact, which animated Wycliffe from the commencement of his public career—who attained to manhood just at this time—the spirit of national independence boldly opposing a course of proceeding which made use of church affairs as a handle for other ends. It was no unchurchly spirit which lay at the bottom of this opposition. The very contrary was the truth. It was no mere phrase-making, still less any hypocritical dissimulation, when Edward III., at the close of the document quoted above, said of himself and his subjects, 'We all desire to render to your most holy person and to the holy Roman Church the honour which is due from us.' Only this honour rendered to the Church was not blind and unconditioned: it was manly and dignified, and was prepared, in case of need, to oppose the head of the Church himself, not only in word but in deed, in matters affecting the Church's temporalities.

In reference to this church-spirit of England, it is a significant and important circumstance, that up to a period later than the middle of the thirteenth century no sects and divisions had ever arisen in the National Church, nor any departures of any sort from the characteristic form of the Church of the West. We find no certain trace to show that during all the mediæval centuries, down to that time, any form of native heresy had ever sprung up upon the English soil.[1] Nor even were foreign heretical sects ever able to find a footing in England, however much, in the twelfth and thirteenth centuries especially, these sects spread and propagated themselves on the Continent. Only two instances are mentioned by the chroniclers of such heretics appearing in England, and in both cases they were immediately put down and extinguished.

Heretical movements.

In the first instance, under the reign of Henry II., in the year 1159, there arrived in the country a party of thirty persons of both sexes, apparently Low Germans, under the leadership of a certain Gerhard; but having soon fallen under suspicion of heresy, they were imprisoned and tried before a Synod in Oxford, by which they were found guilty, and delivered over to the secular arm. Their punishment was to be branded upon the forehead, to be flogged through the streets, and then, in their wounds and half-naked,

Followers of Gerhard.

---

[1] A letter, numbered 113, in Vol. XXIV., p. 1208, of the *Biblioth. Maxima Patrum*, from Peter de Blois, Archdeacon of Bath, to the Archbishop of York, calling upon him to arrest the progress of the enemies of the Church by Councils and severe penalties, might seem to prove a different state of matters, if the description of the heretics referred to were a little more exact. These are manifestly described as *Cathari*, but as to their doings and proceedings nothing definite whatever is stated. It is possible that the reference may be to imported Catharism, of which mention is to be made immediately.

to be driven out in winter into the open fields, where, without food and shelter, outcasts from all society, and by all men unpitied, they were left miserably to perish. But they met their fate with joy notwithstanding; they sang aloud, 'Blessed are ye that are persecuted for righteousness' sake, for yours is the kingdom of heaven.' But the monkish chronicler, heartlessly enough, makes the following comment upon the incident:—'This pious severity not only purified the kingdom of the plague which had already crept into it, but, by striking terror into the heretics, guarded against any future irruption of the evil.'[1] Between forty and fifty years later, however, at the beginning of the thirteenth century, under the reign of John, as a later writer briefly informs us, several Albigenses came into England and were burnt alive.[2]

That such merciless procedure should in the end act as a deterrent may be easily understood; and, in particular, to the Waldenses, who never seem to have made their way into England. At least, Peter of Pilichdorf, who wrote in 1444 against the Waldenses, attests that, with some other countries, England had always remained entirely pure and free from the Waldensian sect.[3] And I find an indirect confirmation of this in the circumstance, that in all the writings of Wycliffe which I have searched through in manuscript, I have never come upon a single trace to indicate that, either in his own time or in earlier centuries, heretics of any kind had made their appearance in England. Even the Waldenses are not once historically referred to by him, or so much as named. It is without all support, therefore, from original sources, when some writers put forth the conjecture that there were secret disciples of the Waldensian doctrines in England in Wycliffe's time, who only came publicly into view when emboldened by his movement and the number of his followers.

If there had been any foundation for this conjecture, the opponents of Wycliffe and his party would certainly not have omitted to make use of such a fact, which they could so easily have turned to their own advantage. They would in that case have pilloried the Lollards

---

[1] *Chronicle of the Augustinian Canon,* William of Newbury, in Yorkshire, 1208. *Historia Rerum Anglicarum Willelmi Parvi,* ad fidem codd. MSS., rec. Lond., 1856. 8vo., Vol. I., 120 f.

[2] Henry of Knighton, Canon of Leicester, in the second half of the fourteenth century, *Chronica de eventibus Angliae,* in Twysden's 'Historiae Anglicae Scriptores.' Lond., 1652. Vol. III., col. 2418.

[3] Petri de Pilichdorf *Contra Sectam Waldensium Tractatus* in Biblioth. Maxima Patrum, Lyon 1677, xxv., especially c. 15, p. 281. Here the author's drift is to show to the Waldenses a number of 'peoples and races and tongues,' where, by God's grace, all are orthodox in the faith, and have remained utterly untouched by this sect, *ubi omnes homines sunt immunes a tua secta penitus conservati;* and among these he mentions England first of all, then Flanders, etc.

as the adherents of a sect already long ago condemned by the Church. But of this, too, there is not a single trace. On the contrary, one of the earliest opponents of the Lollards, in a polemical poem written soon after Wycliffe's death, freely admits that England, which now favours the Lollards, had hitherto been free of all stain of heresy, and of every form of error and deception.[1] In a word, it is irreconcilable with the known facts of history to attempt to bring the inner development of Wycliffe or his followers into connection with any earlier manifestation of heresy on the European continent. And, in England itself, the history of the centuries before Wycliffe has not a single manifestation of the heretical kind to show which was of any continuance or of any importance.

It is no doubt true that in the intellectual, moral, ecclesiastical, and political character of the period in which Wycliffe's youth and early manhood fell, there were elements which exercised influence upon him, and received from him in turn a further development. These, however, were all elements which were compatible with true zeal for the existing Church, and with a sincere devotion to the Papal See; being, on the one hand, a certain national self-inclusion, favoured by insular position, but fostered still more by the spirit of Saxon nationality, which was evoked so powerfully during the thirteenth and fourteenth centuries, till it stood out conspicuously in the compact, united consciousness of the whole nation; on the other hand, a spirit of independence which did not shrink from defending the rights and interests of the nation and the National Church, even against all the power of the Papal See, and to wage open war against the abuses of the Church. In a word, there awoke in the Anglican Church of the thirteenth, and still more of the fourteenth centuries, 'the true Reformation spirit which can never die out in the Church, but must rather from time to time break forth afresh with rejuvenescent strength, in order to remove the ever recurring rust of abuses and mischiefs.'[2]

Awaking of the Reformation spirit.

5.—Richard of Armagh and the Mendicant Orders.

WE must at this point recall the name of an important personage in whom this Reformation spirit had a vigorous vitality—an older con-

---

[1] The poem is printed in the collection *Political Poems and Songs relating to English History,* ed. Thomas Wright (Rolls Series), Vol. I., pp. 231-249, under the title added by the editor, *Against the Lollards.* The date assigned to it, 1381, I cannot for weighty reasons regard as correct. In the seventh strophe, says the author,

O terra jam pestifera,
dudum eras puerpera
omnis sanæ scientiæ,
haeresis labe libera,
omni errore extera,
exsors omnis fallaciæ.

[2] Döllinger, *Kirche und Kirchen, Papsthum und Kirchenstaat.* München, 1861, xxx. f.

temporary of Wycliffe, to whom, as to Grossetête, he often refers, and with whom he has sometimes been placed in a closer connection than can, in our judgment, be historically justified. We refer to Archbishop Richard of Armagh, Primate of Ireland, who had a high celebrity in his day.

Richard Fitzralph studied in Oxford, under Dr. John Bakonthorpe, who was an opponent of the Mendicant Orders, and in whose steps his disciple is alleged to have walked.[1] Fitzralph was recommended to Edward III. as a man of high ability, and was promoted to be Archdeacon of Lichfield; in 1333 he became Chancellor of the University of Oxford; and finally, in July, 1347, Archbishop of Armagh. The only side on which he is still known at the present day is as the practical Churchman, especially in connection with his opposition to the encroachments of the Mendicant Orders. But in his own age and in following times he was also held in high honour as a master of theological science. The reason why nothing is now known of him in this character is, that none of his dogmatic and polemical writings have ever been sent to the press. *Career of Fitzralph.*

But in addition to theological lectures delivered in Oxford, he left important writings behind him. Among these we are told not only of a commentary on the sentences of Peter Lombard, originating in his Oxford lectures, but also of several apologetico-polemical works, directed partly against Judaism—*De intentionibus Judæorum*—partly against the Armenian Church. The latter work, his nineteen books against the errors of the Armenians, called also his *Summa*, was the principal dogmatic work of 'Richard of Armagh,' as he was commonly called, or simply '*Armachanus;*' and Wycliffe himself cites the books against the Armenians with extraordinary frequency. Richard composed this work under Pope Clement VI., about 1350, at the request of several Armenian Bishops. For since 1145 the Armenian Kings had entered into transactions and connections with Rome, which had for their aim a union of the National Church of Armenia with the Roman Church of the west. At the beginning of the fourteenth century several synods of the Armenians were held in Sis, the ancient Issus, in 1307, and in Atan (Adana) in 1316, with a view to this union. In this connection the learned Englishman wrote the extensive work referred to,[2] at the *His writings.*

---

[1] See Appendix I., by Dr. Lorimer.
[2] When King Leo IV. of Lesser Armenia applied to Pope Benedict XII. for assistance against the Saracens, the latter replied, in 1341, that before he could do anything for this object, the Armenians must renounce their many errors. A schedule of these errors was appended to the Brief, extending to the number of 117. From that time attention was directed in the west of Europe to the differences in doctrine and usage of the Armenian Church. Hence the subject and title of Richard's work, *De Erroribus Armenorum.*

instance of the Armenian John, bishop-elect of Khelat, and his brother Nerses, Archbishop of Manaz-Kjerd. Richard accordingly threw his book into the form of a dialogue. John, the bishop-elect, proposes questions, and brings forward objections. Richard himself answers and solves them. In the first six books are handled the Christological and Trinitarian doctrines; the seventh defends the Primacy of Rome; four books—8 to 11—are devoted to the Doctrine of the Sacraments; the twelfth and following to the Doctrine of the Last Things; the five remaining books closing with philosophico-theological investigations of a general kind, which form the basis of the whole work.[1]

We are told that Richard left behind him a translation of the Bible in the Irish tongue, which would have been an important fact if it had been well attested, but the allegation rests upon insufficient evidence.[2]

But we have trustworthy information on the position taken up by the Irish Primate against the Mendicant orders. The following circumstances gave rise to this incident as related by himself:

Fitzralph and the Mendicants. Having occasion to come to London on the business of his Archbishopric, he found that learned men there were engaged in animated discussions upon the question of the poverty of the life of Jesus, and whether He had even begged. This was no doubt an after effect of the debate formerly maintained between Pope John XXII. and a party of the Franciscans. The Archbishop was repeatedly asked to preach in London upon the subject, and in the Church of St. Paul he delivered seven or eight sermons in English, in which he set forth and maintained the propositions following:—

1. Jesus Christ, during His sojourn upon earth, was indeed always a poor man; but

2. He never practised begging as His own spontaneous choice.

3. He never taught any one to beg.

4. On the contrary, Jesus taught that no man should practice voluntary begging.

5. No man can either prudently or holily determine to follow a life of mendicancy.

6. Mendicancy forms no part of the rule of the Franciscans.

7. The Bull of Alexander IV. (of the year 1255) against a certain book (the *Introductorius in Evangelium aeternum*) is not directed against any of the above propositions.

8. For the purposes of confession, the parish church is always

---

[1] Vid. Dr. Karl Werner's *Geschichte der apologet. und polemisch. Literatur der Christl. Theologie.* Schaffhausen, 1864. III., 409. Comp. Hefele's *Conciliengeschichte*, IV., p. 569 f., p. 425.

[2] Joh. Bale, *Scriptorum Britannicorum Centuriæ*, p. 246.

more suitable for the parishioner than any church or chapel of the begging monks.

9. For hearing confessions the parish priest is always preferable to the begging monk.

These nine propositions evidently fall into two groups. The first group, 1 to 7, treats entirely of the moral question, in what 'Apostolical Poverty' consists; in particular, whether begging, in its proper sense, is permitted to Christian men, and is in itself a virtue —yea or nay. The second group, consisting of the last two propositions, relates to the ecclesiastical question, whether it is advisable and right that parishioners should confess in a conventual church to a mendicant monk, instead of going to their parish church and parish priest. In both respects the high-placed dignitary expressed himself in opposition to the Mendicants, to their principles, and to their privileges. No wonder that he was attacked in consequence. The Mendicant Orders raised accusations against him at the Papal Court, and he found himself obliged to undertake a journey to Avignon in 1357, and to prosecute his defence in person before Innocent VI. It is not improbable that the Irish Primate acted not only for himself, but in name and by commission of several English bishops; at least Wycliffe mentions the rumour that the bishops in general had contributed to defray his travelling charges, etc.[1] The address which he delivered at a solemn sitting of the Council, November 8, 1357, in presence of the Pope and Cardinals, affords us some insight into his ecclesiastical views.[2] His contention is simply one for the rights of the pastoral office as against the privileges of the Begging Orders, by which these rights were infringed—a contest which was renewed in France about fifty years later, in 1409 and following years.

The first and by far the larger half of the discourse must be regarded as containing the main gist of the whole. It is this part which has procured for it the title, 'A Defence of the Parish Priests;' for the second part, only a fourth of the whole, is taken up with the proof and justification of the first seven propositions quoted above. *His defence before the Pope.* The preacher lays the main stress of his argument against mendicancy upon the fact, which he proves in a very convincing manner, that the Redeemer, during His life on earth, was neither a mendicant Himself nor ever taught His

---

[1] *Trialogus*, IV., c. 36. Ed. Lechler, p. 575.
[2] *Defensorium curatorum contra eos, qui privilegiatos se dicunt*, printed in Goldast's *Monarchia*, II., pp. 1392–1410, with a better text in Brown's *Appendix ad Fascic. rerum expetend*, etc., Vol. II., pp. 466–486. This speech, however, is said to have been printed in Lyons as early as 1496, and in Paris in 1511, along with a tract in reply to it, to be mentioned further on; vid. D'Argentré, *Collectio judiciorum de novis erroribus*, I., 379.

disciples to be such. His most weighty objection against the principles which he opposes lies, if we are not mistaken, in the assertion that the notion of voluntary mendicancy rests only upon ignorance of the Scriptures, or upon the covetous pretext that the practice is conformable to the life of Christ.[1] But he takes up first the last two of those nine propositions, *i.e.*, the question of Confession and of the privileges of the Begging Orders, and he gives his reason for doing so at the beginning of his discourse. He does so, because a matter which is of common interest to the whole priesthood, yea, to all Christendom, takes precedence of a matter of private interest, whereas the principle of mendicancy is only a private affair of the Begging Orders. To guard himself, however, against misapprehension, as if he meant to assail the Begging Orders *on principle*, he not only enters a caveat at the very commencement of his discourse against any possible suspicions of his orthodoxy, but also against the surmise that his aim was to attack the whole position of the Orders which had received the sanction of the Church. What he aimed at was no more than this, that these orders should be restored to the purity of their original foundation. In other words, it was their reformation he sought, not their suppression.[2]

With regard to confession, the archbishop shows most convincingly that it is much more suitable, and, on moral grounds, much more advisable, that confession should be made to one's own parish priest (*sacerdos ordinarius*) than to a begging monk; for the former stands much nearer than the latter to any member of his own parish coming to confess, and has personal knowledge both of the man and his previous sins; and naturally such a man has more feeling of shame before one whom he sees every day, than before a stranger whom perhaps he sees face to face only once a year. It may also so easily happen, for want of personal knowledge of people, that a monk receiving confessions may absolve persons who are under the ban of excommunication. The speaker attests that in his own diocese, where perhaps there are not fewer than two hundred persons under excommunication for murders, fire-raisings, thefts, and such-like crimes, there are only forty at most of these who come for confession to him, or the confessors under him. People of this description prefer to confess to the begging friars, and are at once absolved and admitted to communion by them.

Mendicants and parish priests.

---

[1] *Unde non video, qualiter ista opinio de observantia mendicitatis spontaneæ fuerit introducta, nisi ignorando scripturam, aut fingendo eam esse Christi vitæ conformem,* ut per ipsam quæstus amplior haberetur; vid. Brown, *Fasciculus*, etc., p. 486.

[2] Brown's *Fasciculus*, etc., pp. 466–468.

On the other hand, the archbishop urges that the parish priest is a more righteous judge, and less subject also to suspicion of avaricious motives, for he has his parish living, which the begging monk has not. Let it only be remembered that the Mendicant orders, since the time when they obtained the privilege of hearing confessions, have built everywhere the most beautiful monasteries and truly princely palaces, which, before that time, they were in no condition to do. It is never heard that they impose alms upon those who confess to them, for the repairs of a parish church or a bridge, or for the upholding of a country road; they prefer to impose them entirely for their own benefit and that of their order.

But he goes still farther. It is not only the abuse of their privileges which is the cause of manifold moral mischiefs, but the very existence and normal effect of these rights viewed by themselves, and apart from all their misuse. These rights are injurious to those who go to confession, because such persons are less ashamed of their sins before strangers, and pay no regard to contrition, which is the chief part of the sacrament of penance, and are led besides to undervalue their parish priests. They are injurious to the parish priests, by estranging from them their own parishioners to such a degree that the latter soon cease to have any personal knowledge of them. The mischief even extends to the spiritual order at large. For the begging monks know how to draw to themselves young men at the universities and elsewhere by means of the confessional; they entice them into their orders, and never allow them to leave again; even during the years of noviciate they permit them to have interviews with parents at most only in presence of a brother of the monastery. One day not long ago, on going out from his inn to the street, the archbishop met with a respectable English gentleman who had made a journey to Avignon for no other purpose but to obtain from the Curia the surrender of his son, whom the begging friars of Oxford had inveigled last Easter, though yet only a boy thirteen years old. When the father hurried to Oxford to rescue him, he was only permitted to speak with his son under the eyes of several monks. 'What is this but man-stealing, a crime worse than cattle-stealing, which is a penal offence?' And this with mere children, before they have come to years of discretion! *[margin: Insidious influence of the Mendicants.]*

And let it not be said such youngsters will serve God afterwards with all the more devotion, and therefore it is allowable to gain them by promises and lies. People 'must not do evil that good may come' (Rom. iii. 8). No lie, in particular, is allowable for a good end, and no man, for any reason of his own invention, is at liberty to set aside any of the commandments. The theft, and the teaching which helps to it, are both mortal sins. Things have come to such a pass in England that laymen no longer send their sons to the universities, but prefer to make farmers of them, rather than run the risk of losing them in that fashion ; and hence it is that, whereas in the preacher's time there where thirty thousand students in Oxford, there are now no more than six thousand. And this is a great mischief for the clergy in particular, though in every faculty alike the secular students (*i.e.*, non-monks) are constantly on the decrease, while the begging orders have been making no end of gains, both in the number of their converts and their members.

Mischiefs wrought by them.

Add to this that it is now almost impossible to purchase good books at the universities, for they are all bought up by the Mendicants; in all their convents are to be found large and valuable libraries. The Archbishop himself had sent three or four of his parish priests at a time to the university, but in every instance one at least of these had left and come back again, because they found it impossible to get a Bible to buy, or any other theological book. And thus, in the end, he thinks, there will cease to be any clergy, and faith will entirely die out in the Church.

How injurious the rights of the begging order were to the Christian people, the preacher depicts from the life. Already, says he, neither great nor small can any more take a meal without the friars being of the party; and not standing at the door, as might be supposed, to beg for alms, but pushing into the houses without ceremony. Yes! and they not only eat with the guests, but carry off bread, and meat, and cheese along with them; and quite in the face of Christ's express command, they go from hall to hall, from house to house.

But lastly, these privileges work mischief even to the Mendicant friars themselves. For they lead them into disobedience of their own Rules, and cause them to fall into greed and avarice and ambitious aspiration after vain honours and dignities. As to the first, the preacher instances several violations of the original Franciscan Rule, which had all arisen from their later-obtained privileges and exemptions. But the friars are also guilty of avarice, for they have acquired only such rights as enable them to accumulate wealth. If it were not their aim to make money, they would at least hand over the burial dues, when funerals occur among them, to the parish churches and the parish priests; but this is what they never do, and their covetousness must be to blame for it. The right of hearing confessions, too, they exercise with the same view. They receive the secret confessions of women, even of princesses; and there are even instances of their finding their way into the boudoirs of the most beautiful women of noble rank. Scandals enough, which come of the abuse of the Confessional!

Although these privileges have been conferred upon them by Papal authority, they cannot continue to make use of them without mortal sin. Neither can they sincerely repent of these sins without making restitution, as far as they can, of the rights which they have taken away from the parish priests. In this connection, as in support of all his other representations, Richard of Armagh repeats the Bible-text which he has prefixed to his whole discourse, 'Judge not according to the outward appearance, but judge righteous judgment' (John vii. 24).

The good man spoke out with frankness and courage. He displays in his sermons much dialectical skill and culture, and a solid and ripe theological erudition. But more than all, he is penetrated by a spirit of intense moral earnestness and of true manhood. Richard of Armagh has the spirit of a Reformer, in the noblest sense; he is a man who fights against modern degeneracy and ecclesiastical abuses with combined wisdom and zeal; with eye uplifted to Christ, and with the sword of the Spirit, which is the Word of God.[1]

Spirit of Fitzralph.

From this point let us cast a look backwards to Grossetête, and another forward to Wycliffe. Richard of Armagh and Robert of Lincoln were in many respects men of kindred spirit, and yet in reference to the Mendicant orders all but antipodes; for the former attacked them and the latter patronised and promoted them. But let the times in which they lived be distinguished, and the two men come nearer in character to each other. At the time when Grossetête became a bishop—in the second quarter of the thirteenth century, the Franciscans (with whom he came into the nearest connection) were in their first period, and were animated by their first love; they

Comparison with Grossetête and Wycliffe.

---

[1] Of course, the Mendicant orders themselves, as a deeply interested party, could not be expected to give an impartial judgment on the proceedings of the archbishop. We learn from the *History of the Franciscans*, by Lucas Wadding, how they sought to explain such an opposition on his part. The archbishop, it was alleged, had set his heart upon getting for his own palace an ornament belonging to a neighbouring convent of the Order, and when this was refused him, and the magistrates of Armagh had taken the monks and their rights under their protection, the archbishop conceived a malicious feeling against them, and did all he could to increase the opposition which had already begun to be stirred up against the Order in England.—*Annales Minorum*, VI., p. 62.

numbered among them many men who were zealous and active for the good of souls. The Bishop of Lincoln rejoiced to find in them instruments and fellow-workers, full of insight and power. That was why he honoured them with his confidence, availed himself of their services, and extended to them his support.

A century passed away, and Richard of Armagh had experiences of the Order of quite another kind. The Mendicants were caressed by the Bishops and Popes; it fared with them as with children who are the pets of their families—they were spoiled. Distinguished by privileges, they became more and more pretentious and encroaching; the Order and its honour, its interests, and its revenues, became now the chief objects of their aims, instead of the honour of God, the good of the Church, and the salvation of souls. Degeneracy, the moral corruption of both the Mendicant orders, was an accomplished fact. In such circumstances, a man who was an honest lover of goodness, and had a clear eye for the real state of matters, must of course take up quite a different position toward these Orders from a man of the same gifts and of like spirit who had lived a hundred years earlier, when they were in their moral bloom and glory. The difference of spirit, therefore, between the two men is more apparent than real.

But we also cast a look forward from Richard of Armagh to John of Wycliffe. It has been conjectured that the latter, in the matter of the Mendicant orders, followed immediately in the footsteps of the former. This conjecture was favourably received, and for a long time has passed as a historical fact. What led to this was the circumstance that Wycliffe, in several of his writings, made repeated and very severe attacks upon these orders. But the writings referred to belong not to the earliest, but precisely to the latest which he produced. In his earlier and earliest pieces I find none of this severe antagonism to the Mendicant monks, but, on the contrary, in many places a sentiment of recognition and high esteem. This will be pointed out more fully hereafter. We have no warrant, therefore, to suppose that Wycliffe took up immediately the threads which had dropped from the hands of Richard of Armagh, when, after more than two years' residence in Avignon, he died there in December, 1359. One thing only is certain, that Wycliffe, in his earnest and presistent warfare against church evils and corruptions—a warfare which he too carried on from love to Christ the Church's Lord, and with the weapons of God's Word—had Richard Fitzralph, in particular, as one of his nearest precursors.

This discourse of the Archbishop of Armagh called forth a reply from a Franciscan doctor of theology in Oxford, Roger Conway,[1] which appeared at latest in 1362, but probably some years earlier, in the Archbishop's lifetime. This production is a very different one from the Archbishop's, both in form and in spirit, for it is not a spoken discourse, but a treatise of twice the bulk, and the whole gist of the monkish doctor is the exact opposite of the Prelate's. The Franciscan's standpoint is entirely that of the scholastic divine and the Church lawyer. In his mode of treating his subject, the throb of personal emotion is scarcely ever perceptible, which makes so pleasing an impression in the Archbishop. He asserts over and over again that the discourse of the Archbishop, whom he treats, however, with great respect, is nothing but a bill of accusation against the begging orders: so much the more vigorously does he himself take up the ground of Law and Right. It is more the 'decretalist,' the master of Church law, whom we listen to than the theologian; whereas in Richard Fitzralph the feeling of the devout Christian, of the true pastor, of the zealous Church prince pulsates throughout. But this purely legal posture of the defender of the Mendicants makes the inevitable impression that, however unconsciously, yet in substance and effect it is only the selfish interests of the orders that he undertakes to defend.

Franciscan reply to Fitzralph.

Here, too, we think we ought to mention another writing which dates from this century, more precisely from 1356, and which, so far at least, deserves to be put side by side with Richard Fitzralph's discourse, as both pieces are directed against the evils and abuses of the Church. We refer to the much-discussed, but, as it seems to us, more discussed than known tract, *Of the Last Age of the Church*, which was long ascribed to Wycliffe himself, and given out as a juvenile piece of his, but upon inadequate grounds, and in disregard of weighty reasons which make against his authorship.[2] The short essay is in substance nothing more than an indictment against the sins of the priests, and particularly against their traffic in offices (simony). This abuse the author considers to be the Third Trouble which comes upon the Church. The first consisted in the Persecutions, the second in the Heresies, the third in Simony. There is now only one more trouble to follow, viz., the Devil at broad noonday—*i.e.*, the Antichrist. This view, and a great deal more in the tract, the author borrows from the writings of Abbot Joachim of Flore; but he bases it as Bernhard of Clairvaux

Treatise on the 'Last Age of the Church.'

---

[1] His name is written Connovius or Chonoe. The piece is entitled *Defensio Religionis Mendicantium*, and is printed in Goldast's *Monarchia*, pp. 1410–1444.

[2] *Vide* Article II. in the Appendix.

also does in his sermons, on the Song of Songs (33) and upon Ps. xcv. 5, 6.

It is not difficult to discover that the author views the Church disorders of the time in a very narrow manner. He has an eye only for abuses and sins attaching to those of the clergy who are in possession of tithes and landed endowments. This shows that his position in the Church is one different from theirs—a position from which this particular side of the Church's evils comes directly under his view; that is to say, he seems to belong to one or other of the Mendicant orders, like the above-named Roger Conway. The author, besides, in his whole style of mind, is a man of contracted views; his mode of thinking is apocalyptic, in the meaner not the grander sense; and he hangs entirely upon authorities such as Abbot Joachim, or rather the pseudo-Joachim writings. This last circumstance helps us to trace with certainty his connection with the Franciscans, particularly with that portion of the Order which was attached to Joachimism, and specially to the apocalyptic views of the so-called 'Eternal Gospel.' At all events, this production was entirely destitute of any strong, living germs of principle from which any future development could spring.

6.—Thomas Bradwardine—His Teaching and Spirit.

VERY different is the case with the teaching of an important contemporary of the foregoing writer, who, like him, belongs to the period immediately preceding Wycliffe's public career.

We refer to Thomas of Bradwardine, a Christian thinker, who knew nothing higher and holier than to do battle for 'the cause of God,' and especially to bring into recognition the free and unmerited grace of God as the one only source of salvation, in the face of an age whose strong leaning, on the contrary, was to build salvation upon human merit. Nor did he entirely fail in gaining the age's concurrence in his teaching. His contemporaries held him in high esteem; they gave him the honourable title of the 'Profound Doctor' (*Doctor Profundus*).[1] The lectures delivered in Oxford, in which he expounded his doctrine, found such high acceptance that many of his auditors, including men of high position, made repeated requests to him to embody his views in a work for publication. And Wycliffe in particular, who could scarcely have known him personally, was full of esteem for

Bradwardine's doctrine of grace.

---

[1] It seems to me very probable that this epithet may have been suggested to his admirers by his frequent use of the word *profound*, to denote the mysteries of truth, *e.g.*, *profundissima haec abyssus, De Causa Dei*, p. 808.

him, which he manifests upon every mention of his name, although he strongly opposes some of his dogmatic views. We believe that we are not mistaken in maintaining that the principles which lay at the basis of Bradwardine's teaching were not without important influence upon Wycliffe. In the fifteenth century, also, his credit still stood very high. A man like John Gerson (died 1429) often quoted him as an authority in his work on *The Spiritual Life of the Soul*.

At the period of the Reformation he seems to have been little known, but at the beginning of the seventeenth century George Abbot, Archbishop of Canterbury (1610–1633) revived the memory of his celebrated predecessor, and had the merit of suggesting and promoting the publication of his principal work, which was prepared for the press by Henry Savile, Warden of Merton College, upon the basis of a collection of six manuscripts.[1] But this service to his earlier fame came too late, for Bradwardine and his work have never obtained, in later times, the high consideration to which they are entitled.[2]

Thomas of Bradwardine[3] was born near the end of the thirteenth century, but where and in what year cannot be determined with certainty.[4] He takes notice himself, on one occasion, that his father lived in Chichester.[5] As, however, it appears, from Oxford documents of the year 1325, that he then held the office of a Proctor of the University, it is concluded, on good grounds, that he must have been born in 1290 at the latest. Further, we have certain knowledge that he went to Oxford as a student, and was there admitted into Merton College, which had been founded in 1274. Here he studied not only scholastic philosophy and theology, but also mathematics and astronomy, with such success as to obtain the highest reputation in all these branches of learning.

It was at this period, also, that an incident occurred to him which

---

[1] *Thomæ Bradwardini Archiepiscopi olim Cantuariensis De Causa Dei, et de Virtute Causarum Libri tres.* Lond., 1618, fol. Edited by Henry Savile, Head of the same College in Oxford (Merton) where Bradwardine had once been a student and fellow.

[2] In Germany, Schroeckh, it is true, in his *Kirchengeschichte*, gave a pretty long extract from the *Causa Dei*, v. 34, pp. 226–240. But from his time down to the present day, if I am not quite mistaken, our most learned Church historians have bestowed little attention upon the work, or as good as none at all. Neander, at least, in his *General History of the Christian Religion and Church*, has passed over Bradwardine in profound silence; while Gieseler, though he gives several important passages from him (*Lehrbuch der Kirchengeschichte*, 3 edit., II., p. 239), has entirely misconceived the fundamental principle of his teaching; as Baur also does, in his *Christliche Dogmengeschichte*, p. 265, 2 edit.

[3] The most authentic account of his life is contained in Savile's Preface to the *Causa Dei*.

[4] The small village in the county of Hereford, not far from the border of Wales, from which Thomas took his surname, is still called Bredwardine.

[5] *De Causa Dei*, III., c. 22.

gave a decisive turn to his inner life, and which we fortunately learn from his own pen. His narrative is as follows:—'I was at one time, while still a student of philosophy, a vain fool, far from the true knowledge of God, and held captive in opposing error. From time to time I heard theologians treating of the questions of Grace and Free Will, and the party of Pelagius appeared to me to have the best of the argument. For I rarely heard anything said of grace in the lectures of the philosophers, except in an ambiguous sense; but every day I heard them teach that we are the masters of our own free acts, and that it stands in our own power to do either good or evil, to be either virtuous or vicious, and such like. And when I heard now and then in church a passage read from the Apostle which exalted grace and humbled free-will,—such, *e.g.*, as that word in Romans ix., "So then it is not in him that willeth, nor in him that runneth, but in God that showeth mercy," and other like places,—I had no liking for such teaching, for towards grace I was still unthankful.[1] I believed also with the Manicheans, that the Apostle, being a man, might possibly err from the path of truth in any point of doctrine. But afterwards, and before I had become a student of theology, the truth before mentioned struck upon me like a beam of grace, and it seemed to me as if I beheld in the distance, under a transparent image of truth, the grace of God as it is prevenient both in time and nature to all good deeds—that is to say, the gracious will of God which precedently wills, that, he who merits salvation shall be saved, and precedently works this merit of it in him, God in truth being in all movements the primary Mover. Wherefore, also, I give thanks to Him who has freely given me this grace (*Qui mihi hanc gratiam gratis dedit*).'[2]

Spiritual awakening.

From this interesting testimony from his own lips, it appears that Bradwardine, while still a student, and even before he had begun the regular study of theology, had experienced a spiritual awakening which brought him off from the Pelagian way of thinking, and led him to the conviction that the grace of God is prevenient to all God-pleasing action, instead of being acquired by such action preceding. This awakening had evidently occurred in connection with such utterances of St. Paul as that in Romans ix. 16, which had suddenly struck upon the young man's soul with a clear light and arresting force, insomuch that from that day forward the all-determining power of grace became the central truth of his Christian thinking.

[1] *Ingratio mihi gratia displicebat.* The word-play here cannot be imitated in English.

[2] *De Causa Dei*, Lib. I., c. 35, p. 380.

It has been already mentioned that Bradwardine held a University office in 1325. We next hear of him delivering lectures for some time as a Doctor of Theology in the University, by which he laid the foundation of his theological renown, and at a later date he became Chancellor of St. Paul's in London. *Doctor and royal Chaplain.* When the war with France broke out, and Edward III. made the campaign in person, John Stratford, Archbishop of Canterbury (1333-1348) proposed him to the King for war chaplain and confessor. In this capacity he accompanied the King in his campaigns in 1339 and subsequent years, and so great was his religious and moral influence upon Edward and his army, upon whom he knew how to press the claims of humanity, that many historians of those wars were convinced that the English victories were more due to the holiness of this priest than to the warlike virtues of the King and the valour of his troops.

In 1348 Archbishop Stratford died, and the chapter of Canterbury chose Bradwardine to be his successor; but the King's attachment to him was such that he could not make up his mind to release him from attendance on his person. *Archbishop of Canterbury.* But upon the death of John Ufford, who was nominated in his stead in May, 1349, before receiving consecration, and the chapter having a second time made choice of Bradwardine, the King at length gave his consent to the arrangement. Thomas of Bradwardine was nominated Archbishop by King and Pope, was consecrated in Avignon in the beginning of July, and returned immediately to England to assume his office. But only a few weeks after, August 26, 1349, he died in the Palace of Lambeth.

Bradwardine's theological views are exhibited in a systematic form in the work already named. It bears the title *Of the Cause of God*, for the author has the consciousness of appearing like an advocate in defence of God's honour, in standing forward to oppose Pelagianism, and to exalt the agency *Bradwardine's 'Causa Dei:' anti-Pelagian.* of God's free and unmerited grace in the conversion and salvation of man. He by no means conceals from himself that in so doing he is swimming against the current of prevailing opinion, for it is his own remark that 'the doctrine is held by many either that the free will of man is of itself sufficient for the obtaining of salvation; or if they confess the need of grace, that still grace may be merited by the power of the free will, so that grace no longer appears to be something undeserved by men, but something meritoriously acquired. Almost the whole world,' he says, 'has run after Pelagius and fallen into error.' But Bradwardine does not allow himself to be disheartened by this state of things. He knows for certain that one man, if the Lord is with him, will be able to chase a thousand foes, yea to put twelve thousand to flight (1 Sam. xviii. 7).

This joyful courage in conflict, this devout confidence of victory in pleading the cause of God's grace as the only source of salvation, cannot fail to remind us of the Reformers, who were essentially heralds of the same grace, and opposers of the delusion that salvation can be earned by human merit. The method, it is true, which the scholastic divine followed was different from theirs, owing to the peculiar character of mediæval culture. The Reformers went to work theologically, Bradwardine philosophically. He gives as his reason for adopting this method, that the later Pelagians had asserted that Pelagius had been overcome purely by church authority and by theological proofs, but in a philosophical and rational way it had never been possible to confute him. Bradwardine's design, therefore, is to make use mainly of philosophical arguments and authorities. In regard to authorities he adheres, in fact, so closely to his declared design, that he gives more space to the sayings of philosophers, old and new, and attaches more stress to them, than he does to his own independent reasonings. However, he also elucidates the question theologically, namely by arguments of Scripture and appeals to the Fathers and Scholastics, with the view, as he says himself, of showing the right sense of many passages of Holy Scripture and the Fathers, which had often been misunderstood and perverted by the Pelagians of ancient and later times.

Waiving, for want of space, any analysis of the doctrinal contents and reasonings of a work so bulky and profound, it may be observed, in general terms, that the scientific success of the performance is less satisfactory than the religious and moral spirit with which it is imbued. For the absolute determinism which Bradwardine sets forth, labours under an inappropriate mixing up of metaphysical and physical ideas with an ethical question, and thus rests the doctrine that salvation is grounded exclusively upon grace upon an insecure foundation.

Scientific defects of the work.

But the spirit which animates him is worthy of all recognition. He is filled with a moral pathos—a lofty earnestness of Christian piety, which cannot fail to make the deepest impression.[1] His drift is to exhibit grace as a free and unmerited gift of God, and to strike down every imagination of human merit

Its spirit.

[1] In proof of this, I point to the fervent prayer with which Bradwardine, towards the close of the work, begins cap. 50 of Book III., p. 808. He invokes the Redeemer thus :—' Good Master—Thou, my only Master—my Master and Lord, Thou, who from my youth up, when I gave myself to this work by Thy impulse, hast

in the work of conversion. It is for this reason that he controverts in particular the favourite dogma of the Scholastics that man can qualify himself to receive grace, in other words, that he can *deserve* grace, if not to the strict extent of full worthiness (*de condigno*), still in the sense of meetness and suitableness (*de congruo*). To acquire merit before God, Bradwardine holds to be impossible for man in any sense whatsoever.[1] He who affirms the contrary turns God, in effect, into a poor trafficker; for he who receives grace on the footing of any kind of merit, has purchased the grace and not received it as a free gift.

Bradwardine sets out, in fact, as pointed out above, from his own experience—from actual life—and he keeps actual experience ever in his eye. And in regard to the authorities for the doctrine of unmerited grace to whom he cares most to appeal, he is thoroughly alive to the fact that it was by their own living experience that they too were brought to the knowledge of that grace. The Apostle Paul, for example, was 'a chosen vessel of grace,' inasmuch as, at a time when he was not thinking of good works at all, nor was even standing aloof from deeds of wickedness; at a time when he was thirsting for Christian blood, and was even persecuting the Lord Himself, suddenly a light from heaven shone round about him, and the grace of Jesus Christ at the same instant preveniently laid hold upon him. He speaks of the Apostle as emphatically a child of grace, who, in gratitude for the same, makes devout and honourable mention of this grace—his mother—in almost all his epistles, vindicating her claims, particularly in his Epistle to the Romans, where he makes grace the subject of a large and acute investigation[2] which fills the Epistle almost from

taught me up to this day all that I have ever learned of the truth, and all that, as Thy pen, I have ever written of it,—send down upon me, also now, of thy great goodness, Thy light, so that Thou who hast led me into the profoundest of depths mayest also lead up to the mountain height of this inaccessible truth. Thou who hast brought me into this great and wide sea, bring me also into the haven. Thou who hast conducted me into this wide and pathless desert, Thou my Guide, and Way, and End, lead me also unto the end. Show me, I pray Thee, Thou most learned of all teachers, show to Thy little child, who knows no outlet from the difficulty, how to solve the knot of Thy Word so hardly knit. . . . But now I thank Thee, serenest Lord, that to him who asketh, Thou hast given; to him that seeketh, Thou hast shown the way; and to him that knocketh, Thou hast opened the door of piety, the door of clearness, the door of truth. For now when Thou liftest the light of Thy countenance upon Thy servant, I believe I see the right understanding of Thy Word,' etc. In one place, after he had been warmly defending Augustine against a misinterpretation of Peter Lombard, and had subjected the scholastic to a somewhat sharp critique, maintaining that the latter interpretation is in direct opposition to the meaning of that Father (Lib. II., c. 10, p. 502), he is almost alarmed at his own boldness, and pleads in excuse for himself 'the zeal for the house of God and catholic truth, which fills him with a vehement ardour against the error of the Pelagians; for it is not against Lombard himself that he has said a word, but against his error, because it is so nearly akin to the false teaching of Pelagius.'

[1] *De Causa Dei*, I., c. 38. p. 319. Compare c. 39, p. 347.

[2] *Ib.* I., c. 43, p. 392.

beginning to end. And quite in a similar spirit he remarks upon Augustine that, 'like the Apostle, he was at first an unbeliever, a blasphemer, and an enemy of the grace of Jesus Christ, but after the same grace had converted him with like suddenness, he became, after the apostle's example, an extoller, a magnificent and mighty champion of grace.'[1] And like the Apostle Paul, like Augustine the great church-father of the west, Thomas Bradwardine too became, by the light from heaven which shone upon him in his youth, an extoller and champion of the grace of God, in opposition to the Pelagian and self-righteous spirit which prevailed in his time.

It was by no means his intention, indeed, in so doing, to place himself in antagonism to the Church of Rome. On the contrary, he *Bradwardine and Rome.* declares expressly his steadfast belief in the doctrinal authority of the Church. He submits his writings to her judgment; it is for her to determine what is orthodox in the questions which he has investigated; he wishes with all his heart to have her support where he does battle with the enemies of God; where he errs, to have her correction; where he is in the right, to have her confirmation.[2] But still, in the last resort, he consoles himself with the help of God, who forsakes no one who is a defender of His cause.[3]

7.—'The Vision of Piers Plowman.'

WHILE the learned Doctor was defending God's cause with the weapons of science, and seeking to bring back his age from the paths of Pelagian error into the one only way of salvation, the same cry for grace was also heard from the conscience of the common people, in their feeling of the urgent need of a better state of things.

About twelve years after Bradwardine's death, this feeling of society found expression in a great popular poem, which yet remains *Author of the 'Vision.'* to be noticed by us as a speaking sign of the times. We refer to *The Vision of Piers Plowman*, which reveals to us, not so much by the social position of its author, as by the circle of readers for whom he wrote and the spirit of which the work is full, the deep ferment which at that time was spreading through the lowest and broadest stratum of the English people. The author himself undoubtedly belonged to the educated class, or rather to the learned class, which was then almost identical with it. He is familiar with the whole learning of his time; he knows the Classics

---

[1] *De Causa Dei*, I., c. 35, p. 311.— *Factus est gratiæ laudator, gratiæ magnificus ac strenuus propugnator.*

[2] *Ib.* Preface, p. 7. Also the end of the work, III., c. 53, p. 872.
[3] *Ib.* p. 8.

and the Fathers, the Scholastics and the Chroniclers, and also the Canon Law; he quotes the Bible according to the Vulgate and the 'Glossa;' quotes likewise Latin Church hymns in the original; in short, he was a scholar, and probably a monk. In the sixteenth century the tradition existed that his name was Robert Longland or Langland, born at Cleobury Mortimer, in Shropshire, educated in Oxford, and then admitted a monk in the Benedictine Priory of Great Malvern, Worcestershire.

Several allusions to localities such as the Malvern Hills and the like, point to the fact that he must have lived in the west of England, on the border of Wales. Perhaps he sprang from the agricultural population; at all events, he shared their feelings, and wrote for them and from their point of view; and this he did to such good purpose, that his poetry went straight to the people's hearts, and continued to be loved by them and committed to memory, and frequently imitated, for several generations, down to the middle of the fifteenth century.

From the first appearance of this poem, the figure of Piers Plowman became, and long continued to be, a favourite one with the friends of moral and religious reform. The great popularity of the work is attested by the very considerable number of manuscripts of it which still exist, most of them written towards the end of the fifteenth century.[1] Add to this the circumstance that these manuscripts are seldom written in a beautiful hand, and are scarcely ever adorned with illuminated initials, which is a pretty plain proof that they were not intended for the higher ranks of society, but for the middle class. A highly remarkable document of the time of the Peasants' War, under Richard II., viz., the 'Call' of the ringleader, John Ball, to the people of Essex, contains several manifest reminiscences of Piers Plowman.[2] The poet himself, however, was as little a sower of sedition as he was a heretic. He preaches constantly the duty of obedience to the higher powers. But the pleasure he takes in lowering the great in the estimation of the people, and in raising the credit of the lower classes, could not fail to make him a great favourite with the multitude. And although he did not attack a single doctrine of the Church, yet his unsparing exposure of the sins of the clergy must have aided the growing public sentiment in favour of reform.

In view of the oppression which prevailed among the nobility, the

Popularity of the Poem.

---

[1] In the British Museum there are eight of these MSS., from ten to twelve in the different libraries of Cambridge, and as many in those of Oxford, etc.

[2] In Walsingham's *Historia Anglicana*, under the year 1381. Ed., Riley, II., p. 33 f.

corruption among the clergy, and the dishonesty among the tradesmen, the simple heart of the peasant appears to the poet to be the only remaining seat of integrity and virtue. It is the husbandman in his mean position, not the Pope and his proud hierarchy, who exhibits upon earth an image of the humble Redeemer. In its language and poetical form, too, the work has quite a popular cast. With the exception of the Latin citations, and some Norman-French phrases which occasionally occur, the language is pure Middle-English; while in form it is the most beautiful example extant of old Anglo-Saxon verse. For it is not rhyme, properly so called, which is here used, but what is called alliterative rhyme. Instead of the Anglo-Saxon alliteration, the Normans, since the twelfth century, had introduced the *romaunce* rhyme, which continued in prevailing use till the middle of the thirteenth century. Later, we find in use a combination of rhyme and alliterative in one and the same line. Still, it is not improbable that during the whole of that time the pure Saxon alliterative continued to maintain itself along with the Anglo-Saxon tongue among the lower strata of the population. Its coming up again to the surface, about the middle of the fourteenth century, appears to be only one aspect of the great social and national movement before referred to which took place at that period. Seen from this point of view, in the literary history of the country, Langland's poem has a special claim upon our attention.

Form and language of the Poem.

The old Saxon alliterative verse was now so much again in favour that it was used in long romances like *William and the Werewolf*, a position which it continued to hold as late as the fifteenth century, at which date it found imitators even in Scotland. The author of *Piers Plowman* is well acquainted indeed, it is true, with common rhyme, and he introduces it occasionally, but only in Latin of the ecclesiastical type. But in his own English composition he employs exclusively alliterative rhyme; his constant usage being the following, that in every connected couplet of lines (each line having two rising and two falling accents), the two most important words of the first line begin with the same letter, while in the second line the first accented word also begins with it.[1]

The poem belongs to the allegorical class, and consists of a long series of visions, in which the poet has revelations made to him in the

---

[1] *E.g.* Vs. 1901 f. The command of God to Saul in his war with the Amalekites, to put every man, woman, and child to death, as well as the cattle, is expressed thus:—

'Burnes and bestes,
bren hem to dethe,
widwes and wyves,
women and children.'

way of dreams, of the condition of human society, and of various truths relating to it. The date of the composition admits of being fixed pretty exactly. That dreadful plague, which, under the name of the Black Death, laid waste the half of Europe in 1348 and following years, was already several years past. Mention is made more than once of the 'Pestilence;' it forms, so to speak, the dark background from which the figures stand out. But a second 'sickness' is also referred to which raged in England in 1360–62, and with this agrees the circumstance that the lines, beginning with number 1735, contain an undoubted allusion to the peace of Bretigny, which was concluded in the year 1360, and formed an important incident in the history of the English and French war. Further, the poet touches in vv. 2499 seq. upon a great storm from the south-west, which occurred on a 'Saturday evening,' to which he alludes also in vv. 4453 seq. We know from chronicles that this tempest, which threw down towers and high houses, and almost all the great trees, took place on January 15, 1362,[1] and the exactness with which the date of that event is fixed by the poet warrants us in assuming that the poem must have been written no long time thereafter, perhaps at the end of 1362.[2]

Its date.

The poet goes forth, in the warm summer time, to wander into the wide world. On a May morning, already fatigued by his walk, he lays himself down on the Malvern Hills beside a well, and falls asleep. There, in a dream, he sees wonderful things—upon a hill in the east a tower, built with great art, the tower of truth; in the west the fortress of care, where dwells the wicked fiend. Upon a charming plain between the two he sees a multitude of men of all ranks and conditions, rich and poor, going about their different works and ways. Clergy, too, are not wanting, begging friars, preachers of indulgences, priests in the service of the King or the nobles, and so forth. With this begins the first of the poet's visions, of which the work, closely examined,

Summary of the first vision.

---

[1] Walsingham, *Historia Anglicana.* Ed., Riley, I., 296.

[2] Our citations are from the edition of the poem, 1856, by Thomas Wright, 2 vols. 8vo, London. This is properly a second edition, following upon that which was prepared by Pickering. The Introduction, from which we have derived several of the facts mentioned above, was drawn up by Pickering, after whose death Thomas Wright, the well-known historian of literature, took charge of the new edition. As early as the sixteenth century two different editions of the Vision appeared —the first, published in 1550, was edited by Crowley, and went through three editions in a single year. Crowley belonged to that estimable class of publishers who in the sixteenth century united in themselves the character of the scholar and author with that of printer and bookseller, and who deserved so well of literature. The other edition, which appeared in 1561, was also published in London by a famous printer, Owen Roger. In 1813 Whitaker published an edition of the book, upon the authority of a MS. which exhibits a peculiar recension of the text.

is found to contain ten, although this number does not at once meet the eye; for the usual division of the text into twenty *passus* taken from the manuscript copies is rather a superficial one. The visions have a tolerable amount of connection with each other, though by no means a very close one.

A variety of allegorical figures step upon the scene; some talking, some acting, and occasionally a sort of drama developes itself. First appears an honourable lady—the Church—and instructs the poet in the significance of the spectacle before him, and especially on the point that truth is the truest of all treasures, and that the chief subject of truth is nothing else but love and beneficence. Then enters in dazzlingly rich array the lady 'Reward,' *i.e.*, earthly reward. To her all ranks and conditions of men do homage. She is on the point of being betrothed to 'Falsehood,' instead of to 'Truth.' Then 'Theology' puts forward his claim to her hand, and all parties repair to Westminster to bring the matter to a judicial decision; but 'Truth' hurries on before to the king's palace, and speaks in the ear of the knight 'Conscience.' The knight speaks with the king, and the king gives command to put 'Reward' in prison as soon as she arrives. But in prison she fares by no means amiss. The judges in Westminster themselves pay court to her, a begging friar visits her, hears her confession, and gives her absolution. At last the king sends for her to his presence, gives her a reprimand, and sets her at liberty upon her promises of amendment; he even proposes to wed her to his knight 'Conscience,' but the knight, while thanking him in the most courtly terms, draws a picture of her character in the blackest colours. She defends herself in a way to win for her the king's grace, whereupon 'Conscience' appeals to 'Reason,' and, in the end the king takes 'Conscience' and 'Reason' to be his councillors.

The poet awakes, but soon falls asleep again, and now begins the second vision. He sees again the same plain full of people, to

Second vision.

whom 'Reason' is preaching a sermon, in which he tells every rank and condition of people his mind. The sinners before him are seized with remorse. They fall upon their knees, and 'Penitence' gives them absolution. And now thousands rise to their feet and set out on a pilgrimage to 'Truth.' But nobody knows the way. At last a ploughman calls out that he knows the way. It is here that Piers Plowman comes upon the scene. He offers to show the pilgrims the road in person if they will only wait till he has ploughed and sown a bit of ground, and in the meantime several help him at his work. When it comes, however, to the ears of 'Truth' that Piers purposes to make a pilgrimage to her, she sends him a letter of indulgence, desiring him to stay at home and work, and informing him that the indulgence is applicable to all who assist him in his work, a message which awakens among all the greatest joy. But, in the end, nothing more is found in the brief of indulgence than these two lines: 'And those who have done good shall go into everlasting life, but those who have done evil, into everlasting fire.' Then the poet awakes again; he reflects upon his dream, and he is convinced that 'Do Good' will be better in the last judgment than a whole pocketful of indulgences, or letters of fraternity.

From the third to the tenth vision the representation principally turns upon the three allegorical persons, 'Do Good,' 'Do Better,' and 'Do Best.' The allegorical action passes over more and more into didactic poetry, 'the Plowman' coming repeatedly upon the scene, but in such a way that under the transparent veil of that figure the Redeemer Himself is here and there to be recognised. *Third to tenth visions.*

The whole drift of the poem is to recommend practical Christianity. The kernel of its moral teaching is the pure Christian love of our neighbour—love especially to the poor and lowly; a love of our neighbour reaching its highest point in patient forbearance, and love towards enemies—a love inspired by the voluntary passion of Christ for us. As the 'Luxemburgers' (a false coin then circulating widely in England) resemble a 'sterling' in the stamp, but are of base metal, so many nowadays bear the stamp of the heavenly King and His crown, but the metal—the soul—is alloyed with sin. The poet accordingly lays bare, on the one hand, the evil works and ways of all ranks and conditions of men, dealing castigation round among all classes with the lash of his satire; while, on the other hand, he commends the good wherever he finds it. That he is by no means a heretic has already been remarked. He assumes without question the whole body of Church doctrine; the doctrine of transubstantiation, *e.g.*, he takes for granted as something self-evident; and however much value he attaches to the conscience and the natural understanding of man, he is by no means a despiser of learning, and especially of theology. But what he demands is, that the seven liberal arts and every science should be cultivated in no selfish spirit, in order to acquire wealth; nor from a motive of vanity, in order to be styled 'Magister;' otherwise men only lose their time in them; but from love to our Lord and to the people. In other words, learning has value in his eyes only when benefit accrues from it to mankind; and *Meaning of the allegory.*

therefore he thinks it a practice to be censured when mendicant friars and masters of arts preach to the people about matters above human comprehension, instead of speaking to them of the Ten Commandments and the seven sins. Such men only wish to show off their high learning, and to make a boast of it; they do not act from sincere love to their neighbour.

On the other hand, he commends all princes and nobles, bishops and lawyers, who in their dignified places are useful to others, and render real service to the world. But 'Truth' gives her 'brief and seal,' not only to men of learning and rank, but also to men of trade and traffic, to assure them that they shall not come short of salvation, if, with all their diligence in trade and money-making, they give out of their gains for the building of bridges, the feeding of the poor, to help in sending children to school, or teaching them a trade, or in setting out poor young women in marriage, and in promoting the cause of religion. Industrious and honest married people are also highly commended; it is they who hold the world together, for from marriage spring both kings and knights, emperors and servants, father-confessors, holy virgins and marytrs. Evidently Piers the Plowman is made the chief figure of the poem, not merely on account of his humble condition in life, but also to do honour in his person to labour, joined with the fear of God. Both points of view are inseparably connected in the poem. Undoubtedly there is something of a democratic spirit in the teaching of the author, but it is a Christian democracy, like that word of the Redeemer, 'To the poor the gospel is preached.' More than once it is remarked by the poet how much better off in that respect people in low condition are than the high-placed and the educated. The seven sins are far more dangerous for the rich than for the poor. Augustine himself (the most enlightened doctor and the greatest of the four, Ambrose, Augustine, Jerome, and Gregory the Great) is appealed to as a witness for this, for the poet has read in one of his sermons the passage, 'Behold the ignorant themselves take the kingdom of heaven by violence.'

Its democratic tendency.

That none come into the kingdom of God sooner than the poor and lowly is a thought which he dwells upon in several parts of the poem. For the Church the poet cherishes deep veneration, but this by no means prevents him from speaking openly of her faults. In one place he makes the general remark, that while uprightness and holiness spring from the Church by the instrumentality of men of pure character and life, who are the teachers of God's law, all sorts of evil, on the other hand,

Its view of the Church and clergy.

spring from her, when priests and pastors are not what they ought to be. What he has chiefly to censure in the priesthood of his time is their worldliness, their sins of selfishness and of simony. Other shortcomings and failings, indeed, are also mentioned, as when the ignorance of many priests is satirised by the introduction of a curate who knows nothing of the 'cardinal virtues,' and never heard of any 'cardinals' but those of the Pope's making, or when 'Indolence' owns frankly that he has been priest and parson for more than thirty winters, but can neither sing by notes nor read the lives of the saints. He can hunt horses better than tell his parishioners the meaning of a clause in *Beatus Vir*, or *Beati Omnes* in the Psalter.

But it is the worldliness of the clergy that the satirist chiefly lashes. His complaint of the abuse that foreign priests should have so much office and power in England, reminds us vividly of Grossetête's demands, as well as of the measures which King and Parliament, twenty years before, had adopted against Papal provisions and reservations. Hardest and bitterest of all are his complaints of the self-seeking and avarice which prevail in the Church.

'Conscience' complains before the king's tribunal of the Lady 'Reward,' on this as well as other grounds, that she has infected the Pope with her poison, and made evil the holy Church. She is in the confidence of the Pontiff, for she and 'Master Simony' seal his bulls; she consecrates bishops, be they ever so ignorant; and she takes care for the priests to let them have liberty to keep their mistresses as long as they live. Time was when men lived in self-denial and privation, but nowadays men value the yellow gold piece more than the cross of Christ, which conquered death and sin. When Constantine endowed the Church with lands and lordships, an angel was heard to cry aloud in Rome, This day the Church of God has drunk venom, and the heirs of St. Peter's power 'are a-poysoned all.'[1]

> 'If possessions be poison,
> And imperfect them make,
> Good were to discharge them
> For holy Church sake,
> And purge them of poison
> Ere more peril befall.'

---

[1] *Passus* xv., v. 10, 607; 10, 659. The poet proceeds upon the mediæval tradition of the Donation of Constantine. Comp. Döllinger, the *Pope-Fables of the Middle Age*. Munich, 1863, p. 61. Like the poet of our 'Visions,' Dante, in the 'Inferno,' canto xix., v. 115, curses that Donation as the source of all the avarice and simony in the Church—

'A hi Costantin, di quanto mal fa matre
Non la tua conversion, ma quella dote,
Che de te pere il primo ricco patre!'

The legend in particular of the angel's voice, *Hodie effusum venenum in ecclesia*, is found in the scholastic divines, chroniclers, and poets of the thirteenth century. See Döllinger, as above.

The suggestions of this passage take the form in another place of
Predictions of reform. a prophecy—the prophecy of a coming king, who will punish with heavy blows all monks and nuns and canons who have broken their rules, and, in league with his nobles, will reform them by force.

> 'And yet shall come a king
> And confess you all
> And beat you, as the Bible telleth,
> For breaking of your rule,
> And amend you monks and monials,
> And put you to your penance,
>   *Ad pristinum statum ire.*
> And barons and their bairns,
> Blame you and reprove.'

If it is the 'monks possessioners,' or landed orders, who are here meant, neither are the Mendicant orders spared in other places, as, *e.g.*, in the passage where a begging friar visits the all-fascinating Lady 'Reward' in person, and gives her absolution in return for a horse-load of wheat, when she begs him to be equally obliging to noble lords and ladies of her acquaintance who love to wanton in their pleasures. 'And then,' says she, 'will I restore your church for you, and build you a cloister-walk, and whiten your walls, and put you in painted windows, and pay for all the work out of my own purse; so that all men shall say I am a sister of your house.'

It is thus that the Visions of Piers the Plowman attack, not indeed the doctrine of the Church of that age, but in the most outspoken manner, all the prevailing sins of the clergy from the highest to the lowest, and in so doing, render distinguished service in helping forward the work of reform.[1]

[1] See Appendix III., by Dr. Lorimer.

CHAPTER II.

WYCLIFFE'S YOUTH AND STUDENT LIFE.

1.—Birthplace and Family.

WE are more accurately informed of Wycliffe's birthplace than of the date of his birth, and we owe this information to a learned man of the sixteenth century, John Leland, who has been called the father of English antiquaries.[1]

In his *Itinerary* he has inserted a notice of Wycliffe's birthplace, which, though only obtained from hearsay, yet as the earliest, and recorded only about 150 years after the great man's death, must always be regarded as of high authority. Leland's remark runs as follows:—'It is reported that John Wiclif, the heretic, was born at Spresswell, a small village, a good mile off from Richmond.'[2]

This notice, it is true, has its difficulties. The first is, that Leland himself appears to contradict his present statement in another of his works, for he says in his *Collections* in mentioning 'Wigclif' in the county of York, that 'Wigclif' the heretic sprang from that place.[3] These two statements appear, at first sight, to contradict each other, and yet, when looked at more narrowly, they are easily reconciled; for in the first-named work Leland is speaking of Wycliffe's birthplace proper; while, in the other, he is rather making mention of the seat of his family. But

Wycliffe and Spresswell.

---

[1] Leland was commissioned in 1533, by Henry VIII., to examine the libraries and archives of all cathedrals and monasteries, colleges, and cities; and he employed six years in travelling all over England and Wales, in order to collect materials for a history of the kingdom. He spent other six years in working up these collections into an account of the antiquities of England, but the work was never finished, for his excessive labours brought on disease of the brain, and he died in 1552. His *Itinerarium*, however, in nine volumes, was published in Oxford 1710–1712.

[2] *Itinerarium* V., 99. [*They say*] *that John Wyclif Hæreticus* [*was borne at Spreswel, a poore village a good myle from Richemont.*] I quote from Lewis, *History of Wiclif*, p. 1, note *a*. The words between brackets do not stand in Leland's original MS., but only in a transcript of Stowe. *Vide* Shirley, *Fasc. Zizan.* Introd. x., note 3.

[3] *Unde Wigclif hæreticus originem duxit. Collectanea*, I., 2, 329. Cited by Vaughan, *Life and Opinions*, I., 232, note 8.

there a still greater difficulty arises from the fact that in the neighbourhood of the town of Richmond, in the North Riding of Yorkshire, no village of the name of Spresswell has ever been known to exist. This fact has given rise to various conjectures, *e.g.*, that Leland, in the course of his inquiries, had heard of a place called Hipswell or Ipswell, and had mistaken its name for Spresswell, or that Spresswell may have been the name of some manor-house or estate of the Wycliffes. It is also thought by some that Leland could not have personally travelled through that district of the county; for, in giving its topography, he has fallen into many mistakes.[1]

But very recently Leland's credit for accuracy on this point has been vindicated, and his account has received a confirmation which sets the matter in the clearest light. Dr. Robert Vaughan, the scholar, who, since 1828, has rendered important services to the history of Wycliffe, has, by means of correspondence with other scholars in the north of England, established the following facts:

Not far from the River Tees, which forms the boundary between the North Riding of Yorkshire and the county of Durham, there was formerly a town of the name of Richmond, of higher antiquity than the existing Richmond, and which is to be found in old maps under the name of Old Richmond.

About a mile from Old Richmond, there was still in existence in the eighteenth century, close to the Tees, a small village or hamlet called Spresswell or Spesswell. An old chapel also stood there, in which were married the grandparents of a man living in that neighbourhood, who vouched for the truth of this information. These were, however, the last pair married in the chapel, for it fell down soon after, and now the plough passes over the spot where it stood.[2]

Only half a mile from Spresswell lies the small parish of Wycliffe,[3] the church of which still stands on the level bank of the Tees, without tower, and partly overgrown with ivy. Upon an eminence, not far from the little church, stands a manor-house, which formerly belonged to the family of Wycliffe of Wycliffe. From the time of William the Conqueror down to the beginning of the seventeenth century, this family were lords of the manor and patrons of the parish church. In 1606 the estate passed, by marriage of the heiress, to the family of Tunstall. Another branch of the family, however, carried on the name, and it is hardly more than half a century since the last representative of the family, Francis Wycliffe, died at Barnard Castle on

---

[1] Shirley, Introd. xi.; Vaughan, *Life and Opinions*, I., 233; and *John Wycliffe, a Monograph*, 1854, p. 5 f.

[2] *Athenæum*, April 20, 1861, p. 529.

[3] In 1853 the population of the little village did not reach 200 souls.

Tees. The tradition both of the locality and the Wycliffes of Wycliffe has always been, that it was from this family that the celebrated forerunner of the Reformation sprang.

It no longer, then, admits of a doubt that Wycliffe was born at Spresswell, not far from Old Richmond. His birthplace belongs to the district which, though not a county itself, but only part of one, is commonly called Richmondshire, forming the north-western portion of the great county of York, or, more exactly, the western district of the North Riding, a hilly, rocky highland, with valleys and slopes of the greatest fertility. The valley of the Tees, in particular, and especially that part of it where Spresswell was situated, is a region of great and various beauty, presenting landscape scenery of equal grandeur and softness.[1]

Scenery and people.

It was, then, a country of strongly marked character upon which the eyes of Wycliffe rested in his childhood and boyish years; but we should lose ourselves in the domain of poetry if we endeavoured to describe the influences which the surrounding scenery exerted upon the opening mind of our hero. We have a surer foothold for the history of the man, in the peculiar character of the population of those northern counties of England. In Yorkshire especially, though also in other counties of the north, as Northumberland, Westmoreland, and Cumberland, the Anglo-Saxon element has maintained itself in greater purity, tenacity, and force, than in the south of England. In the centuries next succeeding the Norman invasion, much more of the old English nature continued to keep its hold in these parts of the kingdom than in the midland and southern counties. It is said that there are families there to the present day, who have remained in uninterrupted possession of their estates from the time of the Norman invasion, and almost even from the period of the Saxon immigration; these old Saxon families, it is added, belonging not to 'the nobility,' but to 'the gentry.' The country people at the present day, in the whole of Yorkshire, and most of all in the remote dales of the interior, still speak an ancient dialect, which, like the Scottish tongue, bears an unmistakable German impress.[2] The whole nature of the Yorkshire people has an antique cast about it. In the rest of England, the Yorkshireman passes for a robust, stouthearted, honest personage—one who is every inch a man.

It was from the bosom of this tenacious old Saxon people that Wycliffe sprang; and the more it holds true that it was precisely the

---

[1] Dibdin, *Observations on a Tour through almost the whole of England.* London, 1801, 4to, I., 261.
[2] Kohl, *Journeys in England and Wales*, 1841, II., 50, 123, 165, 178. *E.g.*, people say *lig* instead of lie; to *speer anybody* (aufspüren), instead of to ask or inquire; *I do not ken*, instead of know.

German element of the English population which formed the strength of the national movement of the fourteenth century, the more important, unquestionably, is the circumstance that a man like Wycliffe, who rendered, in particular, such important services to the development of the English language, should have belonged to a province and people who had always been distinguished by faithful and persistent adherence to the old Saxon nature and ways. And it appears that the Wycliffes belonged precisely to those families of the Yorkshire gentry who have persistently preserved for centuries, not only their estates, but also the characteristics of their Saxon descent.

The Wycliffe family.

The family of the Wycliffes must at one time have been numerous, and of many branches; for documents of the second half of the fourteenth century give information of several different men of this name.[1] In 1368 we find mention of Robert of Wycliffe, as priest of a chapel in Cleveland, in the diocese of York, probably the same priest who, in 1362, was made parish priest of Wycliffe, and in 1363 made an exchange of this office for another. Besides him, we know, from church documents, of another priest of the same period, who bore the same name as our Reformer, written 'John Wyclyve,' who, on July 21, 1361, was appointed parish priest of Mayfield by Archbishop Islip, that being an estate of the See of Canterbury. He remained priest there for nearly twenty years, and in 1380 was made rector of the parish of Horsted Keynes, where he died in 1383, one year before his more illustrious namesake.[2] We shall have occasion, below, to return to this second John Wyclyve.

It is, moreover, a remarkable fact, that the Wycliffes, after the death of their most celebrated member, and in particular from the Reformation down to their extinction, were always distinguished for their fidelity to the Church of Rome. In 1423, a certain Robert Wyclyf, parish priest of Rudby, in the diocese of York, made a will which leaves no room for doubt that the testator was very far from sharing the views of John Wycliffe. At the commencement of the document he commends his soul to 'Almighty God, to Saint Mary, and to all the Saints;' he passes over the Redeemer in entire silence; he makes more than one provision for

Their adherence to Rome.

---

[1] In 1362 a certain Robert of Wycliffe was made parish priest of Wycliffe by Catherine, widow of Roger Wycliffe; and in the following year we find a William of Wycliffe presented to the same place. In the interval, however, the patronage had changed hands, for the patron in 1363 is John of Wycliffe, who, we may conjecture, was the son, now come to his majority, of Catherine, and her deceased husband, Roger Wycliffe.

[2] Whitaker, *History of Richmondshire*, I., 197, quoted by Vaughan, *Monograph*, p. 5; and *Register of the Archbishop of Canterbury*, also quoted by Vaughan, p. 548.

masses for the repose of souls; and leaves several legacies in favour of nuns and Mendicant monks, etc. From the fact that such soul-masses are to be said, not only for himself, but also for the souls of his father, mother, and all his benefactors, it is plain that the parents of the testator must also have been strict Romanists. Among the four churches, for the repair of each of which he left forty shillings, is named the church of 'Wyclyf,' and to the poor of the same parish is also left a sum of forty shillings. These two latter dispositions are unquestionable indications that the testator was connected by birth with that locality.[1]

It seems as if Wycliffe's family, feeling themselves exposed to danger by his keen assault upon the Church of Rome, had become all the more devoted to the Papacy on that account. At all events, even after the English Reformation, the Wycliffes remained Roman Catholic, and with them about half the inhabitants of the village—a division which continues to the present day. The old church on the bank of the Tees belongs to the Anglican Establishment, while the Roman Catholic inhabitants of Wycliffe until recently repaired to a chapel built at the side of the manor house on the neighbouring height. They have now a chapel of their own at some little distance.

Touching the date of Wycliffe's birth,[2] no direct documentary information has come down to us. John Lewis was the first who fixed upon the year 1324; and he has been followed in this date by the great majority of writers without further inquiry, although he never even attempted to produce docu-

Date of birth.

---

[1] *Vide* the Documents from the Episcopal Register of Durham, in Vaughan's *Monograph*, p. 545.

[2] On the orthography of the family name Wycliffe, I may here introduce the following remarks: There was an endless variety of ways of spelling it in the fourteenth and fifteenth centuries, and some of this variety has reappeared among English writers in recent times. Vaughan states that the name is written in nearly twenty different forms; but this is far from being a high enough estimate. I have found as many as twenty-eight varieties in the usage of these centuries. They divide themselves into two chief classes, according as the vowel used in the first syllable is *i* or *y*. The explanation is to be found in the generally wretched condition of orthography in the Middle Ages, which prevailed specially in the names of places, and in surnames taken from these. It was not merely that every author adopted at his own pleasure his own way of spelling such names, while preserving uniformity of usage after choosing it, but one and the same author or copyist allowed himself unbounded liberty and caprice in the writing of the same name, as Walsingham, the chronicler, who writes the name of Wycliffe in at least eight different forms. *Vide* the edition of Riley, I., 335; II., 50, 52, 57, etc.

[Mr. F. D. Matthew, in the *Academy* for June 7, 1884, has proved that the most usual spelling of the first syllable was *Wy*, not the *Wi* which German writers (as Buddensieg) generally give, on the authority of some early documents. The former also better consists with the etymology of the local name (*Gwy*, *Wy*, 'water,' or 'stream'). We therefore adopt it without hesitation in this edition. For the last syllable, *clif* or *cliffe* is immaterial: the latter has the advantage of being usual, and in accordance with analogy. While on the subject of etymology, it may be added that the spelling *Wick* is decidedly objectionable, as suggesting the Saxon *wick*, or 'village,' which has no part in the formation of the word.]

mentary evidence in support of it. Probably he proceeded upon the supposition that when Wycliffe died, at the end of 1384, he may have been a man of sixty; and counting back from that year, he arrived at 1324 as the approximate year of his birth. But we have nothing to authorise the surmise that Wycliffe at his death was exactly sixty years of age. Younger than that he could hardly have been, but he might easily have been older. We know that during the last two years of his life he suffered from the effects of a paralytic attack, and that he afterwards died from a repetition of the shock. If we assume that 1324 was his birth-year, he must have had a stroke at fifty-eight, a comparatively early age; whereas the notices which we have of his latest life by no means give the impression that his vigour had been impaired at an unusually early period. This circumstance taken alone makes it probable that when Wycliffe died he had reached a more advanced age than is usually supposed, and was, at least, well on towards seventy. But besides this, there are some expressions in his writings, where he speaks of his earlier years, which could only have come from a man pretty well advanced in life. Thus, he says in one of his Saints' Days' sermons, 'When I was still young, and addicted myself to a great variety of favourite pursuits, I made extensive collections from manuals on optics, on the properties of light,' etc.[1] That does not sound like the speech of a man of only fifty-four or fifty-six; yet as those sermons, by sure marks, could not have been delivered later than 1380, nor earlier than 1378, Wycliffe could not have been more than from fifty-four to fifty-six years of age at the time, if the common date of his birth is correct. All these indications make it appear probable to us that when Wycliffe died he must have been considerably older than is usually supposed. He must, in that case, have been born at least several years earlier than 1324; but we have no positive data to enable us to fix the precise year.

2.—Wycliffe's Course of Study.

WE have as little historical information on the subject of Wycliffe's earliest education as on that of his birth-year; and it would answer no good purpose to fill up this blank with the suggestions of our own fancy. But so much is implied in the nature of the case, that in the years of his childhood and early youth he grew up vigorously into the old Saxon pith of the family stem to which he belonged, and of the whole people among whom he was brought up.

Training in boyhood.

[1] *Sermons on Saints' Days* ('Evangelia de Sanctis'), No. 53, MS. 3928 of the Imperial Library of Vienna. *Denis*, No. CD., fol. 106, col. 1.

No doubt, also, the historical recollections and folk-lore of the Yorkshire people, especially in connection with certain localities, had very early made a deep impression on the susceptible mind of the boy, and had become a part of himself. For I find the writings of Wycliffe so full of allusions to and reminiscences of the early times of his fatherland, as to justify the assumption that from his youth up he had been familiar with patriotic scenes and pictures. The boy, no doubt, received the first elements of instruction from some member of the clerical body. Probably the parish priest of Wycliffe was his first teacher, and taught him the rudiments of Latin grammar; and doubtless, too, the youth, who must from childhood have had a lively and inquisitive genius, spent his whole time at home till he went to Oxford. For as yet there were no schools in existence to prepare lads for the universities, except the cloister and cathedral schools. The universities themselves had rather the character of public schools and gymnasia than universities proper; at least a multitude, not only of young men, but even of mere boys, were to be found in Oxford and Cambridge, not as the pupils of schools collateral to the university, but as members of the university itself. We know, for example, from the loud complaints of Richard Fitzralph, Archbishop of Armagh, that many boys under fourteen years of age were already considered to be members of the university. *The early university system.*

The functions of the universities in the Middle Ages were far more comprehensive than in modern times. While the continental universities of the present day are generally of use only to young men above eighteen in acquiring for several years the higher education,—mature men ordinarily belonging to the academic body only as teachers or officials, and in comparatively small numbers,—the mediæval universities included in their structure two additional storeys, so to speak, above and below,—an upper storey, that we might call an 'Academy' in the narrow sense—and a lower storey, a species of grammar school and gymnasium. As to the former, the number of grown-up men who belonged to the mediæval universities, not exclusively as teachers of the student youth, but in the general character of men of learning, and as members of the self-governing corporation (Magistri Regentes), was very large and important. The English universities are now the only ones in Europe which have preserved this feature to a great degree unimpaired, in the fellows of their colleges, whose numbers are considerable. On the other hand, in the lower storey, the mediæval universities included a number of lads who for the present could only enjoy the benefit of preparatory training. This latter circumstance must especially be kept in view, when we meet with statistical notices of the attendance at universities like Oxford, which astonish us by their enormous figures.

It would, then, be in itself quite conceivable that Wycliffe might have gone to Oxford even as a boy. This is not, however, probable. For his home, close on the northern boundary of Yorkshire, was so far distant from the University that the journey, in the fourteenth century, must have been an affair of no inconsiderable time and fatigue and even danger; and prudent and conscientious parents would hardly be able to bring themselves to send a son upon such a journey before his fourteenth or sixteenth year; and, in effect, to let him pass away for ever from their parental oversight.[1] It is more probable that Wycliffe was at least fourteen, perhaps as much as sixteen, years old when he went to Oxford. Positive testimonies as to the exact date are wholly wanting; but, assuming that he was born in 1320, and that he did not repair to the University before his fifteenth year, we are brought to 1335 as the approximate year.

Enters Oxford.

At that time, of the twenty colleges and more which exist to-day in Oxford, there were five already founded, viz., Merton, founded in 1274; Balliol, 1260–82; Exeter, 1314; Oriel, 1324; and University College, 1332. These foundations were originally designed purely for the support of poor scholars, who lived under the oversight of a President, according to a domestic order fixed by the Statutes of the Founders. It was only at a later period that they became, in addition to this, boarding-houses for students in good circumstances. Queen's College was not erected before 1340. It took its name from Philippa, Queen of Edward III., who contributed towards its foundation; Robert Egglesfield, one of her court chaplains, being the real founder. It has been commonly accepted as a fact that when Wycliffe went to Oxford he was immediately entered at Queen's College. This he could only have done on the supposition that he did not come up to the University till the year 1340; but we have already shown that an earlier date for that incident is more probable. Apart from this chronological consideration, there is a want of all sure grounds for the assumption that Wycliffe entered into any connection with Queen's College at so early a date. The oldest records of the College go no farther back than the year 1347; and the name of Wycliffe does not occur in them earlier than

Its five colleges.

---

[1] Comp. Vaughan, *Monograph*, p. 16, where travelling and intercourse in England during the fourteenth and fifteenth centuries are graphically described on the authority of ancient sources.

1363; and even then he appears, not properly as a member of the College, but only as a renter of some rooms in the building;[1] a relation to it which appears to have continued for nearly twenty years —down to the time when Wycliffe's connection with the University as a corporation entirely ceased.

If the question thus recurs, into what college Wycliffe was received when he first came to Oxford, we must confess that, in the absence of all documentary evidence, we are unable to answer it with any distinctness or confidence. We know that in the course of years he became a member, and sometimes head of several colleges or halls. Merton and Balliol, in particular, are named in this connection, to say nothing at present of a third hall of which we shall have to speak hereafter. But all the notices we have of this kind relate to a later period—not to Wycliffe as a young scholar, but to his mature years. If mere conjectures might be allowed, nothing would appear to us more probable than that he was entered at Balliol on his first coming to the University. For this college owed its foundation (1260–82) to the noble family of Balliol of Barnard Castle, on the left, or Durham, bank of the Tees, not more than five miles from Spresswell, Wycliffe's birthplace; and that there existed a connection of some kind between the Wycliffe family and Balliol College,[2] appears from the fact that two men, who were presented to the parish of Wycliffe, by John Wycliffe of Wycliffe, as patron, in 1361 and 1369, were members of Balliol College—the one William Wycliffe, a fellow, and the other John Hugate, then Master of the College.[3]

Wycliffe's college.

But we acknowledge that we are here only hinting at a possibility, which, however, will be raised to a probability in the course of an investigation upon which we shall have to enter at a subsequent stage.

But if the college into which Wycliffe entered as a scholar does not admit of being determined with certainty, there is no doubt, on the other hand, as to the 'nation' in the University to which from the first he belonged. It is well known that all the universities of the Middle Ages divided themselves into

Division into 'nations.'

---

[1] *Vide* Extracts from the Bursars' Accounts of Queen's College, as given by Shirley in an Excursus to the *Fasciculi Zizaniorum*, p. 514. Vaughan, indeed, maintained in his *Life and Opinions of John de Wycliffe*, and also in his more recent *Monograph*, that Wycliffe's name occurs in a list of the original members of the college, who entered it in 1340, immediately after its foundation. But Shirley, who lived in Oxford, gives the most positive assurance that no list of members of so early a date exists among the papers of the college, p. xiii.

[2] [See Appendix III., by Dr. Lorimer: 'Balliol College in Wycliffe's Time.']

[3] Comp. *Wycliffe, his Biographers and Critics*, an article by Vaughan in *The British Quarterly Review*, Oct., 1858.

'nations,' according to the countries and provinces, sometimes even the races, to which their members belonged. Thus, in the University of Paris, from a very early period, there were four nations—the French, the English (at a later period called German), the Picard, and the Norman. The University of Prague had, in like manner, from its foundation, four nations—the Bohemian, Bavarian, Polish, and Saxon. In the University of Leipzig, the division into the Meissnian, Saxon, Bavarian, and Polish nations, with which it started at its foundation in 1409 as a colony from the University of Prague, continued until the year 1830;[1] and even at the present day this ancient arrangement continues to be of practical importance in many respects, especially in relation to particular endowments. It was the same with the English Universities in the Middle Ages; but in Oxford there were only two such 'nations,' the northern and the southern (*Boreales* and *Australes*). The first included the Scots, the second the Irish and Welsh. Each nation, as in the universities of the Continent, had its own elected president and representative, who bore the title of Procurator (hence *Proctor*).

That Wycliffe joined himself to the northern 'nation' might of course be presumed; but there is express testimony to the fact that he was a *Borealis*.[2] This is not without importance, inasmuch as this 'nation' in Oxford, during the fourteenth century, was the chief representative, not only of the Saxon or pure Germanic folk-character, but also of the principle of the national autonomy. But this connection of Wycliffe with the 'northern nation' produced a double effect. It had a determinative influence upon Wycliffe's own spirit and mental development; while, on the other hand, as soon as Wycliffe had taken up an independent position, and began to work upon other minds, he found within the University, in this nation of the *Boreales*, no inconsiderable number of men of kindred blood and spirit to his own, to form the kernel of a self-inclusive circle—of a party.

And now, as respects the studies of Wycliffe in the years of his student-life, the sources here also fail to give us as full information as we could have wished. We are especially left in the dark as to the men who were his teachers. It would have been very helpful to know whether he was personally a hearer of Thomas Bradwardine and of Richard Fitzralph. Judging from

<small>Wycliffe's teachers.</small>

---

[1] *The Book of Statutes of the University of Leipzig for the first 150 years after its foundation.* Edited by Friedrich Zarncke. Leipzig, 1861, 4to, 3, 42.

[2] The Chronicler of St. Albans, Thomas Walsingham, commences his account of Wycliffe under the year 1377, with the words: '*Per idem tempus surrexit in Universitate Oxoniensi quidam Borealis, dictus Magister Joannes Wyclef,*' etc. Riley's ed., I., 324.

dates, it is quite possible that he did come in contact with the latter, for Fitzralph was, in 1340 and for some years afterwards, resident in Oxford as Chancellor of the University, and was still, without doubt, delivering theological lectures, for it was not till 1347 that he was made Archbishop of Armagh. On the other hand, it seems very doubtful whether, at the time when Wycliffe was a student, Thomas Bradwardine was still in Oxford, and not rather already in France, in the train of Edward III., as military chaplain. Wycliffe, indeed, more than once makes mention of the *doctor profundus*, but in a way which decidedly leads us to infer only a knowledge and use of his writings, not a personal acquaintance with the man.

But if we are left in the dark on the subject of Wycliffe's principal teachers, we are not altogether without light on the question as to what and how he studied. The knowledge which we possess at the present day of the character of the mediæval universities, and of the scholastic philosophy, is sufficient of itself to give us some insight into these points. For one thing, it is beyond all doubt, that although the Middle Ages made exclusive use of the Latin tongue (not, indeed, in its classical form) as their scientific organ, they were not at all familiar with the Greek language and literature. It may, with full warrant, be maintained that the scholastic philosophers and divines were, as a rule, ignorant of Greek, and attained to any knowledge they had of its Christian and classical literature only by means of Latin translations, and sometimes only through Latin tradition. Men like Roger Bacon, who had some acquaintance with Greek, are rare exceptions.[1] It was only during the fifteenth century that, in consequence of certain well-known events, the study of the Greek language and literature became more general. But even at the beginning of the sixteenth century Greek scholars and teachers like Erasmus and Philip Melancthon were rare enough. Manifestly the revival of Hellenic speech and culture in Western Europe was one of the chief causes of the advent of the modern epoch; as, on the other hand, the prevailing ignorance of the Greek language, and the impossibility of any direct acquaintance with Greek literature, was one of the most essential *momenta* which conditioned the onesidedness and narrowness of mediæval science.

This want we recognise also in Wycliffe. His writings supply manifold proofs of his total ignorance of Greek. This is shown, not only by very frequent mistakes in the writing of Greek proper names

---

[1] It has been usual to ascribe to Gerbert in the tenth, and to Abelard and John of Salisbury in the twelfth century, a knowledge of Greek, but Schaarschmidt, in his *Johannes Saresberiensis*, 1862, p. 108, has proved convincingly that they had no claim to this praise.

and other words which might be attributed to the copyists rather than to the author himself, but also by the etymological explanations of Greek terms which Wycliffe not seldom introduces, which for the most part are beside the mark and erroneous.[1] He is always more successful when, on questions which presuppose a knowledge of Greek, he leans on the authority of others, as, *e.g.*, on Jerome, as *linguarum peritissimus*, *De Civili Dominio* III., c. 11. When Wycliffe quotes a Greek writer, it is his custom, quite frankly, to give at the same time the name of the Latin source from which he derived his knowledge of the Greek work. In short, it is quite plain that in all cases he looked at the Greek only through Latin spectacles. But this defect was, no doubt, entirely owing to the education which Wycliffe had received in his youth, especially as a student at Oxford; for if there had been any possibility at that time of acquiring a knowledge of Greek at the University, Wycliffe was just the man who would certainly not have neglected the opportunity. For how ardently he thirsted after truth, and with what unwearied industry he sought to obtain a many-sided mental culture, we shall presently have occasion to show.

Ignorance of Greek.

Another point is the course of study which was pursued in the Middle Ages. This differed from the course of modern university training, as the latter has developed itself on the Continent, in one very important respect. Much greater stress was laid upon, and, in consequence, much more time was devoted to, general scientific culture; whereas, in the present day, professional studies have the preference, certainly more than is wise and good. At that time a large space was occupied by the study of the 'Liberal Arts.' And these seven *artes liberales*, from which the Faculty of Arts took its name, had to be studied in strict order and course: first, the *Trivium*, including grammar, dialectics, and rhetoric; then the *Quadrivium*, embracing arithmetic, geometry, astro-

The 'Liberal Arts.'

---

[1] Greek proper names are often written in the Bohemian MSS. of Wycliffe's works so erroneously as to be almost unrecognisable, *e.g.*, *Pictagerus* instead of Pythagoras. *De veritate Sacræ Scripturæ*, c. 12. And who would guess that *cassefatum* in the same MS. was meant to be nothing else but κακόφατον? But the false writing of a Greek word is not always to be put to the account of the copyist, for in one place, *e.g.*, the miswritten word *apocrisus* (instead of apocryphus) is immediately followed by an etymological remark which presupposes *s* to have been written instead of *f*. The word, it is said, comes from *apo*=*de*, and *crisis*=*secretum*, because the subject is the secrets of the Church; or, according to others from *apos*=large, and *crisis*=*judicium*. *De Veritate Scripturæ*, c. 2. Another etymological attempt is no better. *Elemosnia* is alleged to be compounded of *elemonia*=misericordia, and *sina*; or of *elia*, which comes from *Eli*=God, and *sina*=mandatum; it signifies, therefore, God's command. *De Civili Dominio*, III., c. 14, MS. [The name *Michael*, again, is apparently derived by Wycliffe from μάχη, 'battle,' which he writes, *micha*, and *El*=God. *Trial.* ii. 10, p. 109.]

nomy, and music. The *Trivium* was also named compendiously the *Artes Sermocinales* or 'Logic,' and not without reason, inasmuch as λόγος designates equally speech and thought; the students in this part of the curriculum being called *Logici*. To the *Quadrivium*, on the other hand, was given sometimes the collective name of 'Physics,' in the old comprehensive sense of science of nature, and sometimes the name of the 'Mathematical Arts.'[1]

That Wycliffe possessed a special faculty and taste for natural philosophy we shall presently point out; but first let us dwell a little longer upon his logical studies. We know from the testimony of John of Salisbury, who died in 1180, that in the twelfth century many who devoted themselves to the sciences never got beyond the *Trivium*, to the majority of whom dialectics was the chief stumbling-block;[2] and we can understand this the more readily when we remember that it was usual in the scholastic age to look upon dialectics as the science of sciences, and even, in a certain degree, as the philosophy of all science (Wissenschaftlehre). In the logic and dialectics of the Middle Ages the formal schooling and discipline of scientific thought joined itself partly to a kind of philosophy of speech, partly to a metaphysical ontology, or to what Hegel has called speculative logic. If we consider, however, the imposing *rôle* which was played in the scientific life and action of the Middle Ages by the Public Acts of Disputation, those tournaments of the learned world, we may well conceive what an indescribable charm dialectics, as the art of disputation, must have had for the men of that time. How close to hand lay the temptation to forget or disdain everything compared with this art, and to look upon it as a world in itself, revolving round itself as its own absolute self-end!

Logical and dialectical studies.

To these logical and dialectical studies Wycliffe, without doubt, devoted himself in his student days with the greatest zeal, as is attested by the numerous writings of this character produced in his mature age. Indeed, we may say that all his writings, upon whatever subject, not excepting even his sermons, confirm this attestation, inasmuch as all of them are stamped throughout with the dialectic genius of the author. But even if this testimony had not been forthcoming, we know that it was the unchallenged and universally admitted

---

[1] *E.g.*, Wycliffe, *Tractatus de statu innocentiæ*, c. 4, quoad artes mathematicas quadruviales. Vienna MS., 1339 f, 244, col. 2-245. Roger Bacon is also wont to include the sciences of the *Quadrivium* under the general term of *Mathematics*.

[2] Comp. Reuter, *Johannes von Salisbury*. Berlin, 1842, p. 9, and Schaarschmidt, *Johannes Saresberiensis*. Leipzig, 1862, p. 61.

brilliancy of his dialectical genius alone which acquired for Wycliffe his high scientific fame.

But he was still far from overvaluing the arts of logic, as if these alone constituted science. The mathematical sciences of the *Quadrivium* had also an extraordinary attraction for him, and it is worthy of consideration how often in his writings, and with what predilection, he refers to this department. At one time it is arithmetic or geometry which must do him service in illustrating certain truths and relations; at another time it is physical and chemical laws, or facts of optics or acoustics, which he applies to illuminate moral and religious truths; and not only in scientific essays, or in sermons preached before the University, but even in his English sermons he makes unhesitating use of such illustrations.[1] But it was not in his riper years that Wycliffe first began to apply himself to the study of natural science; he had begun to do so in his youth, while a student in Oxford, as he himself tells us, in words quoted on a preceding page. The reference there, indeed, is limited to collections which he had made in his younger days from works upon optics, but we may obviously infer that he had occupied himself with other branches of natural science as well, *quando fuit junior*. No doubt it was under the instructions and by the personal example of some teacher in the University that his taste for these studies was first awakened and encouraged; but who this teacher was we ask in vain. Neither contemporaries nor men of later times, nor Wycliffe himself, afford us any knowledge upon the subject. It may, however, with some reason be conjectured that at the time of Wycliffe's student life some disciples of the great Roger Bacon, who lived long in Oxford, and survived till 1292, may still have been working there, and that the enthusiasm for natural science, which we are so often sensible of in Wycliffe, was derived by him through this medium and from that illustrious man, who was called, not without reason, *Doctor Mirabilis*, and who, anticipating his namesake, Francis Bacon, had already, in the thirteenth century, grasped and exemplified the experimental method of science. It is matter of fact that among the learned men who adorned the University of Oxford in the first half and in the middle of the fourteenth century, not a few were distinguished by mathematical, astronomical, and physical knowledge. Thomas

---

[1] So in the 26th of his *Sermons on Saints' Days* ('Evangelia de Sanctis'). Vienna MS., 3928; also in the 51st sermon of the same collection, and in the 24th sermon of another collection, included in the same MS. vol. Explanations of this kind are not uncommon in his learned treatises, *e.g.*, in the *De Dominio Divino*, II., c. 3; *De Ecclesia*, c. 5, etc.

Bradwardine, for example, who died in 1349, mentioned above as a theological thinker, was held in high estimation as a mathematician and astronomer; John Estwood, at one time a member of Merton College, was celebrated about 1360 for his astronomical attainments; as was also William Rede, who built the library of that college, and in 1369 became Bishop of Chichester.[1] These are only a few names selected out of a great number of contemporaries who were all members of the University of Oxford as scholars, or masters and doctors. We are not, then, too bold if we conclude from these facts that in the first half of the fourteenth century there prevailed in that University a special zeal for mathematical and physical studies, which also laid hold of Wycliffe.

But the natural sciences had as little power to enchain him, exclusively and for ever, as logic and dialectics; and Wycliffe passed from the seven liberal arts to Theology. This was, no doubt, the design which his parents had in view when they destined him for a life of study. He was to become a cleric, for the priestly calling was, in the public opinion of that age, the highest in human society. If the Wycliffe family cherished any ambitious wishes for the gifted scion of their house, it was a course of theological education and the standing of priesthood, which in that age, and especially in England, formed the surest stepping-stones to the highest dignities of the State. But we find no warrant either in his life or in his writings for attributing such ambitious designs to himself. What drew him as a young man to theology was, in our judgment, neither an ambition which looked upon the science only as the means of attaining selfish ends, nor a deep religious need already awakened and consciously experienced, which sought the satisfaction of its own cravings in the Christian theology. It rather appears to us, judging from those self-revelations, scattered here and there in his writings, which give us an insight into his student life, that the motive which impelled him, apart from all external considerations, to devote himself to theology, was entirely intellectual and scientific. His passion for knowledge and thirst for truth drew him to theology as the highest science of all, 'the queen of sciences.' From his own writings it is evident that he entered upon the new study with the untiring zeal which had characterised his former pursuits. The scholastic theology, it is true, was entirely wanting in the various historical discipline of our modern theology, and it knew only a small part of practical and exegetical theology, or the wide

Theological studies.

---

[1] Lewis, *History of the Life of Wiclif*, following Leland's *De Scriptoribus Britannicis*.

field of Biblical science. Almost the whole body of theological science took the form of systematic theology. That had been the case since the second half of the twelfth century—*i.e.*, since the *Sentences* of 'the Master,' the Lombard, Peter of Novara, had become the manual of dogmatic instruction.

But we should greatly err if we were to suppose, on this account, that the theological studies of the Middle Ages comprehended, as a general rule, only a small amount of scientific matter. On the contrary, they extended themselves to large fields of knowledge, of which Protestant theology, at least in later times, has taken little or no account. In particular, the Canon Law, since the time when it was collected and sanctioned, formed an extremely comprehensive and important subject of the theological course. Nor must we undervalue the reading of the Fathers, *e.g.*, of Augustine, and of the Doctors, *i.e.*, the Scholastics, which at the same time occupied in some degree the place of dogmatic history. Nor was the practice amiss of dividing the theological course into two stages, which we may briefly describe as the Biblical and the Systematic. The former came first in order. It consisted in the reading and interpretation of the Old and New Testaments. The interpretation took the form of *Glosses*. The whole of mediæval science, in fact, developed itself from Glosses; Dialectics from Glosses on the writings of Aristotle; Law from Glosses on the *Corpus Juris;* and so also Theology from Glosses first on the Bible, and then on the Sentences of Peter Lombard. That the original text of the Bible, through all this process, remained a book sealed with seven seals, and that only the Latin Vulgate was the subject of translation, need not be dwelt upon after what has been said above. To interpretation proper (*expositio*), which consisted in explanations more or less short, verbal, or substantial, sometimes aphoristic in form, and sometimes running on at large, succeeded learned discussions, in the scholastic manner (*quæstiones*), in the form of disputational *excursus*.

As already hinted, the prefixing of the Biblical to the dogmatic course was, besides being commendable in itself, also suitable to the object in view, for the students were in this way taken, before everything else, to the fountain-head, and obtained a knowledge of sacred history and Bible doctrine—if only this Biblical instruction had been of the right kind! But there was lacking *immediate* contact with the original. Men looked into the Bible text only through the coloured spectacles of the Latin version. And that was not all: men were, at the same time, so fettered and prejudiced by the whole mass of ecclesiastical tradition, that the

Course of theology.

possibility of a fair interpretation of the Scriptures was out of the question. The Biblical course, besides, was looked upon, not as the necessary foundation of all that was to follow, but rather as an entirely subordinate and preparatory discipline to Theology properly so called. This appeared in the division of labour which was made in the matter of theological lectures; for bachelors of theology of the lowest degree were allowed to deliver lectures on the Bible, and usually this work was left to them alone; whereas bachelors of the middle and highest degrees (*baccalaurei sententiarii* and *formati*),[1] as well as the doctors of theology, lectured on the Sentences of Peter Lombard, and sometimes on *Summæ* of their own. The 'doctors' would have thought it beneath their dignity to lecture on the Biblical books; the bachelors who were relegated to this work were called in a depreciatory tone only *biblici*, in contrast to *sententiarii*. When Wycliffe, therefore, went forward from this stage to what was considered the higher one, in which he studied what is now called systematic theology, it was chiefly lectures on the *Sentences* of the Lombard to which he had to listen. And here, too, that mode of treatment prevailed which began by glossing the text of the master, and followed this up with different 'quæstiones.' In addition, the numerous 'disputations' which were always held, served to promote the culture of the students. To these was added the reading of patristic and scholastic works. Among the latter, in the time of Wycliffe, the works chiefly in favour, at Oxford at least, were the *Summa* of Thomas Aquinas, the writings of Bishop Robert Grossetête (*Lincolniensis*), and the comprehensive work of Archbishop Richard Fitzralph (*Armachanus*) against the errors of the Armenians. Beyond all doubt, Wycliffe, in his student years, was a diligent reader of all these works, of which he makes so frequent use in his writings.

Further, as no one could have the credit of being a true theologian who was not at home in Canon Law, Wycliffe fulfilled this last requirement in a degree which is best evinced in his yet unprinted works, where he shows himself to have been quite a master of Canonical Jurisprudence; and that he had laid the foundations of this learning, even as a student, we assume with all confidence. Lewis adds that Wycliffe also studied Roman Law,[2] and the Canonical Law of England; and the assumption is indeed probable that he was no stranger to either; as is shown, not only by many of his writings, but also by the practical share which he took at a later period in ecclesiastico-political affairs; but whether he had

---

[1] Comp. Thurot, *De l'Organisation de l'Enseignement dans l'Université de Paris au Moyen-age*, 1850, p. 137.
[2] Lewis, *Life of Wiclif*, p. 2.

thrown himself into the study of these subjects in his youth is a point which we must leave in a state of uncertainty.

We have no positive data to show to what length of time Wycliffe's student course extended, and can only arrive at a probable estimate with the help of our general knowledge of university customs in that age. We know that in England, as well as on the Continent, the university course in the Middle Ages occupied a far longer period than at present. It has been truly said that 'men were not then misers with their time.' To study for ten years was by no means uncommon. Two years, at least, were allowed to the *Trivium*, and as many to the *Quadrivium*, so that four years, to begin with, were taken up by the general sciences in the Faculty of Arts. The study of theology in its two stages lasted, as a rule, for seven years, frequently even longer, although in some cases not so long, but even then for five years at the least.[1] We shall, therefore, scarcely err if we suppose that Wycliffe gave six years to the study of theology; and it can scarcely be too high an estimate if we reckon up his whole term of study to a decade of years. So if we were right in our conjecture, that he entered the University about the year 1335, the end of his curriculum would fall about the year 1345. Later data of his life afford nothing to contradict this computation. At all events, we must assume that he had already taken all the academic degrees in order up to that time, with the single exception of the theological doctorship. Thus, without doubt, he had become *baccalaureus artium*, and two or three years later *magister artium*. And again, after an interval of several years, he must have become bachelor of theology, or, as it was then expressed, 'bachelor of the *sacra pagina*;' but whether he became licentiate of theology before or after the year 1345 must be left undetermined. Herewith we leave Wycliffe's student years, and pass to his manhood.

Length of Wycliffe's student course.

[1] See article *Sorbonne*, in Herzog's 'Theol. Realencyclopädie.' Eng. ed. by Dr. Schaff, vol. III.

CHAPTER III.

QUIET WORK IN OXFORD—1345-1366.

1.—Wycliffe as a Member of Balliol and of Merton.

IN commencing this period of Wycliffe's life with the year 1345, we have before us two full decades of years during which he in no way appeared upon the stage of public life, either in Church or State. For in those chronicles which record the history of England in the fourteenth century, there does not occur the slightest mention of his person during these years. In fact, it is not till ten years later still, that the chroniclers mention him for the first time (1377). For this reason, we designate this stage of his life the period of his quiet work; and of that work during all these twenty years Oxford was the exclusive field.

We have to think of Wycliffe at this time as a member of a college in full standing (*socius, fellow*), as one of the Regent Masters (*magistri regentes*), *i.e.*, as a man taking an active part in the inde-   **A Regent** pendent, and in some sense republican government of   **Master.** his own college and of the whole academic body—a position to which he had been in due order admitted, after passing through certain stages of academic study, and after he had acquitted himself of certain learned tasks (disputations and the like).

The college, indeed, of which Wycliffe became a Fellow, is a question which lies under as much uncertainty as that other which has been discussed in the last chapter, viz.: what college it was with which he had been previously connected as a scholar.

Since the appearance of Lewis's life in 1720, the view has been commonly accepted that he was first a Fellow of Merton College, and afterwards, about the year 1360, was promoted to   **Master of** the presidency of Balliol College.[1] In support of the   **Balliol.** first point, there exists a single documentary proof, which, however,

---
[1] John Lewis, *History*, etc., I. 4. Vaughan, *Life and Opinions*, I. 241. *Monograph*, p. 39.

is not absolutely unquestionable. It consists of an entry in the Acts of Merton College, according to which, in January, 1356, 'John Wyklif' held the office of seneschal or rent-master of the college.[1] This has hitherto been unhesitatingly understood of our Wycliffe; but Shirley maintains, on the contrary, that that notice probably refers to his namesake and contemporary, 'John Wiclif' or 'Wyclyve,' who, according to trustworthy documents, was parish priest of Mayfield. The grounds upon which this scholar relies are the following :— The fact is certain beyond challenge, that the Reformer Wycliffe and no other was Master of Balliol in 1361. Now, the relations which existed between this college and the Wycliffe family, make it natural to presume that he belonged to Balliol from the first; while, on the other hand, it is in the highest degree improbable that the members of this college would have chosen for their Master a man who was member of another college (Merton).[2] The difficulty presented by this last remark will find its solution in an inquiry upon which we shall enter presently; and as to Shirley's ground of doubt, it is obvious to reply that John Wycliffe of Mayfield was also a Wycliffe,[3] and therefore stood as nearly related to Balliol College as our Wycliffe, and to Merton College no nearer than he. Thus the most important element of the question still continues to be the established fact, that our Wycliffe was Master of Balliol in 1362. We are unable, for our part, to recognise any decisive weight in Shirley's argument in opposition to the view which has hitherto prevailed, that Wycliffe was for some time a member of Merton. On the other hand, we believe that we are able to throw some new light on this hitherto somewhat obscure subject, and that not by means of bare conjecture, but of documentary facts.

The difficulty lies chiefly in explaining the frequent change of colleges through which Wycliffe is alleged to have passed, inasmuch as according to the older tradition, he was first admitted to Queen's, then transferred to Merton, and was soon afterwards made Master of Balliol; or even if we set aside Queen's College (the mention of it in connection with Wycliffe's student-life being unhistorical), and assume that he began his course as a scholar of Balliol, then it seems stranger still that he should have left this college and become a member of Merton, only to return to Balliol, and that too in the capacity of Master. But precisely here is the point upon which we think we are able to throw light, from a document which, till now,

---

[1] *The Wycliffite Versions of the Bible,* vol. I., p. vii.
[2] Shirley, *Fasciculi Zizaniorum,* p. 511.
[3] [But possibly of another family, and even of another part of the country. The names may have been originally different, *White-cliff* and *Wy-cliff.*]

has hardly been considered in relation to the subject. We refer to the Papal Bull of 1361, first published by Lewis, not, indeed, in the original, but in extensive extract, in which the incorporation of the parish church of Abbotesley with Balliol Hall (so the college was then called) is approved and sanctioned.[1] This document makes reference, at the same time, to the representation which the members of Balliol had submitted to the Papal See in support of their petition that the incorporation might be confirmed. From this representation we see pretty clearly what had been the financial condition of the college up to that time. For it states that by means of the pious beneficence of the founder of the college, there are indeed numerous students and clerics in the hall, but aforetime each of them had received only eight farthings weekly; *and as soon as they became Masters of Arts, they had immediately to leave the Hall*, so that, on account of poverty, they were no longer able to continue their studies, and found themselves, in some instances, obliged to have recourse to trade for the sake of a living. Now, however, Sir William Felton, the present benefactor of the foundation, formerly patron of Abbotesley, but who had already, in 1341, transferred his right of collation to Balliol College,[2] has formed the design, out of sympathy with its members, to increase the number of scholars, and to make provision for their having the common use of books in all the different faculties; and also, that every one of them shall have a sufficient supply of clothing and twelve farthings a-week; and further, *that they shall be at liberty to remain quietly in the Hall, whether they are masters and doctors or not, until they obtain a sufficient church-living, and not till then shall they be obliged to leave.*

Poverty of Balliol.

From this it is as clear as possible, that up to the year 1360 the extremely limited resources of Balliol had made it necessary that every one belonging to the foundation should leave as soon as he obtained his Arts degree, and that the incorporation of the Church of Abbotesley was intended by the benefactor to help in providing that members of Balliol, even when they became masters or doctors, might in future continue to live in the college as they had done before. If then Wycliffe, as we have reason to presume, was received into Balliol as a scholar, the circumstances of the college at that time must have obliged him to leave it as soon as he had graduated. And now, far from finding objections to identifying this Wiclif, mentioned in the Merton papers as seneschal of that college in 1359, with our own Wycliffe, we are glad to learn from this source what

---

[1] Lewis, *History*, etc., p. 4.
[2] Comp. Samuel Lewis, *Topographical Dictionary*, 5th ed., Lond. 1842; 4to. 'Abbotesley.'

had become of him since the time when, as we may now presume, he was obliged to leave Balliol as a master. And as it was customary in the colleges that every one behoved to be for some considerable length of time a Fellow before he could undertake such a function as that of seneschal, we may infer that Wycliffe had been for several years, probably since his graduation as a master, a member of Merton before he entered upon the office. The circumstances just mentioned serve to show, in addition, how easily it might come to pass that Wycliffe, although he had left Balliol, might yet at a later period be called back again to that college, and even be placed at its head; for as his leaving was by no means a spontaneous act of his own, but was entirely due to the financial situation of the college, it is impossible that it should have given rise to any feeling to his disadvantage, whereas, under other circumstances, such a feeling might have existed, and have stood in the way of his subsequent promotion.[1]

We believe that we have thus been able to clear up a point which has hitherto been obscure. But however this may be, the fact that Wycliffe was Master of Balliol in the year 1361, is in any case completely established. This appears from four different documents which are preserved among the archives of this college, and which have all a bearing upon the fact that Wycliffe, as 'Magister seu Custos Aulæ de Balliolo,'[2] took possession, in the name of the college, of the already mentioned incumbency of Abbotesley in the county of Huntingdon, which had been incorporated with the foundation. From these documents it appears that Wycliffe had become Master or Warden of Balliol before this date; and yet it cannot have been long before, since in November, 1356, the name of Robert of Derby occurs

[1] [A valuable paper by the late Prebendary Wilkinson appeared in *The Church Quarterly Review* for October 1877, on the connection of Wycliffe with the three Oxford Colleges, and is chiefly directed against Professor Shirley's views on the same subject. The author agrees with Dr. Lechler in maintaining the identity of the Reformer not only with John Wiclif, Warden of Canterbury Hall, but also with John Wiclif, Fellow or Postmaster of Merton. On the latter point his arguments can scarcely be regarded as satisfactory. That Wycliffe was Master of Balliol in 1361 proves that he was previously a Fellow: and the two colleges, Balliol and Merton (the head-quarters of the *Boreales* and *Australes* respectively) were bitter rivals. Wood in his *History and Antiquities of Oxford*, referring to the time of Wycliffe, says: 'The members of Merton College *refused, at this time and before, to elect northern scholars into their society.*' In Wycliffe's time, also, the finances of Balliol were in a better condition, from the benefactions of Sir William Fenton and Sir Philip de Somerville (1341). Prebendary Wilkinson is much more successful in his argumentation on the question of the Reformer's Wardenship of Canterbury Hall, and he claims, upon good grounds, 'to have established that Dean Hook was premature in regarding the question as conclusively settled in the negative by Professor Shirley's arguments.'—*Note by Dr. Lorimer, abridged.*]

[2] Shirley gives an exact account of these documents in notes 4 and 5 on p. xiv. of Introduction. [Several of them are transcribed in 'Riley's Report to the Royal Commission on Historical MSS. on the Archives of Balliol College.'—*Lorimer.*]

as Master; nor was even he Wycliffe's immediate predecessor, but one William of Kingston. Three of these documents, dated April 7, 8, and 9, 1361, have immediate relation to the Act of Incorporation itself, while in the fourth, dated July in the same year, Wycliffe, as Master, transmits to the Bishop of Lincoln, John Gynwell, the Papal Bull wherein the incorporation was sanctioned. But before this last date Wycliffe had been nominated by his college, May 16, 1361, as Rector of Fillingham. This is a small parish in the county of Lincoln, lying ten miles north-west of the city of Lincoln. But the fact of this appointment does not imply that Wycliffe immediately left the University, and lived entirely in the country in order to devote himself to pastoral duties. This does not appear to have been contemplated in the nomination. According to law and custom, he still retained his membership in the University, with all its powers and privileges; and without doubt he continued to reside at Oxford. What provision he made for the work of the parish, by the appointment of a curate or otherwise, and whether during the University vacations he resided regularly in Fillingham, in order to discharge his pastoral duties in person—cannot be decided. But it is matter of fact that an entry exists in the *Acts of the See of Lincoln*, to which diocese Fillingham belonged, showing that Wycliffe applied for and obtained in 1368 the consent of his bishop to an absence of two years from his parish church of Fillingham, in order to devote himself to the studies of Oxford.[1] It may be conjectured that he had obtained similar leave of non-residence for a similar period on previous occasions.

Rector of Fillingham.

On the other hand, his nomination to the rectorship of a country parish made it necessary that he should relinquish the Mastership of Balliol. That this really took place, may be inferred from an entry in the account-books of Queen's College, to the effect that Wycliffe, in October, 1363, and for several years afterwards, paid rent for an apartment in the buildings of that college.[2] We know besides, from other sources, that in 1366 a certain John Hugate was Master of Balliol.

---

[1] The entry in the Episcopal Register of Lincoln, Bishop Bokyngham's, 1363–97, is as follows:—'*Idibus Aprilis, anno Domini millesimo CCCmo. LXVIII. apud parkum Stowe concessa fuit licentia magistro Johanni de Wyclefe, rectori ecclesiæ de Filyngham, quod posset se absentare ab ecclesia sua insistendo literarum studio in Universitate Oxon. per biennium.*'

[2] [The remarks made by Buddensieg in opposition to this view (*Zeitschrift für Historische Theologie*, 1874, p. 316) rest upon what I consider to be an erroneous interpretation of the entries in the account-books of Queen's College, quoted by Shirley in the *Fasciculi*, p. 514; for these entries manifestly refer, not to short stays in the college rooms, but to rents of rooms paid by the year, with which sense alone agrees the recurring mention of Wycliffe's *camera*. In a passage of his paper further on, Buddensieg himself understands all the entries in question of a two years' rental.—*Lorimer.*]

During the twenty years which we have in view in the present chapter, Wycliffe's work in Oxford was twofold—partly scientific, as a man of scholastic learning, and partly practical, as a member, and for some time president of a college, and also as *Magister regens* in the general corporation of the University. That he did not apply himself exclusively to pastoral duties in Fillingham may be assumed with certainty. With respect to his scientific labours, he began while only a Master in the faculty of Arts to give disputations and lectures on Philosophy and Logic. From many passages in his extant manuscript works it appears that he gave courses of such lectures with zeal and success. But from the time when he became Bachelor of Theology, he was at liberty to deliver theological lectures in addition; but only, in the first instance, on the Biblical books, not on the Sentences of the Lombard, as already shown. But the Biblical lectures which he delivered proved to be of the greatest use to himself. In teaching the Scriptures to others, he first learned the true meaning of them himself (*docendo discimus*); so that these lectures unconsciously served as a preparation for his later labours as a Reformer.

Work in Oxford.

But Wycliffe had also the opportunity of acquiring practical ability, and of making himself useful, by taking part as a Fellow of Merton College in the administration of that society; and doubtless his popular and beneficial activity in this position contributed essentially to bring about his appointment to the headship of Balliol. The qualities for which he was especially valued in this relation are evident from the document by which the Archbishop of Canterbury, Simon Islip, an earlier fellow-student, appointed Wycliffe to the Presidency of Canterbury Hall. The Archbishop gives as his reason for this nomination, apart from Wycliffe's learning and estimable life, his practical qualifications of fidelity, circumspection, and diligence.[1]

2.—Wycliffe as Head of Canterbury Hall and Doctor of Theology.

IN the meantime, as has just been mentioned by anticipation, Wycliffe had been appointed Warden of Canterbury Hall, a small newly-founded college; but this position also, without any blame on his part, proved to be of only short duration. This point in his biography, however, is attended with more than one historical difficulty, although till 1840 it was universally believed that Wycliffe was for some time head of this new hall.

[1] Lewis, *Life of Wiclif*, Appendix No. 3, p. 290.

Simon Islip, Archbishop of Canterbury, founded a Hall in Oxford which should bear the name of the Archiepiscopal See. Its first warden was a monk of violent character named Wood-hall, under whom there were incessant contentions among the members. To remedy this scandal, the Archbishop removed Woodhall from the headship, and replaced three other members, who were monks, by secular priests. In 1365 he appointed 'John of Wiclif' to be second warden, and intrusted to him the oversight of the eleven scholars, now all seculars. But in the following spring (April 26, 1366), the active Archbishop Islip died, and was succeeded as Primate of England early in 1367 by Simon Langham, a man who had previously been a monk, and continued to cherish a thoroughly monastic spirit. By him Wycliffe was deposed from his wardenship, and the three members who had been introduced with him were removed from the college. Langham also restored Woodhall to the headship, and re-installed the three monks who had been deprived with him. Wycliffe and the three Fellows appealed from the Archbishop to the Pope, but the process proved uncommonly protracted, and ended in 1370 with the rejection of Wycliffe and his fellow-appellants, and the confirmation of their opponents in their several places.

Canterbury Hall.

The termination of this affair exceeds by several years the limit of that period of Wycliffe's life with which we are now concerned; but for the sake of connection we shall dispose of the whole subject here. From the fourteenth century to our own time, this chapter of Wycliffe's history has been turned to use against him by his literary adversaries. They knew how to attribute his antagonistic tendencies, and especially his attacks upon the Pope and the monastic system, to motives of petty personal revenge for the losses which he had incurred on this occasion, and thus to damage his character and fame. We shall, therefore, have to inquire whether this imputation is well grounded or not, keeping before us, here as always, the truth as our highest aim.

We might, indeed, at once dispense with such an examination, if it could be shown that this whole story has been interwoven with the biography of the precursor of the Reformation only through confounding him with another person of the same name. This view of the subject has, in fact, been recently entertained and defended with no little skill and learning by competent scholars, whose aim, it is only fair to state, was by no means to defend Wycliffe against imputation, but simply and solely to bring to light the historical facts of the case.

Two Wycliffes.

The historico-critical difficulties which have here to be solved may be comprised in two questions:—

1. Is 'John of Wiclif,' the Warden of Canterbury Hall, identical with Wycliffe, the precursor of the Reformation, or is he not?
2. Was the appointment of Wycliffe to the headship of the Hall, and of those three secular priests or members of the same, contrary to the terms of the foundation, or not?

We shall be obliged to distinguish these two questions, but we cannot keep them separate in our inquiry.

In August, 1841, there appeared an article in the *Gentleman's Magazine*, known afterwards to be by Mr. W. J. Courthope, a member of the Heralds' College. This article first made the attempt to show that 'John Wyclyve,' the Warden of Canterbury Hall, was a person to be carefully distinguished from the celebrated Wycliffe.[1] The writer had been led to this conclusion in the course of drawing up a local history of the Archbishop's Palace of Mayfield, in Sussex. He discovered, that is to say, in the archives of Canterbury, that on July 20, 1361, a 'John Wyclyve,' or 'Whytclyve,' was appointed parish priest of Mayfield by Archbishop Islip—the same prelate who, four years later, nominated 'John Wyclyve, to the presidency of Canterbury Hall; and it is very remarkable that the deed of this later nomination is dated Mayfield, December 9, 1365. Islip seems to have had his ordinary residence there since the time when he appointed 'John of Wyclyve' to the parish. Further, the tone in which the Archbishop speaks in the deed of the learning and excellent personal qualities of the man whom he nominates to the wardenship presupposes intimate acquaintance, and seems more like the praise of a friend than a merely formal commendation.[2] Another circumstance urged as worthy of consideration is that the name itself in both documents is written *clyve* in the second syllable, whereas the name of our Wycliffe and the Warden of Balliol is found in all the documents written with *clif* or *cliffe*. Last of all, the critic lays stress upon the fact that the Archbishop, in April, 1366, was taking steps to allocate the income of the parish church of Mayfield to the support of the Warden of the Hall, which, however, was prevented by his death. But all this appears decidedly

The Rector of Mayfield.

---

[1] The substance of the article is given in the appendix to Pratt and Stoughton's edition of Foxe's *Acts and Monuments*, vol. II., p. 943, and in Vaughan's *Monograph*, Appendix, p. 547. In the latter, however, 1844 is printed by mistake for 1841.

[2] '*Ad vitae tuae et conversationis laudabilis honestatem, literarumque scientiam, quibus personam tuam in artibus magistratam* (sic, no doubt for *magistratum*) *Altissimus insignivit, mentis nostrae oculos dirigentes, ac de tuis fidelitate, circumspectione et industria plurimum confidentes, in custodem Aulae nostrae Cantuar.—te praeficimus,*' etc.—Wood's *History and Antiquities, Oxon.*, I. p. 184; Lewis, *Life of Wiclif*, p. 290.

to imply that it was the parish priest of Mayfield who was promoted to the Wardenship of the Hall: he was, however, in 1380 transferred to the neighbouring parish of Horsted Keynes, and received a prebend in the cathedral church of Chichester. He died in 1383—only one year before our Wycliffe.

This learned and acute investigation attracted much attention. On the one hand, it commended itself to many, and there were not wanting men of learning who went even farther, undertaking to prove that *three*, or even *four* men of the name of John Wycliffe, all belonging to the clerical order, were living at the same time. These assertions we leave out of account, as resting upon a misunderstanding. But still we ought not to accept, untested, the view that it was John Wyclyve, parish priest of Mayfield, and afterwards of Horsted Keynes, and not the celebrated Wycliffe, who was promoted by Islip to the Wardenship of the new Hall in Oxford, deposed by the Archbishop's successor, and thereby led to carry on a process before the Roman Curia. This view has been accepted and supported with additional arguments by other investigators besides Mr. Courthope, especially by the late Professor of Ecclesiastical History in Oxford, Walter Waddington Shirley.[1] The latter also is of opinion that that John Wyclif who is mentioned as member and seneschal of Merton College in 1356, must likewise have been the Wyclyve of Mayfield, and not our Wycliffe. To this last point, which we believe we have already disposed of, we shall have occasion once more to return. But the question whether John Wyclyve, the head of Canterbury Hall, was, or was not, one and the same person with our Wycliffe remains, as we believe, to this day undecided. Shirley and others answer it in the negative, while Vaughan and the learned editors of the Wycliffe Bible, the Rev. Josiah Forshall and Sir Frederic Madden, affirm it most decidedly.[2]

Let us first examine the grounds which are alleged against the identity of our Wycliffe, and in support of that of the less celebrated Wyclyve of Mayfield, with the Warden of Canterbury Hall.

Wyclyve of Mayfield not Warden.

1. The argument founded upon the *form of the name* is converted, upon closer examination, into an argument in favour of the identification of our Wycliffe with the Warden of Canterbury Hall. By careful investigation among documents of the period, the late Prebendary Wilkinson established the fact that the name of the parish priest of Mayfield is always written Whitcliff, or Whytclyfe, etc., *i.e.*,

---

[1] In a long Excursus to his edition of the *Fasciculi Zizaniorum*, p. 513-528.

[2] It may now however be regarded as settled in the affirmative.

is uniformly written with *t* in the first syllable, while the name of our Wycliffe and of the Warden of that Hall never appears with *t* in the first syllable.'¹ 2. The argument founded upon the circumstance that the Archbishop's deed of appointment is dated at Mayfield is a precarious one, for this fact, taken by itself, by no means necessarily leads to the inference which has been drawn from it. 3. This second ground is combined with a third, viz., that the terms of the deed imply a personal acquaintance of the Archbishop with his nominee. This is undoubtedly the case. But it does not follow that the Archbishop's nominee was the parish priest of Mayfield, with whom, of course, from his residence there for several years, he was perfectly well acquainted. It is quite possible that the Archbishop was also personally acquainted with our Wycliffe; for if it is true that the Wycliffe known to fame was for several years after his student course a member of Merton College, it is extremely probable that he and the said Archbishop, who was also of the same college, were from that time on a footing of mutual acquaintance and regard. —The other points alleged in support of this view we leave aside, as of less importance; but the observations already made justify us, we believe, in maintaining that the grounds which have been alleged against the identity of our Wycliffe with the head of Canterbury Hall prove absolutely nothing.

On the other hand, if we are not quite mistaken, the positive testimonies in favour of the identity are entirely decisive. 1. The oldest testimony in support of it is that of a younger contemporary of Wycliffe. The learned Franciscan and Doctor of Theology, William Woodford,—who wrote against Wycliffe while he was still living, and of whom Wycliffe, so far as I can find, speaks with genuine respect,²—mentions, in a controversial treatise dated 1381, entitled *Seventy-Two Questions concerning the Sacrament of the Altar*, as a well-known fact that Wycliffe was driven from his position at Canterbury Hall by prelates and endowed monks. Still further, Woodford connected Wycliffe's subsequent antagonism to the endowed orders with that incident of his life.³ This testi-

Testimony of Woodford.

---

¹ [This statement is too sweeping. See *Wiclif's Place in History*, by Prof. Burrows, p. 51. We must fall back on the extreme uncertainty of mediæval spelling.]

² Wycliffe calls him *Doctor meus Reverendus Mr. Willelmus Wodford* in his work *De Civili Dominio*, III. c. 18, Vienna MSS., 1340, fol. 141, col. 2. He says of him—'*Arguit contra hoc compendiose et subtiliter more suo. Et revera obligacior et amplius huic doctori meo, quo in diversis gradibus et actibus scolasticis didici ex ejus exercitatione modesta multas mihi notabiles veritates.*'

³ Of this writing, which has never been printed—*Septuaginta duo Quæstiones de Sacramento Altaris*—there is preserved a MS. in the Bodleian, No. 703. Harl. 31, fol. 31. Under Quæstio 50 the author speaks of the polemic of Wycliffe against the monks in the following style :—'*Et hæc contra religiosos insania generata est ex corruptione. Nam priusquam per religiosos possessionatos et prælatos expulsus fuerat de aula monachorum Cantuariæ,*

mony, coming as it does from a contemporary, seems scarcely to leave room for any remaining doubt. It has been attempted, notwithstanding, to diminish the weight of Woodford's testimony by arguing that he could not have had any personal recollection of that incident, for as his latest work was written so late as the year 1433, he must have been still a boy at the time of the event in question; besides which, these *Seventy-Two Questions* were written, it is alleged, in great haste, and at a time of strong excitement and zealous controversy, when every story to the discredit of Wycliffe might be expected to find willing ears. Last of all, Woodford never repeated this allegation in his later writings; and his scholar, Thomas of Walden, never once touches upon it in his great polemical work— from which it may be concluded that the latter had no belief in its truth.[1] To all which we reply that though Woodford was a younger man than Wycliffe, he must have lived in Oxford with him for some considerable time, as is manifest from the language of Wycliffe quoted in note 1 on the preceding page. Woodford, therefore, might very well have had an exact and certain knowledge of the whole affair; and his manner of referring to the subject corresponds well with this supposition, for it is no more than an incidental allusion, as to a well-known fact, introduced chiefly because of Wycliffe's polemics against the endowed orders. Nor can the circumstances that Woodford does not recur to the subject in his later writings, and that Thomas of Walden, who wrote after him, never once mentions it, be of any avail as proof against the truth of a fact vouched for by such testimony. It is well known how precarious arguments *a silentio* are wont in general to be. We are, therefore, still prepared to assign to the testimony of Woodford a decisive weight in support of the fact that our Wycliffe was nominated to the headship of Canterbury Hall, but before two years had passed away was driven from his position.

2. It is remarkable that in Wycliffe's own writings a passage is found where he treats fully of the whole affair;[2] but he handles the matter so much upon its own merits, and so little as a personal affair, that at first sight it might admit of a doubt whether he had

nihil contra possessionatos attemptavit quod esset alicujus ponderis. Et priusquam per religiosos mendicantes reprobatus fuit publice de heresibus in sacramento altaris, nihil contra eos attemptavit, sed posterius multipliciter eos diffamavit; ita quod doctrinæ suæ malæ et infestæ contra religiosos et possessionatos et mendicantes generatæ fuerunt ex putrefactionibus et melancoliis.'—Shirley, p. 517.

[1] Shirley, as above.
[2] Shirley was the first to call attention to this passage, and he has given it, though not at full length, in the 'Note on the two John Wiclifs,' at the end of the *Fasciculi*, p. 526. I had found the passage before I observed that he had already given an extract from it. But I found it necessary to reproduce the context with somewhat greater fulness.

himself really taken any part in the business. In fact, his manner of speaking has even been thought by some to prove that he himself was not the person in question. With all the more exactness must we look into the language which he employs, having regard to the whole connection of the passage. In the section of his book, *De Ecclesia*, containing the passage, he is treating of the property of the Church, and the question in ch. 16 is whether the provision of landed property for the Church is really a necessity and a benefit to her, and not rather a mischief. In particular, the author discusses the question, assuming the 'Donation of Constantine' to be a historical fact, whether Silvester did right in accepting that Donation. This question Wycliffe answers in the negative. But he also examines all the arguments adduced by the opposite side against this negative. Among others, he reviews the fifth objection brought against his opinion, viz., that if Bishop Silvester in Rome committed a sin in accepting the permanent endowment of the Church with lands, then in like manner the colleges in Oxford had sinned in accepting gifts of temporal estates for the support of poor clerics, and it must consequently be the duty of the members of those colleges spontaneously to forego the continued possession of such gifts; yea, that they ought in strict propriety to solicit their promoters and patrons to recall these dangerous endowments. But by such a course essential injury would be done to the religious liberality of the people, and not only to the income of the clergy derived from such foundations, but also to the provision made for the poor. It will be seen that the indirect mode of proof used by Wycliffe's opponents takes the form of reasoning *per deducens ad familiare inconveniens*, *i.e.*, they are fain to deduce from his contention a consequence which touches very nearly the interest both of himself and the corporation to which he belongs (*familiare*), the intolerableness of which or its practical hurtfulness (*inconveniens*) must be obvious.

In his reply Wycliffe denies the pretended logical exigency of this reasoning, as if it followed from his premises that all endowments for the benefit of the University were sinful. He urges that it is possible for a sin of inadvertence to creep in, not only in a thing which is good in itself, but also in a transaction which is morally good in respect to the personal motive from which it springs. And this he proceeds to make plain *in familiariori exemplo*, by an example touching himself still more closely.[1] This example is none other than the incident of *the*

---

[1] The words *in familiariori exemplo* cannot be understood in any other sense. The *comparative* here points back to the preceding *positive, familiare inconveniens*.

foundation of a college in Oxford by Archbishop Islip. He does not mention Canterbury Hall by name, but that this college and no other is meant cannot admit of the slightest doubt. Wycliffe mentions two chief particulars in relation to this Hall: first, its original foundation by Simon Islip, and its endowment with landed property; and next, the upsetting of that foundation by Archbishop Simon Langham, whom he calls Anti-Simon, because, with the same baptismal name as Islip, his way of proceeding was antagonistic to the Archbishop's. To the founder he ascribes a purer motive in his provision for the college even than had found place in the endowment of any English monastery; yet Wycliffe was of opinion that Islip had acted in the matter not without sin, for the incorporation of a parish church, or the alienation of an estate in mortmain, can never take place without sin, both in the giver and the receiver.[1] But as to Islip's successor in the primacy, Wycliffe maintains most distinctly that he sinned much more than Islip himself in upsetting the arrangements in reference to the college. Now, the circumstance that Wycliffe in this passage does not expressly and unmistakably speak of himself as one concerned in the college and the change which it underwent, is insufficient to shake our conviction that he had this personal concern in it notwithstanding. His mode of speaking of himself in the third person we are familiar with in other instances; and that the incident had a special relation to his own person, he gives us clearly to understand in his use of the words *familiarius exemplum.*

Archbishop Islip's intentions.

At the time when he wrote thus fully, ten years had passed away since his removal from Canterbury Hall, for this book *De Ecclesia* was finished, as we undertake to show with precision, in the year 1378. The affair had long ceased to give pain; and although at the time he had felt it keenly, the author was now able to speak of it with perfect coolness, and simply as a matter of fact. Like his opponent Woodford, however, Wycliffe speaks of the incident in a

---

Opponents had pointed to the endowments of the University and its colleges as matters nearly affecting Wycliffe's interest; but Wycliffe replies by pointing to something which touched his personal interest more nearly and more directly still; and it is this comparative *familiariori exemplo*—not Shirley's reading of the MS. *familiari*—which is of decisive importance for our inquiry.

[1] Wycliffe here no doubt alludes, in addition to the estate of Woodford, to the church of 'Pageham' (Pagham in Sussex, on the coast of the Channel), which the Archbishop had incorporated with the foundation of his hall, as appears from several documents which have come down to us. (*Vide* Lewis, pp. 285, 293.) Shirley is right in referring the alleged sin of Archbishop Islip to this act of incorporation, whereas Dr. Vaughan, in an article in *The British Quarterly Review,* October, 1858, erroneously refers Wycliffe's censure to the circumstance that the Primate had, in the first instance, introduced into his foundation both monks and seculars.

manner which implies that it was one well known to all; for, with the exception of the founder himself, he does not mention a single name —neither that of the college nor that of Langham, nor even a single name of any of the members of the college, earlier or later; and he dwells only upon such points as were of substantive importance. On the one hand, he notes that the design of the endowment of the foundation was a truly pious one; that the statutes and arrangements of the house were worthy of praise, and fitted to benefit the Church; and that by the Archbishop's appointment only secular clerics —*i.e.*, learned men not belonging to any of the monastic orders— were to devote themselves therein to science. On the other hand, Wycliffe mentions how after Islip's death his instructions were frustrated, the members who were in the enjoyment of the foundation dispossessed, and several introduced who were by no means in need of such a provision, but, on the contrary, in very comfortable circumstances. But he does not expressly say that the latter were monks, and members of the Benedictine foundation of Canterbury, although this can be gathered from the context; while it is plainly avowed that all the changes in the membership of the college had been carried through by means of false representations (*commenta mendacii, fucus*), and not without simony besides (*symoniace*).

This occurrence, Wycliffe thinks, ought to be a warning to the Bishop of Winchester, to watch carefully lest a similar fate should befall his own foundation. William of Wykeham, one of the leading prelates and statesmen of England in the fourteenth century (died 1404), had occupied himself since 1373 with the foundation of a great college in Oxford; he had already formed a society in that year, for whose maintenance he provided; in 1379 he concluded his purchases of ground as a site for the house; and on April 13, 1386, several years after Wycliffe's death, there took place the solemn consecration of 'St. Mary's College of Winchester in Oxford,' which soon afterwards received the name of 'New College,' under which it flourishes at the present day. The way in which Wycliffe speaks of Wykeham's foundation shows clearly that the fact was not yet an accomplished one, but was still only in the stage of preparation. Otherwise, the advice which he modestly gives the Bishop (*consulendum videtur domino Wyntoniensi*, etc.) would have come too late.[1]

Let us now proceed to examine the second question, Was the appointment of Wycliffe as Warden of Canterbury Hall, and of the

[1] Robert Lowth, *Life of William of Wykeham, Bishop of Winchester*, 1758, pp. 93, 176.

three secular priests, William Selby, William Middleworth, and Richard Benger as members of the same, contrary or not to the provisions of the foundation?[1]

Questions between monks and seculars.

Wycliffe's opponents answered this question, of course, in the affirmative. They asserted that the statutes of the college had prescribed, as a fixed principle, that a Benedictine of the chapter of Canterbury should be warden, and that three other monks from the same chapter should be members; implying that Wycliffe and those associated with him had put forward unwarrantable claims in demanding that the government of the college should lie in the hands of secular priests, and that Wycliffe should be made head. It was actually Wycliffe and his friends, they alleged, who had excluded from the College Henry Woodhall, the existing warden, and those members, who, like him, were Benedictines of Canterbury.[2]

According to Wycliffe's showing, the exact opposite of all this was the truth, viz., that Archbishop Islip had ordained that secular priests alone should study in the college; and it was only after the death of the founder that members of the archiepiscopal chapter, contrary to his will, had placed themselves in possession. These two statements are so directly contradictory as to nullify each other. We must look for information from other sources in order to arrive at a satisfactory conclusion on the subject. And fortunately such information is available in the eight documents relating to these events, which Lewis obtained from the archiepiscopal archives, and published in the Appendix to his *Life of Wiclif*. Two royal edicts in particular are here of importance. In the first, dated October 20, 1361, Edward III. grants his consent to the proposal of Archbishop Simon Islip to found a Canterbury Hall in Oxford, and to attach to and incorporate with this hall, as soon as it should be erected, the church, *i.e.*, the church revenues of Pagham in Sussex. The second royal ordinance, dated April 8, 1372, contains the confirmation of the Papal judgment of 1370, by which Wycliffe and his associates were finally excluded from Canterbury Hall. In both these decrees mention is made of two classes of members of the college, who, according to the intention of the founder, were to live there together—monks and non-

---

[1] [The identity of our Wycliffe with the Warden of Canterbury Hall is indirectly confirmed by the circumstance that Benger, Middleworth, and Selby, who were members of the hall under John Wycliffe, 1365-66, had previously been members of Merton College, like Wycliffe himself, and were afterwards, with the exception of Benger, members of Queen's College, with which Wycliffe also, as is well known, stood in a certain connection.—*Vide* Buddensieg, *Zeitschrift* (comp. p. 101, note 2), p. 336.—*Lorimer*.]

[2] We learn that this was the representation of the case made in the complaint addressed by Wycliffe's opponents to the Papal See, from the mandate of Urban V. of May 11, 1370, by which the process was decided.—*Vide* Lewis, p. 292 f, for the documents.

monks;[1] and in the second decree, consistently with this, a charge of departure from the terms of the original royal confirmation is laid equally against the founder himself, for having subsequently set aside the monkish members in favour of the seculars, and against the Papal decision, in virtue of which, in all time coming, monks alone from the Benedictine Convent of Canterbury should be members.[2] But notwithstanding this charge, Edward III. in the latter edict grants remission for these violations of the fundamental statute of Islip, but not without requiring the Prior and Convent of Canterbury to pay into the King's treasury 200 marks,[3] a *naïve* condition, which confirms in the fullest manner Wycliffe's allegation, that simony had had a part in the game. Thus, it appears that the royal confirmation of the foundation originally proceeded on the assumption that two classes of members should be united in the college, monks and non-monks.

This confirmation, however, was set forth before Canterbury Hall was actually founded, when the Archbishop had first determined upon its plan, and was desirous of paving the way for carrying it out by obtaining the necessary consent on the part of the State. The document, therefore, allows conclusions to be drawn from it only in regard to the original intentions of the founder, but does not prove that when Islip, a year later (1362), actually completed the foundation and carried it into effect, this twofold description of membership was established by statute. In this connection it is in the highest degree noteworthy that the Archbishop himself, in his deed of April 13, 1363, wherein he endows the hall with his estate at Woodford, although referring to the number of the members as twelve, does not, by a single word, give it to be understood that some of them must be monks.[4] Yet that this was indeed his intention would appear from the deed of nomination, March 13, 1362; the Prior and Chapter of Christ Church in Canterbury propose to Archbishop Islip for the headship of the new-founded Canterbury Hall in Oxford three of their brethren of the Benedictine Abbey (Henry Woodhall, Doctor of Theology, Dr. John Redingate, and William Richmond), from whom he may himself appoint the warden. In this document, in fact, they refer to an order made by the Archbishop himself, in virtue of which this nomination should be made by them.[5] There is no room,

Marginal note: Statutes of the college.

---

[1] '*Aula (Cantuariensis) in qua certus erit numerus scolarium tam religiosorum quam secularium,*' etc.—No. 1. in Lewis, p. 285; No. 8, pp. 297, 301.

[2] '*Præter licentiam nostram supradictam. Contra formam licentiæ nostræ supradictæ.*'—Lewis, pp. 298, 299.

[3] '*De gratia nostra speciali, et pro ducentis marcis, quas dicti Prior et conventus nobis solverunt in hanaperio nostro, perdonavimus omnes transgressiones factas,*' etc.—Lewis, p. 229.

[4] '*Quam (aulam) pro duodenario studentium numero duximus ordinandam.*'—Lewis, p. 287, No. 2.

[5] '*Juxta formam et effectum ordinationis vestræ factæ in hac parte.*'—Lewis, p. 291. No. 5.

therefore, to doubt that the Archbishop, in the first instance, desired that at least the head of his college should be taken from the Benedictine order, and more specifically from the Chapter of Christ Church in Canterbury, and that he secured this by his statutes. But it does not appear that any provision was made by the deeds of foundation that, in addition to the dignity of the headship, three places of the membership must also be filled with monks;[1] still, as a matter of fact, there were found in the hall, during the first stage of its existence, in addition to Henry Woodhall, who was its first warden, three other monks from the Benedictine monastery of Canterbury.

How it came to pass that a change in this respect was introduced does not clearly appear. The monk party represent the course of events in this manner: that Wycliffe and his associates (Selby, Middleworth, and Benger), in an overbearing spirit, and without warrant, put forth the claim that the government of the college ought to be in the hands of secular priests, and in particular that John Wycliffe ought to be warden; and they had accordingly expelled the said warden, Henry Woodhall, and the other Benedictines, from the college, and taken possession of the property of the foundation.[2] But that this representation is in contradiction to the actual course of affairs is evident, beyond doubt, from the royal edict of April 8, 1372, before mentioned, in which it is plainly stated, that it was the Archbishop himself who displaced the existing warden and those members who were monks, allowing only those scholars who were not monks to remain, and appointing a man of this class to the wardenship.[3]

Allegations of the monkish party.

Royal warrant.

The testimony of this royal warrant is all the more trustworthy from its apparent impartiality, for with these words is immediately connected the inculpatory remark, that this measure of the Archbishop was in contradiction to the original authorisation which had been conferred on the part of the State. How the Archbishop had influenced this alteration is not intimated. But the words of the document give the impression that Islip had not merely intervened in a passing act, but had intended an essential alteration of the statute. It is at this point that the remark of Wycliffe (*De Ecclesia,*

---

[1] The latter was maintained by Wycliffe's opponents in their representation to the Curia; but that the matter was not placed beyond doubt is plain from the language of the deed, which intentionally left it indeterminate. Compare Lewis, No. 7, p. 292.

[2] '*False asserentes, dictum collegium per clericos seculares regi debere, dictum Johannem fore custodem collegii supradicti.*

Monachos de ipso collegio excluserunt.'—Lewis, ib.

[3] '*Amotis omnino per prædictum archiepiscopum—Custode et cæteris monachis scolaribus—ab aula prædicta, idem archiepiscopus quendam scholarem (secularem?) custodem dictæ aulæ, ac cæteros omnes scolares in eadem seculares* (so to be read instead of *scolares*) *duntaxat constituerit,*' etc.—Lewis, No. 8, p. 298.

ch. 16) comes in, that Islip had appointed that secular clerics alone should study in the college, which also took effect. Taken by themselves, his words might, indeed, lead one to think that Wycliffe is speaking of the *original* statute. But this is not his meaning. The reference is rather to the last ordinance of the Archbishop, making an alteration from the first statute; and the term *ordinance* can undoubtedly have this meaning. If we so take the words, the contradiction which at first sight seems to exist between Wycliffe's representation of the proceeding and that contained in the royal edict entirely disappears. But the statement of the opposite party laid before the Papal Curia, as gathered from the mandate of Urban V., is irreconcilable with both these representations, and must be characterised as a manifest perversion of the facts and a malicious calumny. The result of our investigation, therefore, is the following:—That the appointment of Wycliffe to the headship of Canterbury Hall was contrary to the original foundation-statutes as approved by the State, but that it proceeded upon an alteration of the first statutes subsequently made by the founder himself.

On December 9, 1365, Wycliffe was nominated Warden of Canterbury Hall by Archbishop Islip: not quite five months from that date the worthy Archbishop died (April 26, 1366). His successor, Simon Langham, was enthroned March 25, 1367, and on the sixth day thereafter he nominated John Redingate to be Warden of the Hall. Wycliffe, of course, must have been previously deposed. The new warden was a Benedictine of Canterbury, and one of the original members of the hall. Three weeks later, however, April 22, 1367, the Archbishop recalled this nomination, and re-appointed Henry Woodhall, the former head of the hall, to the wardenship. To the authority of the latter Wycliffe would now, with the other members, be subject.[1] But even so much as this reduced position in the college was not allowed to him. On the contrary, the reorganisation of Canterbury Hall intended by the monkish-minded Archbishop led to the exclusion of all the secular members. Wycliffe and his fellows appealed from the Archbishop to the Pope; but as Langham, in the next year after his being appointed Archbishop, was made Cardinal, and went to Avignon, the issue of the appeal was a judgment by which Wycliffe and his fellows were definitively expelled; and the college was thenceforward exclusively filled with monks from Christ Church at Canterbury.[2]

Wycliffe dispossessed.

---

[1] Lewis, No. 6, p. 292. An extract from a document of the archiepiscopal archives.

[2] '*Decrevit et declaravit, solos Monachos prædictæ ecclesiæ Cant., secularibus exclusis, debere in dicto collegio perpetuo remanere.*'—Lewis, No. 7, p. 295.

This was at all events still more opposed to the original meaning and intention of the foundation than the exclusive occupation of the hall by seculars. For from the first the secular element had far outweighed the other, even if we assume, what is by no means proved, that the original statutes ordained that four members of the twelve should be monks; still more, if the only point fixed by the statutes was that the head of the house should be a Benedictine of Canterbury, the introduction of three other Canterbury monks not being prescribed in the statutes, but proceeding from the free determination of the founder. Wycliffe himself, as we have seen, uses very strong language respecting the contrast between the new Archbishop's measures and the decree (more accurately the last decree) of his predecessor (*eversum est tam pii patroni propositum. Anti-Simon,* etc.). And the royal edict itself appears to look upon Langham's reconstitution of the college as a much more serious contradiction to the original foundation approved by the State than the alteration which was made by Islip himself; for of this latter it is only said that it was done *præter licentiam nostram supradictam*—'beyond or in excess of our foresaid licence'— whereas the exclusion of all secular members is declared to be *contra formam licentiæ nostræ supradictæ*—'in the teeth of our licence,' and not merely beyond or in excess of it. This difference of language is plainly intentional; and it will certainly be allowed that the latter expression is the stronger and more decisive of the two. Here the original statute is the only standard of judgment, for in this edict, issued by the Government, it is only the legality of the different acts in question which is dealt with.

His criticisms on the proceeding.

But Wycliffe does not apply to the question this low formal standard only, but forms his judgment of the last organic change which had been made upon its substantive merits in point of congruity with the ends contemplated by the foundation. And here his judgment is one of entire disapproval, because the newly-appointed members, being already richly provided for, were by no means in need of the bounty of such a foundation. He is here thinking of the extensive landed possessions belonging to the Benedictine monastery of Canterbury, which was organically connected with the archiepiscopal cathedral, while the colleges in Oxford, as in Paris and other universities, were originally and principally intended for the support of the poorer class of students, and of masters without independent means. Wycliffe is here speaking, however, as before remarked, in a purely objective manner, and by no means in such a tone as would warrant us to assume that the painful experiences which he had had to endure in his relations to the oft-mentioned college, had a determining influence upon his ecclesiastical views and work. It is only, however, a thorough exhibition of his public conduct that can throw light upon the question whether there is any truth in the reproach against Wycliffe, that the position of antagonism taken up by him against the Church, especially against prelates and monastic orders, arose from a sense of injury to his own private interests, and was thus inspired by low motives and personal revenge.

Canterbury Hall no longer exists in Oxford as an independent foundation, for after the Reformation the buildings of the hall were incorporated with the stately College of Christ Church, founded by Cardinal Wolsey.

We now return to the year 1366—the limit of the period assigned to the present chapter, which time we have been led to exceed by four or six years, in order to finish the topic now discussed. This year was possibly the date at which Wycliffe reached the highest degree of academic dignity, that of Doctor in the Theological Faculty. Since the sixteenth century it has been assumed, on the authority of a statement of Bishop Bale, that Wycliffe became Doctor of Theology in 1372.[1] In assigning this date, Bale, it may be conjectured, proceeded upon the fact that in the royal ordinance of July 26, 1374, which nominated commissioners for negotiations with the Papal Court, Wycliffe is introduced as *sacræ theologiæ Professor*, and therefore must have been already doctor.[2] And here let me remark, by the way, that the title of professor of theology given to Wycliffe has generally been misunderstood, as though it meant that he had been appointed to a professorial chair. But this rests upon an anachronism. The mediæval universities, down at least to the fifteenth century, knew nothing of professors, in the sense of modern universities. The title *sacræ paginæ*, or *theologiæ Professor*, denotes, in the fourteenth century, not an university office, to be thought of in connection with particular duties and rights, and especially with a fixed stipend, but only an academic degree; for it is synonymous with Doctor of Theology. Such an one had the full right to deliver theological lectures, but was under no special obligation to do so, nor, apart from some trifling dues as a member of the Theological Faculty, had he any salary proper, except in cases where, along with the degree, some church living might be conferred upon him.[3]

Wycliffe a Doctor of Divinity.

---
[1] So Vaughan in his latest work on Wycliffe, the *Monograph*, p. 138.
[2] Lewis, in Appendix No. 11, p. 304.
[3] Comp. Thurot, *De l'Organisation de l'enseignement dans l'Université de Paris au Moyen age*, p. 158.

So much as this we know from the royal document just mentioned—that Wycliffe was a Doctor of Theology in the year 1374. But it is only the latest possible date which is thus fixed; and Bale conjectured with good reason, that Wycliffe must have become a doctor some considerable time before, and suggested the year 1372. Shirley, on the other hand, believes that he is able to make out, with some probability, that Wycliffe was promoted to this degree as early as 1363, a view which he supports by several controversial pieces of the Carmelite John Cunningham, directed against Wycliffe, which he has himself published. And it is, indeed, worthy of note that that monkish theologian, in his first essay, as well as in the introduction to it, speaks of Wycliffe exclusively under the title of *magister*, whereas in the second and third he uses the titles *magister* and *doctor* interchangeably.[1] Now the first of these essays, where the latter title never once occurs, has reference to a tract of Wycliffe, in which he mentions that it is not his intention to go, *for the present*, into the question of the right of property (*de dominio*);[2] while a fragment upon this question, which Lewis gives in his appendix to the *Life of Wiclif*,[3] was probably written in 1366, and the larger work of Wycliffe, *De Dominio Divino*, from which that fragment was probably taken, was written at latest in 1368. Hence Shirley believes that he may indicate the year 1363, as that in which Wycliffe received his degree.

We are unable, however, to concur in this conjecture, because we have positive testimony to show that in the end of the year 1365, Wycliffe was only Master of Arts, and not yet Doctor of Theology. For Archbishop Islip describes him in the document of December 9, 1365, in which he nominates him to the headship of Canterbury Hall, as *magister in artibus*,[4] whereas the whole connection shows that he would certainly have laid stress upon the higher academic degree, if Wycliffe had already possessed it.

The fact then stands thus, that Wycliffe was a Doctor of Theology in 1374, but not in 1365. He must thus have taken that degree some time during the intervening period; but in the absence of documentary authority it is impossible to fix the precise date.

---

[1] Shirley, *Fasciculi*, etc., pp. 4, 14, 43, particularly pp. 73 and 88. Comp. Introduction, p. xvi.
[2] *Ib.* p. 456.
[3] Lewis, No. 30, p. 349.

[4] Lewis, No. 3, p. 290. *Personam tuam in artibus magistratam* — so it should be read with Anthony Wood, not *magistratum*, as Lewis has it. [The above argument of course assumes Wycliffe's headship of Canterbury Hall.]

CHAPTER IV.

WYCLIFFE'S FIRST PUBLIC APPEARANCE IN THE ECCLESIASTICO-POLITICAL AFFAIRS OF ENGLAND.

1.—Wycliffe as a Patriot.

AFTER having followed with attention the course of Wycliffe's purely academic career up to the present point, we can only be astonished to behold him all at once upon the stage of public life. Hitherto we have known him only as a man of science—as a quiet scholar. From his youth to the flower of his manhood, he had only seldom left, so far as we can see, the precincts of the university city of Oxford. He seems even to have visited but rarely his parish of Fillingham, to which he had been presented in 1361, and on each occasion only for a short time. We know, in fact, that he obtained a dispensation from his bishop to enable him to remain at the University, and devote himself without interruption to science.

It is true that as Fellow and Seneschal of Merton College,[1] as Master of Balliol, and as Warden of Canterbury Hall, he had had *The student becomes the man of action.* practical problems of many kinds to solve, and had been much occupied with business of an economic, legal, and administrative description. The judgment of his patron in high place, Archbishop Islip, when he entrusted him with the government of Canterbury Hall, is assurance to us that Wycliffe had already, both in Merton and Balliol, proved himself to be a man of practical talent, and upright, circumspect, and energetic in matters of business. Still, all this activity had been exerted within a narrow circle, and one more or less closely connected with properly scientific life. But now we see the scholar step out from the quiet scenes of the University to take part in public affairs. For it was not merely that Wycliffe began to manifest his interest in the affairs of the kingdom in a Christian and literary way, which he might have

[[1] It will be remembered that this is hardly substantiated. See note, p. 100.]

done without quitting his chamber in the cloistered buildings of his college; but he came personally forward to take an active part in the public business of Church and State. This change of position comes upon us with surprise; but yet we are not to imagine that Wycliffe had altered, but only that he now began to reveal another aspect of his character. For Wycliffe was a many-sided man; one of high mark, who not only entered deeply into all that influenced, on many different sides, his own people and times, but who, in some things, was far in advance of his age—a prophet and type of what was still in the future. And it is only when we study separately the many different qualities which were combined in him, and then again survey them in their innermost unity, that we shall be able to draw a true and faithful picture of his powerful personality.

At this moment it is Wycliffe the patriot whom we have to depict. He represents in his own person that intensification of English national feeling which was so conspicuous in the fourteenth century, when, as we have seen above, Crown and people, Norman population and Saxon, formed a compact unity, and energetically defended the autonomy, the rights and the interests of the kingdom against external influences, and especially in opposition to the Court of Rome. This spirit lived in Wycliffe with extraordinary force. His great works, still unprinted, *e.g.*, the three books *De Civili Dominio*, his work *De Ecclesia*, and others, leave upon the reader the strongest impression of a warm patriotism—of a heart glowing with zeal for the dignity of the Crown, for the honour and weal of his native land, for the rights and the constitutional liberty of the people. How often in reading his works do we come upon passages in which he recalls the memories of English history! The different invasions of the country by 'Britons, Saxons, and Normans,' all stand before his mind's eye (the Danes alone seem already forgotten). Augustine, the 'Apostle of the English,' as he calls him in one place, he mentions repeatedly in his treatises and sermons; he frequently touches upon the later Archbishops of Canterbury, especially Thomas Becket; of kings too, as Edward the Confessor and John, he speaks ever and anon; he refers to Magna Charta with distinguished consideration as the fundamental law of the kingdom, binding equally king and nobles.[1] That Wycliffe had made the law of England a subject of special study, in addition

Wycliffe's national feeling.

---

[1] *De Civili Dominio*, II., c. 5, MS. *In Magna Carta, cui rex et magnates Angliæ ex juramento obligantur*, cap. 15, sic habetur: *Nulla ecclesiastica persona— censum.* This wording and numbering of the passage do not exactly correspond to those of the document now regarded as the original authority. Wycliffe has a second reference to Magna Charta in the same chapter.

to canon and Roman law, has been known since the days of Lewis; and we have come upon several confirmations of this fact. In the same context with the reference to Magna Charta, Wycliffe speaks of the Statutes of Westminster and Statutes of Gloucester; in another place he contrasts, in connection with a particular question, the Roman law (*lex Quirina*), and the English law (*lex Anglicana*), giving preference to the latter.[1] But, so far from taking merely an academical interest in these subjects, and showing only a historical knowledge of them, he manifests a deep concern for the present condition of the nation, and a primary care for its welfare, its liberties, and its honour. Let it not be thought, however, that his intellectual horizon was bounded by the national interests of his own island-people. On the contrary, he had at heart the welfare of all Christendom, and indeed of the whole human race; but the strength of his cosmopolitanism was to be found in his deep and earnest patriotism.

It is not wonderful that such a man—a churchman and distinguished scholar on the one hand, and a thorough patriot on the other—rich in knowledge, full of insight, and inspired with zeal for the public good—should have been drawn into the career of the statesman and the diplomatist. Yet he never lost himself in purely political affairs; it was only where questions and measures combined the ecclesiastical and the political that he gave his co-operation; and, in the end, his undivided strength was concentrated upon the ecclesiastical domain.

But before we follow him into public life, it is necessary to get rid of an impression which has hitherto almost universally prevailed. As
Alleged attacks on the mendicant orders. early as the sixteenth century the literary historians, John Leland and John Bale, put forward the view—which, in the eighteenth, Lewis fully developed in his *History*, and which was, in substance, maintained by Vaughan himself—that Wycliffe commenced his exertions for a reform of the Church with attacks upon the monastic system, especially upon the Mendicant Orders.

The view which is commonly taken is the following:—As early as the year 1360, immediately after the death of the celebrated Archbishop of Armagh, Richard Fitzralph, Wycliffe opened an attack in Oxford upon the Dominican and Franciscan Orders, the Augustinians and the Carmelites, on the ground of their fundamental principle of living upon the alms of the people. Indeed, it has even been represented that when Richard of Armagh died, his mantle descended upon Wycliffe, by whom his work was immediately taken up and

[1] *De Civili Dominio*, I., c. 34.

carried farther. Critical investigation, however, is unable to find any confirmation of this common opinion.

Vaughan, in 1831, had followed Anthony Wood in the confident statement that Wycliffe publicly censured the errors and failings of the Mendicant Orders as early as 1360, and became the object of their hostility in consequence.[1] But in his later work, as the fruit of more careful investigation of the subject, he is no longer able to arrive at the same confident result upon the point. He remarks, with truth, that there is no direct evidence to show that Wycliffe began that controversy at the precise date which he had previously assigned. But he continued to the last, notwithstanding, to be of opinion that Wycliffe began his work as a Reformer with attacks upon the Monastic, and especially upon the Mendicant Orders; he believed, besides, that while the exact date at which Wycliffe began the controversy could not be ascertained, it must yet be fixed at a period not much later than 1360.[2] But on this subject we are unable to agree with him, not only because, like himself, we are unaware of any direct and decisive proof that Wycliffe began his attacks upon the monks even in the years next following 1360, but because, on the contrary, we have in our hands direct proofs that Wycliffe continued to speak of the Mendicant Orders with all respectful recognition during the twenty years which elapsed between 1360 and 1380. We content ourselves here with stating, in anticipation, so much as this—that the reading of the unpublished writings of Wycliffe, among others, yields the most weighty confirmation to the statement of his opponent Woodford, that it was in connection with the controversy opened by Wycliffe on the subject of Transubstantiation, and therefore after 1381 at the earliest, that he began on principle to oppose himself to the Mendicants, who had come forward as his antagonists on that fundamental question.[3] But to this point we shall return hereafter, and we leave it now, in order to fix our attention upon the part which Wycliffe took in the public affairs of England in Church and State.[4]

---

[1] *Life and Opinions of Wycliffe*, I., 262.
[2] *John de Wycliffe*, a Monograph, 1853; p. 64, especially p. 87. Comp. also *Brit. Quart. Rev.*, 1858, October.
[3] Woodford, *Septuaginta duo Quæstiones de Sacramento Altaris*. Prof. Shirley is quite correct in maintaining in his edition of the *Fascic. Zizan* xiii. that the view hitherto held upon this point of Wycliffe's biography is an unfounded one.
[4] See Appendix by Dr. Lorimer.

2.—Wycliffe's Concern in the Rejection of the Papal Claim to Feudatory Tribute.

IN the year 1365, Pope Urban V. had renewed his claim upon Edward III. for the annual payment of one thousand marks, under the name of *Feudatory Tribute;* he had even demanded the payment of arrears extending over a period of no fewer than thirty-three years. For so long a time had the payment of the tribute been discontinued, without any remonstrance from the Papal Court. In case the King should decline to comply with this demand, he was summoned to present himself in person before the Pope as his feudal superior, to answer for his proceeding. The payment in question was imposed in 1213, as we before saw, by Innocent III. upon King John, for himself and his successors; but, in point of fact, it had been paid from the first with the greatest irregularity, and King Edward III., from the time of reaching his majority, had never allowed it, as a matter of principle, to be paid at all. When Urban claimed the payment, this prince acted with the greatest possible prudence; he laid the question before his Parliament. He had often enough been obliged, in order to meet the cost of wars, to ask Parliament to consent to increased burdens of taxation; and all the more acceptable to him was the opportunity of giving into the hands of the representatives of the country the repudiation of an impost which had been in abeyance for more than a generation. Should Parliament adopt this resolution, the Crown was covered by the country. But the burden of taxation was not the principal point of view from which the Parliament looked at the Papal demand; much more than that, the honour and independence of the kingdom was the determining consideration for its representatives; and this all the more, because, on the one hand, the war with France, and the victories obtained in it, had given a powerful stimulus to the national spirit, while, on the other hand, the political rights and liberties of the people had been heightened and secured in proportion to the sacrifices which they had been called to make of property and blood.

The Pope's claim to tribute.

The Parliament assembled in May, 1366, and the King immediately laid before it the Papal demand, desiring its opinion thereon. As may well be conceived, the prelates were the party who were placed in the greatest difficulty by this question, and they begged therefore a day's time for consideration and counsel among themselves. The result was, that they came to a unanimous conclusion, concurring herein with the other estates of the realm.

Resolution of Parliament.

Thus the Lords spiritual and temporal, together with the Commons, arrived at the decision to the effect that King John had acted entirely beyond his right in subjecting his country and people to such a feudal supremacy without their own consent; and, moreover, that the whole compact was a violation of his coronation oath. Further, the Lords and Commons declared that, in case the Pope should carry out his threatened procedure against the King, they would place the whole powers and resources of the nation at the disposal of the King for the defence of his crown and dignity. This language was as intelligible as it was forcible: Urban quickly yielded; and since that day not one word more has ever been said on the part of Rome of her feudal superiority over England, still less of a payment of feudal tribute.

In this momentous national affair Wycliffe also bore a part. That this was the case has long been known, but in what form or way he took his share in it is less clear. Since Lewis wrote his *History* of the Reformer, it has been known that Wycliffe published a polemical tract upon that question of political right, entirely siding with the Parliament; and that he did so in consequence of a sort of challenge which had been addressed to him by name by an anonymous Doctor of Theology, belonging to the Monastic Orders.[1] But how came it to pass that the gauntlet was thrown down to Wycliffe, and to no other? Wycliffe himself, in replying, expresses his astonishment at the passionate heat with which the challenge to answer the arguments of his opponent had been addressed personally to him. Nor is the explanation of the puzzle, which he mentions as having been suggested to himself by others, one which is at all satisfactory to ourselves. Three grounds, he says, had been named to him upon which the man had so acted—(1) in order that Wycliffe might be personally compromised with the Court of Rome, and that he might be heavily censured and deprived of his church benefices; (2) that the opponent himself with his connections might conciliate for themselves the favour of the Papal Court; and (3) that, as the effect of a more unlimited dominion of the Pope over England, the abbeys might be able to grasp in greater numbers the secular lordships of the kingdom, without being checked any longer by brotherly hindrance and control. We may leave untouched the

Wycliffe's vindication of Parliament.

---

[1] A considerable portion of this tract, which is of the highest interest, was included by Lewis in the Appendix to his *Hist. of Wiclif*, No. 30. The text is unfortunately in a very imperfect condition, owing, in part at least, to the state of the MS. from which it was derived. But that the tract may have been written very soon after the May Parliament of 1366, and perhaps still earlier in that year rather than in 1367, is the impression which it leaves upon me as strongly as upon the editors of the Wycliffe Bible, vol. I., p. vii., note 10, and Prof. Shirley, *Fasc. Ziz.* xvii., note 3.

last two reasons, as self-evident; but with regard to the first we must of necessity ask again, How are we to account for the hostility which seized upon Wycliffe's person on this occasion, for the purpose of blackening his character at the Court of Rome, and to bring upon him individually censure and material loss? The controversy between Wycliffe and the Mendicant Orders, alleged to have been commenced at an earlier date, cannot be used for the explanation of this fact,[1] because documentary history knows nothing of such a controversy carried on at that date. Besides, Wycliffe has here to do, beyond question, with a member of the *endowed* Orders, whose interests were by no means identical with those of the Mendicants, but often enough ran counter to them.[2] And when it is urged that Wycliffe must already before that time have signalised himself as an upholder of the independence and sovereignty of the State in relation to the Church, we acknowledge, indeed, that this is extremely likely; but it is still only a conjecture, without any positive foundation, and therefore of no real service to us in solving the difficulty.

Let us look more narrowly at the contents of the tract itself, and see whether it does not itself supply us with a solution of a more distinct and trustworthy kind. The anonymous doctor had taken his stand upon the absolutely indefeasible right of the hierarchy. He had maintained, as regarded persons, that under no circumstances could the clergy be brought before a civil tribunal; and, in regard to Church property, he had laid down the proposition that temporal lords must never, nor under any conditions, withdraw their possessions from churchmen. And with respect to the immediately pending question, touching the relation of the English Crown to the Papal See, he had maintained that the Pope had given the King the fief of the government of England, under condition that England should pay the yearly tribute of 700 marks to the Papal Court;[3] but that as this condition had remained for a time unfulfilled, the King of England had forfeited his right of monarchy.

Claims on behalf of the Pope.

In addressing himself to the task of exhibiting this latter assertion in its true light, Wycliffe begins by assuring his readers that he, as a humble and obedient son of the Church of Rome, would assert nothing which could be construed into unfairness towards that Church, or which could give any reasonable offence to a pious ear. He then

---

[1] As it has been used by Vaughan, *John de Wycliffe, a Monograph*, 1853, p. 105.

[2] This latter fact had been already remarked upon by Vaughan in his earlier work, *Life and Opinions*, etc., I., p. 283.

[3] The tribute amounted to seven hundred marks for England, and three hundred for Ireland, making together the sum of one thousand marks, as usually given.

refers his opponent, for a refutation of his views, to the votes and declarations of opinion which had been given in the Council of temporal lords.[1]

The *first* lord, a valiant soldier, had expressed himself thus: 'The kingdom of England was of old conquered by the sword of its nobles, and with the same sword has it ever been defended against hostile attacks. And even so does the matter stand in regard to the Church of Rome. Therefore my counsel is, let this demand of the Pope be absolutely refused, unless he is able to compel payment by force. Should he attempt that, it will be my business to withstand him in defence of our right.' *Answer of seven Barons.*

The *second* lord had made use of the following argument:—'A tax or a tribute may only be paid to a person authorised to receive it; now the Pope has no authority to be the receiver of this payment, and therefore any such claim on his part must be repudiated. For it is the duty of the Pope to be a prominent follower of Christ; but Christ refused to be a possessor of worldly dominion. The Pope, therefore, is bound to make the same refusal. As, therefore, we should hold the Pope to the observance of his holy duty, it follows that it is incumbent upon us to withstand him in his present demand.'

The *third* lord observed—'It seems to me that the ground upon which this demand is rested admits of being turned against the Pope; for as the Pope is the servant of the servants of God, it follows that he should take no tribute from England except for services rendered. But he serves our land in no sense whatever, either spiritually or temporally; his whole aim is to turn its possessions to his own personal use and that of his courtiers, while assisting the enemies of the country with gold and counsel. We must, therefore, as a matter of common prudence, refuse his demand. That Pope and Cardinals leave us without any help either in body or soul is a fact which we know by experience well enough.'

The *fourth* lord—'I am of opinion that it is a duty which we owe to our country to resist the Pope in this matter. For, according to his principles, he is owner-in-chief of all the property which is gifted to the Church or alienated to her in mortmain. Now, as one-third of the kingdom at least is so held in mortmain, the Pope is head over the whole of that third; but in the domain of civil lordship, there cannot be two lords of equal right, but there must be one lord superior, and the other must be vassal; from which it follows that during the vacancy of a church either the Pope must be the vassal of

---

[1] *In quodam concilio.* The Parliament is no doubt intended, but Wycliffe designedly makes use of a general expression.

the King of England, or *vice versâ*. But to make our King the inferior of any other man in this respect, we have no mind, for every donor in mortmain reserves to the King the right of feudal superiority. During that interval, therefore, the Pope behoves to be the inferior or vassal of the King. But the Pope has always neglected his duty as the King's vassal, and, therefore, he has forfeited his right.'

The *fifth* lord puts the question, 'What then may have been originally the ground upon which that undertaking (of King John) was entered into? Was that annual payment the condition of the King's absolution and his reinstalment in the hereditary right to the crown? For a pure gift, intended as a mere beneficence for all coming times, it could not in any case have been. On the former supposition (viz., that the payment was a condition of absolution), the agreement was invalid on account of the simony which was committed therein; for it is not allowable to bestow a spiritual benefit in consideration of the promise of temporal gains to be bestowed—"Freely ye have received, freely give." If the Pope imposed the tax upon the King as a penitential penalty, he ought not to have applied this alms-gift to his own uses, but should have given it to the Church of England, which the King had wronged, as a compensation for the wrong. But it is not in accordance with the spirit of religion to say—"I absolve thee under condition that thou payest me so much in all time coming." When a man in this way breaks faith with Christ, other men may also break faith with him, if the treaty be immoral. In all reason a punishment should fall upon the guilty, not upon the innocent; and as such an annual payment falls not upon the guilty King, but upon the poor innocent people, it bears the character of avarice rather than of a wholesome penalty. If, on the other hand, the second case be supposed, viz., that the Pope, in virtue of his concordat with King John, became feudal superior of the Royal House, it would then logically follow that the Pope would have power at his will and pleasure to dethrone a King of England, under pretext of having forfeited his right to the throne, and to appoint, at his discretion, a representative of his own person to occupy the throne. Is it not, then, our duty to resist principles like these?'

The *sixth* lord—'It appears to me that the act of the Pope admits of being turned against himself. For if the Pope made over England to our King as a feudal fief, and if, in so doing, he did not usurp a superiority which did not belong to him, then the Pope, at the time of that transaction with King John, was the lord of our country. But as it is not allowable to alienate Church property without a corresponding compensation, the Pope had no power to alienate a kingdom possessed of revenues so rich for an annual payment so trifling; yea, he might at his pleasure demand our country back again, under the pretence that the Church had been defrauded of more than the fifth part of the value. It is necessary, therefore, to oppose the first beginnings of this mischief. Christ Himself is the Lord-Paramount, and the Pope is a fallible man, who, in the opinion of theologians, must lose his lordship in the event of his falling into mortal sin, and therefore cannot make good any claim to the possession of England. It is enough, therefore, that we hold our kingdom as of old, immediately from Christ in fief, because *He* is the Lord-Paramount, who, alone and by Himself, authorises, in a way absolutely sufficient, every right of property allowed to created beings.'

The *seventh* lord—'I cannot but greatly wonder that you have not touched upon the over-hastiness of the King, and upon the rights of the kingdom. And yet it stands to reason that a hasty, ill-considered treaty, brought on by the King's fault, without the country's consent, can never be justly allowed to operate to its permanent mischief. According to the law of the land (*consuetudo regni*), it is necessary, before a tax of this kind is imposed, that every individual in the country, either directly or by his lord-superior, should give his consent. Although the King and some few misguided persons gave their consent to the treaty, they had no warrant to do so, in the absence of the authority of the kingdom, and of the full number of consenting votes.'

To these utterances of several lords in Parliament, Wycliffe, in the tract referred to, adds little more, so far as it is known from the copy furnished by Lewis. He points out, with reason, that the treaty in question was proved, by the arguments developed in these speeches, to be both immoral and without authority. The speeches constitute the chief bulk of the tract, both in matter and space.

Before we proceed to a closer examination of the speeches which the tract communicates, let thus much be observed in a general way, that Wycliffe in this piece, in opposition to the censures cast by the monks upon the recent legislative action of the kingdom, takes up the defence of that action with warmth and emphasis. The question was, whether the State, in certain cases, is entitled to call in Church property, or whether such an act would, in all circumstances, be a wrong. The latter view was maintained by his opponents, the former is the contention of Wycliffe; and this view, we shall find below, he systematically developed and fully established.

Returning to the above speeches, it immediately appears upon an attentive examination, that the question of State-right, whether the payment demanded by the Pope, as feudal superior of the Kings of England, ought to be made without delay, or ought to be decidedly repudiated, is treated in these speeches from the most manifold points of view. The first lord—a soldier—takes for his standpoint the right of the strongest,[1] trusts to his own good sword, and reckons the amount of material force on either side. If this first speech is the outcome of a warrior-like realism, the second is inspired by a Christian idealism; for the speaker grounds his argument upon the ideal of a Pope as the follower of Christ, and would carry back the existing Pope to the condition of evangelical poverty. The third lord takes the standpoint of the country's interests, which it behoves the Pope, as 'servant of the servants of God,' to promote, in order to acquire a right to corresponding services; but this he does neither spiritually nor materially. The fourth lord applies to the question the standard of *positive* law, especially of the feudal law. The Pope, upon his own principles, is the owner of all Church property in England: now lord-paramount of all this he cannot be, for such alone is the King; he must therefore be a vassal, but as he has always disregarded his feudal duty to the throne, his right is forfeited. The fifth speaker enters into an examination of the different motives which may have led to the concordat in question under King John, which he finds in any conceivable view so objectionable as to nullify the concordat; for the transaction was either an unchristian simony, or a moral wrong, or an act of usurpation intolerable to England. The sixth speaker, like the fourth, takes the feudal law for his starting-point, but seeks to prove, that not the Pope, but Christ alone, is to be regarded as Lord-Paramount of the country. Last of all, the seventh lord applies to the question the standard of the constitution of the kingdom, and arrives at the conclusion that the concordat between King John and Innocent III. was invalid from the very first, by reason of its lacking the consent of the country in the persons of its representatives in Parliament.

If we compare, further, the leading ideas of these speeches with the decision of the Parliament of May, 1366, of which, however, only the most general features have come down to us, we immediately see that the two in all essential respects agree. The argument of the seventh lord in Wycliffe's tract is, indeed, entirely identical with the first ground given by Parliament in its Act of Repudiation, and the declaration of

---

[1] We would not say, with Boehringer, in his *Vorreformatoren*, I., *Wycliffe*, p. 63, that the standpoint taken up by this lord was that of natural right, for there is certainly a distinction to be taken between natural right and the right of the strongest.

the first lord with the Parliament's concluding declaration. The conjecture, indeed, has been made, that the whole of these speeches may very well have been merely free compositions of Wycliffe himself, preferring to put the bold thoughts which he wished to express into the mouths of others, rather than to come forward with them directly in his own person; and in doing so he has kept to the Act of Parliament and to the views of its most distinguished members, but not in the sense of reporting speeches which were actually delivered.[1] But why it should not be believed that we have here a report of speeches actually delivered, we fail to perceive. If the ancient accounts of the proceedings in Parliament, notwithstanding their extremely summary character, are nevertheless in remarkable agreement with some, at least, of Wycliffe's somewhat fuller speeches, in respect to the grounds assigned, and the whole tone of confident defiance with which they conclude, this fact is in itself a weighty reason for thinking that Wycliffe here introduces actual Parliamentary addresses.

Was Wycliffe author or reporter of the speeches?

Independently of this argument, it deserves to be taken into account that the whole effect of this polemical piece of Wycliffe depended essentially upon the fact that these speeches had been actually delivered. It may be thought, indeed, that the earls and barons of the kingdom at that period can hardly be credited with the amount of insight, and even occasionally of learning, which is conspicuous in these addresses. But the Parliamentary life of England at that day had already held on its course for more than a century, and could not fail to bring with it an amount of practice in political business by no means to be under-estimated, as well as a development of interest in public affairs, arising from constant participation in their management. The only thing which can be alleged, with some appearance of force, against the view here taken, is the circumstance that some of the thoughts referred to are just such as might have come from the soul of Wycliffe himself, *e.g.*, what the second lord says of the Pope—that before all others it behoves him to be a follower of Christ in evangelical poverty, and the like. But at the present day men often fail to have any correct idea of the wide extent to which, since the thirteenth century, the idea of 'Evangelical Poverty' had prevailed. And it may well be conceived that ideas of Wycliffe's own, too, may at length have penetrated into those circles of English society to which the language now in question was attributed. So much, indeed, as this must be conceded, that the speeches, as they lie before

[1] De Ruever Gronemann, *Diatribe in Joh. Wiclifi Vitam.* Traj. ad Rhen., 1837, p. 93.

us, were grouped together by Wycliffe, and in some particulars so moulded by him as to bear unmistakably here and there the personal impress of the reporter. But this concession need not hinder our belief that the main substance of the several speeches was taken from actual proceedings in Parliament.[1]

If this is so, we cannot avoid the question, From what source did Wycliffe learn so accurately these Parliamentary proceedings? This answer would be very simple, if the opinion expressed by some were well grounded, that Wycliffe was personally present at that session of the Legislature as a hearer.[2] But it is in the highest degree doubtful whether the proceedings of Parliament were at that day open to the public. The Parliament was rather regarded as an enlarged Privy Council of the King, and if we are not mistaken, all traces are lacking of any man who was neither a member of Parliament nor a commissioner of the King, being permitted to be present at its sittings. On the other hand, it has been thought that Wycliffe had received accurate information from one or other of those lords who were personally acquainted with him, and with whom he was associated by similar patriotic sentiments, and that he reported the speeches upon the good faith of his informant. This conjecture is worth listening to; but what if Wycliffe was himself a member of that Parliament? If he was, it would at once be plain how it came to pass that he and no other man was made the object of attack in reference to that Parliament.

Was he a member of Parliament?

At first sight, this may seem to be a conjecture more bold than probable. But, however little known, it is a fact established by documentary evidence, that, from the end of the thirteenth century, elected representatives of the inferior clergy were summoned to serve in Parliament.[3] It is also an ascertained fact, that to the Parliament of 1366, besides bishops, abbots, and lords, six masters of arts were summoned by royal order.[4] With these facts in view, it is quite conceivable that Wycliffe might have had a seat and voice in that

---

[1] We entirely agree with Vaughan on this point, who, both in his earlier and later works on Wycliffe, considers the speeches of the lords to have been actually spoken in Parliament. [So Prof. Shirley (*Fasc. Zizan.* preface, p. xix.) speaks of Wycliffe's tract as 'the earliest instance, I believe, of a report of a Parliamentary debate.']

[2] Vaughan, *Life and Opinions*, etc., I., 291, drew this conclusion from the words in Wycliffe's tract, *Quam audivi in quodam consilio a dominis secularibus;* but the words *esse datam*, used in connection with these, at once exclude this understanding of them.

[3] The piece entitled *Modus tenendi Parliamentum*, dating, according to recent investigations, from before 1295, ed. Hardy, mentions, p. 5, that the bishops were to appoint for every archdeaconry two experienced men as representatives, *adveniendum et interessendum ad Parliamentum.* Comp. Pauli, *Geschichte von England*, IV., p. 670, note I.

[4] Comp. Parry, *Parliaments and Councils of England*, Lond., 1839, p. 129.

Parliament as an elected representative of the inferior clergy, or in virtue of a royal summons. The step, it is true, from abstract possibility to probability, is still a long one. But now I find, in the unprinted works of Wycliffe, one passage at least, from the wording of which it appears clearly enough that he was at one time in Parliament, although some years later. In his book, *De Ecclesia*, he has occasion to remark that the Bishop of Rochester (this, without doubt, was Thomas Trillek) had told him under great excitement, in open sitting of Parliament, that the propositions which he had set forth in controversy had been condemned by the Papal Court.[1] It is true that in this passage we must understand the reference to be to a later Parliament than that of 1366. I conjecture that the incident took place in 1376 or 1377, namely, before the Papal censure of Gregory XI. upon several of Wycliffe's theses was publicly known. But though no more than this is established, that Wycliffe was ten years later a member of Parliament, it becomes not only possible but probable that he may already have been in Parliament some time before that date.

However, I find elsewhere in his own writings a hint that Wycliffe belonged to the May Parliament of 1366. If otherwise, what could be the sense and bearing of his words, when in the same tract which contains his speeches of the Lords, he says in one place,[2] 'If such things had been asserted by me against my King, they would have been inquired into before now, in the Parliament of the English Lords.' If Wycliffe had only published his views in lectures or writings, it would be most improbable that these should become the subject of inquiry in Parliament. At least he could not himself have entertained such a thought, to say nothing of giving it utterance, without betraying an amount of vanity and excessive self-esteem quite foreign to all we know of his character. The case bears a different aspect, when we infer from the above words the seemingly logical conclusion, that Wycliffe was himself a member of the Parliament which was called to discuss that highly important question; and that he had there fully

---

[1] *De Ecclesia*, c. 15. MS. 1294 of the Vienna Library, f. 178, col. 2. *Unde episcopus Roffensis dixit mihi in publico parliamento stomachando spiritu, quod conclusiones meæ sunt dampnatæ, sicut testificatum est sibi de Curia per instrumentum notarii.* The words *dixit mihi* forbid us to understand that the Bishop had only spoken of him in his absence; rather he must have spoken to him and launched his charge against him face to face. Let me only add that the words *publicum parliamentum* do not presuppose *publicity*, in the modern sense of the term, but only lay stress upon the circumstance that, instead of a private communication, the charge was made publicly in the hearing of many witnesses.

[2] *Si autem ego assererem talia contra regem meum, olim fuissent in parliamento dominorum Angliæ ventilata*, in Lewis, p. 350. According to the connection, the emphasis appears to lie not on *ego*, but upon *contra regem meum*.

and emphatically unfolded his views. For indeed, in that case, if the view he took had touched too nearly the honour and the rights of the Crown, it would not have been allowed to pass without decided contradiction on the part of men so patriotic as those speakers were.

Last of all, I believe that there is still another utterance of Wycliffe which should be applied to this incident, although hitherto, indeed, it has been otherwise understood. At the very beginning of the remarkable tract still before us, Wycliffe declares his readiness, in consideration of his being *peculiaris regis clericus*, *i.e.*, in a peculiar sense a king's cleric, to accept the challenge of the opponent, and to defend the law of the land.[1] Lewis and Vaughan, and all who follow the latter, have understood this allusion to mean that Edward III. had nominated Wycliffe to the office of King's Chaplain.[2] But we do not find elsewhere a single trace of evidence by which this conjecture is confirmed. For this reason, it has been thought necessary to give the words another meaning—this, namely, that Wycliffe meant by that expression to distinguish himself as a cleric of the National Church, in opposition to a cleric of the Papal Church.[3] But this explanation does not quite satisfy us, on account of the '*talis qualis*' of the passage. For this expression of modesty is only in place if the three words quoted above denote a certain function or social position, but not so if they indicate only a certain tendency and mode of thought. What sort of distinguished position are we, then, to think of under the title of *peculiaris regis clericus*? I hold it to be not only possible but probable, that under this title the summoning of Wycliffe to Parliament by the act of the King is indicated; that is to say, that the King required his presence in that Parliament as a clerical expert, or, in modern phrase, as a Government commissioner. At least this view may be worth examination as a suggestion, seeing that the meaning of the title used by Wycliffe is still so far from being settled.

But that Wycliffe had a seat and vote in the Parliament of 1366, I venture to maintain as a fact, for which I have produced sufficient grounds. The only adverse consideration which might be alleged against it rests upon the way in which Wycliffe introduces his account of the speeches of the Lords. For his language at first conveys the impression that the author's knowledge of the matter is only by

---

[1] *Ego autem cum sim peculiaris regis clericus talis qualis, volo libenter induere habitum responsalis*, etc., in Lewis, p. 349.
[2] Lewis, 20; Vaughan, *Life*, I., 284; *John de Wycliffe*, 106; Shirley, *Fasc. Zizan.* XIX.; Björnström, *John Wiclif*, Upsala, 1867, p. 36.
[3] Böehringer, as above, p. 32.

hearsay. To this circumstance, however, no decisive weight can be assigned, for the reason that Wycliffe probably wished to avoid the appearance of boasting of having been himself an ear-witness of the speeches, and that he preferred to appeal to the matter as one which was well known and talked about (*fertur*). But if the real state of the case was that which we think we have shown to be probable, we have then an easier explanation, not only of the detailed character of the report of several of the speeches, but also of two additional points—first, of the agreement of several ideas in those addresses with certain favourite views of Wycliffe; for if Wycliffe was a member of that Parliament he would be able to find all the easier access to men in high position, so as to inspire them with his own convictions upon the great question of the day. And secondly, if Wycliffe was then in Parliament, and had exercised some influence upon the decision arrived at, it will then become obvious why he in particular should have been singled out for challenge by the unnamed monk to whom the action of that Parliament was a thorn in the flesh. It has at least been made clear that Wycliffe took part, in a powerful and influential way, in the great Church and State questions of the day, and this in the direction of having much at heart the right and honour of the Crown, and the liberty and welfare of the kingdom.

<small>Part of Wycliffe in the decision.</small>

If in this matter he was compelled to oppose himself to the claims of Rome, we are still without the slightest reason for regarding as mere phraseology his solemn declaration that, as an obedient son of the Church, he had no wish to dishonour her, or to injure the interests of piety. We are unable, however, to concur in the opinion, that Wycliffe's dauntless courage and disinterestedness come out all the more conspicuously from his conduct in this business, because the question touching the headship of Canterbury Hall was at that time pending before the Roman Court. For if it is true, as with other scholars we believe it to be, that the controversial tract before us was drawn up after the May Parliament of 1366, *i.e.*, in the year 1366 itself, or at latest, in the first months of the following year, Wycliffe was still at that date in undisturbed possession of that position. For though Islip had died on April 26, 1366, Simon Langham was not installed Archbishop of Canterbury till March 25, 1367, and it was on March 31 that he transferred the Wardenship of that Hall to the Benedictine, John Redingate. It appears, therefore, more than doubtful whether Wycliffe was, at the date of the composition of this tract, already deposed from his position in the hall; on the contrary, precisely this dignity may have been included

<small>Wycliffe still head of Canterbury Hall.</small>

among the 'Church benefices' of which he was to be deprived, if things went agreeably to the wishes of his adversaries.

3.—Events after 1366.

WYCLIFFE manifested the same spirit on another occasion, some years later. Unfortunately the sources of history are not here so abundant as to enable us steadily to follow the course of his inner development and his external action; and we are obliged at this point to pass over an interval of six or seven years. The years following these were ill-fated for England in her foreign relations.

In May, 1360, after the war with France had lasted for twenty-one years, the Peace of Bretigny had been concluded. In this treaty, the whole south-west of France, with several cities on the north coast, was unconditionally surrendered to the English Crown. On the other hand, England expressly renounced all claims to the French Crown, and to any further acquisitions of French territory. What was ceded to her, however, was a magnificent acquisition in itself. But the Peace of Bretigny became only a new occasion of discord. Soon enough there sprang from it first a tension of feeling between the two nations, then a misunderstanding, and at last an open breach. The brilliant, but fruitless, expedition of Edward the Black Prince to Spain in 1367, with the view of restoring Pedro the Cruel to the throne of Castile, led to a renewed outbreak of hostility with France, who had given her support to the usurper of the Castilian Crown, the Bastard Henry of Trastamara. This expedition brought upon the heir-apparent of the English throne an attack of dysentery, as the effect of the Spanish climate, under which he continued to suffer till, in 1376, he died. When the war with France broke out again in 1369, it was an irreparable misfortune for England that the great general (who had developed, indeed, more military than administrative talent in the government of his principalities of Aquitaine and Gascony) was incapacitated by bodily disease to resume the post of command. Insurrection burst forth into flames in the ceded provinces of France, and was never again subdued. One fortress after another fell into the hands of the enemy. In August, 1372, the city of Rochelle again became French. The English rule over a great part of France was gradually broken up. But this was not all. The English fleet, too, could no longer maintain its superiority; on the contrary, the English coasts were left a defenceless prey to every attack by the enemy's ships. Public opinion in England, as may readily be supposed, became much disconcerted and disturbed. So long as successes and martial glory had been the harvests of war, the nation had willingly borne the necessary sacrifices, both of money and of blood. But when the successes thus obtained vanished away like shadows, when disaster was heaped upon disaster, and when the country itself was menaced by the enemy, complaints became louder and louder, and grievances more and more bitter, till it was at last resolved to take action against the Government itself.

A Parliament met during the Lent of 1371; and when Edward III. laid before it a demand for a subsidy of fifty thousand silver marks in aid of the war, the proposal led, as it would appear, to very animated debates. On the one side, a motion was made, and was also eventually carried, that the richly-endowed Church should be included, to a substantial amount, in the incidence of the new tax; and on the other, the representatives of the Church, as was to be expected, did not fail to offer opposition to such a proposal. They used every effort to accomplish the exemption of the clergy, the rich monasteries, foundations, etc., from the new burden of taxation. It was very probably in that Parliament that one of the lords replied to the representations of some members of the endowed Orders in the form which Wycliffe has preserved in one of his unpublished works.[1] The far-seeing peer, in the course of the discussion, told the following fable:—'Once upon a time there was a meeting of many birds; among them was an owl, but the owl had lost her feathers, and made as though she suffered much from the frost. She begged the other birds, with a trembling voice, to give her some of their feathers. They sympathised with her, and every bird gave the owl a feather, till she was overladen with strange feathers in no very lovely fashion. Scarcely was this done when a hawk came in sight in quest of prey; then the birds, to escape from the attacks of the hawk by self-defence or by flight, demanded their feathers back again from the owl; and on her refusal each of them took back his own feather by force, and so escaped the danger, while the owl remained more miserably unfledged than before.'

'Even so,' said the peer, 'when war breaks out, we must take from the endowed clergy a portion of their temporal possessions, as property which belongs to us and the kingdom in common, and we must wisely defend the country with property which is our own, and exists

---

[1] Wycliffe, *De Dominio Civili*, II., c. I, Vienna MS., No. 1341 (Dénis, CCCLXXXII., not CCCLXXX. as Shirley gives it), f. 155, col. 1. Shirley has given the passage in the Introduction to *Fasc. Zizan.*, p. xxi.

among us in superfluity.' The hint as to the origin of all Church property was plain enough as well as the menace—

> 'And art thou not willing,
> Then use I main force.'

The result was that the clergy had the worst of it. Taxes of unexampled weight were imposed upon them for all lands which had come into their hands by mortmain for the last 100 years, and even the smallest benefices, which had never been taxed before, were subjected to the new war impost.

It cannot be doubted that there was an intimate connection between this financial measure and a new proposition which the same Parliament submitted to the Crown. The Lords and Commons proposed to the King to remove all prelates from the highest offices of State, and to appoint laymen in their places, who could at all times be brought to answer for their proceedings before the temporal courts. This proposal of Parliament was in fact accepted by Edward III. At that time the highest office in the State, that of Lord Chancellor of England, was filled by the Bishop of Winchester, William of Wykeham. The Bishop of Exeter was Treasurer, and the Lord Privy Seal was also a prelate. It does not appear, indeed, that Parliament had any personal objection against Wykeham and his colleagues—the proposal was made upon its own merits, and its chief object was to secure ministerial responsibility. But as early as March 14, the Bishop of Winchester laid down the dignity of Chancellor, and was succeeded by Robert Thorp: at the same time, the offices of Treasurer and Keeper of the Seal were bestowed upon laymen. In February, 1372, we find the whole Privy Council constituted of laymen.[1] This change of ministers derived its chief importance from its distinctly anti-clerical character. Apart from its bearing upon questions of home administration, especially financial, the aim of the measure was also to place the Government in an attitude of emphatic opposition to the encroachments of the Papal Court.

Prelates in State offices.

Under such circumstances, it is no wonder if the demands of the Papacy excited decided resistance on the part of a country exhausted by an unfortunate turn of the war, and even gave occasion to measures of precaution on the part of the Government. No doubt it was felt by very many to be an expression of what lay deep in their own hearts, when Wycliffe

Resistance to Papal exactions.

---

[1] Compare the signatures of all the King's ministers under the protocol on the oath taken by Arnold Garnier, in the Appendix.

stood forward against one of the Papal agents who were traversing the land to collect dues for the Curia, and in the form of a commentary on the obligations which these men took upon themselves by oath, opened an attack upon the doings and traffickings of the Pope's Nuncio as dangerous to the kingdom.

The occasion was this. In February, 1372, there appeared in England an agent of the Papal See, Arnold Garnier by name (Garnerius, Granarius), Canon of Chalons in Champagne, and Eicentiate of Laws. He bore written credentials from Gregory XI. (who had ascended the Papal Chair in 1370), as Papal Nuncio and Receiver of Dues for the Apostolic Chamber. *Arnold Garnier, Papal Receiver.* The man travelled with a train of servants and half-a-dozen horses. He remained for two years and a half in the country, and during that time probably collected no inconsiderable sums. In July, 1374, he made a journey to Rome with the reserved intention of returning to England, for which purpose he was furnished with a royal passport, dated July 25, available until Easter, 1375; and from a letter of Gregory XI. to Bishop Wykeham of Winchester, it appears that Garnier returned to England in due time, to carry forward his work as Nuncio and Receiver.[1] When this agent of the Roman Court arrived, in the first instance, he obtained the consent of the Government to his collectorship only under condition of swearing solemnly beforehand to a form of obligation in which the rights and interests of the Crown and kingdom were guarded on all sides. The Frenchman acceded to this condition without the slightest scruple, and on February 13, 1372, at the royal palace of Westminster, in presence of all the councillors and officers of the Crown, he formally and solemnly took the oath.[2]

But this formality by no means set at rest the misgivings of all patriotic men. Wycliffe was one of these, and by-and-by he wrote a paper on the sworn obligations of the Papal Receiver, *Wycliffe's Paper.* the drift of which was to inquire whether Garnier was not guilty of perjury, in so far as he had taken an oath never to violate the rights and interests of the country, while yet such a violation was entirely unavoidable, if, in fulfilment of his commission, he collected in England a large amount of gold and carried it out of the kingdom.[3]

---

[1] The royal passport is printed in Rymer's *Foedera*, ed. 4. London, 1830, vol. III., 2, f. 1007. The Pope's letter of introduction is printed by Lowth in the Appendix, of original documents, to his *Life of Wykeham*.

[2] The textual form of the oath is printed in Norman French in Rymer, III., f. 933.

The Latin text was prefixed by Wycliffe to the inquiry of which we are to speak immediately; and as the latter would not be intelligible without the former, I have also given the form of the oath in the Appendix.

[3] This paper, which has hitherto been known only by its title, is preserved in

The aim of the inquiry appears to have been to show that there was an irreconcilable contradiction between the permission given by the State to collect moneys for the Court of Rome on the one hand, and the intention to guard the country against all wrong to its interests on the other.

That this short paper was written not later than 1374, is certain, because it speaks of Garnier as being still in England plying his business, and it may have appeared as early as 1372.[1] As to its genuineness, no doubt is to be entertained. Its title, indeed, is not to be found in the catalogues of Wycliffe's writings given by Bishop Bale and other literary historians of the sixteenth and seventeenth centuries, but it stands in a pretty full list of the works and tracts of Wycliffe which is found at the end of a Vienna manuscript (Cod. 3933, fol. 195). An additional testimony to its Wycliffe authorship, not to be undervalued, is the fact, that the paper forms part of another Vienna MS. (Cod. 1337) which contains in all no fewer than fifty pieces, most of them short ones, which are all productions of Wycliffe. This little tract, besides, in thought and style, bears unmistakable features of Wycliffe's characteristic manner. In particular, we observe a remarkable agreement between this tract and the piece last examined, dating several years earlier, in respect to the point of view taken by the writer, and in the sentiment which forms the basis of both. In both tracts, which in modern phrase we might call 'political articles,' Wycliffe stands before us as a patriot, who has the honour and interests of his country very deeply at heart. In both also, especially in the latter, we learn to recognise him as a Christian patriot, and see in the patriotic defender of his country's interests those qualities which in their development were to shape the ecclesiastical Reformer. The difference between the two tracts is partly in form and partly in matter. In form the earlier is defensive, the later aggressive. In substance the later piece goes deeper into Church questions than the earlier, owing to the difference of the two occasions which called them forth.

To elucidate more exactly the peculiar character of the tract at

---

two MSS. of the Imperial Library of Vienna, namely, No. 1337 (Dénis, CCCLXXVIII.), f. 115, and No. 3929 (Dénis, CCCLXXXV.), f. 246. From the latter MS., which leaves much to be wished for in point of accuracy, I give the text in full, with the exception of a portion at the beginning, which is of inferior importance, in the Appendix. The conclusion seems to have fallen away, for the text terminates in an 'etc.'

[1] *Constat ex facto ejus notorie, quod sic facit*, Art. 5. [But that this memorial cannot have been written before 1377 is clear from the circumstance that near its end reference is made to *regi nostro, licet in ætate juvenili florenti*, which can only apply to Richard II., not to Edward III., who died in June, 1377.—*Lorimer*.]

present before us, we bring into notice, before everything else, this feature of it—that it recognises the domestic prosperity of the country, the wealth of the public purse, and the military strength of England, as valuable blessings, which must be defended against all enemies. This mention of the enemies of the kingdom shows clearly enough how much at that time the actual and possible incidents of the French war were occupying all minds, and filling them with earnest anxiety. *Characteristics of the Paper.*

A second characteristic feature which strikes the reader of these pages is the decidedly *constitutional* spirit which pervades them. The Parliament is spoken of as occupying a most important position as the representative of the nation, possessing authority to sit in judgment upon the question of what would be injurious to the national interests. And in the same spirit the author expresses a desire to see the State take under its protection the time-honoured civil rights of the priests and clerics of the National Church, in opposition to the encroachments of the Papal Receiver. *Its constitutional spirit.*

Further, it is not to be overlooked that Wycliffe is conscious of giving expression in the main only to what is felt and thought by no small portion, perhaps by the majority of the population.[1] But equally strong, and still more important than the national and patriotic feeling of the author, is the religious and moral, and even the evangelical spirit which he manifests in dealing with this matter. When Wycliffe puts forward the principle that the assistance of God is far more valuable than the help of man, and that remissness in the defence of Divine right is a more serious sin than negligence in the duty of defending a human right, he makes his reader feel that he is not merely repeating a traditional maxim, but giving utterance to a great truth from the deepest conviction, and with the most intense sympathy, of his heart and conscience. And it is only an application of this general principle when, as if to complete and give the right interpretation of what he has said on the subject of the national welfare, Wycliffe makes the remark that the welfare of the kingdom depends upon the religious beneficence of its people, particularly upon pious foundations in behalf of the Church and the poor. We also feel the moral earnestness of his tone, and especially the conscientiousness with which he insisted on the duty of truthfulness, when, in allusion to the sophistical speeches and excuses employed either by the Papal agents themselves, or by their *Harmony with popular feeling.*

---

[1] *Ut a multis creditur—executio sui officii—si non fallor, displiceret majori parti populi Anglicani; regnum nostrum jam sensibiliter percipiens illud gravamen de ipso conqueritur.*

friends and defenders, he emphatically denounces a species of craft and guile, which, by means of mental reservations, would bring things to such a pass that even the oath would no longer be 'an end of all strife.' Again, we find the principle expressed by Wycliffe with peculiar emphasis in this piece, as often elsewhere, that a common participation in sin and guilt is incurred when one knows of the evil-doings of a second party, and might put a stop to them if he would, but neglects to do it. And it is only the positive side of this thought when it is asserted that the command to inflict brotherly censure (Matthew xviii. 15), makes it a duty to resist a transgressor whose conduct might influence others for evil.

But more characteristic than all else is what Wycliffe says in this tract respecting the Pope and the pastoral office. That the Pope may commit sin had been already asserted, in one of the Parliamentary speeches of the earlier piece: and in the present one that proposition is repeated more strongly still.[1] In connection with this view, Wycliffe also declares himself opposed to the theory which maintains that absolutely everything which the Pope thinks fit to do must be right, and have force of law simply because he does it. In other words, we here find Wycliffe already in opposition to the absolutism of the Curia. He is far removed, however, from a merely negative position. On the contrary, he puts forward a positive idea of the Papacy, according to which the Pope is bound to be pre-eminently the follower of Christ in all moral virtues—especially in humility, patience, and brotherly love. And next, the views which he expresses respecting the pastoral office are well worthy of observation. Whilst severely censuring the Papal collectors for compelling, by help of ecclesiastical censures, those priests who had to pay annates (*primi fructus*) to the Curia, to make their payments in coin instead of in kind (*in natura*), he brings into special prominence, as a crying abuse, the fact, that by this undue pressure put upon them, the priests found themselves under the necessity (as they must have the means of living) of indemnifying themselves at the expense of their poor parishioners, and of neglecting the services of public worship which they were bound to celebrate. From this passing allusion thrown out only in passing, we perceive what a watchful eye he must have kept upon the pastoral office and upon its conscientious execution—a subject to which, at a later period, he gave all the fulness and energy of his love. Last of all, we will only call attention to this further point, that already, in this small and essentially political paper, the principle makes its appearance which

Views in regard to the Pope.

---

[1] *Cum dominus papa sit satis peccabilis.*

Wycliffe afterwards asserted with 'epoch-making' force, viz., that Holy Scripture is for Christians the sole guide and standard of truth. There is a hint, at least, of this principle when Wycliffe says of the payments in question to the Court of Rome that they are obtained by begging, *in a manner contrary to the gospel (elemosina præter evangelium mendicata)*. **Supremacy of Scripture.**

From all this, this small piece, which has till the present time remained unknown, appears to us to be not without value, inasmuch as, on the one hand, it shows us the manner of Wycliffe's intervention in an affair of weighty public importance, and, on the other, lets us clearly see in the undaunted zeal of the patriot the earliest germs of the later strivings of the Church Reformer.

4.—Wycliffe as a Royal Commissary in Bruges, 1374, and his Influence in the "Good Parliament" of 1376.

In the year 1373 the Parliament had once more raised loud complaints that the rights of patrons were ever more and more infringed and made illusory by Papal provisions. To a petition of the Parliament drawn up to this effect, the King gave answer, that he had already sent commands to his ambassadors, who were at that very time engaged in peace negotiations with France, to negotiate also upon this business with the Roman Court. He had in this behalf given a commission to John Gilbert, Bishop of Bangor, with one monk and two laymen.[1] These commissioners proceeded to Avignon, and treated with the representatives of Gregory XI. for the removal of various causes of complaint on the part of the kingdom, especially of the Papal reservations in the filling of English Church offices, encroachments upon the electoral rights of cathedral chapters, and the like. The commissioners received conciliatory promises, but no distinct and definite answer. The Pope reserved himself for further consultation with the King of England, and for a decision at a subsequent date.[2] **Conference with the Pope on provisions.**

The further negotiations thus held out in prospect were opened in 1374, in connection with the peace conferences, which were still going on in Bruges between England and France. At the head of the peace embassy stood a prince of the blood, John of Gaunt, Duke of Lancaster, third son of Edward III., with the Bishop of London, Simon Sudbury. For treating with the commissaries of the Pope on the pending ecclesiastical questions, the **Negotiations at Bruges.**

---

[1] [The monk was one Bolton of Dunholm: the lay commissioners were William of Barton and John of Shepey.]

[2] Walsingham, *Hist. Anglicana*, Ed. Riley, I., 316.

King commissioned the before-named John Gilbert, Bishop of Bangor; and in addition John Wycliffe, Doctor of Theology; Magister John Guter, Dean of Segovia;[1] Simon of Multon, Doctor of Laws; William of Burton, Knight; Robert of Belknap;[2] and John of Kenyngton. The commission, dated July 26, 1374, invested the King's commissaries with plenary powers to conclude such a treaty with the Papal nuncios on the pending points, as should at once secure the honour of the Church, and uphold the rights of the English Crown and realm.[3] It is, on the one hand, characteristic of the views by which the Government of England at that time was guided, that a man like Wycliffe should have been appointed a royal commissioner for these diplomatic transactions with the Roman Court. On the other hand, it was a high honour for Wycliffe that he, and that too as first in order after the Bishop of Bangor, was selected to protect the rights of the Crown and the interests of the kingdom in a treaty with the plenipotentiaries of the Pope. This fact shows us what confidence was felt in his opinion and insight, in his courage and power of action, on the part both of the Government and the country.

On the very next day after the commission had been issued, namely, July 27, 1374, Wycliffe embarked at London for Flanders.[4] It was the first time in his life he had been abroad. Bruges was at that time a great city of 200,000 inhabitants, which, from its important industries, its widely extended trade, the wealth of its burghers, its municipal freedom, and its political power, offered numerous points of attraction to foreigners; especially at a time when an important congress was assembled within its walls. On the side of France two royal princes, the Dukes of Anjou and Burgundy, brothers of the reigning king, Charles V.,

Wycliffe a commissioner.

---

[1] Böehringer, *Vorreformatoren*, I., 45, makes Guter Dean of Sechow, although in all England no town or any other place of residence so named exists. It is rather the city of Segovia, in Old Castile, that is meant. The English priest, John Guter, had no doubt obtained a Spanish prebend through the Duke of Lancaster, who, after the death of his first wife, Blanche of Lancaster, had married Constance, a daughter of Peter the Cruel, King of Castile, and afterwards put forward claims to the crown of Castile and Leon in her right. Compare John Foxe, *Acts and Monuments*, Ed. Pratt and Stoughton, II., 916, Appendix.

[2] When Richard II. ascended the throne in 1377, Robert Belknappe was chief judge on the Bench of the Common Pleas, but was deposed in 1388, and banished to Ireland, for having set himself in opposition to the absolutistic designs of the King.—*Vide* Walsingham, Ed. Riley, II., 174; Knighton, 2694.

[3] Rymer, *Foedera*, III., 2, f. 1007; Lewis, 304.

[4] Under date July 31 he acknowledged receipt of £60, at the rate of twenty shillings per day paid to him out of the Royal Treasury for the costs of his journey and maintenance abroad. See Oxford edition of the Wycliffe Bible, I., p. vii., note 13. It is a mere misunderstanding when Charles Werner, in his *History of Apologetic and Polemical Literature*, III., 1864, p. 560, speaks of Wycliffe making a journey to Rome. He was never even in Avignon, to say nothing of Rome, where indeed he could have had no business to transact at this time, for it was not till 1377 that Gregory XI. left Avignon for Italy.

were present, in addition to many bishops and notables of the kingdom. As English plenipotentiaries appeared, in addition to the Duke of Lancaster, the Bishop of London and the Earl of Salisbury, the Pope sent in behoof of the treaty between France and England the Archbishop of Ravenna and the Bishop of Carpentras; and commissioned several other prelates, with full powers to negotiate with England on still-pending questions of ecclesiastical right. These nuncios were Bernard, Bishop of Pampelona; Ralph, Bishop of Sinigaglia; and Egidius Sancho, Provost of the archiepiscopal chapter of Valencia.[1] There was no lack, therefore, in Bruges of men in high place and of great political or ecclesiastical importance, with whom Wycliffe, as a prominent man among the English envoys, must have come more or less into contact in the transaction of public business, and no doubt also in social intercourse.

We may be sure that the opportunities that he had on this occasion of transacting business and cultivating intercourse with Italian, Spanish, and French dignitaries of the Church—all of them men who enjoyed the confidence of the Pope and the cardinals, were of lasting value to Wycliffe. *Result of his visit.* Here he had it in his power to take many observations on a field of view which could not easily be laid open to his eye among his own countrymen, even among those of them who were most conspicuous for their devotion to Rome. For 'the Anglican Church' (this name is no anachronism) had within the preceding century attained to a certain degree of independence in regard to principles and views of ecclesiastical law, to which the life and spirit of the Italian and Spanish Churches of that period formed a marked contrast. Upon a personality like Wycliffe, of so much independence of mind, and already inspired with so much zeal for the autonomy of his native Church, this residence in Bruges, and the lengthened negotiations with the plenipotentiaries of the Curia, must have made impressions similar to those which Dr. Martin Luther received from his sojourn in Rome in 1510.

But even apart from his relations to foreign notabilities, Wycliffe's sojourn in Bruges had important consequences for him, through the nearer relations into which it brought him with the Duke of Lancaster. This prince at that time already possessed great and decisive influence upon the Government. *Friendship with John of Gaunt.* He was usually called 'John of Gaunt,' for he was born in Ghent, when Edward III., at the beginning of the French war, was in alliance with the rich cities of Flanders, and, with his Queen Philippa, was

---

[1] According to Barnes—*History of King Edward III.*, p. 866 — referred to by Lewis, p. 33.

keeping his court in that city in 1340. The prince's first title was Earl of Richmond, but after his marriage with Blanche, a daughter of the Duke of Lancaster, he became, on the death of the latter, the heir of his title and possessions. After the death of his first wife, in 1369, he entered into a second marriage in 1372, with Constance, the daughter of Peter the Cruel, of Castile and Leon, and assumed by hereditary right the title of 'King of Castile.' But this was never more than a title. He never himself wore a crown; but in the following century three of his descendants ascended the English throne, viz., his son, his grandson, and his great-grandson—Henry IV., Henry V., and Henry VI.—the House of Lancaster and the Red Rose reigning from 1399 to 1472.

Already, however, the father of this dynasty manifested ambition enough to awaken the suspicion that he was aiming at the English crown for himself. In military talent he stood far behind his eldest brother; for the Black Prince was an eminent military genius, whereas John of Gaunt was a brave swordsman, and nothing more. But in political and administrative capacity he was indisputably superior to the Prince of Wales. When the latter found himself obliged to return to England at the beginning of 1371, on account of the obstinate disease which he had contracted in the Spanish campaign, instead of recovering his vigour on his native soil, he had fallen into a chronic condition of broken health and low spirits, which unfitted him for taking any active part in the business of government; whilst his father, too, Edward III., had become old and frail. Lancaster had known how to utilize all these circumstances for his own ambitious ends, and had acquired since his return in the summer of 1374 from the south of France the most decided influence over the King, and the conduct of public affairs. The second prince of the blood, Lionel, Duke of Clarence, had died in 1368. For the present, indeed, Lancaster undertook only the lead of the peace negotiations in Bruges; but it almost appears as if even from Flanders he had governed both the King and the kingdom.

The Duke's ambition.

That it was first in Bruges that the Duke became acquainted with Wycliffe, or entered into closer relations with him, is by no means probable. It was he, no doubt, who was the cause of Wycliffe's being appointed to take part in these ecclesiastical negotiations. In regard, at least, to John Guter, Dean of Segovia, who had perhaps accompanied the Duke to the Spanish campaign in the capacity of Field-Chaplain, it was undoubtedly to the Duke that he was indebted for his nomination upon the commission, as well as for his Spanish prebend; and it

The Duke's share in Wycliffe's appointment.

would have been truly surprising if a statesman like the Prince—a zealous promoter of lay government, a persistent opponent of the influence of the English hierarchy upon the administration—had not already for years directed his attention and his favour to Wycliffe, as a man whose gifts and bold spirit he might be able to use for his own political objects. I quite concur, therefore, in Pauli's conjecture [1] that it was probably Lancaster himself who had brought about the employment of Wycliffe upon a mission of so great importance. But be this as it may, these two men could not fail to be much in contact, and to have constant exchange of ideas with each other, both on matters of business and in social intercourse, during the time that they were occupied with the congress in Flanders. The Duke, indeed, in the first instance, was concerned only in the transactions with France, and his business with the Papal plenipotentiaries was limited to giving his consent to the conclusions arrived at. But, nevertheless, he stood at the head of the whole English legation, and on this account alone, as well as by reason of his personal tendencies and way of thinking, he could not fail to take the liveliest interest in the course of those negotiations which bore upon the ecclesiastical *gravamina* of the country; and among the members of the ecclesiastical commission Wycliffe was at least one of the most free from prejudice and of the deepest insight.

A few years later we see the Duke of Lancaster step forward publicly as Wycliffe's patron and protector. This favour, grounded upon personal knowledge and esteem of Wycliffe, no doubt increased during the conference at Bruges, though it could scarcely have commenced there.

Wycliffe returned to England after the close of the congress, before the middle of September. Neither official documents nor any contemporary or later chronicles have come down to us respecting the proceedings of the congress in the matter of the Church grievances of England, although, no doubt, some papers relating to the subject lie concealed in the archives of Rome.

We can only draw some inferences as to the course of the transactions from the final result. In this respect, indeed, it would seem that the negotiations between the Papal Court and England had reached a similar issue to those between France and England. The chronicler of St. Albans, Walsingham, has nothing good to say of the behaviour of the French at the peace congress. 'Their thoughts,' he says, 'during all that time were craftily running, not on peace, but on war; they were preparing again.

[1] Pauli, *Geschichte von England*, IV., 487.

their old weapons and forging new ones in order to have all the requirements of war in readiness; while the English had no thoughts of this kind, accustomed as they are not to be led by prudence and foresight, but only to be driven like unreasoning brutes by the goad. But no doubt they trusted everything to the wisdom of the Duke, and, thinking that his eloquence would suffice to obtain for them the blessings of peace, they gave themselves up to carousals and all manner of amusements. Thus it came to pass that the English were deceived and baffled, the congress having been broken off without the conclusion of peace.[1] The congress between England and the Curia came to a like fruitless conclusion. The representatives of the Roman See, like the plenipotentiaries of France, appear to have busied themselves with the refurbishing of their old weapons, while they were at the same time preparing new ones. The Convention in which the congress issued was not of a kind to secure for the future a redress of the Church grievances of which the country complained. England undoubtedly fared the worst in the arrangements arrived at; for, although the Pope made some concessions upon single points, these concessions were more apparent than real, and consisted more in matters of detail than in general principles.

On September 1, 1375, Gregory XI. addressed to the King of England six bulls relating to this business,[2] which amounted briefly to this—to recognise accomplished facts, and to leave the *status quo* untouched. Whosoever was in actual possession of a Church living in England should no longer have his right of incumbency challenged on the part of the Curia; whosoever had had his right to a Church office disputed by Urban V. should at once be confirmed in the office; benefices which the same Pope had 'reserved,' in the event of a vacancy, should, in so far as they had not already become vacant, be filled up by the patrons themselves; and all 'annates' or first-fruits not yet paid should be remitted. In addition, it was conceded that the Church revenues of several cardinals who held prebends in England should be subject to impost, to cover the costs of the restoration of churches and other Church edifices belonging thereto, which the holders had allowed to fall into ruin.

The Pope's concessions.

At first sight these appeared to be numerous and important concessions, but when carefully examined they resolved themselves into very little, for they all related to matters which belonged to the past. For the future the Pope remitted nothing of his claims, not even in

[1] *Historia Anglicana*, Ed. Riley, I., 318. [2] Rymer, *Fœdera*, vol. III., p. ii., fol. 1037.

the smallest trifle. Besides, these concessions referred merely to single cases—they regulated only matters of detail, and left the principle entirely untouched. The bulls, it is true, effected one important change—the Pope abandoned for the future his claim to the reservation of English Church livings; but the King was also bound, on his side, to abstain in future from conferring Church dignities by simple royal command. But, first, the Pope herein surrendered his claim only in consideration of a corresponding concession on the side of the Crown; and, secondly, the concession contained no security whatever that the electoral rights of cathedral chapters should remain thenceforward untampered with. And yet this had been one of the chief points aimed at by the country, as represented by Parliament, to obtain ecclesiastical reform. That this decisive point had not been dealt with by the treaty of 1375 is noted with censure by Walsingham himself, notwithstanding his disposition to favour the Church.[1]

Whether the other members of the ecclesiastical commission had fulfilled their duty, may be fairly asked; indeed, in regard to Bishop John Gilbert, who stood at the head of it, it is a highly significant fact that eleven days after the drawing up of the above bulls, September 12, 1375, he was promoted by the Pope to a more important bishopric. *Promotion of Bishop Gilbert.* He had plainly lost nothing of Gregory's favour by his conduct at Bruges. Hitherto he had been Bishop of Bangor; his diocese embraced the most distant north-west corner of the principality of Wales. But now, when the Bishop of London, Simon Sudbury, was made Archbishop of Canterbury, and the Bishop of Hereford, William Courtenay, was promoted to London, Gilbert was nominated to the See of Hereford.

The 'concordat' which had been concluded between England and the Pope had little enough of importance. It would have been incomparably better to advance on the same path which had been trodden in 1343 and 1350, and to stem the evils of the Church by means of national legislation, than to attempt to find a remedy for them by diplomatic transactions *The 'Good Parliament,' 1376.* with the Papal Court. In the very next spring it became manifest that the complaints of the country were by no means silenced. More loudly and boldly than ever did the Parliament declare the national grievances, when it assembled in the end of April, 1376; and that the representatives of the country expressed the true feeling of the people is evident from the fact that this Parliament lived long afterwards in the grateful memory of the nation, under the name of the Good Parliament.[2]

[1] *Historia Anglicana*, Ed. Riley, I., 317.

[2] *Quod bonum merito vocabatur.*—Walsingham, I., 324.

The Parliament represented to the King, in a lengthy memorial, how oppressively and perniciously the encroachments of the Roman See operated.[1] The aggressions of the Pope were to blame for the impoverishment of the kingdom; for the sums paid to him for the Church dignities amounted to five times as much as the whole produce of the taxes which accrued to the King. There was no prince in Christendom so rich as to have in his treasury even the fourth part of the sum which thus iniquitously was taken out of the kingdom. Moreover, the Church brokers, in the dissolute city of Avignon, promoted for money many 'caitiffs' utterly destitute of learning and character, to livings of one thousand marks annual income; while a Doctor of Theology or of Canon Law must content himself with a salary of twenty marks. Hence the decay of learning in the country. And when foreigners, yea, enemies of the country, were holders of English Church livings, without ever seeing their parishioners or giving themselves any trouble about them, did they not bring the service of God into contempt, and do more injury to the Church than was done by Jews or Saracens? The law of the Church prescribed that Church livings should be conferred and held from pure love, without solicitation or payment; and reason and faith, as well as law, demanded that Church endowments which had been founded from motives of devotion, should be bestowed for the glory of God and in accordance with the founder's intention, and not upon foreigners from among the midst of our enemies. God had entrusted the care of the sheep to the Holy Father, the Pope, to be pastured, and not to be shorn. But if lay patrons witnessed the avarice and simony of the churchmen, they would learn from their example to sell the offices to which they have the right of collation, to men who would devour the people like beasts of prey—just as the Son of God was sold to the Jews, who thereupon put Him to death.

Memorial to the King.

A considerable portion of the complaint of Parliament was directed against the Papal Collector,[2] a French subject, who lived in the country together with foreigners hostile to the King, and was ever on the look-out for English offices and dignities, and seeking to spy

[1] Considerable extracts from this petition, although not in a satisfactory arrangement, have fortunately been preserved, and were printed by Foxe in the *Acts and Monuments*, Ed. Pratt and Stoughton, II., 786. What Lewis communicated from other MSS. is not free from errors.

[2] I do not for a moment doubt that the Papal Collector here several times named was the same Arnold Garnier already known to us, for the description given of him by Parliament applies to Garnier in every particular of chief moment. He is a French subject, he has a head office in London, and has already been employed in London for a series of years. The only objection that can be taken is that Garnier's commission in England dated only from February, 1372, so that in the spring of 1376 he had only been four years, not five, in the kingdom. But this difference is too small to shake the identity which I have assumed.

out the secrets of the kingdom, to its great damage. This Receiver, who was at the same time the collector of Peter's Pence, had a great house in London, with clerks and officers, as if it were the custom-house of a prince, and from thence he was accustomed to send to the Pope about twenty thousand marks a year. This same man, in that year, had, for the first time, put forward a claim to the first-fruits of all newly confirmed livings, a claim which had hitherto been limited to offices which had become vacant in the Papal Court. Even if the kingdom at that moment had as great a superfluity of gold as it ever possessed, the Pope's collectors and the agents of the cardinals would soon enough carry off the whole of this treasure to foreign parts. As a remedy for this evil, it was suggested that a law be laid down, that no Receiver or agent should take up his residence in England upon pain of life and limb, and that upon a like penalty no Englishman should become such a Receiver or agent in behalf of others who were residing in Rome. For the better investigation of the facts, especially in relation to the Papal Receiver, inasmuch as the whole clergy were dependent upon the favour or disfavour of the latter, and would not willingly run the risk of drawing upon themselves his displeasure, it was suggested that it would conduce to the end in view, if the Lords and Commons of the present Parliament would call before them the priest of St. Botolph's, John Strensale, resident in Holborn. He could, if strictly required to do so, give them much information, as he had for more than five years been in the service of the said Receiver as clerk.

The Papal Receiver.

It was further set forth, that cardinals and other prelates, some of them, it is true, natives of England, but most of them foreigners who resided in Rome, were occasionally possessed of the best prebends in England. One cardinal was Dean of York, another of Salisbury, a third of Lincoln; another again was Archdeacon of Canterbury, one of Durham, one of Suffolk, and so on; and these cardinals caused to be remitted to them in foreign parts a yearly revenue of twenty thousand marks. The Pope would in time hand over to enemies of the kingdom all the lands belonging to the prebends referred to, if he continued to deal as arbitrarily with the kingdom and the regalia as he had hitherto done. When a bishopric became vacant by death or otherwise, he would translate from four to five other bishops, in order to obtain from each of them the first year's fruits;[1] and the same sort of thing

Foreigners in English benefices.

---

[1] We had matter-of-fact proof of this above. After the death of Archbishop William Whittlesey, in 1374, Gregory XI. nominated the Bishop of London, Simon of Sudbury, to be Archbishop; the Bishop of Hereford, William Courtenay, to be Bishop of London; and the Bishop of Bangor, John Gilbert, to be Bishop of

took place with other Church dignities in the realm. As to the abbeys and convents, a loud complaint was made that all those of them which had hitherto possessed the right of free election of their own superiors had been deprived of this right by the usurpation of the Pope, who claimed it for himself. Last of all, and to come back again to the point of finance, the petition of Parliament called attention to this fact, that the Pope was in the act of raising subsidies from the English clergy in order to buy off Frenchmen who were taken prisoners by the English, for the purpose of aiding him in carrying on wars of his own in Lombardy. In addition to all this, the English clergy were required to bear the cost of every mission which the Pope sent to the country; and all this is done purely out of love to the kingdom and to English gold.

Such was the long array of grievances. Parliament emphatically assured the King that they brought them forward solely from an honest zeal for the honour of the Holy Church; for all the troubles and disasters which had recently befallen the land were only just judgments for the sin of allowing the Church to become so deformed and corrupt. Great transgressions had always been followed by misfortune and ruin, and would always have the like consequences. Let measures, therefore, be devised to provide a remedy, and this all the more since the current year was the jubilee of the fifty years' reign of the King, and therefore a year of grace and joy.[1] For greater grace and joy for the kingdom there could not be, and none which would be more well-pleasing at once to God and His Church than that such a remedy should be provided by the King.

Some positive proposals were made touching the ways and means of accomplishing the end in view. The first step must be to send two letters to the Pope, the one in Latin under the King's seal, the other in French under the seals of the high nobility, pressing for redress in the matters mentioned, a course which had on a former occasion been taken at the instigation of Parliament.[2] Further, it was pressed upon the attention of the Government that they might renew all those ordinances which had already been published against provisions and reservations on the side of Rome. It would also be advisable to decree that no money should be taken out of the kingdom by exchange or otherwise, on

Proposed redress of grievances.

Hereford. On this occasion, therefore, he translated at the least three bishops, and possessed himself of the first year's revenues of four newly-filled sees.

[1] Edward III. succeeded to the crown after the dethronement of his father, Edward II., January 25, 1327. The year 1376 was therefore exactly the fiftieth of his long reign. It was a happy thought that the King's jubilee could not be better celebrated than by carrying out the necessary ecclesiastical reforms.

[2] In May, 1343.

pain of imprisonment. What measures, in addition, were proposed to be taken against the traffic of the Papal collectors have already been mentioned.

To this representation the King sent for reply that he had already on previous occasions provided a sufficient remedy by legislation for the evils complained of; he was, besides, at that very time in communication with the Papal See upon the subject, and would continue to make such communications from time to time until a remedy was secured. This answer sounded lukewarm enough, especially when contrasted with the petition of Parliament, which was so warmly expressed, and adduced at length so many grounds in support of its prayer. But though the patriotic zeal of the latter must have been considerably cooled by this royal decision, the Parliament of the next year, January, 1377, took up the thread again at the point where the former Parliament had suffered it to drop; and, for the sake of connection, this incident may as well be anticipated here. The Commons, in 1377, presented a petition to the King to the effect that the statutes against 'provisions,' which had from time to time been passed, should be strictly carried into execution, and that measures should be adopted against those cardinals who had obtained 'reservations' for themselves in the two provinces of Canterbury and York, with the clause *anteferri*,[1] to the annual value of from twenty to thirty thousand gold crowns. They also renewed their complaints against the Pope's Collector. That office had always previously been held by Englishmen, but now it was in the hands of a Frenchman, who lived in London and kept a large establishment, which cost the clergy three hundred pounds a-year; and this man sent every year to the Pope twenty thousand marks. It would be a means of resisting these innovations and usurpations if all foreigners, so long as the wars lasted, were driven out of the country, and if all Englishmen were prohibited, upon pain of outlawry, to farm these revenues for the Papal Court, or to make remittances of money to the same without a special licence.[2]

<small>The King's reply.</small>

The proposals of the Good Parliament of 1376, the echoes of which we still catch in 1377, are of such a character that I am bold to maintain that they afford strong evidence of the influence of Wycliffe. In proof of this I point first of all to the circumstance that the proceedings of the Papal

<small>Wycliffe's share in the memorial.</small>

---

[1] [*Anteferri, i.e.,* 'to have the *preference* or *precedence* of all other "reservations" which might have been granted on the same benefices.' See Foxe II., p. 916.]

[2] Foxe, *Acts*, etc., II., 789, from the royal archives.

Collector of that time were one of the Parliament's chief subjects of complaint. This collector was certainly no other than that Arnold Garnier to whose doings and traffickings Wycliffe's tract of the year 1377 refers. Further, I bring into view the fact that in the petition presented by Parliament various national calamities, including not only the rapid impoverishment of the country, but also famine and disease among men and cattle, are attributed to the moral disorders which had spread and prevailed in the Church in consequence of the Papal usurpations, and of the blameworthy negligence of the Government and the people.[1] Now, exactly this thought so repeatedly recurs in different writings of Wycliffe that I must designate it one of his favourite ideas. But independently of this, it is much more natural to think that an idea so peculiar was thrown out at first by some personage of mark, and afterwards adopted by a whole body, than that a political body first gave expression to it, and that it was afterwards taken up and appropriated at second-hand by one of the greatest thinkers of the age. Add to all this yet another circumstance, viz., the incident already mentioned of the Bishop of Rochester,[2] in a solemn sitting of Parliament, casting in Dr. Wycliffe's face the accusation that his Theses had already been condemned by the Roman Court. This incident cannot possibly have occurred in an earlier Parliament than that of 1376, for the excited language of the Bishop could not have been uttered after the Papal censure of Wycliffe's nineteen propositions had been published to the world. The speaker's intention evidently was to make public a fact which up to that time had remained secret. Now, the censure of Gregory XI. was formally signed on May 22, 1377. Accordingly it may be thought possible that the scene referred to occurred in that Parliament which assembled January 27, 1377, the year of Edward III.'s death; and in support of this view the consideration would be of weight, that at this date the information of what had been concluded in Rome against Wycliffe might have reached the ear of a member of the English episcopate. But this conjecture does not bear examination. For the language of the Bishop of Rochester could not well have been made use of after Wycliffe's summons to appear before the English prelates, and this summons was issued February 19, 1377. Various circumstances, therefore, make probable the supposition that the reproach of the Bishop against Wycliffe was

---

[1] Tit. 94. Against the usurpations of the Pope, as being the cause of all the plagues, murrains, famine, and poverty of the realm. Comp. Tit. 100.

[2] This must have been Thomas Trillek, who became Bishop of Rochester in 1363, and was still in office at the accession of Richard II., in 1377. Compare Walsingham, *Hist. Anglic.*, Ed. Riley, I., 299, 332.

uttered in some sitting of the Parliament of 1376. This date need not be thought too early for the Bishop's knowledge of what was then going on in Rome against Wycliffe; for it may well be presumed that a step such as that which Gregory XI. took in the bulls of May 22, 1377, must have originated in a suggestion from England made a considerable time before that date, and must have been in preparation in Rome during an interval of considerable length. All this warrants the supposition that Wycliffe himself was a member of the Good Parliament of 1376, by virtue, we may conjecture, of royal summons. And presupposing this fact, we do not doubt for a moment that he was one of the most influential personalities in the mixed affairs of Church and State which formed so conspicuous a part of the business of that Parliament. If, at an earlier period, he had shared strongly in the outburst of national feeling, and of the constitutional spirit which was so characteristic of England in the fourteenth century, still more had he become, in the course of years, one of the leaders of the nation in the path of ecclesiastical progress. This Parliament, indeed, was the culminating point of Wycliffe's influence upon the nation. From that date it rather began to decline, at least in extent of surface, or, so to say, in breadth. On the other hand, the effects which he produced from that time went deeper down into the heart of the English people than they had ever done before.

There was still another direction in which the Parliament of 1376 employed its effort for the improvement of public affairs. In 1371, as before stated, under the influence of a prevailing anti-clerical sentiment, the representatives of the nation had brought forward and carried into effect a proposition that the highest offices of the State should be entrusted to laymen, instead of to bishops and prelates. But in the course of *Coalition against the Lancaster party.* years there had spread a marked discontent with the manner in which the Government was conducted. King Edward III. had become almost worn out with old age. Since the death of his queen, Philippa (1369), one of her ladies, Alice Perrers, had obtained the royal favour in an extraordinary degree, and had not only taken a conspicuous position in the Court, but had also unduly meddled in many affairs of State. The influence of this lady the Duke of Lancaster had now turned to his own account, in order to acquire for himself a preponderating weight with his royal father in the business of government. He was credited, indeed, with designs of a much wider reach. The Prince of Wales, diseased and near his end as he was, was still able to perceive the danger, and, in spite of his forced retirement from the business of State, took into his hand the threads of an intrigue by which the succession to the Crown should be secured to his son Richard, a boy only nine years of age, and the supporters of his younger brother, John of Gaunt, should be thwarted in their designs. He found means to induce the House of Commons and the clergy to form a coalition against the dominant party of the Duke of Lancaster.

Foremost in the management of the affair was Peter de la Mere, Chamberlain of the Earl of March, a nobleman who, in virtue of the hereditary right of his countess, had the nearest presumptive claim to the Throne. This officer of the Court was, at the same time, Speaker of the House of Commons. Upon occasion of the voting of subsidies, the representatives of the counties complained, through their Speaker, of the bad condition of the financial admini-

Temporary success of the coalition.

stration, and even of embezzlement, fraudulent undercharges, and extortion. The persons who were accused and convicted of these malpractices were the Treasurer, Lord Latimer, a confidant of the Duke of Lancaster, and Alice Perrers herself. The former was put in prison, the latter banished from the Court. The Duke himself, who was the party really aimed at, no man was bold enough expressly to name; on the other hand, it was proposed, evidently with the view of preventing further mischief, to strengthen the Privy Council by the addition of from ten to twelve lords and prelates, who should always be near the person of the King, so that without the assent of six, or at least four of their number, no royal ordinance could be carried into effect. This decisive action of Parliament against the party of the Duke of Lancaster was so much after the nation's own heart, that it was principally for this service that the Parliament received the honourable epithet of 'The Good.'[1] While this movement was in progress, Edward the Black Prince died, June 8, 1376—held in equally high esteem as a warrior and as a man of upright and amiable character. The last care of the deceased prince had been to secure the right of his son and heir; and the House of Commons, sharing the same solicitude, presented an urgent petition to the aged King that he would now be pleased to present to the Parliament his grandson, Richard of Bordeaux, as heir-apparent to the Throne; which was done on June 25.

But scarcely was Parliament prorogued at the beginning of July, when all the measures which it had originated were again brought

[1] Lowth, *The Life of William of Wykeham*, p. 81. Pauli, *Geschichte von England*, 4, 489.

to nothing; the Duke of Lancaster once more seized the helm of the State; Lord Latimer recovered again his share in public affairs; and another friend of the Duke, Earl Percy, was named Lord Marshal. Even Alice Perrers came back again to Court. The cabal completely surrounded the aged King. The leaders of the party of the deceased Prince of Wales were compelled to feel the revenge of the small but powerful Court party. Peter de la Mere, Speaker of the House of Commons, was sent to prison, where he remained for nearly two years. The Bishop of Winchester was impeached, and banished twenty miles from the Court, and the temporalities of his see were sequestrated. *Renewed power of Lancaster.*

The question arises, what share Wycliffe had in the efforts of the Good Parliament to secure the rightful succession to the throne, and to purge the Court as well as the administration from unworthy elements. Assuming that he was a member of that Parliament, and co-operated influentially in its ecclesiastico-political proceedings, he could not have remained entirely without a share in its endeavours to secure the succession to the throne, and to reform the Court and the Government. He must have taken his place either on one side or the other. It is true that we hear nothing definite from himself upon the subject, nor very express testimony concerning it from any other quarter. But we may be sure at least of as much as this, that he could not in any case have played a prominent part in the effort to drive the favourites of the Duke of Lancaster from the Court, and to deprive them of all influence in State affairs; for had this been the case, the Duke would certainly not have lent him his powerful protection only half a year later (February 19, 1377). But, on the other hand, it is scarcely supposable that Wycliffe would join the party of Lord Latimer and his colleagues; especially as in this business the interests at stake were of that moral and legal character for which, in accord with his whole tone of thought, he always cherished a warm sympathy. These considerations taken together lead me to the opinion that while Wycliffe did not actually oppose himself to the majority of the Parliament who laboured to effect a purification of the Court and Government, he took no prominent part in the discussion of the subject; a conclusion sustained by the fact that, as a general rule, he was accustomed and called upon to take a personally active share only in matters of an ecclesiastico-political character. *Wycliffe and court politics.*

CHAPTER V.

PROCEEDINGS OF THE HIERARCHY AGAINST WYCLIFFE IN 1377 AND 1378.

1.—Wycliffe summoned before the Convocation.

AT the very time when Wycliffe stood in the highest estimation of his countrymen, and had reached a position of the greatest influence, a storm burst suddenly upon his head.

As a resolute, far-sighted, and experienced patriot, he possessed the confidence of the nation, as well as the favour of the King. Edward III. had already bestowed upon him more than one prebend, and, what was still more important as a mark of his royal grace, had, as we have shown good grounds for believing, repeatedly summoned him to serve in Parliament as a man thoroughly conversant with ecclesiastical affairs. How the men of Oxford had previously distinguished him by office and honours has been already related. After being Seneschal of Merton College, we have seen him in the position of Master of Balliol; and in 1361 he was nominated by this college to the parish of Fillingham. Seven years later he exchanged this parish for that of Ludgarshall, in Buckinghamshire, for no other reason, doubtless, than that the latter was situated in the neighbourhood of the University. On November 12, 1368, Wycliffe entered upon this pastoral charge. In 1375 he obtained a prebend at Aust, a place romantically situated on the south bank of the Severn, and connected with the endowed church of Westbury, near Bristol, where, in 1288, a foundation in honour of the Holy Trinity had been instituted for a dean and several canons.[1] It was not a parish church, but a chapel; the prebend was evidently regarded merely as a sinecure and place of honour, the holder being at liberty to appoint a substitute to read the masses required by the terms of the foundation. Wycliffe, however, seems to have resigned the pre-

Wycliffe's Church preferments.

---

[1] Vaughan states that it was the King who presented him to this prebend (*Monograph*, p. 180), but all that is certain, from documentary evidence, is that Edward III. confirmed the nomination, November 6, 1375.

bend immediately after obtaining it, for in November of the same year, 1375, as appears from an entry in the rolls of Chancery, the prebend was bestowed upon a certain Robert of Farrington.[1]

His nomination to the rectory of Lutterworth, in the county of Leicester, appears, from documentary evidence, to have been an expression of the royal favour. The patronage of this parish did not, indeed, belong properly to the Crown, but to the noble family of Ferrars of Groby, the owners of the land. But as the heir, Lord Henry Ferrars, was still a minor, the right of collation to the existing vacancy devolved on the Crown, and the King presented John Wycliffe in April, 1374.[2] We shall return to this subject in the sequel. At present we only remark further that Wycliffe appears to have resigned his previous charge at Ludgarshall immediately upon his being appointed to the Rectory of Lutterworth. At least, as early after that appointment as May, 1376, a certain William Newbold is named as the parish priest of that village.[3] On more than one occasion Wycliffe expressed himself strongly on the subject of the pluralities held by many priests and prelates; and he had good reason for doing so. The abuse must have gone very far, when even a Pope spoke of the accumulation of Church offices in one and the same person as a mischief to the Church, as Urban V. did in a bull of May, 1365; in consequence of which Papal censure, a sort of statistical inquiry was set on foot, by requiring of every beneficed man to make an official return to his bishop of all the different Church livings which he held.

Rector of Lutterworth.

From such a return made to the Bishop of London by William Wykeham, afterwards Bishop of Winchester, but at that time Archdeacon of London, it appears that he was the holder of not fewer than twelve livings, some of them of very considerable value, whereas he was not in a position to serve one of these spiritual offices in his own person, being obliged to live continually at Court in the capacity of the King's private secretary.[4] This single example speaks loudly enough of the state of things. Wycliffe, therefore, was justified, as matters stood, in strongly censuring such an abuse; but we should have been compelled to challenge his per-

Wycliffe no Pluralist.

---

[1] *Rotuli patentes* 49, Edw. III., 1, m. 11. *Wycliffe Bible*, Pref. p. vii.

[2] That this was the history of the affair is made certain by an entry in the register of the see of Lincoln, in the place where it records the nomination of Wycliffe's successor in the rectory. On this occasion Lord Henry Ferrars exercised personally his right of patronage; and it was stated at the same time that the last preceding nomination had been made by King Edward, by reason of the minority of Lord Ferrars. *Vide* entry in Lewis, p. 44, with note; and in Vaughan, *Monograph*, p. 180, with note.

[3] According to entry in the *Registrum Bokyngham* of Lincoln.

[4] Lowth, *Life of William of Wykeham*, 1758, p. 31.

sonal moral right to complain of it, if he himself had been guilty of the same practice. And doubtless his opponents in this case would not have failed to cast in his teeth the reproach, that he blamed in other men what he allowed in himself. But he never so acted. Never in any instance did he hold, at the same time, two offices involving the cure of souls.

But all this disinterestedness could not protect him from the opposition of the hierarchy. In the course of a single year, 1377, he was twice summoned to appear before the spiritual tribunals; Opposition of the hierarchy. in the first instance, before Convocation, and in the second, before several prelates, as commissioners of the Pope himself. The reason of his summons before Convocation, and the subjects on which he was required to answer, are involved in much obscurity. We find nowhere any documentary information as to the doctrines for which Wycliffe was required to answer before that tribunal. On the other hand, we have some information of the course which the proceedings took on the occasion of this appearance of Wycliffe before his spiritual judges, from which the conclusion is plain that the hostile step now taken against him was closely connected with the political partisanship of the day. The prelates were embittered against the Duke of Lancaster, who was labouring with all his might to put an end to their political influence. For the moment they were no match for him in the political arena; and all the more readily on this account they seized the opportunity of indirectly humbling him in the ecclesiastical province, in the person of a theologian who stood in intimate relations to his person.

The Parliament opened January 27, 1377. A few days later, on February 3, the Convocation—the clerical parliament—also met, Convocation of 1377. and summoned Wycliffe before them. The Bishop of London, William Courtenay, was no doubt the instigator of this proceeding. He was a younger son of the Earl of Devon; a great-grandson of Edward I. on his grandmother's side, closely related to several families of the high nobility, a man of imperious nature and arrogant, hierarchical spirit. He had been promoted, in 1375 from Hereford to the important see of London, a position which he maintained with far more energy than his predecessor, Simon Sudbury, now Archbishop of Canterbury. The nobleman and the hierarch were united in him; and he represented in his own person the coalition of the nobility with the prelacy in opposing the ambitious designs of Lancaster.

In view of the fact that political rather than ecclesiastical motives had to do with the citation of Wycliffe, the Duke considered it his

CONVOCATION IN ST. PAUL'S.

imperative duty to afford him his powerful protection. He resolved to accompany him in person to the assembly of the prelates. On Thursday, February 19, 1377, the Convocation assembled in St. Paul's, and at Wycliffe's side appeared the Duke of Lancester and Lord Henry Percy, the Grand Marshal of England, followed by a band of armed men, and attended by several friends of the learned divine, in particular, by five bachelors of divinity of the five Mendicant Orders, who, by the Duke's desire, were to stand forward in case of need as the advocates of Wycliffe.[1] The Lord Marshal led the way, to clear a passage through the crowd for the Duke and Wycliffe; but even with his aid it proved a difficult matter to get into the cathedral and to press through the church to the Lady Chapel, where the bishops were assembled. This, of course, was not effected without a considerable amount of disturbance in the sacred building, upon which Courtenay declared to Lord Percy that if he had known beforehand the style in which he was going to play the master within the church, he would have barred his entrance. Whereupon the Duke of Lancaster answered the Bishop, in a rage, that he was resolved to be master there, in spite of the bishops.

Wycliffe summoned to St. Paul's.

After much pushing and hustling, they forced their way at last into the Chapel, where dukes and barons were seated with the Archbishop and other prelates. Here, then, stood Wycliffe before his judges, awaiting his examination—a tall, thin figure, clad in a long, light gown of black, with a girdle about his body; his head, adorned with a full, flowing beard, exhibiting features keen and sharply cut, his eye clear and penetrating, his lips firmly closed, in token of resolution—the whole man wearing an aspect of lofty earnestness, and replete with dignity and character.[2]

Scene in the Cathedral.

The Grand Marshal now turned to Wycliffe, and requested him to be seated. 'He had need to rest himself, for he would have many questions to answer.' 'No!' exclaimed the Bishop of London, beside

---

[1] This last circumstance Foxe (*Acts and Monuments*, II., p. 800, Ed. Pratt and Stoughton) takes from the MS. chronicle of a monk of St. Albans, which was lent to him by Archbishop Parker, and from which he derived the whole detailed account of the incident. More recent writers passed over the circumstance in silence, after Lewis had maintained that it is in the highest degree improbable that the Mendicant Friars should have undertaken the defence of a man who had exposed their superstitions and immoral practices. But this last assumption touching Wycliffe's relations to the friars at this date rests upon error. And we have no good reason to doubt the fact as stated by Foxe, especially as he does not say that Wycliffe himself had associated these four friars with him for his defence, but that the Duke had required them to accompany him to the tribunal; and of Lancaster it is well known that he was as pronounced a friend of the Mendicant Orders as he was a sworn enemy of the prelates.

[2] This description of the personal appearance of Wycliffe is taken from several portraits of undoubted originality still existing, all agreeing in the main. [See *note on Wycliffe's Portraits* in the preface to this present volume.]

himself with rage; Wycliffe must not be seated there; it was neither lawful nor becoming that when summoned to answer before his judges he should sit during his examination—he must stand! The dispute between them on this point became so violent as to end in the use of abusive language on both sides, by which the multitude of people who witnessed the scene became greatly excited. And now the Duke struck in, assailing the Bishop with angry words, the Bishop paying him back in full with taunts and insults. The Duke, finding himself overmatched in this line, passed to the use of threats, and declared that he would chastise not only the Bishop of London, but all the prelates of England, for their arrogance. To Courtenay, in particular, he said: 'You talk boastfully of your family, but they will be in no condition to help you; they will have enough ado to protect themselves.' To which the Bishop replied, that if he might be bold enough to speak the truth, he placed his trust neither in his family nor in any other man, but singly and alone in God. Hereupon the Duke whispered to the person who stood nearest to him, that he would sooner drag the Bishop out of the church by the hair of his head than put up with such an affront at his hand. But this was not spoken in so low a voice but that several citizens of London overheard it. They were highly incensed, and cried out that they would never consent to see their Bishop so shamefully handled; they would rather lose their lives than he should be seized by the hair.

As the business, before it was well commenced, had degenerated into a violent quarrel and tumult, the sitting of the court was suspended before nine o'clock in the forenoon. The Duke and the Lord Marshal withdrew with Wycliffe, without the latter having spoken a single word. But the citizens of London, who regarded themselves as insulted in the person of their Bishop, were still more enraged when, on the same day, a motion was made in Parliament that the government of the city should no longer be left in the hands of the Mayor, but should be handed over to a royal commissioner, the imprisoned Lord Latimer. Thus a menace to the municipal liberties and self-government of the capital was added to the affront offered to their Bishop. No wonder that the wrath of the citizens found vent for itself in action as well as in word. On the following day they held a great meeting to deliberate upon the double wrong which had been done them—the imperilling of their autonomy, and the insult to their Bishop. At the same moment it came to their ears that the Lord Marshal had imprisoned one of the citizens in his own house in the heart of the city; they rushed instantly to arms they stormed the house of the Marshal, and set at

Popular commotions.

liberty their imprisoned fellow-citizen. They then searched the house for Lord Percy himself, and not finding him there, rushed off to the mansion of the Duke of Lancaster in the Savoy, where they thought they should find both the lords. But they were a second time disappointed; and to make amends, the crowd vented their rage partly upon a priest, whom they mortally wounded on their way back to the city, and partly upon the Duke's coat of arms, which they had pulled down from his palace, and now hung up in a public place of the city reversed, in token that the Duke was a traitor. They would even have demolished Lancaster's palace had not Bishop Courtenay himself interposed, and entreated them to return to quietness and good order.[1] The Princess of Wales, also, widow of the Black Prince, and mother of Richard, the young heir to the throne, came forward to mediate between the Duke and the citizens. A reconciliation was at length effected, in which the Duke consented that the Bishop of Winchester, who had been banished in disgrace from the Court, and Peter de la Mere, formerly Speaker of the House of Commons, who was still in prison, should be brought to trial before their peers; while on his side the Duke obtained from the citizens the concession that the present Lord Mayor and aldermen of the city should be replaced by others. And further, as the instigators of the riot, and the circulators of abusive rhymes against the Duke could not be found, it was agreed, in satisfaction for these wrongs, that a colossal wax candle should be bought at the expense of the city, and carried in solemn procession, with the Duke's arms attached to it, to St. Paul's, and there kindled before the image of the Virgin Mary.[2]

The citation of Wycliffe before Convocation had thus ended in a totally unexpected manner. Wycliffe himself had never opened his mouth. The incident seems to have passed away without affecting him personally in any way. But the scene which took place in the cathedral, and the popular uproar which resulted from it, brought the already high-pitched irritation between Lancaster and the English bishops to an open rupture, in which Wycliffe was by no means the chief person engaged. To Wycliffe himself it must have been a source of sincere pain that he should have been the occasion of such a scene, and that, too, in a consecrated place. It would certainly have been more agreeable to him, had he been allowed to answer to the accusations which were to be laid against him. But who will hold him responsible for the fact that his person was made use of for ulterior objects, both by his enemies and

Results of the Citation.

---

[1] Walsingham, I., 325. [2] Foxe, *Acts and Monuments*, II., 804. Comp. Walsingham, I., 325.

his friends? In citing him before Convocation, the prelates wished to strike a blow, in his person, at the Duke; while the Duke took up the gauntlet as though thrown down to him, glad to have found an opportunity of humbling the Bishop of London and the English prelates as a body. But that the citizens were exasperated against the Duke on account of his doings in St. Paul's, was no proof that they were also opposed to Wycliffe and his case. Within less than a year afterwards, they espoused his interest in the most earnest way; but I am not disposed to lay stress upon this, as the fact might easily be attributed to the fickleness of the multitude. More weight is due to the circumstance that the sole cause which roused so powerfully the feelings of the citizens was partly the heinous affront offered to their Bishop, and partly their alarm for the safety of their municipal rights and privileges; and neither the one nor the other of these causes of offence can with reason be laid to the charge of Wycliffe.

2.—Papal Bulls against Wycliffe.

ALTHOUGH the citation of Wycliffe before Convocation had been entirely without effect, so far as regarded his own person, there was no abandonment of the designs of his Church adversaries against him on that account. The political friends and patrons of the man were too powerful to allow of the prelates carrying out their wishes for his humiliation. His enemies therefore had recourse to the Papal Court, in order to crush him by means of the highest authority existing in the Catholic Church. No doubt the first steps in this direction had been taken some considerable time before this, and the occurrence in St. Paul's would now afford an opportunity for pushing the matter to a climax.

Wycliffe accused in Rome.

Who were the principal accusers of Wycliffe in Rome? John Foxe's answer to the question is, that they were some English bishops, who collected articles of his and sent them to the Pope.[1] But since Lewis's time it has been regarded as pretty well established that it was the monk party, and especially the Mendicant Orders, who appeared in the Curia against him.[2] We agree with Foxe. The assumption that, so early as the period now before us, a controversy had already broken out between Wycliffe and these Orders can only spring from a confusion of dates. Even had such been the case, it was not single Orders and their representatives who would have been recognised as competent public accusers in matters of doctrine, but

[1] *Acts and Monuments* (Pratt and Stoughton), vol. III., p. 4.

[2] Lewis, 46; Shirley, *Fasc. Zizan.*, xxvii.; Böhringer, *Wycliffe*, 53.

only the bishops of the English Church. We find, in point of fact, that Wycliffe himself considered, not the monks, but the bishops, as the parties who had agitated for a condemnation of his doctrine in Rome.[1]

The Anglican Episcopate, therefore, is, in our opinion, to be regarded as the prime mover of the proceedings of the Roman Court against Wycliffe, as an alleged teacher of heresy; and they took care to prepare and manage the net in which they hoped to entangle him with such skill and precaution, as to make sure that the man whom they dreaded, and who had hitherto been shielded by such powerful protectors, should not be able to escape. They had collected the requisite number of theological propositions which Wycliffe had publicly propounded, either in lectures and disputations delivered in the University, or in his published writings, the dangerous tendency of which, menacing the well-being of Church and State, must, they deemed, be manifest to every eye. But it was also of importance so to weave and intertwine the meshes of the net, that the game should be snared, and finally secured. It seemed that this difficult problem had been skilfully solved; for no fewer than five bulls were issued on one day, all aimed at one and the same point. On May 22, 1377, Gregory XI., who had shortly before *The five Papal bulls.* removed from Avignon to Italy, and on January 17 had made his solemn entry into Rome, put his hand, in the magnificent Church of St. Maria Maggiore, to five bulls against Wycliffe. One of the five, and that which seems to contain the essence of the whole number, is addressed to the Archbishop of Canterbury and the Bishop of London.[2] It conveys to the two prelates apostolic commission and plenary powers, first of all to ascertain, by private inquiry, whether the propositions contained in a schedule appended to the bull had been actually put forth by John Wycliffe; [3] and should this be the case, then to cause him to be put in prison, and to be kept there until they should receive further instructions from the Pope, to follow upon the report made to him of their proceedings.

A second bull contains only a supplement to the principal bull.[4] It is also addressed to the Primate and the Bishop of London, and appoints what course should be taken in case Wycliffe should get secret intelligence of the process with which he is threatened, and should save himself by flight from impending imprisonment. To

---

[1] *De Ecclesia*, c. 15; Vienna MS., 1294, f. 178, col. 2.
[2] Walsingham, I., 350; Lewis, Appendix, 15; Vaughan, *Life and Opinions*, I., 429.
[3] Walsingham, I., 353; Lewis, 316, No. 18; Vaughan, *Life*, etc., I., 457.
[4] Walsingham, I., 348; Lewis, 308, No. 14. *Nuper per nos*, etc.

meet this eventuality, the two prelates are commissioned and endowed with full apostolic powers to issue a public citation to Wycliffe to present himself in person before Gregory XI. within three months. A third bull, also addressed to the same prelates,[1] requires them, either personally, or by theologians of unsuspected orthodoxy, to bring the condemned doctrines of Wycliffe to the notice of King Edward, and his sons, the princes; as also of the Princess of Wales, Joan, widow of the Black Prince, and other great personages of the realm, and privy councillors; to convince them of the erroneous character of these doctrines, and of the dangers which they threatened to the interests of the State; and thus to engage them to assist with all their might in rooting out these errors from the kingdom. The fourth bull, addressed to the King himself,[2] informs him of the commission relating to Wycliffe conveyed to the Archbishop and the Bishop of London; and while warmly commending the zeal which he and his predecessors upon the throne had ever displayed for the Catholic faith, earnestly entreats and charges him to extend his royal grace and assistance to the Archbishop and Bishop in the execution of their commission. Last of all, the fifth bull is addressed to the Chancellor and the University of Oxford,[3] requiring of them in the most emphatic manner, and even upon pain of the loss of their privileges, not only to guard against the setting forth and maintaining of erroneous doctrines, but to commit Wycliffe and his obstinate followers to prison, and to deliver them over to the Pope's commissioners, the Archbishop and the Bishop of London.

The plan of operations, it is plain, had been ripely considered. The attainment of the end in view seemed to be assured, by the promised co-operation of the King and the royal princes, of the Privy Council, the chief nobility, and the University of Oxford. These, it was expected, would all contribute their aid to the two commissioners of the Roman Court in bringing Wycliffe under the Church's power. For that was the point aimed at. It was not meant that the Primate and Bishop Courtenay should conduct the investigation in chief against Wycliffe, and pronounce judgment upon him. To them only a preliminary inquiry was committed, viz., to satisfy themselves, in a manner entirely secret and confidential, that

Plan of procedure.

---

[1] *Super periculosis admodum erroribus*, etc., Walsingham, I., 347; Lewis, 307, No. 13; Vaughan, *Life*, etc., I., 427.
[2] *Regnum Angliae quod Altissimus*, etc. Walsingham, I., 352; Lewis, 312, No. 16; Vaughan, *Life*, etc., I., 430.
[3] *Mirari cogimur et dolere*, etc. Walsingham, I., 346; Lewis, 305, No. 12; Vaughan, *Life*, etc., I., 425; Shirley, *Fasc. Ziz.*, 242. That the date given in this document (May 30, 1376) is false, was discovered by Shirley; *vide* Introduction, xxviii., note 1, after having declared his preference for A.D. 1377, at p. 244, note 17, in the body of his work.

the Theses communicated to them from Rome had really been put forward and maintained by Wycliffe. But the process for heresy proper the Pope manifestly reserved for himself. It was a well-considered policy on the part of the Pope to make his appeal to England's sense of honour, in order to gain the interest of all parties for the object in view. To the King he represented what high reputation England had ever borne for her piety and love to the truth, while both he and his ancestors had always zealously defended the faith. The University of Oxford he entreated to remember that its celebrated name would be dishonoured were it to look on in inactivity while tares were sown and grew up among the wheat in the renowned field committed to its care. Even the two bishops whom Gregory entrusts with plenary powers were not spared a word of admonition. They were reminded that the English bishops of former times ever stood upon their watch-tower, and took careful heed that no heresy should spread around them. But such was now the lack of watchfulness on the spot, that men in far-distant Rome became aware of the secret devices and open attacks of the enemies of the Church, before any measures of defence against them had been taken in England itself. Further, it appeared to the Pope advisable to point out to the bishops the fact that some of Wycliffe's propositions agreed in substance with the views of Marsilius of Padua and John of Jandun, whose book had already been condemned by Pope John XXII.

Let us now examine the condemned articles for ourselves. They are nineteen in number, but they are not arranged in a strictly logical order. This, of course, is not Wycliffe's fault, for it was not he who put them together as they appear in the schedule attached to the Papal bulls, but his opponents. The first five Theses were placed at the head of the collection, with the calculated design that from the very first of the series the statesmen and nobles of the kingdom should receive the impression that Wycliffe held revolutionary views, not only in Church matters, but also in political and municipal affairs, and even called in question the rights of private property and hereditary succession. For in Theses 1–5 the subjects treated of have nothing to do with Church life, but refer exclusively to legal and municipal matters, such as property, right of possession, heritages, and so on. It has always, indeed, been assumed hitherto that the topic here treated is the temporal dominion of the Popes, and the political power and secular property of the Church in general. But this view, generally as it has been received, rests entirely upon misunderstanding and prejudice. Upon an unprejudiced examination, it becomes clear that it is only

Nineteen articles of accusation.

municipal and legal relations which are here in question.[1] Wycliffe's principle is, that all rights of inheritance and property are not to be considered as inherently unconditioned and absolute, but as dependent upon God's will and grace. Then in Nos. 6 and 7 he lays down the bold proposition, 'In the event of the Church falling into error, or of churchmen persistently abusing the property of the Church, kings and temporal rulers are entitled, both legally and morally, to withdraw from them, in a legal and moral manner, the temporal property.'

However strongly the endowment may have been secured on the part of the founder, it is still, in the nature of things, necessarily a conditioned endowment, and one liable to be annulled by certain derelictions of duty. Whether the Church was or was not, in point of fact, in a condition of error, Wycliffe will not himself inquire. He leaves it to princes to inform themselves upon that point; and in the event of the case being such, they may confidently proceed to take action—they are even bound, under the pain of eternal damnation, to withdraw, in this event, its temporalities from the Church. Allied to this, and only treating the subject more as a question of principle, is the last Thesis, the 19th, where he maintains that 'a man of the spirituality,' even the Roman Pontiff himself, may lawfully be set right, and even be accused, by his subjects and by laymen. The group of Theses 8–15 is designed to guard against the abuse of the power of the keys, in 'binding and loosing,' especially in so far as Church discipline and the ban of excommunication should be used to secure certain revenues to the Church, and to deter the laity from meddling with Church property. In the same sense, Wycliffe, in Thesis 14, contests the pretended absoluteness of the Pope's power of the keys, and makes the effective power of the same dependent upon its being used in conformity with the gospel.[2] He is only expressing the same thought in another form as when he says (Thesis 9), 'It is not possible for a man to be put under the ban unless he has before and principally been put under it by himself.' In Nos. 10, 12, 13, Wycliffe declares that only in God's matters, and not in matters of

---

[1] Lewis set the example of referring these articles to ecclesiastical property and jurisdiction, p. 46, and he is followed in this by Vaughan and all later writers. The error attached itself to the words in the first article, *Petrus et omne genus suum*—words which it was thought could only be understood of the Apostle Peter and his successors in the Roman See. But, to say nothing of the extreme strangeness of using the word *genus* for *successores*, Wycliffe often makes use, in his unprinted works, of the name Petrus, as also of the prænomens Caius, Titus, etc., in the way of example. But quite decisive of the point is the fact that in the book, *De Civili Dominio*, I., c. 35, from which I am convinced the article was taken, the connection clearly and necessarily leads to the *general* sense which I have indicated.

[2] No. 15. *Credere debemus, quod solum tunc solvit vel ligat* (sc. Papa) *quando se conformat legi Christi.*

temporal goods and revenues, ought Church censures to the extent of excommunication to be applied. With some appearance of isolation from the rest of the propositions, and yet in a certain degree of connection with the Thesis touching the power of the keys, stands, last of all, the 16th Thesis, which claims for every lawfully ordained priest the full power to dispense every sacrament, and consequently to impart to every penitent remission of all manner of sin.

These nineteen Theses, according to their chief material, fall into three different groups. I. 1–5, concerning rights of property and inheritance. II. 6, 7, 17, 18, concerning Church property and its rightful secularisation in certain circumstances, to which No. 19 is a supplement. III. 8–15, concerning the power of Church discipline and its necessary limits, to which No. 16 also belongs. *Arrangement of the Theses.* We shall fix our attention below upon the connection of thought running through these single Theses; but first we follow the course of external events.

3.—First Effects of the Five Bulls in England.

THE Papal bulls, which were based upon these nineteen Theses of Wycliffe as the *corpus delicti*, were signed in Rome by Gregory XI., as before stated, May 22, 1377; but it was an unusually long time before they were made public in England. Not till December 18, 1377, did the Pope's commissioners named in them—the Archbishop of Canterbury and the Bishop of London—put their signatures to a missive to the Chancellor of the University of Oxford, enclosing the Papal commission addressed to him in the matter; this was seven months, all but four days, after the date of the Papal bulls. How is this delay to be explained? Possibly the bulls had been a long time on their way from Rome. But, as is now well known, the intercourse between Rome and England *Delay in publishing the bulls.* was at that time so constant, and, as a general rule, so rapid, that we cannot think it probable that the arrival of those documents had been really delayed by exceptional circumstances for more than half a year. No doubt they reached their destinations at a much earlier date, and that the delay in the publication and execution of the Pope's commission was entirely the act of the commissioners themselves. Nor is it difficult to understand the reason why. These bulls of Gregory XI. arrived in England at a time when Edward III., given up by his physicians, was approaching his end. *Death of Edward III.* This state of matters was known throughout the kingdom; and on June 21, 1377, the aged monarch breathed his last in his palace at Sheen.

The bull addressed to the King thus became void; and yet, without the help of the State proceedings against Wycliffe could not take the course which Rome desired. The weeks next ensuing, during which all public interest was engrossed by the entry of the boy King into London, and his solemn coronation as Richard II. in Westminster, were of all seasons the least appropriate for bringing before the public this business from Rome. Then, again, everything depended *Events of the new reign.* upon the spirit which was to animate the Government during the King's minority, and upon the position which the regency should take up in ecclesiastical affairs. To all this were added, in August, attacks of the French upon the south coasts of the kingdom, and threatening movements of the Scots in the north. In October, the first Parliament of Richard II. assembled, and in the House of Commons, at least, there prevailed so outspoken a feeling of antagonism to Rome, that it appeared every way advisable to wait till the prorogation of Parliament, which occurred on November 25, before measures were put in operation against Wycliffe. As the most pressing business in this Parliament was the raising of supplies for the war and, above all, for the defence of the kingdom, the attention of the Legislature was once more drawn to the systematic draining of the country for the benefit of the Roman Court and of foreign Church dignitaries, and to all the questions connected therewith; the effect of which was, that the Commons addressed several petitions to the King, in which they renewed their complaints against the Papal provisions and reservations. They proposed to put a stop to these usurpations, which violated the Convention of 1374 between Gregory XI. and Edward, by imposing severe penalties upon all persons who should obtain any Church office through Papal provision, or who should rent from any foreigner land which was an English Church fief. *An anti-Romish Parliament.* They proposed that from February 2 of the ensuing year, all foreigners alike, whether monks or seculars, should leave the kingdom, and that during the continuance of the war all their lands and properties in the country should be applied to war purposes. The income of French clergy alone, accruing from English livings, was estimated at £60,000 a year. In this Parliament also, the question of the right of the State was mooted and discussed with great earnestness. 'Whether the kingdom of England, in case of need, for the purposes of self-defence, is not competent in law to restrain the treasure of the land from being carried off to foreign parts, although the Pope should demand this export of gold in virtue of the obedience due to him, and under the threat of Church censures.'

Upon this question, if we are rightly informed, Wycliffe drew up, by command, an opinion for the young King and his Great Council. In that paper he answered the question with a decided affirmative, appealing to three different standards of laws. *Wycliffe's State-paper.* First, he takes his stand upon the *law of nature*, in virtue of which every corporate body, and therefore also such an incorporation as the kingdom of England, possesses the power of resistance, for its own self-defence. He appealed, secondly, to *the law of the gospel*, according to which all almsgiving (and into this all Church property ultimately resolves itself), in case of necessity, ceases of itself to be a duty binding by the law of love. In support of which latter assertion, he appealed to several expressions of St. Bernard of Clairvaux, in his memorial to Pope Eugene III., *De Consideratione.*[1] Herein Wycliffe also lays stress upon considerations of what is due to the national welfare. If things went on as hitherto, England must be impoverished, and her population decline, while the Curia, by the superfluity of wealth flowing in upon it, would become arrogant and profligate. The enemies of England, by means of her own gold, would be put in a position to make her feel the effects of their malice, while Englishmen would be laughed at by foreigners for their 'asinine stupidity,' etc.[2] Last of all, he appeals to the *law of conscience.* In the second part of the Opinion, he endeavours to remove the apprehension of dangers which might possibly arise from the adoption of the measures in question.

After the Parliament, thus anti-Romish in its temper, was prorogued, no obstacle any longer stood in the way, and it seemed now high time to carry out the Pope's commission, by taking steps against Wycliffe.[3] Accordingly, on December 18, the two commissioners issued a mandate to the Chancellor of Oxford, in which the bull addressed to the University was enclosed. The mandate, which Edmund Stafford presented in person, was to this effect. 1. That the Chancellor, calling to his aid learned and orthodox doctors of *Wycliffe cited to London.*

---

[1] Foxe has incorporated an extract from this memorial with his work, as well in its Latin as its English form. *Acts and Monuments*, III., 54. The complete original is found in MS. in a volume made up of several pieces, in the Bodleian, from which it has been published by Shirley in the *Fasc. Zizan.* He has compared with it a second copy, which is found in one of the Vienna Wycliffe MSS. (Dénis, 358, now numbered 1337, f. 175.) The title of it in the Oxford MS. is, *Responsio Magistri Joannis Wycliff ad dubium infra scriptum quaesitum ab eo per Dominum regem Angliae Ricardum secundum, et magnum suum Concilium, anno regni sui primo.*

[2] Shirley, *Fasc. Zizan.*, 263.

[3] That the commissioners had at their own instance delayed the execution of the Papal commission, which appears to have reached their hands in due time, is evidently presumed by Walsingham when he says, 'How disrespectfully, how negligently they acted in executing their commission, is better passed over in silence than expressed.' *Hist. Anglic.* Ed. Riley, I., 356.

Holy Scripture, should ascertain whether, as a matter of fact, John Wycliffe had set forth the Theses in question, which were contained in the collection drawn up in Rome, a schedule of which was appended to the Papal bull. The result of this inquiry he was instructed to report to the commissaries in a sealed letter. 2. The Chancellor was to cite Wycliffe to appear within thirty days before the Papal commissaries or their delegates in St. Paul's Church in London, there to answer concerning his Theses, and to await consequences. Touching the steps which should be taken in this direction by the Chancellor, the commissaries expected to receive notice in an open letter.[1]

Two things are worthy of remark in this mandate: first, its essential departure from the terms of the Papal bull. Gregory XI. had instructed his commissaries, as we have seen, that in the event of its being found that Wycliffe had actually set forth the Theses in question, they were to cause him to be put in prison, and thereupon wait for instructions from Rome. The mandate, on the contrary, says not a word about imprisonment, but only requires that Wycliffe should be cited to present himself (upon the footing of a man at large) at the bar, and then, it is true, to await what was to follow. This is quite a different thing. But the commissaries must have had very good reasons for departing from the stringent instructions which they had received. Doubtless they were convinced that a prosecution of a man who was in such high favour at Court, as well as among the people, would be not only dangerous, but, as matters stood, quite impossible. They resolved, however, to do something, and so cited Wycliffe to appear before them. Another thing in the mandate is worth consideration—the tone in which the commissaries address the Head of the University. Once and again they impress upon him his duty, from a motive of reverence and submission to the Holy See, punctually and faithfully to carry out the instructions which they sent to him. This sounds suspicious, and leaves the impression that they had some reason to doubt beforehand the disposition of the University to take part against Wycliffe.

In point of fact, the upshot proved that the state of feeling in Oxford was entirely unfavourable to the end contemplated. Thomas Walsingham informs us with great displeasure that the men who were then at the head of the University hesitated long whether to receive the Papal bull with honour or to discard

Feeling at Oxford.

---

[1] The mandate is printed by Lewis in his Appendix, No. 17, p. 314, as also in Wilkins' *Concilia Magnae Britanniae*, III., p. 123; only in the latter the date given is v Cal. Januarii, instead of xv Cal., *i.e.*, December 28, instead of December 18. This is the solution of the discrepancy remarked upon by Hoeffler, in his *Anna von Luxemburg*, p. 53, note 3.

it with total disrespect. The chronicler pours out his feelings in an apostrophe to the University, in which he laments how deeply she has fallen from her former height of wisdom and learning, seeing that now, under a dark cloud of ignorance, she is not ashamed to doubt concerning things which no Christian layman would hesitate for a moment to believe.[1]

The representatives of the University resisted, it appears, for some time the bull which Gregory himself had addressed to them. The case was different with the archiepiscopal mandate which accompanied the bull, for in this nothing was required of them save an inquiry into the question of fact, whether such and such propositions had been actually set forth by Wycliffe, and his citation to appear before the episcopal tribunal. Neither of these requirements touched too nearly either the honour or the rights of the University. It was otherwise with the Papal bull. This reflected upon the honour of the University at its very onset, by sharply animadverting upon its remissness in opposing the erroneous doctrines which had sprung up within it. It appeared, besides, to be an infringement of the rights of the corporation to require of them to take Wycliffe prisoner, and deliver him up to the commissioners, and to do the like with several of his followers, if they should manifest any contumacy. No wonder, if the heads of the University found it opposed to their dignity and even to their rights, that they should be called upon to play, so to speak, the part of constables who, at the bidding of a third party, were to be compelled to make prisoners of members of their own corporation, and deliver them over to a tribunal with which they had nothing to do. Even apart, however, from the formal and legal point of view, sympathy with Wycliffe and esteem for his person were no doubt strong enough in Oxford circles (as the Pope himself presupposed) to have awakened an animated opposition to the Papal demand. What conclusion was arrived at in the end has not been expressly handed down to us; but we may readily conjecture that the University conformed its action to the demands formulated in the more temperate mandate of the commissioners, and as much as possible ignored the commands of the bull itself.

4.—The Process against Wycliffe.

By the mandate to the Chancellor, Wycliffe was cited to appear in St. Paul's in London thirty days after the service of the citation. There appears to have been a subsequent adjournment to a later date, and

---

[1] Walsingham, *Hist. Anglic.*, I., 345.

to a different locality, viz., the Archbishop's palace at Lambeth. Many councils have been held in the chapel of this palace since the days of Anselm of Canterbury, and here Wycliffe was appointed to appear before the Pope's commissioners. When this took place cannot be exactly determined. The month of April, 1378, has generally been assumed as the time, since Lewis attempted to fix this approximate date, which, however, he himself regards as uncertain.[1] It is probable that the date was somewhat earlier, for, according to Walsingham's account, Gregory XI. must have been still alive at the time of this examination.[2] But Gregory died March 27, 1378. It follows that the transaction must have taken place at latest in March, perhaps even in February. This was not much later than the term for which Wycliffe was originally summoned by the Chancellor of Oxford. Wycliffe unhesitatingly presented himself before the Archbishop, Simon Sudbury, and the Bishop of London, William Courtenay. The Duke of Lancaster, who had stood forward in St. Paul's as his defender, was no longer, since the change on the throne, in possession of ascendant influence. But Wycliffe stood in no need of high protection. He possessed courage enough to place himself, without it, before the commissioners of the Pope.

Wycliffe appears at Lambeth.

In defence of the nineteen Theses, condemned by the Curia as erroneous, he put in a written answer, in which he set forth the standpoint which he had taken in these Theses, and at once expounded and vindicated their several meaning.[3] This answer was meant to be communicated to the Pope himself. Such was Wycliffe's own intention, at least, as may be seen from the manuscript passage quoted in the note. Meanwhile, however, the business on this occasion, as before, did not pass over entirely without disturbance. Sir Henry Clifford, an officer in the Court of the widowed Princess of Wales, appeared in the session, and demanded of the commissaries, in name of the Princess, that they should abstain from pronouncing any final judgment respecting the accused. Citizens of London, too, forced a passage into the chapel,

His defence and dismission.

---

[1] *Life of John Wiclif*, p. 58.

[2] Walsingham, *Hist. Anglic.*, I., 356, says in reference to the upshot of the transaction, 'Wiclif escaped, *amplius non compariturus coram dictis episcopis, citra mortem Gregorii Papae.*'

[3] This short 'Defence' is incorporated by Walsingham in his *Chronicle*, I., 357-363. It is also given by Lewis in his *Appendix*, No. 40, p. 382; and by Vaughan, *Life*, etc., I., 432. In the Chronicler its title is *Declarationes*; in Lewis, *Protestatio*. I find that Wycliffe himself, in his work *De Veritate S. Scripturae*, c. 14, f. 40, col. 4 (Vienna MS., 1294), gives to this piece the latter title, *Protestatio*. Another justification of the same nineteen articles, differing in point of form, and purporting to have been presented to the Parliament, is given by Shirley, *Fasc. Zizan.*, p. 245.

and loudly and menacingly took part with the theologian, who was a patriot so much beloved and honoured. This double intimidation, from high and low, the spiritual tribunal was unable to withstand. To save appearances, however, Wycliffe was prohibited any longer from delivering in lectures and sermons the Theses in question, because, as was pretended, they would give offence to the laity. It was not, therefore, because they were in themselves erroneous. Such was the impression, it would seem, which Wycliffe had made by his defence. He was allowed to leave the tribunal as free as he had appeared before it; quite contrary to the intentions which had been formed in Rome, and directly in the teeth of the instructions which had been given to the commissaries.

No wonder that the zealous adherents of Rome were displeased in the highest degree with this result of the process. We have still a lively echo of this feeling in the utterances of the chronicler Walsingham on the subject. In great wrath, *Walsingham's comment.* he pours himself forth against the vain-glorious boastings with which the prelates began the business, and the fear of man with which they closed it. When they were appointed the Pope's commissaries against Wycliffe, they had declared, in the fulness of their courage, that by no entreaties of men, by no threats or bribes, would they allow themselves to be drawn aside from the line of strict justice in this affair, even if their own lives should be menaced. But on the very day of hearing, for fear of the wind which blew the reed hither and thither, their words had become smoother than oil, to the public humiliation of their own dignity and to the detriment of the whole Church. Men who had vowed not to bend to the princes and peers of the realm till they had punished the arch-heretic for his extravagances, were seized with such terror at the sight of a certain knight of the Court of Princess Joan, that one would have supposed that they had 'no horns on their mitres more;' for 'they became as one that heareth not, and who has no word to say against it in his mouth' (Ps. xxxviii. 14). Thus it was that the crafty hypocrite, by his written defence of those godless Theses of his, had the better of his judges, and got clear off.[1]

[1] Walsingham, I., 356; comp. 362. We may here find a place for the remark that the two examinations of Wycliffe before the English prelates, treated of in this chapter, have not always been rightly viewed by historians. Foxe, indeed, in the sixteenth century, and his Romish contemporary, Nicolas Harpsfield, placed the examinations in St. Paul's in the days of Edward III., and at a time antecedent to the appearance of the five Papal bulls. They follow, in this point, the account of Walsingham (which, however, is not entirely consistent with itself, and of other chroniclers of the period between Wycliffe and the Reformation. But Lewis, pp. 46, 56, assumed that both the examinations, at St. Paul's and at Lambeth, took place in consequence of the Papal bulls, and not before, and that not only the later, but the first also took place under Richard II., after King Edward's death. He was followed in this not only by Mosheim, Schröckh,

Thus, then, was a second attack upon Wycliffe happily repelled. The first had been an independent attempt of the English Episcopate; the second had proceeded from the central power of Rome itself, whose instruments for this occasion were two English prelates. On the first occasion, a prince of the blood had made use of his influence in the Government to thwart, in a violent way, the design of the prelates. On the second occasion, a powerful sympathy from different circles in the country served to shield the bold Reformer; the learned Corporation of Oxford bestirred itself to guard in his person its own independence; the mother of the young King put in a powerful word for him; and the burghers of London, although, it is true, in a tumultuous manner, manifested their sympathy with the honoured patriot. We see how widely among the higher and lower strata of the population, esteem for Wycliffe and the influence of his spirit were then diffused. It is true that, in the Chapel at Lambeth, the Papal commissaries formally prohibited him from publishing any more in the pulpit or in the chair the doctrine condemned by the Pope. No formal promise to that effect was, however, given by Wycliffe; and if he resolved to persevere in his own path, in spite of this prohibition, the prelates were destitute of power to arrest his progress.

The two citations compared.

All these considerations apart, the relations of the Western Church at large were assuming such a form just at this time, that an earnest and free spirit like Wycliffe's could only be inflamed still more to press for reformation with all its strength. Not long after the trial in Lambeth, Gregory XI. died, March 27, 1378; and a few months later was developed that great and long-continued Papal schism which exercised an influence of the greatest importance

The Papal schism.

Gieseler, and Neander, but also by English scholars, such as Lowth, Baber, and a writer in the *Westminster Review*, 1854. The last-named author believed that he was able to bring positive proof that Walsingham must have been in error when he placed the appearance of Wycliffe at St. Paul's at the beginning of 1377, instead of the year 1378. But Vaughan, in the *Life*, etc., 2 ed., I., 357, note 23, has proved, by weighty arguments, that that event took place as early as 1377 (February 19), and that the Papal bulls were not issued till a later date, so that the event cannot have been a consequence of the bulls, but much rather the occasion of their issue on May 22, 1377. To Vaughan, undoubtedly, belongs the merit of having placed this subject in a clear light, in regard both to the chronology and to the facts of the case. The following facts are decisive in support of this view:—1. The popular tumult in London, directed against the Duke of Lancaster and Marshal Percy, which was undoubtedly a consequence of what occurred in St. Paul's, is always and persistently placed in the year 1377, and not in the year following, 1378. 2. Lord Percy, in the beginning of 1378, was no longer Marshal, but in 1377 he was, without doubt, invested with this dignity. 3. The day of the week which is assigned by the English contemporary chronicler, viz., Thursday before the Feast of St. Peter's, February 19, corresponds with this day of the month in the year 1377, but not in the year 1378.

upon Wycliffe's inner and outer life.[1] Thus the year 1378 forms a turning-point in his career. A storm which menaced his safety had been turned aside, and on this occasion it had become evident how many hearts were beating in sympathy with him and his efforts. Then befell the great Church schism which shook violently the moral prestige of the Roman Church, so far as it had any such still remaining, which paralysed its power, and stimulated every good man to do his utmost to help the necessities of the case, and to raise up again the fallen Church. It is easy to understand that Wycliffe, after having applied himself till now, almost exclusively, to matters of mixed ecclesiastical and political interest, should henceforth devote himself to interests of a purely ecclesiastical kind, without of course renouncing the character of the patriot. From that time he first stood forward in the specific character of a CHURCH REFORMER.

[1] The Chronicler of St. Albans appears to have felt this himself, when he says of Gregory XI.'s death, '*Cujus obitus non modicum fideles contristavit sed in fide falsos, ipsum Johannem (Wiclif) et ipsius asseclas, animavit.*' Walsingham, I., 356.

CHAPTER VI.

WYCLIFFE AS A PREACHER. HIS EFFORTS FOR REFORM IN PREACHING AND FOR THE ELEVATION OF THE PASTORAL OFFICE.

1.—Wycliffe as a Preacher; his Homiletical Principles.

WYCLIFFE not only made use of scientific lectures from his chair in Oxford, nor only of learned works and small fugitive tracts; he also availed himself of preaching as a means of battling with the evils which he saw in the religious condition of the National Church, of implanting sound Christian life, and of thus serving, according to his ability, the interests of his Church and people.

It is characteristic of the man and his way of acting, that in this extremely important matter he commenced by doing his duty at his own personal post, from which he afterwards extended his influence to wider circles.

This comes out with the greatest clearness from his sermons that have been handed down to us. These divide themselves into two great groups—the Latin sermons and the English. The latter are partly sermons which he may be presumed to have preached to his congregation at Lutterworth, as parish priest, and partly outlines of sermons which he prepared as a kind of model for itinerant preachers of his school; we shall return to these in the sequel. The Latin sermons were, without doubt, delivered in Oxford before the University, perhaps in St. Mary's.[1] This is antecedently probable, but it is also manifest from the form and contents of the sermons themselves. Not unfrequently we find learned matters referred to in them in a way which makes it certain that the audience must have consisted of people of culture and scholastic

Wycliffe's sermons: Latin and English.

---

[1] Comp. Shirley, *Fasc. Zizan.*, 305. *Cum Magister Nicolaus* (Hereford) *in Quadragesima praedicasset publice in Ecclesia B. Virginis in lingua Latina toto clero*, etc.

learning—as, for example, when, in the first of the 'Miscellaneous Sermons,' he speaks of the manifold interpretations then received of the sense of Scripture, and, in particular, of the *sensus tropologicus* and *anagogicus;* when quotations are introduced, not only from the Fathers, but from the Canon Law; and when abstract questions of logic and metaphysics are investigated, such as the relation of the soul to the body, etc. What sort of audience must a preacher have before him when he speaks of the imitation of Christ, as Wycliffe does in the third of his Sermons for Saints' Days, and asks, How does it help us towards the imitation of Christ to pore over the pages of the logicians? or what aid comes from the knowledge of the natural philosophers, acquired at such a cost of labour? or from the well-known method of reason, adopted by the mathematicians? Plainly, the preacher has people of learning before him—the professors and students of the University. This was long ago correctly noted by a reader of the Vienna manuscript of these sermons, who writes on the margin, opposite this passage, the words, '*Magistri et studentes notate.*'[1] The preacher, in fact, in one instance mentions Oxford by name;[2] and one of his sermons from beginning to end is simply an address delivered on the occasion of a doctoral promotion in the University.[3]

The Latin sermons of Wycliffe known to us belong to many different years, as may be gathered with tolerable certainty from several internal marks. Most of these collections, indeed, belong to the latest years of his life, but one of them, containing forty miscellaneous sermons, consists of earlier discourses, all delivered before the year 1378;[4] and these are all instructive and valuable for the insight they give into the course of Wycliffe's development. At present we will say nothing of what is to be learned from this source of the progress of his mind in the matter of doctrine; we will confine ourselves to what we are able to gather with respect to the views he took of the object of preaching, and of the actual condition of the preacher's office at that period.

Latin sermons.

In the last-named collection of Latin sermons, belonging to the period of his academic life and work, he expresses himself in different

---

[1] *Evangelia de Sanctis*, No. 3, fol. 5, col. 2 of the Vienna MS. 3928. (Dénis CCCC.)

[2] Twelfth Sermon, fol. 28, col. 4 of the same MS.:—*Nam frater alienigena, de regno suo portans pecuniam paucam, ut theologiam discat Oxoniae*, etc.

[3] No. 24 in the Twenty-four Miscellaneous Sermons, fol. 185 of the same MS.

[4] The two oldest extant catalogues of Wycliffe's writings, found in two Vienna MSS., dating from the beginning of the fifteenth century, agree in giving this collection the title *XL. Sermones compositi dum stetit in scholis*, in contrast with another collection which is entitled *Sermones XX. compositi in fine vitae suae.* This confirms the correctness of an observation which I had made before this notice was known to me.

passages on the subject of preachers and preaching. Two sermons in particular on the Gospel for Sexagesima Sunday—Luke viii. 4-15, the Parable of the Sower—supply us with important information as to his views on this point.[1]

Before everything else Wycliffe lays stress upon the truth that the preaching of the Word of God is that function which serves, in a degree peculiar to itself, to the edification of the Church; and this is so, because the Word of God is a seed (Luke viii. 11, 'The seed is the Word of God'). In reflecting upon this truth, he is filled with wonder, and exclaims, 'O marvellous power of the Divine Seed! which overpowers strong warriors, softens hard hearts, and renews, and makes divine, men brutalised by sin, and departed infinitely far from God. Plainly, so mighty a wonder could never be wrought by the word of a priest, if the Spirit of Life and the Eternal Word did not, above all things else, work with it.'

Wycliffe on the preacher's office.

But the grander and more exalted the view which Wycliffe takes of the preacher's office, so much the more severely does he condemn the faults and deficiencies of the actual average preacher of his own time. As the worst of these, he censures the evil practice of not preaching God's Word, but reciting stories, fables, or poems that were altogether foreign to the Bible. He refers again and again to this subject in sermons both of his earlier and later years, as well as in treatises and tracts.[2] We have no ground to assume that sermons of the kind he censures were not preached from some Bible text. It is rather to be supposed that the preachers, after giving out a text from the Scriptures for form's sake, were none the less accustomed to draw the main contents of their sermons from other sources. There were not even wanting instances of preachers who were bold

---

[1] This collection of sermons stands beside a collection of Sermons for Saints' Days (written later), and of twenty-four Miscellaneous Sermons (also dating from Wycliffe's last years), and also beside a few short essays, in the Vienna MS., 3928 (Dénis CCCC). The collection of 'forty sermons' (which, however, number only thirty-eight) begins at fol. 193 of the MS., and the two sermons on Luke viii. 4-15 are the eighth and ninth in number of the collection, fols. 206-210.

[2] In the sermon last mentioned (comp. preceding note), Wycliffe reminds his hearers of the exhortation of the Apostle Peter, 'If any man speak, let him speak as the oracles of God;' and declares that men now-a-days in preaching do not preach the Word of God, but *gesta,* *poëmata vel fabulas extra corpus Scripturae,* fol. 208, col. 1. He says the same thing in the sermon preceding, fol. 206, col. 3. In a later collection of sermons, 61 *Evangelia de Sanctis*—in sermon 56 he speaks of *tragoediae vel comoediae et fabulae vel sententiae apocriphae, quae sunt hodie populo praedicatae.* And in the work *De Officio Pastorali,* Leipzig, 1863, v. II., c. 5, p. 37, he says of the Mendicant Monks, *Et tota sollicitudo est eorum, non verba evangelica et saluti subditorum utilia seminare, sed fraudes, joca, mendacia, per quae possunt populum facilius spoliare.* Also in the Treatise, *De Veritate S. Scripturae,* Wycliffe lays down the principle: *Theologus debet seminare veritatem Scripturae, non gesta vel chronicas mundiales.*

enough to dispense with a Scripture text, and to choose something else. Even an Archbishop of Canterbury, Cardinal Stephen Langton, 1228, saw nothing offensive in taking for the text of a short Latin sermon which still exists, a dancing-song in old French, allegorically applying, it is true, ' the Fair Alice,' and all that is said of her, to the Holy Virgin.[1] Things of this sort, however, may have been of comparatively rare occurrence; but in the thirteenth and fourteenth centuries it had become almost a prevailing pulpit-fashion, instead of opening up Bible thoughts, and applying them to life to draw the materials of sermons from civil and natural history, from the legendary stores of the Church, and even from the fable-world of the Middle Ages, and heathen mythology. If a priest, on a Saint's Day, recounted the miracles of the saint as narrated in his legend, this had some claim to be listened to as a piece of sacred history. But the *Gesta Romanorum*, and all manner of tales and fables taken from profane sources like Ovid's *Metamorphoses*,[2] were made use of by preachers, if not for the edification, at least for the entertainment of their hearers.

Faults in contemporary preaching.

The taste for allegorical interpretations and applications, as these gradually came into general use, helped men over every objection to the practice; and the craving for entertainment of this description grew stronger, the less preachers were able to supply the souls of men with wholesome refreshment from the eternal fountain of the Word of God. No wonder that sermons often became a web whose warp and weft consisted of all other threads save those of Bible truth. It was precisely those men of the fourteenth century who were specially trained for the work of popular preaching—namely the Dominicans and the Franciscans—who humoured the corrupt taste of the time, and flavoured their pulpit addresses with such stories and buffooneries. If the multitude were amused for the moment, and the begging friar who tickled their ears got his reward of a collection,[3] the end aimed at was gained, and the Penny-

Methods of the friars.

---

[1] *Sermo Magistri Stephani de Langeduna, Archiep. Cantuar., de Sancta Maria*, in the Arundel MSS. of the British Museum. Wright gives the whole sermon in his *Biographia Britannica Lit.*, II., 446.

[2] An elder contemporary of Wycliffe, Thomas Walleys, an English Dominican (died 1340), published a book, entitled *Metamorphosis Ovidiana moraliter explanata*, which was printed six times at least onwards from the end of the fifteenth century. Comp. *Histoire Littéraire de la France. Quatorzième siècle.* Tom. XXIV., p. 371 and LI. And another Dominican, an Oxford Doctor, John Bromyard, drew up a collection of histories, alphabetically arranged under certain heads, which were all intended for the use of preachers (hence the title of the work: *Summa Praedicantium*); but his histories are in good part taken from the popular storytellers. *Hist. Littér. de la France*, XXIV., 372.

[3] Wycliffe—*De Officio Pastorali*, II. 5—thinks that the people should despise such monks as preachers, for an additional reason—viz., because it was their custom to make a collection immediately after their sermons.

Preacher (as Brother Berthold of Regensburg, as early as the thirteenth century, calls this set of preachers) could go on his way rejoicing.

It is nothing wonderful that even Catholic literary historians, like the learned continuators of the *Histoire Littéraire de la France*, condemn a style of pulpit eloquence such as this; or that even in the beginning of last century a Dominican like the learned Jacob Echard, pronounced the stories with which the brethren of his Order were accustomed to amuse their audiences to be 'stale and absurd.'[1] But if a contemporary like Wycliffe saw these serious evils in their true light, and condemned them in so decided a tone, his judgment must have been enlightened by the Word of God; since he himself shared in other respects in many of the pulpit faults of his own time.

The second objection which he took to the prevailing pulpit fashion of his age, was that even when the Word of God was preached this was not done in the right way. Preachers were in the habit of breaking up the Bible thoughts into the smallest and finest particulars, and of making moral applications of them in a style so loaded with rhetorical ornaments, including even the use of rhyme, that the language of Scripture was thrust into the background, and the language of the preacher came alone to be regarded, as if he were himself the author and discoverer of God's truth. This practice, he remarks, comes from nothing else but the pride of men, every one seeking his own honour, every one preaching only himself, and not Jesus Christ (2 Corinthians iv. 5). On all such preaching Wycliffe pronounces the judgment that it is a dead word, and not the word of our Lord Jesus Christ—not the word of eternal life (John vi. 68). It was this prevailing want of the true seed of the word of life which, in his opinion, was to blame for the spiritual deadness of the people, and for the wickedness which in consequence prevailed in the world.

The Bible ignored.

These were weighty truths, indicating the necessity for much more than a mere reform of preaching, looking, indeed, in the direction of a reformation of the Church at large, yea, of a regeneration of Christendom from the life-seed of the Word of God. Meanwhile, let us limit ourselves to the pulpit, and take a close view of the strictures which Wycliffe makes on the prevalent preaching of his time. Even in cases where the Word of God is preached, and not matters of quite

---

[1] In 1719, the French Dominican, Jacob Echard, published vol. I., and in 1722 vol. II., of a collection, in historical order, of the works of his Order, *Scriptores Ordinis Praedicatorum*, etc., in which he speaks strongly enough of the Dominican style of preaching in the fourteenth century, and censures those *historiolas ineptas et insulsas*, II. 762.

another kind, he censures, as already remarked, the manner in which this is done; and what he disapproves of is twofold—first, the scholastic form of preaching; and, secondly, its rhetorical ornamentation.[1]

As to the former, Wycliffe takes notice of the method of endless logical distinctions and divisions.[2] This practice had found its way into the pulpits from the lecture rooms of the scholastics. It was connected with the universal dialectic habit of the Middle Ages, a habit which appeared in frequent definitions, hair-splitting divisions and subdivisions, and in endless syllogistic processes of proof. Hence arose a series of treatises on Method, in particular of aids to the preparation of sermons, *e.g.*, a treatise by an anonymous author of the year 1390, under the title of *The Art of making Sermons*, in which the syllogism is held up as the ground form to which everything else is to be reduced.[3] Logical subtleties.

As to the other point—the rhetorical and poetical ornamentation with which preachers thought they were bound to set off their sermons. Wycliffe repeatedly returns to it.[4] He goes into this subject very minutely, seeking to expose in their true light the grounds upon which men tried to excuse if not to justify the practice, in order to bring to light the self-conceit which lay at the bottom of all, and to warn preachers against it. Rhetorical artifices.

The first ground which was alleged in support of the practice was that there was a necessity to give up the old style of preaching and introduce a new one, otherwise there would be no longer any difference between a thoroughly schooled divine and a poorly educated mediocre priest. To this ground Wycliffe allows no weight whatever. It savours, he justly remarks, of nothing else but vainglory, and a desire to take precedence of others. 'Not so, beloved. Let us rather follow the example of our Lord Jesus Christ, who was humble enough to confess, "My doctrine is not Mine, but the Father's who sent Me. He who speaketh of himself seeketh his own glory."' Pleas for such methods.

---

[1] In the sermon referred to, p. 178, note 1, fol. 208, col. 1, it is said of the modern preacher: *Praedicando Scripturam dividet ipsam ultra minuta naturalia, et allegabit moralizando per colores rithmicos quousque non appareat textus Scripturae.*

[2] In the same sermon, fol. 208, col. 2— *Inanis gloriae cupidus est qui innititur divisionibus verborum. Illi invicem invident qui nedum divisiones thematis sed cujuslibet auctoritatis occurrentis ingeminant.*

[3] *Ars faciendi sermones.* The tract begins with the proposition—*Haec est ars brevis et clara faciendi sermones, secundum formam syllogisticam, ad quam omnes alii modi sunt reducendi.* Comp. *Hist. Littér. de la France*, XXIV. 365.

[4] He censures the ambitiousness which aims to exalt itself by the use of *grandia verba*, and disapproves of the attempt to give a more beautiful form to the sermon by the *color rhetoricus* and by *colligantia rithmica, i.e.*, rhymes; he goes the length even of maintaining that by this *declamatio heroica*, etc., God's Word is only falsified.

The second ground upon which men took their stand was this: every subject treated of must have a form correspondent with itself. Now, theology is the most perfect of all subjects. It behoves, therefore, to be clothed in the noblest and most beautiful form, and that is the dress of oratory and poetry. Wisdom only becomes perfect when adorned with eloquence. To these ideas Wycliffe opposes himself in the most decided manner. This ornamental style, upon which men so plume themselves, is so little in keeping with God's Word that the latter is rather corrupted by it, and its power paralysed for the conversion and regeneration of souls. God's Word, according to Augustine, has a peculiar and incomparable eloquence of its own, in its very simplicity and modesty of form.

The third ground relied upon was an appeal to the poetical form of several books of the Old Testament, from which it was argued that it is the duty of a theologian to be guided by this precedent, especially as poetry has a charm of its own, and is further of advantage for helping the memory. To which Wycliffe replies—'It is one thing to sing a spiritual song, and another to speak a word of warning. The measure of verse has, it is true, a certain charm, but only a sensuous charm, which rather draws off the soul of the hearer from the spiritual and eternal subject of discourse, and destroys his taste for spiritual nourishment.'

How sound and good, and worthy of being laid to heart even at the present day, these thoughts of Wycliffe are, it is hardly necessary for us to point out at any length. In his criticism of the grounds on which his contemporaries sought to defend the scholastic or rhetorical and poetical style of preaching, there is a positive as well as a negative side, so that we may arrive at very definite views as to Wycliffe's convictions on the true method of setting forth the Word of God. We may here distinguish between the two questions—what to preach, and how to preach it. To the first Wycliffe replies, as is shown by his words above cited, it is *God's Word* that should be preached, for God's Word is the bread of souls, indispensable and wholesome; and therefore, he thinks, to feed the flock spiritually without Bible truth, is the same thing as if one were to prepare for another a bodily meal without bread.[1] God's Word is the seed which begets regeneration and spiritual life.[2] Now, the chief business of a preacher is to beget and to nourish members

What to preach.

---

[1] The twenty-second of the Sermons for Saints' Days (61 *Evangelia de Sanctis*). *Idem est spiritualiter pascere auditorium sine sententia evangelica, ac si quisfaceret convivium corporale sine pane.* Vienna MS., 3928, fol. 42.

[2] *Miscell. Sermons*, No. 8. *Verbum Dei habet vim regenerativam.* In the same MS., fol. 206, col. 3.

of the Church.¹ Therefore it is God's Word he must preach; then only will he succeed. This was why the Church of Christ grew so mighty when the gospel was preached by the apostles, whereas at the present day the Church is continually decreasing for the want of this spiritual seed.² If the prophets of the Old Testament preface their prophecies with 'Thus saith the Lord,' and if the apostles proclaim the Word of the Lord, so must we too preach God's Word, and proclaim the gospel according to the Scriptures.³ There is one point in particular to which Wycliffe draws attention—that believing Christian men, who are really preaching the gospel, must necessarily give the first place to the preaching of the Gospel *history*, for in that holy history lies the faith of the Church, which the congregation is bound to learn and know.⁴ 'The priests learn and teach Holy Scripture for this purpose, that the Church may learn to know the walk of Christ, and may be led to love Christ Himself.' ⁵

To the question, How ought the Word of God to be preached? Wycliffe replies, in general terms, that the truth which edifies ought to be uttered aptly. Of course this, taken alone, does not amount to much. Coming close to the subject, he calls to his aid the general rule, that every means subservient to an end is the better adapted to that end, the shorter and completer the way in which it leads to it (*compendiosius et copiosius*). As now the sowing of God's Word is the appointed means for the glory of God and the edification of our neighbour, it is plain that the sowing is all the more aptly done the more shortly and completely it fulfils that end. Without doubt, this is the case with a plain and simple mode of address (*plana locutio*); and this mode therefore ought to be chosen.⁶ In another place Wycliffe expresses his preference for a 'humble and homely proclamation of the gospel;'

How to preach.

Aptness and simplicity.

---

¹ The twelfth sermon of the same collection has these words—*Praecipuum officium viri ecclesiastici est gignere membra ecclesiae*, etc., fol. 52, col. 1. Again, in ninth sermon, p. 207, col. 4—*Sacerdos Domini missus ad gignendum et nutriendum populum verbo vitae.*

² *Sermons for Saints' Days*, No. 22. *Quando praedicatum est ab apostolis evangelium, crescit ecclesia in virtute; sed modo, ex defectu spiritualis seminis, continue decrescit*, fol. 42, col. 3.

³ In sermon 20 of *Miscellaneous Sermons*—fol. 176, col. 2—Wycliffe says: *Auditus tam praedicantis quam etiam sermonem audientis debet fieri verbo Christi; et hinc est, quod prophetae legis veteris dixerunt, 'haec dicit Deus,' et apostoli praedicaverunt verbum Domini.*

Farther on he mentions that the whole congregation testifies their veneration for the gospel, 'for when the gospel is read the people rise to their feet and remain standing—they remove their hats, cross themselves, listen with attention, and kiss the wall of the church; while the men of rank lay aside their swords. And all this is done to show their devotion before the gospel of Jesus Christ—while men ofttimes deny the gospel by their deeds.'

⁴ In the twenty-second of the *Sermons for Saints' Days*, fol. 42, col. 2.

⁵ *Sacerdotes ad hoc discunt et docent Scripturam sacram, ut ecclesia cognoscat conversationem Christi et amet eum*, fol. 202, col. 4, Sermon 6.

⁶ Sermon 9.

and by this he no doubt meant nothing else than this plainness and simplicity of language.[1] And he proceeds on the same principle when he remarks: 'It was because a flowery and captivating style of address cannot fail to be of little account wherever the right substance of preaching is present, that Christ promised to His disciples (Matthew x. 19) no more than that it would be given to them *what* they should say: the *how* would naturally follow.'[2] That the admonitions which occur in a sermon should be suitable to the state of the audience, is a self-evident deduction from the same principle;[3] and the utterance given to the truth ought to be apposite and fitting (*apte loqui veritatem*). Only one thing must never on any account be wanting—genuine devout feeling—the *fidelis sermonis ministratio*—from which everything in the sermon should be the outcome. 'If the soul is not in tune with the words, how can the words have power? If thou hast no love, thou art sounding brass and a tinkling cymbal.'[4] Still, there is nothing inconsistent with this in the requirement that the preacher should use sharpness of speech (*acuti sermones*) upon proper occasions. Wycliffe remarks that it must not be supposed that sharpness includes in it malice or ill-feeling. Christ contended sharply with the Pharisees, but He did so out of a pious heart and from love to the Church.[5] His last observation on the subject is the crowning one, that 'in every proclamation of the gospel the true teacher must address himself to the heart, so as to flash the light into the spirit of the hearer, and to bend his will into obedience to the truth.'[6]

Such are the positive requirements which Wycliffe lays down for preaching and preachers. Let us see how far he complied with them himself, by examining his Latin as well as his English sermons.[7] *What* does he preach? He strives to preach God's Word, not man's; not worldly things, but the saving truth. This is what we feel to be his spirit everywhere. That he always takes his texts from the Bible, either from the Church lessons or from other parts, freely selected, according to circumstances, is a matter of slight importance. But he is also fond of connecting one text with another—

Wycliffe's topics.

---

[1] *Sermons for Saints' Days*, No. 31, fol. 65, col. 1.
[2] *Ib.*, fol. 61, col. 4.
[3] No. 30 in the same collection, fol. 60, col. 3. *Verba exhortationis sunt congruentiae auditorii applicanda.*
[4] *XL. Miscell. Sermons*, No. 8, fol. 206, col. 2.
[5] *XXIV. Sermons*, No. 4, fol. 138, col. 4.
[6] *Ib.*, No. 20, fol. 176, col. 1.

[7] Vaughan, in his *Life and Opinions*, etc., published some extracts from Wycliffe's English sermons, upon the basis of which Engelhard wrote his *Wykliffe as a Preacher*. Erlangen, 1834. But these sermons, which, in their complete form, had remained till lately in MS., have been recently given to the world in an excellent form by Thomas Arnold from the Clarendon Press, forming three volumes of Wycliffe's *Select English Works*.

e.g., he often combines one Sunday's Gospel with the Gospel for the preceding Sunday, or with the Epistle for the same; and in doing so he dwells with admiration upon the excellencies of the Word of God; observing, in one place, that Scripture truths stand in such an intimate connection with each other, that every one of them lends support to every other, and all of them unite in the revelation of God.[1]

Further, in all cases where he pronounces a judgment upon any doctrine, or upon any ecclesiastical custom and institution, it is always the Bible which he employs as the standard of truth. He goes back to the teaching of the Redeemer; he points to the apostles and their deeds; the authority of the Primitive Church is everywhere appealed to. To bring out the doctrine of the Scriptures (*fides Scripturæ*) as of supreme authority, is his highest aim. His sermons are saturated with Bible thoughts and interwoven with Bible reminiscences. With reference to his advice mentioned above, that the Gospel history especially should be preached to the people, we must not omit to mention that he very frequently narrates, in a clear and simple style, the history contained in the Gospel for the day, interweaving explanatory remarks with the story. After doing so, it is true, he not unfrequently passes on to set forth the 'mystical sense' of the passage. On one occasion he justifies this with the words, 'To get at a meaning of this history, which will be good for the edification of the people, its mystical sense has to be considered.'[2] I find, however, that 'Wycliffe's mystical interpretation,' as he makes use of it in the Latin sermons, sometimes consists in nothing more than a simple bringing out of religious truths, and a moral application to his hearers, and to the present time, of the features of the history which he takes for his text.

His standard of appeal.

There are many things, indeed, freely handled in these sermons, which are far from being Biblical subjects, such as the Standing and the Rights of the Papacy, the Landed Endowments of the Church, Monachism, and particularly the Mendicant Orders, etc. In this way much matter is brought into discussion, which is ecclesiastical and even ecclesiastico-political; and this seems at first sight to be out of keeping with his own principle, that the preaching should have to do with God's Word alone. But when I look into the scope and object of these discussions, I come to the conclusion, that it is always the Bible which the preacher applies to these questions as his rule of judgment, and that he has never any other aim in view than to establish Apostolic doctrines, and to realise

Ecclesiastical topics.

---

[1] *XL. Sermons*, No. 11, fol. 213, col. 1.   [2] Comp. *XL. Miscell. Sermons*, No. 5, fol. 201, col. 1.

again, in the present, the conditions of the primitive Church. It would be an injustice, therefore, to look upon all these parts of his sermons as digressions, by which Wycliffe became untrue to his own principle. There is only one thing about his sermons which must at once be conceded, namely, that the innermost kernel of the gospel, according to the conviction of Evangelical Christendom in our own time, *i.e.*, the doctrine of reconciliation through Jesus Christ, and the way of salvation, especially of the justification of the sinner through faith, is not to be met with in them. This is, however, not the proper place to go into this fact; we shall hereafter return to it in our analysis of Wycliffe's doctrine.

When we examine the sermons of Wycliffe in reference to their form, their manner of presentation, style, and tone, we meet also here with appearances which cannot but seem strange to us, when we think of the principles which he laid down respecting the form of preaching. For we find scholastic formulæ, abstract ideas, formal definitions, learned investigations, syllogistic and dialectical argumentation, all in a measure which we should not have expected from him, in view of the homiletic maxims which he himself expressed. There are, however, two points here which we must not leave out of sight: first, the fact that the Latin sermons, as remarked above, were probably preached in Oxford before the University, or, at all events, before audiences composed of men of learning. In such circumstances the preacher had no need to descend to so plain a style as would have been necessary in addressing a rural congregation. On the contrary, Wycliffe did right to keep in view the requirements of a University church, and the style of preaching to which such hearers were accustomed. No wonder, then, that we find so much in the form of these sermons which, to ourselves, appears more suitable to the lecture-room than the church—to the chair of the professor than to the pulpit. And, secondly, in order to form a just judgment, we ought not to under-estimate the influence which custom and prevalent forms of thought and style exercise, sometimes unconsciously, even upon the most distinguished and independent genius.

On the other hand, however, we remark that even in these sermons there is no lack of that *plana locutio* which Wycliffe recommended to preachers. The style is very often simple and clear, the mode of expression not without vividness, sometimes picturesque and suited to popular taste, and here and there too, especially in controversial passages, not without a touch even of banter and raillery. The tone is by no means uniformly didactic; on the contrary, it rises every now and then into considerable animation—into moral pathos, as in a passage where he speaks of prayer, and commends general prayer in comparison with special petitions. After referring to an argument which was used on the other side, he exclaims, 'Oh! if the Apostle had heard this piece of subtle hair-splitting, how much would he have despised it.'[1]

In the English sermons, we find still more frequently a plain and popular, even a drastic style of speaking, and a moving, heart-felt tone, especially when the preacher anticipates the judgment-seat and the last account. In the sermon on the Second Sunday of Advent we meet with this passage: 'Sad belief (earnest faith) of this third Advent should stir men from sin and draw them to virtue. For if they should to-morrow answer to a judge, and win great rents or else lose them, they would full busily shape for their answer, and much more if they should win or lose their life. Lord! since we be certain of the day of doom that it shall come to us, and we wit not how soon, and there we shall have judgment of heavenly life, or else of deep of hell that evermore shall last, how busy should we be to make us ready for this! Certes, default of belief is cause of our sloth, and thus should we fasten in us articles of the truth, for they will be loose in us as nails in a tree, and therefore it is needful to knock and make them fast.'[2] *His English sermons.*

Lastly, as concerns the tone of these sermons, and the moral spirit which dictates their whole contents, it will not be easy for any one who allows them to work upon him without prejudice, not to receive the impression that there is here a veritable zeal for the glory of God—a pure love to the Redeemer, and a sincere concern for the salvation of souls. There reigns throughout them an earnest striving after the life that is in Christ Jesus, a truly godly mind, whose habit is to view all that is earthly in its relations to a higher world, and to deal with all in the light of eternity. It is impossible not to think that such a preacher, so full of earnest godliness and Christian conscientiousness, must have made a deep impression upon all men who did not deliberately stand aloof from the sphere of his influence. *His earnestness.*

If Wycliffe's work as a preacher in the University was important, it may be supposed that he also did a true and blessed work among his flock at Lutterworth, as a parish priest. In the last years of his life, as we shall see below, he was shut out from the University of

---

[1] *XXIV. Miscell. Sermons*, No. 10, fol. 153, col. 3.

[2] *Sermons on the Gospels*, ed. Arnold, vol. I., Sermon XXVII., p. 70.

Oxford, and was thus able to devote to the pastoral office the whole time and strength which yet remained to him.

First, let us be allowed to introduce here a picture whose original has been conjectured, not without good grounds, to have been none other than Wycliffe himself. Geoffrey Chaucer, the father of English poetry, as he is commonly called, was a younger contemporary of Wycliffe; but, though he satirises the sins and infirmities of his time without sparing even those of the clergy, his spirit was certainly not congenial with Wycliffe's; Chaucer was entirely a man of the world, of æsthetic culture, enlightened, and an enemy to all superstition, but also a stranger to all religious earnestness. He knows, however, how to value what is good and worthy of honour, wherever he finds it. And so, in the prologue to his *Canterbury Tales*, which are an imitation of Boccaccio's *Decameron*, he has interwoven the following beautiful description of a country priest, which includes, at all events, some lineaments of Wycliffe:—

Chaucer's 'Good Priest.'

> 'But rich he was of holy thought and work,
> He was also a learnèd man—a clerk,
> That Christ's Gospel truely would preach,
> His parishens devoutly would he teach.
> Benign he was, and wondrous diligent,
> And in adversity full patient;
> And such he was yprovèd often sithes (times),
> Full loth were him to answer for his tithes,
> But rather would he given, out of doubt,
> Unto his poor parishioners about
> Of his offering, and eke of his substance.
> He could in little thing have suffisance.
> Wide was his parish, and houses far asunder,
> But he ne left nought for ne rain nor thunder.
> In sickness and in mischief, to visit
> The farthest in his parish, much and lit (great and small),
> Upon his feet, and in his hand a staff.
> This noble example to his sheep he yaf (gave),
> That first he wrought and afterward he taught.'

There are several features of this portrait which agree with the character of Wycliffe, and not a single trait can be detected in it which does not suit him. The humility, the contentment, and the unselfishness; the moral spotlessness, the compassionate love, the conscientious and diligent faithfulness in his office, and the Biblical character of his preaching—these lineaments were all his. The learning of the man is also made prominent. Pre-eminently like him also is the oneness of teaching and conduct exhibited in the picture; the doing ever went before the teaching.

Application to Wycliffe.

The remark of Vaughan has, indeed, some force, that in these characteristics of a country priest, the grand features of Wycliffe as a Reformer are entirely wanting.[1] But this circumstance by no means tells against the conjecture that the poet intended to paint Wycliffe simply as a pastor. It is not merely doubtful, but in the highest degree improbable, that Chaucer had any appreciation of the great Reformation-thoughts and strivings of Wycliffe, or ever gave them any recognition in a practical form. Chaucer took up a position in reference to ecclesiastical matters which may most readily be compared with the mode of thought of many of the Humanists at the beginning of the sixteenth century—an open eye and a mocking laugh for all clerical failings and weaknesses, but no heart for the earnestness and the sanctity of the subject. But undoubtedly he had an appreciation of sterling moral excellence in humble life.

2.—Wycliffe's Itinerant Preachers.

If Wycliffe, by his conscientious faithfulness in the pastoral cure, stood forth as a model preacher and pastor, he worked in this way effectually for the elevation of his office, even had he done nothing more. But he did not confine himself to this. Both by word and deed he laboured to promote everywhere the right preaching of the gospel; and the most effective instrumentality which he used for that end was the institution of a *Preaching Itinerancy*.

It has long been known that Wycliffe sent out itinerant preachers of the gospel. Lewis, it is true, only touches upon the subject incidentally, in so far as he mentions one or another English tract in which Wycliffe speaks of 'poor priests,' and in their defence. Vaughan, on the other hand, has gone fully into the subject, and has given a clear and distinct picture of those diligent and devoted men.[2] Shirley also has brought out several interesting details with regard to the whole institution;[3] and the subject is now to a certain extent well understood. There are still, however, certain questions of importance relating to it which have never yet received an answer; indeed, it has hardly yet occurred to any one to propose them. The questions are these:—At what date did Wycliffe begin to send out itinerant preachers? How was he led to entertain the idea of such a step at all? It happens in this case, as

---

[1] *Life and Opinions*, vol. II., p. 139.
[2] *Ib.*, II., 163. *John de Wycliffe—a Monograph.* 1853, p. 275.
[3] In the preface to his edition of the *Fasc. Zizaniorum*, p. xl. He justly remarks there that this feature of Wycliffe's practical Church reform has engaged the attention of his biographers much less than it ought to have done.

so often in history, that an important fact comes suddenly to light. While it was preparing itself in silence, no one thought of it; all at once it stands revealed before the world.

At the end of May, 1382, the Archbishop of Canterbury, William Courtenay, in a mandate addressed to the Bishop of London, speaks of 'certain unauthorised itinerant preachers who, as he had unhappily been compelled to learn, set forth erroneous, yea, heretical assertions in public sermons, not only in churches, but also in public squares and other profane places,' and 'they do this,' as he adds with special emphasis, 'under the guise of great holiness, but without having obtained any episcopal or papal authorisation.'[1] That the Primate means by these men real Wycliffite itinerant preachers, appears with certainty from the twenty-four articles of doctrine annexed to the mandate, all of which, with hardly an exception, belong to Wycliffe. To this same date also belong several English tracts, in which Wycliffe undertakes the defence of the proceedings of the itinerants.

It is clear that in May, 1382, the preaching itinerancy was already in full swing; but we should like to know its first beginnings, and thus get an insight into the motives and causes from which it arose. On that subject Wycliffe himself could best have given us information; but he was not the man to talk about a matter before he took action in it. He contented himself with afterwards justifying and defending what had been done.

It might be supposed that it was first at Lutterworth, in his quiet rural charge, that Wycliffe began to send forth itinerant preachers. In this case the presumption would have readily offered itself that he had sought and found in this new institute a compensation for the wider and more stirring sphere of work from which he had been cut off. To me, however, it appears, on more than one ground, that Oxford was the cradle of the new institution. First of all, it lies in the nature of the case that the sending forth of itinerants could only have developed itself gradually, and in the course of several years. Now, as in May, 1382, public attention was already drawn to it, and the itinerant system had manifestly been already for some time in full operation,[2] this takes us several years farther back, to a date when Wycliffe resided in the University for a good part, at least, of every year. Besides, the work did not consist merely in the sending out of the preachers; they must be prepared

Oxford the headquarters.

---

[1] The document is printed in Wilkins' *Concilia Magnae Britanniae*, III., fol. 158, Comp. the missive of the same prelate, dated two days earlier, and couched in about the same terms, to the Carmelite, Peter Stokes, in Oxford. *Fasc. Ziz.*, p. 275.

[2] *Sane frequenti clamore et divulgata fama ad nostrum pervenit auditum*, etc. *Fasc. Zizan.*, p. 275.

beforehand for their calling. This was the most important point, and the preparation could not be effected in a hurry. In thinking of the necessary course of study, we naturally turn to the University; for in the small town of Lutterworth we can hardly imagine a circle of educated theologians being collected round the parish priest, even though that priest was Wycliffe. It is far easier to suppose that Wycliffe, while still in Oxford, entered into close relations with a number of young men, some of them graduates in Arts, and some youths who were still in their undergraduate course. It is independently probable that a personality of such high distinction, as well in the field of learning as in practical Church work, should have drawn around him not a few susceptible young men who desired to carry on their culture under his guidance.

What we could not fail to conjecture beforehand is found to be confirmed by positive proof. An enthusiastic follower of Wycliffe, William Thorpe, in his examination before the Archbishop of Canterbury, Thomas Arundel, gave the following information concerning the course of his own studies and his relation to Wycliffe:—'I prayed my parents that they would give me licence for to go to them that were named wise priests, and of virtuous conversation, to have their counsel, and to know of them the office and the charge of priesthood. And hereto my father and my mother consented full gladly, and gave me their blessing and good leave to go. And so that I went to those priests whom I heard to be of best name, and of most holy living, and best learned, and most wise of heavenly wisdom, and so I communed with them unto the time that I perceived, by their virtuous and continual occupations, that their honest and charitable works passed their fame which I had heard before of them. Wherefore by the example of the doctrine of them, and specially for the godly and innocent works which I perceived then of them and in them, after my cunning and power I have exercised me then and in this time, to know perfectly God's law, having a will and desire to live thereafter.' To the Archbishop's further inquiry, 'Which are these men holy and wise? Thorpe replied, 'Maister John Wycliffe was holden of full many men the greatest clerk that they knew then living; and therewith he was named a passing ruly [1] man, and innocent in his living.' Besides Wycliffe himself, Thorpe names several of his admirers, such as John Aston, Nicholas Hereford, John Purvey, and others, and then continues thus:—'With all these men I was right homely, and communed with them long time and oft; and so, before all other

---

[1] *I.e.*, of strict principle; the opposite of *unruly*.

men, I chose wilfully to be informed of them and by them; and specially of Wycliffe himself, as the most virtuous and godly wise man that I heard of, or knew.'[1]

The whole account sounds as though Thorpe had enjoyed the instruction of all these men at the same time. If this was so, we can only suppose that Oxford, not Lutterworth, was the place where Thorpe had cultivated his intercourse with those worthy men, and especially with Wycliffe himself; and we are hereby led to the assumption that Wycliffe had already begun in Oxford to train younger men to the priestly office, and in particular to the office of preaching. We shall scarcely err if we assume that Wycliffe, as long as he worked in Oxford as a Doctor of Theology, and was in the habit of preaching frequently, if not regularly, before the University, formed there a training-school of preachers, a sort of priest seminary, which, however, was of an entirely private and voluntary character. I have not a moment's doubt that while he was still in Oxford Wycliffe sent out as voluntary itinerant preachers young men belonging to this circle, who had attached themselves so closely to his person, and had embraced his theological views and convictions as well as his practical Church principles. Perhaps the entrance which the first preachers of his school found among the people, and the warm acceptance which their sermons obtained in the country districts, gave fresh courage to himself and his scholars, so that the first itinerants were followed by ever increasing numbers, and the whole undertaking gradually took root and extended itself. When Wycliffe at a later period withdrew entirely to Lutterworth, he of course did not give up this agency, but carried it on with all the more zeal the more painfully he felt that, by his dismissal from the University, a field of richly blessed work had been closed to his ministry.

Training of itinerants.

But what was this agency meant to do? and what were its practical results? Was it intended that a systematic rivalry and opposition should be made by the itinerants against the parochial clergy? The opponents of the movement naturally viewed it in this light; and even at the present day there are Roman Catholic historians who have admitted this idea to their minds.[2] But how can this view of the subject be even thinkable, seeing that the itinerants, on this supposition, would have pronounced sentence of condemnation upon the venerated master himself, who was never

Itinerants and parish priests.

---

[1] *Acts and Monuments of John Foxe*, ed. Pratt and Stoughton, v. III., 256–258.

[2] *E.g.*, Lingard, *History of England*, v. IV., maintains that the Wycliffe preachers thought very meanly of the whole body of the parish priests.

himself one of the itinerant preachers, but preferred to work precisely in the character of a parish priest among his own flock? Moreover, the hierarchy would certainly not have omitted to accuse the itinerants of hostility to the parochial clergy and the calumniation of their characters; but of this I find not a single trace. All they are accused of is that they promulgate erroneous doctrine, and that they preach of their own will without episcopal sanction. This, indeed, is only an *argumentum ex silentio*. But I am able to appeal, in support of the opposite view, to express testimonies as well, and these from Wycliffe's own mouth. In his little book, *Of the Pastoral Office*, although he accuses the parochial clergy of much degeneracy, of worldliness, of neglect in preaching the gospel, and of the evil custom of non-residence in their parishes,[1] appearing also as the advocate of 'the simple priests,' *i.e.*, the evangelical itinerants, he at the same time stands up for the parish priests, if they only do their duty in some sort. He defends their rights against the encroachments of the mendicant monks; and also, in the face of the incorporation of parish tithes with foundations and monasteries, he roundly and clearly lays down the principle that all parishes should be able to pay for the ministrations which their pastors in humility render to them.[2] In his Latin sermons, again, Wycliffe blames, it is true, those parish priests who are 'dumb dogs, and cannot bark' (Isa. lvi. 10), or who preach only for selfish and ambitious ends;[3] but he expects, nevertheless, great things from true and prudent pastors,[4] and lays upon the heart of the parochial clergy the Redeemer's admonition, 'Watch.' It is their duty to keep watch over their flocks.[5] At the end of the tract, to be mentioned again below, *Why Poor Priests have no Benefices*, Wycliffe expressly assures his readers that these priests pronounce no condemnation upon those pastors who do their duty and teach truly and steadfastly the law of God in opposition to false prophets and the devices of the wicked fiend.[6] According to all this, there is certainly no ground for assuming that the Wycliffite itinerants allowed themselves to run down the parochial clergy as a body; although it cannot, of course, admit of a doubt that with regard to unconscientious and worldly-minded pastors and preachers they were in the habit of expressing themselves in no very measured language.

---

[1] In one place—*De Officio Pastorali*, I., c. 17—he refers to them as *pseudo-pastores*.

[2] In the same treatise, II., 5, he says: *Appropriationes ecclesiarum cathedralium defraudant parochias a praedicatoribus legitimis verbi Dei. Deberet parochiis cunctis sufficere servitium, quod sacerdotes proprii humiliter subministrant.*

[3] *XL. Miscell. Serm.* No. 29, fol. 283, col. 3.

[4] *Sermons for Saints' Days*, No. 56 as above, fol. 117, col. 1.

[5] *XL. Miscell. Serm.* as above, fol. 194, col. 2.

[6] Comp. Vaughan, *Life and Opinions*, II., 169.

The sending forth of these itinerant preachers was a measure which, so far as I can see, passed through several stages of development. In its first stage, the preachers were exclusively men who had already taken orders. This appears from the title which Wycliffe is wont to apply to them. In his work on *The Pastoral Office*, he calls them sometimes 'presbyters,' sometimes 'priests,' and yet in such a way as to indicate clearly by the connection, or by the use of epithets like *faithful* or *simple* priests or presbyters, what description of clergy he means. However much his opponents may have looked down upon such men as 'uneducated' and 'stupid'—a reproach which Wycliffe bravely takes as levelled against himself as well as others [1]—they must yet have been men who had received ordination, otherwise Wycliffe would certainly never have applied to them the name of 'priests.' Yet this designation occurs both in his Latin writings and in his English sermons and tracts.[2] With this also agrees the justification of the free preaching of every priest, which William Thorpe put forth in his examination before Archbishop Arundel, a quarter of a century later, and which, without doubt, may be traced back to the teaching of Wycliffe himself. Thorpe expresses himself in the following terms:—'By the authority of the Word of God, and also of many saints and doctors, I have been brought to the conviction that it is the office and duty of every priest, faithfully, freely, and truly to preach God's Word.[3] Without doubt it behoves every priest, in determining to take orders, to do so chiefly with the object of preaching the Word of God to the people to the best of his ability. We are accordingly bound by Christ's command and holy example, and also by the testimony of His holy apostles and prophets, under heavy penalties, to exercise ourselves in such wise as to fulfil this duty of the priesthood to the best of our knowledge and powers. We believe that every priest is commanded by the Word of God to make God's will known to the people by faithful labour, and to publish it to them in the spirit of love, to the best of our ability, where, when, and to whomsoever we may.'

Thorpe, who was an itinerant of Wycliffe's school, speaks in this

---

[1] *De Officio Pastorali*, II., c. 10, p. 45. *Nobis rudibus*, comp. II., c. 4, p. 36; *dicunt de talibus presbyteris, quod sunt stolidi ac rudes*.

[2] *Trewe Preestis* (True Priests). Sermons published by Arnold, v. I., p. 176; II., pp. 173, 182; *pore prestis* (poor priests), tract *Lincolniensis* in *Miscellaneous Works*, p. 231. *Fifty Heresies and Errors of Friars*, c. 36, p. 393. *Greet sentence of curs expounded*, c. 9, p. 293; comp. *De Ecclesia et membris ejus*, c. 2, in *Three Treatises by John Wycliffe*; ed. Todd, p. xi. "This moveth por prestis (poor priests) to speke now hertily in this mater."

[3] 'That it is euerie priests office and duty for to preach busilie, freely, and truelie the worde of God.' Foxe, *Acts and Monuments*, v. III., p. 260.

passage as a priest himself, and in the name of others like-minded with himself, who were also in priests' orders.

But even in this first stage, when only priests went out as itinerants—two sub-stages must, I think, be distinguished. At the beginning of the movement it was scarcely laid down as a principle, that no one should accept a pastoral charge. *Benefices declined.* Later, men made a virtue of necessity, and the principle was adopted that even if such a charge could be obtained, it was advisable not to accept it. This is the position taken in the tract, *Why Poor Priests have no Benefices*,[1] in which the principle just named is justified on three grounds: 1. Generally speaking, no benefice is to be obtained without simony, whether the right of collation be in the hands of a prelate or a temporal lord. 2. That the beneficed priest, by reason of his dependence upon his ecclesiastical superiors, may be compelled to give up to them, contrary to right, all that portion of his revenues which exceeds his own necessities, and which by God's law and public right ought to be expended upon the poor. 3. A priest without benefice, not being bound to a particular parish, and being free from the jurisdiction of sinful men, is at liberty to preach the gospel wherever he can be of use, and can also without hindrance flee from one city to another, according to Christ's instruction, in case he should be persecuted by the 'clergy of Antichrist.'

In the second stage, an important step in advance was taken. The adoption of lay preaching was resolved upon, as it had been practised before among the Waldenses, with whom lay preaching had been a powerful factor in their whole movement; and yet, so far at least as I know the writings of Wycliffe, he was not at all aware of this precedent, and acted quite independently of it.

That lay preachers appeared among the Lollards after Wycliffe's death does not admit of a doubt; but that even in his lifetime, and with his knowledge and approval, laymen were employed as itinerant preachers, I believe I am able to prove. *Lay preaching.* It is certainly no accidental circumstance that Wycliffe, in sermons of his latest years, in referring to his beloved itinerants, no longer speaks of them as 'poor priests,' or 'simple,' or 'faithful' priests, but on all occasions applies to them the names of 'evangelical men,' or 'apostolic men.'[2] It looks as if, in such places, he intentionally avoided the name of priests, because this was now no

---

[1] Vaughan, in *Life and Opinions*, etc., v. II., p. 164 f., has given large extracts from this tract, which he regards as an indubitable work of Wycliffe; but Arnold, in his *Select Works*, vol. III., p. xx., places the tract— *Whi pore Prestis han nen Benefice*, at least among the works of doubtful authenticity.

[2] *Sermons for Saints' Days*, Nos. 31, 37, 53, fol. 61, cols. 2 and 3; fol. 76, col. 4; fol. 109, col. 1.

longer applicable to all the itinerants; but still more clearly does this appear from a passage in the *Dialogus* or *Speculum Ecclesiae Militantis*. In this tractate, which was written certainly not earlier than 1381, and probably not before 1383, when comparing the beneficed clergy with the itinerants, he makes use of these words: 'And as respects the fruits of preaching, it appears certain that a single unlearned preacher effects more, by the grace of God, for the edification of the Church of Christ, than many who have graduated in schools or colleges, because the former scatters the seed of the law of Christ more humbly and more abundantly both in deed and in word.'[1] But the most convincing passage of all, to my mind, is that which occurs in one of his later sermons, where Wycliffe asserts with great emphasis that for a ministry in the Church the Divine call and commission are perfectly sufficient; there is an installation by God Himself, although the bishop has given in such a case no imposition of hands, in accordance with his traditions.[2]

If the fact was, as we have now, we believe, shown to be probable, that the itinerant preaching began at a time when Wycliffe still belonged to the University, we are justified in further assuming that Oxford was the starting-point, and that the country immediately surrounding this city was the first scene of the new movement. It then spread from thence more widely over the land. From several facts, attested by written documents, it appears that the town of Leicester soon became a second centre of the Wycliffite itinerancy—a fact which was, no doubt, connected with the circumstance that in the last years of his life Wycliffe had his settled residence at Lutterworth, in the county of Leicester. One of the first who appeared as an itinerant preacher was John of Aston. He was followed, also in Wycliffe's life-time, by William Thorpe, already mentioned, and others. These men went forth in long garments of coarse red woollen cloth, barefooted, with staff in hand, in order to represent themselves as pilgrims, and their wayfaring as a kind of pilgrimage, their coarse woollen dress being a symbol of

Spread of itinerancy.

The preachers.

---

[1] *Dialogus*, or *Speculum Ecclesiæ militantis*, c. 27, Vienna MS. 1387 (Dénis CCCLXXXIV.), fol. 157, col. 1; and the like words again occur in full in the short piece, *De Graduationibus scholasticis*, c. 3, MS. 3929 (Dénis CCCLXXXV.), fol. 249, col. 2. The words run thus—*Quantum ad fructum, certum videtur quod unus ydiota, mediante Dei gratia, plus proficit ad aedificandam Christi ecclesiam, quam multi graduati in scolis sive collegiis, quia seminat humilius et copiosius legem Christi, tam opere quam sermone.*

[2] *Sermons for Saints' Days*, No. 8, fol. 17, col. 1. *Videtur ergo, quod ad esse talis ministerii ecclesiae requiritur auctoritas acceptationis divinae, et per consequens potestas ac notitia data a Deo ad tale ministerium peragendum, quibus habitis, licet episcopus secundum traditiones suas non imposuit illi manus, Deus per se instituit.*

their poverty and toil ('poor priests'). Thus they wandered from village to village, from town to town, and from county to county, without halt or rest, preaching, teaching, warning, wherever they could find willing hearers, sometimes in church or chapel, wherever any such stood open for prayer and quiet devotion; sometimes in the churchyard, when they found the church itself closed; and sometimes in the public street or market-place.[1]

Their sermons were, before everything else, full of Bible truth. This was to be expected from them, for these men had all gone forth from Wycliffe's school, had imbibed his principles, and had all formed themselves as preachers upon his model. They had learned to regard as their chief duty 'the faithful scattering of the seed of God's Word;' and their sole aim was to minister sound nourishment to the people.[2] 'God's Word,' 'God's Law,' therefore, was not only their text, but their sole theme; and it agrees perfectly with the picture which we could not fail beforehand to draw for ourselves, when the Leicester chronicler, who tells us that he had more than once been a hearer of their preaching, testifies that the preachers were continually enforcing that 'no man could become righteous and well-pleasing to God who did not hold to "Goddis lawe,"[3] for that,' says he, 'was their favourite expression, to which they were ever appealing in all their addresses.' Wycliffe himself, in his English tract, *Of Good Prechyng Prestis*, declares that

Their sermons Biblical.

---

[1] This description rests upon several attestations of friends and foes—the latter of an official as well as private character. A document both official and of certain date is the missive given above of William Courtenay, Archbishop of Canterbury, of 30th of May, 1382, directed against certain itinerant preachers, alleged to be both unauthorised and heretical, published in Wilkins' *Concilia*, and in Shirley's *Fasc. Zizan.*, p. 275. Among other things it is said—*Quidam, aeternae damnationis filii, sub magnae sanctitatis velamine, auctoritatem sibi vindicant praedicandi—tam in ecclesiis quam in plateis et aliis locis profanis dictae nostrae provinciae, non verentur asserere, dogmatizare et publice praedicare.* Wycliffe himself defends the practice of his friends in preaching everywhere without distinction of place, in the 37th of his *Saints' Day Sermons. Videtur mihi quod sacerdos zelans pro lege Domini, cui negatur pro loco et tempore praedicatio verbi Dei, debet usque ad passionem martyrii, in casu quo non debet esse sibi conscius, praedicationem vel hortationem, in quocunque loco auditorium habere potest,* asserere verbum Dei. *Sic enim Christus non solum in sinagogis sed in castelli* (Matt. IX. 35) *constantius praedicabat. Locus enim non facit sanctum populum, sed e contra* (fol. 75, col. 3).

The Chronicler of St. Albans, Thomas Walsingham, narrates under the year 1377, that Wycliffe, partly to disguise his heresy, and partly to spread it more widely, entered into alliance with other men as associates, living partly in Oxford, and partly in other parts of the kingdom, and he describes them *talaribus indutos vestibus de russeto, in signum perfectionis amplioris, incedentes nudis pedibus, qui suos errores in populo ventilarent,* etc. *Hist. Angl.* ed. Riley, 1863. I. 324. The chronicler Knighton, of Leicester (or his continuator), remarks, col. 2657, that he had himself heard several of these men preach.

[2] *De Officio Pastorali*, II., c. 3, p. 34. *Salubriter populo praedicantes.*

[3] Knighton, *De Eventibus Angliae*, col. 2664. *Talem enim habebant terminum in omnibus suis dictis semper praetendendi legem Dei, 'Goddis lawe.'*

their first aim was directed to this, that God's law should at all times be recognised, taught, practised, and highly regarded.[1]

That these sermons or exhortations [2] were less of a dogmatic than an ethical character, we may gather not only from the name which, after Wycliffe's example, the preachers were in the habit of applying to the Word of God—viz., God's law—but also from the confirmatory statements of Wycliffe and their opponents. In the tract just mentioned, Wycliffe states that the second aim of the 'good preaching priests' was that all gross open sins prevailing among different ranks, and also the hypocrisy and erroneous teaching of Antichrist and his followers, *i.e.*, the Pope and the Popish clergy, should be done away; while, in the third place, they strove to promote true love in all Christendom, and especially in England, and so to help men to reach in safety the blessedness of heaven.[3]

And ethical.

The form and language of these addresses behoved, according to Wycliffe's principles, to be plain and simple.[4] But these men, according to all the notices which we possess of them, must have been in the habit of using language of a very emphatic and trenchant description: and this, as well when they laboured directly for the awakening and moral regeneration of the people, setting eternity before their eyes, and exhorting them to live in Christian brotherhood and peace and beneficence, as when they depicted the prevailing sins of the time, holding up before all ranks their vices and lusts, and especially exposing to reprobation the vices of the clergy—their hypocrisy, sensuality, avarice, and ambition. From the description given of these popular discourses by the ear-witness of Leicester, entirely adverse as he was to the movement, one receives a vivid impression both of the winning attractiveness and unction, and of the arresting and subduing power by which they must have been characterised.[5] When we remember the moral earnestness and the crushing power which we have felt in Wycliffe himself as a preacher, we cannot wonder that his scholars also, men in earnest about 'God's Law,' should have rebuked the prevailing sins

Force of their language.

---

[1] *Of good Prechyng Prestis.* Comp. Shirley, *Original Works of Wycliffe*, p. 45. Lewis—*History*, p. 200—gives the commencement of the piece, which indicates, at the same time, its chief substance. Arnold, in *Select English Works*, III., p. xix., places this piece among the works of doubtful authenticity.

[2] In more than one passage which treats of the Itinerants, Wycliffe puts together *praedicationes* and *exhortationes*.

[3] *Of good Prechyng Prestis.* Comp. Vaughan, *Life and Opinions*, etc., II., p. 187.

[4] *De Officio Pastorali*, II., c. 3, p. 34. *Debet evangelisator praedicare plane evangelicam veritatem.*

[5] Knighton, col. 2664. *Doctrina eorum in quibuscumque loquelis in principio dulcedine plena apparuit et devota, in fine quoque invidia subtili et detractione plena defloruit.* Comp. col. 2660. *Frequenter in suis sermonibus—clamitaverunt, Trewe Prechoures! False Prechoures!*

of the time without reserve and with all sharpness. Of course this severity of speech, especially when it was directed against the hierarchy, offended the latter in the highest degree, and slanders were spread about the preachers to the effect that the only thing they were able to do was to abuse the prelates behind their backs; that they were undermining the whole frame of the Church, and were serpents casting forth deadly poison.[1]

Against these calumnies Wycliffe defended his followers in a tract entitled, *The Deceits of Satan and his Priests*. Almighty God, who is full of love, gave commandment to His prophets to cry aloud, to spare not, and to show to the people their transgressions (Isaiah lviii. 1). The sin of the common people is great, the sin of the lords, the mighty and the wise, is greater, but greatest of all is the sin of the prelates, and most blinding to the people. Therefore are true men by God's commandment bound to cry out the loudest against the sin of the prelates, because it is in itself the greatest, and of greatest mischief to the people.[2] *Defence against calumnies.*

Wycliffe, as we before had occasion to see, published a considerable number of tracts which related exclusively, or at least chiefly, to the itinerant preachers of his school. There are still extant both English and Latin writings of this kind. Those in English are all defences of the preachers, some of them taking the form of controversy with their opponents. To this class belong the following:—*Of Good Preaching Priests*,[3] *Why Poor Priests have no Benefices*, *Of Feigned Contemplative Life*,[4] *Of Obedience to Prelates*,[5] *Mirror of Antichrist*.[6] These writings, it is true, are all placed by Arnold among the works of doubtful authenticity. Among the Latin writings is, *e.g.*, the small tract, *Of Academic Degrees*, including a defence of the itinerant preachers; the sole object of which is to prove that the preaching of the gospel by men who are not graduates is justified by the Scriptures, and allowed by the Church.[7] *Tracts on Itinerancy.*

While the tracts hitherto named treat chiefly of the itinerants, and are intended less for them than for the people, and some of them especially for the learned class (such as the tract last mentioned), there is also a small book which I find *The 'Six Yokes.'*

---

[1] The Archbishop of Canterbury in his Mandate of the year 1382, mentioned above.

[2] *On the deceits of Satan and his priests*, after Vaughan, *Life and Opinions*, etc., v. II., p. 184.

[3] Comp. Lewis, *History*, p. 200; Shirley, *Catalogue*, p. 45, No. 32.

[4] *Of feyned contemplatif Lif*, Shirley. Comp. Lewis, p. 198. No. 107, 42, No. 26.

[5] Shirley, 40, No. 12.

[6] Shirley, 41, No. 17. Vaughan, *Life and Opinions*, II., p. 188 f, under the title, *On the Four Deceits of Antichrist*.

[7] *De Graduationibus scholasticis*, in three chapters, in Vienna MS. 3929 (Dénis CCCLXXXV., fol. 247, col. 2, 250, and in other MSS.).

among Wycliffe's writings, which was composed primarily and directly for those simple preachers themselves. I refer to the tract of *The Six Yokes.* For as to the so-called *Letter to the Simple Priests,* it is neither, as I have been convinced for some years, a real letter in form (although it occurs under this title in two catalogues of Wycliffe's writings made at the beginning of the fifteenth century), nor does it relate to the itinerants, but obviously treats of ordinary parish priests. The whole appears to me to be a fragment taken either from some tractate, or (which I think quite possible) from a Latin sermon.[1]

The tract of *The Six Yokes,* on the other hand, appears to me to have been designed by Wycliffe for those of his friends who devoted themselves to the itinerancy. Its very commencement indicates this: 'In order that unlearned and simple preachers, who are burning with zeal for souls, may have materials for preaching,' etc. I must here remark, however, that the materials of this tract were originally interwoven with several of his Latin sermons, and were only subsequently formed into an independent whole. For I find in the *Saints' Day Sermons* some of the same portions which now form several chapters of the tract.[2] The English sermons, too, lately issued by the Clarendon Press, leave the impression, at least in several places, of being sketches intended by the author for the use of others rather than himself. At the end of the very first of them, for example, occurs the remark, 'In this Gospel may priests tell of false pride of rich men, and of lustful life of mighty men of this world, and of long pains of hell, and joyful bliss in heaven, and thus lengthen their

---

[1] The *Epistola missa ad simplices Sacerdotes* is mentioned in both the Catalogues drawn up in Bohemia, which Shirley printed in his *Catalogue*—the first from the Vienna MS., 3933 (Dénis CCCXCI.), fol. 195; the second from Dénis CCCXCIII., fol. 102. Comp. especially pp. 62, 68, in *Catalogue*. Shirley placed too much confidence in these notices when he printed in his Introduction to the *Fasc. Zizan.* the supposed letter (to which he gave, at his own instance, the name of a circular), p. xli., note. The text which he gives requires, indeed, some not inconsiderable corrections, and yet it proves clearly enough that it has no reference to the Itinerants, and in no case was a letter addressed to that class.

[2] The first chapter of the treatise forms the close of the twenty-seventh sermon in the *Sermons for Saints' Days,* fol. 53, col. 4; fol. 54, col. 2. The second and third chapters make up the greatest part of the twenty-eighth sermon, from fol. 54, col. 4 onwards. The fourth chapter, again, forms the concluding part of one sermon, viz., the thirty-first, fol. 62, col. 3. The fifth chapter makes the second half of the thirty-second sermon, fol. 63, col. 3; fol. 64, col. 3; and even so does the last chapter form the second half of the thirty-third sermon, fol. 65, col. 3; fol. 66, col. 2. It is not, therefore, quite accurate when Shirley observes of the tractate, *De sex Jugis,* that it is an extract from the Sermon II., No 27; for in this sermon only the beginning of the tractate is to be found, at least in the MS. which I have made use of.

There is also observable a difference in the ways in which these several sermons are manipulated to make out the several chapters of the tractate; for while what is used of the first sermon is closely interwoven with the contents of the first chapter, the portions of the other sermons made use of are only mechanically attached to the following chapters—inserted into them, so to speak, like fragments of exploded stone.

sermon as the time asketh.' 'Here may man touch of all manner of sin, and specially of false priests, traitors to God, that should surely clepe (call) men to bliss and tell them the way of the law of Christ, and make known to the people the cantelis (devices) of Antichrist.' Still more characteristic is the concluding remark of the second sermon: 'Here the preacher may touch upon all manner of sins, especially those of false priests and traitors to God, whose duty it is to deal faithfully with the people for their salvation, and to show them the way of the law of Christ, and the deceitful wiles of Antichrist.'[1] These and other passages, of which we could mention several more, lead us to the conjecture that these sermons were composed by Wycliffe, in part, at least, for the benefit of the itinerants of his school, as helps and guides, and furnishing materials for preaching. At all events, the fact is certain that no inconsiderable part of the literary labours of Wycliffe centred in the Institute founded by him for this preaching itinerancy, and was designed to be serviceable to the preachers, either by defending them from attack, or assisting them in their work.[2]

---

[1] *Sermons on the Gospels*, v. 1., 3–6.
[2] [We are without exact information as to when the system of 'Poor Priests' was set on foot by Wycliffe. The prevalence of the Lollard doctrines in after years throughout the district lying immediately to the east of Oxfordshire seems to point to some original centre of activity in that neighbourhood; and as Wycliffe held the living of Ludgarshall from 1368 to 1374, the probability seems to be that the plan was initiated there. After his removal to Lutterworth, it continued in full activity, and is specially noticed by Archbishop Courtenay in a letter to the Bishop of London in 1382. 'Unauthorised preachers,' writes the archbishop, 'under the cloke of great holiness, are setting forth false and heretical doctrines, and perverting many from the Catholic faith,' *Fasc. Ziz.*, p. 275. We may therefore, with sufficient accuracy, assign the chief activity of the movement to the years between 1370 and 1382.]

CHAPTER VII.

WYCLIFFE AS BIBLE TRANSLATOR, AND HIS SERVICE DONE TO THE ENGLISH LANGUAGE.

1.—The Novelty of the Idea of an English Translation of the whole Bible.

IN the preceding chapter we have seen Wycliffe laying down the principle that, in preaching, God's Word must be taught before everything else, because it is the indispensable bread of life, the seed of regeneration and conversion. Nor was it only in theory that he laid down this principle. That he knew how to establish and elucidate it as a matter of doctrine we shall have opportunity to see by-and-by, when we come to represent his whole dogmatic system. He also carried out the principle in life and action: first, in his own person as a preacher; and next, by sending out itinerant preachers to proclaim the Divine Word. The same principle led him also to the work of Bible-translation. Wycliffe was not a man to do anything by halves. When once he recognised a principle to be right, he knew how to carry it out completely on all sides. So here in particular. The principle that God's Word should be preached to the people, he expanded into the principle that Scripture must become the common property of all. As a means to this end, he saw the necessity of the Bible being translated into the language of the country, with the view of giving it the widest possible diffusion among the population.

[margin: The Scriptures for all.]

This was a project so great, so new, and so bold for that age, that we become eager to learn what were the preparatory intermediate stages through which Wycliffe was led onward to the execution of his high purpose. In order to understand the undertaking in its peculiarity and greatness, we must first have before us a clear idea of the state of things before Wycliffe took the first step in the matter.

Sir Thomas More, the well-known statesman under Henry VIII., repelled the charge laid against the hierarchy at the time of the Reformation, that it had withheld the Holy Scriptures from the people during the Middle Ages, by the assertion that it was by no means true that Wycliffe was the first man who had undertaken a translation of the whole Bible into English for the use of the laity, for complete English translations of it had existed long before Wycliffe's time. He had himself seen beautiful old manuscripts of the English Bible, and these books had been provided with the knowledge of the bishops.[1] Nor was More the only one who claimed to have knowledge of English translations of the Bible before Wycliffe; several Protestant scholars of the seventeenth century were of the same opinion. Thomas James, the first librarian of the Bodleian, a very diligent and indefatigable polemic against the Papists, had held in his own hands an English manuscript Bible, which he judged to be much older than the days of Wycliffe.[2] Archbishop Usher followed in the same line, when he assigned this alleged pre-Wycliffite version to be about the year 1290.[3] Henry Wharton, also, the learned editor and completer of Usher's work, even believed himself able to show who the author of this supposed translation was, viz., John of Trevisa, a priest in Cornwall.[4]

Alleged previous versions.

All these suppositions, however, rest upon error, as was seen several years later by the last-named investigator himself, who corrected both his own text and that of Usher.[5] Those manuscripts of the English Bible seen by Sir Thomas More, and later by Thomas James, were, it is certain, nothing more than copies of the translation executed by Wycliffe and his followers. There is documentary evidence to show that at the time of the Reformation there were several manuscripts of this translation in the hands of Roman Catholic prelates. Bishop Bonner, for instance, was possessor of one, which is now preserved in the Archiepiscopal Library at Lambeth, and a second copy, which belonged in 1540 to a Knight of St. John, Sir William Weston, is now in Magdalen College, Cambridge.[6] Besides, if the fact were correct, that there ever existed any older English translation of the whole Bible, some sure traces of it, on the one hand, would not have been wanting, and, on the other, we may feel very certain that, in that case, the Wycliffites

These really Wycliffe's.

---

[1] Thom. More, *Dyalogues*, fol. cviii. cxi. cxiv.
[2] *Treatise of the Corruption of Scripture*, Lond., 1612, p. 74. *Vide* Forshall and Madden's *Wycliffite Versions of the Bible*, vol. I., p. xxi.
[3] *Historia Dogmatica Controversiae de Scripturis et Sacris Vernaculis.* Lond., 1690, 4to, p. 155.
[4] *Auctorium Historiae Dogmaticae* J. Usserii, p. 424.
[5] H. Wharton (under the pseudonym Ant. Harmer), *Specimens of Errors in the History of the Reformation.* Lond., 1693. *Vide* Vaughan, *John de Wycliffe*, p. 334, Note 1.
[6] *Wycliffite Versions of the Bible*, vol. I. Pref. xxi. lvii.

would not have omitted to appeal to that fact in justification of their own undertaking. It is quite clear from their writings, moreover, that they knew nothing of any older translation; but, on the contrary, regarded their own version as the first English version of the whole Bible.[1] Only in one solitary instance, in a tract of the years 1400–1411, is mention made, in defence of the right of possessing the Bible in the English tongue, of the fact that a citizen of London, of the name of Wering, was in possession of an English Bible, which many had seen, and which appeared to be two hundred years old.[2] Assuming that this statement of age was trustworthy, the translation in question could only have been one belonging to the Anglo-Saxon period. Let us now see how the case stands with regard to translations of that era.

All the attempts at Bible translation and commentary which are known to date from Anglo-Saxon times belong to that period which is called, by linguists and literary historians, the *old* Anglo-Saxon period, reaching down to A.D. 1100; while the *new* Anglo-Saxon or Half-Saxon period extends from 1100 to 1250.[3] Now, the old Anglo-Saxon literature is comparatively rich in productions which treat of Biblical subjects, both in verse and prose. The first of the Anglo-Saxons to adopt this line was the monk Caedmon of Whitby, who lived in the seventh century.[4] In his religious poem, called *The Paraphrase*, he sang of the Creation, the Fall, the Flood, the Exodus, and kindred topics. Bishop Aldhelm, of Sherborn, in the eighth century, according to the testimony of Bale, translated the Psalter; and an Anglo-Saxon paraphrase of the Latin Psalter, which was discovered in the Royal Library of Paris at the beginning of the present century, is considered to be in part the work of Aldhelm. The Venerable Bede, also, while producing works for the learned, comprising all the erudition of the age, was not forgetful of the wants of the common people. We know from himself that he made a translation of the Apostles' Creed and the Lord's Prayer into Anglo-Saxon, and presented copies of it to the less educated among the priests with whom he was acquainted;

The Anglo-Saxon.

---

[1] *Wycliffite Versions*, p. xxi., Note 9.
[2] Printed at the time of the Reformation as *A compendious olde treatyse shewynge how that we ought to have the Scripture in Englyshe.* Vide *Wycliffite Versions*, vol. I. xxxiii., Note, and xxi., Note 9.
[3] Max Müller, *Lectures on the Science of Language*, Lect. v. vi., Note. C. Friedrich Koch, *Historische Grammatik der Englischen Sprache*, I., p. 8.

[4] The only MS. of these Poems, dating from the tenth century, and belonging to the Bodleian Library, does not name the author. Francis Junius, who published the first edition of the *Paraphrase* in 1655, in Amsterdam, was the first to put forth the conjecture that Caedmon was the author. New editions have been brought out by Benjamin Thorpe, Lond., 1832, and by Bouterwek, Elberfeld, 1849.

indeed, his latest work was an Anglo-Saxon translation of the Gospel of John, which he had no sooner finished than he expired, in the year 735.[1]

The greatest of the Anglo-Saxon princes, King Alfred, is known to have entertained at least the design of making parts of Scripture accessible to his subjects in the mother tongue. Not long after his time there existed a Saxon translation of the Gospels, of which several MSS. have been preserved; and if the Psalter attributed to Bishop Aldhelm was not really his work, its date, at least, cannot be later than the tenth century. In addition, two Latin MSS. of the Gospels, with interlinear Saxon glosses, reach up to the days of Alfred, who died in 901.[2] Similar glosses upon the Psalter and the Proverbs are known to scholars, which are conjectured to belong to the same century.

King Alfred.

Towards the end of the tenth century, the monk and priest Aelfric had the extraordinary merit of executing a translation of selected parts of the Books of Moses, Joshua, Judges, Kings, and of Esther; and, in addition, of Job and the apocryphal books of Maccabees and Judith; while in his eighty Homilies he greatly promoted Bible knowledge by his renderings of the text, and by quotations from the Bible at large. The writings which have descended to the present time are sufficient to prove that the Anglo-Saxon Church was in possession of a considerable part of the Bible in the mother tongue. But when we reflect how much of this literature must have perished during the Danish incursions and conquests, and, at a later period, in consequence of the Norman invasion, we must form a conception of its extent very different from what is suggested by its existing remains. These Saxon glosses and translations, however, continued to be in use among the Saxon part of the population during the Norman Period—a fact which is established by the circumstance that several of the MSS. in question were not executed till the twelfth century.

Versions in the tenth century.

In little more than a century after the Norman invasion, the Norman population possessed a prose translation of the Psalms, as well as of the Latin Church hymns, in their own language, the Anglo-Norman. This was the case even before the year 1200; and towards the middle of the thirteenth century the Normans had not only a Bible history in verse reaching down to the Babylonish captivity, but also a prose translation of the whole Bible. It is, indeed, a remarkable fact, attested by men of

Norman Versions.

---

[1] Cuthberti *Vita Bedae*.
[2] Namely, the so-called *Durham Book* and the *Rushworth Gloss*, in the Bodleian.

special learning in this field, that the French literature of the mediæval age was extremely rich in translations of the Bible—that it surpassed, indeed, in this respect the literature of all the other European peoples.[1] Still, it must always be borne in mind, with regard to England in the eleventh and twelfth centuries, that the Norman tongue was only the language of the dominant race, of the higher classes, spoken at Court, in the seats of the nobles and bishops, in the courts of justice, the churches, and the garrisons, while the Saxon tongue lived on among the middle and lower strata of the population, the traders, artizans, and peasantry. The Anglo-Norman translations of portions of the Bible could only therefore be of use to the privileged classes, while the mass of the people enjoyed none of the benefit, but, on the contrary, were all the less considered and provided for, the more those classes were satisfied who had the power of the country in their hands.

But from the middle of the thirteenth century the Saxon element grew in strength, both in the population and the language. From that date the English language was developed in three periods: Old English from 1250–1350, Middle English to 1500, New English from the sixteenth century downwards.

As in Anglo-Saxon and most languages, so also in Old English, the earliest attempts in Biblical subjects are of a poetical kind. Such

Old English. is the *Ormulum*, a Gospel harmony in verse without rhyme,[2] a work, however, not of a kind to make way among the common people. Another production somewhat later describes the chief facts of the First and Second Books of Moses.[3] To the end of the thirteenth century belongs a translation of the Psalter in verse, the language of which is simple and full of expression.

The oldest prose translation of a Bible book into Old English dates from the fourteenth century—about 1325—and, what is remarkable, two translations of the Psalms in prose appeared almost simultaneously. The one was executed by William of Shoreham, a

Versions of the Psalms. country parish priest, in the county of Kent; the other was the work of a hermit, Richard Rolle, of Hampole, who died in 1349. The former wrote the Psalter, verse by

---

[1] Reuss, *Revue de Théologie*, II. 3: 'Les bibliothèques de la seule ville de Paris contiennent plus de manuscrits bibliques français que toutes les bibliothèques d'Outre Rhin ne paraissent en contenir d'allemands.

[2] Called *Ormulum*, after the author, whose name was either Orm or Ormin, and who was an Augustinian Canon. Edited, with Notes and Glossary, by Wright, Oxford University Press, 1852, 2 vols. 8vo.

[3] *The Story of Genesis and Exodus*, an early English song, about A.D. 1250. Edited by Richard Morris for the Early English Text Society. 1865.

verse, in Latin and English, the translation being in general faithful and verbal, except that the author often substitutes the words of the gloss in place of the text. The other, the so-called Hermit of Hampole, had written in the first instance a Latin Commentary on the Psalms. This occasioned him afterwards to translate the Psalter, and to publish it with an English Commentary.[1] According to a notice in English verse, found in one of the numerous MSS. of this work, and which dates from the fifteenth century, the author undertook the work at the request of a worthy nun, Dame Margaret Kirkby. The original was still to be seen in the nunnery at Hampole; but many copies of it were alleged to have been tampered with by the Lollards, and altered in the sense of their doctrines— an imputation which the editors of the Wycliffe Bible have found entirely wanting confirmation, although they have examined many MSS. of this translation and commentary on the Psalter.[2] A third translation of the Psalter—which is found in a Dublin MS. of the fifteenth century, and has been supposed to be the work of a certain John Hyde, because the book was at one time his property—appears from the specimens given of it to be nothing more than a revision of the language of the translation of Shoreham.[3]

The whole result for this period, as well of the Anglo-Saxon as of the Norman and the Old English tongues, stands as follows:—

1. A translation of the entire Bible was never during this period accomplished in England, and was never even apparently contemplated.

2. The Psalter was the only book of Scripture which was fully and literally translated into all the three languages—Anglo-Saxon, Anglo-Norman, and Old English.

3. In addition, several books of Scripture, especially of the Old Testament, were translated partially or in select passages, as by Aelfric, leaving out of view poetical versions and the translation of

---

[1] For our first trustworthy information concerning the person and life of this remarkable man we are indebted to the documents published by Mr. Perry in the preface to the *English Prose Treatises* of Richard Rolle de Hampole. Lond., 1866 p. xv. f. *Vide Legenda de Vita Ricardi Rolle*, preserved in the Cathedral Library of Lincoln. According to these, he was born at Thornton, in Yorkshire, studied at Oxford, and returned home in his nineteenth year, where he immediately took to a hermit's life. Later in life he laboured as an itinerant preacher in the northern parts of Yorkshire, and he closed his life in Hampole in 1349.

[2] *Wycliffite Versions of the Bible*, vol. I., p. iv. At all events, one such remark drawn from a single MS. is not sufficient to support the conjecture made by Humphrey Wanley that this translation of the Psalms in its shortest form was a juvenile work of Wycliffe himself.

[3] *Ib.*, vol. I., pp. v. and vi., and particularly Note 1. All the preceding statements regarding the Bible translations which were anterior to Wycliffe rest upon the learned investigations of the editors of the Wycliffe Bible, found in their preface.

the Gospel of John by Bede, which celebrated work has not come down to us.

4. Last of all—and this fact is of great importance—in none of these translations was it designed to make the Word of God accessible to the mass of the people, and to spread Scriptural knowledge among them. The only object which was kept in view was partly to furnish aid to the clergy and to render service to the educated class.

2.—How Wycliffe came to engage in this Undertaking.

CONSIDERING that this was the state of things down to the middle of the fourteenth century, the fact becomes one of a highly important character that only thirty or forty years later a translation of the whole Bible had been executed, and that, too, with the design of becoming the common property of the nation. And this was the work and merit of Wycliffe. To what extent he did the work of translation with his own pen, it will hardly ever be possible to ascertain with perfect certainty; but so much as this is certain, that it was he who first conceived the idea, that he took a personal share along with others in the labour of its execution, and that the accomplishment of the task was due to his enthusiastic zeal and judicious guidance.

Wycliffe's undertaking.

This fact is so strongly attested by manifold testimonies of friends and foes as to be beyond all doubt. Knighton, a chronicler of the period, in a passage which was probably penned before the year 1400, laments the translation of the Bible into English, and ascribes it categorically to Wycliffe. He maintains that Christ gave the Gospel, not to the Church, but only to the clergy and doctors of the Church, to be by them communicated to the weaker brethren and the laity according to their need; whereas Wycliffe has rendered the Gospel from the Latin into English, and through him it has become the possession of the common people, and more accessible to the laity, including even women who are able to read, than it used to be to the well-educated clergy. The pearl is now thrown 'before swine and trodden under foot,' etc.[1] When the chronicler speaks of 'the Gospel' here, we are not to understand him in a restricted sense, as meaning the translation of the New Testa-

Testimony of Knighton.

---

[1] Knighton, col. 2644, *Hic magister Joannes Wyclif Evangelium quod Christus contulit clericis et Ecclesiae Doctoribus, ut ipsi laicis et infirmioribus personis secundum temporis exigentiam et personarum indigentiam cum mentis eorum esurie dulciter ministrarent, transtulit de Latino in Anglicam linguam non Angelicam; unde per ipsum fit vulgare, et magis apertum laicis et mulieribus legere scientibus, quam solet esse clericis admodum literatis et bene intelligentibus; et sic evangelica margarita spargitur et a porcis conculcatur,* etc.

ment only, as distinguished from the Old, or even of the Gospels, in distinction from the other New Testament books. The whole of Holy Scripture was often so designated. This being so, we need no further proof to show that Knighton regarded the translation of the Bible as the work of Wycliffe.

We also find the idea and plan of a Bible translation attributed to Wycliffe in a document of official character. Archbishop Arundel of Canterbury and his suffragan bishops, in the year 1412, *Testimony of Arundel.* addressed a memorial to Pope John XXIII., with the petition that in the exercise of his plenary apostolic powers he would pronounce sentence of condemnation on the heresy of Wycliffe and his party. In this document Wycliffe is charged, among other things, with having contended with all his power against the faith and the doctrine of the Church, and, in order to make his malice complete, with having devised the plan of a translation of the Holy Scriptures into the mother tongue.[1] The language here employed, it may be remarked in passing, is a clear proof of the fact that before Wycliffe's time there was no English translation of the Bible in existence. It is also evident from the words that it was not merely single books, but the whole Bible, that had now been translated. The document, however, speaks only of the idea and the plan of the work, without ascribing to Wycliffe himself its execution in detail.

By the side of these testimonies proceeding from opponents may be placed the language of one of Wycliffe's admirers—John Huss— who says in a polemical tract against John Stokes of the *Testimony of Huss.* year 1411: 'It is plain from his writings that Wycliffe was not a German, but an Englishman.—For the English say that he translated the whole Bible from Latin into English.'[2]

The fact is certain, then, that Wycliffe was the first to conceive the great idea of a translation of the *whole* Bible, and that for the use of the whole people. What, then, we are led to ask, were the intermediate thoughts and preliminary stages by which Wycliffe was led to the conception of this grand design?

As a great number of his writings have come down to us, it is natural that we should first look into these for information on this point. If Luther in his day refers every now and then to his Bible-translation in letters from the Wartburg and later writings, it might

---

[1] Wilkins, *Concilia Magnae Britanniae*, III., p. 350, *Joannes Wycliff—et ipsam ecclesiae sacrosanctae fidem et doctrinam sanctissimam totis conatibus impugnare studuit, novae ad suae malitiae complementum Scripturarum in linguam maternam translationis practica adinventa,* etc.

[2] *Replica contra Jo. Stokes. Quod autem Wicliff non fuit Teutonicus sed Anglicus, patet ex suis scriptis—nam per Anglicos dicitur quod ipse tota Biblia transtulit ex Latino in Anglicum.*

be supposed that Wycliffe, too, must sometimes have had occasion to refer to a work whose importance and greatness lay so near his heart, and that such references might be found to throw light upon the preliminary stages of the undertaking. But, in point of fact, it is very rare to find, either in his Latin or his English writings, any allusions to the work either while in progress or after its completion. The condition of things at that time, it must be remembered, was very different from what it was in the third and and fourth decades of the sixteenth century. In Wycliffe's day men could not conceal from themselves that such an undertaking was attended with danger; and therefore it was the part of prudence not to talk loudly of the matter so long as it was only in progress. Notwithstanding, however, the almost total silence of Wycliffe respecting his own work, one circumstance, at least, seems probable, viz., that it was through the translation of several single books of the New Testament that he was gradually led to contemplate a complete version of the whole Bible.

Wycliffe's course.

The editors of the Wycliffe Bible—Rev. Josiah Forshall and Sir Frederic Madden—are of opinion that the earliest translation of a Biblical book executed by Wycliffe was the Commentary upon the Revelation of St. John.[1] Now, it is true that, as early as the sixteenth century, Bishop Bale included among Wycliffe's works an Explanation of the Apocalypse; and Shirley has admitted the same without hesitation into his list of Wycliffe's genuine writings.[2] But, for my own part, I do not see my way to attribute this Commentary to Wycliffe, especially since the translation of the text contained in the oldest manuscripts of the work does not agree with Wycliffe's translation of it in his complete version.[3]

His supposed earliest Bible work.

The case is different, indeed, with the single Commentaries on the Gospels of Matthew, Luke, and John, as the English version of the Vulgate text given in these writings agrees with the Wycliffe translation in its earliest form. The Preface to the Gospel of Matthew is very much in accordance with Wycliffe's general style; but, in my judgment, the Commentary on the Gospel of Luke cannot be recognised as his work, because in the preface the author writes of himself in a manner which is not at all applicable to Wycliffe. The writer first introduces some words of Scripture, and then proceeds as follows:—'Therefore it is that a poor, insignificant man (a caitiff), who, for a time, has been inhibited from

Single commentaries not Wycliffe's.

---

[1] *Wycliffite Versions*, I., p. vii.
[2] *Catalogue of the Original Works of J. W.*, p. 36.
[3] *Wycliffite Versions*, I., p. viii., Note z.

preaching, from causes known to God, writes the Gospel of Luke in English for the use of the poor people of his nation, who understand little or no Latin, and are poor in wit and worldly wealth, but none the less are rich in good-will to be well pleasing to God.'[1] It is impossible to point out a moment in Wycliffe's life when 'for a time he was hindered from preaching the gospel.' For the allusion here has no appearance of being to a time of sickness, but rather to some hindrance on the part of ecclesiastical superiors. Thus understood, the side hint that the causes of the hindrance are known to God becomes all the more appropriate, as it hints at the wisdom of God's permission of the hindrance. The whole mode of expression appears to me to be such as to indicate one of Wycliffe's itinerant preachers as the writer, but not Wycliffe himself.[2]

Nor does the preface to the Commentary on the Gospel of John speak for the authorship of Wycliffe, when the author gives for his determination to write it the following reasons:—'Our Lord Jesus Christ, very God and very man, came to serve poor meek men, and to teach them the gospel; and for this cause St. Paul saith that he and other apostles of Christ be servants of Christians for the sake of our Lord Jesus Christ. And again he saith, "I am debtor to wise men and unwise;" and again, "Bear ye the charges one of another, and so ye shall fulfil the law of Christ;" that is, of charity, as St. Augustine expoundeth. Therefore a simple creature of God, willing to bear in part the charges of simple poor men well willing to God's cause, writeth a short gloss in English on the Gospel of John, and setteth only the text of Holy Writ, and the open and short sentences of holy doctors, both Greeks and Latins, and allegeth them in general for to ease the simple wit and cost of poor simple men, remitting to the greater gloss written on John, where and in what books these doctors say these sentences.'[3] This description of his own person suggests that the writer desired to remain anonymous; whereas Wycliffe, so far as I know, in all cases took the personal responsibility of what he wrote, not to mention the fact that, while he is always glad to have the support of passages from the fathers and later doctors of the Church, Wycliffe never confines himself to a mere reproduction of the earlier authorities, as is done in the productions now in question, which, in substance, only render in English

---

[1] *Wycliffite Versions*, I., p. ix., Note d. The words run thus:—'Herfore a pore caityf lettid fro prechyng for a tyme for causes known to God,' etc.

[2] Arnold, in his Introduction to the First Volume of *Wiclif's English Sermons*, p. 5, concludes against the Wycliffe authorship of this Commentary on partly the same grounds as those upon which I had come to the same conclusion some years before; only he conjectures that its true author may have been a monk.

[3] 'Herfor a symple creature of God writith a schort glos in Englisch,' etc.

what already stands in the *Catena Aurea* of Thomas Aquinas. However, as I have not been in a position to examine the manuscripts for myself, and can only rest my judgment upon the short extracts which are given in the preface to the Wycliffe Bible, I do not pretend to be able to pronounce an authoritative judgment upon the subject. Only so much as this appears to be beyond doubt—that the writer or writers of these commentaries must have belonged to Wycliffe's school.

The same thing must also be said of the author of a Commentary on the first three Gospels, who gave, in the same way, a translation of the Vulgate text, with commentaries from older fathers and doctors; for 'the Servant of God' who encouraged the author to undertake the work gives utterance to precisely such principles as Wycliffe maintained. In the preface to the Gospel of Matthew the author writes as follows:—'I was stirred some time ago to begin this work by one whom I suppose verily was God's servant, and ofttimes prayed me to begin this work, saying to me that since the Gospel is the rule by the which each Christian ought to live, and divers have translated it into Latin, the which tongue is not known to every man but only to the learned, and many laymen are that gladly would con the Gospel if it were translated into the English tongue, and so it should do great profit to man's soul, about which profit every man that is in the grace of God, and to whom God has sent ability, ought heartily to busy himself.'[1]

Thus far, then, we have found nothing which can be regarded with an adequate degree of confidence as a preliminary labour of Wycliffe in the work of Bible-translation. There is more reason for recognising as a work from Wycliffe's own hand the English translation of the Latin Harmony of the Gospels (entitled *Series Collecta*) which Prior Clement of Lanthony, in Monmouthshire, wrote in the second half of the twelfth century. For (1) this translation has always, from the sixteenth century, especially since Bishop Bale, been attributed to Wycliffe, and never to any other man. (2) It varies very little from Wycliffe's translation of the Gospels. (3) The preface of the translator (to be carefully distinguished from that of the Prior) consists of two parts, the one being identical with the preface to the Commentary on Matthew's Gospel mentioned above, while the other was evidently intended from the first to be the preface to the translation of this

A Gospel Harmony.

---

[1] *Wycliffite Versions*, I., pp. ix., x., and particularly Note f. 'One that I suppose veraly was Goddys servant—seyand to me that sethyn the gospel is rewle, be the whilk ich Cristen man owes to lyf—ilk man that is in the grace of God, and to whome God has sent konnyng, owes hertely to bysy him.'

Gospel Harmony; and this latter bears the unmistakable stamp of thought and expression peculiar to Wycliffe.

The author of the preface takes as his text the saying of Christ, 'Blessed are they who hear the Word of God and keep it;' and he draws from it in particular the conclusion that 'Christians ought to travail day and night upon the text of Holy Writ, especially upon the Gospel in their mother tongue.'[1] 'And yet,' he remarks, 'men will not suffer it that the laity should know the Gospel, and read it in their common life in humility and love.' Hereupon he continues as follows :—'But covetous clerks of this world reply and say that laymen may soon err, and therefore they should not dispute of Christian faith. Alas! alas! what cruelty is this, to rob a whole realm of bodily food because a few fools may be gluttons, and do harm to themselves and others by their food taken immoderately.[2] As easily may a proud worldly priest err against the Gospel written in Latin, as a simple layman err against the Gospel written in English. . . . What reason is this, if a child fail in his lesson at the first day, to suffer never children to come to lessons for this default? Who would ever become a scholar by this process? What Antichrist is this who, to the shame of Christian men, dares to hinder the laity from learning this holy lesson which is so hard (strongly) commanded by God? Each man is bound to do so, that he be saved, but each layman who shall be saved is a real priest made of God, and each man is bound to be a very priest.[3]

'But worldly clerks cry, that Holy Writ in English will set Christians in debate, and subjects to rebel against their sovereigns; and therefore it shall not be suffered among laymen. Alas! how may they more openly slander God, the Author of peace, and His holy law, fully teaching meekness, patience, and charity? . . . Thus the false Jews, namely, high priests, scribes and Pharisees, cried on Christ that He made dissension among the people. O Jesus Christ! Thou that didst die to confirm Thy law, and for ransom of Christian

---

[1] It is to be regarded as a peculiar merit of the Editors of the Wycliffe translations of the Bible that they have given in the Preface so rich an anthology of extracts from English manuscripts. One of the most valuable of these communications, in my opinion, is the second preface, printed in full from two MSS., to the English translation of the Gospel-harmony of Clemens, in vol. I., p. xiv., col. 2, and p. xv., col. I. The sentence last quoted in our text is worded in the original thus—'Cristen men owe moche to traueile nyght and day aboute text of holy writ, and namely the gospel in her modir tunge.'

[2] Here *unmesurabli* is to be read according to the other MS., not *mesurabli*, which the editors have preferred.

[3] *Wycliffite Versions*, vol. I., p. xv., col. I. 'Thanne eche lewed man that schul be saued is a real prest maad of God, and eche man is bounden to be suche a verri prest. But worldly clerkis crien that holy writ in Englische wole make cristen men at debate, and suggetis to rebelle agheyns her souereyns, and therefor it schal not be suffred among lewed men.'

souls, stop these blasphemies of Antichrist and worldly clerks, and make Thy holy Gospel known and kept of Thy simple brethren, and increase them in faith, hope, and charity, and meekness, and patience, to suffer death joyfully for Thee and Thy law. Amen, Jesu, for Thy mercy!'

I repeat, these are through and through genuine thoughts of Wycliffe, spoken with godly warmth in his own simple but sharp and original style. The whole preface is nothing else than a plea for the translation of the Gospel into English, and for its diffusion among the laity. And if this preface was written specially for the translation of the Gospel Harmony, it lets us see that at that date, whatever it was, Wycliffe had already grasped the idea, 'the Bible for the people!' At the same time, this theological vindication of the idea could not fail to lead on to the plan of a *complete* Bible version. It is to be regarded as a kind of temporary substitute for the latter that to that Gospel Harmony in English there was added an appendix containing portions of the Catholic epistles, and selected extracts from other parts of the Bible. This collection presents in the different manuscripts variations in bulk, and also in the arrangement of the several pieces.[1] In how far, however, this appendix is the work of Wycliffe, it has not hitherto been possible to ascertain.

The second half of the fourteenth century witnessed the production of another work of the same kind which is well worthy of attention, viz., a complete translation of all the Epistles of Paul, in which the Latin and English follow each other, paragraph by paragraph, or even verse by verse, in such a way that with a very literal translation there are interwoven occasional explanations of single terms. The circumstance, however, that the full Latin text always stands first, is a clear proof that the work could not have been prepared for the people, but rather for the less educated class of priests.[2]

Version of the Epistles.

All the writings hitherto mentioned were preparatory labours by which the proper goal to which they all tended was more and more nearly reached, viz., a pure and at the same time a complete English version of the whole Bible.

---

[1] *Wycliffite Versions of the Bible*, v. I., pp. xi., xii.

[2] *Ib.*, v. I., p. xiii. In an English tract, which may well have come from Wycliffe's pen, p. xiv., Note, it is expressly said that 'as the parish priests are often so ignorant that they do not understand Latin books so as to be able to instruct the people, it is necessary not only for the ignorant people, but also for the ignorant priests, to have books in the English language containing the necessary instruction for the ignorant people.'

3.—The Wycliffe Translation.

THE New Testament was naturally translated first. Luther followed the same order nearly 150 years later. But the main difference in the two cases was that Luther translated from the Greek original, Wycliffe from the Latin of the Vulgate. There is no need to prove this latter fact. Wycliffe had no knowledge of Greek, and everywhere it is Latin, not Greek, which is spoken of as the language from which the version is made. That the translation of the New Testament was Wycliffe's own work we may assume with a considerable degree of certainty, for this is the point upon which the testimonies of friends and foes, as given above, most undoubtedly agree. Although Huss speaks of the whole Bible as translated by Wycliffe, we shall yet find immediately that a great part of the Old Testament was done by one of his friends; and our attention is thus directed chiefly to the New Testament as Wycliffe's part of the work. Knighton, in speaking of 'the Gospel,' and 'the Evangelical Pearl,' refers of course primarily to the New Testament. Added to this, there is a close resemblance of expression and style in the Gospels as compared with the other parts of the New Testament: and the whole has the appearance of being cast in one mould.

The New Testament.

Prefaces are attached to the several books. These, however, are not original productions, but merely translations of the prologues which usually precede the different books of Scripture in the manuscripts of the Vulgate of the fourteenth century. Whether these prefaces were translated by the same hand as the text is not certain; and there is some reason to suppose that they were not attached to the text at first, but were added afterwards—at least, they are wanting in some manuscripts before the Gospels, and in other copies before the other books. Not unfrequently short explanations of words are admitted into the text. The different manuscripts, however, of this original version of the New Testament vary considerably from one another, as the Biblical text in several of them has undergone a considerable number of corrections and changes.

Prefaces.

The execution of the Old Testament was taken in hand either while the New Testament was still in progress, or shortly after the completion of the latter,—and this not by Wycliffe himself, but by one of his friends and fellow-labourers. The original manuscript of this part of the work has remarkably been preserved.[1] A second manuscript, which was copied from this

The Old Testament.

---

[1] It is preserved in the Bodleian Library, No. 959 (3093), and is distinguished by the circumstance that very often alterations are made in the middle of a sen-

one before undergoing correction, contains a remark which ascribes the translation to Nicholas of Hereford; and this remark, which was manifestly added no long time after, is worthy of full credit. Now, it is a peculiar circumstance that both these manuscripts break off quite unexpectedly in the middle of a sentence,—namely, in the Book of Baruch iii. 20,[1]—a fact which can only be explained by the supposition that the writer was suddenly interrupted in the work. This supposition well coincides with the fact, attested by existing documents, that Nicholas of Hereford, Doctor of Theology, and one of the leaders of the Wycliffe party in 1382, after a sermon preached by him before the University on Ascension Day, was cited, in June of the same year, to appear before a Provincial Synod in London, to answer for his teaching on that occasion.[2]

Nicholas of Hereford.

The result of his examination was that on July 1 sentence of excommunication was passed upon him. Against this sentence he appealed to the Pope, and, according to Knighton's Chronicle, went in person to Rome to prosecute his appeal, but was there thrown into prison, where he remained for some years, when he was at length discharged, and returned to England. It is easy, therefore, to understand how Nicholas of Hereford came to be so suddenly interrupted in the middle of his work; and as it was impossible for him to carry on the work for several years, the fragment remained as it was when he was unexpectedly compelled to lay down his pen.

If these combinations and conjectures rest upon any adequate ground, they furnish us at the same time with the advantage of a fixed date; for, supposing the above facts to be correct, we shall then be able to assume with some confidence that in June, 1382, at the latest, the translation of the New Testament by Wycliffe must have been completed, if his fellow-labourer Hereford had already in the Old Testament advanced as far as the Apocrypha, and was in the middle of the Book of Baruch. The version itself affords proof that it was continued and finished by another hand; not improbably by Wycliffe himself. From Baruch iii. 20 the style is one characteristically different from Hereford's, as we shall have

Date of the work.

---

[1] The second MS. is in the Bodleian, marked *Douci* 369, and ends with the words, 'and othyr men in the place of hem risen. The yunge.' Then on the next tence; not unfrequently a word has been cancelled as soon as it was written, or before it was written fully, in order to put another in its place. *Wycliffite Versions*, I., pp. xvii. and xlvii.

side stands written by another but contemporary hand, '*Explic^t translacōm Nicholay de herford.*' See *Wycliffite Versions*, vol. I., pp. xvii. and l., where a facsimile of these words with the preceding lines is given.

[2] *Fasc. Zizan.*, p. 289. Knighton, *Chronica.*, col. 2656.

occasion to show in the sequel. The prologues to the books of the Old Testament, as in the case of the New Testament, are only a translation of those which were then commonly found in the manuscripts of the Vulgate. For the most part they consist of letters and other pieces of Jerome.

It must have been a heartfelt joy and deep satisfaction for Wycliffe when the translation of the whole Bible was completed, and the great plan accomplished which he had so long cherished and pushed forward with so warm a zeal. This, in all probability, took place in the year 1382. Wycliffe, however, was not the man to betake himself to rest as soon as he had attained any single object, and least of all in this sacred cause. To him the translation of the Bible was not an end in itself, but only a means to an end, that end being to place the Bible in the hands of his own countrymen, and to bring home the Word of God to the hearts of the English people. His next care, therefore, after the translation was ready, was to make it as widely useful as possible. For this purpose copies of it were now made and circulated, not only of the whole Bible, but also of portions, and even of single books. Moreover, in many of these copies there was inserted a table of the Bible lessons for Sundays and all the feast and fast days of the ecclesiastical year, which table is still to be found in several of the existing manuscripts; and, in order to put select portions of Scripture into the hands of many at a cheap price, books were also copied out which contained no more than the Gospels and Epistles. Of this sort are two manuscripts still remaining, which were written at all events before the close of the fourteenth century.

The work completed.

Copies multiplied.

A still more important work now became necessary. As soon as the English Bible was complete and came into use, the imperfections which clung to it began to be manifest; and in truth it was not to be wondered at that it should have considerable blemishes. It was a work of uncommon magnitude, especially for that time, considering that it was executed under unfavourable circumstances by different hands, and in the absence of any firm basis of clear and consistent principles of translation. The portion executed by Hereford, embracing the Old Testament books, had a character of its own, differing much from Wycliffe's version of the New Testament in its method of translation, and in the form of its English idiom. These and other blemishes could least of all escape the notice of Wycliffe himself. It was he undoubtedly who suggested a revision of the whole work, and perhaps undertook it himself. Luther, in like manner, after his complete German Bible

Revision.

appeared in 1534, began ere long to revise it, and never ceased till his death to improve and polish it, partly by his own hand and partly with the assistance of Melancthon, Bugenhagen, Cruciger, and others. No marvel if the case was the same with the English Bible of the fourteenth century.

The revision was a work of time. Wycliffe did not live to see it completed. The revised Wycliffe Bible did not appear till several years after his death, and the improved form which it then assumed was essentially the work of one man, who was a trusted friend of Wycliffe, and in his latest years his assistant in parochial work, John Purvey. This fact has been made not merely probable but certain by the learned editors of the Wycliffe versions of the Bible, who have also shown that the probable date of the completion of the revision was the year 1388—*i.e.*, four years after Wycliffe's death.[1] Before the appearance of the collected edition of the Wycliffe translations just referred to, very confused and mistaken ideas of the oldest English versions of the Bible prevailed. Not to speak of the already-mentioned and now exploded assertion of Sir Thomas More, that long before Wycliffe's day there were in existence complete translations of the Bible in English, it was a common error, since Lewis's day down to 1848, to take the older translation of Wycliffe for the later revised one, and to take the later for the older, *i.e.*, for the genuine or unrevised work of Wycliffe. More than this, down to the year 1848, no part of the older translation had appeared *in print*, with the exception of the Song of Songs, which Dr. Adam Clarke had printed in his Bible Commentary from a manuscript in his own possession.[2] It seems that the older genuine

[marginal note: John Purvey.]

---

[1] To have established this fact, and brought clear light into the manifold darkness which rested upon these subjects, is one of the numerous merits of these two men who, with the liberal support of the delegates of the University Press of Oxford, carried on their investigations for twenty-two years, made a thorough search of the most important public and private libraries of Great Britain and Ireland, and on the basis of a critical comparison of numerous MSS. published the earlier as well as the later translations, along with prefaces. The work has this title, *The Holy Bible, containing the Old and New Testaments, with the Apocryphal books, in the earliest English versions made from the Latin Vulgate by John Wycliffe and his followers; edited by the Rev. Josiah Forshall, F.R.S., and Sir Frederic Madden, K.H., F.R.S., Keeper of the Manuscripts in the British Museum.* Oxford University Press, 1850, 4 vols. large 4to, with a copious Preface in vol. I. (from which we have drawn much of what we have given above), and a Glossary to these translations in vol. IV. The two translations are throughout printed side by side in double columns—the older to the left, the later to the right. The various readings are given in Notes.

[2] Henry Wharton, in the *Auctorium* to Ussher's *Historia dogmatica Controversiae de Scripturis et Sacris vernaculis*, London, 1690, p. 424, had rightly perceived which was the older and which the later translation, and while rightly attributing the older to Wycliffe, had incorrectly assigned the later to John of Trevisa. Dr. Waterland had come to see that the Translation, with the General Preface to the Bible, was the work of John Purvey; but he had not held fast to this view, and had even fallen back to the old opinion that the

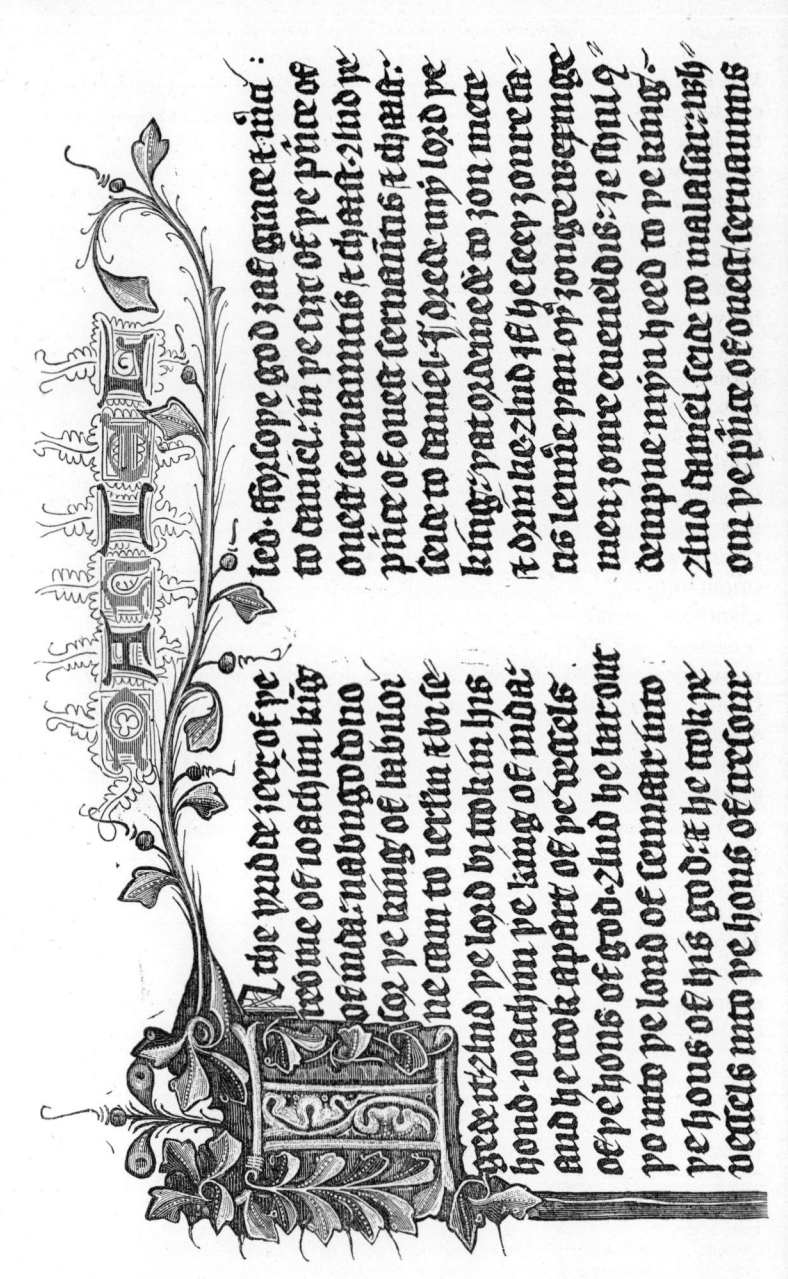

N the þridde ȝeer of þe
rewme of ioachim kig
of iuda, nabugodono-
for, þe king of babiloi
ne cam to ierlm̄ & bisē-
gede it: And þe lord bitoke in his
hond, ioachim þe king of iuda:
and he took apart of þe vessels
of þe hous of god. And þe he took þ
forn into þe lond of sennaar into
þe hous of his god: & he took þ
vessels into þe hous of tresour

led. ¶ Forsoþe god ȝaf grace and
to daniel, in þe siȝt of þe prince of
oneste seruauntis & chast. And þe
prince of oneste seruauntis, seide
forþ to daniel, I drede my lord þe
king, þat ordeynede to ȝou mete
& drinke. And if he seeþ ȝoure fa-
ces leene þan oþ ȝonge men þe ȝng-
men ȝoure euenelois, ȝe shul ȝ
dempne myn heed to þe king.
And daniel seide to malasar, þat
our þe prince of oneste seruauntis

FACSIMILE (Daniel i. 1, 2; 9-11) FROM AN EARLY MS. OF PURVEY'S REVISION, IN THE BRITISH MUSEUM; SLIGHTLY REDUCED IN SIZE.

Wycliffe translation had met with the fate of being so long ignored in consequence of the appearance of the later improved version. For the later form of the text of the translation was eagerly sought after. Copies of it came into the hands of people belonging to all classes of society, and must have been multiplied with extraordinary rapidity, for even at the present day there are still about 150 manuscripts extant which contain Purvey's revised version either in whole or in part, the majority of which were executed within forty years after the year 1388. *Eager reception of the book.*

It would, however, be extremely short-sighted and hasty if we should undervalue or entirely overlook the work of Wycliffe by reason of Purvey's work. Was, then, Purvey's Bible translation anything more than a uniformly executed edition of Wycliffe's work, already published, revised in respect to language and expression? The revision was, indeed, carried through in a consistent manner under the guidance of distinctly conceived principles; but this was a work of far less difficulty than the task of originating the translation itself, especially when we consider the grandeur and the novelty of the first idea of the work, and the tenacious persistency and steady industry which were absolutely required for its execution. Last of all, we point again to the probability before referred to—that it was Wycliffe himself who was first sensible of the need of a revision of the finished translation; and it was only the carrying out of the task which fell to Purvey—whose relative merits, however, we have no wish to undervalue. *Purvey and Wycliffe.*

What, now, is the peculiar character and importance of the earlier version, in so far as it was Wycliffe's personal work? Its peculiarity becomes more clearly visible when we compare the New Testament in the older version with the Old Testament as rendered by Hereford. Hereford's translation is excessively literal, and keeps as close as possible, almost pedantically, to the Latin expression and arrangement of sentences of the Vulgate. This makes the version very often stiff and awkward, forced and obscure. The *Character of the version.*

later recension was the earlier. He was followed in this by John Lewis, Wycliffe's first biographer, when he published, on the basis of two MSS., the later translation of the New Testament as the work of Wycliffe —*The New Testament, translated out of the Latin Vulgate, by John Wiclif, about 1378.* Lond., 1731, fol. This same translation has been twice printed in the present century—in 1810, by H. H. Baber, *The New Testament, translated from the Latin, in the year 1380, by John Wycliff,* D.D.; and in 1841, upon the basis of one MS., in Bagster's *English Hexapla,* 4to. (*The Bible Translations of Wiclif, Tyndale, Cranmer, and others*). On the other hand, the New Testament in the older translation was first published in 1848 by Lea Wilson, after a MS. in his own possession, under the title, *The New Testament in English, translated by John Wycliffe,* circa 1380. Lond., 4to. Last of all, Rev. Josiah Forshall and Sir Frederic Madden have given to the world the two Translations of the whole Bible, with critical exactness, in the work already mentioned.

translator kept only the original in view, in the wish to render it with the utmost possible fidelity; on the spirit and laws of the English tongue he seems scarcely to have bestowed a thought, and as little on the qualities of intelligibility and legibility which it was his business to impart to the translated text. The case is quite different with Wycliffe in the books which he translated, and above all in the New Testament. He ever keeps in view the spirit of his mother-tongue and the requirements of English readers, so that the translation is so simple as to be thoroughly readable. Nay more, it is a remarkable fact that Wycliffe's English style in his Bible translation, compared with his other English writings, rises to an uncommon pitch of perspicuity, beauty, and force.[1]

If we compare Wycliffe's Bible, not with his own English writings, but with English literature in general before and after his time, a still more important result is revealed. Wycliffe's translation of the Bible marks an epoch in the development of the English language just as much as Luther's translation does in the history of the German tongue. The Luther Bible opens the period of the new High German; Wycliffe's Bible stands at the head of the Middle English. It is usual, indeed, to represent not Wycliffe, but Chaucer—the father of English poetry—as the first representative of the Middle English literature. But later philologists —such as Marsh, Koch, and others—rightly recognise Wycliffe's Bible prose as the earliest classic Middle English. Chaucer, indeed, has some rare features of superiority—liveliness of description, a charming way of clothing his ideas, genuine English humour, and a masterly command of language. Such qualities of style appeal more to the educated classes—they are not adapted to make a form of speech the common property of the nation. That which is destined to develope a new language must be something which concerns closely the weal and the woe of man, and which for that reason takes hold irresistibly of every man in a nation, the lowest as well as the highest, and, to use Luther's expression, 'satisfies the heart.' In other words, it must be moral and religious truths, grasped with the energy of a genuine enthusiasm, and finding acceptance and diffusion for themselves in fresh forms of speech. If Luther, with his translation of the Bible, opened the era of the High German dialect, so Wycliffe, with his English Bible, stands side by side with Chaucer at the head of the Middle English. In the latter, moreover, are already found the fundamental characters of the new English, which reached its development in the sixteenth century.

Influence on the English language.

[1] This remark was first made by Sharon Turner in his *History of England during the Middle Ages*. 1830. Vol. v., p. 425. Comp. p. 447.

CHAPTER VIII.

WYCLIFFE AS A THINKER AND WRITER; HIS PHILOSOPHICAL AND THEOLOGICAL SYSTEM.

1.—His Gradual Development as a Thinker and Reformer.

IT makes a great difference in our whole view and judgment of Wycliffe, according as, on the one hand, we assume that from the very beginning of his public work he stood forth with a complete and unified system of thought, or as, on the other, we recognise a gradual development of his thoughts, and progress of his knowledge. The former assumption was entertained until recent times. Wycliffe's earliest biographer, John Lewis, was the first to adopt this view, and it continued to be held even after Vaughan had been able to throw some light upon the inner progress of Wycliffe's ideas. Men imagined they saw Wycliffe stand before them at once a finished man, and missed in him that gradual loosening from the bonds of error, and that slow progress in new knowledge, which in the case of Luther followed the first decided break with his old thoughts. This assumption rests upon error, and especially upon an imperfect acquaintance with the underlying facts. Even from the *Trialogus*, the first of Wycliffe's works which was sent to the press, men might have learned with sufficient certainty that Wycliffe had passed through very considerable changes of opinion. For in more than one place he makes the frankest acknowledgment that on more than one metaphysical question, he had formerly tenaciously upheld the opposite of what he now maintained—that 'he was sunk in the depths of the sea, and had stammered out many things which he was unable clearly to make good,' etc.[1] Still more strongly does he express himself in one of his unprinted writings, where he makes the following free confession: 'Other statements which at one time appeared strange to me,

Wycliffe's views progressive.

[1] *Trialogus*, ed. Lechler. Oxford, 1869. Lib. III., c. 8, p. 155; I., c. 10, pp. 69, 70.

now appear to me to be sound and true, and I defend them; for,' he continues, in the words of St. Paul, 'when I was a child in the knowledge of the faith, I spoke as a child, I understood as a child; but when, in God's strength, I became a man, I put away, by His grace, childish thoughts.' In this place he is speaking especially of the freedom of man's will and agency.[1] And in a similar way he expresses himself in his work on the *Truth of Holy Scripture*, touching his childishly literal understanding of the Bible in his earlier years. 'At last, however,' he continues, 'the Lord, by the power of His grace, opened my mind to understand the Scriptures;' and he even adds the humbling confession—'I acknowledge that ofttimes, for the sake of vain-glory, I departed from the teaching of Scripture, both in what I maintained and what I opposed, when my double aim was to acquire a dazzling fame among the people, and to lay bare the pride of the sophists.'[2]

Other frank acknowledgments of Wycliffe to the same effect could be produced, but these may suffice, and I only add here a few more particulars which are worthy of mention.

Among the collections of Wycliffe's Latin sermons there is one, upon which we have already remarked, that, when compared with the others, supplies some information regarding the progress of the preacher in knowledge. We refer to the older collection of forty miscellaneous sermons.[3] This comes out especially in his doctrine of the *Lord's Supper*, on which we shall have occasion to remark more particularly below. In addition to this, it is unmistakable that on the subject of the *Papacy* and the *Hierarchy*, not only Wycliffe's tone of language, but even his mode of thought, is essentially different, after the occurrence of the Western Schism of 1378, from what it was before that event. Further, on the subject of the *Mendicant Orders*, Wycliffe's opinions in his earlier writings differ widely from those expressed in his later ones. We shall show that there is no good ground for the supposition which has hitherto prevailed among Church historians, and upon which even an investigator like Vaughan proceeds in his latest work

Particular illustrations of his progress.

---

[1] *Responsiones ad argumenta Radulphi de Strode*, Vienna MS. 1338, f. 116, col. 3. *Et aliae conclusiones, quae olim videbantur mihi mirabiles, jam videntur mihi catholicae, defendendo*, etc.

[2] *De Veritate Sacrae Scripturae*, c. 6; c. 2, Vienna MS., 1294, fol. 13, col. 1; fol. 3, col. 1: *De ista vana gloria confiteor saepe tam arguendo quam respondendo prolapsus sum a doctrina scripturae*, etc.

[3] This did not escape the notice of attentive readers, even so early as the Hussite period, as is shown by the remark which is to be read in the margin of the Vienna MS. 3928, fol. 193, from another hand than the transcriber's: *Constet omnibus, quod iste Wycliff XL. sermones illos scribens fuit alius a se ipso hic quam alibi, ut apparet legenti. Quia demptis paucissimis, paene in omnibus his scriptis sequitur ecclesiam in fide et ritibus et modo loquendi catholico.*

upon Wycliffe, viz., that Wycliffe had commenced his conflict with the Mendicant Orders as early as 1360 or the following year, and carried it on for twenty years afterwards.[1] It was in connection with the question of transubstantiation that any controversy of Wycliffe with these particular Orders took its rise. Before that time it was rather against the endowed Orders that he aimed his attacks, while towards Francis of Assisi and Dominic, and the Orders founded by them, he cherished and expressed all manner of respect and sincere recognition.

All these facts constitute a sufficient proof that Wycliffe passed through important changes of opinion, even after he had arrived at mature years, and had made his first appearance upon the public stage; and that on several questions of great moment he gradually arrived at essentially different conclusions from those of his earlier years. It would indeed have been astonishing if a mind so independent and thoughtful—a man whose whole life was spent in labours on behalf of others, and in efforts for God's glory and the public good—had, in the substance of his teaching, adhered stiffly to the standpoints which he had in the first instance taken up. It will accordingly be our aim, as far as possible, to point out the gradual development of Wycliffe's views on all the chief points of his philosophical and theological beliefs.[2]

Such progress to be expected.

We have to regard Wycliffe first as a philosophical, and next as a theological thinker and writer; and though his philosophy and theology continually interlock, conformably to the whole character of scholasticism (for Wycliffe was a scholastic divine), yet it may be conducive to clearness if we give to each a separate treatment.

2.—Wycliffe as a Philosophical Thinker and Writer.

IN order that the distinctive features of Wycliffe's philosophy may be adequately described, a sufficient amount of his writings in this department must first be forthcoming. Here much is lacking; for

---

[1] Vaughan, *Monograph*, pp. 87, 410.

[2] The most accurate and thorough exposition of Wycliffe's teaching hitherto published is that of Dr. E. A. Lewald, formerly Professor of Theology in Heidelberg, *Die Theologische Doctrin Johann Wycliffe's, nach den Quellen dargestellt, und kritisch beleuchtet*, in the *Zeitschrift für hist. Theologie*, 1846, pp. 171, 503, 1847, p. 597. Lewald, while making use of Vaughan's *Life and Opinions*, etc., has chiefly confined himself to the *Trialogus*. He investigates Wycliffe's doctrine in its most important heads, following the order and carefully analysing his reasonings. What may still be regarded as defects in this, in many respects, excellent product of German industry and learning, are, I think, these two: first, that the author does not exhibit sharply enough what constitute Wycliffe's peculiar and distinctive ideas; and secondly, that the exposition binds itself too closely to each section of the *Trialogus* successively taken up, whereby the connection of the different parts of the same doctrine is, in more than one instance, broken up, and repetitions are introduced.

of his philosophical works, in the form of treatises, not a single piece has ever appeared in print, down to the present day; and, what is more serious, a considerable number of them have in all probability perished.¹ Contenting ourselves with what remains available, and turning first to his logical pieces, these, so far as we are acquainted with them, consist of only two short tractates, the one entitled *Logica*, the other *Logicae Continuatio*. Both of these have the peculiarity of limiting themselves to the simplest ideas and principles; whereas the logical treatises of the fourteenth century generally run into excessive length and lose themselves in the extremest subtleties.² In the *Logica* he treats simply of *terminus*, *propositio*, and *argumentum*, each of these forms of thought being defined and exhibited in its simplest varieties. And here we meet with the memoriter-verses on the manifold forms of syllogism which had been in use since the time of William Shyreswood.³

Lack of available material.

Wycliffe's logic.

The *Logicae Continuatio*, again, examines somewhat more largely the different kinds of judgments and processes of proof. That Wycliffe restricted himself in both works to the most general principles of the science, was no doubt done in consideration of what was wanted for young men on their first introduction to the study of logic.

It is next worthy of notice that these treatises on formal logic have a theological and especially a Biblical end in view. In the introduction to the *Logica*, Wycliffe says frankly, 'I have been induced by several friends of God's Word (*legis Dei amicos*) to compose a treatise in explanation of the logic of Holy Scripture. For, as I see many entering upon the study of logic, with the idea that they will be the better able thereby to understand the Word of God, and then leaving it again, on account of its distasteful mixture of heathenish ideas, and also of the hollowness of the study when thus conducted, I propose, with the object of sharpening the faculties of believing minds, to give processes of proof for propositions which are all to be drawn from Scripture,' etc., etc.⁴

Logic subsidiary to theology.

The reader sees that it is entirely with Christian ideas—with Biblical knowledge—that he proposes to concern himself. Yet the result is no sorry mixture of theological and philosophical matter,⁵

---

¹ In the list of lost works of Wycliffe given by Shirley in his *Catalogue*, p. 50, occur not fewer than twenty-four numbers, which appear to have been works of a logical or metaphysical description.

² Comp. Prantl, *Geschichte der Logik im Abendlande*, vol. III. (Leipz., 1867), p. 178.

³ *Ib.*, vol. III., p. 10.

⁴ Vienna MS., 4523, fol. 1, col. 1.

⁵ It is not a *Theologica Logicis inserere*, as the University of Paris expressed its censure in the year 1247. D'Argentré, *Collectio judiciorum de novis erroribus*, I., p. 158. Paris, 1728.

but a purely formal doctrine of the laws of thought. Even in his latest years he laid great stress upon a right knowledge of logic for the understanding of Christian truth, and maintained that the light esteem of Scripture doctrine, and every error in respect to it, had its root in ignorance of logic and grammar. This was not a thought exclusively Wycliffe's own. He shared it with William Occam, whom he names more than once in his manuscript works, and sometimes under his scholastic title of honour, *Venerabilis Inceptor*.[1]

Passing from Logic to Metaphysics, the question which Wycliffe regarded as by far the most important was that of *Universals*. He handles this question not only in several treatises devoted to it, *e.g.*, *De Universalibus, Replicatio de Universalibus, De Materia et Forma, De Ydeis*, but in his theological works, also, he not seldom returns to it as being, in his opinion, a doctrine of great reach and decisiveness in its theological bearings. For Wycliffe was in philosophy a Realist. He takes his stand firmly and with the greatest decision upon that side which maintains the objectivity and reality of Universals; following herein Augustine among the fathers of the Church, and Plato among the ancient philosophers, as his authorities and models. In this point he sides with Plato against the criticism which Aristotle directed against the Platonic doctrine of ideas.[2] However highly he values Aristotle in other respects, calling him, as the Middle Age in general did, *The Philosopher*, and usually leaning upon his authority, he is still distinctly conscious that on this subject he is a Platonist, and essentially at variance with Aristotle—a state of matters which was not at all irreconcilable with the fact that Wycliffe, like all his contemporaries, had no knowledge whatever of the Platonic philosophy from its original Greek sources. He seems to have known Plato only from Augustine and by his mediation; and he was by no means the first who, while of a Platonising spirit, was yet unable to withdraw himself from the authority of Aristotle. The Parisian teacher Heinrich Göthals of Ghent (d. 1293) (Henricus de Gandavo, *Doctor solemnis*), the Averroist Johann of Jandun (d. about 1320), and Walter Burleigh (d. 1337 [3]), to all of whom Wycliffe occasionally refers, had preceded him in the path of an Augustinian Church-Platonism conjoined with Aristotelian method.

---

[1] *E.g.*, *De Universalibus*, c. 15; fol. 57, col. 1; *De Veritate Scripturae*, c. 14; fol. 40, col. 4; fol. 41, col. 3.
[2] *Trialogus*, ed. Lechler, Book I., c. 8, p. 62; I, c. 9, p. 66; Book II., c. 3, p. 83.
[3] Comp. Prantl, *Geschichte der Logik im Abendlande*, III., pp. 183, 273, 297.

That Wycliffe makes use of the double designation *universal* and *idea* in speaking of the same subject, is sufficient to show that he had not overcome the dualism between Aristotelic and Platonic first principles. Nowhere, so far as we know, does he draw a clear and definite distinction between *idea* and *universal*. And yet one difference may be observed to prevail in his use of language upon this subject. When he treats of ideas, his point of view is always one where he looks at matters from a higher to a lower level; whereas the case is often the reverse when he speaks of *universals*. Manifestly, in the one case, the ground taken is *à priori* ground; in the other case it is empirical. It is the Platonic spirit which prevails in the former, the Aristotelic in the latter.

Influence of Plato and Aristotle.

Still Wycliffe is perfectly well aware that the principle which asserts the objective reality of universals is a very disputable one; and he has reflected on the causes which have given rise to the controversy regarding it. Four causes, it appears to him, underlie this great and long-standing divergency of opinion. The first cause is found in the strong impressions made by the world of sense, whereby the reason is darkened. The second cause he finds in a striving after seeming instead of real knowledge, as of old among the Sophists,[1] from which arises much contention, insomuch that men dispute propositions which ought to be conceded as necessary truths. A third cause he finds in the pretentiousness of men, which is always reaching after something peculiar to itself, and stiffly maintaining and defending it. And finally, he discovers a fourth cause in the want of instruction.[2]

Controversy on the reality of universals.

Wycliffe's doctrine of ideas and their reality does not admit of being set forth without the conception of God. For he takes this conception as his starting-point. The Idea is, in his view, an absolutely necessary truth,[3] for truth is nothing else but God's thought, which thought is also immediately a willing and working, a proposing and doing, on the part of God. For God cannot think anything which is external to Himself, unless this thing is intellectually thinkable. What God creates, He cannot possibly create by chance or unwisely; He must therefore think it; and His thought, or the archetype of the creature, is identical with the *idea;* and this same is eternal, for it is the same in time with the Divine

Conception of God.

---

[1] *De Universalibus*, fol. 70, col. 1: *Quidam enim more sophistarum non solum volunt scire sed videri scientes.*

[2] *Ib.*, fol. 70, cols. 1 and 2.

[3] *Trialogus*, Book I., c. 8, p. 61: *Ydea est, veritas absolute necessaria.*

knowledge. In its essence it is one with God, in its form it is different from God, as a ground comformably to which God thinks out what He creates. It has in itself a ground in reason, by virtue of which it determines the Divine knowledge.[1]

In this last expressed proposition lies, as it appears to me, the kernel of Wycliffe's doctrine of ideas, the central point of his Realism. He is not satisfied with regarding human knowledge as a reflex of actual existence; while the Nominalism or Terminism (as Prantl calls it[2]) of Occam looks upon knowledge, in so far as it goes beyond the sensible observation of nature and the empirical self-contemplation of the soul, only as something subjective, and cast in a logical form. According to Wycliffe, in thinking of universals, we conceive what has an independent existence, what has its ground in God's thought and work. But even God's thought, he holds, does not proceed arbitrarily, but conformably to its subject, agreeably to reason, answerably to the reason of things. And hence, in more places than one, he decidedly censures the usual practice of speaking of the thinkability of the unreal, or even of the self-contradictory, as empty subtlety, and a copious source of false reasonings and perverted conclusions.[3] Rather he lays down the proposition that God can only think that which He thinks in point of fact, and He thinks only that which *is—is*, at least in the sense of intellectual entity, in like manner as God, in willing, working, and creating, can only work and produce that which He actually produces, in its own time. For God's knowing and producing are coincident; God's knowledge of any creature, and His production and sustentation of it, are one and the same thing.[4]

The realism of Wycliffe, accordingly, is a principle of great and wide bearing. He is an enemy of all arbitrary, empty, and vague thought; he will not allow it to have the value of thought; as, for example, when a man supposes what might have followed if a certain something presupposed had not taken place (*conclusiones contingentiae*). Only realities can be thought. Thus knowing and thinking are coincident, as well in God as in the human mind, which thinks exactly as much as it knows, and no more.[5] Only, if we would hit Wycliffe's meaning, we must not restrict the real to what is per-

---

[1] *Si (Deus) illud intelligit, illud habet rationem objectivam, secundum quam terminat intellectivitatem divinam.* *Trialogus*, I., c. 8, p. 63.

[2] Prantl, *Geschichte der Logik im Abendlande*, III., p. 343. Comp. Eduard Erdmann, *Grundriss der Geschichte der Philosophie*, I., p. 432. (Berlin, 1866.)

[3] *Trialogus*, I., c. 9, p. 67.—Comp. Lewald, *Theol. Doctrin Wycliffe's*, in the *Zeitschrift für hist. Theologie*, 1846, p. 210.

[4] *Ib.*, I., c. 11, p. 74: *Cum idem sit Deum intus legere creaturam quamlibet, et ipsam producere vel servare.*

[5] *Ib.*, I., c. 10, p. 70: *Intellectus divinus ac ejus notitia sunt paris ambitus, sicut intellectus creatus et ejus notitia.*

ceptible by the senses, and what is a matter of experience at the present moment. Agreeably to his principle, he does not allow of any endless series of ideas, according to which every idea would give rise again to another, and that to a third, and so on for ever. Such a reflex action, evermore mirroring back the idea and reduplicating it, is to him something useless and perverted, a mere stammering talk without sense and substance; whereas we have to occupy ourselves with the realities of things, which objectively determine our knowledge by what they actually are.[1]

It remains to add that Wycliffe loves to give a Biblical as well as a philosophical basis and development to these thoughts by means of the idea of the Logos. He is convinced that his doctrine of ideas is agreeable to Scripture, and he lays stress upon it particularly on that account. For the same reason he holds it advisable to expound this doctrine of ideas only to such as are familiar, at least in some degree, with the thoughts of Scripture; one to whom the latter are still strange may easily take offence at his doctrine.[2] Herein Wycliffe supports himself, with special liking, upon an expression of St. John in the prologue of his Gospel—a passage to which, in several of his writings, and in connection with different thoughts, he continually returns, sometimes by express quotation, and sometimes by a mere allusion.[3] And yet, remarkably, this passage is one which Wycliffe has misunderstood (following, it is true, the lead of the Latin Fathers, especially Augustine, and of several of the scholastics, including Thomas Aquinas); his error lying in throwing into one sentence certain words which properly fall into two. In chapter i. 3, the Evangelist says of the Logos—'All things were made by Him, and without Him was not anything made that was made;' and then in ver. 4 continues—'In Him was life,' etc. But Wycliffe, following the authority of his predecessors, takes the last words of ver. 3, 'quod factum est' (in the Vulgate), along with 'in ipso vita erat' of ver. 4, as forming together one sentence (a mistake which was only possible where the Greek original was not understood); and then he finds the thought of the whole to be this—'Everything which was created was originally, and, before its creation

Idea of the Logos.

---

[1] *Trialogus*, I., c. 11, p. 72: *Falsum est, quod ydeae, alia est ydea et sic in infinitum, cum multiplicando illa verba homo balbutiendo ignorat se ipsum*, p. 73: *Intelligamus res, quae per suas existentias movent objective intellectum nostrum.*

[2] *De Ydeis*, Vienna MS., 4523, fol. 67, cols. 1 and 2: *Ista rudimenta sunt lactea et infantibilia, in quibus oportet juvenes enutriri, ut subtilia ydearum percipiant.*

Cavebo ne rudibus et non nutritis in lacte scripturae sic loquar ne darem scandalum fratri meo, etc.

[3] In the *Trialogus*, I., c. 8., p. 63, he refers to the passage, and in the tractate, *De Ydeis*, just quoted, that saying of St. John is, so to speak, the ever-recurring refrain. He applies the same citation in *De Veritate Scripturæ Sac.*, Vienna MS., 1294, fol. 19, col. 1.

in time, an actual reality—ideally pre-formed, in the eternally pre-existent Logos."[1]

With this passage he connected other Biblical expressions; above all the word of Christ where He testifies of Himself, 'I am the way, the truth, and the life' (John xiv. 6), which last word he interprets, certainly not very happily, as meaning the eternal life of thought. In addition, he appeals to the authority of the Apostle Paul, where (Romans xi. 36) he says 'Of Him, and through Him, and to Him are all things.' In particular, he supposes that when the Apostle was caught up into heaven, and saw visions and heard unutterable words, he had a view vouchsafed to him of the intellectual world—the world of ideas.[2] And then he traces to the instructions of St. Paul the initiation of his great convert Dionysius into those high mysteries which the latter has treated of in his work *On the Divine Names*.[3]

True knowledge is conditioned by Wycliffe, conformably to the above basis of thinking, by the apprehension of the ground of things pre-existing in the eternal reason. If men look at creatures only in their existence as known to them by experience (*in proprio genere*), their minds thereby are only distracted and drawn off from God. If we desire one day to see God in the heavenly home, we must here below consider His creatures in the light of those deep intellectual principles, in which they are known and ordered by Him, and we must turn our eyes towards that eternal horizon under which that light lies concealed.[4] *The ground of true knowledge.*

But not only true knowledge, but also true morality is conditioned, according to Wycliffe's fundamental view, by our grasping and striving after that which is universal. All envy, and every sinful act, has its basis in the want of well-ordered love to the universal. Whoever prefers a personal good to a common good, and sets his aim upon riches, human dignities, etc., places that which is lower and individual above that which is higher and universal: he reverses the right order of things, he loves not truth and peace (Zechariah viii. 19), and therein falls into sin. And thus it is that error in knowledge and feeling with regard to uni- *The principle of morality.*

---

[1] Lewald, *Zeitschrift*, etc. (see p. 225, n. 2), p. 208.
[2] *De Ydeis*, in MS. mentioned p. 230, n. 2, fol. 64, col. 2.
[3] *Ib.*, fol. 65, col. 1.
[4] *Liber Mandatorum*, Vienna MS., 1339, fol. 139, col. *a*: *Cum visio creaturarum in proprio genere sit tam imperfecta et tantum distrahens etiam in viae: —verisimile est, quod non erit in patria. Si ergo voluerimus videre naturam divinam in patria, consideremus creaturas secundum rationes suas, quibus ab ipso cognoscuntur et ordinantur, et convertamur ad orizontem aeternitatis, sub quo latet lux ista abscondita.*

versals (*circa universalia*) is the cause of all the sin that is dominant in the world.[1]

After this glance at Wycliffe's philosophical principles, especially his realistic metaphysics, we pass on to his theological system, in which we shall see again the reflection of the philosophical standpoint which has been indicated above.

3.—Wycliffe's Theological System.

1. *The Sources of Christian Truth.*

IN proceeding to treat of Wycliffe's theological system, we have to inquire first of all into his fundamental ideas of the sources of our knowledge of Christian truth. The nature of the subject, and the theological peculiarity of Wycliffe, both require precedence to be given to this point.

Wycliffe recognises a double source from which Christian knowledge is to be derived—reason and revelation, as we are wont to say;
Reason and revelation. *ratio* and *auctoritas*, as the scholastics express themselves. For in all the scholastics we find this distinction made. They bring forward, for one and the same proposition, first *rationes*, or ground of reason, and next *auctoritates* or testimonies of Holy Scripture, or of the Fathers, Councils, etc. Wycliffe distinguishes, in like manner, between *ratio* and *auctoritas* as the two bases of theological argument and of all Christian knowledge.[2]

Under 'reason' Wycliffe by no means understands anything merely formal—thought, with its inherent laws—in virtue of which it rejects what is contradictory and draws necessary conclusions from given premises, and regulates the formation of ideas, the process of proof, and the like. In one word, by the term *ratio* Wycliffe
Wycliffe's definition of Reason. does not denote merely the formal logic and dialectic. However much stress he lays upon these sciences, in the spirit of his age and of its scholastic philosophy, he by no means contents himself with a merely formal doctrine of thought and a scientific method, but he has a conviction that the reason of man has within itself a certain basis of truth in reference to the invisible, the Divine, and the moral. To this stock of intuitional truth belong the *universals*, or ideas, so far as knowledge or theoretical reason is con-

---

[1] *De Universalibus*, c. 3, Vienna MS., 4523, fol. 69, cols. 1 and 2 : *Sic error intellectionis et affectus circa universalia est causa totius peccati regnantis in mundo*, etc.

[2] *E.g., Trialogus*, I., c. 8, p. 61 : *Nec ratio, nec auctoritas hoc convincit;* and similarly in other places.

cerned. With reference, on the other hand, to action and the practical reason, Wycliffe appeals to the law of nature, which has its seat in the conscience and the natural reason.[1] He looks upon the law of nature as the standard of all laws, so that not only municipal law, but even the moral commandments of Christ, are to be valued according to their conformity to the law of nature.[2] On this subject, indeed, I think I have remarked in Wycliffe a certain wavering of judgment, or more accurately a progress of thought in the direction of recognising the exclusively decisive authority of revelation—*i.e.*, of Holy Scripture. For while in the book *De Civili Dominio* he sets forth the law of nature as the independent standard of all laws, even of the moral law of Christ, I find that in his treatise *Of the Truth of Holy Scripture*—which was written several years later at the least—he recognises the law of Christ as the absolutely perfect law, as the source of all that is good in every other law.[3] But in so saying he has no intention to bring into question that there exists a natural law in the conscience and the reason.

Not only in matters of action and of duty, but also in matters of faith, Wycliffe recognises a *natural light;* only he most distinctly pronounces as erroneous the notion that the light of faith is opposed to the light of nature, so that what appears to be impossible, in the light of nature, must be held for truth in the light of faith, and *vice versa*. There are not two lights thus contradicting each other; but the natural light has since the fall been weakened, and labours under a degree of imperfection; but this God in His grace heals by the impartation of revealed knowledge. Thus it comes to pass that what one man knows by the spiritual light of grace, another man knows by natural light. Hence the different stages of knowledge in respect to the articles of faith among different men.[4] Thus Wycliffe has no doubt that Plato and other philosophers were able to know, by means of natural light, that there is a Trinity in the nature of God;[5] and he makes the attempt himself to prove by grounds of reason the doctrine of the Trinity, the necessity of the Incarnation of

The light of nature.

---

[1] *De Veritate Scripturae Sac.*, c. 12, Vienna MS., 1294, fol. 31, col. 4. Here he is speaking of threats against his own person, and expresses the opinion that a Jew or heathen would, from an inborn sentiment of goodness, abhor those who were guilty of such, inasmuchas they *obviant legi conscientiae et naturaliter insitae rationi*.

[2] *De Civili Dominio*, II., c. 13, Vienna MS., 1341, fol. 207, col. 2: *De quanto aliqua lex ducit propinquius ad conformitatem legis naturae est ipsa perfectior.*

Sed lex Christi patiendi injurias propinquius ducit ad statum naturae quam civilis. Ergo ista cum suis regulis est lege civili perfectior. Comp. c. 17, fol. 236, col. 2.

[3] *De Veritate Scrip. Sac.*, c. 20, fol. 67, col. 1. The love of our neighbour is thoroughly learned and acquired by the law of Christ: *in tantum quod si lex alia docet caritatem aut virtutem aliquam, ipsa adeo est lex Christi.*

[4] *Trialogus*, I., c. 6, p. 55.

[5] *Ib.*, I., c. 6, p. 56.

the Divine Logos, and other doctrines of the gospel.[1] He thus credits reason with an independent power of its own of penetrating deeply into the knowledge of the mysteries of salvation. Herein he occupies the same standpoint with the great majority of the scholastic divines.

His difference from the other scholastics in the view he takes of 'authority,' *i.e.*, of positive revelation, is even more marked than his agreement with them on the subject of reason. On this subject Wycliffe approves himself as a thoroughly independent thinker, and especially as a man imbued with the spirit of the Reformation; for he has already come in sight of the principle that Holy Scripture is the only authoritative document of revelation, that it is the rule and standard of all teachings and teachers. But I find that on this decisive point it was only step by step that Wycliffe attained to the truth.

Apart from reason, the scholastics set forth as a standard principle, 'authority.' Under this idea they range, in miscellaneous array, conclusions of Councils, decrees of the Popes, doctrines of the Fathers, Biblical statements. In their eyes Holy Scripture has no peculiar, exclusive, privileged position, no decisive weight of its own. In other words, the Middle Age, in the generic idea of 'authority,' brings together, in naïve fashion, two different things, which, since the Reformation, have been distinguished from each other, as well as by Roman Catholics as by Protestants, viz., Scripture and Tradition. Criticism was so far incomplete, that these two elements were looked upon and made use of as of like nature and like validity. The Bible itself was regarded as only a part of tradition—a book handed down from one generation to another, just as the works of the Fathers were. Tradition, on the other hand, had come to be regarded as falling under the idea of 'Scripture,' as it was only known through the medium of its written form. We do not mean by this to call in question the fact that the scholastic divines were in general aware of the distinction between the Bible and Church tradition. Evidences of this are, no doubt, to be found in their dogmatic systems, *summæ*, *quodlibets*, etc. But that was a theoretical distinction. In practice, in bringing proof in support of any Roman dogma, the distinction was immediately forgotten; traditional elements and Scripture proofs were all uncritically jumbled together, as though they were all of equal value; they were all alike 'Authorities.'

With Wycliffe in this respect the case was essentially different. It

[1] *Trialogus*, I., c. 7, p. 58; III., c. 25, p. 214.

is true, indeed, as shown above, that he too mentions 'authority' along with 'reason' in a general way, as sources of knowledge and bases of proof in matters of faith; and in dealing with such questions, like other scholastics, he places Scripture and Tradition in line together, under the one banner of 'authority.' But this in his case, when closely examined, is only like a small fragment of egg-shell still adhering to the wings of the newly-hatched chicken. It is merely the force of custom which we recognise in this still lingering use of the technical word 'authority.' For in all cases where he is independently developing his own principles, and maintaining them not merely in theory, but applying them to particular questions of a practical nature, he draws so sharp a line of distinction between Scripture and Tradition that the two can no longer be properly ranged under the common head of 'authority.' For he ascribes to Holy Scripture, and to it alone, 'unlimited authority;' he distinguishes in principle between God's Word and human tradition, and he acknowledges the Scriptures to be in and by themselves the all-sufficing source of Christian knowledge.

Scripture and Tradition.

Nor was it only at a later stage of his teaching that Wycliffe grasped this decisive principle; he gave early expression to it. It was only gradually, it is true, that he reached it, and to what extent this was so, will be shown below. But as early as the date of his collection of 'Miscellaneous Sermons,' which all belong to the period of his academic labours, and at all events to the years preceding 1378, he expresses himself in a manner which shows that he fully recognises the alone-sufficiency of the Word of God, and pronounces it to be unbelief and sin to give up following 'the law of God,' and to introduce in place of it human traditions.[1]

Advance in Wycliffe's views.

With a clear consciousness of the whole bearing and extent of this truth, Wycliffe lays down the fundamental proposition that 'God's Law,' *i.e.*, Holy Scripture, is the unconditional and absolutely binding authority. This principle he expresses in innumerable places in sermons, learned treatises, and popular tracts, and in the most manifold manner, always with the consciousness of bearing witness to a truth of the widest scope. His opponents, too, were quite sensible of the far-reaching and weighty consequences which must result from this principle; and for this reason they did not fail to make it the object of their attacks. It

Sufficiency and supremacy of Scripture.

---

[1] *Miscellaneous Sermons*, XVIII., fol. 222, col. 2: *Infidelis consideratio est, quod periret ecclesia nisi praeter legem Dei humanis legibus regularetur. In hoc enim peccatur infideliter, dimittendo executionem legis Dei, et inducendo traditiones humanas, fomenta litium.*

was in defence of the principle, as well as to illustrate and establish it to the utmost of his power, that Wycliffe wrote one of the most important of his works, under the title, *Of the Truth of Holy Scripture* (*De Veritate Scripturae Sacrae*).[1]

How he understands his own principle will best appear, if we inquire into the way in which he partly establishes and partly applies it. In establishing and proving the principle of the absolute authority of Holy Scripture, Wycliffe looks at his subject from many different points of view. First of all, he sets out from the general truth, that in every sphere there is a *first*, which is the standard for everything else in the same sphere.[2] That the Bible is first and highest in the sphere of religion, he proves by pointing to the fact that Holy Scripture is, as a matter of fact, the Word of God. This last proposition he presents in various turns of expression; at one time he describes Holy Scripture as the Will and Testament of God the Father, which cannot be broken;[3] and at another he asserts that God and His Word are one, and cannot be separated the one from the other.[4]

Proofs of the authority of Scripture.

In other passages, secondly, he describes Christ as the proper Author of Holy Scripture, and deduces immediately from that fact its infinite superiority and absolute authority. As the person of one author is to another, so is the merit of one book compared to another; now it is a doctrine of the faith that Christ is infinitely superior to every other man, and therefore His book, or Holy Scripture, which is His law, stands in a similar relation to every other writing which can be named.[5] This being so, he knows not how to give any other psychological explanation of the indisposition of many to acknowledge the unbounded authority of the Bible compared with every

---

[1] *De Veritate Scripturae Sacrae*, fols. 1–119, col. 2. This work forms part of the so-called *Summa* of Wycliffe, namely, its Sixth Book, and with its thirty-two chapters would fill a printed volume of about thirty sheets. That this work had its origin in theological lectures is certain, both from its contents and form. Its date also is fixed by two passages to have been the year 1378. The book is properly nothing more than a defence of the Bible against the *accusatores* or *inimici Scripturae* of whom the author repeatedly speaks, *e.g.*, c. 12 and 28. From one passage in the first chapter it appears that one leading opponent in particular of Wycliffe and his teaching, along with others of the same views, had given the proximate occasion to this apology for the Bible; and this is the reason, no doubt, why the personality of Wycliffe himself stands out in this particular work with an almost statuesque effect.

[2] *De Blasphemia*, the 12th book of his *Theological Summa*, fol. 126, col. 2: *In omni genere est unum primum quod est metrum et mensura omnium aliorum.*

[3] *De Veritate Scrip. Sac.*, c. 9, fol. 21, col. 4: *Si non licet filio infringere testamentum patris terreni, multo magis non licet catholico dissolvere testamentum infrangibile Dei patris.* Comp. c. 14, fol. 43, col. 3, where he calls Scripture *testimonium Dei, quod voluit remanere in terris, ut suam voluntatem cognoscerent,* etc.

[4] *Wycket*, ed. Oxford, 1828, p. 5: 'For he (God) and his worde is all one, and they maye not be separated.'

[5] *Trialogus*, III., c. 31, p. 239.

other book, in any other way than from their want of sincere faith in the Lord Jesus Christ Himself.[1] And as it was a standing usage of thought and speech in the mediæval period to speak of the Bible as 'God's Law' and 'Christ's Law,'[2] so Wycliffe calls Christ our Lawgiver; he warmly exclaims that Christ has given a law which is sufficient in itself for the whole Church militant.[3] But Holy Scripture is regarded by him as not only the work of Christ, its Author, not only as a law by Him given; it stands yet nearer to Christ: CHRIST HIMSELF is the Scripture which it behoves us to know; and to be ignorant of the Scripture is the same thing as to be ignorant of Christ.[4]

This thought leads directly to a third argument in support of the unlimited authority of Scripture, viz., the *contents* of the Bible. The Bible contains exactly that which is necessary and indispensable to salvation—a thought to which Wycliffe gives expression in the language of the Apostle Peter, 'Neither is there salvation in any other, for there is none other name under heaven given among men whereby we must be saved,' but the name of Jesus Christ.[5]

With this limitation of the contents of the Bible to what is necessary to salvation stands connected the universal application and force of the commands and directions of the Gospel. 'If Christ had gone, in the least degree, more into detail, the rule of His religion would have become to a certain extent imperfect; but as it now stands, layman and cleric, married man and monk, servant and master, men in every position of life, may live in one and the same service, under Christ's rule. The evangelical law, moreover, contains no special ceremonies whereby the universal observance of it would have been made impossible; and therefore the Christian rule and religion, according to the form of it handed down to us in the Gospel, is of all religions the most perfect, and the only one which is in and by itself good.'[6]

---

[1] *Trialogus*, III., c. 31, p. 238: *Non sincere credimus in Dominum Jesum Christum, cum hoc dato ex fide fructuosa teneremus, quod Scripturae sacrae—sit infinitum major auctoritas quam auctoritas alterius scripturae signandae.*

[2] Among the writers of the fourteenth century, I name only Occam, Marsilius of Padua, Peter D'Ailly; and of the fifteenth century, John of Goch, which latter lays great stress upon evangelical liberty, and yet, as little as Occam, finds any difficulty in boasting of the *evangelicae legis libertas*. Goch, *De quatuor erroribus circa legem evangelicam exortis;* in Walch, *Monimenta medii avi*, Fasc. 4, p. 75; Occam, *De jurisdictione imperatoris in causis matrimonialibus;* in Goldast, *Monarchia*, I., p. 24.

[3] *De Officio Regis*, Vienna MS., 3933, c. 9, fol. 46, col. 1: *Legifer noster Jesus Christus legem per se sufficientem dedit ad regimen totius ecclesiae militantis.*

[4] *De Veritate Scrip. Sac.*, c. 21, fol. 70, col. 2: *Ignorare scripturas est ignorare Christum, cum Christus sit scriptura, quam debemus cognoscere.*

[5] *De Blasphemia*, c. 1, Vienna MS. 3933, fol. 118, col. 3. Comp. *De Veritate Scripturae Sac.*, c. 1., fol. 1, col. 2: *In illa consistit salus fidelium.*

[6] *De Civili Dominio*, II., c. 13, fol. 211, cols. 1 and 2: *Nullas particulares cerimonias exprimit, quibus eis universalis observantia vetaretur. Ideo regula ac religio Christiana secundum formam in evangelio traditam est omnium perfectissima et sola per se bona.*

Last of all, he points to the *effects* of Holy Scripture as an evidence of its truly Divine and absolute authority. The sense of Scripture is of more efficacy and use than any other thought or language.[1] The experience of the Church at large speaks for the sufficiency and efficacy of the Bible. By the observance of the pure law of Christ, without mixture of human traditions, the Church very rapidly grew; since the mixing up of traditions with it, the Church has steadily declined.[2] Furthermore, all other forms of wisdom vanish away, whereas the wisdom which the Holy Ghost imparted to the apostles on the day of Pentecost remains for evermore; and all its enemies have never been able effectually to contradict and withstand it.[3]

This principle of the absolute authority of the Scriptures, which Wycliffe knows how to confirm on so many different sides, immediately finds in his hands the most manifold applications.

From the principle of the Divine origin of Scripture immediately follows its infallibility (whereas every other surety, even an enlightened Church doctor, like St. Augustine, easily errs and leads into error),[4] its moral purity,[5] and its absolute perfection in matter and form. In the respect last named Wycliffe more than once calls attention to the fact that Holy Scripture has a logic of its own, and that its logic is firmly based and unanswerable, and that every believer ought to venerate and imitate not only the sense and contents of Scripture, but also its logic.[6] For the Holy Ghost led the apostles into all truth, and delivered to them also, without doubt, a logic of His own, that they might be able to teach others again with the like authority. But the chief inference which Wycliffe deduces from the Divine origin and absolute authority of the Bible is its perfect and entire *sufficiency*. The Bible alone is the ground document of the Church, its fundamental

The doctrine applied.

Infallibility of Scripture.

Sufficiency.

---

[1] *De Veritate Scrip. Sac.*, c. 15, fol. 45, col. 4 : *Efficacia sententiae* (the subject spoken of is the Bible) *est magis utilis . . . . quam sententia vel locutio aliena.*

[2] *De Civili Dominio*, I., c. 44, fol. 141, col. 1 : *Pure per observantiam legis Christi sine commixtione traditionis humanae crevit ecclesia celerrime; et post commmixtionem fuit continue diminuta.*

[3] *Ib.*, III., 26, fol. 252, col. 2 : *Aliae logicae et sapientiae evanescunt, sed os et sapientia, quam dedit apostolis in die pentecostes, manet in aeternum, cui non potuerunt efficaciter resistere et contradicere omnes adversarii.*

[4] *Sermons for Saints' Days*, No. LV., fol. 112, col. 3. *De Veritate Scripturae Sac.*, c. 2, fol. 4, col. 3 : *Locus a testimonio Augustini non est infallibilis, cum Augustinus sit errabilis.*

[5] *De Civili Dominio*, I., c. 34, fol. 81, col. 2 : *Lex humana est mixta multa nequitia, ut patet de . . . . regulis civilibus, ex quibus pullulant multa mala; lex autem evangelica est immaculata.* Comp. *Liber Mandatorum*, c. 10, fol. 114, col. 2 (after Psalm xviii. 31).

[6] *Trialogus*, I., c. 9, p. 65 : *Sicut sacrae scripturae sententia, sic et ejus logica est a fidelibus veneranda*, III., c. 31, p. 242; *Cum logica scripturae sit rectissima, subtilissima et maxime usitanda.* Comp. *Supplementem Trialogi*, c. 6, p. 434. *De Veritate Scripturae Sac.*, c. 3, fol. 6, col. 1.

law, its *charta*. Evidently with allusion to the Magna Charta, the fundamental charter of the civil liberties of his nation, Wycliffe loves to speak of the Bible as the charter of the Church's liberties, as the God-given deed of grace and promise.[1] It is the kernel of all laws of the Church, so that every precept profitable to the Church is contained in it, either expressly or by deduction.[2] Scripture alone has this importance and authority for the Church—a doctrine which corresponds almost literally with the motto of the German Reformation, *verbo solo*,[3] *the Word alone*. To Scripture alone, therefore, is ascribed the prerogative of 'authenticity.' In comparison with it, all other writings, albeit they may be the genuine works of great Church doctors, are 'apocryphal,' and have no claim upon our faith for their own sake.[4]

Not merely in the ecclesiastical sphere and in that of religion and morals, but in the whole circle of human existence, including civil life and the state, all law, according to Wycliffe, ought to order itself according to the Law of God. Every action, every charitable deed, buying, exchange, etc., is only so far right and good as the action is in accord with the evangelical law; and in so far as it departs from that law, it is to the same extent wrong and invalid.[5] Yea, he goes so far as to assert that the whole code of civil law ought to be grounded upon the evangelical law as a Divine Rule[6]—a view which is less evangelical than legal, and reaches farther in its consequences than can be approved, for it leads directly to a complete Theocracy, if not a complete Hierarchy.

Scripture universal in application.

From what precedes flows the rule—Put nothing, whatever it be, upon a footing of equality with Holy Scripture, still less above it. Wycliffe, without reserve, lays down the proposition, 'It is impossible that any word or any deed of the Christian should be of equal authority with Holy Scripture.'[7] To place

Its sole authority.

---

[1] *De Ecclesia*, c. 12, fol. 165, col. 1: *Sine conservatione hujus cartae impossibile est quod maneat dignitas ad privilegium vel aliquod bonum gratuitum capiendum. De Veritate Scripturae Sac.*, c. 12, fol. 32, col. 4, he calls the Bible *carta a Deo scripta et nobis donata, per quam vindicabimus regnum Dei.* Comp. c. 14, fol. 43, col. 4.

[2] *De Veritate Scrip. Sac.*, c. 21, fol. 71, col. 1: *Lex Christi est medulla legum ecclesiae. De Ecclesia*, c. 8, fol. 152, col. 3: *Omnis lex utilis sanctae matri ecclesiae docetur explicite vel implicite in Scriptura.*

[3] *De Civili Dominio*, I., c. 44, fol. 133, col. 1: *Sola Scriptura sacra est illius auctoritatis et reverentiae, quod si quidquam asserit, debit credi.*

[4] *Trialogus*, III., c. 31, p. 239: *Quod Scriptura sacra sit infinitum magis autentica et credenda, quam quaecunque alia. . . . Unde scripta aliorum doctorum magnorum, quantumcunque vera, dicuntur apocrypha*, etc. In the use of this term 'apocrypha' (it is the same with Occam), Wycliffe does not refer to the *genuineness* of these writings, but to their *credibility* and *authority*.

[5] *De Civili Dominio*, I., 35, fol. 83, col. 2.

[6] *Ib.*, c. 20, fol. 45, col. 1: *Totum corpus juris humani debet inniti legi evangelicae tanquam regulae essentialiter divinae.*

[7] *De Veritate Scrip. Sac.*, c. 15, fol. 48, col. 2: *Impossibile est, ut dictum Christiani vel factum aliquod sit paris auctoritatis cum Scriptura sacra.*

above Scripture, and prefer to it, human traditions, doctrines, and ordinances, is nothing but an act of blind presumption. A power of human appointment which pretends to set itself above the Holy Scriptures can only lame the efficacy of the Word of God, and introduce confusion.[1] Yea, it leads to blasphemy, when the Pope puts forward the claim that what he decrees in matters of faith must be received as gospel, and that his law must, even more than the Gospel itself, be observed and carried out.[2] It is the simple moral consequence of the doctrine, that 'Scripture alone is of absolute authority,' when Wycliffe enforces the duty of holding wholly and entirely to Scripture, and Scripture alone—of 'hearing Moses and the prophets'[3] and not even to mingle the commandments of men with evangelical truths. Men who practise such a mixture of God's truth and human traditions Wycliffe calls *mixtimtheologi*, 'medley divines.'[4] He also remarks that it is no justification of a doctrine that it contains, in a collateral way, much that is good and reasonable, for so is it even now with the behests and the whole life of the Devil himself; otherwise God would not suffer him to exercise such power. But Christian law should be only and purely the law of God, which is without spot and giveth life to the soul; and therefore a law of tradition ought to be repudiated by all the faithful, on account of the mixture of even a single atom of Antichrist.[5] By a glance into the history of the Church of Christ, Wycliffe discovers that this departure from the Evangelical Law through the mixture of later traditions was at first very slight and almost unobservable, but that in process of time the corruption became ever ranker.[6]

What we have here to do with is, unmistakably, nothing else but the principle that 'God's Word pure and simple' ought to be taught,

---

[1] *De Civili Dominio*, I., 36, fol. 86, col. 2; *Liber Mandatorum*, c. 22, fol. 180, col. 1: *Potestas jurisdictionis super Scripturam sacram humanitus introducta potest effectum legis Dei casando confundere.*

[2] *De Blasphemia*, c. 3, fol. 125, col. 3.

[3] *De Civili Dominio*, I., c. 11, fol, 24, col. 1. Spiritual rulers are bound *uti pro suo regimine lege evangelica impermixte. De Veritate Scripturae Sac.*, c. 14, fol. 42, col 3: *Videtur mihi summum remedium solide credere fidem Scripturae, et nulli alii in quocunque credere, nisi de quanto se fundaverit ex Scriptura. Ib.*, c. 20, fol. 66, col. 1: *Utilius et undique expeditius foret sibi (ecclesiae) regulari pure lege scripturae, quam quod traditiones humanae sunt sic commixtae cum veritatibus evangelicis, ut sunt modo.*

[4] *De Veritate Scrip. Sac.*, c. 7, fol. 17, col. 3: *Ut quidam doctor traditionis humanae et mixtimtheologusdicit.* Comp. *De Condemnatione XIX Conclusionum*, in Shirley, *Fasciculi Zizan.*, 1858. The opposite to this is *purus theologus; De Ecclesia*, c. 10.

[5] *De Blasphemia*, c. 8, fol. 144, col. 1: *Lex autem Christiana debet esse solum lex Domini et immaculata convertens animas, et per consequens recusari debet a cunctis fidelibus propter commixtionem cujuscunque attomi* (sic) *antichristi.*

[6] *Sermons for Saints' Days*, No. XLIX., fol. 99, col. 1.

and that God's Word, and nothing else, not even any angel, ought to determine articles of faith, as is laid down in the Second of the Lutheran Articles of Schmalkald. In one word, this is the Bible principle of the Reformation—the so-called *formal* principle of Protestantism.

<small>Principle of Protestantism.</small>

Wycliffe himself was well aware of the importance and wide bearing of his Bible principle. That is the reason why he calls his adherents 'Men of the Gospel'—*viri evangelici, doctores evangelici*,[1] etc.—a name which, in the mouth of his admirers and disciples, was applied to himself as a high title of honour. If honorary titles were created for other scholastic divines, which, for the most part, were taken from the special character of their scientific pre-eminence, such as *Doctor subtilis, irrefragabilis, profundus, resolutissimus*, etc., or from their moral purity and elevation, such as *Doctor angelicus, seraphicus*, etc.; so for Wycliffe the title of honour, *Doctor Evangelicus*, which early became current among his friends and followers, and was also transplanted to the Continent (as appears from a number of passages in Wycliffe-manuscripts transcribed by the Hussites), was one of a kind to indicate, in an appropriate way, his high estimation of the value of the gospel—an estimate which he put upon nothing else—and to signalise, in fact, his characteristic Bible principle.

<small>Wycliffe 'Doctor Evangelicus.'</small>

Here also may be the proper place to mention that Wycliffe's knowledge of the Bible was, in fact, astonishing. The remarkable number of Scripture passages which, in a single work, he sometimes explains and sometimes applies, as in the *Trialogus*, is of itself enough to show that he was, in an extraordinary degree, familiar with the Bible. And although his skill in interpretation is not masterly (how *could* it be so at that time?), yet I have not seldom found in the reading of his unprinted works that he often manifests a felicitous tact and exact judgment in the process, and that an appropriate passage of Scripture does not easily escape him when his object is to arrange a train of Scripture proof. But his Bible knowledge is almost more remarkable in cases when it is not his object to quote Scripture, but when, notwithstanding, the whole life and movement of what he writes is in Scripture thought and phrase.

<small>His knowledge of the Bible.</small>

The fact is not without importance that even the enemies of Wycliffe, as before remarked, recognised and controverted his Scrip-

---

[1] *Sermons for Saints' Days*, No. XXXI., fol. 61, col. 2, No. XXXVIII., fol. 76, col. 4. Also in the *XXIV. Miscellaneous Sermons*, No. XIX., fol. 175, col. 1. Under *viri evangelici* in these places, at least in the two last, are chiefly meant Wycliffe's itinerant preachers. But of *doctores evangelici* he speaks in *De Civili Domino*, MS. 1340, fol. 163, col. 1.

ture principle. In particular, it may be in place to mention that one of his opponents accuses him of being, on this point, an adherent of the 'heretic Occam;' in other words, that he had borrowed from Occam the principle of resting exclusively on Scripture—as, in fact, men have ever been inclined, in the case of the manifestation of any tendency which appeared suspicious and erroneous, to identify it with, and to derive it entirely from, some earlier teaching which had been already condemned and branded as unsound doctrine. The fact of this accusation having been made I know from Wycliffe's own words, as in his book, *Of the Truth of Holy Scripture*, he takes notice of the objection, and replies to it.[1] His words are to the effect that three trustworthy men, according to the information of his nameless opponent, had said that Wycliffe did exactly what 'that heretic' Occam and his followers had done before him, viz., he took his stand upon the literal sense of Holy Scripture, and would submit to no other judgment whatever. Farther on, where he answers this accusation, Wycliffe replies, among other things, that he had neither borrowed his principles from Occam, nor originated them himself; instead of that, they are irrefragably grounded in Holy Scripture itself, and are in repeated instances set forth also by the holy Fathers. Now, this assertion of Wycliffe is fully confirmed when we look into Occam's own writings upon the subject. He appeals, indeed, wherever possible, to Holy Scripture (particularly in his controversial pieces against Pope John XXII.), and he knows how to select his proof-passages with intelligence and judgment;[2] but still there is an important difference between him and Wycliffe on the subject of the rank and prerogative of biblical authority. The difference is this, that Occam always appeals to, and claims authority for, Scripture and Church-teaching *in combination*—thinks of the two as being always found in harmony. Evidently he cannot for a moment reconcile himself to the thought that the sanctioned doctrines of the Church itself, as well as the teaching of the Fathers of the Church, must first be tested by the help of Scripture.[3] Whereas Wycliffe

Wycliffe's opponents.

Wycliffe and Occam.

[1] *De Veritate Scrip. Sac.*, c. 14, fol. 40, col. 4. Comp. fol. 41, col. 3.
[2] *E.g.*, *Defensorium contra Joannem papam XXII.*, in *Fasciculus rerum expetendarum*, etc., ed. Brown, 1690, fols. 439–465. *Dialogus* in Goldast, *Monarchia*, Frankfort, 1668, II., fols. 398–957. *Opus nonaginta dierum contra errores Joannis XXII. papae de utili dominio rerum ecclesiasticarum*, etc. Goldast, II., fols. 993–1236.
[3] Occam, in his *Dialogus*, Lib. II., fol. 410, in Goldast, investigates the question of what constitutes false doctrine, and he brings into view the principle as one which had been held by some, while at the same time himself opposing it, that only those doctrines should be held to be orthodox and necessary to salvation which are taught either directly or indirectly in Holy Scripture. With this principle, Wycliffe's, it is true, is identical; but there is nothing to show, notwithstanding, that he had borrowed it from any quarter.

distinguishes quite clearly between Scripture and Church-teaching, and recognises the Bible as the supreme standard by which even the doctrines of the Church and the Fathers are to be tried. In brief, any dependence of Wycliffe upon Occam for his Scripture principle is an allegation which cannot with any show of right be maintained. On the contrary, Wycliffe took a decided step in advance towards the truly evangelical standpoint, the standpoint of the Reformers of the sixteenth century. Wycliffe took this step, in our judgment, quite independently; and it could not have been owing to a mere self-deception that he was conscious of having derived his principle of the absolute authority of the Bible, and the Bible alone, from no other source than from the Scripture itself, by means of his own personal investigations.

Before Wycliffe's time, the Waldenses came the nearest to the Biblical principle of the Reformation, when, in their desire to justify their practice of free lay preaching in opposition to the Romish hierarchy, they appealed from the existing law of the Church to Divine law, to the Word of God, to Holy Scripture. They thus set against Church tradition and Church law the Holy Scriptures as the higher and decisive authority, by which they measured and tested not only the prohibition of lay preaching, but also other ordinances and traditions of the existing Church.[1] Still, it must be remembered that, although the Waldenses were led by their practical necessities to see and to make use of the normal authority of the Holy Scriptures, they failed to grasp and consciously to realise the Bible principle itself *as such;* whereas in the case of Wycliffe we find all this in full measure; and we need not remind the reader again that Wycliffe appears to have had only an imperfect knowledge of all that relates to the Waldenses.

Wycliffe and the Waldenses.

We cannot leave this subject before touching upon several points, which, though not of first-rate importance, are yet by no means of subordinate interest.

The first of these has reference to *the interpretation of Scripture.* And here we have reached the point which we before hinted at, where I believe I am able to show an important advance in the personal development of Wycliffe. The Scripture principle attains to only half its rights, so long as, though the Bible is acknowledged to be the supreme and decisive authority, yet in practice the authority of Church tradition is nevertheless exalted as the standard of Scripture interpretation. For then the tradition which had been before repudiated comes in again by a back door,

Interpretation of Scripture.

---

[1] Dieckhoff, *Die Waldenser in Mittelalter.* Göttingen, 1851, pp. 171, 267.

and under cover of the motto 'Holy Scripture alone,' the authority of the Church, and of traditional Church doctrine, asserts itself once more.

At this latter stage of opinion Wycliffe found himself at a time when, as Doctor of Theology, he recognised as an authority, apart from reason, only the Holy Scripture, not tradition. At the same time he still held two guides to be indispensable to the understanding and interpretation of Scripture, viz., Reason and the interpretation of the Holy Church doctors as approved by the Church.[1] The work in which he so expresses himself respecting Scripture and its interpretation was written at latest in the year 1376. But only a few years later he had already come to see that not even in the work of Scripture interpretation can the tradition of the Church have a decisive weight. In the third book of his treatise *De Civili Dominio*, c. 26, he opposes the opinion that every part of Scripture is of doubtful meaning, because it can only be understood by the help of the doctors of the Church, and these doctors may put us in a difficulty by opposing interpretations; and because it was competent for the Church of Rome to decide that any part of Scripture has a sense the opposite of that which had hitherto been assumed. To which Wycliffe replies, 'No created being has power to reverse the sense of the Christian faith—the holy doctors put us in no difficulty, but rather teach us to abstain from the love of novelties, and to be sober-minded.' But the chief thought which he opposes to this view is that 'the Holy Ghost teaches us the meaning of Scripture, as Christ opened the Scriptures to the apostles.'[2]

Tradition and Scripture interpretation.

Here we see that Wycliffe has already begun to have doubts respecting the right of the Church to speak with a decisive voice in the matter of Scripture interpretation. He means what he says when he asserts that 'the Holy Ghost instructs us in the understanding of Scripture.' The only remaining question is, By what means and in what way do we arrive at certainty that the sense which we find in a given passage, or in Scripture as a whole, is really given to us by the Holy Ghost? It would, in Wycliffe's own judgment, be to enter upon a dangerous path, for an interpreter to be so bold as to claim to be assured by the illumination of the Holy Ghost that he had hit

---

[1] In Pref. to Book I., *De Dominio Divino*, MS. 1339, fol. 1, col. 1: *Innitar . . . in ordine procedendi rationi et sensui scripturae, cui ex religione et speciali obedientia sum professus. . . . Sed ut sensum hujus incorrigibilis Scripturae sequar securius, innitar ut plurimum duobus ducibus, scilicet rationi philosophis revelatae, et postillationi sanctorum doctorum apud ecclesiam approbatae.*

[2] *De Civili Dominio*, III., 26, MS. 1340, fol. 252, col. 2: *Spiritus Sanctus docet nos sensum Scripturae, sicut Christus aperuit apostolis sensum ejus.*

upon the right meaning of Scripture.¹ Wycliffe goes no farther, indeed, than this, that an indispensable means of attaining to the right understanding of Scripture is the enlightenment of the Scripture inquirer by God Himself; for Christ is the true light which lighteneth every man (John i. 9), and hence it is impossible that any man should have light to know the meaning of Scripture unless he is first enlightened by Christ.² He even confesses on one occasion for himself that at an earlier period of his life he had spoken about the Scripture 'as a child' (1 Cor. xiii. 11), and had felt himself greatly at a loss in the defence of Scripture till his eyes had been graciously opened to perceive the right understanding of it, and to arrive at the conviction of its perfect truth.³ And in connection with this he repeatedly insists upon the truth that a devout and virtuous and humble spirit is requisite if a man would understand the genuine sense of Scripture (*sensus Catholicus*). Putting away all pretentious sophistical hollowness, and renouncing all disputing about mere words, a man must search out the meaning of every Scripture writer in *humility*.⁴

How to learn the meaning of Scripture.

Devoutness and humility.

So much on the *personal* spirit of every honest 'disciple of Scripture.' But on the objective matter itself, by far the most important truth taught by Wycliffe, and what he repeatedly insists upon, is the tenor of Scripture teaching as a whole, from which follows the rule of always explaining single passages in a manner consistent with its general sense; in other words, to interpret Scripture by Scripture. It is a part of this truth when he warns against 'tearing the Scriptures in pieces,' as the heretics do. We must rather take them in connection, and as a whole; only then can they be rightly understood, for the whole of Holy Scripture is the one Word of God. It is in harmony with itself; often one part of Scripture explains the others; it is all the more useful to read Scripture diligently, in order to perceive its harmony with itself.⁵ With such views,

Scripture self-interpreting.

---

¹ *De Veritate Scrip. Sac.*, c. 15, fol. 45, col. 1: *Ne pseudo-discipuli fingant se immediate habere a Deo suam sententiam, ordinavit Deus communem Scripturam sensibilem.*

² *Ib.*, c. 9, fol. 23, col. 1. *De Civili Dominio*, III., 19, fol. 162, col. 2: *Nemo sufficit intelligere minimam Scripturae particulam, nisi Spiritus Sanctus aperuerit sibi sensum, sicut Christus fecit apostolis.*

³ *Ib.*, c. 6, fol. 13, col. 1. Comp. c. 2, fol. 4, col. 4: *Nisi Deus docuerit sensum Scripturae, est error in januis.*

⁴ *Ib.*, c. 15, fol. 45, col. 1: *Ad irradiationem confert sanctitas vitae;* c. 9, fol. 22, col. 4: *Virtuosa dispositio discipuli Scripturae*, is viewed as including *auctoritatis Scripturae humilis acceptatio;* c. 5, fol. 12, col. 1: *Sensus auctoris humiliter indagandus.*

⁵ *Ib.*, c. 19, fol. 62, col. 3: *Tota Scriptura sacra est unum Dei verbum.* Comp. c. 12, fol. 31, col. 1: *Tota lex Christi est unum perfectum verbum procedens de ore Dei;* c. 4, fol. 9, col. 4: *Non licet lacerare Scripturam sacram, sed allegare eam in sua integritate ad sensum auctoris.* Comp. c. 6, fol. 15, col. 3: *Haeretici lacerando . . . negant Scripturam sacram*

it may easily be conceived that Wycliffe is no friend of arbitrary interpretation, which played so large a part at that period; he opposes it often enough. And although he now no longer recognises in principle that the traditional interpretation of the Church is the authorised guide, still the *consensus* of the Fathers in the understanding of Scriptures has great weight in his judgment, in any case where it occurs: more than once he lays stress upon the *consonantia cum sensu Doctorum*.[1]

But as Wycliffe sets out from the conviction, which he derived chiefly from Augustine, that Holy Scripture includes in itself all truth —partly mediately, partly immediately—so he maintains, on the one hand, that reason is indispensable to the right understanding of Scripture; and, on the other hand, that the right understanding of Scripture is the only thing which can work in the mind a joyful and unlimited assent to its contents.[2]

<small>Reason and faith.</small>

It is well known that in mediæval times the conviction was firmly held that Holy Scripture contains a manifold—indeed, a fourfold sense. To this traditional opinion Wycliffe nowhere opposes himself. Ever and anon, as in his sermons, he expressly assents to it. It is, however, characteristic of the good sense and sobriety of his thinking that he takes as his starting-point the literal sense of Scripture; and that he claims this sense to be the indispensable, the never-to-be-depreciated, and the abiding basis of all thorough and deep understanding of the Scriptures. He knows right well that a reckless man is in a position to pervert the whole sense of Scripture, if he denies the literal sense and invents a figurative sense at his pleasure. In opposition to this, he lays down the principle that all the counsels of Christ, as all Holy Scripture in general, must be observed to the letter, as every particle of Scripture, in virtue of its incontrovertible contents, is true. The literal sense, indeed, may be taken in two ways: sometimes according to first appearances, as ignorant grammarians and logicians take it; at other times according to that understanding of it which an orthodox teacher

<small>Literal and spiritual sense of Scripture.</small>

---

esse veram, et non concedendo eam ex integro capiunt; e contra autem catholici allegant pro se Scripturam sacram, . . . cum acceptant ejus autenticam veritatem ex integro ad sensum, quem sancti doctores docuerant. Farther, c. 9, fol. 22, col. 3: *Crebra lectio partium Scripturae videtur ex hoc necessarium* (sic), *quod saepe una pars Scripturae exponit aliam. Prodest crebro legere partes Scripturae pro habendo conceptu suae concordantiae.* In the *Miscellaneous Sermons*, No. XL., fol. 213, col. 1, Wycliffe observes: *Sunt enim veritates Scripturae quae sunt verba Dei, sic connexa, quod unumquodque juvat quodlibet.*

[1] *De Veritate Scrip. Sac.*, c. 15, fol. 45, col. 1. Comp. c. 12, fol. 31, col. 4.

[2] Lewald, in *Zeitschrift für Historische Theologie*, 1846, p. 177. *De Veritate Scripturae*, c. 9, fol. 22, col. 4: *Utrobique in Scriptura sacra est conformitas rationi, et per consequens ratio est testis necessarius ad habendam sententiam scripturarum.*

acquires by the instruction of the Holy Ghost. And that, precisely, is the *spiritual sense*, to reach which the doctors of Holy Scripture are specially bound to use all their endeavours.[1]

On this subject I find a thought expressed which is thoroughly to the point, that there is nothing like a gap intervening betwixt the literal and the spiritual sense; but that the latter is immediately connected with the simple sense of the words; and that everything depends on determining the spiritual sense which is couched in the literal sense. And this is what Wycliffe also does in the interpretation which he gives to Scripture. As a rule, he takes his start from the literal sense; and, as remarked above, he knows, on numerous occasions, how to make Scripture passages yield a sense as simple as it is full and rich.

The Curialists in Wycliffe's time were accustomed to found upon Luke xxii. 38—'See, here are two swords,' taken along with the answer of Jesus, 'It is enough'—a Scripture proof of the dogma, that to Peter, and therefore to the Pope as his rightful successor, there appertains a twofold power—the spiritual and the temporal; this double power being signified, figuratively, by the two swords. In opposition to this, Wycliffe observes, with the support of Augustine's rules of interpretation, that such a leap from the literal sense to the spiritual avails nothing, if this figurative meaning is not founded upon other passages of Scripture. Now, he continues, this mystical sense of Peter's double power of the keys has nowhere else any basis in Scripture; and the whole, therefore, is merely a sophistical, false conclusion, originating in the suggestion of a wicked spirit.[2] Bearing in mind this well-founded leaning to the literal sense of Holy Scripture, Wycliffe's favourable judgment of Nicolas of Lyra, who was his contemporary (d. 1340), may be readily understood. In adducing some of his interpretations, he calls him a 'modern, indeed, but a thoughtful and pregnant interpreter of Scripture according to the letter.'[3] As a proof of the great attention which Wycliffe pays to the usage of language (*usus loquendi*), even in small particles, let the circumstance be mentioned here, that in investigating the question of man's ability for good, apart from grace, he

Illustration: the 'Two Swords.'

---

[1] *De Veritate Scrip. Sac.*, c. 2, fol. 4, col. 3: *Et sic posset proterviens totum sensum Scripturae subvertere negando sensum literalem et fingendo sensum figurativum ad libitum. De Civili Dominio,* III., 19: *Omnia Christi consilia—sicut et tota Scriptura—ad literam observanda,* etc. *Et iste sensus est spiritualis, circa quem doctores sacrae paginae debent specialiter laborare.* Comp. c. 9, fol. 56, col. 2.

[2] *De Quatuor Sectis Novellis*, MS. 3929, fol. 232, col. 4: *Non valet saltus a literali sensu Scripturae ad sensum misticum, nisi ille sensus misticus sit alicubi fundatus.*

[3] *De Veritate Scrip. Sac.*, c. 12: *Doctor de Lyra, licet novellus, tamen copiosus et ingeniosus postillator Scripturae ad literam, scribit,* etc.

remarks upon the distinction between ἀφ' ἑαυτῶν and ἐξ ἑαυτῶν (2 Cor. iii. 5); and then, after a comparison of passages bearing a resemblance to each other in point of expression, he adds the observation that the Apostle Paul, on good grounds, was careful in his use of prepositions and adverbs.[1] On weighing this observation well, we immediately perceive that, if logically carried through, it would form the basis of a rational system of grammatical interpretation. We are not entitled to suppose, of course, that Wycliffe was aware of any such bearing of the thoughts which he expressed; but the expression appears, nevertheless, worthy of remark, as a slight indication of his fine observation and careful interpretation of terms.

Careful attention to language.

To the question in what relation to each other Wycliffe placed the Old and New Testaments, the only answer that can be given is that while he exhibits, on more than one side, the difference between the two revelations, he is yet not clearly aware of their fundamental difference. In repeated instances he has occasion to speak of the distinction between the two Testaments. Not seldom does he mention, in connection with his censure of the encroachments of the hierarchy upon the civil province, that the New Testament does not meddle with that sphere.[2] But in one place he examines the distinction in question upon its purely scientific side, under several heads, viz., as to their respective contents, authorship, kind and manner of revelation, degree of perfection, etc.[3] And here Wycliffe, it is true, also speaks to the effect that in the Old Testament the prevailing thing is *fear;* in the New Testament, *love*.[4] This appears to be quite apposite. He fails, notwithstanding, as already said, in the right insight into the radical and essential difference between law and gospel. He makes use, indeed, of these two simple and weighty designations of the two Testaments; and also characterises quite accurately the spirit of the man who stands under the law, and of the man who lives in the state of grace. But the single circumstance that he so often, and without the least misgiving, speaks of the evangelical *law* (*lex Evangelica*), and describes Christ as our *lawgiver* (*Legifer*), is a sufficient indication to us that he had not yet become fully conscious of the essential difference between Moses and Christ, law and gospel,

Relation of the two Testaments.

Defective views.

---

[1] *De Dominio Divino*, III., c. 5, fol. 84, col. 2 : *Apostolus autem de ratione notabili respexit praepositiones et adverbia*.

[2] *De Officio Pastorali*, II., c. 7, p. 39 : *Christus renuit judicium seculare, quod approbat in lege veteri.*

[3] *Liber Mandatorum*, c. 7–9, MS. 1339, fol. 104, col. 1 ; fol. 112, col. 1.

[4] *Ib.*, c. 7, fol. 105, col. 2 : *Brevis est differentia legis et evangelii, timor et amor.* Comp. c. 8, fol. 107, col. 1 : *Lex nova tanquam amorosa est lege timorosa perfectior.*

law and grace. The deeper reason of this we shall find below, in his doctrine of the way of salvation. It lies in this, that he had not yet come in sight of the *material* principle of Protestantism—justification by faith alone. We have, accordingly, no ground for understanding the title of honour which was given him of *Doctor Evangelicus* in the full sense of a decidedly Pauline theology, and of a truly evangelical doctrine of salvation. If Wycliffe had been a *Doctor Evangelicus* in his doctrine of the way of salvation, as he was in his doctrine of the sole authority of Scripture, he would not, humanly speaking, have remained a mere precursor of the Reformation, but would have been himself a Reformer.

That Wycliffe recognised the right of all Christians to the use of the Bible is a point which it is hardly necessary to dwell upon here, after having seen above, in the sixth and seventh chapters, how emphatically he inculcated the duty of preaching God's Word, and how he had translated it into English in order to make it accessible to the people. We may remark, however, that the deep veneration which he felt for the Word of God, and the knowledge which he had acquired of its infinite value, were enough to lead him to the conclusion that the Bible was a book for every man. This thought he expresses often enough in the clearest manner, not only in the treatise *Of the Truth of Holy Scripture*, where this was most to be expected, but also in other writings. In the work just mentioned he says in one place, the 'Holy Scripture is the faultless, most true, most perfect, and most holy law of God, which it is the duty of all men to learn to know, to defend, and to observe, inasmuch as they are bound to serve the Lord in accordance with it, under the promise of an eternal reward.'[1] In *The Mirror for Temporal Lords*, he demands for all believing people immediate access to the Holy Scriptures, chiefly on the ground that Christian truth is made known more clearly and accurately there than the priests are able to declare it; while many of the prelates besides are quite ignorant of Scripture, and others of them intentionally hold back from the people certain portions of Scripture doctrine.[2] And in his English tract, the *Wyckett*, he exclaims with emotion, 'If God's Word is the life of the world, and every word of God is the life of the human soul, how may any Antichrist, for dread of God,

The Bible a book for all.

---

[1] *De Veritate Scripturae Sac.*, c. 7, fol. 17, col. 4: *quam omnes homines tenentur cognoscere defendere et servare, cum secundum illam tenentur sub obtentu aeterni praemii Domino ministrare.*

[2] *Speculum Secularium Dominorum,* c. 1. *Vide* my essay, *Wiclif und die Lollarden, Zeitschrift für histor. Theologie,* 1853, p. 433, note 30. Comp. Lewald, *Theologische Doctrin des Johann Wycliffe,* in the same *Zeitschrift,* 1846, p. 180.

take it away from us that be Christian men, and thus suffer the people to die for hunger in heresy and blasphemy of men's laws, that corrupteth and slayeth the soul?'[1]

4.—Doctrine of God and the Divine Trinity.

IN the first four chapters of his *Trialogus*, Wycliffe goes into the proofs of the existence of God. He occupies himself partly with the ontological proofs, in which he closely follows Anselm of Canterbury in his *Proslogium*, partly with the cosmological proofs. In the former he starts from the idea of 'The Highest Thinkable,' and comes to the conclusion that this highest thinkable also exists. In the latter he starts from the idea of a cause, and arrives at the existence of a last and highest cause.[2] As Wycliffe in this place appropriates to himself trains of thought which had already been made use of by previous thinkers, and appears to be peculiar only in the reflections which he makes upon them, it is not necessary for me to enter farther into them here, and I content myself with referring to the exposition of them given by Lewald.

The Divine existence.

In his inquiry into the attributes of God, on the other hand, we come in sight of a peculiarity of Wycliffe's doctrine, which we may briefly indicate as *positivity*, in the philosophical sense, or as realism. The subject discussed is the nature of our idea of the infinitude of God. Wycliffe starts from the axiom that God is the absolutely perfect Being. Following Anselm of Canterbury and his *Proslogium*, he lays down the twofold principle—(1) God is the highest that can be thought; (2) God is the best which exists;[3] and in the inquiry into God's attributes he always proceeds upon the ruling principle that God is all which it is better to be than not to be.[4] But according to all this an idea of God may be formed quite different from Wycliffe's idea of Him. The infinitude of God may be thought of in a vague and absolutely indefinite sense, or in the sense of a positive and substantive perfection. Wycliffe takes the latter view with distinct consciousness and decision. He insists on its being understood, not merely in a negative but positive sense, that God is immeasurable and infinite, as God possesses a positive perfection in this respect.[5]

The Divine attributes.

Infinity.

---

[1] *Wycket*, Oxford, 1828, p. 5.
[2] *Trialogus*, I. c. 1–4, pp. 39–52. Comp. Lewald, *Theologische Doctrin Wyclife's* in *Zeitschrift für histor. Theologie*, 1846, p. 188.
[3] *Ib.*, I., c. 4, p. 50: *Deus est, quo majus cogitari non potest,* p. 49: *Deus est optima rerum mundi.*
[4] *Ib.*, I., c. 4, p. 52: *Deus est quidquid melius est esse quam non esse.*
[5] *Ib.*, c. 5, p. 54: *Non solum negative sed positive conceditur Deum esse infinitum, . . . cum Deus habeat positivum perfectionis in istis denominationibus.*

The precise meaning of this will become clear when we take up single attributes of God. As to God's *omnipotence*, Wycliffe decidedly rejects the idea of a wholly unlimited power of doing. It does not follow from God's omnipotence that He has the power to become less than He is, or the power to lie, etc. Neither is it allowable to conclude, on the other hand, that God's power is a limited one because He is unable to do what men do, namely, to lie, or to sin in any way; for to lie, or to sin, does not mean the doing of something, but abstaining from the doing of the good.[1] Wycliffe regards it as the act of a mistaken imagination when men suppose that God is able to bring into existence an infinite world for Himself; he puts in the place of an alleged unlimited and boundless power the idea of a power conditioned and limited by no other power, the *greatest positive* power of all.[2] In other words, he conceives of the Divine omnipotence as a power self-determining, morally regulated, ordered by inner laws (*potentia Dei ordinata*, in opposition to *potentia absoluta*).[3] He thus arrives at the proposition that God's almighty power and His actual work of creation and causation are coincident with and cover each other.

<small>Omnipotence.</small>

In a similar way he expresses himself respecting the Divine *omniscience*. This appears to him to be in every respect a *real* or actual wisdom. God's wisdom is a thing of absolute necessity, for He necessarily knows, first of all, Himself, and also all of which He is the Creator. But the conclusion which Wycliffe draws from the Divine all-knowledge is a peculiar one, viz., that all which ever was, or shall be, *is*. This he proves in the following way: Whatever was or shall be, God shall know it. If He shall know that it is, then He knows *now* that it is, for God cannot begin or cease to know anything; but if God knows anything as being, that thing *is*. Therefore if anything was or shall be, so is it.[4] Further, Wycliffe rejects the distinction which men were inclined to make between God's power to know and His actual knowing, and instead of this lays down the proposition, God *can* know nothing unless what He knows is fact. For if God *can* know it, He knows it *now*, for He cannot make a beginning or an end of knowing; and God knows nothing but what is, at least in the sense of the *ens intelligibilis*.[5]

<small>Omniscience.</small>

---

[1] *Trialogus*, c. 5, p. 53. Comp. Lewald, pp. 196, 215.

[2] *Ib.*, I., c. 2, p. 42: *Deus est maximae potentiae positivae*, etc.; comp. c. 10, p. 69: *Sicut Deus ad intra nihil potest producere, nisi absolute necessario illud producat, sic nihil ad extra potest producere, nisi pro suo tempore illud producat.* Again, p. 71: *Omnipotentia Dei et ejus actualis creatio vel causatio adaequantur.*

[3] *De Dominio Divino*, III., c. 5, MS. 1340, fol. 30, col. 1: *Phantasiantes de Dei potentia absoluta.*

[4] *Trialogus*, I., c. 5. p. 52.

[5] *Ib.*, I., c. 9, p. 67.

With this again connects itself Wycliffe's view of God's *eternity*. He deduces this eternity from the consideration that if there existed any *measure* (*mensura*) which was antecedent to God, then God Himself could not be the first and highest cause, from which it appears that eternity is the proper name for the measure of the Godhead. Accordingly, he regards eternity expressly not as a mere attribute which indwells in God, but as identical with God Himself. But eternity in itself is absolutely indivisible—it has no *before* and *after*, like time.[1] From this last proposition he then deduces the Divine unchangeableness. God cannot change His thoughts, His understanding and knowing. What He thinks and knows, He knows eternally. If He were to change His thoughts according to the change of their object, He would then be in the highest degree changeable in His thoughts. Yea, God's thought would be constructed out of observations made from moment to moment.[2] With this again is connected the doctrine of what he calls *the deep Metaphysic*—*i.e.*, his own realistic philosophy, viz., that all which ever has been or shall be is present to the Divine mind, *i.e.*, in the sense of real existence.[3]

Eternity.

The doctrine of the Divine Trinity Wycliffe evidently took up simply in the form in which it had been in part conceived by the ancient Church, and in part handed down by the scholastic doctors before him. We should in vain seek in his writings for any peculiar and original treatment of this article, especially on the basis of Scripture teaching. There is only a single point of this Trinitarian doctrine, as it seems to me, in which he felt a peculiar interest—the doctrine of God the Son, as the Logos. From all that Wycliffe says, as well in the *Trialogus* as occasionally in other writings, on the subject of the Trinity, it appears indubitable that he presupposes, and proceeds upon as conclusively established, the whole body of Church dogma as it was sanctioned in the fourth century, and was finally completed by Augustine. He operates with the technical terms of the Latin Church Fathers—*Nature* and *Person*, as fixed by ecclesiastical sanction; and yet he is not altogether unacquainted with the definitions of the Greek theology. Still, so far as he occupies himself with such definitions, he by no means penetrates into the subject any deeper than others had done before him.[4]

The Trinity.

---

[1] *Trialogus*, I., c. 2, p. 42: *Aeternitas, quae est omnino indivisibilis, et cum sit ipse Deus, non accidentaliter sibi inest, nec habet prius et posterius sicut tempus.*

[2] *De Veritate Scrip. Sac.*, c. 19, fol. 62, col. 2: *Deus non potest mutare sensum—vel intellectum suum, sed omne quod sentit, intelligit . . . aeternaliter illud cognoscit.* Wycliffe appeals in support of this partly to Holy Scripture, *e.g.*, Mal. iii. 6, etc., partly to authorities such as Augustine, Anselm, Bradwardine.

[3] *Ib.*, c. 6, fol. 19, col. 3.

[4] *Trialogus*, I, c. 6, especially p. 59.

Further, as to what concerns the speculative proof of the doctrine of the Trinity, Wycliffe, it is true, devotes to it much attention. In the *Trialogus*, the sophistical opponent Pseustis censures it as an undue pretension of the reason, and as an injury done to faith and its exclusive light, that so specific an article of faith as that of the Trinity should be proved by arguments of reason.[1] Wycliffe himself, speaking in the character of Phronesis, adheres to the belief that the reason is able to attain to a knowledge of this truth. He finds no difficulty in maintaining that Plato and other philosophers had grasped it. But he laid particular stress, notwithstanding, upon the assertion that a *meritorious* knowledge (*meritorie cognoscere*), i.e., a saving knowledge of the mystery of the Trinity, is possible only to that faith which springs from Divine grace and illumination.[2] As to grounds of reason for the doctrine, however, Wycliffe remarks that it is self-evident that here any such proof of the 'why' is out of the question, and that only the 'that'—the Divine fact itself—can admit of such proof; in other words, the Divine Trinity cannot possibly be grasped and proved from its relation to any cause higher than itself, because God Himself is the highest and last cause; rather this truth can only be proved from facts which are the effects wrought by the Triune God.[3] But when we look more narrowly at the proofs themselves, which Wycliffe partly indicates and partly states at length, we find that they are merely the same which were first brought forward by Augustine in his great work on the Trinity, founded upon natural analogies—memory, cognition, will, and the like—and which among the scholastics had already been appropriated to his own use by Anselm in his *Monologium*.

The Trinity proved by reason.

As already observed, Wycliffe interests himself by far the most in the idea of God the Son as the Logos. For in this idea of the Logos lies at the same time Wycliffe's doctrine of ideas; in other words, the doctrine of Realism. The Logos—the substantive Word—is the inclusive content of all ideas—of all realities that are *intelligible* (capable of being realised in thought), and is thereby the mediating element or member between God and the world. And yet in the Logos both the God-idea and the world-idea are immediately one. We need not wonder, therefore, if in Wycliffe we sometimes stumble upon propositions which verge too nearly on Pantheism, such as this: 'Every existing thing is in reality God

Doctrine of the Logos.

---

[1] *Trialogus*, I., c. 6, p. 54.
[2] *Ib.*, p. 56.
[3] *Ib.*, c. 7, p. 58, applying the Aristotelian distinction between proofs which come to a διότι, and such as come to a ὅτι, or, as Wycliffe expresses himself, *demonstratio propter quid*, and *demonstratio, quod est*. Comp. Lewald, p. 199.

Himself, for every creature which can be named is, in regard to its "intelligible" existence, and consequently its chief existence, in reality the Word of God' (John i. 3). But hardly has he used this language when he becomes conscious that this thesis has its dangerous side, and therefore immediately guards himself against the conclusion which might be drawn from it, that God is the only existence.[1] His words are, 'But this gives no colour to the conclusion that every creature whatever is every other creature whatever, or that every creature whatever is God.' Here we see that to give support to Pantheism is not at all his meaning or design; and if, notwithstanding, he approaches it here too closely, it should not be lost sight of, in excuse for him, that Augustine himself, in whose footsteps he treads in the doctrine of the Logos and in that of ideas, has not always known how to avoid Pantheistic conceptions.

Pantheistic tendencies disclaimed.

5.—Doctrine of the World, of the Creation, and of the Divine Dominion.

FROM the preceding, we may already conjecture what Wycliffe's views will be on the subject of *the world;* for his ideas of the attributes of God, such as omnipotence and omniscience, could not be determined without having regard to the things of the world. Thus it does not surprise us that Wycliffe declares the Creation to have been an act of God which was remote from all arbitrariness of determination—an act which in its own nature was necessarily determinate. The School of the Scotists, following the lead of Duns Scotus himself, conceived of the Divine Will and creative work as a matter of freedom and of unconditioned discretion, and maintained, in logical consistency with this view, that God could have done otherwise than He has actually done. He does not choose to do anything because it is the best, but it is the best because He chooses to do it; and God might have created the world otherwise than He has created it.[2]

Creation.

In direct opposition to such views, Wycliffe takes the side of the Thomists, and maintains that it was impossible for God to have

---

[1] *Liber Mandatorum*, c. 9, fol. 110, col. 1: *Omne ens est realiter ipse Deus; dictum enim est in materia de ydeis, quod omnis creatura nominabilis secundum esse intelligibile et per consequens esse principalissimum est realiter verbum Dei* (John i.). *Nec ex hoc est color, quod quaelibet creatura sit quaelibet, aut quaelibet sit Deus.* Comp. *Trialogus*, I., c. 3, p. 47.

[2] Comp. Erdmann, *Gundriss der Geschichte der Philosophie*, I., 1866, p. 424.

made the world larger or fairer, or more rapid in its movement, etc., than it is.[1] Like Thomas Aquinas, he lays great stress upon the aphorism expressed in the Book of Wisdom (xi. 22), that God ordered everything by measure, number, and weight.[2] He believes that he discerns therein not only a fact of experience, but also an inner law of the Divine Will and creative action, according to which they are free only in this sense, that they are at the same time determined by an inward necessity.

Scotist and Thomist views.

Still, it does not follow from this that Wycliffe meant to say that the existence of the world is a necessity, that God *must needs* have created it. In one passage the only thing he says at all to this effect, and that with a certain timidity of tone, is that God could not for ever have withheld Himself from creating any being, because otherwise He would not have been in the highest degree communicative and good.[3] At all events, that is only a *moral* necessity, conditioned by the goodness and love of God—His own special attributes. But Wycliffe concedes so much as this, that every creature of God, in so far as we regard its intelligible nature, is as necessary and as eternal as God Himself, for its intelligible nature is coincident with God Himself—with the substantive Logos.[4]

On the other hand, he draws a sharp line of distinction between God and the world in respect to their mode of existence. God alone is eternal, immutable, without *fore* and *after*. The world is temporal, *i.e.*, it has a mutable existence, including in it a *fore* and an *after*. Wycliffe supposes, besides, as Albertus Magnus had done before him, a third medium existence, which he calls *aevum* or *aevitas*, and which belongs to pure, spiritual beings, as angels, and the blessed in heaven; and here, too, there is no succession of time. Hereby *aevitas* is distinguished from time; but how it is to be distinguished from eternity cannot be gathered from his explanations.[5] Time and eternity form a decisive difference between the world and God. 'It is one thing for a thing to exist always, and another for a thing to be eternal; the world exists always, because at every time, and yet it is not eternal, because it is created; for the moment of creation must have a beginning, as the world had.'[6]

God and the world contrasted.

---

[1] *De Dominio Civili,* III., c. 5, fol. 29, col. 1 : *Impossibile fuisset ipsum fecisse mundum majorem, pulcriorem,* etc.

[2] *Trialogus,* IV., c. 40, p. 390, and *De Dominio Civili,* in the passage just quoted : *Christus ponit cuncta in mensura, numero, et pondere.*

[3] *De Dominio (in communi),* c. 7, fol. 123, col. 1 : *Concedunt quidam, quod Deus non posset perpetuo continere non producendo aliquam creaturam, quia tunc non esset summe communicativus ac bonus,* etc.

[4] *Trialogus,* II., c. 1, p. 76.

[5] *Ib.,* I., c. 2, p. 79.

[6] *Ib.,* I., c. 1, p. 76 : *Aliud est rem semper esse et eam aeternaliter esse, . . . instans creationis oportet incipere sicut mundum.*

Accepting the ideas of the Aristotelian metaphysics, as taken up and further developed by scholastics like Thomas Aquinas, Wycliffe distinguishes in the creation and in all single existences, substance and form, *i.e.*, the substratum capable of receiving determination, and the being which determinates it. It is only both these united which make a creature to be what it is; and these three, including the resultant creature, answer to the Trinity. The determinating form answers to the Logos; the substantive matter answers to God the Father; and their union into one points significantly to the communion of the uncreated Spirit.[1]

Substance and form.

Instead, however, of going further into the cosmology of Wycliffe, it may be more worth while, as this cosmology contains little that is peculiar to himself, to learn what he teaches on the subject of THE DIVINE DOMINION.

This is a part of his teaching which is quite as characteristic as it has been hitherto little known. The latter circumstance is very easily explained by the fact that the works to which Wycliffe committed his views upon this subject have not only never been printed, but are also nowhere to be met with in England, and have come down to us in the Vienna manuscripts alone. The three Books of *The Divine Dominion* (*De Dominio Divino*) form a preliminary work to the great theological collective work of Wycliffe, the *Summa in Theologia;* and in the repeated perusal of the books *De Dominio Divino* I have received the impression that we have here lying marked out before us the path of transition by which Wycliffe passed over from the philosophical to the properly theological period of his life and authorship. The work itself is of a mixed nature—metaphysical investigations and biblico-theological inquiries passing over into each other. The author, also, specially values, not only scholastics like Anselm of Canterbury, but also the Fathers of the Church, for their philosophical reasonings in support of Christian doctrines. The preface to the work gives occasion to the conjecture, as Shirley was the first to remark, that Wycliffe began it not long after his promotion to the Theological Doctorate.[2]

'De Dominio Divino.'

The question at once arises: How came Wycliffe, at this stage of his development, to make precisely this idea of dominion the pole of his philosophico-theological thinking? I am not able to give a direct answer from his own mouth, but, from certain hints and indirect proofs, I think I am able to gather that two facts in the history of his century became points of

'Dominion' Wycliffe's central idea.

---

[1] *Trialogus*, II., c. 4, p. 87.
[2] Introduction to *Fasciculi Zizaniorum*, p. xvi.

attachment for Wycliffe's thinking, and served to direct his thoughts precisely to this idea of Dominion. One of these was the struggle between Church and State which took place on the threshold and in the former half of the fourteenth century—namely, the conflict between France, under Philip the Fair, and Pope Boniface VIII.; and then the conflict between the Emperor, Louis of Bavaria, and Pope John XXII. These conflicts, the former of them especially, disclosed a new bent of the public mind in Europe, and turned much more upon questions of principle than the earlier wrestling-matches between *sacerdotium* and *imperium* under the Emperors of the Staufen race. Men perceived more distinctly than ever before, that the question in dispute was whether the State should be in subjection to the Popedom, and the latter should become an absolute world-monarchy, or whether the State or sovereign power, within the sphere of civil life and affairs, should be independent of the Popedom. It was a question of lordship. It had to do with *dominion*.

The other fact was the collision between the Papacy and the stricter party of the Franciscans, which, together with the ecclesiastico-theological discussions which took their rise from it, did not pass away without leaving impressions on Wycliffe. Here the question in dispute, which was answered in the affirmative by Occam and others, was, Ought the Franciscan Order to be poor and without property? It was a dispute about *dominium*, in the sense partly of personal and partly of corporate property and rule.

These facts appear to have led Wycliffe to take the idea of *dominium* as the kernel or germ of a whole system of thought. But as a man of deep penetration, he took a more comprehensive view of the subject, and treated it on a much grander scale, than his predecessors, who stood nearer to those conflicts in actual life, and had therefore investigated the questions involved with a much more direct practical interest, indeed, but also from a more restricted point of view. For example, the representatives of the State idea, or the party of Philip the Fair and Louis the Bavarian, contended for the autonomy of the State in purely civil affairs; but Wycliffe goes farther, and recognises, as attaching to the State, both a right and a duty even in the internal affairs of the Church. He widens the *dominium* of the State. Again, the contention of the Franciscans was that the obligation of poverty should be laid only upon the monks, or more strictly upon the Mendicants, and should be stringently enforced. Wycliffe goes farther in this matter also, and would have, in place of dominion, a ministry of humility in poverty imposed upon the clergy at large, upon the spiritual office in general. He takes a deeper view of the subject, and treats it with a more penetrating insight; and herein placed himself in antagonism to a conception which everywhere prevailed in the Middle Age. Through the feudal system all the relations of life had been converted into forms of landed possession, all offices into the form of fiefs, into a sort of territorial property and subordinate *dominion*.[1] A natural consequence of this was that the majority of the masters of Canon Law regarded the spiritual office as a dominion. Wycliffe, on the contrary, recognises it, not as a mastery, but as a service. In his view, it is not a *dominium*, but a *ministerium*.

To come nearer to the subject itself, the plan of Wycliffe's great work—the *Summa in Theologia*—comprehending twelve books on the main subject, besides three preliminary books, is laid out in such a way that the doctrine of the *Dominium* forms the kernel of the whole subject. For he treats, first of all, in the three preliminary books[2] of the Divine dominion, in such wise that the First Book, after some observations of the most general kind, investigates the Subject of the dominion, or who is its lord; the Second Book, the Object of the dominion, or upon whom it is exercised; the Third, the Acts of the dominion, or wherein it consists. In the *Summa* itself, the First Book—*Liber Mandatorum* or *De Preceptis*—develops the rightful foundation of all human dominion, viz., the commandments of God. The Second Book—*De Statu Innocentiae*—defines the nature of the dominion which prevailed in the state of innocency as a dominion of man exclusively over nature, and not over his equal. The Third, Fourth, and Fifth Books treat of Civil Dominion. Wycliffe then enters upon the properly ecclesiastical territory. The Sixth Book—*De Veritate Scripturae Sacrae*—establishes the standard authority of the Bible. The Seventh Book is *De Ecclesia*. The Eighth—*De Officio Regis*—discusses the question of Christian Magistracy, or the relation between Church and State. The Ninth Book—*De Potestate Papae*—illustrates the Roman Primacy; and the last three Books treat of the chief evils under which the Church is suffering, viz., the Tenth, *De Simonia*; the Eleventh, *De Apostasia*; the Twelfth, *De Blasphemia*.

---

[1] Augustin Thierry, *Lettres sur l'histoire de France*, 7th edition. Paris, 1842. Lettre IX., p. 148.
[2] *De Dominio Divino:* Lib. I., in 19 chapters, the last of which has remained a fragment; at least this applies to all the three Vienna MSS. which contain this book. Lib. II. contains in the MSS. only five chapters, and Lib. III. only six; both books break off in the middle of the treatment.

In the preliminary work, *Of the Divine Dominion*, Wycliffe illustrates first of all the Idea of Dominion in general. He remarks that it has four sides: the *subject* ruling; the *object* ruled over; the *relation* of the ruler to the ruled; and the *law* whereon the rule is founded. He decides for the following definition, 'Dominion is the relation of a rational being, in virtue of which he is set over another as his servant,'[1]—manifestly an unsatisfactory definition, if judged by a logical standard, as it is only verbal, not substantive, and expresses *idem per idem*. He then gives a survey of the different species of dominion, according to its subjects, its objects, and its foundations. There are three kinds of rational beings, and therefore also three kinds of dominion—divine, angelic, and human. There are also three different objects of dominion, and therefore the distinction between monastic, municipal, and kingly rule. And there is a like difference in the foundations of dominion—natural law, evangelical law, and human law—and thus there is a natural dominion, an evangelical dominion—which is nothing else but a *ministerium*, a service in love in the stead of Christ—and human dominion, *i.e.*, the dominion of force or compulsion.[2]

'Dominion' defined.

No dominion, of whatever kind it is, is absolutely eternal, as it, of course, must first begin with the existence of the ministering creature. God Himself is not called 'Lord' before He has created the world. But God's dominion begins with the creation, and as a consequence of it. To uphold the creatures and to rule them are prerogatives belonging to Him, on the very ground that He is Lord.[3]

The Divine dominion excels every other in all respects—in virtue of its *subject*, inasmuch as God in no way stands in need of the creature put under Him; in virtue of the *ground* upon which His dominion rests, viz., His infinite power as Creator, on which account, also, God's dominion never comes to an end; lastly, in respect to the *object* of His dominion, for the creature must be subject to God whether he will or not.[4]

The Divine Dominion chief of all.

Wycliffe also takes up the question whether the service of God admits of a more or a less, which he answers in the negative; for every creature owes God service with his whole being. Here, however, he remarks that, besides such beings who stand directly under the

---

[1] *De Dominio Divino*, Lib. I., c. 1, fol. 1, col. 2: *Potest dominium sic describi: dominium est habitudo naturae rationalis, secundum quam denominatur suo praefici servienti.*

[2] *Ib.*, I., c. 3, fol. 5, col. 1.

[3] *Ib.*, I., c. 2, fol. 3, col. 6. The observation upon the Divine name 'Lord' is founded upon Genesis ii. 2, where the Vulgate translates the two Hebrew names which here, for the first time, occur together, יְהֹוָה אֱלֹהִים by *Dominus Deus*.

[4] *Ib.*, c. 3, fol. 5, col. 2. Comp. c. 1, fol. 2, col. 1: *Quaelibet creatura necessario servit Deo, ut sibi canit ecclesia: 'Serviunt tibi cuncta, quae creasti.'*

dominion of God—the individual creatures—there are also things which stand under it only indirectly or mediately, *e.g.*, errors and sins. These, indeed, do not themselves serve God; but the persons who commit sin and are the slaves of sin are subject notwithstanding, in the main, to the supreme God.[1] Wycliffe repeatedly returns to this difficult point. In the chapter, especially, where he inquires into the *extent* of the Divine dominion, he enters into a very full and searching investigation respecting the relation of the human will to the absolute dominion of God over all which is and comes to pass.[2] It is, however, not appropriate to enter into this investigation here; we shall find a more suitable place for it below.

The Second Book, as remarked above, treats of the Objects of the Divine Dominion. Here Wycliffe's realistic view of the universe comes at once into view. All dominion applies to what is created, consequently God's dominion connects itself with the order in which the creatures were made. And, as *being* is created before everything else, so God's dominion has first of all to do with created being. God has dominion over the general at an earlier stage than over anything individual which can be named.[3]

Objects of the Divine Dominion.

Finally, the Third Book inquires into the single acts by which dominion is exercised. Of these there are sixteen, of which there are three which belong exclusively to the Divine dominion—creating, upholding, and governing; and thirteen which have a relation to human dominion, while some of them likewise belong to God and the Divine government.[4]

The first among these acts is that of Giving. Wycliffe treats of this first; but as the manuscript before me is incomplete, and breaks off at the close of the sixth chapter, he does not get much beyond this act; for in these few chapters he investigates only the idea of Giving, with the corresponding idea of Receiving;[5] also that of Granting and Recalling, as also that of Lending and Borrowing.[6] Meanwhile we may console ourselves over the fragmentary condition of this Book with the thought that enough of what is characteristic is found in what of it still remains to us. Wycliffe begins his treatment here with the observation that the act of giving belongs, in the highest measure, to God, for God's giving is of all the

Acts of Divine Dominion.

---

[1] *De Dominio Divino*, c. 4, fol. 9, col. 2.
[2] *Ib.*, c. 10, 14–18.
[3] *Ib.*, Lib. II., c. 1, fol. 59, col. 1. As the author at this point immediately enters more deeply into his favourite doctrine of the reality of universals, our MS. breaks off at the fifth chapter before he has returned to his proper subject. Still I see, from the commencement of Book III., that in Book II. he had treated of the ideas of creation, conservation, and government.
[4] *Ib.*, Lib. III., c. 1, fol. 69, col. 1.
[5] *Ib.*, c. 1–3.
[6] *Ib.*, c. 4–6.

richest, and to the creature the most useful—the richest, inasmuch as God never gives to His servants anything without giving to them His chief gift—Himself.[1]

Further, the inquiry respecting the kinds of granting, lending, and so forth, leads up to the idea of merit; and here the author lays down the principle that merit and the means of attaining to merit are absolute gifts of God. He is beforehand with us, awakens us, moves us to the acquiring of merit. But from this again Wycliffe deduces the consequence, not to be undervalued, that no creature can merit anything before God unless it be in consideration of congruity (*de congruo*), but under no circumstances in consideration of worthiness (*de condigno*).[2] To this negative proposition, to which plainly the chief importance attaches, Wycliffe often returns afresh, in order to lay special emphasis upon it, and to prove it in the most convincing manner—a thought in which the evangelical ground-truth does not indeed come purely into daylight, but still comes into view in some degree. We shall by-and-by refer again to these ideas more at length in their own place.

The idea of merit.

In the doctrine of the good and evil angels Wycliffe has little that is peculiar. He accepts the Patristic and Scholastic ideas with regard to differences affecting them, *e.g.*, the difference between the morning-knowledge and the evening-knowledge of the angels—*i.e.*, their foreknowledge and their knowledge from experience. He attaches special importance to the occasions of various kinds which are made use of by the evil spirits, for the temptation and seduction of men; as well as to the conflict with the powers of darkness which at the end of all things will take the form of a tremendous, decisive struggle between the Church of Christ and the Antichrist.

Good and evil Angels.

6.—Doctrine of Man and of Sin.

In his treatment of the Doctrine of Man, Wycliffe mixes up an extraordinary amount of matter which is either of a philosophical kind, or entirely belongs to the natural sciences, especially anatomy and physiology—*e.g.*, the anatomy of the brain,[3] or the question in what way the perceptions of the senses take place.[4] From his manner of speaking on such subjects we see that Wycliffe

Wycliffe's Anthropology.

---

[1] *De Dominio Divino*, c. 3, fol. 71, col. 2: *Deus non dat suis famulis quodvis donum, nisi principaliter det se ipsum.*
[2] *Ib.*, III., c. 4, fol. 78, col. 2: *Nulla creatura potest a Deo mereri aliquid nisi de congruo, sic quod nihil penitus de condigno.* Fol. 79, col. 1: *Creatura penitus nihil a Deo merebitur ex condigno.*
[3] *Trialogus*, II., c. 6, p. 94.
[4] *Ib.*, II., c. 7, p. 97.

possessed not only extensive knowledge in the field of the natural sciences—on the scale, of course, of his own age—but also a sound and accurate judgment on such matters. But this is not the place to take notice of his observations in this field, nor yet of his philosophical expositions respecting the distinction of a double soul in every human being; concerning the mental faculties (cognition, will, and memory; following Augustine), and touching the immortality of the soul.[1] We limit ourselves rather to what is important in a theological sense; and here it is worthy of remark that Wycliffe, as I see from several passages in his unprinted works, finds in the Redemption, quite justifiably, the key to the Creation; and throws a reflex light from the eschatology of Scripture upon its anthropology, in holding fast to the Biblical idea of the *whole* man as a Unit made up of Soul and Body.[2] The greatest importance, however, seems to attach to all that portion of his treatment of 'Man and Sin' which belongs to the moral sphere, viz., the doctrine of the will, the question concerning the Freedom of the Will, and concerning Evil and Sin.

In reference to the human will, Wycliffe lays great stress upon its freedom, for to him it is clear that the moral worth or worthlessness of action is conditioned by the freedom of the will.

Freedom of the Will.

He maintains that 'God has placed man in so great a condition of freedom that He can demand from him absolutely nothing else than what is "meritorious" (*i.e.*, what is of moral worth), and therefore under the condition that man performs it freely.'[3] And yet Wycliffe, quite unmistakably, has a leaning to the Augustinian view. Among all the Fathers Augustine is the man to whom he is at all times most indebted, for whom he cherishes the profoundest respect, and whose disciple he was held to be by his own adherents, who, for this reason, sometimes gave him the name of 'Joannes Augustini.'[4] Wycliffe, moreover, looked upon Thomas of Bradwardine—the *Doctor profundus*—as a teacher with whom he was sensible of standing in intellectual affinity;[5] and manifestly he felt himself one with him not only in a general sense, in virtue

---

[1] *Trialogus*, II., c. 5, p. 90, and c. 8, p. 101. Wycliffe himself, however, in his sermons, does not entirely avoid entering into philosophical questions of this kind, *e.g.*, in No. XXIX. of the *Sermons for Saints' Days*, fol. 57, col. 4.

[2] *E.g.*, in the sermon just now mentioned, fol. 58, col. 1.

[3] *De Ecclesia*, c. 13, fol. 168, col. 3.

[4] According to the testimony of Thomas Walden, *Doctrinale antiquitatum fidei*, I., c. 34, Venetian edition, 1571, vol. I., fol. 105, col. 2: *Sui discipuli vocabant eum famoso et elato nomine Joannem Augustini.*

[5] In the *De Dominio Divino*, c. 14, fol. 139, col. 1, Wycliffe calls *Armachanus* (Archbishop Richard Fitz-Ralph), and the *Doctor profundus*, '*duo praecipui doctores nostri ordinis;*' which, I suppose, could only be intended to mean that these were men with whom he was conscious of being at one in his views.

of his zeal for God's honour and cause,[1] but also in his fundamental view of the all-sufficing grace of God in Christ, and of God's all-determining will. But notwithstanding this, he is so fully convinced of human freedom, that in its defence he places himself in opposition even to a *Doctor profundus*. He agrees with him, indeed, in the main principle that everything which takes place does so of necessity, and, further, in the doctrine that God co-operates in every act of will in the sense of previously determining it;[2] but, notwithstanding this, Wycliffe does not intend in any way to prejudice the freedom of choice of the human will; in particular, he repudiates the conclusion drawn from the main principle, that if any one sins, it is God Himself who determines him to the act.

And here we come to Wycliffe's doctrine of evil. In every action he distinguishes two things, the *act* of a being created by God, and the *feeling* from which the act proceeds. The act itself —the doing of the creature—is good, and is determined by God, who, therefore, so far co-operates in producing it. But the feeling from which the act springs may be a bad, ill-ordered feeling, morally evil and sinful; in causing this perversion of the soul, this evil condition of the will, God in no way co-operates.[3] It is only the intention, the feeling which prompts an act, which makes the act a sin; and that intention or feeling is not from God.

Doctrine of Evil.

Wycliffe here applies the distinction between substance and accident to the subject of evil.[4] 'Every action,' he says, 'which is morally evil, is evil only *accidenter*.' But evidently this investigation of the question is not of a character to solve its knots. For, first of all, there is a multitude of actions, *e.g.*, of deceit, of betrayal, of malice, in which a line of distinction can only be drawn in a forced and artificial way, between the active power of a created being, on the one hand, and the bad or morally censurable intention and feeling of the act, on the other. But, further, the question must be asked, How then does it stand with regard to actions which are moral, pious, and well-pleasing to God? Does God co-operate in such actions only to the extent of aiding the active power of His creature, and not also towards the production of the pious feeling itself? And if the latter is the true view, viz., that God's co-operation extends, in such

God not the author of sin.

---

[1] '*De Causa Dei*' was the title which Bradwardine gave to his principal work. Comp. p. 67 above.
[2] *De Dominio Divino*, I., c. 14, fol. 139, col. 1—a passage in which Wycliffe entirely follows Bradwardine's course of thought.
[3] *Obliquitas animi, malitia voluntatis*. *De Dominio Divino*, I., c. 14, fol. 139, col. 2.
[4] *Ib.*, *Omnis actus—malus moraliter est accidenter solum malus.*

cases, both to active power and feeling—as we must assume to be the case, according to the words of the Apostle quoted by Wycliffe in another place, 'Not that we are sufficient of ourselves to think anything as of ourselves' (2 Corinthians iii. 5)—then arises the question, How comes it that God Himself, in this case, awakens and determines the thoughts and feelings, but does not do so in the other case? And either there appears to be a marvellous inequality, if not arbitrariness, in the Divine procedure, or we are brought back again to the thought that God wills and determines ultimately also the free volition of evil in the creature, because He determines all, and, as the ultimate cause, is the Maker of all.

This is precisely the point on which Wycliffe consciously and deliberately departs from the doctrine of Bradwardine. He gives a decided negative to the view held by the latter, that in the act of sin there is a necessity which excludes all freedom of choice, inasmuch as the distinction between God's permission and His positive will and pleasure is, as Bradwardine alleges, a nullity; and the truth rather is that God's will precedes every action of man, and infallibly determines it, so that no will of the creature is in itself really free. Wycliffe finds here in the *Doctor profundus* an error of which he seeks an explanation in a false antecedent proposition, viz., that every volition in God is an eternal, absolute substance.[1] The thought that God Himself occasions the evil volition in the soul of man is repugnant to the feeling and thinking of Wycliffe, not only on the ground that the sinner would then be in a position to excuse himself with more than a mere appearance of reason, but chiefly on the ground that,

Wycliffe and Bradwardine.

---

[1] *De Dominio Divino*, c. 16, fol. 144, col. 1. He begins by remarking that this subject is one of those things which are, according to 2 Peter iii. 16, hard to be understood, and that not all the Doctors had entertained right notions about it: *Ideo restat ulterius declarandum: si ponatur in actu peccati necessitas ultra contingentiam ad utrumlibet, sicut videtur multis Doctorem pro°undum dicere, ymo quod Deus velit beneplacite hominem peccare; ... quia, ut dicit, omnis Dei permissio, est ejus beneplacitum, cum tam potens dominus non permittit aliquod* (aliud, MS. 1339) *nec aliqualiter, quod non placet. Maximum autem fundamentum in ista materia est de actu volitionis divinae, quod non subsequitur sed praecedit naturaliter quemlibet actum vel effectum. ... Ex isto quidem videtur sibi* (Thomas Bradwardine) *libro* III., 4 *capitulo, quod omnis actus est inevitabilis creaturae, et per consequens nulla volitio creata est pure libera* (per se pure libera, MS. 1339). *Nec mirum, si variet ab aliis in ista materia, quia* III. *libro, c.* 6, *ponit quotlibet volitiones in Deo esse aeternas essentias absolutas. Ideo cum modicus error in principio* (primo, MS. 1339) *scilicet in quaestione, quid est* (quidem, MS. 1339) *hujusmodi voluntatum, facit variationem maximam in opinione de passionibus communiter; non mirum, si variet a sapientibus, qui ponunt, omnes volitiones hujusmodi non esse absolutas substantias,* etc. And here he names Thomas Aquinas (I., Pars Summae, Quaest. 15 and 16), the Doctor subtilis (Duns Scotus), as well as Dominus Armachanus, Lib. xvi., c. 5, *De quaestionibus Armenorum.* In the following chapter, 17th, he came back once more to Bradwardine, in controverting the doctrine maintained in the *De Causa Dei*, II., c. 30, of the inevitability of every act of creature will in presence of the Divine will.

on that pre-supposition, the dark shadow would fall on God Himself, of being privy to sin and consenting to it, and therefore guilty of it. Wycliffe says, in distinct terms, that if that were a correct view, every murderer, robber, or liar would be able to say with reason, 'God determines me to all these acts of transgression, in order to perfect the beauty of the universe.'[1] It is precisely such blasphemous consequences, so dishonouring to the holiness of God, that Wycliffe intends to obviate, and therefore he makes a reservation of autonomous freedom—not absolute, indeed, but relative, and placed out of reach of all compulsion—to the innermost sphere of feeling and of volition.[2]

With this result, however, in reference to moral volition and action, stands connected a view of the whole world of being and becoming, according to which evil is not a being but a not-being; not a positive action, but a defect or negation. *Evil a negation.* This idea of the negativity of evil, Wycliffe, as he himself hints in one place, borrows from no less an authority than Augustine himself. And, in point of fact, however strongly Augustine lays stress upon the power of sin, especially in his controversial writings against the Pelagians, he nevertheless speaks of sin in other places as having only a negative existence. Such, in effect, is the significance of the thought that sin is only an occasion of good—a thought which scholastics like Anselm, Albertus Magnus, and others, have also appropriated from Augustine.[3] But Augustine also expresses himself in the most direct manner to the effect that sin is not a doing, but a defect or omission of doing;[4] it is not anything positive, and therefore has no *causa efficiens*, but only a *causa deficiens ;* or, otherwise, it is not an *affectio*, but a *defectio*, etc. This doctrine of the negativity of evil was, in the case of Augustine at least, a consequence of his internal struggle with Manichæism. In order to avoid the concession of an independent existence of evil in opposition to God, he endeavours to represent it as a thing which has in truth no real or substantive being of its own—an unreality, a non-entity.

---

[1] *De Dominio Divino*, I., c. 15 ; fol. 141, col. 2 : *Deus me necessitat ad omnes istos actus nefarios pro perfectione pulcritudinis universi.*

[2] Immediately after the last quoted words follows the reply : *Hic dicitur, quod creatura rationalis est tam libera, sicut creatura aliqua potest esse (licet non possit aequari libertati summi opificis), cum sit tam libera, quod cogi non poterit* (sic), *licet tam Deus quam bonum infimum* (a lower good, the possession or enjoyment of which excites desire) *ipsam necessitare poterit ad volendum.* Comp. c. 18, fol. 151, col. 2. *De Veritate Scrip. Sac.*, c. 23, MS. 1294, fol. 76, col. 4. *Cum praedestinatione et praescientia stat libertas arbitrii.*

[3] Augustine, *De Libero Arbitrio*, III., 13, Opp. Venet., 1729, I., 625. *Enchiridion*, c. ii. *Quid est aliud quod natura dicitur nisi privatio boni.* Comp. Anselmi, Cant., tract., *De concordia praescientiae et praedestinationis . . . cum libero arbitrio*, Qu. I., c. 7. Alberti Magni *Summa Theol.*, Tract VI.

[4] Augustine, *De Civitate Dei*, XII., 7. Opp., Tom. VII., Venet. 1732, p. 306.

This Augustinian thought Wycliffe, in fact, made his own. Even in the pulpit (in his Latin sermons) he does not shrink from setting forth this speculative doctrine of sin. From the saying of Christ, 'If I had not come and spoken to them, they had not had sin,' he takes occasion to handle the metaphysics of sin, and to maintain its negativity quite in the manner of Augustine.[1] He expresses the same thought both in his earlier and later writings. For example, in his work, *De Dominio Divino*, he lays stress upon the assertion that sin, as such, is a defect, a want, not positive action;[2] and in the *Trialogus* he repeatedly takes occasion to say that sin is not a being, but a non-being—a defection;[3] that sin, even original sin, is only an occasion of good;[4] that there does not exist an idea of evil or sin[5] (*non habet peccatum ideam*), and that therefore it is out of the question to speak of sin being caused or wrought by God. There is, therefore, a forth-putting of God's will and power and government in respect to evil, only in so far as God turns the evil into an occasion of good,[6] partly in visiting it with punishment, partly when He takes occasion from sin to institute salvation and redemption. In this he goes so far as not even to shrink from maintaining that it is better that there should be a law (the law of the flesh, Romans vii.) opposing itself to God, than that the universe should be without such opposition, for thereby is the Providence of God revealed, and His glorious power.[7] Even in his Sermons he is not afraid to give expression to these thoughts; not, indeed, without guarding his hearers from the false inference that it might be lawful to do evil that good might come out of it (Romans iii. 8); for in the case of obstinate sinners, their sins serve only to land them in unutterable miseries, and to the redeemed their guilt is of benefit only in the sense of being the occasion of the Mediator's fulness of grace.[8]

---

[1] In the 30th of his *Sermons for Saints' Days*, fol. 60, col. 2: *Non habet causam nisi in quantum sapit bonum, sicut non dicitur esse, sed potius Deesse secundum aliam rationem. . . . Nec valet excusatio capta a beato Augustino, quod peccatum non habet causam efficientem sed deficientem.*

[2] *De Dominio Divino*, I., c. 14, fol. 40, col. 1: *Secus est de effectu et defectu secundum conditiones oppositas: nam omnis effectus, in quantum hujusmodi, placet Deo secundum Esse primum, quamvis secundum Deesse . . . sibi displiceat.*

[3] *Trialogus*, I., c. 10, p. 71: *Peccatum, quod est defectus hominis*, etc.

[4] *Trialogus*, c. 11, p. 74; III., 22, p. 205. Comp. III., 26, p. 222.

[5] *Ib.*, I., c. 9, p. 67: *Non habet peccatum ideam.* Comp. c. 11, p. 74: *Cum peccati non sit idea*, etc. Comp. Lewald, *Zeitschrift für historische Theologie*, 1846, p. 217.

[6] *Ib.*, III., c. 22, p. 205: *Creaturæ mala facit defectum, de quo Deus facit gratiose bonum.* Comp. c. 4, p. 141.

[7] *Liber Mandatorum sive Decalogus*, c. 5, fol. 100, col. 2: *Melius est, esse legem Deo adversantem, ad manifestandam ejus providentiam et gloriosam potentiam, quam esse, quod tota universitas sine repugnantia fundaretur.*

[8] *Miscel. Sermons*, No. XXV., fol. 234, col. 3.

We shall only mention, in brief, that Wycliffe treats of the state of innocence in Paradise, of the fall of the first man, and of original sin, entirely in the sense of Scripture and the doctrine of the Church, keeping specially close to Augustine. In his view, Adam was the representative of the whole human race, the germ of which he already carried within himself—a view which came all the more naturally to him, as he was deeply imbued with the *realistic* mode of thought. As he regarded the *genus* humanity as a *real* collective personality, it became easy to him to see represented in Adam, the first transgressor, his whole sinful posterity.[1] And yet in this matter Wycliffe is not without a mode of thinking which is peculiar to himself. Personality stands so high in his regard that he is not content with looking upon the first sin as the collective act of the whole human race, but he attempts to conceive of original sin as a personal act of every individual human being, *i.e.*, in the *intelligible* sense.[2] Further, in intimate connection with this subject, he pronounces most decidedly against the doctrine which regards the *semen generativum* as the bearer of the self-propagating *peccatum originale*. However much he sides with Augustine and differs from Pelagius in other things, he does not hesitate openly to acknowledge that the latter has proved convincingly that the *semen generativum* is not the conveyer of original sin. Wycliffe himself pronounces with emphasis that not what is corporeal, but the mind is the conveyer of it.[3] This does not rest, indeed, upon any original reflection of Wycliffe himself, for Thomas Aquinas had already given expression to the same thought.[4] But it is, nevertheless, a fact bearing somewhat significantly on Wycliffe's character as a theologian that he preferred the mental to the corporeal view of the subject, and that he laboured to place above everything else the moral personality of every individual man.

7.—Doctrine of the Person of Christ and the Work of Redemption.

WYCLIFFE speaks of the person of Christ as the God-man in innumerable passages, and he takes occasion to do so when treating of

---

[1] *Trialogus*, III., c. 24–26.
[2] *Ib.* III., 26, p. 220: *Quilibet ex traduce descendens a primo homine in principio suae originis habet proprium peccatum originale*, etc. Comp. Lewald, in *Zeitschrift für historische Theologie*, 1846, pp. 231, 517.
[3] *Ib.*, p. 221: *Ideo, sicut bene probat Pelagius, peccatum originale non in illo semine subjectatur, quamvis illud semen sit signum vel occasio sic peccandi; . . . patet, quod . . . peccatum illud in spiritu subjectatur.*
[4] Thomas Aquinas, *Summa*, Secundae Pars I., Qu. 83. Art. 1, ed. Venet., 1478. Comp. Lewald, as above, p. 517.

the most different points of the Christian doctrine and life. But all his inquiries into the personality of the Redeemer, Divine and human in one, in so far as they are of a doctrinal character, suffer under a certain monotony and stiffness. He simply repeats in a stereotyped fashion the traditional Christology of the Church, together with the proofs alleged in support of it by the Fathers and the Scholastics. But of profound original reflection on the godly mystery we find no trace; his thoughts upon it never flow in the channel of speculation.

Deity of Christ.

Wycliffe emphasises the truth that Christ was a true Man, that He is, in fact, our Brother; and he defends the doctrine of the true humanity of the Redeemer against dialectical objections.[1] On the other side, he bears testimony to the true Godhood of Christ as the Logos on so many occasions, not only in sermons but also in treatises, both scientific and practical, that it hardly seems necessary to adduce single passages in proof of the statement. It will suffice to mention that Wycliffe maintains with all distinctness the pre-existence of Christ, the eternity of His personal Being.[2] And further, the idea of the incarnation of God, the union of both natures in the one person of the God-man, as well as all questions respecting the possibility and necessity of the incarnation, were all taken up into his system by Wycliffe entirely in the form in which they had been settled in the course of the Christological contests of the fourth and fifth centuries, and in which they had been speculatively carried out by Augustine, Anselm of Canterbury, and others.[3] On these points, and all which stands in connection with them, we are not able to discover anything characteristic or peculiar in his mode of thought or treatment.

The Incarnation.

And yet Wycliffe's Christology has one remarkable distinctive feature, viz., that he always and everywhere lays the utmost possible emphasis upon the incomparable grandeur of Jesus Christ as the only mediator between God and men, as the centre of humanity,[4] and our one only Head. He is in truth quite inexhaustible in the task of bringing these truths into full expression by means of the most manifold ideas and figurative illustrations. He loves especially to set forth Christ as the centre of humanity. In the passages of his festival sermons

Christ the Centre of Humanity.

---

[1] *Trialogus*, III., 29, p. 230, cf. IV., 39, p. 386.
[2] *Ib.*, III., 30, p. 235: *Personalitas Christi est aeterna, et suae humanitatis assumptio aeternaliter praeparata*, etc.
[3] *Ib.*, II., 7, p. 99; cf. III., 30, p. 235: *unio hypostatica naturarum*. III., 25, p. 215: *necesse fuit Verbum divinum incarnari*, etc. Comp. Lewald, *Zeitschrift für historische Theologie*, 1846, pp. 519, 523.
[4] *Ib.*, III., 11, p. 164. Comp. *Sermons for Saints' Days*, No. XVII., fol. 33, col. 2. *Miscel. Sermons*, XXV., fol. 234, col. 3.

referred to below, he says, Christ in His Godhood is an *intelligible* circle, whose centre is everywhere, and its circumference nowhere. In His Manhood He is everywhere in the midst of His Church; and as from every point of a circle a straight line reaches the centre, so the Christian pilgrim, in whatever position of life he may find himself, comes straight to Christ Himself as the centre; whereas the modern Sects (the Mendicant Orders) find themselves, so to speak, as at the angles of a rectilinear figure, outside the circumference of those who are in a state of salvation. Wycliffe also makes use of the most manifold thoughts and figures to express the truth, that Christ is the one incomparable Head of redeemed humanity. He chooses his illustrations for this purpose sometimes from the secular and political, and sometimes from the spiritual and ecclesiastical sphere. Thus, in a sermon preached on All Saints' Day, he calls Christ the best of conquerors, who teaches His soldiers how to conquer a kingdom for Him by patience.[1] In like manner, he calls Him 'our Cæsar,' 'Cæsar always Augustus,' etc.[2] The figure of a giant marching forward exultingly he applies also to Christ, resting originally upon a Bible passage (Psalm xix. 6), and allegorically applied long before Wycliffe's day (*e.g.*, by Gregory VII. in his letters), but employed by Wycliffe with a special preference to the Redeemer.[3] But still more frequently does he derive his figures and descriptions from religious and Church life, when he would express the fundamental thought that Christ is the true Head, and the only authoritative Superior of redeemed, believing men. In this sense he calls Christ 'the Prior of our Order,'[4] or 'the Common Abbot,' 'the Highest Abbot of our Order.'[5] The expression, in like manner, is borrowed from the Monastic sphere, when, in comparison with other founders and holy patrons, such as St. Francis and others, Christ is called 'our Patron.'[6] The idea, again, is borrowed

---

[1] *Sermons for Saints' Days*, XXXIX., fol. 77, col. 4: *Christus conquestor optimus docet suos milites per fugam et patientiam conquirere sibi regnum.*

[2] *De Statu Innocentiae*, c. 1, fol. 238, col. 1. *De Civili Dominio*, III., c. 25. *Liber Mandatorum*, c. 8, f. 106, col. 2, *Christus qui existens Caesar semper Augustus semper meliorando procedit*. *De Veritate Scripturae s.*, c. 28, f. 98, col. 1.

[3] *De Divino Dominio*, III., 4, f. 81, col. 1. *De Civili Dominio*, III., c. 7, f. 37, col. 1. *Miscel. Sermons*, No. III., f. 134, col. 1. In the latter passage is combined with the Biblical image of the victorious giant, the antique image of Atlas bearing up the world, inasmuch as Christ (Heb. i. 3) upholdeth all things by His mighty word.

[4] *De Civili Dominio*, II., c. 8, fol. 179, col. 1: *Christus, qui est prior nostri ordinis atque principium.*

[5] *Trialogus*, IV., 6, p. 263; c. 33, p. 364. *De Ecclesia*, c. 5. *De Sex Jugis*, c. 2. *De Civili Dominio*, II., 13; fol. 212, col. 1. *Sermons for Saints' Days*, No. VI., fol. 12, col. 1. *English Sermons on the Gospels*, No. XXX. 'God made Him . . . priour of al his religioun; and he was abbot, as Poul seith, of the best ordre that may be.' *Select English Works*, ed. Arnold, vol. I., p. 77. The expression, somewhat strange to us, occurs also elsewhere, *e.g.*, in John Gerson.

[6] *Ib.*, IV., 35, p. 371: *sequi Christum patronum*, etc.

from the general constitution of the Church, when Wycliffe says of Christ, with a conscious allusion to 1 Peter ii. 25, that 'the Bishop of our souls[1] and our eternal Priest, from whom we have consecration, is one who far surpasses our bishops on earth.' He even gives to the Redeemer, inasmuch as He is a Royal Priest, the title of Pope.[2]

But not only from human ties and relations, whether civil or ecclesiastical, does Wycliffe borrow his comparisons when his object *Supremacy of Christ.* is to picture forth the solitary grandeur of the Redeemer; he also summons to his aid the invisible world, and again and again exclaims that Christ is the Saint of all saints. This description rests upon the passage in Daniel ix. 24, where the promised Messiah is spoken of under this name; and Wycliffe makes frequent use of it.[3] What he means by the appellation, he develops clearly enough when he goes on to remark that 'to all saints, whosoever they be, is due remembrance, praise, and veneration, only in so far as they derived all of good which they possessed, and proved by deeds and sufferings, from Christ Himself, who is the only source of salvation; and in so far as they walked in the imitation of Christ.'[4] In accordance with this is the judgment which he gives on the subject of the invocation of saints, and the festivals and devotional services observed in their honour; these, he says, can only be of use in so far as the souls of men are kindled by them into love for Christ Himself. But it often results from the multitude of saints whose intercession is thus sought, while yet Christ is the only true Mediator and Intercessor, that the soul is drawn away from Christ, and love to Him is weakened.

In all this, it is true, there is nothing set forth which is new and important in a scientific and dogmatic sense; but the devout spirit which it breathes, and the whole posture of the author's heart toward God, enforces the decisive apostolic truth, 'Neither is there salvation in any other; there is none other name under heaven given among men whereby we must be saved.' Where the grand truth of 'salvation in Christ alone' is so consciously

---

[1] *Miscellaneous Sermons*, No. VII., fol. 148, col. 4: *Episcopus nos consecrans et excedens nostros episcopos est episcopus animarum et sacerdos in aeternum*, etc.

[2] *Ib.*, No. VIII., fol. 149, col. 1: *Illi ergo episcopo* (Christo) *fuit gloria et imperium, cum sit simul rex et imperator, cum sit simul rex et imperator et sacerdos sanctissimus sive papa. De Ecclesia*, c. 2, fol. 8, col. 2: *Quilibet laicus fidelis tenetur credere, quod habet Christum sacerdotem suum, rectorem* (parish priest), *episcopum atque papam*, etc. *De Civili Dominio*, III., 22, fol. 196, col. 2. He calls Christ, in order to distinguish Him from the Roman Pontiff, *Summus Pontifex longe majoris auctoritatis . . . cui oportet amplius obedire.*

[3] E.g., *De Statu Innocentiae*, c. 2, fol. 239, col. 1. *Saints' Days Sermons*, No. I., fol. 1, col. 1. Comp. *Trialogus*, III., 30, p. 234. [Auth. Ver. 'the most Holy;' which Wycliffe understands of Christ.]

[4] *Trialogus*, III., 30.

and clearly, as it is here, set over against the piebald variety of saint-worships, Church-authorities, foundations, and institutions in which men sought salvation side by side with Christ, we recognise a knowledge, a feeling, and an action truly *reformational*. And undoubtedly Wycliffe is distinctly conscious of regarding Christ as the only Mediator, as alone the source of salvation.[1] Thus he lays down the following principle, that 'If we had Christ alone before our eyes, and if we served Him continually in teaching and learning, in prayer, work, and rest, then should we all be brothers, sisters, and mothers of our Lord Jesus Christ' (Mark iii. 35).[2] He looks upon himself and those who were like-minded with him, as those who before all things seek the honour of Christ, who contend for the grace of God and Christ's cause, who carry on a warfare against the enemies of the cross of Christ; in a word, as the party of Christ.[3] And when Wycliffe, as was shown above, in the most emphatic manner and on many sides, affirms the sole standard authority of the Bible, this, the *formal* principle of his system, *verbo solo*, has a connection of the most intimate and essential kind with its *material* principle, viz., that 'Christ alone is our Mediator, Saviour, and Leader,' not only in itself, but also in reference to Wycliffe's own personal consciousness of this connection. For to him Christ and the Bible are not two separated powers, but in the most intimate sense one, as we have already seen above (p. 237).

Christ the only Mediator.

This characteristic thought of Wycliffe—Christ alone the source of salvation—rests, indeed, not only upon the idea of the *person* of Jesus Christ as the God-man, but quite as much upon the doctrine of the *work* of Christ. Proceeding, then, to develop Wycliffe's view of the redemptive work of Christ, the first fact that presents itself to us is that he contemplates Christ in a threefold character, as Prophet, Priest, and King. It is not precisely the phrase, current among ourselves, of the 'threefold office' of Christ, which we meet with in Wycliffe; but his representation of the threefold personal dignity of the Redeemer comes in substance to the same thing.[4]

Threefold work of Christ.

---

[1] *Trialogus*, III., 30, p. 234: *Nullus homo potest—sine illo ut fonte salvari.*

[2] *De Civili Dominio*, II., 13, fol. 212, col. 1.

[3] *Saints' Days Sermons*, No. VII., fol. 13, col. 1: *Totus honor Dei gratiae ex integro tribuatur.* No. III., fol. 6, col. 2: *Christus —fortificat pugnantes pro causa sua*, etc. When in No. II., fol. 3, col. 1, Wycliffe says of St. Paul that he lifts the banner of his Captain, in glorying only in the Cross of Christ, the words admit of being justly applied to Wycliffe himself. In the *Liber Mandatorum*, c. 26, fol. 206, col. 2, he remarks that *pars Christi sit parte adversa potentior;* and in the same treatise, c. 28, fol. 214, col. 2, he speaks of *doctores detegentes sensum scripturae* as *Christi discipuli.*

[4] *De Civili Dominio*, II., c. 8, fol. 179,

1. As to what concerns Christ as a *Prophet*, we meet here again with a one-sidedness of view which has been already mentioned. It is that by which the Gospel is predominantly regarded in the light of a new law, Christ being the Lawgiver. Wycliffe, indeed, as was shown above in the investigation of his *formal* principle, knows how to place in a clear light the manifold difference between the two covenants, and the infinite superiority of the new over the old; but notwithstanding this he places the Redeemer in so far on the same line with Moses, as he holds Christ to be a lawgiver. Occasionally, indeed, he comes very near to the truth, but only in an almost unconscious way; as when he answers the question, why Christ, our Lawgiver, did not deliver the new law in a written form, as Moses delivered the old one. To this, his answer is threefold. First, it behoved Christ, as the perfectly sinless One, to conform His life to the state of unfallen innocence, in which men knew and fulfilled God's will in a purely natural way, without the help of writing or paper. Secondly, his work was, in the power of his Godhead, to write the commandments of life upon the inner man created after His own image. Thirdly, if Christ had occupied Himself with the business of writing a record, the holy Evangelists would never have undertaken it, and would never have accomplished that miracle of unity in diversity (*concordia tante distantium*) which we see in their narratives.[1]

Prophet and Teacher.

When, however, Wycliffe designates Christ as a Prophet and Teacher, it is by no means only His spoken word that he has in view, but also quite as much the example which He exhibited in His actions and sufferings; for, as he observes, 'the works of Christ are the best interpreters of His law.'[2] He Himself is 'the Book of Life,' and 'all the doings of Christ are an instruction for us.'[3] It is on these grounds that he demands that the life of Christ should be placed before the eyes of men of all classes, in schools, in sermons, and in churches,[4] because it is a life which comes home to every man, and is known to the whole Church as a city set on a hill. To mention here shortly only one particular, Wycliffe is

Example.

---

col. 1: *Ille enim, qui est sacerdos in aeternum, propheta magnus atque magister, exhortatus est saluberrime crebrius praedicando; sed cum sit rex regum, exercuit tam auctoritative quam ministerialiter correptionem humanitus coactivam.* Comp. the words quoted in note [2] p. 270: *Illi ergo episcopo . . . papa.*

[1] *Liber Mandatorum,* c. 6, fol. 102, col. 1.

[2] *Trialogus,* IV., 16, p. 300: *Opera Christi sunt interpres optimus legis suae.* Comp. III., 31.

[3] *De Civili Dominio,* I., 28, MS. 65, col. 1: *Omnis Christi actio est nostra instructio.*

[4] *De Veritate Scripturae Sac.,* c. 29, fol. 101, col. 4: *Vita Christi, tanquam communissima et toti ecclesiae notissima super verticem montium posita, est in scolis, in sermonibus atque ecclesiis omni generi hominum detegenda.*

accustomed to hold up with special preference one feature of the character of Jesus, His humility and gentleness, and another from the history of His life, His poverty. In one of his sermons he remarks that it is to Christ that men must look for a perfect example, for 'He is our sinless Abbot; whereas the saints, even the Apostles Peter, Paul, and John, and the rest, were not free from sin, and error, and foolishness, as we know from Scripture itself.'[1]

Here we may be allowed to add what was Wycliffe's manner of thinking respecting the holy Virgin. In his sermons preached on the Festivals of Mary, he could not do otherwise than speak of her. On the Festival of the Purification, Wycliffe touches the question whether she was absolutely without sin, and closes with words to this effect—that in no case is it necessary to salvation to believe that Mary was free from original and all actual sin. Yea, it is a pharisaic folly to contend so much upon such a question. The most advisable course is not to give any categorical decision either way. His personal view of the matter is that the holy Virgin was *probably* without sin.[2] From this it is evident enough that Wycliffe, who acknowledges clearly and emphatically the sinlessness of the Redeemer, was at least not disposed to recognise the sinlessness of Mary as a matter of dogma. In a sermon preached on the Festival of the Assumption, he also discusses the question whether Mary was taken up to heaven corporeally, or only spiritually. In doing so he weighs the reasons for and against the alleged Assumption in an unprejudiced and cool tone, but so as to incline the scale to the negative of that opinion. He remarks that God has kept such things secret from us in order that we may humbly confess our ignorance, and may hold fast all the more earnestly the things which are more necessary to the faith.[3]

The Virgin Mary.

2. Christ as 'everlasting Priest' (Hebrews vii.), and the power of His reconciliation, Wycliffe commends with a warmth altogether peculiar. He never fails to lay a simple and truly devout emphasis upon Christ's Passion. In a Passion sermon he remarks that Christ is saying every day in our hearts— 'This I suffered for thee, what dost thou suffer for Me?'[4] Particu-

Priest and Sacrifice.

---

[1] *Saints' Days Sermons*, No. VI., fol. 12, col. 1: *Petro, Paulo, evangelistae Johanni et ceteris citra Christum Scriptura imponit grave peccatum, et per consequens errorem et stultitiam, . . . ideo abbas noster Christus impeccabilis est videndus.*

[2] *Ib.*, No. VIII., fol. 14, col. 2.

[3] *Miscellaneous Sermons*, No. XXVI., fol. 235, cols. 3 and 4: *Adhuc Deus celavit a nobis puncta talia, ut recognoscentes humiliter nostram ignorantiam, fidei necessarioribus fortius insistamus.*

[4] *XL. Miscellaneous Sermons*, No. XVIII., fol. 222, col. 4: *Christus dicit in nobis cottidie: Hoc passus sum pro te, quid pateris pro me?* Comp. the well-known words, 'This I did for thee, what doest thou for Me?'

larly worthy of notice is what he says of the infinite power and eternal importance of the Passion of Christ and the reconciliation accomplished by Him. Again and again he affirms that the effect of the Passion of Christ extends as well to later ages as to the ages preceding it, and therefore reaches forwards to the world's end, and backwards to the world's beginning. Were this not so, then never would a single member of the human family since the fall of the first man have become morally righteous or a saved man.[1] No one can be saved unless he is washed in the blood of Christ (Revelation i. 5). The blood of Christ, in virtue of His spiritual nature, is so constituted that it penetrates to the kernel of the mind and purifies it from sin both original and actual.[2] The boundless power of the sufferings of Christ Wycliffe describes in such terms as to say that they would suffice for the redemption of many worlds;[3] and he places the state of grace, which has its ground in the redemption of Christ, higher than the state of innocence in Paradise. Christ, he affirms, has gained more for mankind than Adam lost.[4]

This, however, is to be understood only of the *intensive power* of the grace of God in Christ, not of the extensive reach of the reconciliation. For Wycliffe, like Augustine, limits the work of redemption to the elect, and does not hesitate to say that Christ has not redeemed all men, for there are many who will remain in the everlasting prison of sin.[5]

Only one point more may be mentioned in this place, viz., the continual mediation and intercession of Christ, which Wycliffe warmly affirms, on the ground of Scripture (1 John ii. 1), in opposition to the pretended intercession of the saints.[6]

3. The dignity of Christ as 'King of kings,' Wycliffe chiefly mentions, in so far as he deduces from it the duty of worldly rulers to

---

[1] *Trialogus*, IV., 12, p. 288: *Non dubito quin passio Christi tam ad posterius tempore* (sic) *quam ad anterius in fructus efficacia se extendit.* Miscellaneous Sermons, No. 1., fol. 193, col. 2: *Sicut virtus meriti Christi se extendit usque ad finem mundi post ejus completionem, sic virtus ejusdem meriti se extendit usque ad principium mundi ante ejus impletionem. Et nisi sic esset, nunquam fuisset persona humani generis, post praevaricationem primi hominis, justa moraliter sive salva.*

[2] *XXIV. Miscellaneous Sermons*, No. VIII., fol. 148, col. 4.

[3] *De Ecclesia*, c. 3; fol. 11, col. 2: *Christus salvavit totum mundum humani generis, cum apposuit medicinam passionis, quae suffecit redimere multos mundos.*

[4] *De Veritate Scripturae Sac.*, c. 30, fol. 107, col. 3: *Humanum genus est in majori gratia, per reparationem Domini nostri Jesu Christi, quam fuisset, posito, quod nemo a statu innocentiae cecidisset,* etc.

[5] *De Civili Dominio*, III., 25; fol. 246, col. 1: *Patet, quod Christus non redemit omnes homines a damnatione ad regnum, cum multi sunt qui non resurgent in judicio, sed manebunt in perpetuo carcere peccatorum.* Comp. *De Veritate Scripturae Sac.*, c. 30. *Tertii dicunt, sicut ego saepe locutus sum, quod Christus solum redemit praedestinatos, quos ordinavit ad gloriam.*

[6] *Trialogus*, III., 30, p. 236.

serve Christ and to further His kingdom. In relation to which he calls to remembrance the fact that Christ more than once made use of His royal power, as when in His own Person He drove the buyers and sellers out of the temple.[1]   *Christ the King.*

8.—Doctrine of the Order of Personal Salvation.

To the question concerning the personal application of the salvation wrought out by Christ, Wycliffe gives the same general answer as the Church doctrine of his time and as Scripture itself; the way in which the individual becomes a partaker of salvation is by conversion and sanctification.

With regard to conversion, Wycliffe recognises that it includes two things—turning away from sin, and a believing appropriation of the saving grace of Christ; in other words, repentance and faith. Repentance he regards as an indispensable condition of the forgiveness of sins and of a real participation in the merits of the Redeemer. He acknowledges without reserve that 'no man would be in a condition to make satisfaction for a single sin, if it were not for the unmeasurable mercy of the Redeemer. Let a man, therefore, give proof of fruitful repentance before God, and forsake past sins, and by virtue of the merits of Christ and through His mercy, his sins shall be blotted out.'[2]   *Repentance and conversion.*

But the repentance which he holds to be indispensable must not only be sincere and heartfelt, must not only have respect to sin itself, and not merely to its punishment, must not only be a 'godly sorrow,' as the apostle calls it, but it must also be a 'fruitful' repentance; it must verify itself in an actual and abiding forsaking of sin. In other words, Wycliffe here views the penitence and turning from sin included in conversion as one and the same with the work of sanctification, in which self-denial, or the constant avoidance of sin, forms the one side, while the love of God and our neighbour forms the positive completing side. But precisely this blending together of initial repentance, with the subsequent and abiding giving up of sin, is a defect which Wycliffe has in common with the teaching which prevailed in his time; and this defect corresponds with another of much greater moment in reference to faith.

---

[1] *Trialogus*, IV., 18, p. 306.
[2] *XXIV. Sermons*, No. VI., fol. 143, col. 4: *Verum concluditur, quod pro nullo peccato suo posset homo satisfacere, nisi esset immensitas misericordiae Salvatoris. Poeniteat ergo homo Deo fructuose, et deserat peccata praeterita, et virtute meriti Christi et suae gratiae sunt deleta.*

Passing on to the idea of faith, as constituting the other side of the work of conversion, Wycliffe distinguishes, as had been usual since Augustine set the example, a threefold use of the term. By 'faith' is understood—(1) The *act* by which a man believes; (2) the *condition of soul* in which a man believes; (3) the *truth* which a man believes.[1] Further, he makes the distinction, also a favourite one, between *explicit*, or conscious faith, and *implicit*, or unconscious faith; meaning by the latter the faith which a good Christian, who explicitly believes in the Catholic Church in general, extends to every particular item of doctrine which is included in the Church's whole belief.[2] When we hear Wycliffe say that 'Faith is the foundation of the Christian religion, and without faith it is impossible to please God;'[3] or when he lays down the principle that faith is the primary foundation of the virtues, and unbelief the first mischief which leads to sin, which was the reason why the Devil enticed men first of all into unbelief,[4] we might naturally be led to suppose that Wycliffe must have grasped the idea of faith at its very kernel, and must have understood it to mean a heartfelt turning of the soul to God—a most inward laying hold of the reconciliation in Christ. And yet this is not the case. After careful investigation, the result which I have arrived at is this, that Wycliffe views faith as being, on one side, a knowledge and recognition of certain truths of Christianity, and, on the other side, a moral acting in imitation of Christ from a motive of love; whereas that element of faith which, to a certain extent, forms the connecting link between these two, viz., the heartfelt turning of oneself to, and laying hold of, the redeeming love of God in Christ, is almost overlooked. For in places where Wycliffe describes faith more closely, the kernel of it appears to be something intellectual—a knowledge of the truth, which, however, has for its consequence and fruit a course of moral action. In particular, he adduces, as a proof of the necessity of faith, the fact that all those

---

[1] *Trialogus*, III., 2, p. 133. *De Ecclesia*, c. 2, fol. 133, col. 4: *Fides nunc sumitur pro actu credendi, quo creditur, nunc pro habitu credendi, per quem creditur, et nunc pro veritate, quae creditur, ut docet Augustinus* XIII° *De Trin.* (c. 2 and 3).

[2] *Ib.*, *Alia est fides, quae est credulitas fidelis explicita, et alia fides implicita, ut catholicus, habens habitum fidei infusum vel acquisitum explicite credit ecclesiam catholicam in communi, et in illa fide communi credit implicite . . . quodcunque singulariter contentum sub s. matre ecclesia.*

[3] *XL. Sermons*, No. XII.; fol. 214, col. 1: *Fides est fundamentum religionis Christianae, sine qua impossibile est placere Deo.*

[4] *De Veritate Scripturae Sac.*, c. 21, fol. 71, col. 4: *Sicut primum fundamentum virtutum est fides* (Heb. xi.), *sic primum detrimentum alliciens ad peccandum est infidelitas*, etc. And some lines before he says, it is certain, *non esse quenquam possibile peccare, nisi propter defectum fidei. Trialogus*, III., 2, p. 135. *Cum impossibile sit quenquam peccare, nisi de tanto in fide deficiat.*

who have reached the years of youthful ripeness are obliged to learn their *credo*.[1] And in a connection quite different from this, where faith is his subject, Wycliffe lays it down as a principle, 'that it is absolutely necessary to salvation that every Christian should believe, at least implicitly, every article of the faith.'[2] He does not intend by this to say a word in favour of easy belief or credulity. He is much too sensible and critical for that. Even in his sermons the critical side of his character reveals itself.

Turning now to the other side of faith, Wycliffe evidently assumes that the kernel of faith is a state of *feeling*—a moral activity—when, in accord with the theology of his age and agreeably to Aristotelian metaphysics, he lays particular stress upon the *fides formata*, and defines faith to be a steadfast cleaving to God or to Christ in love (*per amorem caritatis perpetuo adhaerere*).[3] In so defining it, Wycliffe, hand-in-hand with his theological contemporaries, passes immediately beyond the moment of conversion, and takes his standpoint within the work of sanctification; in other words, he mixes up conversion and sanctification, faith and works. And, for this reason, we can hardly expect to find Wycliffe doing homage to the Pauline Reformation-truth of the justification of the sinner by faith alone. There are not wanting, indeed, expressions which, at first sight, verge upon this truth, *e.g.*, when referring to Hebrews xi., he describes faith as 'the ground of the justification of man before God,'[4] or when he enumerates the functions of faith as follows:—(1) It animates all the regenerate in the path of virtue; (2) it urges and strengthens pilgrims to do battle with their enemies; (3) it covers the enemy with defeat. And here it is interesting to note that Wycliffe grounds the first of these statements upon Romans i. 17, and Habakkuk ii. 4, 'The just shall live by his faith.'[5]

Faith and feeling.

---

[1] *XL. Miscell. Sermons*, No. XII., fol. 214, cols. 1–3. The connection of thought in this passage is significant: *Nemo potest placere Deo nisi ipsum diligendo; sed nemo potest Deum diligere, nisi ipsum per fidem cognoscendo.*

[2] *De Civili Dominio*, I., c. 44, fol. 143, col. 2: *Oportet—omnem Christianum de absoluta necessitate salutis quemlibet articulum fidei saltem implicite credere.*

[3] *Trialogus*, III., 2, p. 133: *Fides (ut dicunt scholastici) alia est informis,—et alia est fides caritate formata. De Veritate Scripturae Sac.*, c. 10, fol. 25, col. 1: *Nisi habuerint fidem formatam, damnabuntur tanquam vacui inutiles;* c. 2, fol. 133, col. 4: *si habuerit fidem caritate formatam. XXIV. Sermons*, No. XVII., fol. 169, col. 1: *in Christum credere—sibi (Christo) per amorem caritatis perpetuo adhaerere. De Veritate Scripturae Sac.*, c. 21: *Credere in Deum est credendo ipsum sibi adhaerere firmiter per amorem.*

[4] *De Veritate Scripturae Sac.*, c. 10, fol. 25, col. 3: *Probat apostolus Hebr. xi., quod fides sit fundamentum justificationis hominis quoad Deum.*

[5] *XL. Sermons*, No. XII., fol. 214, col. 3: *Inter alia, in quo* (sic) *fides est utilis, prodest generaliter ad haec tria:* 1, *omnes regeneratos in via virtutum vivificat;* 2, *viantes ad invadendum inimicos excitat et confortat;* 3, *protegendo impugnantes confundit.* . . . . . Habakkuk ii. 4: '*Justus meus ex fide vivit*,' etc.

But the nearer he approaches to the truth, the more evident does it become that Wycliffe, in his estimate of faith, still occupies the standpoint of mediæval scholasticism, and has not even a presentiment, to say nothing of an understanding, of what faith was to the mind of the Apostle Paul. In the perusal of his writings I have scarcely met with a more characteristic passage than the following, which occurs in a sermon on the purely Pauline passage, Romans x. 10, 'With the heart man believeth unto righteousness, and with the mouth confession is made unto salvation.' Wycliffe remarks, in the course of his sermon, that 'as life precedes all living actions, so faith goes before all other virtues. It is for this reason that the apostle, in Hebrews x., says, in the words of the prophet, "The just shall live by faith;" as if he would say that the spiritual life of the just springs out of faith. In order that a man may be righteous, it is necessary that he should believe what he knows. And as faith under favourable circumstances works great things, inasmuch as it is impossible that so great a seed, when sown in fruitful soil, should not spring forth and work to good effect, it is for this reason the apostle adds, "With the mouth confession is made unto salvation."'[1] Wycliffe, it is manifest, failed to seize the evangelical idea of faith. One might almost say that in his case, as in that of other scholastics, as Thomas Aquinas, Duns Scotus, and others, the very organ needed for this was wanting. He has, therefore, no faculty of perception for the truth of justification by faith alone. On the contrary, he is inclined to put 'righteousness before God' to the account of good works along with faith, and for this reason does not even deny to these all 'merit.'

Faith and justification.

This leads us from the work of conversion to the work of sanctification; and, on going more closely into the latter, we come, at the same time, in sight of Wycliffe's fundamental thoughts on the subject of morals. And, if we are not mistaken, his ethical system is worthy of a more careful study than it has ever hitherto received.

Wycliffe's ethics.

To the question respecting the highest good, *summum bonum*, Wycliffe replies that there are three kinds of good, which are graduated according to their value, thus:—The good things of for-

---

[1] *XXIV. Sermons*, No. xx., fol. 175, col. 3: *Sicut vita praecedit omnes alios actus secundos, sic fides virtutes alias, et hinc dicit apostolus Hebr. x. ex testimonio prophetae:* '*Justus ex fide vivet;*' *ac si intenderet, quod vita spiritualis justorum originatur ex fide. . . . Ideo dicit apostolus:* '*Corde creditur ad justitiam,*' i.e., *quod homo sit justus, requiritur ipsum credere intellectum. Et cum fides, habita opportunitate, operatur magna, si est, cum impossibile est tantum semen in terra fructifera non in bonam operam ebullire, ideo subjungit apostolus, quod* '*ore confessio fit ad salutem.*'

tune, which possess the smallest value; the good things of nature, which have a medium value; and lastly, the good things of virtue and grace, which are of the highest worth.[1] *Virtue the summum bonum.* The highest good, then, is to him coincident with virtue, which virtue is conditioned by grace. The good things of virtue are, at the same time, the good things of grace. The standing in grace is the condition of Christian freedom, and freedom from sin is the summit of all freedom.[2] In the standing of grace the Christian has a right to all things; not in the sense of municipal right, but in virtue of grace, *titulo gratiae*.[3]

Coming closer to Wycliffe's doctrine of virtue, we have, it is true, at first, the well-known old song of the four philosophical or cardinal virtues—righteousness, courage, prudence, and modera- *Division of the virtues.* tion (this is Wycliffe's usual way of arranging them), and of the three theological virtues—faith, hope, and love.[4] But, on a closer examination, ethical ideas peculiar to himself, and characteristic of his mode of Christian thought, are not altogether lacking. These I find in what Wycliffe says of humility and of love. Humility he recognises as the basis of all virtue; as in pride he discovers the first sin. In the third book of the *Trialogus* he gives an outline of the fundamental prin- *Humility the basis of virtue.* ciples of his ethics (c. i.-xxiii.). In particular he treats (c. ix.-xxiii.) of the seven mortal sins and their opposite virtues, and there he places pride foremost among the sins, and humility foremost among the virtues. And why so? Because the root of every kind of pride lies in this, that man does not humbly believe that all that he has comes to him from God.[5] Pride is the first step to apostacy. When man is proud, he is guilty of an implicit blasphemy, for he denies by implication that he has any one above him to whose laws he owes obedience.[6] On the other hand, humility, according to oft-repeated expressions of Wycliffe, is the root of all virtues, yea, even of Christian piety. The more humility a man has, the nearer is he to Christ.

---

[1] *Saints' Days Sermons*, No. v., fol. 8, col. 1: *bona fortunae, quae sunt minima, bona naturae, quae sunt media, bona virtutis et gratiae, quae sunt maxima*.

[2] *Trialogus*, III., 29, p. 229, *De Ecclesia*, c. 11, fol. 161, col. 2: *Libertas a peccato est maxima, sine qua non est aliqua vera libertas.*

[3] *De Ecclesia*, c. 14, fol. 174, col. 1, on mentioning the pretended 'Donation of Constantine,' Wycliffe says of Silvester: *Fuit dominus super astra et omnia inferiora homine in natura, sed non titulo civili, imo titulo gratiae, quo justi sunt omnia.*

[4] *Trialogus*, III., 1 and 2, p. 128.

[5] *Ib.*, III., 10, p. 163: *Tota radix cujuslibet speciei superbiae stat in isto quod homo errat non credendo humiliter, quod quidquid habuerit est a Deo.*

[6] *De Christo et ejus Adversario*, c. 10, fol. 74, col. 3: *Superbia est primus pes, per quem peccator a Deo decidit, ut patet de Lucifero,* etc. XL. *Miscellaneous Sermons*, No. VI., fol. 8, col. 1: *Superbia est implicite blasphemia... Quum homo superbit, negat implicite se habere superiorem, legibus cujus obediat.*

Humility—*i.e.*, the heartfelt and practical acknowledgment that we are God's servants, and that to Him alone belongs the glory—is, so to speak, the mild atmosphere in which all other virtues can alone grow and flourish.[1] This view of humility as the basis and root of all virtue rests unmistakably upon a religious sentiment, and upon a dogmatic conviction which gives to God alone the glory, and which sees in Christ alone the salvation of mankind. These ethical thoughts of Wycliffe are thus a mirror of his religious and dogmatic individuality.

The true centre of all Christian virtue Wycliffe declares to be the love of God and our neighbour. Without love to God with all the heart and all the soul, there dwells no moral virtue in man. No one can reach the blessed home without it; it is the wedding garment without which we cannot stand in the final judgment.[2] Love to God is the chief lesson which man learns in the school of the virtues; and no action has value except that which is animated by the love of God above everything else.[3] In his treatise, *Of the Ten Commandments*, Wycliffe investigates psychologically, in imitation of St. Bernard, the different gradations of the love of God; and he declares to be the highest stage of it that state of feeling which, in virtue of a certain relish of the Divine sweetness, passes beyond all created things and goes forth in love to God Himself, purely for His own sake; while there is also a love of God which seeks a recompense for its affection, which loves Him not for what He is in Himself, but in view of reward.[4] From the pure love of God springs the love of our neighbour.[5] On this subject Wycliffe calls attention to the fact that love has its own order according to which it is bound to love, in the first place, the members

Love the principle of Christian virtue.

---

[1] *Trialogus*, III., 11, p. 164: *Humilitas est aliis virtutibus fundamentum. Quicunque est humilior, est Christo propinquior; religio in humilitate fundata. De Graduationibus Scholasticis*, c. 2, fol. III, col. 3: *Radix religionis Christi est humilitas. XL. Miscellaneous Sermons*, No. VI., fol. 202, cols. 3 and 4: *Fides et humilitas connexae sunt fundamentum religionis Christianae. Humilitas est quasi aura temperata, in qua oportet omnia plantaria aliarum virtutum conseri, si debeant crescere in Christiano.* In his English writings, sermons, etc., Wycliffe insists often enough, and with the greatest emphasis, upon meekness, *e.g.*, in the 121st sermon in Arnold's edition, I., 399, he says, 'Ever as a man is more meek, evere the betere man he is.' And *meek, meekness* signify with Wycliffe, according to his Bible translation—*vide Wycliffite Versions of the Bible*, vol. IV., 10—not softness or gentleness, but humility.

[2] *Ib.*, III., 2, pp. 132, 136.

[3] *De Civili Dominio*, III., 26, fol. 247, col. 2: *Ars praecipua, quam in schola virtutem addiscimus, est ars diligendi Deum. XL. Miscel. Sermons*, No. I., fol. 194, col. 2: *Nullus actus hominis meritorius est, nisi in quo Deus supereminenter diligitur.* In one of his English sermons Wycliffe says, 'Humility is the foundation of all virtues, and Love their summit which reaches to heaven.' *Select English Works*, vol. I., p. 64.

[4] *Liber Mandatorum, sive Decalogus*, c. 31, fol. 126, col. 2.

[5] *Trialogus*, III., 2, p. 136: *Consistit autem caritas in amore, quo Deus debite diligitur et tota sua fabrica.*

of its own household, &c. (1 Timothy v. 8). Honest love manifests itself, according to circumstances, by candid remonstrance and earnest censure (like as God Himself chasteneth those whom He loveth), while that weak indulgence which allows everything to take its own way is nothing else but a blind love and a false compassion.[1] The principle, that the love of our neighbour should begin with what stands nearest to it ('Charity begins at home,' according to the modern proverb), is connected with another held by Wycliffe, that it is the duty of every man conscientiously to fulfil the requirements of his position and calling, be that calling what it may. The more faithfully and conscientiously he discharges his nearest duty, the more certainly, by virtue of a certain concatenation in things, will he be useful to others and advance their welfare.[2]

This thought stands in unmistakable opposition to the one-sidedness of a narrow, monkish mode of feeling and thinking on moral subjects, which considered the contemplative life and seclusion from the world as the surest means of virtue. Wycliffe, on the contrary, sets out with the design of restoring the active life of the Christian man in the most various callings to its true moral rights—so often ignored in his day; and how he did this in respect to civil life and the State we shall show below. *The true Christian life.*

When the question is put, What is the moral standard which the individual should apply in any given case, when he is concerned to know what is well-pleasing to God, or what is conformable to the love of God and our neighbour—we are pointed by Wycliffe to the example of Christ, the imitation of which will lead us in an unerring and sure path. Christ says to each one, 'Follow Me;' and every man who desires to be saved must follow Him, either in suffering or at least in moral conduct.[3] To give a particular instance, Wycliffe, on one occasion, deduces from the incident in the Gospel concerning 'the woman that was a sinner' in the house of Simon the Pharisee,[4] rules as to the way and manner in which a servant of Christ should conduct himself in inter-

---

[1] *Saints' Days Sermons*, No. LVI., fol. 114, col. 4: *Ordo caritatis exigit, quod homo primo in ordine diligat suos domesticos*, etc. *De Ecclesia*, c. 15, fol. 177, col. 2: *Patet, quod de lege caritatis et spiritualis elemosinae—tenetur praepositus, subjectos corripere. Unde inter omnia peccata, de quibus magis timeo in superioribus regni nostri, sunt caeca pietas, falsa misericordia*, etc.

[2] *Liber Mandatorum* (*Decalogus*), c. 23, fol. 186, col. 2: *Faciat ergo quodlibet membrum ecclesiae, quod incumbit officio sui status, et de quanto facit solicius* (*sic* from *sollicite*), *de tanto quadam naturalitate cuilibet membro capaci prodest amplius*, etc., cf., fol. 187, col. 1.

[3] *Saints' Days Sermons*, No. III., fol. 4, col. 2: *Omnem salvandum oportet sequi ipsum vel in passione vel saltem in moribus. Et si sit virtuosus, quomodo Dei virtus causans et exemplans virtutem suam non erit dux, quem sequitur in moribus?*

[4] *Ib.*, No. XVIII., fol. 36, col. 3.

course with sinners. He lays down this principle, 'The nearer the life of a Christian comes to Christ, the more rich it is in virtue. It follows that men's departure from the principles of the Christian religion is owing to their having too high a value for many teachers who stand in opposition to Christ, to the neglect of the doctrine and example of the best Master and Leader.'[1] Manifestly, Wycliffe sets up here an ideal standard; but he is clearly conscious of doing so, and censures, in the sharpest manner, the practice of attempting to reduce at pleasure the moral standard, and of pretending that the *commands* of Christ are indeed binding upon every man, but not so His counsels, for these last are obligatory only upon heroic Christians like the saints, but not upon people of an average sort. Such an allegation would tend to extinguish the religion of Christ, for then every man might set aside all Christ's counsels together, and maintain that they were not binding upon him, for he was one of the weak. Wycliffe, on the contrary, lays down the principle that 'Every counsel which Christ has imparted is binding upon every one to whom it is given.'

With this view stands connected the circumstance that Wycliffe pronounces a moral neutrality to be entirely inadmissible, yea, unthinkable: like for 'as no man can be neutral in regard to virtue and vice, so neither can the life and walk of any man be neutral.'[2] He rightly looks upon the moral character of a man as a complete whole, whose prevailing principle gives or takes away the worth of every single feature and act. Wycliffe is far removed from that *atomistic* view, which, as with Pelagius and others, regards every single act as an isolated phenomenon. He prefers, on the contrary, a comprehensive way of looking at the subject, which recognises the moral life as constituting a whole made up of many parts. 'As the earlier drops have a preparatory effect, and the last drop completes the hollowing of the stone, so sins which have full swing in the middle of a man's life prepare the way for his despair at last.' Wycliffe admits, indeed, that any one may do a work which is in itself good (*opus bonum de genere*) while living in a state of mortal sin; but he holds that in that case the work is a sin, and the doer of it even incurs, in the act, a mortal sin, as, *e.g.*, when a parish priest, while living in an unconverted and dissolute state of life, administers the sacraments

Character to be regarded as a whole.

---

[1] *De Veritate Scripturae Sac.*, c. 29. fol. 101, col. 4: *De quanto vita Christiani est Christo propinquior, de tanto est virtuosior. Et patet correlarie, quod declinatio a religione Christiana ex hoc oritur, quod nimis attenditur ad multos magistros Christo contrarios, doctrina et sequelæ magistri et ducis optimi praetermissa.*

[2] *Ib.*, I., 43, fol. 123, col. 1: *Sicut nemo potest esse neuter quoad virtutem et vitium, sic nulla conversatio hominis potest esse neutra.*

correctly, does good to the poor, etc., etc. Not only *what* a man does is to be considered, but how he does it, and from what feeling and motive. Wycliffe is fond of expressing this in the words of St. Bernard, 'God recompenses not the good thing which is done, but that which is done in a good way; God rewards not the *what* but the *how*.[1] And from this it further follows, that every pilgrim upon earth has need to test his own life most carefully in reference to this point, whether he is living in the hope of salvation, and has a standing thereby in the state of grace.'

After this survey of the ethical thoughts of Wycliffe, we return to his views, before touched upon, respecting the way in which the sinner attains to righteousness before God. Bringing together all he says on this subject, his opinion amounts to this—that man can obtain righteousness before God, forgiveness of sins, and hope of eternal life, only through grace, but not without his own moral work and sanctification. Now, it is true that he is wont to express this in a way which looks as if he had stood at no great distance from the delusion that heaven can be *earned* or merited by men.[2] But we must be on our guard not to mete Wycliffe's theology with the measuring line of the Reformed Confessions. For, in the first place, he goes to work with quite a different apparatus of ideas from an evangelical theologian of the present day. Ideas such as *meritum* and *demeritum* (for he makes very frequent use of these correlative ideas) he derived, like the Scholastics before him, from the Latin Fathers, chiefly in the sense of moral worth and unworth. The proper idea of *merit, i.e.*, of an independent performance, conferring a full legal claim upon God's recognition and recompense, in the form of eternal blessedness, he designates according to scholastic usage *meritum de condigno;* while the *meritum de congruo* obtains validity and recognition in consideration only of what is fair and reasonable, not of strict right.[3] Then,

Justification.

Doctrine of merit.

---

[1] *De Civili Dominio*, I., 43, fol. 202, col. 1; fol. 203, col. 1: *Sicut malum de genere potest bene fieri (e.g.*, execution of criminals), *sic bonum de genere potest male fieri*. Glossa Bernhardi, '*Deus*,' inquit, '*non est remunerator hominum sed adverbiorum*,' hoc est tantum dicere; non remunerat Deus bonum quod fit, sed quod bene fit. Comp. *De Officio Pastorali*, I., 10, p. 18: *Ideo dicunt loquentes communiter, quod Deus est remunerator adverbiorum*. Farther, *De Veritate Scripturae Sac.*, c. 14, fol. 116, col. 4: *Non solum debet attendi, quid homo faciat, sed qualiter et qua intentione, cum Deus sit remunerator adverbiorum, quae faciunt maxime ad moralitatem, quam oportet fundari in gratia et caritate, quae non possunt inesse, nisi insit moralitas.*

[2] The expressions, *mereri praemium in alio seculo, meritum, opera meritoria*, are of such frequent occurrence with Wycliffe, that the slightest doubt can evidently never have occurred to him of the propriety of applying them to Christians. They are also repeated so often that it appears superfluous to quote passages in proof of the fact.

[3] Wycliffe defines *meritum* in one place to be something done by a rational creature which is worthy of reward; and he remarks that, as the same man may

secondly, when it comes to the application of these ideas to the actual state of things, Wycliffe contends, quite categorically, against all thoughts of proper merit in the full sense of the word, *i.e.*, *meritum de condigno*. We have already quoted above an unmistakable utterance of his to the effect that under no circumstances can a creature merit anything of God in virtue of its own worthiness,[1] and he expresses repeatedly the same thought with the greatest emphasis. He declares it to be a vain imagination, when the case is put that 'nature'—*i.e.*, the will-power naturally inherent in man—is able to perform anything good without the co-operation of grace; in his judgment this would amount to God's making a creature of His own equal to Himself. In connection with this point he gives a detailed interpretation of the words of St. Paul in 2 Corinthians iii. 5, 'Not that we are sufficient of ourselves to think anything as of ourselves, but our sufficiency is of God.' He holds that St. Paul, in these words, saves, on the one hand, the freedom of the will, and the power of acquiring a merit *de congruo*, but denies, at the same time, that we are able, without prevenient grace, to merit anything *de condigno*; *i.e.*, he declares that we merit absolutely nothing in the sense of legal claim.[2]

<small>Grace the source of goodness.</small>

Thirdly, When we come still nearer to the actual facts of the case, no fewer than four different questions come under discussion. (1) Can man make satisfaction for sin by good works? *i.e.*, Can he merit the forgiveness of sins thereby? (2) Can he, by his moral behaviour, merit the gift of grace requisite to conversion? (3) Can he, after conversion, merit by good works eternal life or blessedness? (4) Is there in reality such a thing as supererogatory merit? The first question Wycliffe answers in the negative. His straightforward confession upon this point is this—'I do not believe that even the smallest sin committed against the Lord can be effaced by any merit; it must be done away in the main or principally by the merit of this Man (the Redeemer).[3] Quite similarly he speaks on this subject in one of his sermons. 'I do not

<small>Four questions concerning merit.</small>

---

be both father and son, so the same act may be *de condigno* in relation to one set in authority, who rewards without any grace, and *de congruo* in relation to a Lord who rewards only of grace. *De Dominio Divino*, III., fol. 87, col. 1.

[1] *De Dominio Divino*, III., 4, fol. 79, col. 1: *Creatura penitus nihil a Deo merebitur ex condigno*, cf. 78, col. 2.

[2] *Ib.*, III., 5, fol. 84, col. 1, on 2 Corinthians iii. 5: *In quo dicto videtur mihi, quod apostolus more suo profunde primo innuit, nos posse cogitare aliquid 'a nobis,' et per consequens salvatur nobis liberum arbitrium cum potentia merendi de congruo; secundo per hoc, quod negat nos posse aliquid cogitare 'ex nobis,' explicat, quod non possumus mereri aliquid sine praecedente gratia, et sic nihil simpliciter de condigno.*

[3] *Ib.*, III., 4, fol. 30, col. 2: *Non—reor peccatum vel minimum commissum contra dominum per aliquod meritum posse tolli, nisi per meritum hujus viri principaliter sit ablatum.*

see how any sin can be done away by means of *meritum de condigno* in the sinner, since infinite grace is required (he refers to the individual's standing in grace) in order to satisfaction for sin.'[1] The passage also already quoted from the sixth of his Twenty-four sermons contains the same thought, that the infinite compassion of the Redeemer and His all-availing merit alone make possible the forgiveness of sins; while it is by no means excluded that some moral performance of the individual sinner may be requisite, if his own committed sins are to be forgiven him.

1. Man cannot make satisfaction for sin.

As to the second question, Can man by his moral behaviour merit the gift of grace for conversion? it is well known that many scholastics were accustomed to answer it in the affirmative— in assuming that God grants to those who are honest in their endeavours after a better life the grace which is needed in order to conversion. He does this, indeed, not *de condigno*, as if He were bound in law to do it; but *de congruo*, inasmuch as it is fair and meet that honest strivers should be met so far with the needed help. What position does Wycliffe take up in relation to this teaching? He rejects it with the utmost decision as a vain imagination [2] (*vanitas*). He declares himself clearly and roundly in opposition to the supposition that, before his conversion, man can do anything by his moral behaviour to win God's gift of the grace of the Holy Spirit needful to conversion. In other words, he rejects the erroneous notion that converting grace is conferred by God as at least a half-merited reward. Indeed, Thomas Aquinas had also declared himself against the supposition that any one could merit this grace *de condigno*, but the milder view of the possibility of meriting the grace *de congruo* he had passed over in silence.

2. Nor merit saving grace.

The third question is as follows—Can man, after his conversion, merit eternal blessedness by good works? To this question, also, Wycliffe replies in the negative, in so far as any *meritum de condigno* is thought of. On this point we simply recall the expressions already adduced above, to which we only add what follows by way of confirmation. Wycliffe is honestly striving to set aside all vain self-approbation, which gives the glory not to God, but to itself. For this reason he lays stress upon the words of Christ—'When ye have done all, then say, We are unprofitable

3. Nor earn eternal blessedness.

---

[1] *XXIV. Sermons*, No. II., fol. 132, col. 3 : *Ego non video, quomodo ex condignitate meriti peccantis deleri possit quodcunque peccatum, cum ad satisfactionem requiritur gratia infinita specialis.*

[2] *Trialogus*, III., 7, p. 153 : *Et patet vanitas nostrorum loquentium, qui ponunt quod gratia talis datur homini. . . de congruo, ut facilitet hominem ad merendum.*

servants.'[1] The holy life of Christ alone is deemed by him to be absolutely meritorious, and the principle which first lends life, *i.e.*, power and weight, to every other merit.[2] And in another place he brings out the thought that every moral virtue, every truly God-pleasing action, is conditioned by the gracious working of God, by the 'power from on high,' while its availment and weight in God's eyes is dependent on this, that God is pleased, in the riches of His grace, to accept it.[3] There cannot, then, well exist any doubt regarding so much as this, that Wycliffe consciously and distinctly rejects the notion that the converted Christian can effect any moral performance or achievement, in virtue of which he acquires a lawful right to the coming blessedness—*a meritum de condigno.* Herein he agrees with Thomas Aquinas, except that the latter acknowledges such a merit as existing in cases where this meritorious work is ascribed to the Holy Ghost.[4] This, indeed, does not exclude, but in fact indirectly concedes, the truth that there does exist a moral merit, improperly so called—*a meritum de congruo*—or works meritorious in the widest sense. The latter are what are meant when Wycliffe says, on one occasion, 'If the husbandman already has joy in the hope of the fruit of his sowing, how much more may a pilgrim, who may believe that he has done many meritorious works, rejoice in the hope of the fruits which these will yield to him!'[5]

The fourth question—Whether such a thing as supererogation really exists? answers itself from what precedes. For if human merit,

Supererogatory merit impossible. in the strict and proper sense of the word, is not, generally speaking, recognised, much less, of course, can there be anything to say for a pretended surplus merit (*meritum supererogatum*). It is no wonder, therefore, that Wycliffe pronounces the notion of a boundless treasure of supererogatory merit, to administer which is the function of the Church, and in part

---

[1] *De Dominio Divino*, III., fol. 89, col. 2. Here Wycliffe lays down the principle that worldly rulers should ever remember that they are the servants and stewards of God, and he continues as follows: *Si ergo istam sententiam haberemus prae oculis, tunc non inaniter gloriaremur, quasi hoc haberemus ex nobis, sed cum timore distribueremus bona domini solum dignis, ascribentes Deo honores* (sic) *et non nobis, qui solum sumus dispensatores et 'servi sibi inutiles.'*

[2] *Ib.*, III., 4, fol. 80, col. 1: *Ejus* (Christi) *quidem conversatio summe meritoria in plenitudine temporis ordinata est principium vivificans quodlibet aliud meritum subsequens vel praecedens.*

[3] *Trialogus*, III., 2, p. 132: *Quomodo quaeso posset homo mereri beatitudinem, vivendo et agendo secundum beneplacitum Dei, nisi Deus ex magna sua gratia hoc acceptet? Ideo quidquid homo egerit vel natura creata in ipso genuerit, non dicitur virtus moralis meritoria praemii vel laudis perpetuae, nisi illa virtus ab alto venerit, et per consequens ex gratia Dei sui.*

[4] *Summa*, II., 1 Quaest. 114, 3.

[5] *Saints' Days Sermons*, No. XXXIV., fol. 67, col. 2: *Si agricultor in spe gaudet de fructu sui seminis, quanto magis viator, qui debet credere, se fecisse multa opera meritoria, debet eorum fructibus spe gaudere.*

of every Pope for the time being, to be nothing less than a 'lying fiction.'[1]

According to all this, Wycliffe absolutely rejected the notion that man is able to acquire any moral merit in the full sense of the word, whether in order to make satisfaction for sin, or to attain thereby to conversion or eternal blessedness. On the other hand, it must be conceded that he recognised a merit in an improper sense — a co-operation of man's own moral power, partly in the matter of forgiveness of sin, and partly in reference to the hope of the eternal blessedness.

When Melanchthon, in a short critique upon Wycliffe, pronounces, among other things, the judgment that he was totally ignorant of the righteousness of faith, *i.e.*, of the doctrine of justification by faith alone,[2] we cannot do other than acknowledge this judgment to be exact and just. It was reserved for Luther, first of all men, to be called of God to separate by felicitous tact this kernel of saving truth from the husk, and to make it the central doctrine of the Evangelical Confession.[3]

Wycliffe and the Reformation doctrine.

9.—Doctrine of the Church as the Communion of the Saved.

IF we ask for Wycliffe's most general and most comprehensive idea of the Church, he meets our inquiry with a view which is wide enough to embrace both what is visible and invisible, both the temporal and the eternal. 'The Church,' he says, 'is threefold, of the *triumphant* (*triumphantium in coelo*); of the *militant* (*militantium hic in mundo*); and of the *sleepers* (*dormientium in purgatorio*).' The first division embraces the angels and the blessed saints in heaven; the second, the Christians who are alive on earth in conflict with the world; the third embraces those who are fallen asleep, in so far as they have not yet reached the estate of blessedness, but are still in Purgatory. More than once Wycliffe compares these three parts of the whole Church

The Church universal: threefold division.

---

[1] *XXIV. Sermons*, No. VII., fol. 146, col. 2: *Cautela subtilissima a fratribus inventa stat in mendaci fictione thesauri infiniti supererogati meriti ecclesiae triumphantis, quem Deus ponit in potestate distributiva cujuscunque papae caesarii.* Comp. *Trialogus*, IV., 32, p. 158. *Supponunt, quod in coelis sint infinita sanctorum supererogata merita . . . et super totum illum thesaurum Christus papam constituit*, etc.

[2] Preface to *Sententiae veterum de coena Domini*, in a letter to Frederick Myconius, about March, 1530, *Corpus Reformatorum*, vol. II., 32: *Prorsus nec intellexit nec tenuit fidei justitiam.*

[3] [This statement regarding the defect in Wycliffe's doctrine seems to require some qualification. See note in Appendix.]

to the threefold division of Solomon's Temple, as set forth in the well-known sequence—

> Rex Solomon fecit templum,
> Cujus instar et exemplum
>   Christus et ecclesia.
> Sed tres partes sunt in templo
> Trinitatis sub exemplo;
>   Ima, summa, media.

This division of the Church, however, is not a thought peculiar to Wycliffe; it is acknowledged by himself to be an ancient division, and he regards it simply as a Catholic doctrine.[1] Ancient, indeed, it is not, but, no doubt, mediæval, and everywhere current among the scholastic divines. There is nothing, therefore, characteristic of Wycliffe in this division, any more than there is in his idea of the oneness which it assumes of the Church on earth with the Church in heaven and in Purgatory.

There is, however, one peculiar feature in his fundamental idea of the Church. Not that this peculiarity was anything new, or belonged only to Wycliffe (he has it, as he was well aware, in common with Augustine),[2] but it is one of very great importance, and runs like a scarlet thread through the whole system of Wycliffe's thinking—we mean the thought that the Church is nothing else than *the whole number of the elect*. It is to this thought that we have to direct our attention before every other, for this concerns the eternal ground of the Church, while all other parts of the discussion relate to its temporal manifestation and life.

The Church the body of the elect.

According to Wycliffe, the eternal ground or basis of the Church lies in the *Divine election*. He always defines the Church to be the communion or the whole body of the elect.[3] In other words, he places himself in deliberate opposition to the idea of the Church

---

[1] *De Christo et ejus Adversario*, c. 1, fol. 70, col. 1: *Secundum catholicos, ecclesia est praedestinatorum universitas, et sic est triplex ecclesia scilicet, ecclesia triumphantium in coelo, ecclesia militantium hic in mundo, et ecclesia dormientium in purgatorio.* Saints' Days Sermons, No. XLVIII., fol. 97, col. 3; *XXIV. Sermons*, No. XII., fol. 157, cols. 3 and 4. In both sermons I find the above sequence introduced. Comp. Daniel, *Thesaurus Hymnologicus*, vol. v., p. 106.

[2] Comp. *De Veritate Scripturae Sac.*, c. 1, fol. 2, col. 1; *De Ecclesia*, c. 1, fol. 145, col. 2.

[3] *Trialogus*, IV., 22, p. 324: *Vere dicitur ecclesia corpus Christi mysticum, quod verbis praedestinationis aeternis est cum Christo sponso ecclesiae copulatum*, etc. *De Civili Dominio*, I., 43, fol. 116, col. 1. *Necesse est supponere unam veritatem metaphysicam . . . . scilicet quod ecclesia catholica sancta apostolica sit universitas praedestinatorum . . . . et istam ecclesiam necesse est esse sponsam capitis, quam ratione praeordinationis ac promissionis non potest ipsam* (sic) *deserere. Liber Mandatorum (Decalogus)*, c. 23, fol. 184, col. 1: *Omnes Christiani praedestinati simul collecti constituunt unam personam, quae est sponsa Christi. De Ecclesia et membris ejus*, c. 1, p. 4, 'And this chirche is moder to eche (each) man that shal be saved, and conteyneth no membre but only men that shulen be saved.'

which prevailed in his time, and expressly disapproves of those notions and forms of speech according to which men took the Church to mean the *visible* Catholic Church—the organized communion of the hierarchy. Wycliffe, on the contrary, seeks the Church's centre of gravity in the past eternity, in the invisible world above; for to him the Church is essentially Christ's body or Christ's bride, according to the well-known apostolic figures. A soul is incorporated with Christ, or betrothed to Christ, not by any act of man, not by any earthly means and visible signs, but by the decree of God, according to His eternal election and fore-ordination.[1] The Church, therefore, has in the visible world only its manifestation, its temporary pilgrimage; it has its home and its origin, as also its end, in the invisible world, in eternity. Every individual devout Christian owes all that he possesses in his inner life to the regeneration which is the fruit of election.[2] It is only by virtue of the gracious election of God that the individual belongs to the number of the saved, and is a member of the body of Christ, a child of the Holy Mother Church, of which Christ is the Husband.

It is self-evident that, with such a view of the Church as this, Wycliffe could not but regard as radically false the prevailing notion, according to which the Church and the clergy were looked upon as one and the same thing, all the members of the clerical order being included in the Church, and all non-clergy excluded from it,[3]—an error involving immense consequences, against which Luther in his day had still to contend. But the idea of the Church as the whole body of the elect is not only, on the one hand, wider than that conception of it which identified the Church with the clergy; it is also, on the other hand, narrower and more exclusive than this conception—narrower inasmuch as it shuts out from the communion of the Church the ungodly, the hypocrites, and the half-hearted, even when they fill the offices, high or low, of the Church. Further, as Wycliffe carries back conversion, salvation, and membership of the Church to the election of grace, *i.e.*, to the eternal and free decree of God in Christ, he, at the same time, is far removed

The Church not the clergy.

---

[1] *Trialogus*, IV., 22, p. 324, where this doctrine of the Church is significantly enough attached to the treatment of the sacrament of marriage.

[2] *XXIV. Sermons*, No. XII., fol. 158, col. 1: *De nativitate ex semine praedestinationis*, after 1 John iii. 9.

[3] In the English tract under the title *Octo in quibus seducuntur simplices Christiani*, in Wycliffe's *Select English Works*, ed. Arnold, III., 447, Wycliffe says: 'Whanne men speken of holy Chirche, thei understonden anoon prelatis and prestis, monkis, and chanouns, and freris, and alle men that han crownes (that have the tonsure) though thei lyven nevere so cursedly agenst Goddis lawe, and clepen not ne holden seculeris men of holy churche, though thei lyven nevere so trewely after Goddis lawe, and enden in perfect charite. But netheles alle that schullen be savyd in blisse of hevene ben membris of holy Chirche, and ne moo.'

from the assumption, which up to that time was universal, that participation in salvation and the hope of heaven were conditioned exclusively by a man's connection with the official Church, and were dependent entirely upon the mediation of the priesthood. There is thus included in Wycliffe's idea of the Church the recognition of the free and immediate access of believers to the grace of God in Christ; in other words, of the general priesthood of believers.

After thus indicating in general terms the extreme bearing and the 'Reformational' importance of Wycliffe's idea of the Church, let us now look at it from a nearer point of view. There is included or implied in the idea of 'the whole body of the elect' an unexpressed antithesis which not only runs through all the present, but also reaches back into eternity, to the Divine election, and forwards into the eternal future both of the blessed and the condemned. The eternal purpose of God Wycliffe conceives of as a twofold enactment: God has fore-ordained some to salvation and glory, in virtue of His election (*praedestinatio*); to others He has appointed everlasting punishment, in virtue of His foreknowledge of their sin (*praescientia*). The former Wycliffe calls *praedestinati*, the latter ordinarily *praesciti*, 'foreknown;' only in one instance do I find him using instead the expression *reprobi*.[1] He purposely and persistently avoids speaking of a Divine purpose of rejection (*reprobatio*, or such like), following, in this, in Augustine's steps. Yet it is not his meaning, that the Divine adjudication of eternal punishment and damnation is conditioned entirely and purely by God's omniscient prevision of men's own spontaneous choice of evil, and their final continuance in sin. For Wycliffe is well assured of the principle that in the nature of things it cannot be the creature which is the cause of any action or even any knowledge in God, but that the ultimate ground of these must lie in God Himself.[2] Yet it by no means follows from this, in his judgment, that the guilt of sin, on account of which a man is punished eternally, should be attributed in any wise to God's ordination or decree. His meaning rather is this, that when predestination to punishment is viewed passively, it is seen to be the result of the concurrent working of several causes—(1) God Himself; (2) the *esse intelligibile* of the creature; (3) the future entrance of sin or crime.[3]

[1] In a passage of his *Saints' Days Sermons*, No. XLVII., given in note 1 on page 292.

[2] *Trialogus*, II., 14, p. 122: *Praedestinationis aut praescientiae divinae est causa indubie ipse Deus, cum nulla creatura causat, formaliter intelligendo, hos actus sive notitias Deo intrinsecas atque aeternas.*

[3] *Ib.: Intelligendo autem passive praedestinationem vel praeparationem ad poenam, videtur, quod illae sunt a Deo, ab esse intelligibili creaturae, et a futuritione criminis concausatae.*

The final issue, accordingly, *i.e.*, the eternal reward or punishment, is, on the one hand, it is true, brought about by the moral action of man or his transgression (*factum meritorium sive demeritorium*); but, on the other hand, this action of man in the present is preceded by a conditioning cause in eternity, viz., God's election, or fore-ordination in respect to the future action of His creature. But when God ordains a punishment or act of this kind (*ordinat punitionem vel actum hujusmodi*), He has an end in view which is morally good, which subserves the best interests of the Church, and contributes to the perfection of the world.[1]

It needs no lengthened investigation to make it clear that Wycliffe has by no means succeeded by these statements in solving all the difficulties which confront his view of election and the fore-ordination of God. For, assuming his view, only two cases are thinkable. Either the self-determination of a man (as foreknown by God) on the side of evil, and an impenitent persistency in it, is a really free act; and then God's eternal prevision of it and His decree of damnation awaiting the sinner must be thought of as conditioned by the self-determination of the creature emerging in its own time; in other words, the Eternal in this case must be determined by the temporal; the infinite God in His knowing and willing must be thought of as dependent upon His own finite creature. Or, alternatively, the Divine election and eternal ordination of what comes to pass is absolutely free and independent and all-conditioning; and then the logical sequence cannot be escaped, that the transgression of the creature, the sin of man, comes of God's own will and ordering—a conclusion which would throw a dark shadow of blame upon God Himself, and do away with the responsibility of man.

The Divine sovereignty.

It is to be remarked further, in regard to Wycliffe's doctrine of the election of the saved, and the eternal foreknowledge of those who fall into the state of eternal punishment, that he does not ground it, as Augustine does, upon the doctrine of original sin, and the utter impotency of fallen man for moral good, but exclusively upon the idea of the omnipotence of God, and His all-conditioning work in regard to all that comes to pass.

Wycliffe's fundamental idea of the Church as 'the whole body of the elect,' includes, as already remarked, an *antithesis* which runs through the present and actual, as well as through the eternal past and future. He gives clear and sharp expression to this himself. 'There are two classes of men,' he observes,

Two classes of mankind.

---

[1] Comp. the whole 14th chap. of 2d Book of the *Trialogus*, and the Analysis of the same in Lewald, *Zeitschrift für Historische Theologie*, 1846, pp. 222-225.

'who stand over against each other, since the world's beginning to the world's end. The first class, that of the elect, begins with Adam, and descends through Abel and all the elect to the last saint who, before the final judgment, shall contend for the cause of God. The second class is that of the reprobate, which begins with Cain and descends to the last man whom God has foreseen in his persistent impenitence.' To the latter Christ addresses the words, 'Woe unto you, for ye build the sepulchres of the prophets,' etc. (Luke xi. 47), in which special reference is made to Abel's blood, and the afflicted lot of all the prophets and righteous men.[1] Here Wycliffe has in view the whole history of mankind, not the Church of Christ exclusively. As to the latter, the fundamental conception of it as the whole number of the elect draws a separating line somewhere also; and the only question is whether this line is drawn within the Church or outside of it. There are some authors well acquainted with Wycliffe's writings who are of opinion that his conception of the Church draws the separating line outside and around the Church; and that precisely this is the fundamental error of his teaching on the subject of the Church, viz., his maintaining that only those who are saved souls are members of the Church on earth, while the ungodly, on the contrary, are in no sense of the word Church members.[2] In this judgment we cannot entirely concur. At the beginning of the English tract adduced in support of this view by Dr. Todd, of Dublin, Wycliffe, it is true, makes use of language which appears to warrant it.[3] And in other places besides we have the same principle expressed in the most decided manner, as one agreeable to Scripture and confirmed by many testimonies of the Fathers—*i.e.*, that only the elect man is a member of the Church.[4] And it is only an application of this doctrine when Wycliffe, speaking of worldly-minded and immoral bishops, says of them—'They are indisputably no members of the Holy Church, but members of

---

[1] *Saints' Days Sermons*, No. XLVII., fol. 94, col. 1. *Duo genera a principio mundi usque ad finem contraria, primum electorum ab Adam incipiens et descendens per Abel et cunctos electos usque ad sanctum novissimum ante diem judicii militantem; secundum genus reproborum a Caym incipiens et transiens per alios reprobos usque ad praescitum novissimum; et illis Christus dirigit hunc sermonem.*

[2] Dr. Todd has taken this view in his notes to Wycliffe's tract, *De Ecclesia et membris ejus*. Vide *Three Treatises by John Wyclyffe*, Dublin, 1851, p. clvii.

[3] *De Ecclesia et membris ejus*, c. 1, p. 543, note 2, end.

[4] *Supplementum Trialogi*, c. 2, p. 415: *Patet ex fide Christi scripturae et multiplici testimonio sanctorum, quod nullum est membrum sanctae matris ecclesiae nisi persona praedestinata. De Ecclesia*, c. 19, fol. 189, col. 4: *Supposito ex fide Scripturae elaborata a sanctis doctoribus, quod solum praedestinati sunt membra sanctae matris ecclesiae, restat dubium ulterius: si praesciti gerant ordines et officia illius ecclesiae? Et videtur ex dictis, quod non*, etc. In the same Book, c. 3, Wycliffe appeals, in support of this view, particularly to Thomas Aquinas: *Non enim vidi in S. Thoma vel alio Doctore probabili, quod totum genus (humanum) sed pars ejus praedestinata sit sancta mater ecclesia . . . et universalis ecclesia*, etc.

Satan, disciples of Antichrist, and children of the synagogue of Satan.'[1] Here we have a strong antithesis, not between the Church and the world outside of Christendom, but between holy Mother Church and the 'Church of the malignants,' *ecclesia malignantium*, a term borrowed from Psalm lxiv. 2 in the Vulgate version;[2] and between the members of the Holy Church and the members of Satan and the disciples of Antichrist.[3] The harshness of this dualism may seem strange to us, as though it were an utterance of excited feeling and very violent antagonism. We shall, however, judge it more mildly when we remember that even with a Pope like Gregory VII. the very same dualism between members of Christ and members of the devil or members of Antichrist was quite a common usage of speech. The application of the language, it is true, is exactly opposite in the hands of Gregory VII. and Wycliffe, but that makes no difference with regard to the dualism itself.

But still, on the other hand, I find that Wycliffe not very unfrequently gives expression also to another view, according to which his fundamental conception of the Church as the whole body of the elect draws a separating line through the heart of the Church itself. In other words, Wycliffe at times makes use of language which shows that he distinguishes within the circle of the Church between true members and only apparent members, which is an approximation to the distinction made by the Reformers of the sixteenth century between the *visible* and the *invisible* Church. Thus, in a sermon on the marriage feast and the guest without a marriage garment, he says of the apostles that they filled the Church militant with the elect and the foredoomed (*praedestinatis et praescitis*); and in another sermon he observes, on the words of Christ (John x. 26), 'Ye are not of My sheep,' that there are two flocks in the militant Church, the flock of Christ and manifold flocks of antichrist; and the shepherds, too, are of opposite kinds;[4] and by the Church militant Wycliffe always under-

The real and the visible Church.

---

[1] *Saints' Days Sermons*, No. II., fol. 3, col. 1 : *Omnes episcopi, qui ad temporalia, ad mundanos honores in familia, in apparatibus, vel expensis ministerio Christi superfluis anhelant, omnes inquam tales apostotant* (sic) *cum antichristo et solvunt infidelitur — totum decalogum ; et tales indubie non sunt membra sanctae matris ecclesiae. Vita eorum mundana ostendit patule, quod sunt membra diaboli et discipuli antichristi.* Comp. *Trialogus*, IV., 32, p. 325 : *Filios sanctae matris ecclesiae. . . . filios synagogae Satanae* (after Rev. ii. 9).

[2] E.g., *Supplementum Trialogi*, c. 2, p. 416 ; c. 8, p. 447.

[3] *XX. Sermons*, in *Select Works*, ed. Arnold, I., 50 : 'There ben (are) here two manere of chirche, holy Chirche or Chirche of God, that on no manere may be dampned, and the cherche of the fend, that for a time is good, and lastith not ; and this was nevere holy Chirche, ne part therof.'

[4] *Miscell. Sermons*, No. XXXIII., fol. 243, col. 2 : *Et impleverunt* (sc. *apostoli*) *ecclesiam militantem de praedestinatis et praescitis*. And *XXIV. Serm.*, No. IV., fol. 136, col. 4 : *Sunt autem greges duplices in ecclesia militante, scilicet grex Christi et greges multiplices antichristi*, etc.

stands the Church upon earth. Thus, in his view, there is not only a separating line, drawn like a tangent to the circle outside the Church, to serve as a boundary line, but there is another also, drawn like a chord through the Church itself. Wycliffe adopted from Augustine the distinction between the *true* body of Christ and the *mixed* or *simulated* body of Christ, *permixtum, simulatum*.[1] It was his contest with the Donatists which led Augustine to this distinction. He holds, indeed, firmly to the truth that only true believers—the elect—belong to the Church in the proper sense, and form the true body of Christ; but still he concedes that these true members of the Church are for the present mixed with the unconverted, as wheat and chaff are mixed together on the thrashing-floor (*permixtum*). He acknowledges that in the present life the unconverted, to all appearance, form also a part of the Church (*corpus simulatum*). Thus Augustine recognises, indeed, the whole body of elect and truly converted men as the proper kernel of the Church, and yet does not shut his eyes to the fact that in actual experience that kernel exists only with a shell-like surrounding of seeming Christians—a view which coincides with the Reformation doctrine that the Church in the proper sense of the word is the congregation of believers.[2] And inasmuch as Wycliffe accepts that Augustinian distinction, he recognises the unconverted, the only apparently holy, as being also members of the Church in a wider or improper sense, and thus draws a separating line through the Church itself.

The visible Church a mingled body.

The fact is, that Wycliffe never quite escaped a certain wavering of opinion between these two ideas. I cannot find that he was attached to one of the two only in an earlier stage of his thinking, while giving his preference to the other in a later stage; at least, the last quoted passages of his sermons belong to very different periods of his life—the one to a collection of sermons preached in his earlier years, the other to another collection belonging to his latest life [3]—and in both alike he avers that even within the Church militant the elect of God and the adherents of Antichrist exist side by side. This wavering, however, serves to prove that Wycliffe cannot have made the idea of the Church the subject of very mature reflection in a dogmatic sense; he attached more importance to the practical side of the subject.

Advance in Wycliffe's Church views.

---

[1] Augustine, *De Doctrina Christ.*, III., c. 32.
[2] *Confessio Augustana*, Art. VII.: *Est autem ecclesia congregatio sanctorum, in qua evangelium recte docetur et recte administrantur sacramenta.*

[3] The *XL. Miscellaneous Sermons* belong to the earlier years, the *XXIV. Sermons* to the very latest period of Wycliffe's life.

This much is certain, that the real members of the Church, or of the true body of Christ, are, according to Wycliffe's fundamental principle, exclusively those who have been chosen of God unto salvation, and who therefore persevere in the standing of grace to the end; from which it necessarily follows that no man knows with certainty the extent of the Church, or who does, or does not, belong in fact to it. No one knows of another whether he is an elect man and a child of the Church or no; and Wycliffe thinks that this ignorance is a real advantage to us; it keeps us from hasty judgments respecting the spiritual condition of those among whom we live; for no one has a right to pass judgment upon a man, saying either that he is a true member of the Church, or condemning and excommunicating him. No man may canonise another as a saint or pass an opposite sentence upon him, unless on the ground of having received a supernatural revelation upon the subject.[1] Nor only so; Wycliffe also holds to the purely Roman Catholic view, that no Christian can even be sure of his own standing in grace, and so be able to arrive at an assured conviction of his own proper membership in the Church of Christ; he may have an opinion as to the probability of his state, but assurance is by no means to be reached on the question.[2] A man may, indeed, know that he is in a state of grace for the present; but the main point concerns the question whether he will continue therein to the end; and of this no one can be certain for the future.[3] But the probability that any one is of the number of God's elect, and therefore a real child of the Church, rests upon a life of piety and morality, upon good works and the imitation of Christ.[4] Every pilgrim upon earth should have the hope of eternal blessedness, and therefore should be able to rest in the calm belief that he has a standing in grace which makes him well-pleasing to God; and for this reason it is needful that he should carefully examine himself, whether he is conscious of any mortal sin, and whether, without misgiving, he is able to believe that he has a standing in love.[5]

Wycliffe on Christian assurance.

---

[1] *Trialogus*, IV., 22, p. 325: *Ex istis videtur, quod non solum quantitatem ecclesiae sed ejus quidditatem communiter ignoramus*, etc.

[2] *De Ecclesia et membris ejus*, c. 7, L. ed. Todd: 'Certis this pope wot not him silf,' *i.e.*, whether he is one of the members of Christ.

[3] *Trialogus*, III., 6., p. 150: *Concedi debet, quod multi praesciti sunt in gratia secundum praesentem justitiam, praesciti tamen nunquam sunt in gratia finalis perseverantiae*, etc.

[4] *Ib.*, IV., 22, p. 325: *Reputare tamen debemus recte nobiscum viventes esse filios sanctae matris ecclesiae, et contrarie viventes esse filios synagogae Satanae. Supplementum Trial.*, c. 2, p. 416: *Non enim supponeret, quod sint tales* (real members of the Holy Church), *nisi ab evidentia capta ex opere, quo sequerentur dominum Jesum Christum.*

[5] *De Veritate Scripturae Sac.*, c. 14, fol. 33, col. 3.

The thought is no doubt one of great importance—that a Christian, in regard to his own standing in grace, as well as to the membership of others in the Church of Christ, can only find in the moral fruits of grace a true standard of measurement, and distinctive marks which are really certain. It establishes the right, at all times, to apply the moral standard in testing the actual life of the Church, as it is in the present; and this moral feature is one which we find, from Wycliffe downwards, in all the Precursors of the Reformation.

10.—The Worship of the Church.

WE pass on now to the *temporal existence and life of the Church*, and direct our attention (1) to its Worship.

One important side of the worship of the Church—viz., the preaching of the Word—we do not think it necessary to speak of in this place at any length, as we have already shown (chapter vi.) what Wycliffe's judgment was regarding the manner of preaching which was prevalent in his day. We only remind the reader in a word that there were two things which he censured in the sermons of his age : first, that men did not as a general rule preach the Word of God, but other things; and secondly, that when the Word of God was preached, this was not done in a way calculated to make its influence felt as a 'Word of eternal life.'

Preaching

With regard to the other parts of Divine service, Wycliffe again and again censures its degeneracy in the direction of an extreme sensuousness. 'Would that so many ceremonies and symbols,' he exclaims in one place, 'were not multiplied in our Church,'[1] for in such ritual he recognises a relapse into Judaism, which seeks after signs, and a departure from the spiritual nature of Christianity. 'There lies a danger for the Church militant in this practice of Judaising, which values in a carnally sensuous spirit those symbols and the human traditions connected with them more highly than the spiritual things which they signify; and even of giving heed to the Word of God more with the bodily eye than with the eye of the mind and by the light of faith.'[2] When the monks appealed, in defence of the splendour of their cloister churches, to the glory of Solomon's temple, as a proof that the basilicas ought to be more beautiful still in the period of grace,

Sensuousness in worship.

---

[1] *De Ecclesia*, c. 2, fol. 134, col. 2 : *Utinam non multiplicarentur tot cerimoniae et signa in nostra ecclesia!*

[2] *Ib.*, c. 19, fol. 192, col. 1 : *Sed in isto stat periculum militantis ecclesiae, quod judaizando secundum sensum carnalem signa illa cum traditionibus humanis plus suis signatis praeponderet, vel etiam legem Dei plus attendat judicio sensus corporei, quam oculo mentis vel etiam lumine fidei.*

Wycliffe in one passage replies that one can only marvel that the monks should imitate so closely that idolatrous and luxurious king in the Old Testament, and not the example of Christ, the Head of the Church and the King of kings, who had Himself foretold the destruction of the Temple of Jerusalem.[1] And on another occasion he gives a reply still more severe: 'Those senseless Galatians (Galatians iii. 1) wished to burden the Church with the ceremonies of the Mosaic law, and to leave on one side the counsels of Christ; and yet it is the inner man that should be adorned with virtues, as every moral virtue is infinitely better than all the riches or all the ornaments of a body without a soul.'[2]

What most offended Wycliffe's eye in the sensuous degeneracy of Christian worship was the numerous images and pictures in churches, and the veneration paid them. He was prudent enough, indeed, to admit that images, though prohibited in the law of Moses, are not in themselves forbidden in the Christian Church. He acknowledges it also to be indisputable that they may be made with a good design, when they are intended for the purpose of stirring up the believing to a devout adoration of God Himself. But, on the other hand, he recalls the fact that in the early Church images were not used in such great numbers as they are at present. Nor does he hesitate to assert that their use operates mischievously on men's minds in more than one direction. It leads, *e.g.*, to error in the faith, and to the idea that God the Father and the Holy Ghost are corporeal, when the Trinity is represented by artists in such a way that God the Father appears as an old man who holds between His knees God the Son hanging upon the cross, while God the Holy Ghost alights in the form of a dove upon them both, and such like. Very many, besides, have fallen into the error of taking an image for something animated, and solemnly bowing to it, which indisputably is idolatry. Many also have been led to believe in miracles performed by the image, a superstition resting upon mere delusion, or at most a diabolical deception. 'And by such delusions of an adulterous generation which seeketh after a sign (Matthew xvi. 4) are the people of Christ blinded more and more; and therefore must we preach against all such costliness, beauty, and other arts, which are employed more for the purpose of extracting money from deluded strangers than to promote the religion of Christ among the people.'[3]

Images in churches.

---

[1] *Saints' Days Sermons*, No. XVI., fol. 32, col. 1.
[2] *De Blasphemia*, c. 6, fol. 134, col. 4: *Sed isti insensati Galatae volunt monstrose onerare Christi ecclesiam cum cerimoniis legis antiquae, dimissis Christi consiliis,* etc.
[3] *Liber Mandatorum (Decalogus),* c. 14.

'The effect of every image should only be this, to awaken the mind and heart of a man to attend to heavenly things; but when this effect has been produced, the sooner the imagination of the man drops all attention to the qualities of the image, the better, for in the continued dwelling of the imagination upon these qualities lies concealed the venom of idolatry. As, now, the first and greatest commandment forbids us to pray to any work of man, insomuch that it was prohibited to the Jews to make any images whatsoever, it manifestly behoves us to be constantly on our guard against the poison under the honey,[1] *i.e.*, against an idolatrous worship of the image instead of the Divine Being so represented.' 'The people, therefore, must be faithfully warned of the danger which lies in this matter, especially as merely nominal Christians, men of an animal nature, dismissing all faith in spiritual things, are wont at the present day to feed their senses to excess in religion, as, *e.g.*, their eyes with the sumptuous spectacle of the Church's ornaments, their ears with bells and organs and the new art of striking the hour of the day by the wonderful chimes, not to mention many other sensuous preparations by which their other senses are moved, apart altogether from religious feeling.'[2]

By far the greater number of images were representations of the saints, their acts, and their martyr deaths. What Wycliffe thought of saint-worship has been much better known hitherto than his opinion respecting images, for he has given sufficient expression to his views upon it in the *Trialogus*. Vaughan remarked with truth that Wycliffe became step by step more clear and decided in his repudiation of saint-worship,[3] and we are in a position to confirm this general statement by particular proofs. Thus, *e.g.*, it appears worthy of remark that in a sermon of his earlier life, preached on the Feast of the Assumption of Mary, he is teaching, quite unsuspectingly, that the mother of our Lord is to her worshippers a mediatrix full of mercy. 'Even fellow-pilgrims upon earth, moved by brotherly love, help one another in

Saint-worship.

The Virgin Mary.

---

fol. 133, col. 2, particularly 134, col. 1: *Et de ista deceptione generationis adulterae signa quaerentis populus Christi continue plus caecatur*, etc.

[1] *Liber Mandatorum* (*Decalogus*), fol. 134, col. 2: *Ideo de quanto expeditius post expergefactionem ad coelestia imaginativa hominis dimittit accidentia imaginis, de tanto est melius, quia in mora imaginandi latet venenum idolatriae; ... patet, quod summa diligentia cavere debemus venenum sub melle, adorando idolatrice signum loco signati.*

[2] *Ib.*: *Videtur mihi periculum diligentius exponendum, specialiter cum nomine tenus Christiani tanquam animales vel bestiales dimissa fide credendorum spiritualium nimis hodie pascunt sensus, ut visum spectaculis ornamentorum ecclesiae sumptuosis, auditum campanis organis et novo modo discernendi horas diei per campanam mirabiliter tintinantem, et sensibilia, quibus irreligiose moventur sensus alii, sunt parata.*

[3] *Life and Opinions*, II., p. 293.

the time of need, but the blessed Virgin in heaven beholds our necessities, and is still fuller of love, still richer in compassion; and all the more faithfully does she care for our needs, as she knows that she has attained to so high honour in order that she might become the refuge of sinners.' What would men have more?[1] The preacher makes only one condition, that we be the imitators of Mary's virtues, especially of her humility, purity, and chastity, for she loves much only those who are like herself. When, however, the objection is raised that any one who exercises these virtues will certainly obtain the eternal reward even without Mary's help, Wycliffe replies, 'It seems to me to be impossible that we should obtain the reward without the help of Mary. There are, however, degrees in her help. No one goes away from her quite unaided from her boundless resources; even those who have done no good thing as yet shall have experience of her power to soothe; because of her humility and intercession for mankind they shall be more mildly punished. For she was herself in some measure the cause of the incarnation and passion of Christ, and so of the whole redemption of the world. There is no sex or age, no rank or position of any one in the whole human race, which has no need to call for the help of the Holy Virgin.'[2] These are thoughts which vie with the most ardent glorifications of Mary and her merits.

In his later years Wycliffe's judgment was entirely different. There were two questions here which engaged his further reflections—first, the right of the Church to canonise certain personages; and next, the moral value of the devotions and rituals which are offered to the saints.

The first question occupied Wycliffe, as we are able to see, for some length of time. I find traces of this in his work *De Civili Dominio*. But here he still expresses himself with caution, even with a certain degree of reserve; for he maintains only the *possibility* that the Church in her canonisations may deceive both herself and others, either through the love of money, or from the inordinate love of those persons who stand in near relation to the individuals con-

---

[1] *XL. Miscell. Sermons*, fol. 235, col. 2; fol. 36, col. 2, particularly 236, col. 1 : *Tertium, quod debemus credere de matre Domini, quod ipsa est suis et veris cultoribus propitia procuratrix. Nam viatores ex impetu caritatis suffragantur egentibus. Sed b. virgo Maria videt in verbo* (coelo?) *nostram egentiam, et est magis caritativa et magis misericors. Ideo credendum est, quod fidentius procurat contra nostram egentiam et eo specialius, quo noscit se adeptam tantum honorem, ut sit refugium peccatorum.*

[2] *Ib.*, fol. 236, col. 2 : *Hic videtur mihi, quod impossibile est nos praemiari sine Mariae suffragio. . . . Imo illi, qui nihil meruerunt, sentient ejus levamen, cum occasione suae humilitatis et interpellationis pro humano genere mitius punientur. Ipsa enim fuit quodammodo causa incarnationis et passionis Christi, et per consequens totius salvationis mundi.*

cerned, or through illusions of the devil. He puts, also, the case that many holy monks stand higher in blessedness than certain saints whose festivals the Church celebrates. Still, however, it surpasses the judgment of man to decide upon this subject in individual cases, and therefore men must defer to the determination of the Church. It may, indeed, well be that the holders of the Primacy receive special inspiration from heaven in this matter.[1] Wycliffe takes a step in advance of this in his work *De Ecclesia*, when he observes that 'certainly no Christian can believe that it is necessary to salvation to believe of this or that person whom the Church canonises, that he is in glory on that account, especially in respect to certain modern saints.'[2] But most strongly of all does he speak in the *Trialogus*, when he puts into the mouth of others the assertion that it is nothing less than a blasphemous pretension of the Romish Curia when, apart from any special revelation, it pronounces persons to be saints, of whose holiness it can know as little as the 'Prester John,' or the Sultan. And the hearing of witnesses in such a matter cannot possibly supply any proof.[3] Here the authority of the Church to confer canonisation is denied in the most distinct and decided way.

Canonisation.

The second question concerns the moral value, or the contrary, of the devotions and festivals celebrated in honour of the saints. On this subject Wycliffe took up, in his later life, a position essentially different from that which we have seen him occupying in his earlier years; for now he lays down, with entire decision, the principle that a devotion or a festival offered to any saint is only of value in so far as it is fitted to promote and to heighten the feeling of pious devotion towards the Saviour Himself.[4] Again, he is only expressing the same thought when he says that the blessed saints in heaven look down with contempt upon the perverted praise which men offer to them, and upon the many commemorations and numerous festivals, often of a very worldly character,

Festivals in honour of saints.

---

[1] *De Civili Dominio*, III., c. 10, fol. 67, col. 1: *Contingit etiam, quod multi ss. monachi et fratres sint in beatitudine altiores quam dati sancti, quorum festa solemnisat ecclesia, verumtamen discretio hujus in particulari excedit humanum judicium. Ideo standum est determinationi ecclesiae.*

[2] *De Ecclesia*, c. 2, fol. 134, cols. 1 and 2: *Absit christianum credere, quod de necessitate salutis oportet omnem fidelem credere explicite de isto et quocunque, quem ecclesia nostra canonizat, ut eo ipso sit beatus. De aliis autem modernioribus qui canonizantur ratione parentelae, questus vel muneris, non oportet nos apponere tantam fidem,* etc.

[3] *Trialogus*, III., 30, p. 237: *Insuper videtur multis, quod curia ista sic canonizans sanctos blaspheme praesumit, cum subducta revelatione tam plane ignorat sanctitatem defuncti, quam plane ignorat Johannes presbiter vel Soldanus.*

[4] *Saints' Days Sermons* (delivered later than 1378), No. I., fol. 1, col. 1: *Non valet festum vel devotio cujuscunque sancti citra dominum, nisi de quanto in ejus devotionem supereminenter persona solemnisans accenditur.*

with which men desire to honour them; and they withdraw their assistance from all such worshippers.[1] In so saying, he expresses also an unfavourable judgment on the excessive number of saints' days, which he looked upon as in no way promoting the good of the Church. 'As the apostles, without any such saints' days, loved Jesus Christ more than we do, it appears to many orthodox Christians a rash and dangerous thing to institute so many saints' festivals, and they deem that it would be better not to have so many celebrations burdening the Church.'[2] 'It would be no sin in a parish priest,' he says, 'if, in dealing with people who did bodily labour on one of the saints' days appointed to be kept holy by the Church, but having no confirmation of their sanctity from Holy Scripture, he did not censure nor punish them as transgressors of the Ten Commandments; in forbearing to do so, he would, on the contrary, be preserving the liberty of the Christian Church within the limits prescribed by Christ Himself.'

In these circumstances it would have surprised us if Wycliffe had not also spoken with disapproval of the veneration of relics as well as of the custom of pilgrimages, both of which practices were so closely connected with saint-worship; and in fact he has done so in an unmistakable way, although sometimes with much caution. His language, however, is sufficiently strong when he remarks that 'a culpable blindness, an immoderate and covetous worshipping of relics cause the people to fall into gross error, as the punishment of their sin. Whence, in many countries, the love of money brings things to such a pass, that in numerous churches a portion of the body of some one who has been canonised as a confessor or martyr is more honoured with pilgrimages, and costly oblations, and ornaments of gold and precious stones lavished upon his grave, than the body of the mother of God, or the Apostle Peter, or Paul, or any other of the acknowledged saints.'[3] 'For my part, I condemn no act of this kind; but at the same time there are few or none which I can positively

---

[1] *Saints' Days Sermons*, No. II., fol. 3, col. 1: *Cum sancti viatores graviter ferunt exaltationem sui, multo magis beati despiciunt illam laudem eorum perversam; et sic beati creduntur contemnere multas canonisationes; et ita cum beati contemnunt quoscunque Deus contemserit, necessario subtrahunt suffragia a sic eos colentibus.*

[2] *Ib.*, No. I., fol. 1, col. 1: *Cum apostoli sine talibus festis sanctorum plus nobis dilexerunt Jesum Christum, videtur multis catholicum* (pure Christian truth), *tot sanctorum festa instituere esse temerarium; unde videtur quibusdam, quod melius esset non fore tot solemnitates ad onus ecclesiae,* etc.

[3] *De Ecclesia*, c. 19, fol. 192, col. 4: *Unde talis culpanda caecitas, inordinatus ac cupidus cultus circa reliquias faciunt in poenam peccati populum multum falli. Unde in multis patriis cupido pecuniae facit in multis ecclesiis, quod pars personae, emtae ut canonizetur pro confessore vel martyre, plus honoretur peregrinatione, sumptuosa oblatione et sepulcri ornatione auro et lapidibus preciosis, quam corpus matris Dei,* etc. Comp. *Sermons on the Gospel*, No. XXXII., *Select Works*, I., 83.

commend, because those who go on pilgrimage, worship relics, and collect money, might at least occupy themselves more usefully, if they omitted these practices. From the Word of God it even appears to be the duty of all such persons to employ themselves better at the present time, and consequently that they are guilty of great sin in failing so to employ themselves. I say nothing of the sins which occur on these occasions, and how the practice itself is a pharisaical one, savouring of the Old Testament, but without any ground in the new law.'

It is a remarkable fact, psychologically, that in the same sermon on the Feast of the Assumption which so decidedly seems to favour Mariolatry, there already occurs a reference to the errors which develop themselves from the veneration of relics. As stated above, Wycliffe is, in this sermon, investigating the question whether Mary went up corporeally to heaven, or was taken up after her death, and shows his leaning to the latter view. He then adds the remark, 'and because the contrary might have happened in consequence of erroneous worship and covetousness of the clergy, it seems to me probable that God so ordered it that the bodies of Moses, of the Virgin Mary, of the Evangelist John, and of many other martyrs, should remain unknown to us on account of the errors which might result from such veneration.' On the other hand, in a sermon delivered in the last year of his life, on the feast of John the Baptist, Wycliffe expresses the thought that God and the Church triumphant regard the worshipping of corporeal relics at large with no approbation; and then he continues as follows:—'It would be to the benefit of the Church, and to the honour of the saints, if the costly ornaments so foolishly lavished upon their graves were divided among the poor. I am well aware, however, that the man who would sharply and fully expose this error would be held for a manifest heretic by the image-worshippers and the greedy people who make gain of such graves; for in the adoration of the eucharist, and such worshipping of dead bodies and images, the Church is seduced by an adulterous generation.'[1] The difference of tone between the two last-mentioned passages is so marked as to show clearly enough what important progress Wycliffe must have made in the interval in his insight into the dark side of

---

[1] *Saints' Days Sermons*, No. XXII., fol. 43, col. 3. The following words occur at the end of the Sermon, fol. 44, col. 1: *Unde ad honorem foret sanctorum et utilitatem ecclesiae, quod distributa forent pauperibus jocalia* (jewels) *sepulcrorum, quibus stulte . . . sunt ornata. Scio tamen quod acute et diffuse detegens hunc errorem foret a cultoribus signorum et avaris reportantibus ex talibus sepulcris lucrum, manifestus haereticus reputatus; nam in cultu et veneratione eucharistiae, tali cultu mortuorum corporum atque imaginum, per generationem adulteram ecclesia est seducta.*

saint-worship. Only one thought on the subject of pilgrimages may yet be touched upon here; it is this—that Christian people would do better to stay at home, and keep God's commandments in private, than to make pilgrimages and bring gifts to the thresholds of the saints.[1]

In a similar spirit Wycliffe expresses himself on the subject of masses for the dead, and all that concerns them. He attaches little importance to them, and though he does not exactly deny that such masses and prayers for the departed, and foundations in their memory, may be of some benefit to them, he yet affirms with all emphasis his conviction that in all circumstances the good which a man does in his lifetime, should it be only the giving of a cup of cold water, out of love and for the sake of Christ, is of more use to him than the spending of thousands on thousands of pounds by his executors after his death for the repose of his soul.[2]

Another side of the life of the Church on earth in regard to which Wycliffe's judgment may be of importance for us, is *the moral condition and character of the Church.*

Everywhere Wycliffe sets out from ethical ideas, and applies to all conditions and actions the standard of morals. There are occasions when he speaks under the influence of strong feeling on the different aspects of this subject. At such times his discourse has a tone of deep earnestness, and becomes truly impressive, even incisive.

The judgment which he pronounces upon the religious and moral condition of Christendom, when he tries it by the standard of the first commandment, is sufficiently unfavourable. He finds that idolatry and creature worship are in the ascendant everywhere. 'It is clear as day,' says he, 'that we so-called Christians make the creatures to be our gods. The proud or ambitious man worships a likeness of that which is in heaven (Exodus xx. 4), because, like Lucifer, he loves, above all things, promotion or dignity in one form or another. The covetous man worships a likeness of that which is in the earth beneath. And

Prevailing forms of idolatry.

---

[1] *De Civili Dominio*, III., 10, fol. 67, col. 1: *Melius occuparetur populus domi in praeceptorum Dei observantia, quam in peregrinatione et oblatione visitando sanctorum limina.*

[2] *XL. Miscellaneous Sermons*, No. VI., fol. 203, col. 3: *Licet mortuis prosint suffragia ecclesiae, verumtamen quantumlibet opus meritorium . . . . factum a superstite est sibi magis utile, quam foret, ipso mortuo, quantumlibet magnum suffragium; sic quod plus prodest homini viventi dare in caritate 'calicem aquae frigidae' pro Christi nomine, quam pro ipso mortuo, in purgatorio punito, darentur ab executoribus millies mille librae.* Liber Mandatorum (Decalogus), c. 23, fol. 816, col. 2: *Si quaeritur de praestantiori modo juvandi mortuos, dicitur quod juvando vivos amplius indigentes, ut seminando opera misericordiae tam corporalia quam spiritualia secundum spiritum consilii. Non enim oportet imprudenter in uno globo una die celebrare tot missas, facere tot distributiones aut simul tot jejunctiones.*

although, arrayed in sheep's clothing, we hypocritically confess that our highest of all service is in the worship of God, yet it would very well become us carefully to inquire whether we faithfully carry out this confession in our actions. Let us then search and examine whether we keep the first and greatest commandment, and worship God above all. Do we not bend and bow ourselves before the rich of this world more with the view of being rewarded by them with worldly honour or temporal advantage, than for the sake of their moral character or spiritual help? Does not the covetous man stretch out now his arms and now his hands to grasp the gold, and does he not pay court untiringly to the men who have it in their power to hinder or to help his gains? Does not the sensual man, as though he were making an offering to the idol Moloch, cast himself down with his whole body before the harlot? Does he not put upon such persons worldly honour? Does he not offer to them the incense of purses of gold, in order to scent the flow of sensual delight with the sweetest perfumes? Does he not lavish upon his mistress gift upon gift, till she is more wonderfully bedizened with various ornaments than an image of the Holy Virgin? And does not all this show that we love the flesh, the world, and the devil more than God, in that we are more careful to keep their commandments than His? What violence do we hear of the Kingdom of Heaven suffering in our times (Matthew xi. 12), while the gates of hell are bolted? But, alas! broad and well trodden is the way which leadeth to hell, and narrow and forsaken the way which leadeth to heaven! This it is which makes men, for lack of faith, love what is seen and temporal more than the blessings which they cannot see, and to have more delight in buildings, dress, and ornaments, and other things of art and men's invention, than in the uncreated archetypes of heaven.' In the end Wycliffe concludes that at least the greatest part of Christendom is infected with the prevailing idolatry, and in reality treasures the work of its own hands more highly than God the Lord.[1]

Taking all things into view, Wycliffe arrives at the conviction that the moral condition of the race was sinking lower and lower. As **Corruptions of the age.** the world is forsaking the law of Christ, and in conformity to human maxims is surrendering itself to the lust of secular things, it cannot but be that offences and scandals will arise.[2] And when he compares the various classes of wicked men, it appears to him that there is a threefold gradation of evil among

---

[1] *Liber Mandatorum* (*Decalogus*), c. 15, fol. 136, col. 1; fol. 137, col. 2.
[2] *De Civili Dominio*, II., 17, fol. 238, col. 1: *Mundo quidem, relicta Christi lege, declinante secundum traditiones humanas ad cupiditatem temporalium, necesse est ut contumeliae et scandala oriantur.*

them. The common people are bad, the secular rulers are worse, and the spiritual prelates are worst of all.[1]

It may be anticipated from this language that Wycliffe would not be blind to the moral corruption of the clergy of his own age. On the contrary, it is quite clear to him that the Church has much more to fear from enemies within than without, and especially from 'a clergy who are given up to avarice, and therefore enemies to the Cross of Christ and the Gospel.'[2] These few words alone are sufficient to show that while his eye was open to all the religious shortcomings and all the moral faults of the clergy of his time, he looked upon their worldly-mindedness and love of wealth as the real root of all their evil. But this topic does not admit of being fully treated except in connection with the whole body of his teaching on the subject of the constitution of the Church.

II.—Constitution of the Church.

THE first foundation-principle of the Roman Catholic Constitution is the division of the Church into two ranks—clergy and laity—or the division between the teaching and hearing Church—the governing and obeying Church. A distinction which the Reformation *à priori* abolished by putting the idea of office in the place of a distinction of rank, or, in other words, by maintaining the universal priesthood of believers.

Clergy and laity.

This fundamental principle of the Church of Rome Wycliffe does not deny with any clear consciousness of the opposite conception, but nevertheless he puts forth views which are indirectly opposed to it. For the personal responsibility, and the consequent liberty of conscience of the private members of the Church, are principles which he is far from ignoring; on the contrary, he requires that every Christian should have knowledge of the truth, should in a sense be a theologian, for faith is the highest theology. The difference in knowledge between Church member and priest is only one of degree.[3] He goes further still. Not only does he think the case

---

[1] *De Ecclesia*, c. 5, fol. 142, col. 3 : *Omnes praesciti constituunt unum corpus. . . . Ex quo patet, quod oportet esse unam generationem, quae fuit mala in vulgaribus, pejor in secularibus praepositis, sed pessima in praelatis.*

[2] *De Civili Dominio*, II., 2, fol. 156, col. 1 : *Si non fallor, longe plus infestatur ecclesia ab inimicis domesticis, ut clero avaritiae dedito et sic cruci Christi ac legi evangelicae inimico, quam a Judaeis paganis forinsecus.*

[3] *De Veritate Scripturae Sac.*, c. 24, fol. 78, col. 2 : *Omnem Christianum oportet esse theologum, quia necesse est omnem Christianum addiscere fidem ecclesiae, vel scientia infusa vel cum hoc scientia humanitus acquisita ; aliter enim non foret fidelis, fides autem est summa theologia. Ideo oportet omnem catholicum esse theologum ; sed sacerdotem, in quantum superior, secundum quandam excellentiam.* Comp. *De Civili Dominio*, I., 44, fol. 130, col. 2 : *Omnis homo debet esse theologus et*

possible that theologians and priests might take a wrong direction in doctrine and life, while the laity remained steadfast in the truth, but he maintains the existence of this state of matters as a matter of actual fact. Upon occasion of his opposing the doctrine of Transubstantiation, he observes that God always preserves *natural knowledge* among the laity, and keeps up among some of the clergy the right understanding of the Faith, as in Greece and elsewhere, as seemeth to Him good.[1] He does not even shrink from laying down the principle, however much offence it may excite, that the laity have the right, in case their spiritual rulers fail to do their duty, or give themselves up to certain vices and evil ways, to withhold from them the Church's revenues—a principle which undoubtedly rests on the assumption that the laity are in a position and are entitled to judge respecting the life of their spiritual superiors, and the way in which they execute the duties of their office.[2]

Rights of the laity.

To maintain such a principle would have been an astounding pitch of boldness if the Canon Law itself had not been on its side, and papal precedents had not conceded to the congregations of the Church that right. And these facts Wycliffe knew right well how to avail himself of in his own support. We mention only the measure which Gregory VII. had recourse to in his day in order to carry through his reforms, and, in particular, to abolish the marriage of priests. For this end he laid his injunctions upon the congregations —that is, upon the laity—that they should no longer hear masses read by married priests, that they should cease to visit the churches where such priests officiated, and should, so to speak, put a mark of infamy upon them—all by papal command.

Wycliffe, it is true, makes an application of the principle different

---

legista ; nam omnis debet esse Christianus, quod tamen non potest esse nisi legem mandatorum Dei cognoverit, II., c. 13, fol. 210, col. 2. Every Christian is bound to follow the counsels of Jesus Christ, at least some of them, *ad quod judicandum erit discretus sibi ipsi judex optimus.*

[1] *Trialogus,* IV., 5, 261 : *Sed Deus sicut semper servat notitiam naturalem in laicis, sic semper servat sensum catholicum in quibusdam clericis, ut in Graecia vel alibi, ubi placet.* In his piece, *Cruciata* (Wyclif Society, 1883), vol. ii. pp. 619, 620, Wycliffe maintains that it is possible that a time may come when the militant Church may consist only of poor believers, scattered in many lands, of people who follow Christ more faithfully in their moral walk than Pope and Cardinals.

[2] *De Veritate Scripturae Sac.*, c. 25, fol. 82, col. 4 : *Ex istis colligi potest sententia, quam saepe inserui, licet sit mundo odibilis, quod licet laicis in casu tam subtrahere quam auferre bona ecclesiae a suis praepositis. Et voco praepositos quoscunque, qui debent juvare suos subditos spirituali suffragio, . . . ut patet de episcopis et clericis,* etc. In the sequel Wycliffe refutes, fol. 86, col. 2, the objection that laymen are not at all entitled to sit in judgment upon the life and official conduct of their spiritual superiors. This idea he repudiates with the remark, that this would be as much as to say that it was not competent for the laity to concern themselves about their own salvation.

from that of Hildebrand, but the principle in both cases is the same, *i.e.*, that unfaithful and unconscientious clergy deserve the reprimand and actual repudiation of the laity. Wycliffe emphasises the right of the laity so strongly that he puts it forward as a formal duty, the neglect of which cannot be justified. A member of the congregation who omits such a reprimand makes himself a partner of the sin of his spiritual rulers;[1] while laymen who withhold the temporalities of the Church from an unworthy object, take them from him not as a spiritual ruler or Church minister, but as an enemy of the Church.[2] And Wycliffe does not think of such a case as a mere possibility which might occur in single exceptional instances, but believes that abuses of all kinds—the incorporation of benefices with foundations—the granting of indulgences—the neglect of necessary censures—may be pushed to such a length that the so-called clergy would become an utterly worldly body.[3] But, on the other hand, he holds it as no inconceivable thing that the Church might consist for a time of lay members alone.[4]

From the foregoing it appears clearly enough that Wycliffe by no means accepted of the Romish division of the Church into two ranks—the clergy and the laity—according to which the laity had only to hear and obey, and were destitute of all independent judgment and free decision in ecclesiastical matters. On the contrary, he recognises the general priesthood of believers, although he never makes use of this phrase. His conception of the Church as 'the whole body of the elect' is itself an indirect proof of this, for it is as clear as day that, measured by this conception, the chasm which exists between the 'elect' and the 'foreknown' must be thought of as incomparably greater than that which is placed between a cleric and a laic. And, undoubtedly, an 'elect' man—a believing and earnest Christian ('trew man'), layman though he is, yet stands before God infinitely higher than a priest, or a bishop, or even a pope, if the latter, however highly placed in 'the mixed Church,' in virtue of priestly consecration and hierarchical order, is yet only in name a Christian

Universal priesthood of believers.

---

[1] *De Veritate Scripturae Sacrae*, 26, fol. 88, col. 2: *Non excusatur parochianus tali praeposito innuitive consentiens; quin participat peccatis praepositi, qui sic fovet.*

[2] *Ib.*, fol. 88, col. 4: *Laici legitime auferentes bona ecclesiae ab indigno non auferunt ab eo tanquam praelato vel ministro ecclesiae, sed, ut vere debent credere, ab ecclesiae inimico.*

[3] *Ib.*, c. 24, fol. 80, col. 2.

[4] *De Civili Dominio*, I., 43, fol. 127, col. 2. Wycliffe remarks here that when men comfort themselves with the thought that 'Peter's little ship' can never go down, it will depend upon the way in which this is understood, whether it is not a piece of sophistry. The Church militant may exist sometimes among one people and sometimes among another, and sometimes among a very small number of persons. *Nec video, quin dicta navi. Petri possit pure pro tempore stare in laiciss*

and priest, but in truth an enemy of the Church and a limb in the body of the wicked fiend.

This dualism between 'elect' and 'foreknown,' between members of Christ and members of Antichrist, runs through the whole ascending scale of the hierarchy. To the pastoral office, as we have already shown in chapter vi., Wycliffe devoted the most unremitting pains, as well in the practical fulfilment of his own calling as in the labour of thought and the exercise of his influence upon others, by speech and writing. In particular, his whole tractate, *Of the Pastoral Office*, is devoted to it; but, in addition to this, there is scarcely one of his writings, large or small, in which he does not return to the subject, describing the actual condition into which the office had fallen, and striving to the end that it should again become what it ought to be. With great outspokenness he brings to light the negligences and sins of the 'false shepherds.'[1] Above all, he complains of their neglect of the chiefest duty of the office—the preaching of God's Word; they take no heed to feed the sheep; the pastors are often dumb dogs.[2] Oftentimes and bitterly enough he rebukes the total worldliness of many pastors, who neglect the service of God in order to serve noblemen, or waste their time in hunting, drinking, boon companionship, and such like; men so utterly earthly-minded that they can be compared only to moles; they give themselves up wholly to money-gathering, partly by preaching only for gain, partly by fleecing the poor, of whom they are supposed to be the protectors.[3]

Corruptions in the clerical body.

Let it not be supposed, however, that Wycliffe had the same bad opinion of all the parish priests. He was himself a conscientious curate of souls, and may very well have known many like himself in the land. He knows well how to make the right distinctions. 'There are three kinds of pastors,' he observes in one place: 'some who are true shepherds both in name and in truth, and some who are only shepherds in name. And these latter again divide themselves into three classes—there are some, namely, who preach and do the work of a shepherd, but chiefly for worldly fame or profit; and these Augustine calls "hirelings." Men of the second class fail to fulfil their pastoral office,

True and false shepherds.

---

[1] *De Veritate Scripturae Sac.*, c. 23, fol. 77, col. 2, and fol. 78, col. 1 (*pseudopastores*) after Ezekiel xxxiv.

[2] *De Officio Pastorali*, II., c. 1–4, p. 31. *Liber Mandatorum*, c. 30: *Clerici caecantur ignorantia proprii officii, quod est praedicatio verbi Dei*. XL. Miscellaneous Sermons, No. XXIX., fol. 238, col. 3: *Quidam sunt canes muti non valentes latrare*, etc.

[3] *Liber Mandatorum*, c. 10, fol. 114, col. 2; c. 26. fol. 205, col. 1. *De Civili Dominio*, I., 25, fol. 59, col. 1. XXIV. Sermons, No. V., fol. 141, col. 2. XL. Miscellaneous Sermons, No. XXIX., fol. 238, col. 3. *Select Works*, I., 11; II., 60.

but at the same time inflict upon their flocks no visible damage or wrong; and yet they are described by Christ as thieves and robbers (John x. 8), because in virtue of their office they defraud their parishioners of a full return for those Church revenues which are the inheritance of the poor. But the third class not only rob the poor openly of their goods without rendering any corresponding service, but like wolves they also attack and destroy their flocks, and incite them in many ways to sin; and these are "the ravening wolves" (Matthew vii. 15). But a "shepherd" enters into office through the door, which is Christ, in order to serve God and His Church in humility, and not for the sake of earthly gain or worldly advantages. Such an one leads the sheep upon the way which conducts to heaven, by the example of a holy life; he heals the sick, by application of the sacramental means of grace; he feeds the hungry, by reaching to them the food of holy preaching; and finally he gives drink to the thirsty, by opening up to them the wisdom of the Scriptures with the help of the reading of holy exposition.'[1]

On the subject of the Celibacy of the Priesthood, Wycliffe gives repeated expression to his views. In several places he characterises the Church law which enjoins it as an ordinance plainly unscriptural, hypocritical, and morally perni- *Clerical celibacy.* cious. Neither Christ nor His apostles forbade the marriage of priests; they rather approved it.[2] He points not only to the usage of the most ancient Church to consecrate married men as bishops, but also to the still existing practice of the marriage of the clergy in the Greek Church.[3] And as concerns the present, he confesses himself unable to see why in all parts of Christendom allowance should not be given to married men to continue in the priesthood, especially if no candidates of equal qualifications for the priesthood should be forthcoming. In particular, he urges that it would undoubtedly be the lesser evil of the two, that men who are living in honourable matrimony, and who are ruling equally well the Church and their own houses, should be consecrated to the priesthood without disturbance to their married life, than that priests should be living, indeed, out of the married state, but should be practising unchastity in spite of their vows, with wives and widows and virgins.[4]

---

[1] *De Veritate Scripturae Sac.*, c. 23, fol. 75, cols. 2 and 3.
[2] *Of Weddid Men and Wifis;* in *Select English Works of John Wyclif*, ed. Arnold, Oxford, 1871, III., 189. On the *Seven Deadly Sins,* ib., c. 29, 163.
[3] *De Veritate Scripturae Sac.*, c. 24, fol. 81, col. 2 : *In primitiva ecclesia ordinati sunt monogami in episcopos, . . . et sic continuata est talis copula in Orientali Christianismo.*
[4] *Ib.*, fol. 81, col. 3: *Numquid credimus communius malum fuisse conjugatos literatos et castos gubernationi ecclesiae*

Hypocrites, it is true, who set the ordinances of men above the word of Scripture, abhor the marriage of a priest as poison, while allowing themselves in uncleanness of the most shameful kind. And yet Scripture nowhere forbids the marriage of a priest, but prohibits unchastity to all men, the laity included, without exception.[1] But even apart from such sins and vices, Wycliffe is of opinion that in all cases it would be better that a priest should live as a married man, than that while remaining out of matrimony he should live a wholly secular life, addicted to ambition and the love of money.[2] Let this be as it may, Wycliffe never allows himself to be shaken in his conviction that the pastoral office, more than any other, when rightly exercised, is the most useful, and for the Church the only indispensable, office; that all the other grades of the hierarchy may fall into disuse, but that the cure of souls in the congregations of the Church must always be continued and steadfastly upheld.[3]

This last declaration is in accord with Wycliffe's view of the higher gradations of the hierarchy, especially with his conviction, to which he had before given expression, that between priest and bishop there is no difference arising from consecration —that, on the contrary, every priest regularly ordained possesses full power to dispense in a sufficient manner all the sacraments. Among the nineteen propositions of Wycliffe which Pope Gregory XI. rejected in 1377, this one now stated is already found; and I find that it was extracted from his work, *De Civili Dominio*.[4] This conviction was not only always held fast by him from that time forward, but was developed still more boldly and logically, as may be seen from his later writings; and he was confirmed in it partly by Holy

Presbyter and bishop originally the same.

---

et domus suae intentos, stante conjugio ordinari presbyteros, quam nos extra conjugium post votum continentiae cognoscere omne genus mulierum ut meretrices, conjugatas atque viduas et virgines, imo proprias filias speciales?

[1] *Responsiones ad Argumenta Radulphi de Strode*, MS. 1338, fol. 120, col. 4.

[2] *De Officio Pastorali*, II., 11, p. 46: The disciples of Christ are turned into Pharisees, who strain out gnats and swallow camels. *Nam conjugium secundum legem Christi eis licitum odiunt ut venenum, et seculare dominium eis a Christo prohibitum nimis avide amplexantur.* Quite similarly *De Officio Regis*, c. 2, fol. 8, col. 1. Comp. *De Civili Dominio*, II., 13, fol. 105, col. 1: *Unde, si non fallor, minus malum foret clericum uxorari, quam circa mundum esse sollicitum.*—Of Weddid Men and Wifis; in *Select Works*, III., 190.

[3] *Saints' Days Sermons*, No. XLVI., fol. 93, col. 3: *Ratificari quidem debet status residentium curatorum, et subtrahi totum residuum.*

[4] In the schedule added to the Papal Brief of May 22, 1377, No. 16 reads as follows:—*Hoc debet catholice credi, quilibet sacerdos rite ordinatus habet potestatem sufficienter sacramenta quaelibet conferendi et per consequens quemlibet contritum a peccato quolibet absolvendi.* And the original passage to which this refers is plainly the following (*De Civili Dominio*, I., 38, fol. 93, col. 1): *Hoc ergo catholice credi debet, quod quilibet sacerdos rite ordinatus habet potestatem sufficientem quaelibet sacramenta conferendi . . . absolvendi, nec aliter potest papa absolvere. Nam quantum ad protestatem ordinis omnes sacerdotes sunt pares, licet potestas inferioris rationabiliter sit ligata.*

Scripture and partly by the history of the Church. From Scripture he derived the knowledge that the Church of the apostles recognised only the distinction between Presbyters and Deacons, but made no difference between Presbyter and Bishop, which in the apostolic age were identical.[1] And the history of the Church revealed to him the further fact, that even for some considerable time after the apostolic age, the equality of the presbyterate and the episcopate continued to subsist—a fact for which Wycliffe appeals to the testimony of Jerome, and which was known to the Middle Age chiefly from the *Corpus Juris Canonici*, which contained the passage from Jerome just referred to.[2]

Wycliffe, it is true, had an erroneous idea of the manner in which this original equality of the two offices passed into the stage of the superiority of the bishop above the presbyter, and into the further development of the hierarchy in all its gradations. But if his conception of this differed from what, according to the testimony of history, actually took place, the blame of his error lay not in himself, but in the time when he lived—when the unhistorical and mythical traditions of the Middle Age were still in possession of unchallenged prevalency.[3] Wycliffe, that is to say, proceeds on the assumption that Constantine the Great not only endowed the Bishop of Rome, in the person of Silvester I., with rich temporal possessions, but also with new power and dignities—a consequence of which was the elevation of the bishops above the presbyterate not only in the Roman See, but everywhere in the Church, and the development of a graduated hierarchy, culminating in the Papal Primacy itself.[4] Hence Wycliffe in numberless places speaks of the *imperial* plenary power of the Pope—*e.g.*, *Trialogus*, IV. 32 ; *Supplementum Trialogi*, c. 10—

Development of the hierarchy.

---

[1] *Trialogus*, IV., 15, p. 296 : *Unum audacter assero, quod in primitiva ecclesia ut tempore Pauli suffecerunt duo ordines clericorum, scilicet sacerdos atque diaconus. Secundo dico, quod in tempore apostoli fuit idem presbyter atque episcopus; patet* 1 Timothy iii. *et ad* Titum i. Comp. *Supplementum Trialogi*, c. 6, p. 438 : *ut olim omnes sacerdotes vocati fuerunt episcopi. De Officio Pastorali*, I., 4, p. 11 : *Apostolus voluit episcopos, quos vocat quoscunque curatos.*

[2] *Ib.*, IV., 15, p. 296. Comp. *Decreti Pars*, I., *Distinct.*, 95, c. 5, and *Hieron. Comm. in Ep. ad Tit.* i. 5, Opp., vol. VII., 694, ed. Vallarsi Venet. 1766.

[3] Comp. Döllinger, *Die Papstfabeln des Mittelalters*, 2, Aufl. p. 186.

[4] *Saints' Days Sermons*, No. XLVI., fol. 93, col. 3. *Tertio introducta est secundum ordinationem Caesaream praesidentia episcoporum.* Comp. *Trialogus*, IV., 15, p. 296. *Verum videtur, quod superbia Caesarea hos gradus et ordines adinvenit.* He names immediately before Pope and Cardinals, patriarchs and archbishops, bishops and archdeacons, officials and deans, besides the other officers, *quorum non est numerus neque ordo.* In like manner in many other places, *e.g.*, *Saints' Days Sermons*, No. XL., fol. 81, col. 3 : *Licet Constantinus Imperator decrevit, suum episcopum atque clerum esse superiorem in mundana gloria quam reliquos in privatis aliis provinciis, et licet Antichristus sequens in hoc errore ampliavit istam haeresim, tamen fidelis debet recognoscere fidem Christi dictam*, Galatians ii. 6.

whereby he took occasion to exalt himself, allowed himself to be blinded, etc. And when Wycliffe speaks of Cæsarean bishops (*Episcopi Caesarei*) the alleged donation of Constantine is, in like manner, present to his mind as that which was the first occasion of the original equality of bishops and presbyters being disarranged, and a power being attributed to bishops which did not belong to them, and was without warrant. Wycliffe's ideas of the Papacy are assumed to be known with exactitude, and yet, up to the present time, they have been known only from his latest writings, and, on this account, only very incompletely. In looking into his earlier writings as well, I find that his opinions on this subject underwent a considerable change; so much so, indeed, that we are able to trace a steady progress in his judgment respecting it.

The Papal primacy.

I think I am able to distinguish three stages in this development. These admit of being distinguished from each other both chronologically and substantively. In point of time, the first stage reaches down to the outbreak of the Papal schism in 1378; the second stage embraces the years from 1378 to 1381; and the third extends from thence to Wycliffe's death in 1384. In substance the successive stages may be clearly and briefly discriminated thus — first, the recognition within certain limits of the Papal primacy; next, emancipation from the primacy in principle; finally, the most decided opposition to it. I have now to point out this in detail.

The first stage, beginning with the earliest appearance of Wycliffe in ecclesiastico-political questions and extending to the year 1378, is marked by a recognition of the Papal primacy within certain limits. Here Wycliffe is still far removed from attacking the Papacy as such in its very core and essence. As the central power of the Church, he still accords to it a real recognition and a sincere reverence, but only within certain limits, on the maintenance of which he lays great stress; and in this is discerned the free, reformative tendency which is characteristic of even his earliest opinions. What are these limits? They are of two kinds: First, in relation to the State, they bar all attacks of the Papacy upon it, whether on questions of finance or of civil jurisdiction. Here belong the investigations which Wycliffe at the outset of his public career set on foot respecting the claims of the Papacy to the payment of a feudal tribute on the side of England, and other questions of the like kind. Of the same character was the part he took in the transactions at Bruges in 1374–75. In this direction he speaks here and there with great caution and reserve, though some-

Growth of Wycliffe's views.

times also with emphasis.[1] As a rule, it is in reference to the financial spoliation of countries that Wycliffe expresses himself in a sharper tone—calling it downright theft—a robbery of the Church.[2] Then, as concerns the purely ecclesiastical and spiritual domain, Wycliffe in so far imposes a limit upon the Papacy as he denies its pretended necessity in order to salvation, and its unconditioned plenary power. It is itself an indication of this opinion that he maintains the moral right of entering into a scientific inquiry into this plenary power.[3]

In more than one place he disputes with clearness and decision the proposition that the office and Church authority of the Pope is absolutely indispensable and necessary to salvation.[4] Wycliffe reaches the same result which Melancthon expressed in the words, that the Pope may be recognised to be the Head of the Church *jure humano*, but not *jure divino*. Holding such views as these, Wycliffe could not, of course, possibly concede the infallibility and the plenary power of the Pope in spiritual things. On the contrary, he declares quite explicitly that the Pope may err in judgment. God alone is without sin, and His Word alone is infallible.[5] An 'elect man' may believe that the Pope and the Roman Church are guilty of injustice in putting him under a ban; and this assertion he bases on the proposition that it is possible that not only the Pope but the whole Roman Church may fall into mortal sin and be damned; it follows that he may also abuse his power by

Papal fallibility.

---

[1] *E.g.*, In *De Civili Dominio*, II., 4, fol. 164, col. 2, he mentions, it is true, the investiture of John Lackland with the crown of England on condition of the payment of feudal tribute, the transfer of the crown of Castile from Peter the Cruel to Henry the Bastard by Urban V. (1366); but he remarks immediately upon these and other cases, in which the Pope claimed the right, as Peter's successor, to dispose of kingdoms, that it was not his business to inquire whether the Pope thus acted from fatherly affection or in love to his allies, or to censure the abuses of secular princes (*non est meum discutere*). One of the most emphatic passages is that in Book I., 19, fol. 160, col. 1, where he remarks that the greatness of the Pope stands in his humility, poverty, and readiness to serve. When he becomes degenerate and secularised, and an obstinate defender of his worldly greatness, then it seems to the author that the Pope becomes an arch heretic, and must be put down from his spiritual dignity as well as his earthly dominion.

[2] In *Liber Mandatorum*, c. 26, fol, 205, col. 1, he treats of this subject under the commandment 'Thou shalt not steal.'

[3] *De Veritate Scripturae Sac.*, c. 11, fol. 30, col. 3.

[4] In one of his earliest writings (*De Civili Dominio*, I., 43, fol. 123, col. 11), he maintains that no person in the Romish Church is absolutely necessary to the government of the Church; and in the book *De Veritate Scripturae Sac.*, which he wrote in 1378, he treats it as a mere fiction when it is pretended *esse de necessitate salutis credendum, quod papa quicunque sit caput universalis ecclesiae*, etc., c. 20, fol. 65, col. 4.

[5] *De Civili Dominio*, I., 35, fol. 84, col. 1. Wycliffe observes that he who maintains that all bulls and instruments of the Pope are absolutely right and just gives it indirectly to be understood that the Pope is without sin, and therefore God (*implicat, papam esse impeccabilem, et sic Deum; potest ergo errare in judicio*). Comp. 3, 43, fol. 120, col. 1.

putting men under the ban unlawfully, from motives of avarice and ambition. Even Peter three times sinned after his consecration and the conveyance to him of representative power; still more, therefore, may a later successor in his office be capable of sinning. These are views which are still held by many decided Episcopalians, *e.g.*, among the Gallican clergy. But although Wycliffe contested with head and heart the doctrines of the Curialists and flatterers of the Pope touching his absolute power,[1] he was still very far, during this first stage of opinion, and as late as 1378, from impugning the prerogatives of the Roman Church. On the contrary, he expressly concedes them, and defends himself in the most earnest manner against every suspicion of his sentiments in this respect.[2]

We must not forget, indeed, on this point, that the Pope and the Roman Church are always two distinct things; as, in fact, Luther still held fast his veneration for the Roman Church at a time of his life when he had already taken up a sufficiently decided position against the Pope. But even towards the Pope himself Wycliffe at that stage still cherished a confidence which is really touching. I am able to produce in proof of this an expression of Wycliffe which has hitherto remained unknown. After the election of Urban VI., on April 8, 1378, the news of his first speeches and measures was quickly conveyed to England, and these evidently made upon Wycliffe a quite extraordinary impression. How he rejoiced in every sign of good intention and moral earnestness in that quarter! He conceived the hope that the man who had just ascended the Papal chair would prove a reformer of the Church. Under the fresh impression of the news he breaks out into the words, 'Blessed be the Lord, who in these days has given to His Church, in Urban VI., an orthodox head, an evangelical man, one who in the work of reforming the Church, that it may live conformably to the law of Christ, follows the due order by beginning with himself and the members of his own household. From his works, therefore, it behoves us to believe that he is the head of our Church.'[3] Wycliffe's soul is filled with true enthusiasm and joy.

Election of Urban VI.

---

[1] *E.g., De Ecclesia*, c. 12, fol, 164, col. 3: *Blasphemant quidam extollentes papam sophistice super omne quod dicitur Deus*, etc. Comp. *De Veritate Scripturae Sac.*, c. 20, fol. 65, col. 4: they break out *in blasphemiam summe execrabilem, quod dominus papa—sit paris auctoritatis cum Christo humanitus, cum sit Deus in terris*, etc.

[2] *De Veritate Scripturae Sac.*, c. 14, fol. 43, col. 3.

[3] *De Ecclesia*, c. 2, fol. 133, col. 2: *Benedictus Dominus matris nostrae, qui nostrae peregrinanti juvenculae* (an image of the Church from the Song of Solomon) *diebus istis providit caput catholicum, virum evangelicum, Urbanum sextum, qui rectificando instantem ecclesiam* (the Church of the present), *ut vivat conformiter legi Christi, orditur ordinate a se ipso et suis domesticis; ideo oportet ex operibus credere, quod ipse sit caput nostrae ecclesiae.* Comp. c. 13, fol. 178, col. 4.

He believes that in Urban VI. may be recognised a Pope of evangelical spirit and true Christian earnestness, who has *Sanguine hopes.* a clear knowledge of the moral disorders of the Church at the present time, and who possesses both the courage and the self-denial to begin the necessary reform with himself and the Curia. One might, indeed, be disposed to attach the less weight to this language, on the ground that it is only the presumed evangelical and reforming spirit of Urban that he so joyfully salutes. But what fills him with such exalted feeling and hope is precisely the circumstance that it was in a Pope that he saw such a spirit. On one point alone he has still his misgivings—whether this worthy head of the Church will persevere in the good way to the end.[1]

What Wycliffe had foreboded came only too soon to pass. Urban's efforts for reform, however well-meant, were carried out in so highhanded a manner, and with such reckless severity, that *Disappointment.* they gave offence to a number of his cardinals in such a degree as not only to alienate them, but even to convert them into open enemies. In the end, in August, 1378, under pretence of doubts regarding the regularity and validity of his election to the See—which they alleged had been forced upon them by terrorism—they proceeded to the election of a rival Pope in the person of the Cardinal of Geneva, Clement VII. With this step began the Papal schism which continued for nearly forty years. The consequences were that the one Pope excommunicated the other; they fought each other with all the weapons they could think of, and the *The Papal schism.* whole of Western Christendom was rent asunder. This is not the place to follow out the moral and religious effects of this mischievous event. We have to examine here only the effect which it had upon Wycliffe, on his view of the Papacy, and on his moral attitude towards it. We have remarked above that, from the year 1378, Wycliffe emancipated himself from the Papal primacy in principle, and this is what we have now, with more particularity, to show.

This second stage of his conviction and judgment in reference to the Papacy was reached only gradually, as we might beforehand expect. In the time immediately succeeding the outbreak of the Papal schism, he was still inclined to recognise Urban VI. as the legitimate Pope—as, in fact, all England remained attached to him and to his successors in Rome as long as the schism lasted, and

---

[1] *De Ecclesia,* c. 2, fol. 133, col. 2: *Ista autem fides de nostro capite tam gratiose et legitime nobis dato est credenda cum quadam formidine de corona suae finalis perseverantiae. . . . Nec dubium, quin nos omnes tenemur subesse sibi* (sc. Urbano), *de quanto tanquam verus Christi vicarius mandat magistri sui consilia et non ultra.*

refused to recognise the French anti-Pope. But notwithstanding this, Wycliffe even thus early expressed his opinion, that, in case Urban also should fall into evil ways, it would then be better and healthier for the Church to dispense with both Popes together. To this date, probably towards the close of 1378, I believe I may assign several declarations made by Wycliffe, partly in one of his scientific writings, and partly in a Latin sermon delivered by him, no doubt, in Oxford.[1]

When Urban VI., however, allowed himself to adopt the extreme measures against Clement VII. and the cardinals and national churches that supported his cause, of not only laying them under the ban of excommunication, but also of using against them all other possible means of hostility, Wycliffe went farther, and casting off his allegiance to Urban, took up a position of entire neutrality. He now declared it to be probable that the Church of Christ would find herself in better case, and in particular would enjoy a greater degree of peace than she did at present, if both the Popes were set aside or condemned, as it might be concluded from the lives of both that they had little or nothing in common with the holy Church of God.[2] By the experiences resulting from the Papal schism Wycliffe was brought step by step to the conclusion of cutting himself off from all moral connection with the Papacy as such.

Wycliffe's neutrality.

The third stage was only a further development and culmination of the second. Having already gone so far, Wycliffe found it impossible to remain in a position of bare neutrality. It was inevitable, from the nature of the case, that an eversharpening antagonism, and a warfare against the Papacy growing continually more uncompromising, should develop itself. And to this the controversy concerning the Lord's Supper, in which Wycliffe began to engage in the year 1382, essentially contributed. The more violently he was calumniated and attacked by the friends of the Papacy on account of his criticism on the Doctrine of Transub-

His final position.

---

[1] *De Ecclesia*, c. 15, fol. 178, col. 1: *Si nos Anglici gratis tantum obedimus papae nostro Urbano VI. tanquam humili servo Dei, sicut schismatici obediunt Clementi propter dominium et potestatem secularem: quis dubitat, quin ut sic habemus rationem meriti amplioris?* Saints' Days Sermons, No. X. (on Matthias's Day) fol. 19, col. 1. The preacher maintains that the election of Matthias to be an apostle was legitimate and well done. 'Would that men nowadays would proceed in like manner in elections, especially to high places.' That was not the case in the election of Robert of Geneva (Clement VII.), although it certainly was so in the election of Urban VI. *Ideo maneat Urbanus noster in justitia verus Petri vicarius, et valet sua electio. . . . Quod si Urbanus noster a via erraverit, sua electio est erronea, et multum prodesset ecclesiae, utroque istorum carere.*

[2] *Cruciata* (Wyclif Society) vol. ii. p. 621: *Probabiliter creditur, quod utroque istorum subtracto de medio vel damnato, staret ecclesia Christi quietius quam stat modo, cum multi supponunt probabiliter ex vitis eorum, quod nihil illis et ecclesiae sanctae Dei.*

stantiation, all the more did the Papacy itself appear to him to be a limb of Antichrist. To this period of his life belong all the strong assaults upon the Church which have been heretofore known to the world from his *Trialogus* and several popular writings in English. But these attacks become better understood, both psychologically and pragmatically, only when we think of them as a climax gradually realised. All the usurpations of the Papacy hitherto censured and opposed by Wycliffe were now seen by him, for the first time, in the light of a corruption of Christianity of the widest extent, and immeasurably deep, for which he could find no more appropriate name than Antichristianism. The systematic spoliation of the national churches, the haughty pride, the worldly character of the Papal Government, the claims to hierarchical domination over the whole world—all these features of the degenerate Papacy were attacked by Wycliffe after this date as well as before, but were now for the first time seen by him in their connection with what was the worst feature of all—with an assumption of Divine attributes and rights which seemed to him to stamp the Pope as the Antichrist. The Papacy Antichrist.

The Pope's claims to absolute power, and to a heaven entirely special to himself, appeared to Wycliffe all the more astounding, because he held fast to the fundamental principle that, in point of right, there are only deacons and priests in the Church of Christ, and that the whole graduated hierarchy within the priesthood had no other basis than the illegitimate smuggling of secular arrangements into the Church, and grants obtained from imperial patronage. It is, therefore, says Wycliffe, truly ridiculous or rather blasphemous when the Roman Pontiff, without any foundation whatever, says, 'It is our will, so must it be.'[1] From this time forward, however, he speaks of the Papacy much more as a God-blaspheming institution than as a subject of ridicule. In earlier years, indeed, Wycliffe had censured absolutist ideas of Papal dignity and power, but only as the ideas of individual administrators and flatterers of the Pope. But now he regards the assumption of such absolutism as the very kernel of the Papacy itself. For the claim to the dignity of a vicegerent of Christ upon earth, taken along with the strongest contrast to Christ in all respects—in character, teaching, and life—was a combination which appeared to him to be only fully expressed in the idea of the Antichrist; and this name Blasphemy in Papal claims.

---

[1] *Saints' Days Sermons*, No. LVI., fol. 116, col. 3: *Revera tam derisorium vel blasphemum est, quod Romanus presbyter dicat sine fundatione: 'Nos volumus ita esse!'* Comp. 117, col. 1.

Wycliffe applied to the Pope in numberless passages of the writings of his latest years. He now not only called both Popes alike 'false Popes,'[1] and stigmatised Clement VII. in particular as Antichrist; he also applied this name to the Papacy generally, that is, to all the Popes collectively; for, says he, 'they come in the name of Christ, and declare themselves to be His immediate vicegerents, and claim unlimited power in spiritual things, while their whole position rests exclusively upon the imperial grant of Constantine.'[2] But with special frequency he applies to the Pope the well-known words of the Apostle Paul (2 Thessalonians ii. 3) concerning 'the apostacy,' when the 'Man of Sin' is revealed who opposeth and exalteth himself above all that is called God, or that is worshipped. 'Now,' he remarks, 'it is nothing else but blasphemy when the Pope puts forward claims to Divine rights and Divine honours, and almost raises himself above Christ, whose position upon earth he pretends to represent.'[3] No wonder that Wycliffe, when he once went so far as this, did not shrink even from the thought that the Papal office itself is of the wicked one, seeing that no Divine warrant exists for more than the pastoral care of souls, and an exemplary walk in humility and sanctity, along with faithful warring in the spiritual conflict, but none at all for any worldly greatness and dignity.[4] The veneration,

---

[1] *Supplementum Trialogi*, c. 9, p. 450: *Manifeste patet, quod uterque istorum pseudopaparum tanquam membrum diaboli in causa stultissima provocat homines ad pugnandum*, etc.

[2] *Trialogus*, IV., 32; *Supplementum Trialogi*, c. 4, pp. 423, 447, 450. He carries out these thoughts even in sermons—*e.g.*, in *Saints' Days Sermons*, No. XLIV., on Matthew xxiv. 5, where the subject is false prophets and false Messiahs: *Omnes isti pseudo-papae 'veniunt in nomine Christi' dicentes, se esse immediatos vicarios ejus, sic quod infinitum plus possunt de dispensatione quoad spiritualia, quam alius Christianus. . . . Sed fundamentum tacitum stat in donatione Caesarea et concessione quadam Constantina.* Comp. *Select Works*, II., p. 394.

[3] *De Blasphemia*, c. 1, fol. 117, col. 2: *Videtur multis ex fide Scripturae et facto hominum, quod in Curia romana sit radix hujus blasphemiae, quia 'homo peccati antichristus insignis loquitur, quod sit summus Christi vicarius, in vita et opere inter mortales sibi simillimus. Trialogus*, IV., 32, p. 359: *Extollitur—super omne quod dicitur Deus, quod declarat apostolus competere antichristo*, etc. *De Apostasia*, c. 1, MS. 1343, fol. 37, col. 1: If the Pope breaks his covenant (*liga*) by which he is bound conscientiously to follow Christ in his acts, *non apostolicus sed apostaticus habeatur*.

[4] *XXIV. Sermons*, No. IX., fol. 152, col. 1: *Breviter totum papale officium est venenosum; deberet enim habere purum officium pastorale, et tanquam miles praecipuus in acie spiritualis pugnae virtuose procedere, et posteris, ut faciant simpliciter* (similiter?), *exemplare. Sic enim fecit Christus in humilitate et passione, et non in seculari dignitate vel ditatione. Et haec ratio, quare praelati versi sunt in lupos, et capitaneus eorum sit diabolus vita et opere antichristus*, etc. Wycliffe even goes so far as to have no difficulty in maintaining that no man upon earth is better fitted to become Antichrist and vicar of Satan than the Roman Pontiff himself, *ut sit vicarius principalis Satanae et praecipuus antichristus*, just because he can easily deceive the Church with hypocrisy and every kind of lie. *De Blasphemia*, c. 3, fol. 126, col. 1. The idea of Antichrist becomes in the end so common with him that he uses the name as convertible without more ado with the name of the Pope. He speaks of legates *a latere antichristi*, and more in the same style—*e.g.*, *Saints' Days Sermons*, No. V., fol. 8, col. 2: *legatos cum bullis miss sao latere antichristi*.

therefore, which is rendered to the Pope, appears to him to be an idolatry, all the more detestable and blasphemous (*plus detestanda atque blasphema idolatria*), because hereby Divine honour is given to a limb of Lucifer, who, because of his active wickedness, is a more abominable idol than a painted block, etc.[1]

The roughness and unmeasured tone of this polemic may have in it, at first sight, something offensive. But we shall judge it more mildly if we remember that it was by no means a new thought, one never heard of before in its special application to the Papacy, which Wycliffe now expressed. We point to the fact mentioned above that Gregory VII., as appears from his collected letters, was accustomed to distinguish between the 'Members of Christ' and the 'Members of the Devil or of the Antichrist.' Of course it was the enemies of his own aims and designs whom Gregory looked upon as the members of Antichrist: but it was only an application of the same thought from an opposite standpoint, when the opposition party in the Church gave the name of Antichrist to a holder of the Papal dignity himself. And this was what was done in high places in an instance lying close at hand. The same cardinals who opposed themselves to Urban VI., before proceeding to the election of a rival Pope, issued a manifesto against Urban, wherein they roundly declared that Urban ought to be called Antichrist rather than Pope. Is it to be wondered at if Wycliffe followed in the footsteps of their eminences, and declared to be the Antichrist, first the Pope set up by themselves, Clement VII., and afterwards Urban VI., and finally the Popedom at large? He operated with ideas traditionally handed down to him, and he carried the application of these to the highest place in Christendom, but only under the pressure of conscience, and for the honour of Christ as the only Head of the Church.

His strong language anticipated.

In setting forth the doctrine of Wycliffe regarding the Church, it would be a serious omission not to include his thoughts on the subject of the MONASTIC ORDERS.

Wycliffe's controversy with the Mendicant Orders takes so prominent a place in his writings, especially in the *Trialogus*, that it became usual, even at an early period, to look upon this antagonism as one of the most distinctive features of his thought and practical activity. In particular, since the days of Anthony Wood and John Lewis,[2] it has been received as an established fact that Wycliffe put himself forward

Controversy with the Mendicant Orders.

---

[1] *De Blasphemia*, c. 2, fol. 123, col. 3.
[2] Wood, *Antiquitates Oxonienses.* Lewis, *History of the Life and Sufferings of John Wiclif*, 1820, p. 6.

as the adversary of the Mendicant Friars as early as 1360, *i.e.*, at the very commencement of his public career. Even Dr. Vaughan, to whom we are so much indebted for our knowledge of Wycliffe, concedes no more than this in his latest work upon his life—that no documentary proof is to be found in the extant writings of Wycliffe to show that he had at so early a date as 1360 engaged in any discussion respecting these orders; but, notwithstanding this admission, he still represents the matter in such a manner as to imply that Wycliffe, from the very commencement of his work, appeared as their opponent.[1] It was Professor Shirley who was the first to discover that the prevailing assumption was groundless, and in fact contradicted by one of Wycliffe's contemporaries. For a well-known opponent of his, William Woodford, states expressly, that before he drew upon himself the disapprobation of the Mendicants by his erroneous teaching concerning the sacrament of the altar, he had never meddled with them, but had afterwards often made them the objects of his attacks.[2] When Woodward adds that Wycliffe's hostilities against the Friars were therefore prompted by personal vexation, we may regard such an imputation of motive as purely subjective on our informant's part, without the weight of the facts which he gives as purely historical being thereby at all diminished. Shirley, therefore, takes at least a first step towards a correction of the hitherto prevailing view, when he pronounces the tradition to be a fable which relates that on the death, in 1360, of Richard Fitzralph, the active Archbishop of Armagh, Wycliffe inherited, so to speak, his spirit and work, and took up and carried forward the conflict which he had so earnestly urged against the Begging Orders. This correction, however, of Shirley's, has not yet attracted so much attention as could be wished; and Shirley himself, besides, with the materials at his command, has only been able to prove a negative in opposition to the tradition hitherto received. A *positive* exposition of Wycliffe's whole mode of thought and feeling on the subject of Monasticism can only be furnished by means of those chief writings of Wycliffe which still exist only in manuscript.

Mistakes as to its commencement.

From these documents the following well-established results are obtained. As matter of fact, there is no truth in the tradition that Wycliffe, from the very first, was in conflict especially with the Mendicant Orders. On the contrary, I find in his earlier writings evidence to show that to a

Progress of Wycliffe's views.

---

[1] Vaughan's *Monograph*, p. 87.
[2] Shirley, *Fasc. Zizan.*, Introduction, xiv. The passage of Woodford occurs in his unprinted 72 *Questiones de Sacramento Altaris*, Qu. 50, dub. 7.

certain extent he regarded them with moral esteem and sympathy. The same writings, on the other hand, are not free from hostility against the endowed orders—*e.g.*, the Benedictines. At a later period, say from the year 1378, he began to attack the former also in part, and finally, from 1381, he carried on against them a systematic war. These three periods correspond to those which have been pointed out in reference to Wycliffe's position on the question of the Papacy. In the *first period*, in writings where he develops his 'Scriptural theology,' without any application to Roman Catholic dogma, but rather around the central idea of *Dominium*, and in which he is chiefly occupied with *Temporalia*, it is chiefly the endowed Monastic Orders that he keeps in view. It was principally men belonging to these orders who stood forward to oppose his views; and of course he did not fail to meet them with suitable rejoinders. For example, in his book, *Of the Truth of Holy Scripture*, which must have been written in 1378, I find that Wycliffe speaks almost exclusively, or at least mainly, of monks of these orders, as men who deny both in word and deed the doctrine of Scripture, and are apostates from it. It is also only members of these orders whom he speaks of as his personal opponents, who spare neither trouble nor money to blacken him in the eyes of the Papal Court, in order to obtain the Pope's condemnation of certain doctrines which he has set forth. It is manifest that the reference here is to several of the nineteen propositions which were condemned in 1377 by the decree of Gregory XI.[1] In other places also he names as persons who derogate from the Word of God and its authority 'the modern theologians,' 'the monks of the endowed orders' (*religiosi possessionati*), and 'the Canonists' (*sacerdotes causidici*).[2] In the enumeration of these three classes the Mendicants are conspicuous by their absence. But this is not all. I find even language which amounts to positive proof that Wycliffe at that time was inclined to give a preference to the Rule of the Mendicants over that of the endowed orders, as well as over the religious and moral standing of

The endowed orders first attacked.

---

[1] *De Veritate Scripturae Sac.*, c. 20, fol. 65, col. 3: *Religiosi autem possessionati, ut defendant* (instead of defending) *in vita et verbis legem Scripturae patenter apostatant, cum laboribus et expensis laborant ad Curiam romanam pro damnanda sententia dicente, multas cartas humanitus adinventas de hereditate perpetua esse impossibiles. Et tamen Oxoniae tam publice quam procuratorie dicunt testamenta Dei et legem Christi impossibilem et blasphemam. Quodsi legem Scripturae diligerent plus quam cartas proprias de dotatione in perpetuam elemosynam, laborarent forte in contrarium*, etc.

[2] *Ib.*, c. 20, fol. 65, col. 2: *Videtur,— quod magis culpandi sunt nostri theologi, nostri religiosi possessionati, et nostri sacerdotes causidici*, etc. Wycliffe is wont to give this name, *causidici*, to the reverers of canonical law, whose spirit was more juristic than theological, particularly the advocates of Papal absolutism.

the richer portion of the parochial clergy. In one passage he even places Francis of Assisi with his mendicancy side by side with the Apostles Peter and Paul with their hand-labour, in opposition to the worldly possessions and honours of the clergy of his time.[1] And in other places he expresses himself in such terms as to show that he looks upon the Foundations both of Francis and Dominic as a species of reformation of the Church, yea, as a thought inspired by the Holy Ghost Himself. It is possible, however, he concedes, that the Mendicants too may become degenerate and worldly like the rest.[2]

From 1378 we date a period of a few years in which Wycliffe began to attack the Mendicants upon single points of error and abuse.

Beginning of the conflict with the Mendicants. But from the year 1381, when he began to make a definite application of his theological principles, and especially of his Scripture principle, to the Roman Catholic dogmatic system in a critique of its doctrine of the Sacraments, and in particular of the dogma of Transubstantiation, not only did his judgment respecting the Papacy become, as we have seen, much more severe, but he also opened at the same time a conflict with the Mendicant monks, which went on from that time till his death with ever-increasing violence. It may well have been— indeed, we cannot doubt—that Wycliffe was in some measure influenced by the fact, that it was the Mendicants who charged him with heresy for his doctrine of the Lord's Supper. But certainly this was not the sole occasion of the controversy. Manifestly another co-operated in producing the effect, viz., that Wycliffe had now come to recognise in the Begging Friars the most zealous promoters of Papal absolutism, and the most systematic defenders of errors and abuses in the Church. Now it was that he reached the standpoint which we have long been familiar with in the *Trialogus*. Whether it is the scholastic system which he exposes in its nakedness (*sophistae theologi*), or the practical worldliness of the Church; whether he has to do with scientific ideas, or with life and manners—always it is

Grounds of opposition. against the new orders (*sectae novellae*), or the private religions (*religiones privatae*), as he calls the Mendicant Orders, in opposition to the religion of Christians in general, that he

---

[1] *De Civili Dominio*, III., 23, fol. 200, col. 1: *Veritas quam saepe inculcavi, scilicet quod status religiosorum viventium secundum paupertatem evangelicam est perfectissimus in ecclesia sancta Dei.* Ib. II., 13, fol. 208, col. 1. In this latter place he speaks of such an one who is utterly disinclined to give up worldly power and splendour for the sake of Christ, and maintains that such a man's faith is plainly not of the right sort. Such a man has no fancy to go a-fishing with Peter, nor to make tents with Paul, *nec mendicare cum Francisco*. There is only one thing that troubles him—that he is not ruler of the world like Augustus.

[2] *Ib.*, III., 2, fol. 7, col. 2: *Necesse fuit Spiritum S. fratres de ordine Dominici et Francisci statuere ad aedificationem ecclesiae*, etc. Comp. c. 1, fol. 5, col. 1.

deals his blows. Not only in passages where he censures the proceedings of the Friars themselves, or the vices which attached specially to their monasteries, but also in places where he blames the usurpations of the Papacy, the sins of the clergy, and the theological errors of his time, all concentrates itself in a violent invective against the Begging Orders. These appeared to him in that age nearly in the same light as that in which we regard the order of the Jesuits of the present day—as the most ready instruments of Papal despotism, the promoters of an anti-scriptural theology, etc. But, instead of following his controversy with them through its various phases, let a single point be here mentioned, which is significant of the evil opinion which Wycliffe had formed of them as a body. He sees in Cain the Bible original of the four Mendicant Orders, and he is of opinion that when the blood of Abel cried from the earth to heaven for vengeance on the fratricide, that heinous deed was a type of the wickedness of these fraternities. This somewhat odd thought is connected with a certain play upon the letters of the name CAIM (so written instead of Cain), viz., that these four letters are the initials of the names of the four Orders—the Carmelites, the Augustinians, the Jacobites or Dominicans, and the Minorites or Franciscans.[1] *An acrostic.*

Wycliffe, however, did not allow himself to be carried away so far by his controversy with the Begging Friars as to see in them nothing but error and wickedness, and to expect from them only what was evil in all time to come. On the contrary, he makes the following explicit declaration:—'I anticipate that some of the friars whom God shall be pleased to enlighten will return with all devotion to the original religion of Christ, will lay aside their unfaithfulness, and with the consent of Antichrist, offered or solicited, will freely return to primitive truth, and then build up the Church, as Paul did before them.'[2] This thought of Wycliffe was an uncon- *A striking prediction.*

---

[1] *Trialogus*, IV., c. 33, p. 362. Comp. *Supplementum Trialogi*, c. 8, p. 444. *De Officio Pastorali*, II., c. 16, *castra Cainitica*. Hence the name he gives to the mendicant monks at large, *Caïnitae*, in *Suppl. Trial.*, c. 6, p. 437, and to the whole institution—*Caymitica Institutio*; *Trial.*, IV., 17, p. 306. In his English tracts, Wycliffe calls the cloisters of the begging monks 'Cain's castles'—*e.g., The Church and her Members*, c. 5, *Select Works*, III., 348 ; and *Fifty Heresies and Errors of Friars*, c. 2, p. 368. The name *Jacobites* for the Dominicans sprang from the circumstance that their first monastery in Paris stood near the gate of St. Jacques. The fastening of the name upon them as a mark of Cain was very ill taken by the monastic orders and their friends, which it would be easy to prove from Woodford and Walsingham, if it were worth the pains.

[2] *Ib.*, IV., 30, p. 349 : *Suppono autem, quod aliqui fratres, quos Deus dignatur docere, ad religionem primaevam Christi devotius convertentur, et relicta sua perfidia, sive obtenta sive petita antichristi licentia, redibunt libere ad religionem Christi primaevam, et tunc aedificabunt ecclesiam sicut Paulus.* A similar but much vaguer expression I find in the treatise *De Apostasia*, c. 2, fol. 51,

scious prophecy of the Reformation. For let us remember that not only Luther himself was an Augustinian, but that a number of his most active fellow-workers belonged to houses of that order;[1] that Eberlin of Günzburg, and Francis Lambert of Avignon, were Franciscans; that the other Mendicant Orders in like manner contributed no unimportant promoters of the work; while the last prophet of Reformation was the Dominican, Savonarola.[2] Let us further keep in view that the founders of the Reformation, Luther himself before all, owed their evangelical insight, in the main, not to themselves, and not to others, but as a matter of fact to God Himself; and that their own personal enlightenment and conversion led the way to, and qualified them for, the task of renovating the Church. Let us also reflect on the fact that the Reformers of the sixteenth century, more or less consciously, aimed at nothing else but the restoration of primitive apostolic Christianity; and that in the person of Luther especially, the Pauline spirit revived and worked out not only a purification of the Church, and an effectual edification of it, but also its elevation to a higher level of faith and life. Taking all this together, and comparing it with that presentiment of Wycliffe, we cannot fail to see in the Reformation a remarkable fulfilment of what he presaged; and we have no difficulty, in view of the promise of Christ, that the Holy Spirit would show His servants things which were to come (John xvi. 13), in regarding the above declaration of Wycliffe as a prophecy, the like of which the history of Christ's Church has many more to show. True, indeed, the fulfilment in more than one particular went beyond Wycliffe's personal and conscious thought when he penned those words; in particular, his *sicut Paulus* was no doubt far more fully realized in the Reformation than the writer had ever imagined. But that such a prophetic presentiment of the Reformation fruits which were to spring from the bosom of the Mendicant Orders should have come from the pen of so determined and implacable an enemy of these Orders, was a fact all the more astonishing and remarkable.[3]

col. 1: *Si—placet benefacere istis sectis, tribuetur eis abscondite seorsum elemosyna, ut dissolvantur colligationes impietatis, et reducantur ad perfectionem religionis primaevae.*

[1] Comp. C. A. Cornelius, *On the Co-operation in Reformation Efforts of the Augustinians in the Netherlands, the Lower Rhineland, and Westphalia; Geschichte des Münsterischen Aufruhrs*, 1855, I., 33. Friar Barnes in London, also, from whom, in 1528, two Wycliffites out of Essex purchased a printed English New Testament, was an Augustinian. Strype, *Ecclesiastical Memorials*. Oxford, 1832, I., 2, p. 54.

[2] Comp. Leopold Ranke, *Deutsche Geschichte in Zeitalter der Reformatum*, II., 66.

[3] Neander was the first to call attention to this passage, as a prediction that the Reformation would proceed from the Mendicant Orders. Böhringer, *Wycliffe*, p. 568, and Oscar Jäger, *John Wicliffe*, Halle, 1854, p. 57, have observed, in opposition to Neander's view and my own,

This is perhaps no unsuitable place to add something touching Wycliffe's views in other parts of his works on the necessity and means of a reformation of the Church. He declares in many places that such a reformation is a pressing and indispensable necessity. And upon what ground? Because the Church as she is is not what she ought to be. For the Church is departed from the Institution and the Word of Christ—from the Bible—is corrupted from its original condition in apostolic times.[1] If we inquire into the view he took of the historical course through which the Church passed in its progress of corruption, it must, on the one hand, be confessed that in many particulars of the subject he thinks unhistorically, *e.g.*, when he traces back the whole secularisation of the Church exclusively to Constantine the Great—a notion which he shares, indeed, with Dante and other enlightened minds of his century. But, on the other hand, he accurately discerns that the corruption and depravation of Christianity came in quite gradually, and progressed step by step. In answer to the plea of a false conservatism that the Church from time immemorial had stood in the

Wycliffe on Church Reform.

---

expressed in *Zeitschrift fur historische Theologie*, 1853, p. 452, that this is going too far. But if, as Jäger himself admits, we see 'in Wycliffe's whole personality a comprehensive fact-prophecy of the Reformation,' is there anything impossible or even improbable in the idea that there should have been also a word-prophecy of it? And if Wycliffe says no more than *I suppose*, and not *I prophesy*, does it follow that there is no question here of prophecy at all?

[1] It cannot be attempted to bring together all the passages in which Wycliffe has given expression to these views. A few may suffice, *instar omnium*. Beginning with external matters, it is to such he refers when, in the *Liber Mandatorum*, c. 8, fol. 108, col. 1, he says that the stiff demand of the Church for its temporalities far oversteps the example of the primitive Church (*ultra exemplum primitivae ecclesiae*). The Apostolical Church, that Church of martyrs, was also a Church of poor confessors (*ecclesia pauperum confessorum*), but on that very account it did a much greater work than the richly-endowed Church of later times. *De Civili Dominio*, III., c. 22, fol. 193, col. 1. That Wycliffe, in the matter of worship, affirmed that the Church had departed from ancient usage, to which the use of so many images and saints was unknown, has been already noticed above, *vide* p. 296. The hierarchical despotism to which the Popes had reached, he paints in the strongest colours. *De Officio Regis*, c. 7, fol. 37, col. 3. But not only in life, but in doctrine also, has this departure taken place from the Word of God and the true Christian standard, and it is here that he lays the main stress. *Saints' Days Sermons*, XXI., fol. 41, col. 4: At the time of the first advent of Christ the synagogue was manifestly corrupt. Scriptural doctrine was hidden away or perverted—human traditions multiplied, etc. At His second advent the antichrist will be still more deeply and manifoldly apostate. But the priests and Pharisees of the Old Testament were more excusable than the Romish Church—*non enim tantum a lege Mosaica declinaverant, quantum nostri prelati declinant tam vita quam scientia a lege et regula Christiana*. They deceive others, indeed, and themselves by assuming that they are the Holy Church to which Christ has promised that it shall endure to the end. But in the Old Testament times men had indulged in like false confidences. 'The temple of the Lord are these' (Jeremiah vii. 4). But the principal cause of this falling away from true Christianity lies here, as Wycliffe sets forth in *De Veritate Scripturae Sac.*, c. 29, fol. 101, col. 4, that men have set aside the one only Lord and Master, and have given heed to many other masters who are opposite to Christ—that the corrupt traditions of men have been followed, and not the gospel of Jesus Christ.

faith which the Church of Rome teaches, and that therefore it is
heresy and impiety to depart from this religion,[1] he points not only
to the earlier Roman Church,[2] but goes much farther back, and lays
down the principle that the errors of the present age ought not to be
measured by the nearest and latest error which has received Church
approval, but by the institution and life of Christ as the primary
standard. Men would then perceive immediately how far our priests
depart from the first rule or measure, in their law and life and preaching of the gospel.[3] Considering the whole subject broadly, notwithstanding the fact that the secularisation of the Church had begun
through the alleged Donation of Constantine, the first
thousand years of Church history appear to him as the
millennium of Christ (*millenarium Christi*); but from that date
Satan was let loose, and a millennium of lies set in (*millenarium mendacii*).[4] Wycliffe, moreover, is persuaded that upon the inclined
plane on which Christianity now finds itself, it will descend lower
still, even to the deepest point. 'The Antichrist (here the personal
Antichrist himself) will not come before the law of Christ is cast
away avowedly as well as in secret.'[5] Still, even here, contemplating
the deepest and latest apostacy, God's Word stands out clearly
before his mind, not only as the measure of the Church's fall, but
also as the principal means of her restoration.

The two millenniums.

If now we further inquire what were Wycliffe's thoughts touching
the means by which a reformation of the Church was to be
brought to pass, it follows, from what has already been
stated, that this reformation, according to his ideas,
could only be, on the one hand, a purification of the Church from

Methods of reform.

---

[1] *Saints' Days Sermons*, No. XL., fol. 8, col. 4.

[2] *Prior Romana ecclesia, cui magis debemus credere.* XXIV. *Sermons*, No. I., fol. 128, col. 4. He refers here to the eleventh in comparison with the twelfth and fourteenth centuries.

[3] *Saints' Days Sermons*, No. XXI., fol. 65, col. 2: 'Because the Antichrist is aware of the great importance of the institution of Christ, he has managed that it should be departed from only gradually, but craftily; and under his blinding influence, worldly-minded people have been thus led to look upon errors which were still not excessive, as of no consequence, or as no errors at all.'

[4] XXIV. *Sermons*, No. I, fol. 130, col. I: *Aliter errarent tam ecclesia quam doctores de millenario Christi, qui sic esse credendum docuerant. Saints' Days Sermons*, No. XL., fol. 80, col. 4: *Istis ducentis annis et amplius fuit cursus talis antichristi cum sectis suis—nam par tantum temporis et amplius diabolus est solutus*. In the *Trialogus*, the period when the devil was set loose is assumed to be well known—almost as much so as an established chronological fact, *e.g.*, b. III., c. 7, p. 153; c. 31, p. 240; b. IV., c. 2 and 33, pp. 249, 362: *Ante solutionem Satanae, post solutionem Satanae,* etc. This apocalyptic view was everywhere prevalent in the Middle Age. To quote only one document in illustration of this fact, I refer to the letter from Liege, which was addressed to Paschalis II. during the Investiture controversy. There the same thought occurs more than once—Satan is loose, and has great wrath—*Satanas solutus . . . jam divisit regnum et sacerdotium*.

[5] *De Veritate Scripturae Sac.*, c. 15, fol. 45, col. 2: *Antichristus non veniet antequam lex Christi sic dissipata tam intellectu quam affectu*.

the errors and abuses which had invaded her, and, on the other hand, a restoration of primitive Christianity in its purity and perfection.[1] Now, as Wycliffe, along with many true Christians of that century, regarded the secularisation of the Church as its worst evil, and saw this secularisation chiefly in the worldly possessions of the Church, so it seemed to him that the most indispensable means of reform, and, as he hoped, the richest in blessing, would be the unburdening of the Church of her worldly goods and property.

Innumerable times, and almost from every conceivable point of view, Wycliffe returns to this thought, either in the form of calling for the withdrawal and secularisation of the Church's endowments, if need be by force, or in the form of suggesting a voluntary renunciation by the bishops, abbots, and others, of all their worldly dignities and possessions, in conformity with the example of Christ and the standard of His Word.[2] It is due to truth that we should express frankly our conviction that in this thought Wycliffe deceived himself. We share with him, indeed, the belief which he expresses in these words: 'It is impossible that the Lord should forsake His priest, or suffer him to want for food or clothing; and therewith, according to the apostles' rule (1 Timothy vi. 8), should he be content.' But Wycliffe was unquestionably mistaken when he so confidently assumed that the single external measure of a secularisation of the Church's endowments would result in the return of the clergy and the Church at large to the Christianity of the apostles. That was not only a too sanguine hope, resting upon notions all too ideal, but it proceeded from a reformation zeal which was over-hasty and deficient in depth of insight. It seems never to have occurred to Wycliffe that by the dissolution of monasteries and the calling in of Church property the selfishness of Christendom would be awakened, passions stirred, and pious endowments alienated from their original objects.

Secularisation of Church revenues.

---

[1] *De Blasphemia*, c. 1, fol. 118, col. 4: *Purgatio gloriosa ecclesiae ab antiqua blasphemia*, etc. *De Ecclesia et membris ejus*, ed. Todd, c. 6, p. xli.: *Purging of the chirche. De Civili Dominio*, III., 22, fol. 193, col. 2: *Ecclesiae ad primam perfectionem restitutio. De Ecclesia*, c. 3, fol. 135, col. 1: *Correctio nostra secundum statum primaevum*.

[2] A single passage for a thousand may here find a place. In the *Saints' Days Sermons*, No. XXXVI., fol. 72, col. 4, Wycliffe says: *Medicina necessaria ad extinguendum venenum diaboli foret, totum clerum exproprietarium facere, et ordinationem Christi quoad suam ecclesiam innovare*, etc. Comp. *De Officio Pastorali*, II., 11, p. 45; *Trialogus*, IV., 28, p. 310; *Dialogus*, c. 34, fol. 159, col. 2: *Si autem ipsi episcopi . . . et alii dotati praepositi conciperent in hoc vitam et legem Christi, et sic gratis renunciarent omnibus mundanis dominiis, foret illis magis meritorium et gloriosior triumphus ecclesiae militantis super diabolum et alia membra sua*. The whole tractate *De Officio Pastorali* turns in like manner upon the thought that it would be more wholesome for the parish clergy, and, at the same time, quite sufficient for their worldly comfort, to live upon the voluntary gifts of their congregations; food and clothing would not be wanting to them.

In order to have a full knowledge of Wycliffe's idea of Church reform, we must direct our attention also to the personal question, 'Who can, and should undertake the reform?' To this question he replies, 'Every one can do something to help in it. Some should help by declaring reasons for it taken out of God's Word; others should help by worldly power, such as the earthly lords whom God has ordained; and all men should help by good lives and good prayers to God, for in Him is to be found help against the wiles of the wicked fiend: so should Popes, bishops, and begging monks give help in this work by reforming themselves.'[1] He assigned no small share in the work, as already indicated, to earthly princes and lords, or, in one word, to the State. He maintains that worldly lords have not only power to take away the Church's temporalities when she is habitually at fault (*habitualiter delinquente*), but that they are even bound to do it.[2] Wycliffe, indeed, means by this that the Church and cloister endowments should be applied to other pious uses, especially to the relief of poverty. He holds it, therefore, to be advisable that the king should call a synod, in order to proceed in the matter with the aid of its advice, in a manner most suitable to the object in view.[3] And not only does he hold that princes and lords have authority to withdraw monastic and Church endowments and to dissolve monasteries,[4] but he believes that it is their duty also to deprive clerics of their office who, in a spirit of worldliness, have estranged themselves from the pure religion of Christ.[5] And how much in earnest he was in the opinion that princes and lords are not only empowered to adopt such measures, but are even bound in duty to have recourse to them, in virtue of the obligation laid upon them to protect the Church and their own subjects, appears from the manifold calls which he makes upon them to take action, and especially from the fact that he charges them with blindness and indifference to the Church's interests; that they in truth are chiefly to blame that the wholesome reform of the Church is so long delayed.[6] Still,

Restraints on secular despotism.

---

[1] *The Church and her Members*, ch. 6; *Select English Works*, III., 351.

[2] *Trialogus*, IV., 18, p. 311: *Nos autem dicimus illis, quod nedum possunt auferre temporalia ab ecclesia habitualiter delinquente, nec solum quod licet illis hoc facere, sed quod debent*, etc. *De Civili Dominio*, c. 22, fol. 183, col. 2: *Licet dominis temporalibus auferre a religiosis* (monks) *collatas elemosinas progenitorum suorum* (*i.e.*, endowments) *in casu quo habitualiter eis abusi fuerint*.

[3] *De Civili Dominio*, III., 22, fol. 196, col. 2: *Si . . . sit rationabile, ut retrahatur elemosyna regis nostri in alios pios usus, non oportet currere Romam ad habendum consensum sui pontificis . . . ne tamen illud fiat indiscrete, congreganda est synodus auctoritate regis*, etc.

[4] *Ib.*, 193, col. 2: *Claustrorum dissipatio . . . posset verisimilius esse eorum* (claustralium) *correctio*, etc.

[5] *Ib.*, c. 19, fol. 163, col. 1: *Expediens est . . . seculares dominos auferre a clericis onus ministerii hujusmodi, si viderint eos a religione Christi aversos*, etc.

[6] *De Simonia*, c. 5, fol. 21, col. 1: *Nec dubium, qui caecus torpor dominorum*

on the other hand, he desires to prescribe certain limitations, as a bar against despotism and arbitrary power. He lays it down as an express principle that no priest or cleric should be subjected to punishment by the secular arm in the shape of the loss of his endowments, except by full authority of the Church, when his ecclesiastical superior fails in his duty, and only in case of his having fallen away from the true faith.[1] If the clergy would do their duty by brotherly punishment and censure, the need of chastisement by the secular arm could be entirely dispensed with.[2] On the other hand, when Churchmen are notoriously delinquent, it would be a sin to defend them, especially against pious princes, when they, in the exercise of their catholic duty, apply coercion to them in a way in which prelates have no power to do.[3]

This view of the right and the duty of princes, to proceed in certain circumstances against clerics with pains and penalties—not in consequence of any civil offences, but for unfaithfulness to their ecclesiastical office and for departure from the faith—is sufficient of itself to show that Wycliffe was no adherent of the Romish view of the relation between Church and State. But it is in other ways unmistakable that he is already under the influence of the modern idea of the State, as this began to develop itself since the thirteenth and fourteenth centuries.[4] Not only so, he

secularium sit in causa, quare tam gloriosus fructus et emendatio ecclesiae retardatur. In the *Saints' Days Sermons,* fol. 117, col. 2, the Fifty-sixth closes with the wish, 'O that kings would wake up and shake off this faithlessness of the antichrist, and in divine things take the sense of Scripture pure and undefiled!'

[1] *De Civili Dominio,* II., 8, fol. 177, col. 2: *Nullus sacerdos vel clericus debet per coactam ablationem bonorum corripi per brachium seculare, nisi auctoritate ecclesiae, in defectu spiritualis praepositi, et casu quo fuerit a fide devius.*

[2] *Ib.,* fol. 178, col. 2.

[3] *Ib.,* I., 39, fol. 95, col. 2: *Et quum notabiliter delinquunt, peccatum esset ipsos defendere, specialiter contra pios principes catholice coërcentes, qualiter praelati non sufficiunt.*

[4] I bring into view here two particulars —first, The way in which Wycliffe emphasises the inherent rights of the crown, according to which the claim of the Pope to the first fruits of a prelacy, and also the pretended exemption of the clergy in their person and property from the king's jurisdiction, are both irreconcilable with the *integritas regaliae regis nostri. De Ecclesia,* c. 15, fol. 176, col. 2. Comp. *De Officio Regis,* c. 4, fol. 15, col. 2: *Omnis rex dominatur super toto regno suo; omnis clericus regis legius* (vassal or liege) *cum tota possessione sua est pars regni; ergo dominatur super omnibus istis.* Secondly, The way in which Wycliffe sets forth the dignity of the king as derived immediately from God, and as independent of the Church, and even of the Papacy. The governing power of the king is conferred by God, and acknowledged by the people. *De Officio Regis,* as above, fol. 176, col. 3: *Rex, in quantum hujusmodi, habet privilegium concessum a Deo et acceptum a populo ad regnandum.* The king, therefore, is a vicar of God, as good as the Pope, who should exhibit divine justice in his actions; *ista exemplaris justitia in Deo, debet esse exemplar cuilibet ejus vicario tam papae quam regi,* etc. *Rex enim est Dei vicarius.* This is properly the basis of thought in this whole book. In connection with this subject, Wycliffe more than once supports himself upon a thought of Augustine, *Epist.* 185, according to which a king is a representative of God, but a bishop a representative of Christ. *Trialogus,* IV., 15, p. 297 ; *Saints' Days Sermons,* No. XL., fol. 81. col. 4, in the latter of which two places *episcopus* is the word used, in the former *papa.* Comp.

has in his mind an *ideal* of the State; and that is the 'Evangelical State'—which he evidently figures to himself as a commonwealth or commune, in which not rigid right and private property, but love is in the ascendant, and all things are in common[1]—an idea which cannot be absolved from the charge of sanguine idealisation.

But besides the State, Wycliffe assigns to all true evangelically minded Christians an important part in bringing about that reform of the Church which was so urgently needed, and so much to be aimed at. By such helpers he means the 'men of the Gospel' (*viri evangelici*)—the 'evangelical doctors'—or the 'apostolic men,' as he also calls them. These are the men on whom he places his reliance. He is well aware what a single man, if true and steadfast, can accomplish. But he also bethinks himself of the power which lies in united forces, and therefore he requires of evangelical men, that when locally separated they should in will and action stand together as one man, and steadfastly defend the word of Christ which they have among them.[2] His language sounds, in fact, like the trumpet call of a leader who is collecting a party, and leading them in closed ranks into the battle. And Wycliffe in truth has the consciousness of being such a leader in the struggle for Church reform. Indeed, in an important passage of the Appendix to the *Trialogus*, now first published, he acknowledges

Co-operation of all Christians.

The spirit of a leader.

De Blasphemia, c. 7, fol. 140, col. 3. As a fruit of the contest between Church and State, which went on from the end of the thirteenth century between Boniface VIII. and Philip the Fair, we especially must regard the judgment expressed by Wycliffe in *Liber Mandatorum*, c. 26, fol. 205, col. 2, in the following terms :—The king in temporal things stands above the Pope, and therefore the Pope must acknowledge him as in this respect the higher upon earth, though in spiritual things the Pope has the superiority: *Rex autem est in temporalibus supra papam; . . . ideo quoad istud oportet papam superiorem in terris cognoscere, licet in spiritualibus antecellat.* Wycliffe defines the relation between Church and State, between temporal and spiritual government, sharply and clearly, as follows :—Secular princes govern their subjects directly and immediately in reference to the body and temporal goods, but only mediately, or in the second line (*accessorie*), in relation to the soul, which latter interest, however, in the order of the two objects or ends of government, should be the first. On the other hand, the priests of Christ exercise government chiefly and directly in relation to spiritual gifts, *e.g.*, the virtues; yet along with this, and in the second line, in relation to temporal things. But each jurisdiction must lay hold of the other and render it support. As the Church has two estates, clergy and laity—so to say soul and body—so she has two sorts of censure and discipline—spiritual, in the shape of admonition; corporeal, in the shape of compulsion; of which the former takes effect by the preaching of the law of Christ and conviction of reason, and belongs to the doctors and priests of Christ, while the latter takes effect by the deprivation of the gifts of nature and temporal goods, and is exercised in the hands of the laity. *De Civili Dominio*, II., 8, fol. 178, col. 1; fol. 179, col. 1.

[1] *De Civili Dominio*, II., 16, fol. 235, col. 2: *Tunc necessitaretur respublica redire ad politiam evangelicam, habens omnia in communi.*

[2] *Saints' Days Sermons*, No. XXXI., fol. 65, col. 2: *Viri quidem evangelici debent in voluntate et in conversatione tanquam vir unus concurrere, quanquam loco distiterint* (MS. destituerint), *et legem Christi sibi praesentis constanter defendere.* *Doctores evangelici*, *De Civili Dominio*, III., 19, fol. 163, col. 1.

quite openly that he has formed the design 'to lead back the Church to the ordinance of Christ, and pure conformity to His Word.'[1] Nor does he conceal from himself that in such an undertaking he will meet with the most violent opposition, and perhaps will encounter a martyr's death; for not alone Antichrist (the Pope) and his disciples, but the devil himself and all his evil angels are full of hate against the institution of Christ having any place on the earth.[2] A thought which is by no means an isolated one in his writings, and which vividly reminds us of Luther, who knows himself to be constantly in conflict with the wicked fiend. But in view of this mighty and imminent battle, Wycliffe is strong and of good courage, not only because he can depend on the good comrades who have hitherto stood side by side with him in God's cause, and will, he believes, abide by him to the end, having nothing in common with apostates,[3] but chiefly in the firm assurance that it is God's cause and Christ's cross for which he is contending, and that God's cause in the end must always carry off the victory. 'O that God,' he exclaims in one place, 'would give me a docile heart, persevering steadfastness, and love to Christ, to His Church, and to the members of the devil who are rending that Church asunder, that I might out of pure brotherly love encounter them (*ipsa corripiam*). What a glorious cause is this for me in which to end the present miserable life! For this same was the cause of the martyr-death of Christ.'[4] And in another passage, which has long been well known, he says: 'I am assured that the truth of the Gospel may indeed for a time be trampled upon in particular places, and may for a while abide in silence, through the menaces of Antichrist; but extinguished it can never be, for the Truth Himself says, "Heaven and earth shall pass away, but My words shall never pass away."'[5]

Prepared for martyrdom.

Assured of final success.

---

[1] Supplementum *Trialogi*, c. 8, p. 447: *Tunc foret facilius . . . errores corrigere, et statum ecclesiae ad ordinationem Christi pure secundum legem suam reducere, quod attendere desidero.* Comp. *Dialogus*, c. 18: *Intendimus purgationem et perfectionem cleri, quam scimus non stare in multitudine personarum, sed in observantia status, quem Christus instituit.*

[2] *Hoc tentans pro parte Christi habebit plurimos adversantes, quia non solum antichristum et omnes ejus discipulos, sed ipsum diabolum et omnes suos angelos, qui summe odiunt, quod Christi ordinatio stet in terris*: Saints' Days Sermons, No. III., fol. 6, col. 1.

[3] *De Apostasia*, c. 2, fol. 52, col. 1: *Confido de bonis sociis, qui mihi confidenter in causa Dei astiterant, quod . . .* *usque in finem assistent, quia nihil illis et dictis apostatis.*

[4] *De Veritate Scripturae Sac.*, c. 23, fol. 78, col. 1: *O si Deus dederit mihi cor docile, perseverantem constantiam et caritatem ad Christum, ad ejus ecclesiam et ad membra diaboli ecclesiam Christi laniantia, ut pura caritate ipsa corripiam! Quam gloriosa causa foret mihi praesentem miseriam finiendi! Haec enim fuit causa martyrii Christi.* Comp. the beautiful conclusion of Book II. *De Civili Dominio*, c. 18, fol. 251, col. 2: *Concedat Deus nobis clericis arma apostolorum et patientiam martyrum, ut possimus in bono* (the evil with good) *vincere adversarios crucis Christi! Amen.*

[5] *Trialogus*, IV., 4, p. 258. Comp. *Dialogus*, c. 25, fol. 156, col. 1: *Dicam*

But in the last resort his hope for the accomplishment of the necessary reformation of the Church rests upon the help of God and the workings of His grace. However true and steadfast believing men may be to God's cause, God alone has power to awaken and to enlighten men for this work, and with Him alone stands our help against the coming of the evil one.[1] It is for this reason that he even concedes the possibility that the reformation of the Church, for which he so earnestly longs and confidently hopes, may be brought to pass in ways of which he has no conception, and by a miracle of God, with whom is no respect of persons, for among every people and in every land he who loves Him is accepted of Him.[2] These last words sound almost like a far-off presentiment of the event, that the decisive battle of souls for the reform of the Church of Christ would be fought out in another land than his own, and in the midst of another people. At all events, Wycliffe is conscious that the fulfilment of his dearest hope is for himself a mystery, and will come to pass in the end only by a miracle of God's power.

His help in God.

Taking all this into one view—what Wycliffe thought and said of the necessity of a reformation, of the ways and means by which it was to be effected, and of the personalities by whom it was to be introduced—it is impossible for us not to receive this as our total impression—that his soul is full of longing and pressure after a God-pleasing restoration of the Church's purity; the vision of it is continually before his eyes, for this he enlists his whole powers—for this, if it should be God's will, he is resolved to endure persecution and even a martyr's death. It cannot, therefore, admit of a doubt that Wycliffe was a Church reformer of the true evangelical type.

'Sehnsucht und Drang.'

12.—Doctrine of the Sacraments.

Of the doctrinal system of Wycliffe, there still remains for us to examine that chief head wherein he placed himself in strongest

---

ergo istam sententiam pro bono papae atque ecclesiae, et si occisio vel alia poena inm eveniat, rogo Deum meum dare virtute ad constanteret humiliter patiendum.

[1] *De Blasphemia*, c. 1, fol. 119, col. 1 : Verum potens est Deus illuminare et excitare mentes paucorum fidelium, qui constanter detegant et moneant, si digni sumus, ad destructionem hujus versutiae antichristi. Sic enim incipiendo a femina convertit per paucos apostolos totum mundum.

[2] *Ib.* (one of Wycliffe's latest writings), c. 1, fol. 120, col. 4 : Ideo videtur tutius a generatione ista saltem in mente aufugere et ad protectionem Christi confugere, relinquendo destructionem antichristi cum suis satrapis Dei miraculo. Scimus quidem, quod oportet, ut viis nobis absconditis istud eveniat ; sed scimus, quod personarum acceptio non est apud Deum, sed in omni gente vel loco, qui ipsum dilexerit, acceptus est illi.

opposition to the teaching of the Church of Rome—namely, the doctrine of the Lord's Supper and of the Sacraments generally. We shall, however, handle the doctrine of the other sacraments with comparative brevity, because we are able to refer upon this subject to the full and satisfactory treatment which it has received from Lewald.[1] Several points, however, need more precise definition and some degree of correction.

I. *Of the Sacraments in general.*

Here the three following questions come under consideration:— 1. What is the notion and nature of a sacrament? 2. What are the several sacraments? or, in other words, how many sacraments are there? 3. What view is to be taken of the efficacy of the sacraments?

With regard (1) to the *notion* of a sacrament, it is to be premised that Wycliffe has devoted the first half of the fourth book of the *Trialogus* to the doctrine of the sacraments, in the first chapter of which he treats of the sacraments in general, and especially of the notion of a sacrament.

He sets out from the generic idea of the *sign*; a sacrament is a sign; to every sign there corresponds a thing signified, the object of which the former is a sign. But this, as Wycliffe him- *Sacraments as* self allows, is so general an idea, that it must be said that *signs.* everything which exists is a sign; for every creature is a sign of the Creator, as smoke is a sign of fire. God Himself is also a sign— viz., of everything which can be named; for He is the book of life, wherein everything that can be named is inscribed (an allusion to the doctrine of the ideas of all things in God). This generic notion of a sign, therefore, is too general. Wycliffe accordingly advances to a more precise definition of the notion—a sacrament is a sign of a *holy thing*.[2] But this definition also appears to our Thinker to be too wide, for every creature is a sign of the Creator and of its creation— therefore a sign of a holy thing. If we advance still further, and define a sacrament with yet more precision as 'the visible form of an invisible grace,' so that the sacrament bears in itself a resemblance to, and becomes a cause of the grace, even this definition appears to Wycliffe to allow of every possible thing being called a sacrament; for every creature perceptible by the senses is the visible appearance of the invisible grace of the Creator, carries in itself a resemblance

---

[1] Vide *Zeitschrift für historische Theologie*, 1847, pp. 597–636.
[2] *Trialogus*, IV., c. 1, p. 244: *Signum; sacrae rei signum; invisibilis gratiae visibilis forma, ut similitudinem gerat et causa existat.*

to the ideas embodied in it, and is the cause of their resemblance and of the knowledge of the Creator (who is known to man from the creature). Here we find again those metaphysical ideas which lie at the foundation of all Wycliffe's thoughts and views of God and the world.

2. From what he has observed regarding the idea of the sacrament results, of itself, his judgment concerning the *number* of the sacraments. The sacramental idea, according to his view, is much too wide to allow of his conceding that only the so-called seven sacraments are really such. In other words, Wycliffe holds that there are more than seven sacraments.[1] He thinks, *e.g.*, that the preaching of the Divine Word is as truly a sacrament as any one of those seven well-known actions. He makes it clearly understood that he looks upon it as an arbitrary limitation—as an artificially constructed dogma—when no more than the *septem sacramenta vulgaria* are recognised as sacraments.[2] It is a mere irony when he complains that it is owing to his poverty of faculty that he conceives that many things on this head of doctrine rest upon too weak a foundation; nor has he yet become acquainted with the labels which must be affixed if the name of sacrament is to be limited to these seven in one and the same sense.[3]

Sacraments more than seven.

While Wycliffe in most places inclines to the opinion that the seven sacraments had no exclusive right to be regarded as such, *i.e.*, that seven is too small a number for them, in case we set out from the generic idea which is common to them all, he nevertheless also indicates an opinion that the number seven is too large, namely, when tried by the standard of Scripture authority. This thought, indeed, he does not express in plain terms. He only hints at it—at one time by the order in which he treats of the several sacraments, placing the Lord's Supper and Baptism first in order, while leaving the remaining five to follow; while, in another place, he observes expressly that the right order of the sacraments is determined by the measure in which they have for their warrant the express foundation of Scripture.[4] In particular, he

Scriptural restriction of their number.

---

[1] *Trialogus,* IV. c. I, p. 244: *Quomodo ergo sunt solum septem sacramenta distincta specifice?* . . . p. 245: *Mille autem sunt talia sensibilia signa in scriptura, quae habent tantam rationem sacramenti, sicut habent communiter ista septem.*

[2] *Ib.,* p. 246.

[3] *Ib.,* p. 245: *Nec didici pictatias, ex quibus adjectis hoc nomen sacramentum limitari debet univoce ad haec septem.*

[4] *Ib.,* c., 11, p. 281: *Secundum ordinem, quo sacramenta in scriptura sacra expressius sunt fundata.* The difference among the sacraments in this respect was never entirely forgotten even in the Middle Age, at least not in scientific theology. Baptism and the Lord's Supper were always recognised as sacraments of the first rank, so to speak, inasmuch, especially, as they were instituted personally and directly by the Redeemer Himself—a fact which was prominently put forward by Alexander of Hales.

says of the Lord's Supper, which he places first in order, that he does so, among other reasons, because it has the strongest Scripture warrant of all;[1] whereas of extreme unction, which is the last of the seven to be examined by him, he remarks that it has too weak a foundation in that passage of Scripture (James v. 14) upon which it is commonly rested.[2] When, notwithstanding this, he abstains from entering into any proper critique of the other sacraments, with the exception of Baptism and the Lord's Supper, but follows, on the whole, the same manner of teaching which had been in fixed use since Peter the Lombard, this circumstance was owing to the fact that Wycliffe's attention, within the area of this whole *locus* of doctrine, was directed to *one* definite point and concentrated upon it.

3. The third question touches the *efficacy* of the sacraments.

That by virtue of God's ordinance a certain efficacy, a real communication of grace, is connected with a sacrament, Wycliffe has an assured belief. He observes how, in contrast with actions and arrangements of human origination, such as the Pope's election, which have no promise of God that He will endow them with grace, God has given the covenanted promise really to communicate grace with the sacraments of Baptism and Penance, which are obviously named only by way of example.[3] And on another occasion he lays down quite generally the principle that 'all sacraments, when rightly administered, possess a saving efficacy.'[4] True, this saving efficacy is conditional; and what are the conditions and limitations, according to Wycliffe, within which they have this effectual working? One condition, the most undoubted of all, and recognised in the teaching of the evangelical Church, is already mentioned in the passage last quoted, viz., that the sacraments exert a saving efficacy only when rightly administered (*rite ministrata*), *i.e.*, only then do they serve to the real communication of Divine strength when they are administered conformably to their first institution. Wycliffe is likewise thoroughly aware of the truth that a further condition of the gracious working of every sacrament lies in the mind and spiritual state of the receiver.

Sacramental efficacy.

On this subject there is room for doubt on a single point only, whether Wycliffe required a positive preparedness and receptivity in

---

[1] *Trialogus*, IV., c. 2, p. 247.

[2] *Ib.*, c. 25, p. 333.

[3] *De Civili Dominio*, I., 43, fol. 120, col. 2: *Sacramenta baptismatis et poenitentiae, cum quibus Deus pepigit realiter conferre gratiam, . . . quodcunque officium humanitus limitatum, cum quo Deus non determinavit se conferre gratiam.*

[4] *De Ecclesia*, c. 19, fol. 192, col. 1: *Non nego, quin necesse sit, nos in vita intendere signis sensibilibus, in quibus stat modo suo christiana religio, cum debemus credere, quod omnia sacramenta sensibilia, rite administrata habent efficaciam salutarem.*

the form of a penitent, believing, and devout spirit, as a condition of the sacrament possessing a saving efficacy; or whether he held it to be sufficient that the receiver should not oppose a positive hindrance thereto, by an ungodly state of mind and feeling. Expressions occur which seem to favour the latter idea; but in by far the most numerous instances Wycliffe demands a positive receptivity on the part of the person to whom the sacrament is administered, if a gift of grace and a blessing are to flow to him therefrom.[1] Manifestly he is not satisfied with the conditions first formulated by Duns Scotus, that only no barrier should be put in the way of the efficacy of the sacrament by mortal sin in the receiver, or by the set purpose to commit such; but he prescribes a truly penitent and pious frame of mind as a condition of the blessing which should accrue to the receiver.

Preparation of the recipient.

These explanations stand in a certain connection with the other question, whether the saving efficacy of a sacrament is conditioned by the worthiness and 'standing in grace' of the priest who dispenses it. It is usual to assume, and for some time back it has been the settled opinion, that Wycliffe answered this question in the affirmative. This assumption has even passed into the confessions of the evangelical Lutheran Church.[2] This, however, is no proof of the point. The German Reformers, if I am not quite mistaken, came into possession of this thesis, as one alleged to have been held by Wycliffe, from no other source but the Council of Constance. In the list of those articles of Wycliffe upon which this Council pronounced its condemnatory judgment, under the third head were set forth no fewer than four articles all bearing upon the principle in question.[3] But it is well known with how little conscientiousness and trustworthiness this Council went to work upon the question whether a certain article had been really set forth and defended by Wycliffe or by Huss. If we go still farther back, I find that the enemies of Wycliffe, in his lifetime, on only

Worthiness of the administrator.

---

[1] *De Veritate Scripturae Sac.*, c. 12, fol. 33, col. 3: He speaks of *capaces*, communicants to whom the sacrament is of profit; and in *De Ecclesia*, c. 19, fol. 193, col. 3, he speaks of the faith of the communicants, of *fideles, pii fideles*, to whom the Lord's Supper brings blessing, although the ministrant priest be wicked.

[2] The Augsburg Confession, indeed, in Art. 8, expressly mentions only Donatists and the like as those *qui negabant licere uti ministerio malorum in ecclesia, et sentiebant ministerium malorum inutile et inefficax esse*. But the *Apology* expresses itself, in Art. 4, p. 150, ed. Rechenberg, more clearly and fully. It remarks in the style of an authentic interpretation: *Satis clare diximus in Confessione, nos improbare Donatistas et Viglevistas, qui senserunt homines peccare accipientes sacramenta ab indignis in ecclesia*. Even here, indeed, Wycliffe himself is not named, but in all probability the 'Wycliffites' are meant in the sense of including their master, not the reverse.

[3] Orthuinus Gratius, *Fasciculus Rerum Expetend. ac Fugiend*, 1535, fol. cxxxiii. Mansi, *Conciliorum Nova Collectio*, vol. XXVII., 632.

one occasion brought under discussion the particular thesis which is now before us, namely, in the list of twenty-four articles which Archbishop Courtenay procured to be condemned at the so-called Earthquake Council held on May 24, 1382. Among these is condemned as heretical the article (No. 4), that a bishop or priest, being guilty of mortal sin, has no power to ordain, or consecrate, or baptize.[1] It is to be remarked, however, that Wycliffe is not here named expressly as the holder of this doctrine. Among the eighteen articles of Wycliffe, which a provincial Synod under Archbishop Arundel of Canterbury, in February, 1396, declared to be in part erroneous, in part heretical, there is not found any article to this effect, although that whole series of articles, with few exceptions, relates precisely to the doctrine of the sacraments.

Thomas of Walden, however, makes mention of a doctrine of this kind. He opposes it as a Donatistic error and as a wrong against all the sacraments taken together, when Wycliffe puts it as doubtful whether Christ supports and owns in the administration of the sacraments a priest whose walk is contrary to the life of Christ.[2] But it must be remembered that it was not till 1422, and the following years, that Walden wrote his great polemical work—nearly forty years therefore after Wycliffe's death, and several years after the Council of Constance, which he himself attended. And this enemy of the Wycliffites, when dealing with the question now before us, has unmistakably in view the form of the first of those articles which the Council had set forth as Wycliffe's doctrine 'of the sacraments in general.'[3] Still, of course, the matter can only be brought to a decision by the authentic language of Wycliffe himself. Now, so far as my knowledge of the writings of Wycliffe reaches, there is not to be found in them a single expression in which the saving efficacy of the sacraments is made dependent, in language free of all ambiguity, upon the moral and religious worthiness of the administrant priest. True, he says, in one place of the *Trialogus*, when treating of the doctrine of the Mass—so often as Christ works with a man, and only in this case, does He bring the sacrament to effect; but Wycliffe immediately adds, 'and this must be assumed and pre-supposed of our priests.'[4] Still more clearly

Misconceptions of Wycliffe's view.

---

[1] Wilkins, *Concilia*, III., 157 ; Lewis, p. 107.
[2] *Doctrinale Antiquitatum Fidei Ecclesia Cath.*, Venet. 1571, III., 11.
[3] The proposition runs thus in the Acts of the Council: *Dubitare debent fideles si moderni haeretici conficiunt vel rite ordinant vel ministrant alia sacramenta. Quia non est evidentia, quod Christus assistit tali pontifici, propter hoc quod tam hianter super illam hostiam sic mentitur, et in sua conversatione dicit contrarium vitae Christi.*
[4] *Trialogus*, IV., c. 10, p. 280 : . . : *quandocunque Christus operatur cum homine, et solum tunc conficit sacramentum, quod reputari debet de nostris sacerdotibus et supponi.*

does he express himself in reference to baptism, to the effect that children who have rightly received water baptism are partakers of baptismal grace, and are baptized with the Holy Ghost.[1]

It is true, indeed, that if we start with the idea of the Church as the whole body of the elect, which Wycliffe lays as his foundation, and then draw out with logical strictness the conclusions which ensue, we shall then arrive at the view that a minister of the Church who does not belong to the elect cannot therefore be a rightly conditioned steward of God's mysteries and means of grace. But we must be on our guard against drawing abstract consequences from that principle. Wycliffe himself proceeds with caution and moderation in this respect. He declares, *e.g.*, in his work on the Church, that it is a point of undoubted certainty to him that no *reprobate* man is a member or office-bearer of the holy Mother Church; and yet immediately after he remarks that such a person may nevertheless possess certain offices of administration within the Church, to his own condemnation and to the utility of the Church.[2] If the official ministrations of a priest who is not in a state of grace can yet be to the utility of the Church, this evidently implies the saving efficacy of the means of grace dispensed by him. The efficacy, therefore, is independent of the worthiness of the dispensing minister.

Administration by reprobates.

Most decisive of all is an expression occurring farther on in the same chapter, in which Wycliffe declares his conviction that a reprobate, even when he is in a state of actual mortal sin, may administer the sacrament to the utility of the faithful entrusted to him, although it be to his own damnation.[3] From this and other similar passages

---

[1] *Trialogus*, IV., c. 12, p. 286: *Reputamus . . . absque dubitatione, quod infantes rite baptisati flumine sint baptisati tertio baptismate* (scil. baptismo flaminis), *cum habent gratiam baptismalem.*

[2] *De Ecclesia*, c. 19, fol. 189, col. 4: *Hic videtur mihi indubie, quod nullus praescitus est pars vel gerens officium tanquam de s. matre ecclesia; habet tamen intra illam ecclesiam ad sui damnationem et ecclesiae utilitatem certa officia*, etc.

[3] *Ib.*, fol. 190, col. 3: *Videtur autem mihi, quod praescitus, etiam in mortali peccato actuali, ministrat fidelibus, licet sibi damnabiliter, tamen subjectis utiliter sacramenta.* Wycliffe expresses himself to the same effect, and quite unmistakably in *De Veritate Scripturae Sac.*, c. 12, fol. 33, col. 3 : *Nisi Christianus fuerit Christo unitus per gratiam, non habet Christum Salvatorem, nec sine falsitate dicit verba sacramentalia, licet prosint capacibus.* And in an English Tract : *How preiere of good men helpith moche*, he says, c. 4, 'In prayer, it is true, everything depends upon the spirit and character of the praying man;' but the case is otherwise with the sacraments and their administration: 'Thes Antichristis sophistris schulden knowe well, that a cursed man doth fully the sacramentis, though it be to his dampnynge, for they ben not autouris of thes sacramentis, but God kepith that dygnyte to hymself.' *Select English Works*, III., 227. In the work *De Dominio Divino*, III., c. 6, Wycliffe had already set forth the principle roundly and fully, that the efficacy of the means of grace upon the congregation was not injured by the moral character of the ministrant, fol. 251, col. 3 : *Et si praedico appetitu indebito coactus ex commodo temporali, adhuc cum credita sint mihi ex officio eloquia praedicandi, adhuc est officium utile auditori, cum ministerium sacramenti non inficitur ex ministro.*

it appears with a clearness which does not admit of doubt that Wycliffe requires indeed of every office-bearer of the Church who has to administer the sacraments, that for the sake of his own salvation he should be a veritable member of the body of Christ; but he by no means on this account makes the efficacy of the sacraments for the soul's health of those to whom they are dispensed, dependent upon the spiritual condition of the ministrant priest. Wycliffe sees clearly enough that it would be to ascribe much too great an importance to the powers of a minister of the Church, and to attribute to him what belongs solely to God as His sovereign prerogative, if it should be supposed that through the sinfulness of an unconscientious priest, the congregation would incur the loss of the blessing which God communicates by virtue of the means of grace. Wycliffe knew much better how to distinguish between the objective and subjective in Christianity, between the grace of God in Christ, which is hidden in word and sacrament, and the spiritual condition of the acting and dispensing Church minister, than has for a long time back been supposed. The accusation of a Donatistic mode of thought which Melancthon brought against the Wycliffites is, therefore, so far as it was aimed at Wycliffe personally, and not only at his followers, to be set aside as unfounded and unjust, on the ground of a more accurate understanding of Wycliffe's actual teaching.

II. *Of the Lord's Supper.*

Wycliffe always placed the Lord's Supper high above the other sacraments, as the holiest and most honourable of all. He was convinced that no other sacrament has so strong a foundation in the Word of God. But, holding it in such reverence, he watched over its scriptural purity with the greatest care, and when he came to see that the Eucharistic doctrine which was prevalent in the Church of his time was perverted and corrupt, he set himself to oppose it with unsparing severity and indefatigable zeal. It was the doctrine of Transubstantiation against which he contended with all his power.

The Lord's Supper the chief sacrament.

Coming nearer to the subject, we find three questions which require to be answered.

1. How was Wycliffe led to the examination of this particular question?

2. With what arguments did he attack the doctrine of Transubstantiation?

3. What is his own view of the presence of the body and blood of Christ in the Lord's Supper?

1. How was Wycliffe led to a critical examination of this question? It has long been known that it was in the year 1381 that Wycliffe came forward with an incisive attack upon the Romish scholastic doctrine of 'The Change of Substance;'[1] that this attack became from that date the centre of his reformational exertions, in so far as these had reference to the doctrinal system of the Church; and that his antagonism to this doctrine became the chief target aimed at by his enemies, both in scientific argument and by actual persecutions.

Progress of Wycliffe's convictions.

As may be supposed, it was only gradually, and not without vacillations and inward struggles, that Wycliffe arrived at the point of opening an earnest attack upon the doctrine of the Mass which had been long sanctioned in the Church, and which was still the culminating point of the whole Roman Catholic worship. But it has not hitherto been possible to arrive at any exact understanding of the course of thought which brought him at last to this result.[2] Let us see whether more light upon the question is to be gained from the documents which are now lying before us.

First of all, we are able positively to prove that Wycliffe for a long time did not stumble at all at the doctrine, but received it in simple faith in common with other doctrines of the mediæval Church. He confesses, in a controversial piece which appeared to belong to the year 1381, that he had for a long time suffered himself to be deceived by the doctrine of 'accident without substance.'[3] We have found more than one passage of his earlier works in which he still adheres to the doctrine without any misgiving. Especially do such passages occur in his work, *De Dominio Civili*. The usual doctrine of the change of substance in the Supper, of the 'making' of the body of Christ by priestly consecration, is plainly assumed by him in naïve fashion in a passage describing Christ as eternal priest, prophet, and king, where he says, among other things, 'He was a priest when in the Supper He made His own body (*corpus suum conficiens*).'[4] Still clearer is a remark occurring in the first book of the same work. He is there censuring the practice of departing from Biblical language in

His early belief in the doctrine of the Mass.

---

[1] Not so early as 1379—as Böhringer makes it, *Kirche Christi*, II., p. 340; it was not till two years later that he first stood forward against that dogma.

[2] Vaughan, in *Life and Opinions*, etc., vol. II., 58, limited himself to the remark, 'Of the steps which determined his hostile movements relating to it, we are only partially informed.' He knew of nothing further to say than that Wycliffe was led to this result by his studies of Scripture.

[3] *Responsiones ad argumenta cujusdam emuli veritatis*, MS. 3929, c. 16, fol. 114, col. 3: *Confiteor tamen, quod in haeresi de accidente sine subjecto per tempus notabile sum seductus.*

[4] *De Dominio Civili*, II., c. 8, fol. 179, col. 2: *Sacerdos fuit in cena corpus suum conficiens.*

a spirit of undue exaltation of the creature, *e.g.*, when men say, 'The priest absolves the penitent,' instead of saying, 'He declares him before the congregation to be absolved by God's forgiving mercy'—the act of absolution being impossible for any creature to perform. The case is similar, when, in the Supper of the Lord, the priest is said 'to make the body of Christ'—for by this is to be understood that the priest, in a ministerial way, by the virtue of the holy words, and not of his own authority, brings it to pass that the body of Christ is present under the accidents of bread and wine.[1] These words express with the most entire precision what is decisively characteristic in the doctrine of Transubstantiation—namely, that by virtue of the consecration, bread and wine are alleged to be changed into the body and blood of Christ, so that only the sensible properties of bread and wine remain present—the accidents, without the substance or their underlying basis. Nothing can be clearer or more unambiguous than this language, from which it is certain that up till 1378 (for in this year at the latest must this work of *De Dominio* have been composed) Wycliffe still held without any misgiving the doctrine of the Mass.[2]

We have now two certain dates—the year 1378 and the year 1381. At the former date, Wycliffe still adheres to the scholastic doctrine of Transubstantiation with unbroken confidence; at the latter he enters into conflict with it publicly and decidedly. In the interval, therefore, of from two to three years, the change took place in his convictions; and the shortness of the interval gives additional interest to the inquiry, how this change came to pass.

The belief in Transubstantiation renounced.

In order to obtain a satisfactory answer to this question, there is unfortunately no adequate amount of documentary material at our command. One solitary expression of Wycliffe is all that has as yet been found which throws any light upon that transition stage. It occurs in a sermon on John vi. 37. Here, among other matter, the preacher explains the words of the Redeemer, ver. 38: 'I came down from heaven not to do Mine own will, but the will of Him that sent Me.' Upon this he remarks that it is not the meaning of Christ in these words to deny that He has a personal will of His own, but only to say that His own will is at the same

The transition stage.

---

[1] *De Dominio Civili*, I., c. 36, fol. 85, col. 2: *Proportionabiliter de eucaristiae confectione . . . et sibi similibus est dicendum; sacerdos enim 'conficit corpus Christi,'* i.e., *facit ministratorie, quod corpus Christi sit sub accidentibus per verba sacra.*

[2] No doubt the same dogma is assumed as often as we meet with expressions such as *Christum conficere*, and the like, *e.g.*, *De Civili Dominio*, II., c. 18, fol. 249, col. 2: *sacerdos, qui debet quottidie praeparare templum Christo, quem conficit.*

time the will of His Father. For that, he adds, is the way in which Holy Scripture expresses itself, so that often in negative sentences a word, such as 'only' or chiefly,' requires to be supplied, *e.g.*, Mark ix. 37, 'Whosoever shall receive Me, receiveth not (only) Me, but Him that sent Me;' Ephesians vi. 12, 'We wrestle not (only or chiefly) against flesh and blood, but against principalities, against powers.' This usage of speech must be also kept in mind in interpreting the words of Ambrose, to the effect that after the consecration of the host, the bread remains no longer, but what had been bread must be called the body of Christ. By this, according to Wycliffe's explanation, we are to understand, that what remains after consecration is *in the main* or *chiefly* only the body of Christ. Why, then, should it be denied that the bread remains after consecration, in consequence of the fact that it is chiefly the body of Christ that is present?[1]

In this passage manifestly the positive side of Wycliffe's new view regarding the Lord's Supper appears. The negative as yet exists only in germ, which in the course of years developed itself into the sharpest opposition to the scholastic doctrine of Transubstantiation —especially to the assumption of 'accidents' without 'substance.' But the positive side of his new view is here distinctly expressed; and we recognise clearly this twofold proposition—1. After consecration, the bread is still bread as before; 2. After consecration, the Body of Christ is present in the Supper, and that, too, as the principal thing therein.

These thoughts occurring in the transition stage of Wycliffe's convictions are characteristic in more than one respect. The following

[1] *Saints' Days Sermons,* No. LX., fol. 127, col. 1. These sermons, and particularly the sermon in question, the last of the series, belong, as is known by several indications, to the year 1380. To aid in the understanding of the passage, it is further to be presumed that it relates to the interpretation and sense of an expression of Ambrose, *De Sacramentis,* IV., c. 4 (which was admitted into the *Corpus juris canon. De Consecratione, Distinctio,.* II., c. 55). The words of the father are these, '*Et sic quod erat panis ante consecrationem, jam corpus Christi est post consecrationem.*' It is a passage which was often discussed in the Middle Age, and one which Berengar of Tours, *De Sacra Coena,* often occupied himself with. Comp. Vischer's Edition of Berengar, Berlin, 1834, pp. 132, 178. Wycliffe calls his own interpretation of Ambrose's words, *glosa Ambrosii,* and defends it against the charge of being heretical. He takes his stand upon the language of Holy Scripture : *Et notitiam istius modi loquendi vellem haereticos illos attendere, qui abjiciunt glosam istam Ambrosii tanquam haereticam, quod post consecrationem hostiae non remanet panis, sed quod fuit panis, dicendum est esse solummodo corpus Christi. Hoc est, secundum glosam verborum Ambrosii dicendum est, esse solum principaliter corpus Christi. Est enim modus loquendi Scripturae, subintelligendo adverbium 'simpliciter' exprimere hujusmodi negativas.* Then follow the passages, Mark ix. 37; Ephesians vi. 12; John vi. *Nunquam ergo glosa sufficiens pro evangelio sufficit et Ambrosio, qui in modo loquendi fuerat assiduus ejus sequax.* [In this sentence there is certainly an error of the copyist; it should perhaps be read: *Numquid ... sequax?* or *Nonne,* etc.] *Quomodo ergo negandum foret, quod panis remanet post consecrationem, ex hoc, quod remanet principaliter corpus Christi?*

three points come out clearly from them:—1. The motive principle of his subsequent attack upon the scholastic doctrine by no means lay in a preponderant inclination to deny or pull down, but, on the contrary, in an earnest striving after *positive* truth in Divine things. 2. In laying down the proposition that after consecration the bread remains what it is, it was far from his intention to profane a holy thing, to divest the sacrament of its deep significance; he wished to put in the place of a baseless and unreal notion a solid and substantial idea. Besides, it is not to be overlooked that the proposition in question does not stand in the position of a chief proposition, but comes in only as a corrective, subsidiary proposition in connection with the other proposition which follows it. The truth that after consecration the body of Christ is present and forms the chief element in the sacrament, gives by no means a warrant to the inference that in virtue of the consecration the bread ceases to be bread. 3. How this presence of the body of Christ in the Supper is conceived of cannot be fully understood from some short words occurring in one division of a sermon. In any case, the declaration before us furnishes no sufficient ground to assume that Wycliffe, notwithstanding his opposition to the doctrine of Transubstantiation, always and absolutely held fast to the presence of the body and blood of Christ in the sacrament. For as we have now before us the transition stage of his opinions, it is at least supposable that Wycliffe, after he had once attacked the Church doctrine, gradually advanced in the same direction. We shall do well to keep this in view in our further investigations of the subject. But first we have to answer our second question—2. What reasons Wycliffe brought into the field in opposition to the doctrine of the change of substance?

He opens his inquiry into the doctrine in the *Trialogus* with these words:—' I maintain that among all the heresies which have ever appeared in the Church, there was never one which was more cunningly smuggled in by hypocrites than this, or which in more ways deceives the people; for it plunders them, leads them astray into idolatry, denies the teaching of Scripture, and by this unbelief provokes the Truth Himself oftentimes to anger.'[1] Here he proceeds to examine the doctrine from several points of view, and rejects it from every one.

---

[1] *Trialogus,* IV., c. 2, p. 248: *Inter omnes haereses, quae unquam in ecclesia pullularunt, nunquam considero aliquam plus callide per hypocritas introductam et multiplicius populum defraudantem ; nam spoliat populum, facit ipsum committere idolatriam, negat fidem Scripturae, et per consequens ex infidelitate multicipliciter ad iracundiam provocat veritatem.* Comp. c. 5, p. 261: *Antichristus in ista haeresi destruit grammaticam, logicam et scientiam naturalem; sed quod magis dolendum est, tollit sensum evangelii.*

Before everything else, it is with Wycliffe a weighty objection to the dogma that it is contrary to Scripture. How it could ever have come to be received as true, Wycliffe can only explain by the overvaluing of tradition and the undervaluing of the Gospel itself.[1] He sets out from the fact that, according to all the fundamental passages of Holy Scripture which treat of the institution of the Supper (Matthew xxvi., Mark xiv., Luke xxii., 1 Corinthians xi.), 'Christ declares the bread which He took into His hand to be in reality His body (*realiter*); and this must be truth, because Christ cannot lie.'[2]

1. Contrary to Scripture.

In particular Wycliffe brings into prominence the fact that the Apostle Paul, in 1 Corinthians x. 16, and in chapter xi., describes the Supper with the words, 'The bread which we break.' Who would be so bold as blasphemously to maintain that 'a chosen vessel' of God, so great as he, applied a false name to the chief sacrament, especially as he knew that false doctrines concerning this same bread would arise? If Paul knew that this sacrament is not bread, but an 'accident' without 'substance,' he would have acted with too much heedlessness towards the Church, the Bride of Christ, in calling the sacrament so often by the name of bread, and never by its true name, although prophetically knowing that so many errors on this subject would arise in after times.[3] Further, Wycliffe appeals to the way and manner in which Scripture often expresses itself. When Christ says of John the Baptist that he is Elijah, He does not mean that, by virtue of His word, John has ceased to be John, but that, continuing to be John, he has become Elijah in virtue of the ordination of God. And when John himself, being asked whether he was Elijah, denied that he was, this is no contradiction to that word of Christ; for John understands the alleged change as relating to the identity of his person, while Christ understands it of the material character which he bore.[4] And when Christ says, 'I am the true vine,' Christ is neither become a material vine, nor has a material vine been changed into the body of Christ; and even so also is the material bread not changed from its own substance into the flesh and blood of Christ.[5] According to all this,

Testimony of St. Paul.

Illustrations.

---

[1] *Trialogus*, IV., c. 6, p. 262: *Istam ... reputo causam lapsus hominum in istam haeresim, quod discredunt evangelio, et leges papales ac dicta apocrypha plus acceptant.* Comp. c. 7, p. 268: *cujus causa est, quod praelati ... non sint propter legem antichristi in lege Domini studiosi.* Comp. c. 5, p. 261: *Antichristus in ista haeresi ... quod magis dolendum est, tollit sensum evangelii.* See also *Responsiones ad argumenta cujusdam aemuli veritatis*, c. 16, MS. 1338, fol. 114, col. 3: *Fides Scripturae, cum rationes humanae hic deficiunt, est specialiter attendendum (sic).*

[2] *Ib.*, IV., c. 2, p. 250.

[3] *Ib.*, IV., c. 4, p. 257. *XXIV. Miscell. Sermons*, No. 1., fol. 130, col. 2.

[4] *Ib.*, IV., c. 4, p. 256, and more fully, c. 9, p. 274.

[5] *Wyckett*, p. 18, Oxford, 1828.

Wycliffe is persistent in maintaining that the scholastic doctrine is contrary to Scripture, for according to Scripture, in the sacrament after consecration *true bread* is truly the body of Christ, and therefore not the mere appearance of bread or the accident of the same. On the other hand, he asserts that nowhere in the whole Bible, from the beginning of Genesis to the end of the Apocalypse, does a word stand written which speaks of the *making* of the body of Christ, excepting to this effect—that He, the only-begotten Son of the Father, took unto Himself flesh and blood of the Virgin Mary.[1]

But not only does Wycliffe declare the doctrine to be contrary to Scripture, he misses also the testimony of tradition in its support, and lays great stress upon the fact that the doctrine handed down from the better age of the Church stands opposed, as well as Holy Scripture, to the Roman dogma, which is in fact of comparatively recent date. Even the Curia itself, in the period preceding the 'letting loose of Satan,' adhered to the Scriptural doctrine; and the holy doctors of the ancient Church knew nothing of this modern dogma. In particular, Wycliffe mentions that Jerome, that excellent Scripturist and divine, held the Biblical idea of the Lord's Supper; and on another occasion he observes that the doctrine of 'accidents without subject' was as yet no part of the Church's faith in the days of Augustine. It was not till Satan was let loose (*i.e.*, two or three hundred years back) that men set aside Scripture teaching and brought in erroneous doctrines.[2] God, however, knows even at the present day how to uphold the orthodox doctrine of the Supper where it pleases Him, *e.g.*, in Greece and elsewhere.[3]

2. Unsupported by early tradition.

In addition to Scripture and the tradition of Christian antiquity, Wycliffe also appeals to the concurrent testimony of the senses and of sound human understanding in proof of the fact that the conse-

---

[1] *Wyckett*, p. 11: 'In all holy scripture from the begynnyng of Genesis to the end of the Apocalips there be no wordes wrytten of the makyng of Christes bodye,' etc.

[2] *Trialogus*, IV., c. 2, p. 249: *Ipsa Curia ante solutionem diaboli cum antiqua sententia ... planius concordavit ... et sic est de omnibus sanctis doctoribus, qui usque ad solutionem Sathanae istam materiam pertractarunt.* Comp. p. 250, and c. 3, p. 254. *XXIV. Miscell. Sermons*, No. 1., fol. 128, col. 3 : *Et ista est sententia Jeronimi in Epistola ad Elvidiam, qui indubie plus scivit de sensu evangelii, quam omnes sectae modernae noviter introductae. Dialogus*, c. 15, fol. 153, col. 1. The reader is reminded of what was remarked above, of Wycliffe's view of the course of the history of the Church at large, viz., that the first thousand years of that history was the millennium of Christ, since which date Satan is loosed.

[3] *Trialogus*, IV., 5, p. 261. *De Eucharistia*, c. 2, fol. 6, col. 2 : *Novella ecclesia ponit transsubstantiationem panis et vini in corpus Christi et sanguinem ;* fol. 7, col. 1 : *Ecclesia primitiva illud non posuit, sed ecclesia novella, ut quidam infideliter et infundabiliter sompniantes baptisarunt terminum,* etc.

crated bread is bread after consecration as it was before.[1] Yea! even irrational animals, such as mice, when they eat a lost consecrated wafer, know better than these unbelievers do, that the host is bread, just as it was before![2] This appeal to the instinct of the brutes, however, appears to be only a humorous episode, for no serious stress is anywhere laid upon it.

3. Opposed to the testimony of the senses.

Much more value is attached by Wycliffe to the dialectical testing of the ideas, taken intrinsically, with which scholasticism here goes to work. As the effect of consecration, it alleges, bread and wine are changed into the body and blood of Christ in such a manner that the substance of bread and wine is no longer present; that only appearance, colour, taste, smell, etc.—in a word, only the accidents of bread and wine, without the substance of them, are present (*accidentia sine subjecto*). In opposition to this, Wycliffe observes that 'accidents,' such as softness or hardness, toughness or bitterness in the bread, neither exist independently nor in other accidents, and therefore presuppose a substance in which they inhere, such as bread or some other. In the same way the wine in the cup, at first sweet and pleasant to the taste, becomes after some time sour and unfit to drink: this change proves that there must be some substance to which the qualities of the wine can adhere. It is a contradiction—an unthinkable idea—a fiction as in a dream, when men maintain 'accidents without a substance.'[3] He goes further, and assumes the offensive against the upholders of the dogma of the change of substance; he demands of them, *what* then is properly the element which remains after consecration? and as the defenders of the doctrine in that age, especially the learned men of the Mendicant Orders, gave different answers to this question—one saying it is quantity, a second quality, and a third nothing,[4] so Wycliffe recognises in this disagreement a symptom of the untruth and untenability of the whole doctrine, and applies to it the word of Christ, 'Every kingdom divided against itself is brought to desolation'[5] (Matthew xii. 25). And even granting that

4. False metaphysics.

Substance and accident.

---

[1] *Trialogus*, IV., 4, p. 257: *Ideo vel oportet veritatem Scripturae suspendere, vel cum sensu ac judicio humano concedere, quod est panis.* Comp. c. 5, p. 259: *Inter omnes sensus extrinsecos, quos Deus dat homini, tactus et gustus sunt in suis judiciis magis certi ; sed illos sensus haeresis ista confunderet sine causa,* etc.

[2] *Ib.*, p. 257, c. 5, p. 260: *Mures autem habent servatam notitiam, de panis substantia sicut primo, sed istis infidelibus istud deest.*

[3] *Saints' Days Sermons*, No. LIX., fol. 124, col. 1: *Facit miraculosa ipsa accidentia per se esse; cujus somnii causam ego non video, nisi quia deficiunt eis miracula sensibilia, . . . fingunt false insensibilia miracula,* etc. Wycliffe repeatedly calls the proposition in question a fiction, *e.g., Trialogus*, IV., 3, p. 253.

[4] *Ib.*, No. XLVII., fol. 96, col. 2: *Nescit ista generatio, quid sit sacramentum altaris . . . dicit unus, quod est quantitas, et alius, quod est qualitas, et tertius, quod est nihil.*

[5] *Trialogus*, IV., 6, p. 263. Comp.

the idea of 'accident without a subject' were possible and tenable, what would be its use?[1] Why must the bread be annihilated in order that Christ's body may be present? When any one becomes a prelate of the Church or a lord, he does not cease on that account to be the same individual; he remains in every respect the same being, only in a higher position. Does the manhood of Christ cease because He became God? So also is the substance of the bread not destroyed on account of its becoming the body of Christ, but elevated to something of a higher order.[2] And what sort of blessing is that whose working is alleged to be of a destructive and annihilating character? For, according to these men, by consecration they destroy the substance of the bread and wine; whereas Christ, even when He pronounces a curse, does not annihilate the substance of anything, as, *e.g.*, of the fig-tree.[3]

But with the greatest emphasis and moral earnestness Wycliffe opposes the doctrine, on account of the consequences which it leads to, and especially of the idolatry which springs from it, partly through the adoration of the consecrated host, and partly through the blasphemous self-exaltation and deification of man implied in the pretended power of the priests 'to *make* the body of Christ,' the God-man. We only touch, in passing, the allusions of Wycliffe to the spoliation practised by the priests upon the people by means of the masses;[4] but much more frequently and urgently does he combat the idolatrous practice of rendering to the consecrated host truly Divine worship and devotion. He allows no force to the defence brought forward by some theologians of the Mendicant Orders, that the host is not worshipped, but only venerated, on account of the presence of the body of Christ. They must in reason admit that the people, who as a matter of fact worship the host as the body of Christ, are destitute of the light of faith, and idolatrous.[5] In the presence of the Christian faith, which recognises the triune God as God alone, Wycliffe can only regard the worship of the host as unscriptural and utterly without warrant; and

5. Consequences of the doctrine.

XXIV. *Miscell. Sermons*, No. 1., fol. 130, col. 2 : *Et reperi multos in fide sua diabolica variari, sic quod vix duos reperi in eandem sententiam consentire.*

[1] *Trialogus* IV., 5, p. 258 : *Deus nec destruit naturam impeccabilem nec confundit notitiam naturaliter nobis datam, nisi subsit major utilitas et probabilitas ratioins.*

[2] *Ib.*, IV., 4, p. 255.

[3] *Ib.*, IV., 6, p. 264 : Comp. *Sermones de Sanctis*, No. XII., fol. 22, col. 2 : *Sed dicunt, se esse consecratores accidentium,*

et virtute suae benedictionis panem oblatum destrui, nod sacrari.

[4] *Ib.*, IV. 5, p. 261 : *O quis posset fratres et alios apostatas excusare, quod . . . nolunt . . . populum docere, de quo . . . accipiunt tantum lucrum;* c. 6, p. 264 : *Praelati praesumunt propter pecuniam benedicere a Domino maledictis.*

[5] *Ib.*, IV., 7., p. 279 : *Nec prodest fratribus negantibus istam hostiam adorari sed propter assistentiam corporis Domini venerari. . . . Ideo oportet hos fratres dicere, quod populus adorans hanc hostiam ut*

this all the more, because the object to which this Divine honour was addressed was alleged to be only an accident without underlying essence.¹ In fact, it is worse, he remarks, than the fetish-worship of the heathen, who worship throughout the day whatever object they chance first to see in the early morning, when many so-called Christians habitually honour as very God that *accident* which they see in the hands of the priests in the Mass.² Wycliffe's indignation against the idolatry committed in the worshipping of the host is all the stronger because he cannot escape the conviction that the authors of this deification of a creature are perfectly well aware of what their God really is.³ Such priests, accordingly, he does not scruple to call plainly the priests of Baal.⁴ Not seldom he adds to his protest against the worship of the host a personal reservation and a general observation. The reservation is to the effect that for his own person Wycliffe conforms to the custom of the Church (in kneeling before the host), but only in the sense of addressing his devotion to the glorified body of Christ, which is in heaven.⁵ The general observation is, that with the same right as the consecrated host every other creature might lay claim to Divine honours ; yea, with superior right—first, because the host, according to the modern Church doctrine, is not a substance, but only an accident; and secondly, because in every other creature the uncreated Trinity itself is present, and this, being the absolute Spirit, is infinitely more perfect than the body of Christ.⁶

The essence of idolatry.

---

corpus Domini sit idolatra de lumine fidei desolatus. It is worthy of remark that zealous defenders of the Roman doctrine of the Supper were still shy of committing themselves to the proper worship of the elements. Two centuries later the Council of Trent had no longer any hesitation in claiming for the *sanctissimum* the full worship which is due to the true God. Sessio XIII., *Decr. de ss. Eucharistiae Sacramento*, c. 5 : *Nullus dubitandi locus relinquitur, quin omnes Christi fideles pro more in catholica ecclesia semper recepto latriae cultum., qui vero Deo debetur, huic sanctissimo sacramento in veneratione exhibeant. Concilii Trid.* . . . *canones et decreta*, cura Guil. Smets, ed. 4, Bielefeld, 1854, p. 58.

¹ *Wyckett*, Oxford, 1828, p. vi. : ' For where fynde ye, that ever Christ or any of his disciples or apostles taught any man to worshipe it (*sc.* the secret hoost—sacred host) ?'

² *De Eucharistia*, c. 1, fol. 4, col. 2 : *Et forte multi christiani nomine infidelitate paganis pejores ; nam minus malum foret, quod homo id quod primo videt mane, per totum residuum diei honorat ut Deum, quam regulariter illud accidens, quod videt in missa inter manus sacerdotis in hostia consecrata, sit realiter Deus suus.* In his confession on the Supper, Wycliffe calls his opponents *cultores accidentium.* —Lewis, *History*, p. 328.

³ *Trialogus*, IV., c. 4, p. 258 : *Certus sum, quod idolatrae, qui fabricant sibi Deos, satis noscunt, quid sint in suis naturis, licet fingant, quod habeant aliquid numinis a Deo Deorum supernaturaliter eis datum.*

⁴ *De Blasphemia*, c. 15, fol. 165, col. 4 : *Sic indubie faciunt* (*i.e.*, blasphemiam Christo imponunt) *hodie sacerdotes Baal, qui dicunt se esse accidentium factores.* Comp. 167, col. 3 : *illud accidens, quod sacerdotes Baal consecrant. Confessio,* in Lewis, *History*, 332, and in *Fasciculi Zizaniorum*, 134 : *sacerdotes Baal*, in opposition to *sacerdos Christi.*

⁵ *Trialogus*, IV., c. 10, p. 281 : *Visa hostia adoro ipsam conditionaliter, et omnimode deadoro corpus Domini, quod est sursum;* as above, c. 7, p. 269 : *Et tamen nos ex fide Scripturae evidentius et devotius adoramus hanc hostiam vel crucem Domini vel alias imagines humanitus fabricatas.*

⁶ *Ib.*, IV., c. 7, p. 269 : *Certum est,*

Last of all, the most emphatic protest is made by Wycliffe against the delusion that the priest *makes* the body of Christ by his action in the Mass. This thought appears to him to be nothing less than horrible; first, because it attributes to the priests a transcendental power, as though a creature could give being to its Creator—a sinful man to the holy God;[1] again, because God Himself is thereby dishonoured, as though He, the Eternal, were created anew day after day;[2] and lastly, because by this thought the sanctuary of the sacrament is desecrated, and an 'abomination of desolation is set up in the holy place.'[3]

6. Blasphemous priestly claim.

---

quod in qualibet creatura est Trinitas increata, et illa est longe perfectior, quam est corpus. The reading *corpus Christi* is evidently a gloss. *Confessio*, in *Fasc. Zizan.*, p. 125: *Nam in quacunque substantia creata est Deitas realius et substantialius quam corpus Christi in hostia consecrata. XXIV. Miscel. Sermons,* No. I., fol. 131, col. 2: *Ipsi autem dicunt, quod est (scil.* hoc sacramentum) *accidentium congregatio, quorum quodlibet in natura sua est infinitum imperfectius, quam materialis substantia signanda.*

[1] *Wyckett,* ed. Oxford, 1828, VI. : 'And thou then, that art an earthely man, by what reason mayst thou saye, that thou makest thy Maker?' and p. 16 : 'By what reason then saye ye that be synners, than ye make God?'

[2] *De Eucharistia,* c. 1, fol. 2, col. 2 : *Nihil enim horribilius, quam quod quilibet sacerdos celebrans facit vel consecrat quotidie corpus Christi. Nam Deus noster non est Deus recens.*

[3] In *Trialogus,* IV., c. 7, p. 268, it is remarked, but still with some reserve, that what is said in Matthew xxiv. 15 of 'the abomination of desolation in the holy place,' seems to have its ulterior application to the consecrated host. Whereas in the English popular tract called the *Wyckett,* the thought that Transubstantiation is the abomination in the holy place foretold by Daniel xi. 31, xii. 11, is the thread which runs through the whole. The tract takes its title *Wyckett* from the Redeemer's language concerning the strait gate and the narrow way which leadeth unto life ; for the tract sets out from that language and comes back to it at its close. Its substance is in brief the following :—'Christ hath revealed to us that there are two ways, one leading to life, the other leading to death ; the former narrow, the latter broad. Let us therefore pray to God to strengthen us by His grace in the spiritual life, that we may enter in through the strait gate, and that He would defend us in the hour of temptation. Such temptation to depart from God and fall into idolatry is already present, when men declare it to be heresy to speak the Word of God to the people in English, and when they would press upon us, instead of this, a false law and a false faith, viz., the faith in the consecrated host. This is of all faiths the falsest.' The latter thesis is proved by a series of reasons which constitute the largest part of the tract. It closes with the exhortation to earnest prayer, that God may shorten this evil time, and close up the broad way and open up the narrow way by means of Holy Scripture, so that we may come to the knowledge of God's will, serve Him in godly fear, and find the road to everlasting bliss. Thus the warning against the doctrine of change of substance in the Eucharist forms the substance of the whole tract, and this doctrine is contested as 'the abomination of desolation in the holy place'—*i.e.,* the profanation of the sanctuary by heathenish idolatry. 'Truly this muste needs be the worst synne, to say that ye make God, and it is the abhominacion of dyscomforte that is sayd in Daniel the prophete standynge in the holy place' (pp. 2, 16). Comp. p. 17. This small tract is conjectured by Shirley to have been originally a sermon (*Catalogue,* p. 33), and appeared in print first in Nuremberg, 1546 ; and this original edition is closely followed by the edition prepared by Mr. Panton, a successor to Wycliffe in the parish of Lutterworth, which appeared in Oxford in 1828. I am inclined to believe, however, that the use of the name of 'Nuremberg' was only a feint, and that the tract may really have been printed in England ; for the original edition, so far as my researches go, is not to be found either in Nuremberg nor in any other library of Germany, a fact which would be quite unaccountable if it had really proceeded from a German press. Add to this the circumstance that 1546, the last year of Henry VIII.'s life, was a year marked

If we cast another glance over the whole of Wycliffe's controversy on the subject of the Romish doctrine of the Supper, we perceive that his **Denial of the cup to the laity.** attacks are exclusively directed against the doctrine of the change of substance, with all its presumptions and consequences. The denial of the cup to the laity is never once expressly mentioned by him in any of his works, printed or still in manuscript. In Wycliffe's time the practice had not yet received the sanction of the Church. And as little has he applied any searching critique to the doctrine of the sacrifice of the Mass. I find even an express recognition and approval of the idea of the Mass sacrifice in a work which certainly belongs to his latest years, and throughout opposes the doctrine of the change of substance. The connection, however, lets it be seen without difficulty that the sacrifice meant is only the thank-offering of a grateful feast of commemoration, not the effectual oblation of a sacrifice of atonement.[1]

The Holy Supper had been alienated from its institutional purity by three chief corruptions—the denial of the cup, the change of substance, and the sacrifice of the Mass. These three **Threefold corruption of the Eucharist.** particulars Luther, in his principal reformational work, *De Captivitate Babylonica*, 1520, designated as a threefold captivity of the sacrament. Its first captivity relates to its perfection or completeness of parts—it is a Romish despotism to deny the cup to the laity; the second captivity is the scholastic doctrine of the change of substance; the third consists in converting the Mass into a sacrifice and a meritorious work.[2] As these corruptions had crept in gradually in the course of centuries, so also the recognition of them as such, and the re-discovery of the original truth of the case, was only reached step by step. First, the doctrine of the change was attacked, then the denial of the cup, and last the doctrine of the sacrifice of the Mass, with all the errors and abuses therewith connected.

by many persecutions of Protestants by Protestants, so that the concealment of publications and the intentional misleading of inquisitorial search by the fiction of foreign printing places might well be thought advisable. These reasons for thinking that the tract may have been printed in England itself find a strong confirmation in the whole style of the original edition, the typography of which, as Mr. Thomas Arnold has kindly communicated to me in answer to my inquiries, and as he has been assured by learned bibliographers, points either to the English presses of the 16th century or to those of Antwerp. [Editions of the *Wyckett* have also been published by Dr. Vaughan, *Tracts and Treatises of John de Wycliffe* (Wycliffe Society, 1845), and by the Religious Tract Society (*British Reformers*, vol. I.)]

[1] *De Eucharistia*, c. 1, fol. 2, col. 3: *Sicut laudative, non effective benedicimus tam Deo quam Domino, sic et benedicimus corpori Christi et sanguini, non faciendo illum esse beatum vel sanctum, sed laudando et promulgando sanctitatem, quam in corpore suo instituit; et sic ymmolamus Christum, et ipsum offerimus Deo patri.*

[2] *De Captivitate Babylonica Ecclesiae Praeludium*, in *Lutheri Opera lat. ad Ref. Historiam Pertinentia*, curavit Henr. Schmidt, Francof. ad Moen. 1868, vol. v., 28: *Prima ergo captivitas hujus sacramenti est quoad ejus substantiam seu integritatem*, etc.

And in every instance new leaders and captains must needs step into the field. It was the doctrine of the change of substance, along with all its presumptions and consequences, that Wycliffe, from the moment when new light upon the subject came to him, attacked with an indefatigable zeal and a holy earnestness of conscience inspired by his concern for the honour and glory of God.[1]

In this he was followed by the numerous host of his disciples. From the end of the fourteenth to the third decade of the sixteenth century, the protest against Transubstantiation continued to be a characteristic peculiarity of the English Lollards. In the fifteenth century the Hussites contended against the denial of the cup,[2] and, with the fiery zeal characteristic of them, regained for themselves the *calix*, which became their ensign. Last of all, Luther, with all the might of his genius, and his conscience filled with the Word of God, assailed the conception and usage of the Supper as a Mass sacrifice and a good work. The denial of the cup he also regarded, as before stated, as a captivity of the sacrament; but he expressed himself on that point with moderation;[3] and milder still was his judgment on the doctrine of the change of substance, although he denied that it had any ground in Scripture, and regarded it likewise as a captivity of the sacrament.[4] But the most godless abuse and error of all, and one bringing in its train many other abuses as its consequence, he declared to be the conversion of the Mass into a meritorious work and a sacrifice.[5] Now, it was on precisely the same grounds which moved Luther to protest against the sacrifice of the Mass, that Wycliffe, one hundred and forty years before, saw himself constrained to stand forward against the

Lollards and Hussites.

---

[1] In all his writings from 1381 onwards, in Latin and English, learned and popular, also in his sermons, Wycliffe continually recurs to this doctrine, which had now become the hinge or the pole of all his thoughts, and he lives in the conviction that 'for this righteous contention, when this brief, poor life is over, the Lord in His mercy will most bountifully reward him.'—*Trial.*, IV., c. 6, p. 262.

[2] *Documenta Mag. Joannis Hus* . . . ed. Franciscus Palacky, Prague, 1869, p. 124, a letter to his friends in Constance, No. 78, June 16, 1415; and to Hawlik in Prague, June 21, No. 80.

[3] *De Captivitate Babylonica Ecclesiae. Opp. lat.*, V. 29: *Itaque non hoc ago, ut vi rapiatur utraque species, quasi necessitate praecepti ad eam cogamur. . . . Tantum hoc volo, ne quis romanam tyrannidem justificet, quasi recte fecerit, unam speciem laicis prohibens*, etc.

[4] *Ib.*, p. 29: *Altera captivitas ejusdem sacramenti mitior est, quod ad conscientiam spectat. Hoc solum nunc ago, ut scrupulos conscientiarum de medio tollam, ne quis se reum haereseos metuat, si in altari verum panem verumque vinum esse crediderit.*

[5] *Ib.*, p. 35: *Tertia captivitas ejusdem sacramenti est longe impiissimus ille abusus, quo factum est, ut fere nihil sit hodie in ecclesia . . . magis persuasum, . . . quam missam esse opus bonum et sacrificium. Qui abusus deinde inundavit infinitos alios abusus*, etc. This language becomes still stronger in the piece *Of the Abuse of the Mass*, written in 1521. Jena, ed. 1585, fol. 152, 'that the priesthood and mass-offering is no doubt the work of the devil, wherewith he has misled and deceived the world.'

doctrine of Transubstantiation; viz., because it had no foundation in Scripture, because it led men astray into idolatry, and because it brought after it a whole chain of errors and abuses. Like Luther, however, he did not go to work in a merely negative and destructive way. He put forward a positive doctrine of the Lord's Supper.

3. What is the positive view which Wycliffe adopted of the presence of the body and blood of Christ in the Holy Supper?

In place of the Romish theory of the change of substance, he lays down the twofold proposition: in the sacrament of the altar there is (*a*) true bread and true wine; (*b*) but at the same time the body and blood of Christ.

The first proposition, from the time when he began independently to examine the doctrine of the Supper, Wycliffe always lays down *Wycliffe's* with distinctness, establishes with clearness, and defends *positive view.* without any vacillation. The grounds upon which he rests it, we have already seen from his criticism of the opposite doctrine. He takes his stand first of all upon Holy Scripture, inasmuch as Christ's words of institution, and the language of St Paul in agreement therewith, speak of the real bread (and the wine) as the body of Christ (and the blood). The proposition is next confirmed by the testimonies of many fathers and teachers of the first thousand years of the history of the Church;[1] and Wycliffe further throws light upon it by the analogy of a central truth of the Christian faith.

Analogy from He places his doctrine of the Supper in the light of the *the Incar-* foundation truth of the person of the God-man. The *nation.* orthodox doctrine of the person of Christ is that He is both God and Man, both Creator and created—neither solely creature, nor solely Creator. In like manner, the sacrament of the altar is both earthly and heavenly—at once real or very bread, and the real or very body of Christ.[2] This latter is, according to his showing in

---

[1] In the *Confessio Magistri Jo. Wiclif*, in Lewis' Appendix, p. 329 (comp. Vaughan's *Life and Opinions*, etc., II., 432. *Fasc. Zizan.*, Shirley, p. 126), seven witnesses are produced with their statements, Ignatius, Cyprian, Ambrose, Augustine, Jerome, the Roman Church itself in a Decretal under Nicholas II., and the Canon of the Mass, as expressive of the use of the Church. The same citations, word for word, I find in Wycliffe's book, *De Apostasia*, c. 17, fol. 114, col. 2.

[2] It is an apt and happy thought of Wycliffe to put the doctrine of the Lord's Supper and that of the person of Christ in parallelism with each other. For both these articles of doctrine stand, in point of fact, in a near relation and alliance.

On one occasion Wycliffe goes into this parallel in a sermon, viz., the 59th of the *Saints' Days Sermons*, fol. 123, col. 4: *Sicut Christus est duarum naturarum, et haeretici circa ejus personam dupliciter errarunt, sic est de materia de sacramento altaris. Quidam autem haeretici posuerunt, Christum esse verum Deum vel angelum, et non hominem sive corpus, sed assumpsisse corpus fantasticum ad communicandum cum hominibus* (Docetism). *Alii autem sensibilius crediderunt, quod Christus fuisset vere et pure homo, sic quod non Deus. . . . Et proportionaliter, sed gravius, delirant haeretici . . . ipsum sacramentum credunt non esse corpus fantasticum, sed unum accidens sine subjecto, quod nesciunt, sive nihil.* This is as

several places, the true and orthodox view of the sacrament (*catholici dicunt*), whereas the view which maintains that in the Supper there is present exclusively the body of Christ, and not bread, at least only the accidents, and therefore only the appearance of bread, is heretical, and infected with a certain Docetism which is even worse than the ancient Docetism in reference to the humanity of Christ.

The second proposition, which forms, in connection with the first, the Wycliffe doctrine of the Supper, could not but be touched upon already in what precedes. It declares that 'the sacrament of the altar is Christ's body and blood.' But how is this meant? The question is a difficult one to answer. That Christ's body and blood are in the sacrament Wycliffe had always maintained; but *how* he conceived of the relation between the body and blood and the consecrated bread and wine has, down to the present time, remained obscure. Is his meaning possibly this—that the body of Christ is only *represented* by the consecrated bread; in other words, that what is visible in the Supper is merely a figure—a sign of the invisible? or does Wycliffe mean to maintain a *real existence*, the actual or very presence of the body of Christ in the Supper? In other words, does Wycliffe's view stand related intellectually to Zwingli's or to Luther's? This is the question.

Now it is indeed indisputable that Wycliffe in repeated instances expresses himself as though his view was that the visible in the sacrament of the altar was simply and only a sign and figure of the invisible. He says, *e.g.*, 'The sacramental bread represents or exhibits, in a sacramental manner, the body of Christ Himself,' or, 'The bread is the figure of Christ's body.'[1] He who

The crucial question.

Luther's view or Zwingli's.

much as to say that the theory of Transubstantiation is still worse than Docetism. In the English *Confession concerning the Eucharist* (*Select Works*, III., p. 502), Wycliffe says positively: 'Right so as the persoun of Crist is verrey God and verrey mon—verrey Godhed and verrey monhed—right so—the same sacrament is verrey Gods body and verrey bred.' Also in *De Apostasia*, c. 10, fol. 73, col. 1: Wycliffe sees this parallel: *Unde sicut errant haeretici de Christo, alii quod est pure creatura, et alii quod est creator et non creatura, sic est duplex haeresis de sacramento altaris: ut illi dicunt, quod est panis et vinum qui praefuit* (=antea fuit), *sed in natura imperfectius quam terrae furfureus vel venenum, alii autem remissius haeretici dicunt, quod hoc sacramentum non est terrena substantia collecta de terrae fructibus, sed omnino identice corpus Christi. Catholici autem dicunt, quod sicut Christus est duplex substantia, scilicet deitas et humanitas, et sic creator et creatura, sic sacramentum altaris in natura non abjectum accidens, sed terrena substantia—et in signatione, figura vel modo quo aptius vocari potest, est sacramentum corporis Christi, ad quem sensum fidelis omnino debet attendere.*

[1] *Trialogus*, IV., c. 7, p. 267: *Sic autem dici potest quod panis ille sacramentalis est ad illum modum specialiter corpus Christi.* 'Ad illum modum,' *i.e.*, in such a way that the bread sets forth in figure the body of Christ. Immediately thereafter Wycliffe remarks that opponents could have nothing to object to this, in so far as they see that the sacrament is the body of Christ, *i.e.*, sacramentally signifies or figures the body itself. In this sense the *Wyckett* strongly expresses itself—'So the breade is the fygure or mynde (*i.e.*, minding or remembrance) of Christes bodye in earth,' p. 14, ed. Oxford.

looks at such expressions superficially may naturally think himself justified in assuming that Wycliffe held a view which approximates to the Zwinglian opinion. That would, however, be a hasty judgment. For, not to look as yet at the expressions used by him of a distinctly opposite meaning, it is by no means said in the passages given above, that the visible in the sacrament is nothing more than a sign, or figure, or memorial of the invisible, of the body and blood of Christ. Add to this that the connection in which these passages stand, especially in the *Trialogus*, has always a polemical bearing, and is by no means intended to set forth directly and categorically the view entertained by the author himself. But what is of decisive weight is the circumstance that, in by far the largest number of places, Wycliffe expresses himself positively as believing in a real presence of the body and blood of Christ. It certainly does not amount to much when in one place he declares his readiness to believe in a deeper sense of the sacrament than the figurative one, if he shall be taught it by the Word of God or by sound reason (*si ex fide vel ratione doctus fuero*),[1] for this readiness is one very stringently conditioned: but, on the other hand, there are not wanting expressions in which Wycliffe very plainly discards the view that the bread is only a figure of the body of Christ, and declares, on the contrary, that the bread is Christ's body. In one passage he reminds the reader that the question relates to a subject of the faith which has been revealed to us, and that men therefore must give heed to the teaching of Scripture upon it; and, just as it is admitted, on Scripture grounds, that this sacrament *is* the body of Christ, and not merely a sacramental figure of His body, so must it be unconditionally conceded, upon the same authority, that the bread which is this sacrament is in very truth the body of Christ.[2] In another work (*De Apostasia*) Wycliffe says that those who deny that the bread in the sacrament is the body of Christ, fall into the error of Berengarius, who placed himself in opposition to the Word of God and the four great doctors of the Church.[3] Accordingly, we venture to maintain with all decision that Wycliffe does not satisfy himself with the idea of a presence of Christ's body, represented by signs, and sub-

The real presence.

---

[1] *Trialogus*, IV., c. 7, p. 267: *Paratus sum tamen, si ex fide vel ratione doctus fuero, sensum subtiliorem credere.*

[2] *Ib.*, IV., c. 4, p. 255: *Et sicut virtute verborum fidei scripturae conceditur, quod hoc sacramentum est corpus Christi, et non solum quod erit vel figurat sacramentaliter corpus Christi, sic concedatur eadem auctoritate simpliciter, quod iste panis, qui est hoc sacramentum, est veraciter corpus Christi.*

[3] *De Apostasia*, c. 7, fol. 64, col. 1: *Si autem negatur, panem illum, qui est sacramentum, esse corpus Christi, inciditur in errorem Berengarii . . . quod est contra fidem scripturae et quatuor magnos doctores.* Comp. *Confessio*, in Lewis, p. 324: *Simul veritas et figura.*

jectively apprehended by the communicant, but believes and teaches a true and real objective presence of the same in the Supper.[1]

Wycliffe, then, believed in a real presence of Christ's body in the Supper; but not in the sense of a corporeal or local presence. He denies this with the utmost decision. In a substantial, corporeal, and local manner the body of Christ is in heaven, but not in the sacrament. Only the bread (the host) is substantially, corporeally, locally, and quantitatively present in the sacrament, but not Christ's body.[2] Of course the question then arises, If not in a corporeal and local manner, then in what manner is Christ's body (and blood) present in the sacrament, as it is still maintained to be really present? To this question Wycliffe does not omit to supply an answer. He distinguishes a threefold manner of presence of Christ's body in the consecrated host, an effectual, a spiritual, and a sacramental presence : *effectual* (*virtualis*), as He is in His kingdom, everywhere, doing good, dispensing the blessings of nature and of grace ; *spiritual*, as He graciously indwells in the souls of the faithful ; *sacramental*, as He is present in a peculiar manner in the consecrated host. And as the second manner of presence pre-supposes the first, so again the third manner presupposes the second.[3] The glorified body of Christ is operative and spiritual. Christ, in His human nature, is present at every point of the world, therefore also in the host ; but the distinctive manner of presence, which belongs exclusively to the latter, is the sacramental presence of the body of Christ.[4]

Not corporeal or local.

But what does this last mean? So must we needs ask once more; and here Wycliffe's answer is simple—This sacramental presence is a miracle. It rests upon the Divine ordinance—upon the words of institution. By virtue of the sacramental words a supernatural change takes place, by means of which bread and wine

The Presence spiritual only.

---

[1] *Confessio*, in Lewis, p. 324 (in Vaughan, *Life and Opinions*, II., 428, in *Fasc. Zizan.*, ed. Shirley, p. 116): *Modus essendi, quo corpus Christi est in hostia, est modus verus et realis.* Hence he appeals to the church-hymn which Thomas Aquinas is known to have composed, *Pange lingua;* for the words—

'Verbum caro panem verum
  Verbo carnem efficit,
Fitque sanguis Christi merum,
  Etsi sensus deficit'—

he interprets entirely in favour of his own view. *De Apostasia*, c. 3, fol. 53, col. 2; so also in *XXIV. Miscell. Sermons*, No. 1., fol. 130, col. 1.

[2] *Ib.*, p. 324 : *Sunt alii tres modi realiores et veriores, quos corpus Christi appropriate habet in coelo, scil. modus essendi substantialiter, corporaliter et dimensionaliter. . . . Nullo istorum modorum trium est corpus Christi in sacramento, sed in coelo.*

[3] *Ib.*, p. 323, text after Shirley, p. 115 : *Credimus enim, quod triplex est modus essendi corporis Christi in hostia consecrata, scilicet virtualis, spiritualis et sacramentalis.* Comp. *Trialogus*, IV., c. 8, p. 272, where the same thought is expressed, but less clearly than in the passage of the Confession just quoted.

[4] Luther also makes use of the epithet *sacramental* to express the peculiar and, in its kind, unique union between the body of Christ and the eucharistic elements.

remain indeed what they are in their own substance, but from that moment are in truth and reality Christ's body and blood.[1] Not that the glorified body of Christ descends out of heaven to the host, wherever it may be consecrated in church; no! it remains above in heaven fixed and immovable, and only in a spiritual, invisible manner is it present in every morsel of the consecrated host, as the soul is present throughout the body.[2] Therefore we are able to see the body of Christ in the sacrament, not with the bodily, but only with the spiritual eye—that is, with the eye of faith; and when we break the consecrated host we break not the body of Christ—we handle Him not with the bodily touch—we do not chew and eat Him corporeally, but we receive Him spiritually.[3] The host is not itself Christ's body, but undoubtedly this latter is in a sacramental manner concealed in it.[4] In scholastic language, it is not a question of identification or of impanation. Both of these ideas Wycliffe rejects,[5]—not only the former, according to which two things differing in kind and number were alleged to become one and the same in kind and number, but also the latter. The idea of impanation was sustained by that of the incarnation. Just as the Son of God became man without ceasing to be God, or without the human nature passing into the Divine, but in such wise that the Godhead forms with the manhood one inseparable God-manhood; so analogously, it was thought, did the body of

[1] *De Apostasia*, c. 8, fol. 65, col. 1: *Sic in translatione ista supernaturali remanet tam panis quam vini essentia, et cum sic miraculose corpus Christi et sanguis, sortitur nomen excellentius secundum religionem, quam ex fide scripturae credimus; tamen vere et realiter ex virtute verborum sacramentalium fit corpus Christi et sanguis. Quomodo autem hoc fiat, debet fidelis sedulo perscrutari. Ego autem intelligo hoc fieri per viam sacramentalis conversionis, aut quocunque alio nomine ista mutatio catholice sit detecta.*

[2] *Trialogus*, IV., c. 8, p. 272: *Non est intelligendum, corpus Christi descendere ad hostiam in quacunque ecclesia consecratam, sed manet sursum in coelis stabile et immotum; ideo habet esse spirituale in hostia et non esse dimensionatum et cetera accidentia quae in coelo. De Eucharistia*, c. 1, fol. 2, col. 1: *Ipsum* (corpus Christi) *est totum sacramentaliter et spiritualiter vel virtualiter ad omnem* (sic) *punctum hostiae consecratae, sicut anima est in corpore.*

[3] *De Eucharistia*, as above: *Et concedimus, quod non videmus in sacramento illo corpus Christi oculo corporali, sed oculo mentali, scilicet fide.* Shortly before he cites the objection brought against the Christian faith by its enemies, that 'the priests break the body of Christ, they break, therefore, His neck and His limbs, and that we should do this to our God is shocking.' To which Wycliffe replies— we break the holy sign or the consecrated host, but not the body of Christ, for that is a different thing: *frangimus sacramentum vel hostiam consecratam, non autem corpus Christi, cum distinguuntur; sicut non frangimus radium solis, licet frangamus vitrum vel lapidem cristallum. Et haec videtur sententia cantus ecclesiae, quo canitur—*

Fracto demum sacramento
Ne vacilles, sed memento,
Tantum esse sub fragmento,
Quantum toto tegitur—

from the 10th Strophe of the Sequence of Thomas Aquinas: *Lauda Sion Salvatorem*, cf. Daniel, *Thesaurus Hymnologicus*, vol. II., p. 97.

[4] *Ib.*, fol. 2, col. 4: *Visa hostia debemus credere, quod ipsa non sit corpus Christi, sed ipsum corpus Christi est sacramentaliter in ipsa absconditum.*

[5] *Trialogus*, IV., c. 8, p. 269.

Christ become bread in the Supper; not in the sense of the bread ceasing to be bread, but in the sense of the glorified body of Christ entering into a perfect union with the real bread. This theory Wycliffe sets aside as well as the other of the identification of the bread with the body of Christ.[1] Neither 'impanation' nor 'identification' was Wycliffe's doctrine, but only a sacramental presence of the body of Christ in and with the consecrated host, wrought by virtue of the words of institution— what he also calls a 'spiritual,' *i.e.*, an invisible presence. He expresses his doctrine of the Supper compendiously in the proposition, 'As Christ is at once God and man, so the sacrament of the altar is at once Christ's body and bread—bread in a natural manner, and body in a sacramental manner.'[2] Still more compactly does he concentrate his thoughts in the short sentence: 'The sacrament of the altar is the body of Christ in the form of the bread.'[3]

Impanation and Transubstantiation rejected.

Returning to the characteristics touched upon above, according to which the presence of the glorified body of Christ in the Supper is a 'spiritual,' as well as 'effectual' and 'sacramental' presence—like the indwelling of the soul in the body —it follows from this idea, as already mentioned, that we see Christ's body in the sacrament not with the bodily, but only with the spiritual eye — that we do not touch Him corporeally, and therefore, also, cannot receive and enjoy Him corporeally, but only spiritually. To this point Wycliffe more than once refers, emphasising it intentionally, and drawing from it without reserve the

The Presence spiritually realised.

---

[1] It rests entirely on a misunderstanding when the Carthusian prior, Stephen of Dolan, in his *Medulla Tritici seu Anti-Wikleffus*, Pars. IV., c. 3, vide Pez, *Thesaurus Anecdotorum Novissimus*, vol. IV., fol. 316, expresses the opinion that Wycliffe himself first broached both the idea and the technical expression of *impanatio: Confingis tibi* (so he apostrophizes Wycliffe) *adinventionis terminos novo perversitatis loquendi modo . . . . impanationem videlicet corporis Christi tibi fabricans*, referring to the words in *Trialogus*, IV., 8, p. 271. Woodford, before Stephen, knew better than this, when he quotes the word *impanari* from a controversial treatise against Berengar, written by Guitmund, Bishop of Aversa, and states that this was one of the phrases made use of by Berengar. Vide *Woodfordus adv. Jo. Wiclefum*, in *Fasciculus Rerum, etc.*, by Ortuinus Gratius, 1535, fol. 96, col. 2, ed. Edward Brown, 1690, London, fol. 192.

[2] *Saints' Days Sermons*, No. LIX., fol. 124, col. 2: *Veritas quidem est et fides ecclesiae, quod, sicut Christus est simul Deus et homo, sic sacramentum est simul corpus Christi et panis, panis naturaliter et corpus sacramentaliter. Trialogus*, IV., c. 4, p. 258: *Hoc sacramentum venerabile est in natura sua verus panis et sacramentaliter corpus Christi. Confessio*, in Lewis, 328: *Ponimus, venerabile sacramentum altaris esse naturaliter panem et vinum, sed sacramentaliter corpus Christi et sanguinem.*

[3] *De Apostasia*, c. 18, fol. 116, col. 2: *Supponendum est, sacramentum altaris esse corpus Christi in forma panis.* Of *Feyned Contemplatif Lif*, MS. in Lewis, p. 91: 'The Eucharist is the body of Christ in the form of bread.' In English *Confession of Wiclif*, in Knighton's *Chronicle: De Eventibus Angliae*, ed. Twysden, London 1652, vol. III., p. 2650. We give the words according to the original MS., accurately printed in *Select English Works*, vol. III., p. 500: 'I knowleche, that the sacrament of the auter is verrey Goddus body in fourme of brede.'

conclusion which is its necessary outcome.[1] He remarks that the believer's desire is to partake of the body of Christ not corporeally, but spiritually; and therefore it is that the Omniscient has connected that spiritual manner of presence with the host which is to be eaten by the believer, and has set aside another manner of the presence because it would be superfluous. Only unbelievers, or persons of a Jewish spirit, join in the 'murmuring' of those who (John vi. 60, 61) were dismayed and said, 'It is a hard saying,' because they understood Him to speak of a body which it behoved them to eat corporeally.[2] In more than one place Wycliffe appeals to the word of Christ in John vi. 63: 'It is the Spirit that quickeneth—the flesh profiteth nothing.'[3] I might even go the length of maintaining that this expression appears to him, together with the words of institution, 'This is My body,' as the fundamental passage on the subject of the Lord's Supper. The corporeal eating of the bread in the sacrament and the spiritual eating stand as wide asunder from one another, in his opinion, as the heaven from the earth. A swine or a shrew-mouse is able to consume it carnally,[4] but both are incapable of enjoying it spiritually, because to them faith and soul are wanting.

As Wycliffe makes the actual receiving of the body of Christ in the sacrament dependent upon faith, he must necessarily, as a logical thinker, have held that only believing communicants are partakers in fact of the body and blood of Christ; while the unbelieving receive exclusively only the visible signs, and not the invisible body of Christ. Up to the present time, it is true, no passage had been found in which this latter thought was expressed in clear and unambiguous terms.[5] But in the sermon

Only the believing partake truly.

---

[1] *De Eucharistia*, c. 1, MS. 1387, fol. 3, col. 1: *Nota ulterius ad acceptionem corporis Christi, quod non consistit in corporali acceptione—vel tactione hostiae consecratae, sed in pastione animae ex fructuosa fide.*

[2] *Confessio*, in Lewis, p. 325: *Cum ergo fidelis non optaret comedere corporaliter sed spiritualiter corpus Christi, patet quod Omnisciens aptavit illum modum spiritualem essendi corporis sui cum hostia, quae debet comedi a fideli,* etc.

[3] *XXIV. Miscellaneous Sermons*, No. 1., fol. 128, *De Eucharistia*, c. 1, fol. 3, col. 1. *Confession of the Sacrament*, in Lewis, p. 328; in *Fasc. Zizan.*, ed. Shirley, 124; John vi. 63, *dicit Christus: Caro non prodest quicquam, cum nec sumptio corporalis, nec manducatio corporalis corporis Domini quicquam prodest.* —*Wyckett*, Oxford, 1828, p. vii.

[4] *Ib.*, No. 1., fol. 129, col. 4: *Et patet, quod, quantum differt coelum a terra, tantum differt manducare panem sacramentalem spiritualiter et manducare ipsum corporaliter. Stat enim, suem vel soricem manducare ipsum carnaliter, sed non possunt manducare spiritualiter, cum non habent fidem vel animum, quo manducent.* In *De Eucharistia*, c. 1, fol. 2, col. 1, Wycliffe remarks that as a lion, when he devours the body of a man, does not devour his soul along with it, although it is everywhere present in the body; so an animal can, it is true, consume a consecrated host, but not the body of Christ, in the sacrament.

[5] Lewald, indeed, mentions it as a thought of which Wycliffe is fairly convinced, that only the believer enjoys the body of the Lord. *Zeitschrift für histo-*

on the Sixth Chapter of St. John's Gospel, which has already been repeatedly quoted, I find also this thought clearly stated. Wycliffe distinguishes sharply between corporeal and spiritual tasting of the sacramental food; and in accordance with this, he not only maintains that any one who has not received the sacramental food may, notwithstanding, truly partake of the flesh and blood of Christ by means of faith —*e.g.*, John the Baptist; but he also declares his belief that the non-elect do not in fact partake of Christ's body and blood, any more than Christ receives them—and as little as the man who has partaken of indigestible food can be said to have really consumed it.[1]

Taking a survey once more of Wycliffe's whole investigation of the Lord's Supper, to which he almost constantly returned during the last four years of his life, whatever might be the point of Christian doctrine he was discussing at the time, and which he treated of in sermons and popular tracts, as well as in disputations and scientific works, it is impossible not to be impressed with the intellectual labour, the conscientiousness, and the force of will, all equally extraordinary, which he applied to the solution of the problem. With a courage derived from the sense of duty and from the might of truth, he nobly dared to undertake the dangerous conflict with a doctrine which he had come to look upon as a heresy opposed to the teaching of Scripture, dishonouring to God, and the source at the same time of numerous errors, abuses, and mischiefs. His attack upon the dogma of Transubstantiation was one so concentrated, and delivered from so many sides, that the scholastic conception was shaken to its very foundations.[2]

Wycliffe's devotion to the subject.

The animated strife which was directed against Wycliffe, and the strong measures which were taken by the hierarchy against him and his party, are the loudest testimonies to the importance of the attack that called forth this resistance. Although Huss and the Hussites—the Calixtines at least—did not continue Wycliffe's opposition to Transubstantiation, his early

Importance of Wycliffe's protest.

---

rische Theologie, 1846, p. 611. But the sentence from an Easter sermon of Wycliffe quoted in an essay of the well-known Hussite Jacobell (Jacob of Mies) —in Von der Hardt, *Constantiense Concilium*, vol. III., fol. 926—is not sufficient to prove that thought, especially when the connection in which the sentence stands is observed. The sermon from which Jacobell took the sentence is the twentieth of the *XL. Miscellaneous Sermons*. The sentence itself occurs in fol. 226, col. 2.

[1] *XXIV. Miscellaneous Sermons*, No. I., fol. 129, col. 1: *Nec dubium, quin saepe contingit hominem non cibatum sacramentaliter, verius manducare hoc corpus, ut patuit de Baptista*, ... col. 3: *Sed sicut homo proprie non comedit cibum indigestibilem, sic praesciti nec Christum comedunt, nec ipse illos, sed tanquam superflua et indigestibilia mittit foras.*

[2] Even Cardinal Peter d'Ailly (died 1425) expressed the opinion that the assumption of true bread and wine in the sacrament, and not of mere *accidentia*, would have much more in its favour, and would infer fewer superfluous miracles, if only the Church had not decided against it. *Vide* Luther, *De Captivitate Babylonica*, p. 29, Opp. Lat. ed. Schmidt, 1868.

labours in this field bore fruit in the sixteenth century. The theory which he had so violently shaken fell to the ground in consequence of the German and Swiss Reformations; and it is well worth remarking that Luther's opinion on Transubstantiation, although he regarded it as a milder kind of bondage of the sacrament, yet agrees in many parts with that hostile criticism which Wycliffe had developed against it a hundred and forty years before.[1]

As to Wycliffe's positive doctrine of the Lord's Supper, it will hardly be denied either that it is thought out with an uncommon amount of acuteness, or that it does justice to the holiness of the sacrament and its dignity as a real means of grace. It consists, to recur to it once more, of a twofold proposition. The *first* proposition, 'The sacrament of the altar after consecration, as well as before, is true bread and true wine,' requires no further elucidation, especially as it has found recognition in all the Protestant confessions. The *second* proposition, 'The sacrament of the altar after consecration is the body and blood of Christ,' affirms the real presence of the body and blood of Christ, but not on that account a local and corporeal, but a sacramental and spiritual presence of the same, similarly as the soul is present in every part of the human body. When it is affirmed here with emphasis that the body of Christ in the Supper can only be spiritually seen, received, and enjoyed, but not corporeally, because it is only present spiritually, and when, in consequence, it is asserted that only to believers a real participation of the body of Christ in the Supper is attributed, while to the unbelieving, on the contrary, such participation is denied, it is at this point that the difference of Wycliffe's eucharistic doctrine from Luther's becomes most apparent. For it is certain that Luther, at least from the time of his controversy with Carlstadt, taught a corporeal receiving of Christ's body and blood, and, as connected with this, a partaking of the body of Christ on the part both of worthy and unworthy communicants. In close connection with the corporeal receiving held by Luther, and as a necessary preliminary to it, stands Luther's doctrine of the ubiquity of the body of Christ; whereas Wycliffe firmly and distinctly maintains the contrary view—that the body of Christ remains in heaven, and does not descend into every consecrated host. But notwithstanding these points of difference, Wycliffe's doctrine of the Eucharist, with its real but spiritual presence of Christ's body, stands nearer to the Lutheran doctrine of the Supper than it does to the Zwinglian, or even to the Calvinistic doctrine; in so far, at all events,

[1] *De Captivitate Babylonica*, pp. 29, 30.

as Wycliffe understands an immediate presence of the body and blood of Christ, instead of assuming only a communion with Christ's body and blood effected by the Holy Ghost (*Spiritus sancti virtute*).[1] Wycliffe's doctrine of the Supper deserves at least sincere recognition and high estimation, on account of the harmonious union which it exhibits of the power of original laborious thought with the energy of a mature and solid Christian faith.

[1] *Calvini Institutio Relig. Christ.*, IV., c. 17, §§. 31, 33, *e.g.*, in the latter passage: *Fit incomprehensibili Spiritus sancti virtute, ut cum carne et sanguine Christi communicemus.*

CHAPTER IX.

THE EVENTS OF THE LAST YEARS OF WYCLIFFE'S LIFE, 1378–1384.

1.—The Papal Schism and its Effect upon Wycliffe.

IN the Fourth Chapter we followed the personal incidents of Wycliffe's life down to the beginning of the year 1378. In this year and the preceding one the hierarchy had attacked him—in 1377 the English episcopate, and in 1378 the Roman Court itself, under Gregory XI. On both occasions Wycliffe had personally appeared, but on both his enemies were unable to effect anything against him. In the one case the Duke of Lancaster had stepped in to his protection, not without violence; in the other the Princess Regent had shielded him, while the citizens of the capital had stood by him with their sympathies. For three full years from this time he remained exempt from all serious annoyance.

Temporary freedom from molestation.

An event took place soon after Wycliffe's last examination which seemed likely to induce on his part a desistance from all further opposition to the Church. On March 27, 1378, Pope Gregory XI. died in Rome—a year and two months after his festive entry into the city. On the twelfth day after this event, the Archbishop of Bari, Bartholomew of Prignano, was elected Pope, and took the name of Urban VI. The strong moral earnestness which marked his very earliest proceedings produced so favourable an impression in England, and upon Wycliffe especially, that he indulged the joyful hope that the new Pope would put his hand energetically to the necessary reform of the Church.[1]

Death of Gregory XI.

But Wycliffe's joyful expectations were of short duration. Only too soon several of the cardinals were so much disgusted by Urban's well-meant but inconsiderate zeal, and by his haughty, imperious bearing, that in the middle of May they withdrew to Anagni, where their opposition to his measures became more

Urban the Sixth.

[1] *De Ecclesia*, c. 2, fol. 7, col. 2.

and more determined. Towards the end of July, 1378, the French cardinals assembled at Anagni drew up a public letter to Urban VI., in which they declared his election to have been illegal, **The Papal schism.** because it had been compelled by the terrorism of the Roman mob, and called upon him to renounce his pretended Papal dignity, which he had usurped contrary to law.[1] And when this attempt proved futile, as was to be expected, and was answered by Urban in a letter of the most fanatical and peremptory kind,[2] the cardinals who had remained true to the opposition took the final step of electing, on September 20th, at Fondi, in the Neapolitan territory, a rival Pope, in the person of the Cardinal Bishop Robert of Cambray, Count of Geneva, who took the name of Clement VII.

Both parties had sued for the favour of England, even before the election of the rival Pope. When Parliament met in October, 1378, in Gloucester, legates appeared from Urban VI. complaining of the injustice which he had received at the **Appeals to England.** hand of many of the cardinals; and commissioners also, from the opposition party of the College of Cardinals, bringing several writings, which attempted to win over to their side the English Church.[3] These writings, indeed, took no effect, for the Church of England continued to adhere to Urban VI.; but this was a foretaste of the fruits of the coming schism, which was to extend throughout the whole of Western Christendom, and to continue for the next thirty years.

In earlier centuries the schisms created in the Church by the election of rival Popes had produced in the minds of men the most profound impressions. The world's faith in the unity **Effect of the** and immutability of the Church, its confidence in the **schism.** sanctity of the Pontiff in Rome, had been shaken to pieces. When men beheld the vicegerents of Christ contending with envy and hate for power and honour and dominion, they began to have suspicions that all the life and efforts of the rest of the clergy were in like manner nothing but a striving after higher offices and earthly advantages.[4]

It may be readily understood that the effects of a schism like that which had now broken out were more powerfully felt than those of all previous schisms of the same kind, in proportion to **Wycliffe's** its passionate character and its all-embracing extent. **position.** How deeply must a man of Wycliffe's zeal for the honour of God

---

[1] The literal rendering of the letter in Walsingham's *Historia Anglicana*, ed. Riley, I., 382.
[2] Comp. Walsingham, I., 385.
[3] *Ib.*, I., 380.

[4] Comp. on the schism which took place about the year 1044, Voigt's *Hildebrand, as Pope Gregory VII., and his Age*, 2 ed., 1846, p. 2.

and the well-being of His Church, and who was so acute an observer of all ecclesiastical facts, have been affected by the event! High and joyful as the hope had been which he had entertained on hearing the accounts of the first measures of Urban VI., his disappointment was equally severe when in the end Urban, not less than his rival, Clement VII., injured and destroyed the unity of the Church by unbridled passion and by hostile actions. I find that Wycliffe, in consequence of this schism, advanced steadily in his views of the Papacy at large. The event became a most momentous turning-point in the development of his convictions, and in his position as a Reformer. His opinions concerning the Popes, the Papacy, and the right of the Papal primacy, from the commencement of the schism became more keen, more firmly based on principle, more radical. In the time immediately succeeding the outbreak, Wycliffe continued to recognise Urban as the rightful Pope, not only because his election had been regular, and had been carried through with honest intentions, but also because Urban himself was a man of truly upright character.[1] This latter ground, it is true, was of such a kind that, under certain presuppositions, it might lead to the most opposite results. This was expressed by Wycliffe himself, when (possibly towards the end of 1378) he remarked: 'If ever Urban departs from the right way, then is his election a mistaken one; and in this case it would be not a little for the good of the Church to do without both the Popes!'

The sentiment which was here put only contingently was one which Wycliffe by-and-by, under the impression made upon him by the realised results of the schism, accepted definitively as just and true. When he was compelled to see with his own eyes that both Popes, in order to maintain their position against each other, had no scruple in using all kinds of weapons in the strife; that each put under the ban of excommunication not only his rival himself, but all his supporters; and that both parties alike, whenever possible, levied war upon each other,[2] he arrived at last at the conviction that it was not only allowable, but a plain duty, to separate himself from both Popes alike. This was something very different from the neutrality which at the beginning

Separation from both Popes alike.

---

[1] *Saints' Days Sermons*, No. x., fol. 19, col. 1. This is the standpoint which we find also in the *Trialogus*. In two places there, Book IV., c. 36, 37, pp. 373, 377, he speaks of Clement VII. (*Robertus Gilbonensis*), but on both occasions in such a way as to characterise both him and his party as heretical and unchristian. Whereas Urban VI., although his name does not expressly occur, is assumed to be the rightful, and a really good Pope.

[2] Of the two Popes, Urban VI. was the first who threatened to overrun his enemy with a crusade, which he did in a Bull of November 29, 1378.

of the schism was observed by many lands and incorporate bodies in Western Christendom. When the kingdom of Castile adhered to its neutrality till May 19, 1381; when the University of Paris still held the same attitude in the early months of 1379,[1] the intention of the parties was only to guard against over-haste, with the purpose in the end of recognising the Pope who should prove to have been lawfully elected. It was still felt that a Pope was indispensable. People were on their way to submit themselves to one of the two rival Popes; only, under the circumstances, they restrained themselves so far as to reserve their judgment as to which was the true Pontiff. Wycliffe, on the other hand, was on his way to breaking loose from the Papacy itself, both on moral and religious grounds, so strongly was he repelled by the proceedings of both the rivals alike. Each of them declared his opponent publicly, most solemnly, in God's name, to be 'a false, pretended Pope,' damned him as a schismatic, and, as much as in him lay, cut him off from the Church. Wycliffe's judgment of them was distinctly this—They are both in the right (in their judgment of one another), and they are both wrong (in their claims); they are both in point of fact false Popes, and have nothing to do with the Church; for their doings and their lives testify that, far from being members of the body of Christ, they are apostates and limbs of the devil.[2] Not only in scientific works like the *Trialogus*, or in lectures intended for the learned, but even in sermons, he spoke out without reserve against the violence of both parties towards each other. It was nothing less than unchristian, and a thing before

---

[1] Comp. Schwab, *Joannes Gerson*, Würzburg, 1858, p. 113.

[2] This is the standpoint taken by Wycliffe in one of the latest of his known writings, viz., in the Supplement to the *Trialogus;* while in the *Trialogus* itself his position is this, that he looks upon Clement VII. as an illegitimate and inherently unworthy Pseudo-Pope, while quietly, and by implication, recognising Urban VI. In the Supplement, on the contrary, he condemns both Popes as Antichrists, as monsters (*monstra*, c. 4), as incarnate devils (p. 425); he praises the Lord Christ, who is the Head of the Church, that He has split the usurped head, the Pope, into two, and he laments only the stupidity of the Church that she does not withdraw herself from both these pretended and antichristian heads, but rather regards it as her duty to the faith to adhere to one of the two. The fourth chapter of the *Trialogus*, p. 423, treats for the most part of this subject alone. Clement VII., in Wycliffe's opinion, may, comparatively speaking, be the worse Pope of the two; but it may be taken as a probable truth that neither the one nor the other is a real member of the Church, for their walk and work are opposed to Christ and the apostles; it would be better for the Church if she had no Pope at all, and held singly and alone to the Bishop of our souls in the triumphant Church above. In the 9th chapter, p. 448, he pronounces both to be 'manifest Antichrists,' and warns the believers (in allusion to the word of Christ in Matthew xxiv. 23 and 26) in these terms: 'Believe it not that one or either of them is a Pope, and go not a crusading to slay the sons of the Church,' etc.; and in the tract on the crusade, entitled *Cruciata*, c. 8, he expresses himself in quite a similar way (see the passage from it quoted above, culminating in the assertion, *quod nihil illis* (Urban VI. and Clement VII.) *et ecclesiae Dei*—neither the one nor the other has anything to do with the holy Church of God, vol. II. (Wyclif Society) p. 621.

unheard of, that, with the object of securing the death of the rival Pope and his supporters, it was declared to be allowable for every Christian in the West of Europe to put his fellow-Christian to death; for every man held with one or other of the two rivals.[1] When Urban VI. issued a Bull in 1383, on the strength of which Bishop Spencer, of Norwich, undertook a crusade to Flanders, the effect of the schism in stirring up wars was brought home to Englishmen in common with other nations; and Wycliffe raised a loud protest against such proceedings in a Letter to the Archbishop of Canterbury, in his 'Outcry touching the Crusade,' and in other pieces.[2] But still worse, in his opinion, was the fact that even civil war was actually kindled, or at least threatened, by the opposing Popes and their fanatical adherents. Hence the reference in one of his sermons to the fact that the mendicant monks of England were in communication with Clement VII. (the French Pope), and were favourers of his party.[3] One fact alone in these melancholy circumstances appeared to him to be a judgment of God and an instance of His Providential working, namely, that the two anti-christian chiefs were striving to no other end than to injure each other. Wycliffe thought the best and wisest course was to stand by, and look quietly on, until the two halves of Antichrist should destroy each other.[4]

The new crusade: Wycliffe's protest.

We see how neutrality towards the two Popes was converted into a renunciation in principle of the Popedom itself, which ended in the conviction that the Papacy is the Antichrist, and its whole institution from the wicked one. From the year 1381 we find this opinion repeatedly expressed by Wycliffe. The thought and the expression gradually became quite habitual with him. From the day when this immense change took place in his convictions Wycliffe's theological position and his ecclesiastical action became ever more and more decided and energetic. The work of Bible translation, which, with the help of some friends, he had already taken in hand, was now pushed forward with increased zeal and emphasis, so that the English translation of the entire Bible was completed in all probability in 1382. It was probably, too, in the years between 1378 and 1382 that the training and sending forth of

The Papacy as Antichrist.

---

[1] *XXIV. Miscell. Sermons*, No. XI., fol. 156, col. 4.
[2] *Litera Missa Archiepiscopo Cant.*, fol. 105, col. 2; *Cruciata*, throughout (Wyclif Soc.), vol. II., pp. 588–632.
[3] *XXIV. Sermons*, No. XIV., fol. 162, col. 4. The dependence of Pope Clement VII. upon the support of the French Crown converted, in fact, the Papal schism into a national question for England.
[4] *De Quatuor Sectis Novellis*, c. 1 (Wyclif Soc.), vol. I., p. 243: *Benedictus Deus, qui ... divisit caput serpentis, movens unam partem ad aliam conterendam. ... Consilium ergo sanum videtur permittere has duas partes Antichristi se ipsas destruere.*

Wycliffe's evangelical itinerant preachers began. At the end of May, 1382, the Archbishop of Canterbury mentions, in a mandate to the Bishop of London, the operations of 'uncalled' travelling preachers, who were alleged to be spreading erroneous doctrines; and a letter to the Archbishop from members of the University of Oxford who were opponents of Wycliffe—also in the year 1382—mentions the great number of his adherents in the province of Canterbury in such a way as to suggest that it must have been by the preaching of his Itinerants that his reformational views were so largely spread abroad.[1] If we are not mistaken in this supposition, it becomes all the more interesting to notice a remark made incidentally in the same document, to the effect, that the results of which the writers of the letter complain had been accomplished 'within a few years'—a hint which, in fact, may be taken as a confirmation of our suggestion, that the sending out of Itinerants had been commenced by Wycliffe since the year 1378. At all events, the Itinerancy was in full and effective operation in 1380 and following years, when, in the spring of 1382, the Supreme Church judicatories of England found it necessary to take official action against them.

2.—Wycliffe's Attack upon the Doctrine of Transubstantiation.

SUCH action of the hierarchy seemed to be all the more necessary because Wycliffe had recently begun to attack even the doctrines of the Church. This was the effect, on the one hand, of the Scripture principle which he had arrived at long before, by the power of which his criticism gained the requisite internal freedom; but, on the other hand, we shall scarcely err if we recognise in it, at the same time, the effect of the great Papal schism, inasmuch as this allowed him the necessary freedom of external action. Wycliffe for a long time devoted his ardent attention to the doctrine of the Lord's Supper; and at length, in the year 1379 or 1380 at the earliest, he arrived at the result that the doctrine of Transubstantiation is unscriptural, groundless, and erroneous. As soon as he had formed this conviction he gave expression to it without reserve, as well from the pulpit, in the hearing of the people, as from the

Opening of the attack.

---

[1] The passage runs thus: *Doctor quidam novellus dictus Joh. Wycliff, non electus sed infectus agricola vitis Christi, jam intra paucos annos pulcherrimum agrum vestrae Cantuariensis provinciae tot variis seminavit zizaniis, totque pestiferis plantavit erroribus, tot denique suae sectae procreavit haeredes, quod, sicut probabiliter credimus, absque mordacibus sarculis et censuris asperrimis explantari vix poterunt aut evelli.* Wilkins, *Concilia Magnae Britanniae,* 1737, vol. III., fol. 171.

chair, before the learned world. In the summer of 1381 he published twelve short theses upon the Lord's Supper and against Transubstantiation, which he undertook to defend against the world.

These theses were the following:[1]—

1. The consecrated host which we see on the altar is neither Christ nor any part of Him, but the efficacious sign of Him.

<small>The twelve theses.</small> 2. No pilgrim upon earth is able to see Christ in the consecrated host with the bodily eye, but by faith.

3. Formerly the faith of the Roman Church was expressed in the Confession of Berengarius, that the bread and wine which continue after the benediction are the consecrated host.

4. The Eucharist, in virtue of the sacramental words, contains both the body and the blood of Christ, truly and really, at every point.

5. Transubstantiation, Identification, and Impanation—terms made use of by those who have given names to the signs employed in the Eucharist—cannot be shown to have any foundation in the Word of God.

---

[1] *Vide* the original text under the title *Conclusiones J. Wiclefi de Sacramento altaris*, printed from a MS. in the Bodleian, in Lewis, *History*, etc., ed. 1820, p. 318; in Vaughan (from Lewis), *Life and Opinions*, 2 ed., II., 425; *John de Wycliffe*, p. 560; *Fasc. Zizan.*, Shirley, p. 105; from which last we transcribe:

Conclusiones Wycclyff de Sacramento Altaris.

1. Hostia consecrata quam videmus in altari, nec est Christus, nec aliqua sui pars, sed efficax ejus signum.
2. Nullus viator sufficit oculo corporali, sed fide, Christum videre in hostia consecrata.
3. Olim fuit fides ecclesiae Romanae in professione Berengarii, quod panis et vinum, quae remanent post benedictionem, sunt hostia consecrata.
4. Eucharistia habet, virtute verborum sacramentalium, tam corpus quam sanguinem Christi, vere et realiter, ad quemlibet ejus punctum.
5. Transubstantiatio, identificatio, et impanatio, quibus utuntur baptistae signorum in materia de eucharistia, non sunt fundabiles in Scriptura.
6. Repugnat sanctorum sententiis asserere quod sit accidens sine subjecto in hostia veritatis.
7. Sacramentum eucharistiae est in natura sua panis aut* vinum, habens, virtute verborum sacramentalium, verum corpus et sanguinem Christi, ad quemlibet ejus punctum.
8. Sacramentum eucharistiae est in figura corpus Christi et sanguis, in quae transubstantiatur panis aut* vinum, cujus remanet post consecrationem aliquitas, licet quoad considerationem fidelium sit sopita.
9. Quod accidens sit sine subjecto non est fundabile; sed si sic, Deus annihilatur, et perit quilibet articulus fidei Christianae.
10. Quaecunque persona vel secta est nimis haeretica, quae pertinaciter defenderit quod sacramentum altaris est panis per se existens, in natura infinitum abjectior ac imperfectior pane equino.
11. Quicunque pertinaciter defenderit quod dictum sacramentum sit accidens, qualitas, quantitas, aut earum aggregatio, incidit in haeresim supradictam.
12. Panis triticeus, in quo solum licet conficere, est in natura infinitum perfectior pane fabino vel ratonis; quorum uterque in natura est perfectior accidente.

That only a single MS. of the *Conclusiones* is known to exist is the more to be regretted, than in more than one place there is strong reason to suspect that the readings are erroneous, *e.g.*, it can scarcely be believed that Thesis 8 is correctly given, for as in Thesis 5 the idea of *transubstantiatio* is rejected as unbiblical, it is impossible to see how this idea can again be made use of in Thesis 8—*Corpus Christi et sanguis, in quae transubstantiatur panis aut vinum.* In Thesis 12 also, the phrase *infinitum perfectior* may have arisen from the *infinitum abjectior* of Thesis 10, for in the connection where it stands it is unsuitable and out of place.

* Shirley reads *et* in articles 7 and 8.

6. It is contrary to the opinions of the saints to assert that in the true host there is an accident without a subject.

7. The sacrament of the Eucharist is in its own nature bread and wine, having, by virtue of the sacramental words, the true body and blood of Christ at every point of it.

8. The sacrament of the Eucharist is in a figure the body and blood of Christ into which the bread and wine are transubstantiated, of which latter the nature remains the same after consecration, although in the contemplation of believers it is thrown into the background.

9. That an 'accident' can exist without a subject cannot be proved to be well grounded; but if this is so, God is annihilated, and every article of the Christian faith perishes.

10. Every person or sect is heretical in the extreme which obstinately maintains that the sacrament of the altar is bread of a kind *per se*—of an infinitely lower and more imperfect kind even than horses' bread.

11. Whosoever shall obstinately maintain that the said sacrament is 'an accident,' a quality, a quantity, or an aggregate of these things, falls into the before-said heresy.

12. Wheaten bread, with which alone it is lawful to celebrate, is in its nature infinitely more perfect than bread of bean flour or of bran, and both of these are in their nature more perfect than 'an accident.'

These theses, boldly attacking a doctrine of such immense importance in the Roman system as Transubstantiation, made a prodigious sensation in Oxford. In conservative and hierarchical circles in the University it was said that the orthodox faith of the Church was assailed; that devout feeling among the people was impaired; and that the honour of the University would suffer if such new doctrines were allowed to be held forth within it.[1] The Chancellor of the University at the time, William of Berton, sided with those who disapproved of Wycliffe's proceeding. He called together a number of doctors of theology and laws, with the view of obtaining from them a judgment concerning the theses which Wycliffe had published, and also touching the procedure which should be taken by the University in case of need. Two of these trusted counsellors were doctors of laws; among the ten doctors of theology there were only two who did not belong to the monastic orders; the rest were for the most part members of the mendicant orders, viz., three Dominicans, of the Franciscan, Augustinian, and Carmelite orders one each, and of the endowed orders one Benedic-

[1] *Fasc. Zizan.*, Shirley, p. 105.

tine and one Cistercian. It is a fact full of significance for the social relations of the University at that time, that the majority of these doctors were monks, and that exactly the half of these monks were mendicant friars. The result of their deliberations was an unanimous advice that a decree should be issued pronouncing the substance of the theses to be erroneous and heretical, and prohibiting their being publicly taught. The Chancellor accordingly drew up a mandate, in which, without expressly naming Wycliffe, he declared two theses set down in the mandate (containing pretty nearly the substance of the twelve theses given above)[1] to be plainly contradictory to the orthodox doctrine of the Church, and further prohibited the publishing and defending of the said two theses in the University, on pain of suspension from every function of teaching, of the greater excommunication, and of imprisonment; prohibiting also, on pain of the greater excommunication, all members of the University from being present at the public delivery of those theses in the University.[2]

The Chancellor inhibits Wycliffe.

This order was immediately published. The beautiful Augustinian Monastery in Oxford contained several apartments which were used in lecture-rooms.[3] When the officers of the University entered one of these to read the mandate of the Chancellor, Wycliffe himself was seated in the chair and speaking on this very subject of the Lord's Supper. The official condemnation of his doctrine came upon him as a sudden surprise; and yet it is related of him that he immediately uttered the declaration, that neither the Chancellor nor any of his colleagues had the power to alter his convictions.[4] Later on, Wycliffe, according to the same informant, appealed from the Chancellor and his advisers, but not, as might be supposed, to the Bishop of Lincoln, in whose name the Chancellor exercised a certain ecclesiastical authority over the University; still less to the Pope; but to the King, Richard II. He was under the necessity, however, of abstaining from all oral disquisitions upon the Lord's Supper in the University, from that time forward. But as

Silenced at Oxford.

---

[1] *Primo, in sacramento altaris substantiam panis materialis et vini, quae prius fuerunt ante consecrationem, post consecrationem realiter remanere. Secundo, ... in illo venerabili sacramento non esse corpus Christi et sanguinem essentialiter nec substantialiter nec etiam corporaliter, sed figurative seu tropice; sic quod Christus non sit ibi veraciter in sua propria persona corporali.*

[2] Wilkins, *Concilia Magnae Brit.*, vol. III., 170. Lewis, Appendix, No. 20, p. 319. Vaughan, *Life and Opinions*, II., Appendix, No. III., p. 425. *Fasciculi Zizaniorum*, p. 110.

[3] Dugdale, *Monasticum Anglicanum*, London, 1830, vol. VIII., fol. 1596.

[4] This statement from an enemy's pen is found at the end of the document which contains the mandate itself. But when Vaughan (*Monograph*, p. 247) represents the matter as though the Chancellor had been present in person, and Wycliffe had appealed from him face to face, this representation does not agree with the original account.

he was still left at liberty to defend his convictions in a literary form, he published a large *Confession* on the subject in Latin,[1] and also a popular tract in English entitled *The Wicket*. Not only in these, but in other writings, great and small, learned and popular, he continued to prosecute the treatment of this subject, collaterally at least with other themes; for after the year 1382 scarcely a single work of Wycliffe appeared in which he did not recur, and sometimes in more places than one, to this weighty point of doctrine.

Appeals to the king.

3.—The Peasants' Revolt in 1381.

THE measures taken by the Chancellor of Oxford to prevent the sanction of the University from being given to Wycliffe's doctrine of the Lord's Supper were followed in the next year by official action on the part of the heads of the Church. This procedure was, however, partly due to a political event which took place in the year 1381, namely, the great insurrection of the peasantry in England. The adversaries of Wycliffe chose to connect this peasants' war with himself, his doctrine, and his party, and charged him with being the intellectual author and proper ringleader of the revolt. In so doing they rested chiefly upon a confession which John Ball, one of the leaders of the peasants, was alleged to have made before his execution, and from which it appeared that Wycliffe was the chief author of the insurrection.[2] It is worth the pains to go into this subject with some care, in order to inquire whether the event can with any truth and right be set down to Wycliffe's account.

Charge against Wycliffe.

The fact is beyond doubt that the insurrection of 1381 was occasioned by the growing pressure of taxation, by the new poll-tax in particular, and by the provoking severity which was used in the collection of these taxes. To this was added the strong desire and determination of the peasants, who were still in a state of serfdom, to obtain an emancipation which the inhabitants of the cities had already for a long time enjoyed. Acts of resistance to insolent and vexatious tax-collectors fell like so many sparks upon the heaped-up combustibles, and kindled the flames of a social revolution of a mixed democratic and socialistic character.

Causes of insurrection.

---

[1] *Confessio Magistri Johannis Wycclyff*, in Lewis, No. 21, pp. 323–332; in Vaughan, *Life and Opinions*, II., pp. 428–433. *Monograph*, pp. 564–570. *Fasciculi Zizan.*, pp. 115–132.

[2] Walsingham, *Historia Anglicana*, ed. Riley, vol. III., p. 32. *Fasciculi Zizaniorum*, p. 273.

The outbreak seems to have taken place almost simultaneously both south and north of the Thames, in the counties of Kent and Essex. A baker at Fobbing, in Essex, was bold enough to resist the collector, and in Dartford a tile-burner murdered the insolent tax-officer with one of his tools. The first weak efforts of the authorities to put a stop to such deeds of violence were not sufficient to strike terror, but only excited the rioters to still more outrageous measures. On May 30th, when one of the king's judges and a jury were assembled to try some of the Essex insurgents, a mob rushed upon the jurymen, cut off their heads, and marched with these through the county. At the same moment the revolters in Kent collected in a mob under Wat the Tyler, and broke open the Archbishop's prison to release John Ball, the priest, who thereupon became, along with another priest, who called himself Jack Straw, the leader, agitator, and mob-orator of the movement.

The rebel mobs of Essex and Kent united their masses and marched upon London in the beginning of June with a strength, it is alleged, of 100,000 men. The neighbouring counties were infected by the movement, and everywhere mobs of rebels wasted the houses and lands of the nobles, burnt all deeds and documents, and put to death all judges, lawyers, and jurymen upon whom they could lay hands. Every man was summoned to unite with the peasants in the struggle for freedom, as they understood it. The existing laws should be upturned, a new set of laws must be introduced; they would hear of no other taxes in future save the fifteenths, which had been paid by their fathers and forefathers. The worst outbreaks took place in London itself and its suburbs on Corpus Christi day, June 13th, and the following days. The mobs of peasantry, strengthened by the city populace, reduced to ashes the magnificent palace of the Duke of Lancaster in the Savoy, and destroyed all the valuables which it contained. On Friday, June 14th, they seized the Archbishop of Canterbury, Simon Sudbury, who was also Chancellor of the kingdom, along with several other high officers of State, all of whom they condemned as traitors to lose their heads on the block; and while these and other scenes of blood were enacted in London, the neighbouring counties were overrun, and numerous houses of the nobles and many rich religious foundations, including St. Albans, destroyed.

March on London.

The young King, Richard II., only fifteen years old, with his ministers and the whole Council, could command neither courage nor strength enough to make a stand against the storm until on Saturday, June 15th, the undaunted Mayor of

Death of Wat Tyler.

London, John Walworth, of Smithfield, boldly arrested Wat Tyler at the moment when he was approaching the king with an insolent air; whereupon some knights of the king's train set upon him and put him to death. From this moment both soldiers and citizens regained their courage, and in a short time the nobles and armed burghers were able to crush the disorderly masses of the insurgents, to put down the revolt, and to re-establish quiet and good order in the land. The privileges which had been wrung from the king by the rebels were revoked on June 30th and July 2nd, and not only the leaders themselves, but hundreds also of their misguided followers, were apprehended, and, after trial and sentence, punished with death.[1]

We can readily understand how Wycliffe's adversaries pointed to these events with a certain malicious satisfaction, and gave out that these were the fruits of his destructive opposition to the doctrines and institutions of the Church, and especially of the itinerant preachers, his adherents, who went about everywhere stirring up the people. *Groundless calumnies against Wycliffe.* But this was an accusation which was utterly groundless. We lay no special stress upon the fact that Wycliffe himself, in one of his writings still remaining in manuscript, expresses the most deep-felt disapprobation of the peasant war, with its rough deeds of violence and its cruel excesses.[2] For it might be replied that this proves nothing. Wycliffe's opposition to the Church might have had its influence upon the peasantry, and yet it might be reasonably expected that he would utterly disapprove of the cruelties of the rebels.

His adversaries appealed, at least at a later time, to certain confessions which John Ball was said to have laid before his judges. How does the case stand with this confession? In the absence of the official records of the trial themselves, we *Confession of John Ball.* are pointed chiefly to a document which was drawn up at least forty years later,[3] from which we learn that after the suppression of the revolt, when John Ball was condemned at St. Albans, by the chief

---

[1] Vaughan, *John de Wycliffe, a Monograph*, p. 252. Pauli, *Geschichte von England*, v., p. 522. Walsingham, *Historia Anglicana*, ed. Riley, vol. i., 453.

[2] *De Blasphemia*, without doubt written in 1382, c. 13, fol. 158, col. 4: *Patet nobis Anglicis de isto lamentabili conflictu, quo archiepiscopus prior* (Simon Sudbury) *et multi alii crudeliter sunt occisi. . . . Temporales possunt auferre temporalia ab ecclesia delinquente, quod foret tolerabilius, quam quod rurales auferant vitam carnalem a capitali praeposito ecclesiae delinquente . . . et haec videtur nimis crudelis punitio*. In the popular tract *Of Servantis and Lordis, how eche shall kepe his degree*, the poor priests, *i.e.*, the itinerants, are defended against a charge of disseminating a spirit of anarchy and disobedience. *Vide* Lewis, *History*, etc., p. 224.

[3] *Fasc. Zizan.*, Shirley, p. 273. It was plainly the author's design to incorporate with his work, word for word, the protocol of the answers of Ball as it lay before him, but the protocol itself is unfortunately no longer extant.

judge, Robert Tresilian, to be hanged and quartered, he sent for William Courtenay, Bishop of London, Sir Walter Lee, knight, and the notary, John Profet, and in presence of these gentlemen made the confession that he was for two years a hearer of Wycliffe, and had learned from him the false doctrines which he had preached, especially on the subject of the Lord's Supper. The itinerant preachers of Wycliffe's school, he said, had bound themselves to go over all England until they had promulgated his doctrines throughout the land. He had also given the name of Wycliffe as the instigator of the movement, and in the next degree the names of Nicholas Hereford, John Aston, and Lawrence Bedeman.

But these allegations are destitute of the importance which is attributed to them; and, indeed, their truth is doubtful, for several reasons. *The confession examined.* For example, the statement of Ball that he was for two years a hearer of Wycliffe may be perfectly true, but what follows from that? What a multitude of hearers and disciples may Wycliffe have had in the crowded University of Oxford since the time when, as a doctor of theology, he began to deliver lectures! Certainly all these did not become his followers in the sense of having formed his school, so that their opinions and actions could with reason and justice be attributed to him as their head. Add to this, that in view of the notorious hostility of Bishop Courtenay against Wycliffe, it may readily, and with probability, be suspected that the prisoner, who was already under sentence of death, was induced to say something which he knew that high dignitary of the Church would be glad to hear. It seems, in particular, as if the mention of Wycliffe's doctrine of the Lord's Supper had not been made without a leading question from the bishop. But such an allusion to the Lord's Supper was utterly out of place here; for it was not till the early part of 1381 that Wycliffe, as we know, began to attack the doctrine of Transubstantiation; and at that date John Ball was already in the prison of the archbishop, where he remained until the rebel peasants released him. It is therefore unsupposable that the latter should have learned the heresy touching the sacrament of the altar from Wycliffe, and openly have preached it.

The chronicler Walsingham mentions that John Ball had preached for twenty years and more in different places, in a style which showed *Ball and Wycliffe.* that his aim was to gain popular favour; for he was wont to rail against the lords, both spiritual and temporal. Nobody, he preached, need pay tithes to the parish priest, unless the payer was better off than the priest; every man was at liberty to withhold tithes and gifts from the Popish priests if he lived a better moral life than the priest himself, etc.[1] This statement of the annalist of St. Albans is confirmed by an official document. As early as the year 1366, Simon Langham, Archbishop of Canterbury, issued a mandate against the 'pretended priest,' John Ball, who was 'preaching many errors and scandals.' The clergy should forbid the members of their flocks from attending his preachings, and Ball himself would have to answer for his proceedings before the archbishop.[2] Now, before the year 1366, Wycliffe had not yet in any way become the object of public attention. It is besides to be noticed that when in this same year the archbishop had occasion, from the rumours which reached his ears, to take proceedings against Ball, the latter had been carrying on his practices for a considerable time previously; and thus we are carried back to the year 1360 or thereabouts, and therefore to the same period to which Walsingham refers. But the further back we go with the date at which that exciting mob-preacher first began to attract notice, the less does his mode of thought admit of being attributed to the influence of Wycliffe.[3] All the more worthy of attention is the view taken by another contemporary and historian, that John Ball, instead of being Wycliffe's scholar, was rather his precursor.[4] From all which it follows that the personality of this man, and his statements before his execution, by no means avail to prove that Wycliffe was the real author and instigator of the English peasant war of 1381.

On the contrary, several facts go to disprove the existence of any such connection. There is, first of all, the declared hostility of the insurgent peasants and their leaders to Duke John of Lancaster—a fact which is quite irreconcilable with the supposition that Wycliffe, whose high patron this prince was acknowledged to be, stood in any connection, even of a mediate and remote kind, with that movement. The insurgents took an oath from every one who joined them to recognise no one as king who bore the name of John—which could refer to nobody else but Duke John of Lancaster.[5] They suspected him of ambitious designs, and believed him capable of nothing less than high treason. It was for that reason

Their connection disproved.

---

[1] Walsingham, *Historia Anglicana*, ed. Riley, II., p. 32.
[2] Wilkins, *Concilia Magnae Britanniae*, III., 64. Unfortunately this mandate does not contain the slightest indication of the nature of the doctrines which Ball set forth.
[3] This was rightly apprehended by Lewis, who remarked (*History*, etc., p. 223, note *a*) that in all probability Ball was an older man than Wycliffe, at least not young enough to have been a scholar of his.
[4] Henricus de Knighton, *Chronica de Eventibus Angliae*, in *Historiae Angl. Scriptores*, ed. Twysden, fol. 2644: *Hic habuit praecursorem Jo. Balle*, etc., also fol. 2656: *Hic magister J. Wiclyf in suo adventu habuit Johannem Balle suae pestiferae inventionis praemeditatorem*, etc.
[5] Walsingham, *Hist. Anglicana*, ed. Riley, vol. I., 454.

that on June 14, 1381, they set fire to the duke's palace in the Savoy, destroyed all the valuables they found there, and put the prince to death in effigy, by placing a valuable doublet of his upon a lance, and shooting at it with arrows.[1] But, not content with this, they had designs against his person and the whole of his possessions. Before the outbreak of the insurrection he happened to be engaged in negotiations on the Scottish border, and he remained in Scotland after the treaty of peace was concluded, as long as the storm lasted.[2] In the meanwhile two strong leaders of insurgent peasants marched to the north, destroyed the castles belonging to the duke at Leicester and Tutbury, with everything they found in them, and lay in wait for some time, though to no purpose, for his return to the kingdom. All these incidents prove so deep an embitterment against the man who for years had been the declared protector of Wycliffe, that the leaders of the movement could not possibly have belonged to Wycliffe's party.

1. The insurgents' antipathy to John of Gaunt.

A second fact must not be overlooked. The movement of the serf-peasants and their leaders was directed against the privileged classes of the kingdom and all landed proprietors, as well as against all laws, rights, and legal documents favourable to these classes of the population. It was for this reason that they searched everywhere for papers, bonds, and deeds, in order to destroy them, and to create a new law of property upon the footing and basis of absolute freedom and equality. The storm broke forth upon the clergy and the rich Church foundations and cloisters, not because they were spiritual and ecclesiastical bodies, but solely and entirely because they belonged to the land-holding and privileged classes. This is another feature of the English peasant revolt which bears direct testimony against its having anything to do with Wycliffe and his tendencies. For his contention from the first was against the Papacy and the hierarchy, upon the ground that these latter made encroachments upon the rights of the State and the country, and were guilty of violations of their religious and ecclesiastical duties; whereas the rights of the State, and also the position and dignity of the temporal lords, were at all times warmly supported by him, and defended to the utmost of his power. He would have been fully entitled to say to the sowers of sedition and the democratic clamourers for equality, 'You are men of a different spirit from us.'

2. Antagonism to the privileged classes.

A third fact is the partiality of the insurgent peasantry for the

---

[1] Walsingham, *Hist. Anglicana*, ed. Riley, vol. I., 457.

[2] *Ib.*, vol. II., 41.

Begging Friars. Though they attacked the great abbeys and richly endowed foundations, the excited mobs dealt indulgently with the cloisters of the Dominicans, the Franciscans, and the rest of the Mendicant Orders. They evidently looked upon the monks of these Orders as people like themselves, with whom they had certain interests in common, because they, too, were of poor and humble condition. This sympathy with the Begging Orders was openly expressed in the confession of one of the most prominent leaders of the movement, Jack Straw, who, next to Wat Tyler, was the greatest man among them.[1] When he lay in prison under sentence of death, on being required by his judge, the Lord Mayor of London, to make a sincere confession respecting the designs which his party had contemplated, he made the following among other statements:—'We would have ended by taking the life of the king, and by exterminating from the face of the earth all landholders, bishops, landed monks, endowed canons, and parish priests. Only the Begging Friars would have been spared, and these would have been sufficient to keep up divine service throughout the whole country.'[2] This preference of the peasantry for the Mendicant Orders is another thing which speaks decidedly against the view that Wycliffe may have been the intellectual author of the insurrection. It is now ascertained, indeed, that Wycliffe was not, from the first, an adversary of the Begging monks, as has hitherto been supposed; but that it was only after the controversy on the doctrine of Transubstantiation that an antagonism rapidly developed itself between him and these Orders. But, notwithstanding this fact, the high appreciation of the pastoral office which Wycliffe always retained, and his long-continued efforts to raise the tone of the preacher's function, make it impossible to suppose that a revolutionary movement which menaced the pastor's office, and would have substituted the Begging Orders in its room, was in any way originated or occasioned by him.[3] The preference for these

3. Partiality to the Mendicant Friars.

Testimony of Jack Straw.

---

[1] Walsingham, *Historia Anglicana*, ed. Riley, vol. II., 9 : *qui fuit, post Walterum Tylere, maximus inter illos.*

[2] *Ib.*, p. 10 : *Postremo regem occidissemus, et cunctos possessionatos, episcopos, monachos* (the landed monks of the older orders), *canonicos, rectores insuper ecclesiarum de terra delevissemus. Soli Mendicantes vixissent super terram, qui suffecissent pro sacris celebrandis aut conferendis universae terrae.*

[3] Comp. Pauli, *Geschichte von England*, IV., p. 547. *Westminster Review*, 1854, VI., p. 170: 'If there was any underhand agency at work, it seems more probable that the heads of the Mendicants were the movers.' Of very great interest in connection with this subject is a document printed in *Fasc. Zizan.*, p. 292. It is a letter addressed to Duke John of Lancaster by the heads of all the Mendicant monasteries of Oxford, in which they pray the duke to vindicate and protect them against injurious suspicions. The blame of the Peasants' Revolt is charged upon them and their Order, first, because they are alleged to suck out the substance of the land by their mendicancy, and this impoverishment of the people is one cause of the

Orders, which marked the movement, had by no means a religious ground, but rested on a purely social and secular basis—the poverty which was common to both parties. An able theologian has remarked that the peasant wars before the Reformation were essentially different in character from those which came after it. In the former, the feeling which lay at the bottom was the purely human feeling of hatred against unjust oppression; in the latter, there was present at the same time a powerful religious sentiment—the faith that men were fighting in the interest of pure Christianity.[1] This remark we believe to be true.

Motives of the different peasant wars.

4.—Preparations for Persecution on the part both of the Church and the State.

ALTHOUGH it could not without injustice be maintained that Wycliffe had had anything to do, even in an indirect way, with the outbreak of the peasants' revolt, his enemies, notwithstanding, eagerly seized this opportunity of blackening his character and of representing his opposition to certain doctrines and institutions of the Church of his time as the source of the social revolution which had filled everybody with terror.[2] It was an evil omen for Wycliffe that just at that time the man who, perhaps more than any other, leaned to this opinion, rose to the highest dignity in the English Church.

On that dreadful Corpus Christi day, June 13, 1381, when the insurgent hordes of the peasantry perpetrated in London the worst misdeeds, they beheaded in the Tower the Archbishop of Canterbury, Simon Sudbury. He was a man of sense and mild character. In the following October William Courtenay, Bishop of London, was elected his successor. He was the fourth son of the Earl of Devonshire, and was related in blood to several of the highest families in the realm, his mother being a granddaughter of Edward the First.[3] In spirit he was a genuine hierarch—a zealot for the Papacy, and an energetic, domineering Churchman, and had already, in the year 1377, as we have seen—when Bishop of London—set on foot an inquiry against

insurrection; secondly, because the begging of the monks has set a bad example, and the serfs and peasants have been moved by it to desert their work and indulge in idleness, issuing at last in rebellion; and thirdly, because the well-known influence of the Begging Friars upon the larger part of the nobility as well as of the people, has led to the present state of excitement and irritation. The man who, more than any other, has spread such odious charges against these Orders is the doctor of theology, Nicholas of Hereford. The letter is dated February 18, 1381, but this must mean 1382, for the revolt itself did not take place till May of 1381.

[1] Häusser's *Geschichte des Zeitalters der Reformation*, Berlin, 1868, p. 107.

[2] This appears plainly enough from the confession of John Ball, which may be conjectured to have been drawn from him by the Bishop of London.

[3] Lewis, *History*, etc., p. 58, note *d*.

Wycliffe. This 'pillar of the Church,' as his admirers called him, was now Primate of all England. As Wycliffe, in the meantime, had proceeded further and further in his ecclesiastical opposition, and not only in preaching, writing, and academic action, but also by means of the Itinerant Preachers' Institute, had prosecuted his reformational efforts far and wide throughout the country, the new archbishop deemed it to be his imperative duty, without delay, and by all available means, to adopt measures with the view of breaking down the increased power of the opposition party, and putting an effectual stop to their attempts.

His plan of operations was evidently the fruit of cool and mature deliberation, so as to make his victory and success all the more infallible. The order of procedure was to be this: that, in the first instance, the *doctrines* and *principles* of Wycliffe and his adherents should be condemned by ecclesiastical authority; and that, in the second instance, the persons who professed these doctrines should be attacked and compelled to recant, or else, in the event of obstinacy, should be persecuted and struck down without mercy. First deal with the *subject*, and then with the persons. That was the idea; and so men made sure to gain their end. The archbishop designate was able to think over his future proceedings all the more deliberately as, after his appointment, he abstained, on principle, from all official action as Primate till he received the pallium from Rome; and this was not the case till May 6, 1382—a full half-year after his nomination by the Crown.

Now, therefore, he proceeded rapidly to action. The first measure was aimed, as before arranged, against the doctrines; and here no hindrance could stand in the way, for in the sphere of doctrine the ecclesiastical power could act with a free hand. The archbishop summoned an assembly of ecclesiastical notables for May 17, 1382, in London. This assembly consisted of ten bishops, sixteen doctors of laws, thirty doctors of theology, and four bachelors of laws.[1] The archbishop had selected at his own pleasure the men whom he could trust, to examine and decide the questions which he intended to lay before them—all men, of course, of acknowledged Roman orthodoxy and papistical views.[2] The sessions took place in the hall of the Dominican Monastery in Blackfriars.[3] During the sittings of the as-

---

[1] These numbers are taken from the document printed in *Fasc. Zizan.*, p. 291.

[2] The archbishop says of them, in a document printed in Wilkins' *Concilia*, III., 157, *quos famosiores et peritiores credidimus, et sanctius in fide catholica sentientes.*

[3] *Apud Praedicatores, Fasc. Zizan.*, p. 272; *apud Dominicanos*, Foxe, *Rerum in Ecclesia Gestarum Commentarii*, 1559, p. 19. The English edition, 1563, p. 13, rendered this erroneously by 'grey friars' (Franciscans), which has passed into many later accounts—*e.g.*, Vaughan, *Life and*

sembly it happened that a terrific earthquake shook the city, and filled every one with consternation. The event made so deep an impression upon some members of the assembly that they looked upon it as an evil omen, and advised that the design of the meeting should be given up. But Archbishop Courtenay was not the man to be so easily shaken in his purpose. He declared that the earthquake was rather to be regarded as a good and encouraging omen, and he knew how to calm again the minds of the assembly.[1] He represented to the Churchmen that the earthquake was an emblem of the purification of the kingdom from erroneous doctrines. As in the interior of the earth there are enclosed foul airs and winds, which break out in earthquakes, so that the earth is purged of them, though not without great violence, even so there were many heresies shut up in the hearts of the unbelieving, but by the condemnation thereof the kingdom would be purged, though not without trouble and great agitation.[2] Wycliffe himself speaks of the earthquake as a judgment of God upon the proceedings of the assembly, which he was in the habit of calling the 'Earthquake Council;' or, at other times, as a gigantic outcry of the earth against the ungodly doings of men—like the earthquake at the passion of the Son of God.[3]

The earthquake.

Opinions, II., 70; *John de Wycliffe*, p. 269; Pauli, *Geschichte von England*, IV., p. 548.

[1] This earthquake is mentioned not only in chronicles, but also in poems of the time, which have come down to us, and in several places by Wycliffe himself. The day of its occurrence is given variously. Lewis and Vaughan name May 17, the day of the first meeting of that ecclesiastical assembly. But documents like the *Fasc. Zizan.*, p. 272, and historians like John Foxe (*Acts and Monuments*, ed. Pratt and Stoughton, III., 19) mention St. Dunstan's Day, May 19. Walsingham (*Hist. Anglic.*, ed. Riley) gives a day still later, *duodecimus calendas Junii*, or May 21. [The mention of the Saint's day by Foxe is no doubt weighty evidence. But other authorities (the *Godstow Chronicle*, *Eulogium Historiarum*, III., 356—Rolls Series—and even *Fasc. Zizan.*, p. 288) give the Wednesday before Whitsunday, or May 21, supporting Walsingham's date.]

[2] *Fasc. Zizan.*, p. 272. The construction of the words *fuit depuratum* seems to prove that the earthquake cannot have taken place at the beginning of the sittings, but towards the close. Vaughan, however, gives a different construction to the phrase. *Monograph*, p. 265.

[3] *Trialogus*, IV., c. 27, p. 339; c. 36, pp. 374 and 376: *Multi fideles pie reputant, quod in ista damnatione, ad ostendendum defectum attestationis humanae, fuit insolite motus terrae. Quando enim membra Christi deficiunt ad reclamandum contra tales haereticos, terra clamat.* Even in his sermons Wycliffe contended against the Earthquake Council, *e.g.*, in the 11th of the *XXIV. Miscell. Serm.*, fol. 157, col. 1: *Fratres—dampnarunt ut haeresin in suo concilio terrae motus, quod solum praedestinati sint partes s. matris ecclesiae.* Comp. *Fasc. Zizan.*, p. 283; also *Wiclif's English Confession on the Lord's Supper*, which is preserved by Knighton in Twysden, III., 2747. Both Lewis, p. 103, and Vaughan, *Monograph*, p. 571, reproduce the whole piece simply as it appears in the printed chronicle, in which the words now in question are without meaning. But Arnold has recently published the piece in vol. III., *Select English Works*, in a critically amended form, upon the authority of a MS. in the Bodleian Library, containing *Wiclif's Confession*, and after collation with two MSS. of Knighton's *Chronicle*. According to this corrected form, the passage in question reads as follows:—'And herefore devoute men supposen, that this counseil of freris at London was with erthe dyn. For thei putt an heresye upon Christ and seyntis in heven; wherfore the erthe trembled, faylande monnis voice answerande for God, as hit did in tyme of his passioun, when

Of the transactions of the assembly we have no records. We only know the conclusions which it arrived at, and these only from the *Mandates* of the Archbishop, in which he published them for the information and use of the Church. These *Mandates* contain in an appendix twenty-four Articles, which had been in part publicly set forth in the University of Oxford, and in part spread abroad by itinerant preachers in the country. The judgment passed upon these Articles, after deliberation with the Council, was to the effect that they were in part heretical, and in part erroneous.[1] The first ten, which were pronounced heretical, were the following:—

Conclusions of the Council.

he was dampned to bodily deth.' This earthquake is mentioned by Wycliffe in yet another of his English tracts, *The Seven Werkys of Mercy Bodyly*, c. 6. 'Ther cownsel of trembulynge of the erthe.' *Select English Works*, III., p. 175.

[1] Wilkins, *Concilia Magnae Britanniae*, vol. III., 157. Lewis, *History*, p. 357. Walsingham, *Historia Anglicana*, II., 58. Foxe, *Acts and Monum.*, III., 21. *Fasciculi Zizaniorum*, ed. Shirley, pp. 277-282.

Conclusiones hereticae, et contra determinationem ecclesiae, de quibus supra fit mentio, in haec verba sequuntur.

1. Quod substantia panis materialis et vini maneat post consecrationem in sacramento altaris.
2. Item, quod accidentia non maneant sine subjecto post consecrationem in eodem sacramento.
3. Item, quod Christus non sit in sacramento altaris identice, vere, et realiter in propria praesentia corporali.
4. Item, quod si episcopus vel sacerdos existat in peccato mortali, non ordinat, conficit, nec baptisat.
5. Item, quod si homo fuerit debite contritus, omnis confessio exterior est sibi superfluus vel inutilis.
6. Item, pertinaciter asserere non esse fundatum in evangelio quod Christus missam ordinavit.
7. Item, quod Deus debet obedire diabolo.
8. Item, quod si Papa sit praescitus, et malus homo, ac per consequens membrum diaboli, non habet potestatem supra fideles Christi ab aliquo sibi datam, nisi forte a Caesare.
9. Item, quod post Urbanum sextum non est alius recipiendus in Papam, sed vivendum est more Graecorum, sub legibus propriis.
10. Item, asserere quod est contra sacram Scripturam, quod viri ecclesiastici habeant possessiones temporales.

Conclusiones erroneae, et contra determinationem ecclesiae, de quibus superius memoratur, in haec verba sequuntur.

11. Quod nullus praelatus debet aliquem excommunicare, nisi prius sciat ipsum excommunicatum a Deo.
12. Item, quod sic excommunicans, ex hoc sit haereticus, vel excommunicatus.
13. Item, quod praelatus excommunicans clericum qui appellavit ad regem et consilium regni, eo ipso traditor est Dei, regis, et regni.
14. Item, quod illi qui dimittunt praedicare, seu audire verbum Dei, vel evangelium praedicatum, propter excommunicationem hominum, sunt excommunicati, et in die judicii traditores Dei habebuntur.
15. Item, asserere quod liceat alicui etiam diacono vel presbytero praedicare, verbum Dei absque auctoritate sedis apostolicae, vel episcopi catholici, seu alia de qua sufficienter constet.
16. Item, asserere quod nullus est dominus civilis, nullus est episcopus, nullus est praelatus, dum est in peccato mortali.
17. Item, quod domini temporales possint, ad arbitrium eorum, auferre bona temporalia ab ecclesiasticis habitualiter delinquentibus, vel quod populares possint, ad eorum arbitrium, dominos delinquentes corrigere.
18. Item, quod decimae sunt purae eleemosynae, et quod parochiani possunt, propter peccata suorum curatorum eas detinere, et ad libitum aliis conferre.
19. Item, quod speciales orationes applicatae uni personae per praelatos, vel religiosos, non plus prosunt eidem personae, quam generales orationes, ceteris paribus, eidem.
20. Item, quod eo ipso quod aliquis

1. That the substance of material bread and wine doth remain in the sacrament of the altar after consecration.

Ten 'Heresies.' 2. That the 'accidents' do not remain without the 'subject' in the same sacrament after consecration.

3. That Christ is not in the sacrament of the altar identically, truly and really in His proper corporeal person.

4. That if a bishop or a priest be in mortal sin, he doth not ordain, consecrate, nor baptize.

5. That if a man be duly contrite, all exterior confession is to him superfluous and invalid.

6. That it hath no foundation in the Gospel that Christ did ordain the Mass.

7. That God ought to obey the devil.

8 That if the Pope, according to the Divine foreknowledge, be a reprobate and an evil man, and consequently a member of the devil, he hath no power over the faithful of Christ given to him by any, unless peradventure it be given him by the Emperor.

9. That after Urban VI. none other is to be received for Pope, but that Christendom ought to live, after the manner of the Greeks, under its own laws.

10. That it is contrary to Holy Scripture that ecclesiastical persons should have any temporal possessions.

The following fourteen articles were condemned as erroneous :—

11. That no prelate ought to excommunicate any man except he first know him to be excommunicated of God.

Fourteen 'Errors.' 12. That he who doth so excommunicate is thereby himself either a heretic or excommunicated.

13. That a prelate or bishop excommunicating a cleric who hath appealed to the king or the council of the realm, in so doing is a traitor to the king and the realm.

14. That they who cease to preach or to hear the Word of God or the gospel, for fear of such excommunication, are already excommunicate, and in the day of judgment shall be counted traitors to God.

---

ingreditur religionem privatam quamcunque, redditur ineptior et inhabilior ad observantiam mandatorum Dei.

21. Item, quod sancti instituentes religiones privatas quascunque, tam possessionatorum quum mendicantium, in sic instituendo peccaverunt.

22. Item, quod religiosi viventes in religionibus privatis, non sint de religione Christiani.

23. Item, quod fratres teneantur per laborem manuum, et non per mendicationem, victum suum acquirere.

24. Item, quod conferens eleemosynam fratribus, vel fratri praedicanti est excommunicatus ; et recipiens.

15. That it is lawful for any deacon or presbyter to preach the Word of God without the authority or licence of the Apostolic See, or of a Catholic bishop, or of any other recognised authority.

16. That a man is no civil lord, nor bishop, nor prelate, as long as he is in mortal sin.

17. That temporal lords may at will withdraw their temporal goods from ecclesiastics habitually delinquent; also that the commonalty (or tenants, *populares*) may at will correct lords (or landlords, *dominos*) when they transgress.

18. That tithes are pure alms, and that parishioners may, for the offences of their curates, detain them and bestow them on others at pleasure.

19. That special prayers, applied to any one person by prelates or religious men, do no more profit the same person than general prayers would, *caeteris paribus*, profit him.

20. Moreover, in that any man doth enter into any private religion whatsoever, he is thereby made more unapt and unable to observe the commandments of God.

21. That holy men who have instituted any private religions whatsoever (as well of seculars having possessions as of begging friars who have none), in so instituting, did err.

22. That religious men living in private religions are not of the Christian religion.

23. That friars are bound to get their living by the labour of their hands, and not by begging.

24. That whosoever doth give any alms unto friars, or to any friar that preacheth, is excommunicate; as also is he that taketh.

It will be observed that the first ten articles—condemned as *heretical*—began with three theses relating to the Lord's Supper.

It is manifest that Wycliffe's criticism of the doctrine of Transubstantiation had excited the greatest attention. The doctrine of the Sacraments in general, however, forms the point of union in which all the theses of the first class meet, for the 5th thesis relates to confession, and the 4th, with 8–10, to the sacrament of Holy Orders. The 7th thesis—*Deus debet obedire Diabolo*—did not perhaps proceed from a dishonest use of logical inference on the part of opponents, or from a fanatical misapprehension of Wycliffe's meaning; it was rather a thesis of his own, set forth, indeed, in a paradoxical form, but meaning that God has permitted evil to exist in the world, and must therefore have regard to its existence in His government of the world, or must shape His action

Summary.

accordingly, for even Christ submitted Himself to temptation by the devil.[1]

The theses of the second class, which are only censured as erroneous, all belong to the sphere of the external order of the Church. For to that heading belong the questions touching excommunication (11–14), the office of teaching, and the right to preach (14, 15), tithes and Church property (17, 18), monastic orders and cloister-life (20–24), as well as prayers offered by prelates and monks for particular persons (19). The 16th thesis is related to the 4th and 8th in the first class. The 17th thesis, in manifest allusion to the event of the preceding year, viz., the revolt of the serf-peasants, contains a hint, which could scarcely be misunderstood, that the frightful violences and cruelties of the rebels were in some measure connected with the inflammatory doctrines of the itinerant preachers.[2]

In the mandates issued by the archbishop on the basis of the conclusions of the Council, neither Wycliffe nor any other of his friends and adherents were mentioned by name—neither in the mandate to Peter Stokes, the Carmelite doctor of theology in Oxford, the Primate's commissary there, nor in that sent to the Bishop of London, to be by him communicated to all the suffragan bishops of the Province of Canterbury. The mandates declared that 'men without authority, children of perdition, have usurped the office of preachers, and have preached, sometimes in churches, and sometimes in other places, doctrines heretical and unchurchly—yea, and undermining the peace of the kingdom. To stem the evil and to hinder its spread, the archbishop had called into his counsels, with the consent and advice of several bishops, men of experience and ripe ecclesiastical learning, by whom the theses were maturely weighed and examined, and who had concluded that they were in part heretical, and in part, at least, erroneous and unecclesiastical.' So far the two mandates are identical. But at this point they separate: the archbishop's commissary in Oxford is directed to publish the prohibition that, from that day forth, no man shall be permitted to set forth in lectures, or to preach or defend in the University, the errors now censured, and no man suffered to listen to, or in any way to favour the setting forth of the same; but

Marginal note: The Archbishop's mandates.

---

[1] In the Introduction to *Fasc. Zizan.*, lxiv., Shirley has given from a MS. in Trinity College, Cambridge, the passage of a Latin sermon in which Wycliffe mentions the condemnation of the Article, and vindicates the truth contained in it. And in the English tract, *De Apostasia Cleri, Select Works*, III., 437, Wycliffe remarks that Christ Himself submitted to Judas Iscariot: 'Crist obeshede and servede to Scarioth.' Comp. Arnold's note on these words.

[2] It is for this reason that Wycliffe in the *Trialogus* emphatically defends himself against the judgment of the Council, and explains the real meaning of his Article IV., c. 37, p. 377, while he justifies the 19th Art. in the 38th chap., p. 389.

every man, on the contrary, must flee from and avoid every upholder of these doctrines, under pain of the greater excommunication. This mandate was dated May 28, 1382, from Oxford.[1] Two days later was dated the mandate of the Primate to the Bishop of London. It enjoins the bishop, upon his obedience, to communicate to all his brother bishops in the Province the archbishop's injunction that every bishop shall publish three times over, in his own cathedral and the other churches of his diocese, an intimation and prohibition to the effect that, on pain of the greater excommunication, which every bishop has to pronounce in case of need, no one in future shall preach, or teach, or hold the condemned theses, or listen or show favour to any man who preaches them.[2]

In order to give greater publicity to the conclusions arrived at, and to engage the sympathy of the people upon their side, an extraordinary act was appointed. On Friday of Whitsun week, May 30th, a solemn procession passed through the streets of London, including clergy and laity, all arranged according to their several orders and conditions, and all barefoot, for it was meant to be an act of penitence. It concluded with a sermon against the condemned doctrines, preached by the Carmelite, John Cunningham, a doctor of theology; who finished by reading in the pulpit the mandate of the primate whereby the twenty-four theses were condemned, and all men were threatened with the ban who should in future adhere to these tenets, or listen to them when set forth or preached by others.[3] *Act of humiliation.*

The first step was thus taken, and now it remained to carry it out to practical effect. But the second step was not so easy to take as the first. What had to be done was, to bring under the yoke of the judgment which had been pronounced on the new doctrines the persons who were attached to these doctrines —that is to say, to force them to a recantation—to crush those who should prove refractory, and to annihilate the existence of the party. But these were aims which could not be carried out by the Church alone. The help of the State was required. The new archbishop *Help of the State invoked.*

---

[1] Wilkins, *Concilia*, III., 157. *Fasc. Zizan.*, p. 275; comp. p. 282. Lewis, *Append.*, No. 31, p. 356.

[2] *Ib.*, III., 158: Knighton, *De Eventibus Angliae*, Book V. of his Chronicle in Twysden's *Historiae Anglicanae Scriptores*, X., fol. 2652, gives the text of the archiepiscopal mandate to the Bishop of London, as incorporated in the mandate of the Bishop of Lincoln, July 12, 1382, to the archdeacons of his diocese. Knighton had the copy before him which had been sent to the Archdeacon of Leicester, and it was to this archdeaconry that the parish of Lutterworth belonged. Wycliffe himself, as parish priest, must have received a copy of this mandate from the Archdeacon of Leicester through the rural dean of Guthlaxton. The text of the archbishop's mandate is given by Foxe (*Acts and Monuments*, III., 23) in English.

[3] Foxe, *Acts, etc.*, III., 37.

attempted to interest the latter in the business, and to make sure of its support for the end he had in view.

In the parliament which met in May, 1382, the archbishop moved to obtain its consent that orders should be issued from the Chancellor of the kingdom to the sheriffs and other royal officers to imprison such preachers, as also their patrons and followers, as a bishop should indicate to them by name for this purpose. He represented to the House of Lords that it was a well-known fact that different ill-disposed persons were going through the realm, from county to county and from town to town, in a well-known dress; and, under the aspect of great holiness, were preaching from day to day, without authority from the proper ordinary or credentials from any other quarter, not only in churches and churchyards, but also in market-places and other public thoroughfares, where much people were wont to resort. Their sermons were full of heresies and manifest errors, to the great injury of the faith and the Church, and to the great spiritual peril of the people and of the whole realm. These men preach also things of a calumnious kind, in order to sow strife and division between different classes, both spiritual and secular, and they excite the minds of the people, to the great danger of the whole kingdom. If these preachers are summoned by the bishops for examination, they pay no regard to their commands, do not trouble themselves in the least about their admonitions and the censures of the holy Church, but rather testify their undisguised contempt for them. They know, besides, how to draw the people by their fine words to listen to their sermons, and they hold them fast in the errors which they preach with a strong hand, and by means of imposing crowds. It is, therefore, he urged, indispensably necessary that the State should lend the assistance of its arm to bring to punishment these itinerant preachers as a common danger to the country.[1]

Appeal to Parliament against Wycliffites.

The Lords in Parliament gave their consent to the statute proposed; but the consent of the Commons was still lacking. Whether it was that the concurrence of the latter was not asked for, or that the Commons, when asked, decidedly refused it, cannot be ascertained from the extant Parliamentary records. If the proposed statute had become law, it would have become the duty of every king's officer in the counties, upon the application of a bishop to that effect, to send instantly to prison any man who was accused by the hierarchy as suspected of heresy, and to keep him there under strict durance until such time as he had

Lords and Commons.

[1] Foxe, *Acts, etc.*, III., 37.

cleared himself of the charge in the eyes of the Church. The meaning of which was nothing else but this, that the power of the State, so far as it was at the command of the county officials, should at all times and everywhere be at the disposal of the bishops—to make the State the obedient servant of the Church, and the officers of the king the policemen of the bishops.

In point of fact, the young King, Richard II., was induced to admit among the statutes of the kingdom an ordinance of May 26th, wherein, with the pretended consent of Parliament, it was ordered that upon certification from the bishops the king's commands should be issued by the Chancellor of the kingdom to the sheriffs and other State officers of counties for the imprisonment of itinerant preachers, as well as their favourers and adherents.[1] The ordinance sounded like a law which had been made by the joint consent of the Crown and the states of the realm. And yet it was nothing of the kind. It was a mere royal ordinance, given out for a statute of the realm. And this fact did not remain without notice, for in the next sitting of Parliament—October, 1382—the Commons presented a petition to the king, in which they roundly and clearly declared that that 'statute' had never received the consent or approval of the Commons, and moved for the annulling of the same. They were by no means disposed, either for themselves or their posterity, to consent to a greater dependence upon the prelates than their forefathers had known in past times. The consequence was that the offensive 'statute,' wrongfully so called, was withdrawn by the king.[2]

Royal ordinance.

But, apart from that pretended law of the land, the king, by desire of the archbishop, issued also a patent, dated June 26, 1382, wherein, 'out of zeal for the Catholic faith, whose defender he is, and purposes always to remain,' he conveys to the archbishop and his suffragans special plenary power to imprison the preachers and defenders of those condemned theses, and to detain them either in their own or in other prisons, at their pleasure, until they give proofs of repentance and make recantation, or until the king and his Privy Council should have taken some other action in the matter. At the same time the patent obliges all vassals, servants, and subjects of the king, upon their allegiance, and on pain of forfeiting all their estates, not to give any favour or support to those preachers or their patrons; but, on the contrary, to

Powers given to the prelates.

---

[1] Foxe, *Acts, etc.*, III., 37. 'It is ordained and asserted in this present Parliament,' etc.

[2] The French original of the petition in Cotton, *Abridgment of the Parliamentary Rolls*, vol. III., p. 141; translated in Foxe's *Acts and Mon.*, III., 38.

assist the archbishop and his suffragans and their officers in the exercise of these plenary powers.[1]

This patent differs in form from the statute, in so far as the former is only a royal ordinance, which was issued as an act of administration, whereas the statute claimed to be a legislative Act. It differed also in substance from the statute, inasmuch as it only empowered the bishops to put and keep accused persons in prison by the hands of their own officers and servants, so that the officials of the State had nothing directly to do in the matter; whereas the statute made it incumbent upon the State to carry out directly the judgments of the ecclesiastical courts. How it came to pass that the patent was issued after that statute, it is not easy to see, especially as the former, as an addition to the latter, might almost be dispensed with, or at all events must seem to be the weaker measure of the two. As the Lower House, some months later, publicly took objection to the constitutional validity of the statute, the conjecture is an obvious one, that immediately after the publication of the statute, public opinion had declared itself against it—that even some of the county authorities, to whom the imprisonment of itinerant preachers had been proposed agreeably to the provision of the statute, may possibly have declined to carry out the proposal, because they contested its force in law. If this was the case, a necessity would then arise for having recourse to some other expedient; and hence, perhaps, a renewed application of the archbishop to the king, and as the fruit of this the patent of June 26th. At all events, with these powers assailable, a persecution, adequate to what was desired, could now be set in operation.

5.—The Wycliffe Party intimidated by the measures of the Archbishop.

THE preliminary arrangements with the State had now been made as far as practicable. Action could now be taken either to bend or to break the leaders and adherents of the ecclesiastical opposition. The archbishop thought that no time should be lost.

He had already made use of the Church Council of May, 1382, and its condemnation of the articles submitted to its judgment, for the purpose of intimidating Wycliffe and his party. Occasion had been given him to do so by the state of parties in the University of Oxford.

Proceedings at Oxford.

---

[1] The patent is printed in full in Foxe's *Acts, etc.*, III., 39, and has here, as in the *Collection of Patents*, vol. I., 35, the date June 26th, of the 6th year of Richard II. In Wilkins' *Concilia* the same patent is given in Latin, but bears date July 12th. As the latter text is taken from the Episcopal Archives of Ely, the difference of the date may be explained by supposing that in the latter archive the day was noted when the patent arrived in Ely.

Since the beginning of 1381 party feeling there had been more than ordinarily violent. Wycliffe's attacks upon the Papacy, as well as his preaching itinerancy, which had now for some years been in operation, and of which Oxford was the head-quarters, had materially increased the hostility of the opposing parties in the University. The peasants' rebellion, too, had had an indirect influence, at least, upon the position of the two factions. The petition of the Mendicant Monasteries in Oxford to the Duke of Lancaster, mentioned in a former chapter, is an incontrovertible proof of this influence.[1] In particular, that document reveals the fact that Dr. Nicholas Hereford, a well-known friend and colleague of Wycliffe, was the most energetic spokesman of the party in the University which was opposed on principle to the Mendicant Orders. To these ecclesiastico-political antagonisms were added collisions in the domain of doctrine itself. When Wycliffe stood forward with his criticism of the doctrine of Transubstantiation, it was theologians of the Mendicant Orders who first controverted his teaching. In the Oxford Council of 1381, as we have seen, those doctors of theology who did not belong to the Orders of the Augustinians or Dominicans, the Carmelites or Franciscans, were an almost invisible minority. Naturally enough, with Wycliffe and his party the opinion gradually grew into an axiom that 'Begging Monk' and 'thorough-going defender of Papistical doctrine and modern errors' were one and the same thing. As men's minds were now pitted against each other, and the two parties engaged in attacks, not only in the schools and lecture-halls, in disputations and other academic acts, but also in pulpits and in the intercourse of daily life, the excitement became every day more intense. It even occurred that several members of the University were found with arms concealed under their clothes in the halls, and even in the churches.[2] All the more urgent appeared the necessity of interference, even in the interest of peace and order, to say nothing of the need of doing something to uphold the doctrine and life of the Roman Catholic Church.

On Ascension Day, May 15th, Nicholas Hereford had preached one of his bold sermons in the cemetery of St. Frideswide, in which he openly espoused the cause of Wycliffe, and, if we may believe the report of an opponent, gave utterance to many things of an offensive and even inflammatory character.

Hereford's sermon.

---

[1] *Fasc. Zizan.*, p. 292.
[2] *In quo die* (10 Juni, 1382) *visi sunt duodecim homines armati sub indumentis in scholis*. *Fasciculi Zizan.*, ed. Shirley, p. 302. *Post sermonem intravit* (Philippus Repyngdon) *ecclesiam S. Fredeswidae cum viginti hominibus subtus pannos armatis*, p. 300.

It was probably here that he expressed among other things the opinion that Archbishop Sudbury had been put to death, and justly so, because he was understood to have resolved upon taking proceedings against Wycliffe. He had also, some months earlier, taken every opportunity to declaim against the Begging Friars, in connection with the peasants' revolt of the previous year. He asserted that their begging was to blame for the impoverishment of the country, for by it the population was drained more than by taxes and other public burdens—and further, that the bad example which the Mendicants gave by their laziness was the occasion of the serfs and peasants leaving their accustomed labours and rising in revolt against their masters, etc. These representations seem to have found willing ears in Oxford, and a dangerous agitation against the Mendicant Orders began to spread. Hence the necessity under which the latter had found themselves to address the Duke of Lancaster, and to cast themselves upon the protection of that powerful prince.[1]

These inflammatory harangues of the resolute but too excitable Hereford gave particular offence to the Mendicants, and were the cause of his being singled out for attack before all the other friends of Wycliffe. To make suitable preparations for this, it was requisite for his opponents to obtain the necessary basis of facts. But this had its difficulties. For Nicholas Hereford, with all his boldness of attitude, seems to have acted with prudence and foresight. At least, he had not issued anything in writing—neither book nor pamphlet. His enemies were aware of this, and called it wretched cowardice, heretical secrecy, etc.[2] To reach him, no other course remained open at last but to take down from his mouth any doubtful expressions which dropped from him, and to have them legally attested.[3] This was done at the suggestion of Dr. Stokes, the archbishop's commissary.

It seemed to the enemy to be high time to take measures for silencing the Wycliffe party when it became known that Robert Rigge, the chancellor, had appointed Philip Repyngdon to preach before the University on Corpus Christi Day, June 5, 1382. Philip Repyngdon was a member of the stately Augustinian Priory of St. Maria de Pratis in Leicester, and a bachelor of theology in Oxford. Hitherto he had modestly kept himself out of public view, and was even regarded with favour by the

Repyngdon appointed to preach.

---

[1] *Fasc. Zizan.*, p. 292.
[2] *Sed ille Nicolaus velut miser fugiens, nunquam voluit librum vel quaternum communicare alteri doctori, sed modo haereticorum et multoties meretricio processit. Ib.*

[3] *Fasc. Zizan.*, p. 296: *Haereses et errores et alia nefanda redacta sunt in certam formam per notarios, ad instantiam cujusdam doctoris in theologia, fratris, Petri Stokys Carmelitae.*

Popish party. But he had recently preached a sermon in the hospital of Brackley, in Northamptonshire, in which he disclosed himself as an adherent of Wycliffe's doctrine of the Lord's Supper; and after his promotion to the title of Doctor of Divinity, in the beginning of the summer, he commenced his first lectureship in the University in that capacity by extolling the merits of Wycliffe. In particular, he undertook to defend Wycliffe's ethical doctrines at all points. After such proceedings it was natural that the adherents of the scholastic Church doctrine should look forward with some uneasiness to Repyngdon's preaching before the University on such an occasion as Corpus Christi. There was reason to fear that he would use the opportunity to strike a keynote in favour of Wycliffe, and openly to attack the doctrine of the change of substance in the Sacrament, for the very reason that it was the Feast of Corpus Christi. They therefore addressed themselves to the archbishop, with an earnest request that without delay, and before the festival arrived, he would order the condemnation of Wycliffe's Articles to be published in Oxford.[1]

This request was complied with without delay. On May 28th, as already mentioned above, a mandate of the archbishop issued to Dr. Stokes, with instructions to publish in the University the judgment which had been pronounced on the twenty-four Articles, and to prohibit the defence of them.[2] Two days afterwards the Primate addressed a letter to the chancellor, Robert Rigge, in which he censured him in the tone of an inquisitor, for having shown favour to Nicholas Hereford, who was under strong suspicion of heretical opinions, and for having appointed him to preach an exceptionally important sermon. He gives him, at the same time, emphatic advice to abstain in future from giving any countenance to such men, otherwise he must be himself regarded as belonging to the party. On the contrary, let him give his assistance to Dr. Stokes in the publication of the archbishop's mandate against the Articles, and let him cause the mandate to be read by the bedell of the Theological Faculty in the theological lecture rooms at the lectures next ensuing.[3]

Dr. Stokes's mission.

But the chancellor did not allow himself to be intimidated. He said that Dr. Stokes, in his intrigues with the archbishop, was trenching upon the liberties and privileges of the University; that no bishop nor archbishop had any jurisdiction over the University, not even in a case where heresy was in question. The autonomy of the learned corporation asserted itself,

The Chancellor's resistance.

---

[1] *Fasc. Zizan.*, p. 296.   [2] *Ib.*, pp. 275–282.   [3] *Ib.*, p. 298.

we see, against the threatening attempt of the hierarchy to encroach upon the freedom of teaching in the University. But the chancellor did not venture to give expression to these principles in public. On the contrary, after consultation with the proctors and some other members of the University, he publicly announced that he would give his assistance to Dr. Stokes. But in point of fact he put as many difficulties in the commissary's way as he could (at least so says an opponent), and found means to induce the mayor of the city to hold in readiness a hundred armed men—plainly with the view of putting a stop to any disturbances which might ensue; although there were some who imputed to him the design of making away with Dr. Stokes, or at least of compelling him to desist, in case he persisted in the attempt to execute his commission.[1]

Meanwhile the festival of Corpus Christi was approaching. On Wednesday, June 4th, the day before the feast, Dr. Stokes handed to the chancellor a copy of the mandate which the archbishop had sent to him, along with the letter which was directed to the chancellor himself. The chancellor took them both into his hands, but gave expression to some doubts upon the matter; he had as yet, he said, no letter and seal to show that it was his business to assist Dr. Stokes in the execution of the archbishop's commission. It was not until the Carmelite, on the very day of the festival, showed him, in full assembly, the archbishop's letter patent with his private seal attached, that the chancellor declared himself ready to assist in the publication of the mandate; yet under reservation of first advising with the University thereupon, and obtaining its consent thereto.[2]

Stokes's preliminary proceedings.

On Corpus Christi day, the members of the University, with the chancellor and proctors at their head, and accompanied by the Mayor of Oxford, proceeded to the cemetery of St. Frideswide for solemn divine service, which was celebrated in the open air. Dr. Repyngdon preached the festival sermon. He seems to have made no direct attack on the doctrine of the change of substance; and he had good reasons for taking this course on that occasion. But he spoke out his conviction unreservedly that Wycliffe was a thoroughly sound and orthodox teacher, and had at all times set forth the doctrine of the Universal Church touching the Sacrament of the Altar. Among other things, he said that in sermons princes and lords should have honourable mention before the Pope and bishops, otherwise preachers acted contrary to Scripture; he also

Repyngdon's sermon.

---

[1] *Fasc. Zizan.*, p. 298.   [2] *Litera fratris Petri Stokys*, etc., in *Fasc. Zizan.*, p. 300.

referred to Wycliffe's itinerant preachers, calling them 'holy priests.' Of the Duke of Lancaster the preacher declared that he was resolved to take all evangelically-minded men under his protection. There were people who characterised this sermon as seditious.

After sermon the assembly passed into the Church of St. Frideswide, and opponents spread the report that nearly twenty men, with concealed weapons, entered with the rest. Stokes, the Carmelite, suspected that it was his own life which was aimed at, and did not venture to leave the church again. The chancellor waited for the preacher in the porch, congratulated Repyngdon upon his sermon, and accompanied him from the church. The whole Wycliffe party was overjoyed at the discourse.[1] But Dr. Stokes was in such fear of his life that he had not the courage to publish the archbishop's mandate.[2] In the meanwhile the controversy publicly went on in lectures and disputations.[3] From those days date, in my judgment, those disputations in Oxford, extending over several days, of which we read, between the champions of the hierarchy on the one side, and Hereford and Repyngdon on the other. It was significant of the time that the latter were obliged to take up a defensive position, however ably and triumphantly they represented their cause. How much these learned discussions, aided as they were by being open to the public, enchained the attention of the general community, we see from a poem which was composed, at all events, in 1382—not earlier than July and not later than October—and which has come down to our times.[4]

Menacing measures.

Continued disputations.

The chancellor of the University himself was now summoned before the archbishop, to clear himself from the suspicion of heresy. On June 12th, the octave of the Feast of Corpus Christi, along with

---

[1] *Fasc. Zizan.*, p. 299; comp. 307.
[2] Letter from Dr. Stokes to the Archbishop, 6 Juni, *Fasc. Zizan.*, p. 300.
[3] *Ib.*, p. 302.
[4] The dates given above may be gathered from the facts that the appeal of Hereford and Repyngdon to the Pope is mentioned at the end of the poem; and this appeal was made at the beginning of July, from which it follows that the piece could not have been written earlier than that date. But, as Repyngdon recanted on October 23rd, the poem cannot have been written later than in October. The poem, which is distinguished by a remarkable refrain, is in its contents in part a complaint, and in part an honourable commemoration of the Reformation efforts of Wycliffe and his friends. The complaint describes the melancholy condition of England, menaced without, rotten within, and sinking deeper and deeper in its moral and religious life. For this state of things the writer blames all ranks, but especially the Begging Friars, and the Benedictines as well. To uplift the Church again, God has raised up Wycliffe and his disciples, who tell both the landed and the Mendicant orders the truth. But the latter have opposed themselves to the witnesses of the truth, and, coming forward one after another, have attacked them in disputations. But Hereford and Repyngdon defended themselves so victoriously that nothing remained for the friars at last but to take refuge in the archbishop, who thereupon took steps against Wycliffe's friends until they appealed to the Pope.

two others summoned at the same time — Dr. Thomas Brightwell and John Balton, Bachelor of Theology—Dr. Rigge appeared before an assembly of ecclesiastics, presided over by the archbishop, in the Dominican Monastery of London. Here the chancellor was examined touching several facts which seemed to bear out the suspicion that he was a favourer of Wycliffe's party, especially of the Doctors Hereford and Repyngdon, and participated in their opinions.[1] It was difficult for him to contest these facts. It was found that he and the proctors for the year —Walter Dash and John Huntman—had, in point of fact, favoured Wycliffe's doctrines. Hereupon the twenty-four Articles were laid before them, upon which the censure of the assembly of May 21st had been pronounced. Dr. Rigge at once assented to this judgment, while Dr. Brightwell and John Balton only expressed their concurrence in it after some hesitation and mental conflict.[2] It was further laid to the chancellor's charge that he had disregarded the respect and deference which were due to the archbishop, in having taken no notice of the Primate's letter directed to him in person; for which he begged upon his knees the archbishop's pardon, and received the same upon the intercession of the Bishop of Winchester, William of Wykeham;[3] and now it was required of him to publish in person that ecclesiastical censure of the twenty-four Articles which he had been unwilling, a few days before, so much as to assist Dr. Stokes in publishing. He even received a written injunction touching John Wycliffe himself, Nicholas Hereford, Philip Repyngdon, John Aston, and Lawrence Bedeman, no longer to suffer them to preach before the University, and to suspend them from every academic function, until they should have purged themselves from all suspicion of heresy.[4]

The Churchmen now thought themselves quite sure of the University. One unwelcome incident, however, occurred to cool somewhat their satisfaction. When Dr. Stokes was called to account on the same day for not having, up to that time, carried out the archbishop's instructions touching the mandate, he frankly acknowledged that he durst not publish the document, for fear of his life; upon which Courtenay replied, 'Then is the University a patron of heresies, if she will not allow orthodox truths to be published.'[5]

On Saturday, June 14th, Chancellor Rigge returned to Oxford.

[1] *Fasc. Zizan.*, pp. 304-308.
[2] Wilkins, *Concilia Magnae Britanniae*, vol. III., p. 159. *Fasc. Zizan.*, p. 288, fol. 308.
[3] *Fasc. Zizan.*, p. 308.
[4] *Ib.*, pp. 309-311.
[5] *Ib.*, p. 311.

and did not fail, in accordance with the obligation laid upon him, to make known to Hereford and Repyngdon that he had no choice but to suspend them from all University functions. But that he was, notwithstanding, still of the same mind, an incident which occurred soon after showed. A monkish zealot, Henry Crump, of the Cistercian Monastery of Bawynglas, in the county of Meath,[1] had been promoted doctor of theology in Oxford, and was delivering lectures in the University at that time. This man indulged in violent attacks upon the Wycliffe party, and applied to them the heretic name of Lollards, which had recently come into use, but until that time had never been publicly employed; upon which the chancellor energetically interfered. He summoned the doctor to appear before him, and when the latter failed to present himself, he declared him guilty, pronounced judgment upon him as a disturber of the peace, and suspended him from all University functions—a sentence which was solemnly published in the University Church.

Suspension of Hereford and Repyngdon.

But the Cistercian did not take all this quietly; he hastened immediately to London, and laid a complaint against the sentence not only before the archbishop, but also before the chancellor of the kingdom and the Privy Council.[2] The consequence was that the chancellor and proctors were summoned to appear before the Privy Council; and some weeks later Crump's suspension was annulled by royal ordinance, and his complete rehabilitation enjoined. But the archbishop did not omit to turn this opportunity to good account. He exerted himself to obtain from the Government an instruction to the heads of the University similar to that which he had addressed to them himself—viz., that they should not fail to take measures against the Wycliffe party. Meanwhile the archbishop, as Grand Inquisitor (*inquisitor haereticae pravitatis per totam suam provinciam*), had summoned to his tribunal the Doctors Hereford and Repyngdon, and also the bachelor of theology, John Aston. The same appeared (June 18th), in a chamber of the Dominican Monastery in London, before the archbishop and many doctors of theology and laws, in order to be examined on the often-mentioned 'Articles.' The two doctors craved time for reflection; Aston asked for none, but gave his declaration at once, to the effect that he would in future keep silence touching the Articles laid before him. Hereupon he was prohibited from preaching in future in the province of Canterbury. He did

Case of Henry Crump.

---

[1] *Fasc. Zizan.*, p. 349, in a document of the Bishop of Meath. [2] *Ib.*, p. 311; comp. 315.

not deny that he was aware that the archbishop, by a special mandate, had inhibited every man from preaching who had not been properly called to that function. But as he maintained that he had not incurred the ban by his itinerant preaching, which had been continued in the face of the mandate, he too was summoned to appear a second time on June 20th, Hereford and Repyngdon being also summoned to appear on the same day.[1]

On Friday, June 20th, the adjourned examination took place in the same monastery.[2] The assembly consisted of the archbishop, *Examination of the accused.* ten bishops, thirty doctors, and thirteen bachelors of divinity, sixteen doctors, and at least four bachelors of law. Hereford and Repyngdon handed in a written declaration touching the condemned Articles, in which they expressed their views on every one of them in succession. This declaration was so worded as to guard their Church orthodoxy, while at the same time, by a guarded interpretation of the Articles, they sought to establish Wycliffe's soundness in the faith.[3] No wonder that to the archbishop this written declaration seemed to be wanting in straightforwardness. There ensued, therefore, a further examination upon eight of the Articles. But here, too, no understanding was arrived at, because on all points, especially in reference to the doctrine of the Lord's Supper, the accused declined giving any more definite or distinct answer than they had given already in their written reply. Hereupon the assessors of the Inquisitorial Court unanimously declared that the answers of the two theologians were more evasive and reserved than sincere and satisfactory. The archbishop accordingly required them once more, in a solemn tone, to make an unreserved declaration; and when this proved ineffectual, dismissed them from the bar with the intimation that they were to appear once more after eight days, to receive judgment.[4]

John Aston was then called forward. He had shortly before drawn up a brief confession of his faith in English, and circulated it *John Aston.* in London in many copies as a fly-leaf. The object of this was to win over public opinion, and to convince his readers that he was a good, believing Christian.[5] But now the

---

[1] Wilkins, *Concilia*, III., 160; *Fasc. Zizan.*, p. 289. The date of the latter document has to be corrected by substituting xiv. cal. Julii for xiv. cal. Junii. Shirley's conjecture, note 2, on p. 289, is erroneous.
[2] *Fasc. Zizan.*, p. 319.
[3] The 'Explanation' in full form in Latin is to be seen in Wilkins, III., p. 161; *Fasc. Zizan.*, pp. 319-325. In Old English, Knighton's *Chronicle*, fol. 2655; John Foxe, *Acts and Monuments*, III., 32.
[4] Wilkins, III., 163; *Fasc. Zizan.*, pp. 326-329.
[5] *Confessio Magistri Johannis Astone*, in *Fasc. Zizan.*, p. 329. Knighton gives this Confession in Old English, though in part incorrectly, in his *Chronicle*, Book v., fol. 2656.

archbishop required him to give a frank declaration touching the condemned Articles. Aston, a practised itinerant preacher, then began to make answer in the English tongue, which was very displeasing to the archbishop because of the laity who were present. Courtenay required him to speak in Latin. Aston continued, notwithstanding, in the mother tongue, and delivered a bold, and (in the estimate of the spiritual judges) insulting speech, without going, however, into the scholastic questions laid before him on the subject of the Lord's Supper. In the end he was convicted of harbouring the condemned opinions, and declared a teacher of heresy.[1]

On June 27th, Hereford and Repyngdon appeared before the archbishop, at his country seat at Oxford. They were, however, dismissed again without anything being done, and cited once more to appear at Canterbury on July 1st, on the alleged ground that the archbishop at that time had none of his theological and legal assessors about him. *Hereford and Repyngdon excommunicated.* If the archbishop on this occasion had put them to useless trouble, they allowed him to wait to no purpose for them on July 1st. The archbishop appeared at nine o'clock in the chapter-house of his cathedral with nine doctors and bachelors of theology, and ordered the accused to be called. When they failed to appear, he adjourned the proceedings to two o'clock in the afternoon; and when they remained absent also at that hour, he passed sentence upon them of contempt of court, and laid them under the ban of excommunication.[2]

Both of them now appealed to the Pope; but the archbishop declared this appeal to be insolent, without justification, and invalid, and appointed public proclamation of the ban pronounced upon Hereford and Repyngdon to be made with all solemnity on July 13th, in sermons at St. Paul's Cross in London. A cross was erected, candles were lighted, extinguished, and thrown on the ground, etc.[3] The chancellor in Oxford received commands to cause the ban to be published with like ceremonies in St. Mary's Church, and in a simpler form in all the lecture-rooms of the University, along with a summons to both to appear before the archbishop's tribunal.[4] And even all this was not enough—the like publication of the ban and the summons was ordered to be made also in all the churches of towns and larger villages throughout the province of Canterbury.[5]

---

[1] Wilkins, *Conc. M. Brit.*, III., 163. *Fasc. Zizan.*, pp. 290-331.
[2] *Ib.*, III., 164. Foxe, *Acts and Mon.*, III., 40.
[3] *Ib.*, III., 165. The Mandate of the Archbishop to the Preacher at St. Paul's, July 12th.
[4] Mandate of same date to the chancellor in Wilkins' *Concilia*, III., 166.
[5] Mandate of July 30th to the Bishop of London, *Ib.*, III., 167.

Archbishop Courtenay was not content, however, with ecclesiastical measures. He used his influence with the king and Government to engage the power of the State in the affair, and to put down the heresy also with the temporal sword. On the same day on which the mandates of the archbishop were issued to the chancellor of Oxford and the preachers at St. Paul's Cross, a royal patent was drawn up, addressed to the chancellor and proctors of Oxford, by which the duty was imposed upon them of making an inquisition at large (*inquisito generalis*) among the graduates of theology and law in the University, in order to discover such as might adhere to the condemned Articles; and further, within eight days they were to drive forth and banish from the University and the city 'every member who receives, bears favour to, or has any intercourse with, Dr. John Wycliffe, Nicholas Hereford, Philip Repyngdon, John Aston, or any one else of the same party.' Nay, more: search must be made without delay in all the halls and colleges of the University for books and tracts of Wycliffe and Hereford; and all such writings must be confiscated and sent in without correction to the archbishop. All which must be faithfully carried out, under pain of the loss of all the University's liberties and rights. The Lord Lieutenant of Oxfordshire and the mayor of the city, with all other king's officers, were also enjoined to lend a helping hand in carrying out this royal order.[1]

General inquiry ordered.

A day later, on July 14th, was issued a second royal letter to the chancellor and proctors of the University of Oxford, whereby, as already stated, the academic suspension of the Cistercian Henry Crump was annulled, and his restoration to his former position was commanded. This brief at the same time prohibited the University from taking any action against Crump or the Carmelites, Peter Stokes and Stephen Patrington and others, on account of their attacks upon the condemned Articles, and the teaching of Wycliffe, Hereford, and Repyngdon.[2]

The Crown had thus done its utmost in the use of its administrative power to crush the opposition free-thought party, the adherents of Wycliffe. The archbishop on his side had promulgated the ecclesiastical decisions not only in the University of Oxford, but through all the dioceses of the land.

Repressive measures complete.

In the meantime the persecution of the itinerant preachers and of

---

[1] *Breve regium*, in Rymer, *Foedera*, VII., 363; Wilkins' *Concilia*, III., 166; *Fasc. Zizan.*, 312.

[2] *Ib.; Fasc. Zizan.*, 314; Lewis, p. 365; Foxe, III., 43.

all the principal friends and admirers of Wycliffe was proceeding. The Bishops of London and Lincoln in particular— Robert Braybrook and John Buckingham—distinguished themselves by their zeal in this work. In the extensive and populous diocese of Lincoln were Oxford, Lutterworth, and Leicester, the three chief centres of Wycliffite effort; and in the capital of the kingdom and the surrounding country there were also to be found many 'evangelical men.' But the chief instruments of persecution in both dioceses were the mendicant friars. Wycliffe himself mentions this fact, with bitter complaints against the diabolical malice of these monks, who were unceasingly at work in London and Lincoln to extirpate the true and poor preachers, principally for the reason that the latter had discovered and exposed their cunning practices to the people.[1] The Bishop of Lincoln received from the archbishop a letter of commendation and thanks for his indefatigable zeal against 'the Antichrist' and his adherents.[2] One of the itinerants who were summoned in the diocese of Lincoln, examined, and at last condemned to recant, was the priest, William Swinderby. This man appealed at first, when he was summoned by the bishop, to the king, and had the wish in particular to be examined by the Duke of Lancaster. But this helped him little. The case even came before Parliament, but the Parliament did not take up the subject, leaving it to the ordinary himself for decision. The ordinary obliged Swinderby to promise upon oath that he would never more in future preach and teach the Articles which were laid before him. He was, at the same time, required to make a public recantation, in a form which was drawn up for him, and this in the Cathedral of London, in the Collegiate Church of Leicester, and in four parish churches of the diocese of Lincoln.[3]

In the meantime, by command of the archbishop, search was made in Oxford and in the country for Hereford and Repyngdon, Bedeman and Aston.[4] During the summer months they remained in concealment, and were able to baffle the pursuit of their enemies; but in the course of October the three

---

[1] *Trialogus*, IV., c. 37, p. 379: *Tam Londoniis quam Lincolniae laborant assidue ad sacerdotes fideles et pauperes extinguendum, et specialiter propter hoc, quod eorum versutias caritative in populo detexerunt.*
[2] Wilkins, III., 168.
[3] *Processus domini Joh. Lincolniensis episcopi contra Willelmum Swynderby Wycclevistam*, in *Fasc. Zizan.*, pp. 334-346. This is a full transcript, dated July 11, 1382, and sent by the Bishop of Lincoln to those clergy of his diocese in whose churches Swinderby was condemned to make the recantation required of him.
[4] Information of the Chancellor Robert Rigge sent to the archbishop, dated July 25, 1382, in Wilkins, III., 168.

last-named were apprehended, one after the other, and ended by making their submission and agreeing to recant. The first to set this example was Laurence Stephen, or Bedeman;[1] next, Repyngdon, on October 23rd, presented himself before the archbishop and several bishops and doctors in the Dominican Monastery of London. He endeavoured to clear himself of the charges laid against him, and declared his assent to the synodal judgment of May 25th, whereby the twenty-four Wycliffe Articles were condemned; whereupon he was absolved by the Primate from the ban, and restored to his former position, and to his University rights.[2] His recantation was sealed at a provincial synod, held in Oxford in November, by a confession of his faith, which he signed with his own hand on the 24th of that month.[3] Last of all, John Aston, too, made up his mind to a recantation, which he solemnly professed before the same synod in Oxford, probably on November 24th, and was therefore also absolved and restored to his position and rights.[4]

The only one of Wycliffe's friends who now remained firm was Nicholas Hereford. If we are to accept, indeed, the account of Knighton in his Chronicle, Hereford must have recanted about the same time. But upon accurate examination this assumption is found to be erroneous; it is in fact confuted by a piece of information which we owe to the same narrator.[5] He informs us, namely, that Hereford went to Rome, and submitted the twenty-four Articles to Pope Urban VI. for his definitive decision. After mature examination by several cardinals and other theologians, the Pope simply confirmed the judgment which had been pronounced in England. But Urban, mindful of the thanks he owed to the English Church for its adherence to him, instead of sentencing Hereford to death at the stake, was pleased to commute the sentence to imprisonment for life. In the summer of 1385, however, he was unexpectedly released from prison and enabled to return to England, upon occasion of the Pope's being besieged in Nocera by King Charles of Sicily, when the Romans, discontented at the long absence of the Pope, raised a tumult in the city, and among other doings broke open the Papal prison and set free the prisoners.

Hereford still firm.

---

[1] Under date October 18, 1382, the archbishop issued a mandate restoring him to his rights in the University, which presupposes his recantation to have been previously made.

[2] See the relevant document of October 23, 1382, in Wilkins, III., 169.

[3] Wilkins, III., 172.

[4] *Ib.*, III., 172. Comp. in same vol., fol. 169, the archbishop's attestation of absolution and rehabilitation, dated Oxford, November 27, 1382.

[5] Knighton, fol. 2655. *A recantation of Hereford in English;* which, however, cannot belong to the year 1382, but must date from a later period, because it names the year of grace 1382 as the date of a former declaration of its author. Still, we have no ground for suspecting it to be spurious, as Vaughan does, *Life and Opinions,* II., 89.

In this whole narrative there is nothing of inherent improbability. It is, on the contrary, confirmed by the fact that from June 27, 1382, Hereford was not seen in England for several years, as well as by the curious fact, formerly mentioned, that his Translation of the Old Testament was abruptly broken off, and so remained unfinished. On January 15, 1383, the archbishop applied to the king for the assistance of Government against Hereford, because he was still setting the ban pronounced upon him at defiance.[1] In 1387, several years after Wycliffe's death, Hereford is again mentioned as the leading itinerant preacher of the Lollards.[2] It is scarcely credible, if he had remained all these years in the kingdom, that he could have escaped for so long a time the search of his persecutors.

His after career.

Thus had Archbishop Courtenay, at the date of October, 1382, *i.e.*, within five months of his entry upon the actual discharge of his high office, so far succeeded in his designs that the opposition party in the University of Oxford was fairly intimidated and reduced to silence. The most important members of the party were either driven out of the country, or had bowed themselves in submission and made formal recantation. A very considerable success, certainly, to be obtained in so comparatively short a time!

Triumph of Courtenay.

6.—The Cautious Proceedings of the Hierarchy against Wycliffe himself.

ONLY one man still stood firm and erect upon the field; and that was none other than Wycliffe himself; the bold, manful, and indefatigable leader of the party. How was it that the recognised head of the party should have remained unassailed? Judgment, it was true, had been pronounced against his 'Articles.' They had been branded by the Church authority partly as errors, partly as heresies; and it might be said the name was nothing compared with the thing—the principles were the chief matter, and these had been condemned without reserve and without mercy. True, also, measures against Wycliffe himself had not hitherto been wanting. The archbishop had, July 12, 1382, sent an order to the Chancellor of Oxford that no one in the University should be permitted to attend the preaching of Wycliffe or his adherents, or in any way to favour them;[3] and in a second order it was commanded that public intimation should be given

Wycliffe unassailed.

---

[1] The order is given by Foxe, *Acts, etc.*, III., 47.
[2] In a mandate to the Bishop of Worcester of August 13, 1387, Wilkins, III., 202.
[3] Wilkins, III., 160.

that the archbishop had suspended John Wycliffe, with Hereford, Repyngdon, Aston, and Bedeman, from all scholastic functions, until they should be exonerated by himself from all suspicion of erroneous doctrine. But this did not touch directly the person of Wycliffe, especially as at that time he no longer had his principal residence in Oxford, but in his parish of Lutterworth; and of course it was only his honour, not his personal condition, that was affected when, in addition, a royal order to the Chancellor and Proctors of Oxford (July 13, 1382) prohibited all manner of favour being shown to John Wycliffe and the other leaders, and appointed search to be made for the writings of Wycliffe and Hereford.[1]

The question therefore again presents itself, How is it to be explained that, at a time when persecution was so systematically carried out against the friends of Wycliffe, he should have remained personally unmolested? The enigma is attended with great difficulty, inasmuch as his enemies were clearly aware of his personal importance and influence as the leader of his party; they spoke of him as the Antichrist who was doing his utmost to undermine the faith.[2]

It has been sometimes thought that the difficulty may be removed by the observation that the measures adopted against the party applied principally to Oxford, while Wycliffe had already for some time left the University and confined himself to Lutterworth.[3] But this goes but a very little way to clear up the matter; for, on the one hand, Wycliffe appears even now to have still possessed the right of delivering lectures, conducting disputations, and preaching before the University; otherwise the suspension from all academical acts which the archbishop pronounced upon him would have had no meaning;[4] and, on the other hand, the measures referred to were meant to apply to the whole province of Canterbury, howsoever and wheresoever the alleged errors might come into view. It may well, however, be supposed (and this is perhaps the true solution of the difficulty) that it was part of the well-weighed plan of operations adopted by the archbishop, that after condemnation had been pronounced upon the doctrines and principles of the party, the personal persecution should only be directed at first against Wycliffe's adherents and friends, in order that after these had been intimidated and reduced to submission,

Reasons for forbearance.

---

[1] Wilkins, III., fol. 160.
[2] *Illum Antichristum, de quo scribitis pro posse fidei subversorem*, in a letter of Archbishop Courtenay to the Bishop of Lincoln, Wilkins, III., 168. It can scarcely be doubted that the above expressions, which the archbishop borrows, from the letter of his suffragan, refer to Wycliffe.
[3] Vaughan, *Monograph*, p. 286.
[4] *Fasc. Zizan.*, p. 389.

Wycliffe himself might be all the more easily overpowered when deserted by all, and left standing alone.

In the end, however, he was summoned to appear in person before the Provincial Synod which assembled in Oxford, November 18, 1382, and was again adjourned to the 24th of the same month. The fact is not placed beyond all doubt, but has still a balance of probability in its favour, that Wycliffe presented himself before this assembly in the Church of St. Frideswide, and, in the trial to which he was submitted, gave expression to and defended his convictions with freedom, and faithfulness, and unshrinking courage.[1] Another fact, however, con-

Wycliffe before the Oxford Synod.

---

[1] Lewis, p. 117, says, 'I do not find that Dr. Wiclif was at all before this convocation.' Herein he manifestly relies upon the circumstance that the protocol of the sessions (Wilkins, III., 172) does not say a single word about Wycliffe. But Vaughan justly remarks (*Monograph*, Appendix, p. 572), that the protocol throughout contains very meagre minutes of the proceedings. These proceedings relate to the sworn recantations of Repyngdon and Aston, as well as to the examination of the Carmelite Stokes and the Cistercian Henry Cromp. But if Wycliffe made his answers before the council with intrepidity, and the bishops, notwithstanding, could not see their way to decide upon a final condemnation of his person, it is not difficult to explain why such an issue as this, which there was not the slightest reason to be proud of, should rather have been passed over in silence in a half-official minute. While nothing is to be gathered from this document, either for or against the fact in question, we have two other authorities who expressly attest that Wycliffe, when summoned, appeared before the council and made answer for himself. These are the chronicler Knighton and Anthony Wood. It is true, indeed, that when we carefully compare the two, the information of the latter appears to rest exclusively upon that of the former, which is, indeed, of much older date, for the account given by the Churchmen who were present in the council coincides with Knighton's narrative, as also Wood's narrative does, save only that Wood, as a historian of the University, names the chancellor and doctors, as may be easily understood, immediately after the bishops, while the Canon of Leicester puts them in the second place. And there is another circumstance which speaks for Wood's dependence upon the chronicler, that the former as well as the latter, and with quite as little justification too, looks upon the confession of Wycliffe as a recantation. The circumstance, on the other hand, that Wood makes mention of six men who wrote against that confession, of whom Knighton says nothing, is by no means a proof, as Vaughan thinks (p. 573), that Wood had other authorities besides Knighton, in favour of the chief point of Wycliffe having presented himself before the council, for it proves no more than this, that Wood found that particular literary notice in some other source than the Leicester *Chronicle*. All this being so, we have, in fact, only one original authority for the appearance of Wycliffe before the council. But still this authority declares clearly, and with precision, that Wycliffe was summoned by the archbishop to Oxford, that he appeared before him and six bishops, as well as before the chancellor and numerous doctors, and before clergy and people, to answer to the charge of heresy which was brought against him (*De Eventibus Angliae*, fol. 2649). He asserts, it is true, that Wycliffe made a complete recantation (*eis conclusionibus sive opinionibus omnino renuncians, nec eas tenuisse neque tenere se velle protestans*). But this judgment is contradicted by the English Confession on the Lord's Supper, which Knighton has inserted in his *Chronicle*, word for word, in this very place. The document does not contain a single trace of retractation, or of even the correction of what he had before said on the subject, but only a clear exhibition and emphatic assertion of the doctrine of the Lord's Supper which he declares to be the pure doctrine of Scripture, and at the same time the primitive doctrine of the Church, whereas the doctrine of the Sacrament, as a mere accident without substance, he calls a 'modern error.' The *Chronicle* of Leicester has found, notwithstanding, men of easy faith and full of prejudice who have maintained, on this mistaken authority.

nected with the trial is of undoubted historical certainty, viz., that no sentence was pronounced upon him as its issue, either condemning him to make a recantation of his doctrine, or inflicting upon him any other ecclesiastical censure. The silence of his adversaries as to any such issue is itself, in such a case as this, a convincing proof of the fact; for assuredly they would not have failed to trumpet forth the event in high triumph, if they had obtained so unexpected a success, and had forced the renowned and admired head of the opposition to undergo the humiliation of a public recantation. Add to this another fact, that when it was afterwards pretended that he had made such a recantation, they found themselves obliged to put forward as a proof of this a piece of writing —viz., his English Confession—which, properly understood, sets forth Wycliffe's doctrine of the Eucharist in language so clear and unmistakable, and in a tone of such fearless decision, that it is marvellous that it should ever have been appealed to for such a purpose; which, however, would never have been done if any document had ever come from Wycliffe's hand of such a kind as to show that he had submitted to the Caudine yoke of the hierarchical inquisition.

What was it that influenced the hierarchy to abstain from demanding from him such a recantation, to connive at his offence, and to allow the bold, free-spoken man to go back to his Lutterworth flock untouched, and in full possession of all his ecclesiastical promotions? Are we to suppose that they were overawed by dread of the Duke of Lancaster, who had always been his powerful patron? Archbishop Courtenay, it is true, could scarcely have forgotten the scene in his own Cathedral of St. Paul which had touched his honour so deeply; when the duke took upon him the defence of the Oxford doctor in so high-handed a style, and with insulting threats directed against his own episcopal person.[1]

Caution of Wycliffe's enemies.

even in the present century, that Wycliffe at that provincial council sought and obtained rest from further persecution by a cowardly disguising of his real convictions, *i.e.*, Lingard, *History of England*, IV., 260. Hefele, on the other hand, in his *Conciliengeschichte*, VI., 828, has, with justice, acknowledged that Wycliffe, in the confession in question, remained true to his convictions, and even warmly attacked the Roman Catholic doctrine of the Supper. There is only one excuse for this misinterpretation of the piece; if the bishops had reasons for letting Wycliffe's declaration pass as though they were satisfied with it, and saw in it a sort of recantation, it is all the more easy to understand that the chronicler, in case he did not go to the bottom of the matter, might unwarily consider the document in question as a recantation. Nor may it remain unnoticed that Knighton, in addition to this, fell into another error of a chronological kind. He is plainly under the erroneous impression that it was this council at Oxford which first pronounced that judgment upon the Articles of Wycliffe, which, in fact, had already been pronounced upon them in May, 1382. Comp. also the observations of Arnold in *Select English Works*, III., 501.

[1] Comp. chap. v, above. Vaughan, *Monograph*, p. 287, is disposed to think that this was the consideration which chiefly weighed with the archbishop.

But in the interval the duke had been so sensibly affected by the events of the preceding year, when his life was threatened at the hands of the revolted peasantry, that his haughty bearing and power had been much broken down. He had, besides, for some time back —no doubt under the influence of the same circumstances—kept himself free from participation in Church affairs, and had warned Wycliffe to be on his guard—a fact which could not have remained unknown to the archbishop. It can hardly, then, be supposed that it was from any reference to the duke that Courtenay should have resolved to proceed cautiously with Wycliffe. It must rather have been the thought of Parliament and of the state of public opinion that induced him to adopt this prudential course.

It was on Tuesday, November 18, that the Convocation had met in Oxford, and on the following day the Parliament assembled in Westminster. To this Parliament Wycliffe addressed himself in a Memorial which, it might be presumed, would not fail to attract some measure of public attention. *Memorial to Parliament.* At least Wycliffe himself expressed the hope that it would lead to a discussion. In its whole substance the 'Complaint' was drawn up in such a way as to keep steadily before men's minds the legislative point of view. Four points were examined in it: 1, Monastic vows; 2, The exemption of the clergy and Church property; 3, What view was to be taken of tithes and offerings; 4, That the pure doctrine of Christ and His apostles touching the Lord's Supper should be allowed to be publicly taught in the churches.[1] The last point is handled in the briefest manner; and it was good tact in Wycliffe not to go any deeper into doctrine, for King and Parliament were not the proper authorities to decide upon dogmatic questions. But all the more fully does the author examine the first point, devoting almost one-half of the Memorial to the proof of the proposition that monastic vows are nothing but inventions of sinful men, and are destitute of all obligatory force. A twofold fundamental thought runs through the whole document; first, the conception of the pure religion of Christ, without any additions of men; and next, the conception of Christian liberty. When the author urges the right of publicly setting forth the Scripture doctrine of the Sacrament, and when, in opposition to the fetters of monastic vows, he claims

---

[1] This memorial to Richard II. and Parliament, beginning with the words—'Plese it to oure noble and most worthi King Richard,' of which two manuscripts are still extant, the one perfect, in Corpus Christi College, Cambridge, and the other imperfect, in Trinity College, Dublin (comp. Shirley's *Catalogue*, p. 45), was published by Dr. Thomas James in 1608, along with a tract of considerable length against the Mendicant Orders. It is published in Arnold's *Select English Writings*, III., 507–523, upon the basis of the Cambridge MS.

for himself and others the liberty of following the pure and simple rule of the Redeemer; when he contests the right of compulsory tithing, approving of tithes and offerings only as voluntary gifts, it is always a love of Christian liberty by which he is inspired. There can be no doubt that this Memorial, as a summary statement and defence of Wycliffe's ideas, was well fitted to find acceptance among the representatives of the country.

To this must be added the well-warranted mistrust, and the only too intelligible irritation of the House of Commons, occasioned by the unconstitutional and arbitrary measure of the preceding session, when a bill for the imprisonment of the Wycliffe Itinerants by the officials of counties, which had been passed only by the Lords, and had never even been brought before the Lower House, had been admitted into the collection of the Statutes of the realm. What must it lead to, men demanded, if the Crown and the Peers of the realm, over the heads of the Commons, lent their aid to the bishops in encroaching upon the liberty of the people, and forcing them, in a style never before heard of, under the yoke of the prelates? If such an irresponsible proceeding were to pass unnoticed, what would become at last of the legislative power of the Commons? The Commons, therefore, addressed a strong representation to the Government against the pretended 'statute' which had never obtained their consent, and pressed for its annulment—a demand which was, in point of fact, conceded.[1] It may readily be supposed that this question must have been warmly discussed among members of Parliament and in patriotic circles before the opening of the Parliamentary session; and as it was the prelates who were chiefly aimed at in this popular agitation, it is easy to understand how the archbishop, calling to mind the fate which had been prepared for his predecessor Sudbury, may have found it advisable to proceed cautiously with a man so highly regarded in the country, and of such immense influence, as Wycliffe; and especially on the very eve of the opening of Parliament, rather to wink at his offences, than to add intensity to the ill-feeling which already existed by adopting a course in which all considerations of policy and prudence were set aside.

Spirit of the Commons.

7.—The Last Two Years of Wycliffe, and his Death.

WYCLIFFE was left at liberty to return in peace to his quiet cure in Lutterworth; and during the two full years which intervened between that date and his death he experienced no further personal disturb-

[1] Comp. chap. v. above.

ance at the hands of the English hierarchy. The brief term of life still allotted to him he filled up with tranquil but many-sided and indefatigable labour. Before everything else he devoted himself with conscientious faithfulness to his pastoral work. A large number of the English sermons preached by him which have come down to us belong, without doubt, to these last years of his life.[1] He found himself, however, necessitated by age and declining health and strength to engage an assistant pastor—a chaplain; and in this capacity John Horn was associated with him for two years. In addition, John Purvey was Wycliffe's constant attendant and confidential messmate—a helper of kindred spirit to his own, and a fellow-labourer in all his widely extended work.[2] To him, without doubt, we are indebted for the transcription, collection, and preservation of so many of Wycliffe's sermons. In the great work of the English translation of the Bible, next to Nicholas Hereford, John Purvey was the most active and meritorious of Wycliffe's co-workers. When this work was completed in its first form, and Wycliffe became sensible of the need of submitting it to further revision and improvement, it was undoubtedly Purvey upon whom the largest share of this labour fell; and he continued the work after Wycliffe's death, till it was at last happily completed in the year 1388.[3]

Wycliffe at Lutterworth.

Horn and Purvey.

It may also be assumed, with some degree of probability, that during these years the preaching itinerancy, although menaced by the measures of the bishops, was still carried on, though in diminished proportions, and with some degree of caution; and, so long as Wycliffe lived, Lutterworth continued to be the centre of this evangelical mission. But the narrower the limits became within which this itinerancy could be worked, the more zealously did Wycliffe apply himself to the task of instructing the people by means of short and simple tracts in the English tongue, as a compensatory mode of reaching them. The largest number of these tracts—at least half a hundred—which have have come down to us belong to these latest years of Wycliffe's life.[4] Setting aside translations of portions of the text of Scripture, these tracts may be divided into two chief groups. The one consists of shorter or longer explanations of single heads of the Catechism; the other of discussions of the doctrines of the Church. The latter,

Itinerancy.

Wycliffe's tracts.

---

[1] Comp. chap. v. above.
[2] That Purvey (Purney) was Wycliffe's assistant is pretty evident from Knighton's *Chronicle*, col. 2660: *Magistri sui dum adhuc viveret commensalis extiterat . . . atque usque ad mortis metas comes individuus ipsum cum doctrinis et opinionibus suis concomitabatur indefesse laborans.*
[3] Comp. chap. VII.
[4] Comp. Shirley's *Catalogue*, pp. 40-49, and *vide* Appendix II.

for the most part, have a polemical character, while the former are in a more positive form, didactic and edifying. To indicate more closely their contents in a few cases, several tracts of the first group treat of the Ten Commandments, of works of mercy, of the seven mortal sins; several discuss the duties belonging to the different stations and relations of life, while others treat of prayer, and explain the *Pater Noster* and the *Ave Maria*. There are also tracts on the Lord's Supper and on Confession and Absolution. To the second group—all treating of the Church, with its offices and members, institutions and functions—belong all those tracts which we have before mentioned, as defences of the itinerant preachers, and attacks upon their opponents. Others treat of the pastoral office itself, chiefly of the function of preaching, but also of the execution of the pastoral work at large, and of the life and conversation of the priests;[1] and one tract of this set is specially designed to show that it is the duty of earthly rulers and lords to hold the clergy to their duty in all these respects.[2]

Ever interesting himself vividly in all that stirred his countrymen and fatherland, Wycliffe could not remain unmoved when a crusade

Projected crusade. set forth from England which had no other object in view but to fight for the cause of Urban VI. against the supporters of the rival Pope in Avignon, Clement VII., and, if possible, to overthrow the latter.[3] At the head of this crusade was placed, not a nobleman skilled in war, but a prelate of the Church. During the peasants' revolt in 1381, Henry le Spencer, Bishop of Norwich, was the first man who had the courage to oppose himself to the movement, not only when it began, but as long as the flood continued to rise, and when no one else had the spirit to resist it. He

Bishop Spencer. happened to be at his manor-house of Burlee when he heard that the people had risen in Norfolk. In a moment he set off to convince himself whether the fact was really so. Putting on his armour, at the head of a small following of eight lances and a few bowmen, he attacked a crowd of rebels, among

---

[1] *E.g.*, *De Apostasia Cleri* (Shirley's *Catalogue*, p. 46), published by Todd, 1851. *Select English Works*, III., 430.
[2] No. 35, Shirley's *Catalogue*, p. 44. *Select English Works*, III., 213.
[3] Theodore Lindner, in *Theologische Studien und Kritiken*, 1873, 151, has given it as his opinion that the anonymous author of a series of writings designed to put an end to this Papal Schism, which were republished by Ulrich von Hutten, in 1520, must have been one of Wycliffe's followers, and conjectures that the whole series was written in 1381. But no trace is to be discovered in these writings of the specifically Wycliffitic spirit, and its party peculiarities. We have even reason to doubt whether England at all was the birthplace of this series of pieces, so full of puzzles. To say the least, most of the particulars which occur in them, and which are mentioned in a tone of personal feeling, are of such a character that they must be referred to French personalities and events.

whom were two of the ringleaders, whom he ordered to be beheaded upon the spot, and sent their heads to be set up in Newmarket. As he marched through the county, his forces increased at every step, for his resolution inspired new courage in the terrified knights and nobles. At North Walsham he came upon a fortified and barricaded camp of the rebels. This he immediately carried by storm under a blast of trumpets, himself leading the attack on horseback; and, lance in hand, he dispersed the whole body, cut off their retreat, and after a great number had been slain took their leaders prisoners. Those who fled to the churches for safety, trusting to the right of asylum, were slain even at the altar with swords and lances. Among the leaders was John Lister, a dyer of Norwich, who had allowed himself to be styled King of Norfolk. The bishop in person sat in judgment on the ringleaders at Norwich, and condemned them to the gallows. A chronicler applauds him for this—'that his eye spared no one, and that his hand was stretched out with joy for vengeance.'[1] From that day the Bishop of Norwich had a high reputation as a man of heroic fearlessness and energetic action; he was even accredited with the talent of military command. No wonder that he was trusted to take the lead of a martial expedition which was to be a crusade.

Perhaps it is not too bold a conjecture that Henry le Spencer had himself taken the initiative of the movement, and at his own instance had obtained a commission from Urban VI. to lead a crusade against the 'Clementines,' the adherents of the rival Pope. The Pope sent forth more than one bull, in which he empowered the Bishop of Norwich to collect and take the command of an army which should wage a holy war against Clement VII. and his abettors on the Continent, especially in France. Extensive powers were conferred upon the bishop for this end against Clement VII. and all his supporters, both clergy and laity. He was free to adopt all manner of measures against them—to banish, suspend, depose, and imprison, and also to seize their estates. Whosoever should personally take part in the crusade for a year, and whosoever should provide a crusader at his own cost, or whosoever should assist the undertaking with his purse and property, should receive a plenary absolution and the same rights and privileges as a crusader to the Holy Land.[2]

The Pope and the crusade.

These bulls the bishop communicated to the members of Parliament in the session which met in November, 1382, and published

---

[1] Knighton, col. 2638. Walsingham, *Historia Anglicana*, II., 6.

[2] Walsingham, II., 71, particularly p. 76.

them by the dispersion of copies in all parts of the kingdom, which he caused to be posted up on the church doors and the monastery gates, that they might be patent to the knowledge of all.[1] The bishop also, in virtue of 'apostolic authority,' drew up and issued Letters of Indulgence.[2] And now an agitation was set on foot throughout the realm with a view of gaining the largest possible number to take a personal share in the crusade, and of inducing others to aid it, at least, with money and money's worth. For some time the fruit of these efforts does not appear to have everywhere come up to the bishop's wishes and needs. In a circular to the parish priests and chaplains of the diocese of York, he complains of the meagre result, and presses upon them the duty of calling the attention of their parishioners to an opportunity so favourable for their souls' salvation, and of moving those who were remiss, whether rich or poor, by judicious handling in the confessional, to do what was in their power for the enterprise; all opposers of the undertaking it would be their duty to call before them, and to give intimation thereof to the bishop or his commissaries, as well as to send in accurate returns of all the contributions obtained.[3] Circulars to the same effect were no doubt sent at the same time to the clergy of other dioceses. In addition, by a special commission from the Bishop of Norwich, the Mendicants of different Orders put forth the most strenuous exertions in the pulpit and the confessional to awaken enthusiasm for the approaching crusade, and to call forth rich offerings in its behalf. They had in their hands one mighty key to the hearts of men—the promised absolution from all guilt and penalty; an absolution, however, which was only to be obtained at the price of contributions to the holy war.

The undertaking was meant to be made the common affair of the whole English Church and nation. Archbishop Courtenay worked for it—at the instance, no doubt, of the Pope himself—by various mandates, which he issued simultaneously, April 10, 1383, to the bishops of his province, and to the whole parish clergy of the kingdom, to the effect that in all churches prayers should be offered at mass and in sermons for the crusaders and the success of their enterprise; that every Wednesday and Friday solemn processions should be made on behalf of the crusade; and all the parishioners should be exhorted to join in the prayers.[4]

---

[1] Walsingham, II., 72.
[2] *Ib.*, 79. Gives one such indulgence, word for word.
[3] *Ib.*, 78. The circular is dated Feb. 9, 1382; but this should have been 1383, for at the beginning of 1382 the business could not have been so far advanced; besides, the 13th year of his episcopal consecration agrees only with 1383.
[4] Wilkins, *Concilia*, III., 176.

A second mandate enjoined collections for the same object;[1] and the third contains the credentials and recommendation of three agents and receivers of the Bishop of Norwich, appointed for the collection.[2] No wonder that, when such extensive measures were adopted to secure success, an extremely large sum was in the end collected for the war-chest of the crusade. The sums obtained, not only in gold and silver, but also in money's worth, in jewels, ornaments, and rings, in silver spoons and dishes, contributed alike by men and women, and especially by ladies of rank and wealth, were incredibly great. One lady of rank is said to have contributed one hundred pounds of silver, and many persons gave far beyond their means, insomuch that even a clerical chronicler is of opinion that the national wealth, in so far as it lay in private hands, was endamaged.[3]

But the treasures of grace which were offered in return for contributions were also worth something: for the pardons which were offered by Papal authority were of virtue both for the living and the dead. It passed from mouth to mouth that one of the bishop's commissaries had said that at their command angels descended from heaven to release souls in purgatory from their pain, and to translate them instantly to heaven.[4] In another key, but with the same object of making the crusade popular, the archbishop, in his mandate of April 10, 1383, seeks to stir up national feeling and English patriotism in support of the undertaking, by reminding the country that it is directed against France, the hereditary enemy of England; for France was the chief patron of the rival Pope; and by reminding it further, that the well-being of the State is inseparably connected with the interest of the Church; while, in order to do away with the offence which every unprejudiced mind could not but take against the conduct of the war being put into the hands of a prelate, the archbishop gives the assurance that the only object of the war is to secure peace.[5]

Appeals to the people.

Upon such proceedings as these, Wycliffe could neither look with favour, nor preserve silence respecting them. More than once he not only threw gleams of side light upon the crusade, but also discussed it thoroughly. In the summer of 1383 he published a small tract in Latin, bearing the title, '*Cruciata;*

Wycliffe's 'Cruciata.'

---

[1] Wilkins, *Concilia*, III., 177.
[2] *Ib.*, 177.
[3] Knighton, *De Eventibus Angliae*, Lib. v., col. 2671: *Et sic secretus thesaurus regni, qui in manibus erat mulierum, periclitatus est.* Comp. Walsingham, II., 85.
[4] *Ib.*, 2671. The blasphemous extravagance of the language reminds one of Tetzel.

[5] Wilkins, *Concilia*, III., 177: *Praecipue contra Francigenas, ipsorum schismaticorum principales fautores, et domini nostri regis et regni Angliae capitales inimicos pro pace ecclesiae acquirenda et defensione regni . . . quod neque pax ecclesiae sine regno neque regno salus poterit nisi per ecclesiam provenire,* etc.

or, Against the War of the Clergy.'[1] In this pamphlet he illustrates the subject on different sides, and condemns the crusade and everything connected with it in the severest manner; first, because it is a war, then because a war of which the Pope is the instigator is, under all circumstances, contrary to the mind of Christ; and, further, because the whole quarrel between the contending Popes has to do at bottom only with worldly power and mastery, which is a thing entirely unbefitting the Pope, and wholly contrary to the example of Christ. That every one who does anything to aid this crusade shall obtain remission from all guilt and punishment is a lie and 'an abomination of desolation in the holy place.' The Mendicant monks who promote this affair in their sermons, and take upon themselves the labour of collecting for it, are nothing else but enemies to the Church; they and all the cardinals and Englishmen in the Papal Court who plunder the country in this manner must, before everything else, make restitution of this unrighteous lucre, if they would ever obtain forgiveness of their sins.

I know no writing of Wycliffe in which, with a greater absence of all reserve, and in more incisive language, he laid bare, and did battle against the anti-christian spirit which lay in the great Papal schism in general, and particularly in the stirring up of an actual war for the purpose of annihilating one of the rival Popes by force of arms and the shedding of blood.[2] He characterises the crusade as a persecution of true Christians, and as an inversion of the faith. It is a proof of the ascendency of the devil's party, that kings and other powers tolerate the Pope's command to banish and imprison every man who opposes his party or does not actively support it. There are now few men or none at all who have the courage to expose themselves to such martyrdom; and yet never since the time of Christ has there been a better cause for

---

[1] *Cruciata, seu Contra Bellum Clericorum:* Such is the title of a tract in ten chapters [printed by the Wyclif Society, 1883; vol. II., p. 577], of which MSS. are only now extant in Vienna, where no fewer than six copies are to be found. Shirley's *Catalogue*, No. 75. In MS. 3929, which I have used, the name of the author is given at the end. *Explicit Cruciata venerabilis et evangelici Doctoris Magistri Joannis Wyklef.* [References in the following notes are to the printed edition.]

[2] *Cruciata*, c. II., p. 594: 'As Satan,' says Wycliffe, 'poisoned the human race by one sin, the sin of pride, so he has a second time poisoned the clergy by endowing them with landed property, contrary to the law of Christ, and by the publication of a lie concerning the forgiveness of sins and indulgences, he has thrown the whole Western Church into a state of disorder, as now, with two rival Popes, our whole Western Christendom must take side with either the one or the other, and yet both of them are manifestly Antichrists' (*et uterque ipsorum sit patule Antichristus*). But the strongest thing in the piece is the view which pervades it throughout, that at bottom there are only two parties existing at present in the Church—the party of the Lord Christ, and the devil's party (*pars Domini . . . pars ista diaboli*), c. III., p. 600.

which men could have suffered a martyr's death; and never was there a more glorious victory to be won by the man who has the courage to stand up on the Lord's side. It is not enough that so many thousands of men should lose their lives, and that England should be sucked dry by the fraudulent spoliations of hypocrites; the worst of all is that many of those who fall in the crusade die in unbelief while taking part in this anti-christian persecution, while the Antichrist pretends that they are absolved from all sin and penalty and enter at once into heaven.[1]

How is this miserable mischief to be remedied, which threatens in the end to bring the whole Church into confusion? To this question Wycliffe replies: 'The whole schism is a consequence of the moral apostacy from Christ and His life of poverty and purity.' If it is to be mended, the Church must be led back to the poor and humble life of Christ and to His pure Word. In conformity with this view, his thought in the first instance is of princes and rulers. He thinks that emperors and kings have done foolishly in providing the Church with lands and lordships; this they must set right again to the utmost of their power, and so restore peace. Wycliffe compares, in his rough manner, the schism of the two Popes to the quarrelling and worrying of two dogs over a bone, and thinks that princes should take away the bone itself—that is, the worldly power of the Papacy—for surely they do not bear the sword in vain.[2] But *all* Christ's knights should in this cause stand true at the side of Christ's faithful poor; all good soldiers of Christ should stand shoulder to shoulder; this would enable them to win a great victory and renown. Yes! the whole of Christendom should take upon itself toil and trouble in order to put down wickedness, and restore the Church to the condition of apostolic purity, and to put an end to the means by which Antichrist misleads the Church.'[3]

This memorial, written in the summer of 1383, enables us to perceive, in the clearest manner, that Wycliffe was not in the least intimidated by the inquisitorial proceedings which Archbishop Courtenay had taken against him and his friends in the preceding year. He still speaks out in the most fearless and emphatic way

---

[1] *Cruciata*, c. III., p. 600: *Pauci vel nulli sunt, qui audent se exponere martyrio in hac causa; et tamen scimus, quod a tempore Christi non fuit melior causa martyrii, nec gloriosior triumphus illi, qui in causa domini audet stare. Non enim quietatur ista persecutio in multis millibus corporum occisorum, nec solum in fraudulentis spoliationibus hypocritarum, ut specialiter patet in Anglia, sed, quod est gravius, in subversione fidei et perfida exaltatione partis diaboli, sic quod multi occisorum quos Antichristus dicit sine poena ad coelum ascendere, moriuntur infideliter in hac persecutione perfida jam regnante.*

[2] *Ib.*, c. II., p. 591: *Videtur quod eorum interest prudenter auffere hoc dissensionis seminarium, sicut canibus pro osse rixantibus ... os ipsum celeriter semovere.*

[3] *Ib.*, c. II., p. 596.

against both the Popes, and against the crusade commanded by Urban VI., favoured by the archbishop, and undertaken by an English bishop. In a writing directly addressed to the Primate himself, which must have been penned at the same date, Wycliffe plainly told him that he could not learn from Scripture that that crusade in defence of the Pope's cause was a lawful measure, for only those works of man which are done from love have the Lord's approval; and neither the slaying of men nor the impoverishment of whole countries can be the outcome of love to the Lord Jesus Christ. And thus it is plain that there exists no valid and defensible ground for the endurance of martyrdom, for the impoverishment of the people, and for an undertaking causing so much anxiety and mischief.[1]

Letter to the Archbishop.

Of the crusade itself let it only be briefly remarked here, that the Bishop of Norwich embarked in May, 1383,[2] and, advancing from Calais, took several towns in Flanders. But after this rapid and successful beginning he lost time by laying siege to the city of Ypres; and after that he met with nothing but misfortune. His conquests were no sooner won than they were lost again, until at last he was fain to surrender Gravelines, which he had taken, in order to secure his unopposed return to England at the beginning of October. The crusade came to an ignominious end. Nor was that all. At the bar of Parliament, which met at the end of October, the bishop and the chief officers of his staff had to answer to various charges which were laid against them, and the king withheld from him his temporalities, which were not restored again till 1385.[3]

Collapse of the crusade.

It was a melancholy satisfaction to Wycliffe that the crusade against which he had warned the nation came to such a wretched conclusion. In its utter failure he saw a judgment of God; only one thing was not yet clear to him, whether the whole of God's judgment was exhausted, or whether further punishment was yet to follow.[4]

---

[1] *Litera missa Archiepiscopo Cantuariensi*, Vienna MS., No. 1387, fol. 105, col. 1: *Dixit tertio idem sacerdos et tenuit, quod nescit ex scriptura, quod ista crucis erectio pro defensione causae papae sit licita, vel quod approbative processit a domino Jesu Christo. Istud autem ex hoc evidet, quod solum opera hominis ex caritate facta a domino approbantur. Sed probabile est, quod nec ista plebis occisio nec terrarum depauperatio processit ex caritate domini Jesu Christi, specialiter cum non sit fides nostra, quod iste papa est caput vel membrum sanctae matris ecclesiae militantis. Et sic videtur, quod ista non sit stabilis causa martyrii, depauperationis* (MS.: *depauperatio*) *populi et laboris tam anxii et damnosi.*

[2] Walsingham, *Hist. Anglicana*, ed. Riley, II., 88.

[3] *Ib.*, II., 104, 109, 141. Comp. Pauli, *Geschichte von England*, IV., 544.

[4] In the piece, *De Quatuor Sectis Novellis*, Vienna MS., 3929 [printed by the Wyclif Society, vol. III., p. 233], Wycliffe comes to speak of this Crusade, and says: *Nec scimus, si iste ultimus transitus nostratum in Flandriam, quem fratres multi istarum sectarum quatuor regularunt, sit a Deo punitus ad regulam,*

It must have been in this year 1383, or the year following, that Wycliffe's citation to Rome took place—if such a citation were indeed an historical fact. His biographers all agree in narrating that Pope Urban VI. summoned him to appear before his tribunal, but that Wycliffe excused himself in a letter addressed to the Pope himself, on the ground of his declining health, while giving, at the same time, a frank confession of his convictions.[1] But it is passing strange that not one of them points to any contemporary account attesting the fact of such a citation. Of those 'chroniclers' to whom we are indebted for authentic data concerning Wycliffe's person and life, there is not one who has so much as a single word respecting the Pope's summons. The assumption of such a fact appears rather to rest entirely upon inferences drawn from a production of Wycliffe's own pen, which, however, cannot in any case be regarded as an indubitable testimony to the fact in question. This is the so-called letter of Wycliffe to Pope Urban VI.[2] But this piece, when examined without prejudice, is neither a letter in form, nor in substance an excuse for non-compliance with a citation received. Not a single trace can be discovered in it of the form of a real letter—neither an address at the beginning, nor any other epistolary feature from beginning to end. Nor among the alleged letters of Wycliffe is this by any means the only one which has been erroneously included in this category;[3] while of all the letters which are indisputably such, there is not one which is without the characteristic address at least.[4] Indeed, the way in which the piece mentions the Pope is positive proof against the supposition that it was a letter addressed to the Pope himself. Not less than nine times is the Pope mentioned in this short composition, but, without exception, he is always spoken of in the third person; he is never addressed directly. More than once Wycliffe refers to

Citation of Wycliffe to Rome.

'Letter to Urban VI.'

---

vel adhuc ejus punitio sit futura, c. x., p. 281. Under these four sects, Wycliffe understands the endowed priests, monks, canons, and Mendicant orders.

[1] Foxe, *Acts and Monuments*, ed. 1844. III., 49; Lewis, *History*, 122; Vaughan, *Life and Opinions*, II., 121; *John de Wycliffe, a Monograph*, 320.

[2] The piece in Latin is extant in five Vienna MSS., and in English in two Oxford MSS., and in a transcript besides of the 17th century. Comp. Shirley's *Catalogue*, p. 21, No. 55. The English text, as Arnold rightly judges, is a version from the Latin, which, in any case, is the original. The English form of the text is printed in Lewis, p. 333; in Vaughan, *Life and Opinions*, II., 435; *Monograph*, 576; *Select English Works*, III., 504. The Latin text in *Fasc. Zizan.*, 341.

[3] Shirley, in *Catalogue*, p. 21, enumerates eight letters; but in my opinion only the half of these deserve that name. For a long time I have had no doubt of the fact that the alleged *Epistola ad Simplices Sacerdotes* is no letter; *vide* chap. VI.

[4] The Letter to the archbishop has the address, *Venerabilis in Christo pater et domine;* and the letter itself begins thus: *Vester sacerdos pauper et humilis sub spe paterni auxilii, pandit vestrae reverentiae ostia cordis suae*, etc., Vienna MS., 1387, fol. 105, col. 1.

him as '*our* Pope,'[1] which is an indication that the writer had his countrymen before his mind; and when we add to this the circumstance that the discourse, which from the beginning to beyond the middle proceeds in the first person singular, and sounds like an entirely personal confession, passes over, towards the close, into the first person plural, and in two instances assumes the tone of a collective injunction,[2] the conjecture may not seem too bold, that we have before us either the fragment of a sermon, or of a declaration addressed to English readers.

If we look about for any particular occasion which may have given rise to the document, it may be conjectured, with most probability, that Wycliffe put forth this declaration at the time when his friend Nicholas Hereford set out for Rome to make his answer before the Pope. Perhaps, also, what the writing really contains of the nature of excuse stands connected with the occasion which we have surmised, and is explained by it. Possibly Hereford himself may have wished and proposed that Wycliffe should undertake the journey to Rome along with him; or possibly Wycliffe's undertaking it might have been a step approved of by many of his friends as a proof of faith and courage, insomuch that it was hoped that if Wycliffe himself should appear in Rome, a favourable issue for the common cause might be reasonably anticipated. On either supposition Wycliffe might see occasion to express his mind upon the subject; and certainly his words referring to the point sound more like a justification of himself to like-minded friends, than an excuse addressed to ecclesiastical superiors who had cited him to their bar; but least of all do they sound like a reply to a summons which had issued to him direct from the Pope and the Curia.[3]

Occasion of the letter.

---

[1] Thrice it speaks of *Romanus pontifex*, thrice of *papa aut cardinales*, twice of *papa noster*, once of *papa noster Urbanus sextus*.

[2] *Rogare debemus; . . . igitur rogemus Dominum cujuslibet creaturae; et rogemus spiritualiter. . . .*

[3] [There are several points in the history of Wycliffe and the first Wycliffites on which it was natural to expect that some additional light might be obtained from the Papal archives in Rome. One of these was Wycliffe's alleged citation to appear in person before the tribunal of Urban VI., to which it has long been supposed that he sent a declinature on the score of age and infirmity, a supposition for which, as the reader has seen, Professor Lechler sees no adequate ground. A second point was the part which Wycliffe took, in 1374, in the negotiations at Bruges with the Papal Legates, with respect to which our author had expressed his expectation that some original papers hitherto unknown might possibly be preserved in the archives of the Vatican. To which historical points may with equal reason be added the curious incidents in Nicholas Hereford's life recorded by Knighton, and resting exclusively on his authority, viz., his appeal to Pope Urban VI. against the sentence of Archbishop Courtenay, his condemnation and imprisonment in Rome, and his unexpected release from prison and return to England.

Having become aware in 1876 that our Public Records Office had an agent in Rome employed in searches among the archives of the Vatican on matters connected with the history of Great Britain, I brought under the notice of Sir Thomas Duffus Hardy the first of the historical

These thoughts respecting the possible occasion of this remarkable writing claim to be nothing more than conjectures. But that the piece is not a letter to Pope Urban VI. is a point of which I have no manner of doubt.[1] On the presumption of this negative fact all the judgments which have been hitherto pronounced upon the piece itself come to nothing, whether of admiration for its bold, incisive, and ironical tone, according to some, or of censure for its dissembling and disrespectful spirit, according to others. If the writing, as we are convinced upon the evidence of its own contents, was really an address to men of the same convictions as himself, then neither was its author particularly courageous in making use of such sharp language, nor can he be charged with a disrespectful tone or a want of tact in his proceeding.

Its characteristics.

Although this alleged citation to Rome must be relegated to the category of groundless traditions, still, Wycliffe's life, in his latest years, was always in danger. He was well aware of this, and stood prepared to endure still further persecution for the cause of Christ, and even to end his life as a martyr. In the *Trialogus* he speaks more than once on the subject—*e.g.*, where he says : ' We have no need to go among the heathen in order to die a martyr's death ; we have only to preach persistently the law of Christ in the hearing of rich and worldly prelates, and instantly we shall have a flourishing martyrdom, if we hold out in faith and patience.'

---

questions above referred to, and more recently I have called his attention to the other two. In both instances Sir Thomas accepted, with the greatest readiness, my suggestion that search should be made by his agents in Rome, and he lost no time in communicating first with Mr. Stevenson and afterwards with Mr. Bliss ; and from both these gentlemen the instructions sent by him received immediate and painstaking attention ; but, I regret to add, without any satisfactory result. The Bulls of Gregory XI., in the matters negotiated at Bruges, are of course to be seen in their places in the *Bullarium* of that Pope ; but not a single notice has yet been discovered in the records of the Vatican to add anything to our previous knowledge either of Wycliffe or Hereford.

Of course my only reason for recording here this purely negative result is to make others aware, that an opportunity which looked so promising of obtaining further light on a subject of so much historical interest has not been overlooked, in the preparation of the present English edition of Professor Lechler's work, and to save time and trouble to future inquirers in the same field of research.—*Note by Dr. Lorimer.*]

[1] To this assertion, it is true, is opposed the external testimony of the MSS., which, since the second decade of the 15th century, can be shown to have entitled the piece either *Epistola Missa Papae Urbano Sexto* (so the Vienna MS., 1387), or in some other similar way. But still there was an interval of thirty years between the time when Wycliffe wrote it and the execution of these transcripts ; and in this interval many of the shorter writings of Wycliffe had a similar history —*e.g.*, the alleged *Epistola Missa ad Simplices Sacerdotes.*

[The opinion of Dr. Lechler on the 'Citation' must be taken with some reserve. In the tract *De Citationibus Frivolis*, printed by the Wiclif Society, vol. II., p. 556, we find a reference which it is difficult to understand on any other supposition than that Wycliffe was cited to Rome, and prevented by infirmity from compliance : *Et sic dicit quidam debilis et claudus citatus ad hanc curiam, quod prohibitio regia impedit ipsum ire, quia Rex regum necessitat et vult efficaciter quod non vadat!*]

It was for some time received in certain circles as a fact, that Wycliffe had either been banished from the country by the sentence of a tribunal, or betook himself into voluntary exile, from which, however, after some time, he must have returned. Foxe thinks that it may be gathered from Netter of Walden that Wycliffe was banished, or at least that he kept himself somewhere in hiding.[1] In an expanded form the legend relates that Wycliffe went into spontaneous exile, and made a journey into Bohemia. The Bohemians were already infected with heresy, but Wycliffe in person, it was alleged, was the first man who established them in the opinion that little reverence was due to the priesthood, and no consideration at all to the Pope. But I do not find in the chroniclers and other writers of the fourteenth and fifteenth centuries a single trace of this legend; it seems to have come into existence first in the sixteenth century. If I am not mistaken, it was the Italian Polydore Vergil who was the first to bring forward this fable. He had come to England, in 1509, as a Papal emissary, where, by the favour of Henry VIII., he obtained high preferment in the Church, but afterwards returned in advanced age to his native country, where he died in 1555, in Urbino, the place of his birth. In his English history, he told the above story with an air of confidence,[2] although it appears to have been nothing better than a conjecture of his own brain, devised to furnish an explanation of the connection between Wycliffe and Hussitism, by means of a story which resembles very much the fantastic inventions of the Middle Age.

This utterly baseless statement of the Italian was rejected, as it deserved, by Leland, his contemporary, and characterised by him as 'a vanity of vanities' and a dream. But the most important of Leland's writings, including his work on the British writers, were not printed till a hundred and eighty years later; and so his rejection of Vergilius's bold invention remained unknown to most writers, which accounts for the story having still found credit here and there —as with Bishop Bale, from whom it passed over to Flacius and others.[3]

---

[1] *Acts and Monuments*, III., pp. 49, 53.
[2] Polydori Vergilii Urbinatis *Anglicae Historiae Libri*, XXVI., Basileae, 1533. At the end of Book XIX., p. 394, the author speaks of Wycliffe, of whom he says, at the end of the passage: *Ad extremum homo nimium confidens, cum rationibus veris cogeretur ad bonam redire frugem, tantum abfuit ut pareret, ut etiam maluerit voluntarium petere exilium quam mutare sententiam: qui ad Boëmos, nonnulla haeresi ante inquinatos, profectus, a rudi gente magno in honore habetur, quam pro accepto beneficio confirmavit, summeque hortatus est in ea remanere sententia, ut ordini sacerdotali parum honoris, et ad Romanum Pontificem nullum respectum haberet.*

[3] The Father of English Antiquaries, John Leland (died 1552), says in his *Commentarii de Scriptoribus Britannicis*, ed. Ant. Hall, Oxford, 1709, II., 379: *Quid hic respondebo vanissimis Polydori Vergilii vanitatibus, qui . . . disertis et*

It is a fact to which there attaches not the slightest doubt, that Wycliffe spent the last years of his life, without a break, in his own country, and in the town of Lutterworth, where he was parish priest. There is no probability even in the allegation that he was fain to keep very quiet, in order not to draw upon himself the attention of his adversaries. On the contrary, it is proved by the writings which he published during the last three years of his life, including the *Trialogus* and numerous Latin and English tracts, in which, for the most part, he wields a sharp pen and adopts a resolute tone, that his energy was by no means diminished nor his courage abashed.

Priest at Lutterworth.

The gracious protection of God was over him. His enemies must needs leave him undisturbed. This inactive course, indeed, may also have been recommended to them by the circumstance (which cannot have remained unknown to them) that Wycliffe had suffered a paralytic stroke towards the close of 1382,[1] and was totally disabled thereby from appearing again upon the public stage, although his mental power and force of character remained unimpaired. Yet even the personal credit of Wycliffe as a believing Christian remained unassailed up to his death. It is true, indeed, that a number of Articles which were imputed to him were condemned as errors, and, in part, as heresies; and in several mandates of the heads of the Church he was designated by name as under suspicion of erroneous teaching. But no judgment had ever been pronounced upon his *person* by his ecclesiastical superiors; Wycliffe was never in his lifetime judicially declared to be a teacher of error or a heretic; he was never even formally threatened with the ban of excommunication. He continued not only in possession of his office and dignity as rector of Lutterworth, but also in high estimation as a Christian and priest with his parishioners and his countrymen, till he was seized with a second stroke, and two days afterwards was permitted to breathe his last in peace.

Paralysed.

While the year and the day of the Reformer's birth must remain unknown, the date of his death admits of being determined with precision. Differences, indeed, are not wanting in the accounts which have come down to us. Walsingham

Wycliffe's death.

accuratis verbis asserit Vicoclivum, ut alia somnia praeteream, voluntarium exilium petiisse, ac magno postea apud Boëmos in pretio fuisse? etc. The modern Vergilius was generally considered in England a liar, as is shown by the biting expression of the celebrated epigrammatist, Owen (died 1622):

Virgilii duo sunt, alter Maro, tu Polydore Alter. Tu mendax, ille poëta fuit.

[1] This fact is attested by Dr. Thomas Gascoigne: *Et iste Wycleff fuit paralyticus per duos annos ante mortem suam.* See Lewis, p. 336.

gives 1385 as the date,[1] and Oudin, the literary historian, determines for 1387.[2] Two testimonies, however, are extant—the one of an official and the other of a private character, which are quite decisive upon the point. The first is an entry in the Episcopal register of Lincoln, made in the time of Bishop Bockingham—in the days of Wycliffe's immediate successor in the rectory, and indeed as early as the year 1385. It is probable that a question had arisen respecting the right of collation to the benefice, occasioned by the fact that Wycliffe had been nominated to the living by King Edward III. An inquiry, therefore, had been made by commissaries upon the subject; an entry was engrossed in the register recording the result of their investigation; and this record establishes the fact that the nomination of Wycliffe to the parish had been made by the king on account of the then minority of the patron. It is in connection with this that the death of Wycliffe, on December 31, 1384, is officially specified;[3] and we can hardly imagine any proof more documentary, older, or more trustworthy.

The other testimony referred to, though only that of a private individual, has all the force of a declaration upon oath from the mouth of a contemporary, of even an eye-witness. Thomas Gascoigne, Doctor of Theology, and Chancellor of the University of Oxford from 1443 to 1445, who died in 1457, received and wrote down a communication respecting the death of Wycliffe in the year 1441 from the mouth of the priest, John Horn, then eighty years of age, under solemn asseveration of the truth of what he communicated. The declaration was to this effect, that Wycliffe, after having suffered for two years from the effects of a paralytic stroke, on Innocents' Day of the year 1384, while hearing mass in his parish church at Lutterworth, sustained a violent stroke, at the moment of the elevation of the host, and sank down on the spot. His tongue in particular was affected by the seizure, so that from that moment he never spoke a single word more, and remained speechless till his death, which took place on Saturday evening—

Date of the event.

Silvester's Day, and the eve of the Feast of Christ's Circumcision.[4] This declaration was confirmed on oath by the

---

[1] *Historia Anglicana*, ed. Riley, II., 119; *Hypodigma Neustriae in Anglica, Normanica*, etc., ed. Camden, Frankfort, 1602, fol. 537. He is followed by Capgrave (died 1464), *Chronicle of England*, London, 1858, 240.

[2] *Commentarius de Scriptoribus Ecclesiae Antiquis*, Lips., 1722, vol. III., 1048.

[3] The words bearing upon this point run thus: *Inquisitores dicunt, quod dicta Ecclesia* (Lutterworth) *incepit vacare ultimo die Decem.* (Decembri) *ultimo praeteriti* (1384) *per mortem Joannis Wycliff ultimi rectoris ejusdem.* The whole passage (see above, chap. 5) was first published by Lewis from the *Registrum Bokyngham*, and afterwards by Vaughan, *Monograph*, 180.

[4] For this valuable communication we are also indebted to Lewis, who printed

aged priest, John Horn, who must have been a young man of three-and-twenty in the year of Wycliffe's death;[1] and it is entirely credible in every respect. In reference to the death-day itself the two testimonies corroborate each other perfectly; only Horn, as an eye-witness, supplies information, in addition, as to the day on which, and in what circumstances, Wycliffe suffered the second stroke which ended in the fatal issue. It was *in die Sanctorum Innocentium*—*i.e.*, December 28th—during the mass in Lutterworth Church. A correction is thus supplied for the malicious remarks of several hostile chroniclers, to the effect that Wycliffe had the stroke on Thomas Becket's Day, when he had the intention to preach and to make a blasphemous attack upon the saint.[2] The Feast of St. Thomas was kept in the English mediæval Church December 29th; whereas Wycliffe, according to the testimony of John Horn, was struck with paralysis on the 28th. Walsingham's design in misplacing the day was evidently that he might be able to say that Wycliffe was righteously smitten down on the day of St. Thomas, whom he had often blasphemed, and that his death as righteously befell on the day of St. Silvester, whom he had often exasperated by his attacks.[3] This whole pragmatic interpretation, so far as it refers to Becket, is exploded by the fact that Wycliffe was paralysed on the 28th day of December instead of the 29th, while the representation given of Wycliffe's violent attacks upon Becket and Silvester is proved to rest upon an entire misunderstanding.[4]

---

in full Gascoigne's *Deposition*, written with his own hand, from a MS. in the British Museum, *History*, Appendix, No. 25, p. 336. Vaughan has also printed it again, *Monograph*, p. 577.

[1] *Et mihi juravit sic dicendo: sicut respondebo coram Deo, novi ista fuisse vera, et quia vidi, testimonium perhibui.* We may therefore receive all that is contained in the testimony as fully certified; and we have no reason to hesitate between this account and another given by some annalists, as if the day of the last paralytic seizure were not quite certain. Compare Vaughan, *Monograph*, p. 468, 'On the 28th, or, as some say, on the 29th of December,' etc.

[2] Walsingham, vol. II., p. 119: *Die Sancti Thomae, Cantuariensis Archiepiscopi et Martyris . . . Johannes de Wiclif, dum in Sanctum Thomam, ut dicitur, eodem die in sua praedicatione, quam dicere praeparaverat, orationes et blasphemias vellet evomere, repente judicio Dei percussus, sensit paralysim omnia membra sua generaliter invasisse,* etc. He is followed here, word for word,

by Capgrave, *Chronicle of England*, London, 1858, 240.

[3] Walsingham, *Hypodigma Neustriae*, in Camden, *Anglica, Normanica*, etc. Frankfort, 1602: *Et quidem satis juste die S. Thomae percussus est, quem multotiens lingua blasphemaverat venenata, et die Silvestri temporali morte damnatus es', quem crebris invectionibus exasperaver.i.' in dictis suis.*

[4] I find Thomas Becket not unfrequently mentioned in the MS. books and sermons of Wycliffe, *e.g.*, *De Civili Dominio*, I., 34, 39; II., 2, Vienna MS. 1341, fol. 79, col. 2: fol. 94, col. 2; fol. 157, col. 1; *Saints' Days Sermons*, No. V., fol. 8, col. 1; fol. 9, col. 2; *De Ecclesia*, c. 14, fol. 172, col. 3. Compare Wycliffe's English sermons on the Gospels, *Select English Works*, I., 330. And Wycliffe always speaks of Becket, if not indeed with unlimited veneration, yet with sincere respect. He rejects the view which prevailed among some of his contemporaries that Becket had died in a contest about Church property, and he maintains by documentary proofs that

Nor is the representation historically exact which is given by Vaughan, both in his earlier and later works on Wycliffe, to the effect that the Reformer was struck with palsy while 'employed in administering the bread of the Eucharist,' or 'while engaged in the service of the church at Lutterworth.'[1] This is not merely an imaginative touch to the picture, such as may be allowed to an historian, but a contradiction to the only trustworthy account which we possess of Wycliffe's last illness, according to which he was not reading but hearing mass at the moment of his last seizure.[2] It is an additional inaccuracy to assert that Wycliffe was deprived of consciousness by the stroke.[3] Horn says nothing of unconsciousness, but only of a violent shock under which he fell to the ground; he mentions in particular only the paralysis of his tongue. Speechlessness and unconsciousness are two different things; and it is at least conceivable that the sufferer may have come to himself again sufficiently to be sensible of the sympathetic love and care which were devoted to him in his last days by his friends, and to express his gratitude, without words, by looks and gestures. Indeed, Gascoigne's description of his condition rather conveys the impression that it was not one of unconsciousness, for he repeatedly mentions his speechlessness as a circumstance calling for remark, which it would not have been if he had been reduced to a condition of entire unconsciousness.[4] On St. Silvester's Day—

Details.

the contest which Becket carried on was for the jurisdiction of the Church, its autonomy in opposition to the State. The case was very different with Pope Silvester in Wycliffe's eyes, for it was Silvester, according to the historical view which Wycliffe shared with large numbers of minds in the Middle Age, who, by accepting the alleged Donation of Constantine the Great, laid the foundation for the territorial patrimony of the Pope, the wealth of the clergy, and the secularisation of the Church. Wycliffe, notwithstanding, was at all times far from condemning Silvester, as if in that act he had been guilty of an unpardonable sin. He judged the act itself, indeed, of accepting the patrimony to be a sin, but he was also willing to presume that Silvester had acted in the matter with a good intention, and that this sin was forgiven him by God, at least in his last hour. Comp. *Trialogus*, III., c. 20; IV., c. 17. *Supplementum Trialogi*, c. 1, 2, pp. 196, 303, 407. *Saints' Days Sermons*, No. VI. (on St. Silvester's Day), fol. 10, col. 2; fol. 12, col. 1. Nowhere do I find him casting unmeasured blame upon Silvester. The malicious observation of the Popish chronicler mentioned in the text is therefore entirely destitute of truth.

[1] *Life and Opinions*, II., 224: 'He is said to have been employed in administering the bread of the Eucharist when assailed by his last sickness.' And in *John de Wycliffe, a Monograph*, 468, it is said: 'While engaged in the service of the church at Lutterworth he was seized with palsy.'

[2] *Audiens missam in ecclesia sua de Lyttyrwort circa elevationem sacramenti altaris decidit percussus magna paralysi*, says Gascoigne, from the report of John Horn, in Lewis, 336.

[3] Vaughan, *Life and Opinions*, II., 224: 'The paralysis deprived him at once of consciousness.' He expressed himself more cautiously at a later date, *John de Wycliffe*, 468: 'He does not speak, nor even seem to be conscious.'

[4] Gascoigne's words are: *Percussus magna paralysi, et specialiter in lingua, ita quod nec tunc nec postea loqui potuit usque ad mortem suam; in introitu autem sui in ecclesiam suam loquebatur, sed sic ut percussus paralysi in eadem die loqui non potuit, nec unquam postea loquebatur.*

December 31st—1384, John of Wycliffe was delivered out of this paralytic condition by death.

Adversaries of his work pursued him with fanatical outpourings of contumely even beyond his grave. Here are the words of a chronicler who has been frequently named before— 'On the Feast of the Passion of St. Thomas of Canterbury, John Wycliffe—that instrument of the devil, that enemy of the Church, that author of confusion to the common people, that idol of heretics, that image of hypocrites, that originator of schism, that son of hatred, that corner of lies—being struck by the horrible judgment of God, was struck with palsy, and continued to live in that condition until St. Silvester's Day, on which he breathed out his malicious spirit into the abodes of darkness.'[1] There is no need at the present day to use any protest against words so full of venom as these; but at the point where such and so great a man withdraws from the stage of history, we feel it to be a duty to gather up again the various features of intellect and heart which have come before us in tracing the course of his life, and once more to present them in the form of a complete portrait.

Representations of Wycliffe's enemies.

8.—Character of Wycliffe and his important place in History.

THE importance of Wycliffe, as seen from an age five hundred years later than his own time, is in no respect less imposing than it seemed to his contemporaries, in so far as they were not preoccupied by party prejudice against him. But the judgment of the present time must needs differ from that of his own period, as to where the chief importance of his personality and work lay. To the men of his own age his greatness and his chief distinction lay in his intellectual pre-eminence. Not only his adherents, but even his opponents, looked upon him as having no living equal in learning and scientific ability—to all eyes he shone as the star of the first magnitude.[2] But these judgments referred

Wycliffe's fame in his own age.

---

[1] Walsingham, II., 119.

[2] When opponents give expression to such a judgment, it has, of course, the greatest weight. Now Knighton, or his continuator, the Leicester Chronicler, is a man who manifests his dislike to Wycliffe and his party upon every occasion; and yet he cannot avoid bearing this testimony to him: *Doctor in Theologia eminentissimus in diebus illis. In Philosophia nulli reputabatur secundis, in scholasticis disciplinis incomparabilis.* *Hic maxime nitebatur aliorum ingenia subtilitate scientiae et profunditate ingenii sui transscendere. Historiae Anglicanae Scriptores*, vol. III., col. 2644. And the Carmelite John Cunningham, an opponent, who more than once stood forward against him in his lifetime, is reported by his disciple, Thomas Netter of Walden, to have been an admirer of Wycliffe's distinguished learning (*admiratur in Wiclefo doctrinae excellentiam*, Lewis, p. xxiii.). On the side of his

exclusively to *scholastic* learning in philosophy and theology; and Wycliffe's mastery as a scholastic lost immensely in value with scholasticism itself, in the eyes of later generations. We frankly confess, notwithstanding, that in our opinion this depreciation has been carried too far, and that Wycliffe's scientific importance is wont, for the most part, to be undervalued unduly.[1] This fact admits of explanation from various circumstances. First of all, the very unsatisfactory condition in which the text of the *Trialogus* existed till recently was answerable for much of the disfavour into which Wycliffe fell as a writer. Much also in his writings which appears faulty in our eyes is to be put to the account, not of the man himself, but of his age, and of the usages, not always the best, of the scholastic style. The utterly unclassical Latinity, the lumbering heaviness of the style, the syllogistic forms and methods in which inquiries were conducted—these and other features are all characteristics which were common to scholastic literature in general. Even the practice observable in Wycliffe of often repeating himself to an extraordinary degree, not only in different works upon the same subject, but even in the course of one and the same work, was a common fault which he shared with many other scholastic writers of the period. A reader who keeps all this in view will be on his guard against censuring too severely faults and imperfections which Wycliffe had in common with the age in which he lived.

Undue reaction.

Drawbacks in his writings.

On the other hand, this very mastery of Wycliffe as a scholastic deserves a more just recognition in the present age than it usually receives. The high intellectual position which was accorded to him was needed to protect him from the malignant attacks which threatened him as a 'Biblicist,' and a severe critic of Roman doctrine. This, to be sure, was only a secondary benefit of his scientific eminence; but undoubtedly the extraordinary acuteness of his dialectics, the intellectual force of his criticism, and the concentrated unity of the principles which form the immutable basis of his thinking, are worthy of a more unreserved recognition than is now usually accorded to them.

His varied ability.

The many-sidedness of his mind also deserves to be considered.

---

followers, it may suffice to point to the testimonial (so much discussed) of the University of Oxford, which celebrates his *sententiarum profunditas*, and pronounces of him, that *in logicalibus, philosophicis ac theologicis ac moralibus et speculativis inter omnes nostrae universitatis (ut credimus) scripserat sine pari.*

Wilkins, *Conc. Magnae Britanniae*, III., 302. See below, p. 455.

[1] We are not able to agree with Vaughan when, with all his esteem for Wycliffe, he says (*Life and Opinions*, I., 319) that 'his scholastic treatises possess, at the present day, only a very limited value, even for the students of history.'

He has an eye for the most different things—a lively interest for the most manifold questions. Upon occasion of an inquiry on the subject of slavery, for example, he comes to speak of the laws of optics;[1] at another time the thought of mental intuition and the idea of the operations of grace lead him to refer to the laws of corporeal vision.[2] On one occasion he illustrates the moral effect of sin by which the soul is separated from the fellowship of the blessed, by pointing to chemical analysis, by which the most different elements of a compound body are detached from one another and separated in space.[3] How love waxes cold (Matthew xxiv. 12) he illustrates in a sermon by a reference to physical laws, and to the colder atmosphere of the mountain summits.[4] To describe moral watchfulness, he calls in the explanations of naturalists respecting the physiological genesis of sleep.[5] Geometrical and arithmetical relations he frequently introduces in connection with the investigation of certain ideas; and he has a special partiality for the treatment of subjects relating to national economics. The fact that in his references to the natural sciences his notions are now and then fantastical and far from clear, cannot with justice lay him open to any suspicion of ignorance on such subjects; for who would demand of him—a man who had no pretensions to be a professed physicist—that he should have been four or five centuries in advance of his own time? It is certainly well worth remarking how mathematical, physical, naturalistic, and social ideas all pour in a full stream into his many-sided and richly furnished mind.

Scientific knowledge.

Another characteristic feature of Wycliffe is the critical spirit which inspires him. It cannot be denied, indeed, that he, too, innocently repeats several sagas and legends which passed for sterling coin in the Middle Age, *e.g.*, that the Apostle John changed forest leaves into gold, and pebbles on the sea shore into precious stones.[6] In this respect, as in others, Wycliffe pays tribute to his own time. For the Middle Age has a certain fantastical legendary spirit of its own, by which things shape themselves to it in grotesque forms, like the mirage which conjures up distant objects as if they were near at hand, but in reversed position. Historical events and relations received thereby a romantic colouring. The age lacked true historical sense—it was wanting most of all in critical endowment. To this legend-world of the

His critical spirit.

---

[1] *De Civili Dominio*, I., c. 33, fol. 78, col. 1.
[2] *Saints' Days Sermons*, No. LII., fol. 106, col. 3.
[3] *De Ecclesia*, c. 5, fol. 142, cols. 3 and 4.
[4] *Saints' Days Sermons*, No. XXX., fol. 58, col. 4, to fol. 59, col. 1.
[5] *Ib.*, No. XLIX., fol. 99, col. 1. Comp. *Miscell. Sermons*, No. I., fol, 194, col. 1.
[6] *De Ecclesia*, c. 9, fol. 155, col. 1.

Middle Age belongs in particular the Saga of the Donation of Constantine.[1] The endowment of the Papal see with territory and people, the landed possessions of the Church, and her entire secularisation—all these evils which Wycliffe fights against had their source, according to the view which he shares with the centuries before him, in the supposed donation of the Emperor.

It cannot be denied, notwithstanding, that Wycliffe was endowed with a remarkable gift of criticism. In proof of this, we must not lay *Church traditions examined* too much stress upon the fact that when the authority of one of the Fathers is brought into the field against him—as, *e.g.*, of Augustine himself—he does not at once acknowledge himself to be defeated, but first of all investigates, by a thorough examination, whether the meaning of Augustine, in the quoted place or elsewhere, is really entirely opposed to himself.[2] Of higher importance is the circumstance that Wycliffe mentions Church legends occasionally with undisguised doubts of their truth —*e.g.*, the legend that the child whom the Redeemer on one occasion called to Him and placed in the midst of His disciples (Matthew xviii.) was St. Martial, whom Peter at a later period sent into Gaul.[3] But the most decisive fact here is this, that Wycliffe, instead of accepting at once and without more ado the whole condition of the Church as to doctrine, ordinances, and usages, just as it stood and was recognised in his time, turned upon it all a scrutinising glance, and subjected the whole to a rigid examination. However undeniably Wycliffe shares in the weak points of scholasticism, he is still free enough from prepossession, and has still enough of the critical vein to see how much useless straw the ordinary scholastic was still addicted to threshing. It is nothing unusual with him to express his contempt of the many subtleties (*argutiae fictitae*) in which men still dealt so much, and the multitude of baseless possibilities with which they still occupied their heads. He earnestly calls upon men to renounce all such utterly superfluous labour of the brain, and to occupy themselves instead with solid and useful truths (*veritates solidae et utiles*)[4]— all of them thoughts tending towards an emancipation from scholasticism—to a reformation of science.

Still further, it is frequent with him to distinguish between what has come down from antiquity and that which is of later date, which

---

[1] Comp. the interesting investigation of Döllinger in his *Papst-Fabeln des Mittelalters*, ed. 2, Munich, 1863, 61.

[2] *De Ecclesia*, c. 8, fol. 151.

[3] *Saints' Days Sermons*, No. XXVI., fol. 50, col. 3 : *Iste autem parvulus somniatur fuisse Martialis. . . . Sed dimisso isto ipsis, qui credere illud volunt, tenendum est*, etc. Comp. *XXIV. Sermons*, No. X., fol. 155, col. 1 ; *De Ecclesia*, c. 22, fol. 201, cols. 1–3.

[4] Comp., *e.g.*, *Trialogus*, III., c. 27, p. 225.

the men of the last centuries, the moderns, had introduced. But 'old Christian,' with him, means what belonged to the original, the Primitive Church—*ecclesia primitiva*, and precisely for this reason the ultimate standard for him is the Bible—'the law of Christ,' as he calls it. From this purely Protestant spirit of criticism sprang his free and manly contention against various usurpations of the Papacy and abuses of the hierarchy, against many particulars of the Roman Catholic worship, and even against several articles of Roman doctrine, *e.g.*, the doctrine of Transubstantiation. To conduct such a criticism, a holy zeal for the truth and honour of God, moral resolution, and manly courage, were indispensable. In a word, the critical genius of Wycliffe was not merely an efflux of scientific power and independence, but also a fruit of moral sentiment and of Christian character. *Appeal to primitive faith.*

It is not, however, in his intellect that Wycliffe's personality centres, but in his will and character. With him, so far as I see, all thinking, every intellectual achievement, was always a way to an end—a means of moral action and work—it never terminated in itself. And this serves to explain, apart from the fact that Wycliffe shared in many of the faults of his time, many of the weak sides of his performances as an author. There are, speaking generally, two kinds of natures, one manifesting itself in art, the other in practical action. Natures of the former class seek their satisfaction in the works which they complete—the painter in his pictures, the sculptor in the plastic forms which he produces, the musician in his harmonic creations, the poet in his poetry, and the prose writer in his prose. That every part of the work should make the wished-for impression; that the whole should make an unity complete in itself; that the form should so shape itself in harmony with the substance as to give full satisfaction to the mind; and be at once lovable and fair, elevating and attractive: to these ends is directed all the effort of the artist. That is the reason why one sketch after another is made and thrown away, and attempt follows upon attempt; the thinking mind, the critical eye, the improving hand, the smoothing file never rest till a perfect work stands before the artist.[1] To these artistic natures, certainly, Wycliffe does not belong, but as certainly to the men of practical action and work. It is not beauty of form, not its harmony and the full expression of it—in a word, not the work itself as a completed performance which floats before the eye of such men; it is in action and work themselves that they seek *Wycliffe's practical aims.*

---

[1] Comp. Schleiermacher's thoughtful remarks in the second of the *Monologues*, 4 ed., Berlin, 1829, p. 29.

their satisfaction—in the service of the truth, in the furthering of the good, in work for man's weal and God's glory. To this class of natures Wycliffe belonged. At no time was it his aim to give to his addresses, sermons, scientific works, popular writings, etc., an artistic shape, to polish them, to bring them to a certain perfection of form; but to join his hand with others in the fellowship of labour, to communicate to others what he knew, to serve his native country, to promote the glory of God, the kingdom of Christ, and the salvation of souls. That was what he wanted to do, and to serve God therein was his joy and satisfaction. If only what he said was understood; if his spoken word was only kindling to men's souls, whether spoken from the chair or the pulpit; if his written word was only effective, and his action was only followed by any good fruit, then it troubled him little that his style was thought to be without finish or without beauty, or perhaps even wearisome; in the end he neither knew nor cared how it stood with his productions in these latter respects.

It is true that the repetitions which Wycliffe allowed himself go far beyond the permissible limit. And even this is not all. His *His literary method.* treatment of a subject generally moves in a very free and easy manner; a strict logical disposition of his matter is missing often enough. He frequently allows himself to digress from his proper subject, and is obliged to remind himself at last that he has lost sight for a time of his main topic.[1] The structure of his sentences is extremely loose—a circumstance which adds much to the difficulty of arriving at his true and exact meaning; and the diction has rarely anything closely allied to the thought, well-weighed, or carefully chosen. In one word, the style and presentation are lacking in precisely those qualities of well-proportioned and harmonious form, artistic inspiration, æsthetic perfection, which we account classical.

But, in compensation for these defects, Wycliffe always communicates *himself* as he is, his whole personality, undissembled, true, and full. *His strong individuality.* As a preacher, as well as a writer, he is always the whole man. Scarcely any one has stamped his own personality upon his writings in a higher degree, or has carried more of morality into his action than Wycliffe. Wherein, then, consists the peculiarity of his personality?

Wycliffe was not a man of feeling, but a man of intellect. Luther was a genial soul. On one occasion he begs his readers to take his

---

[1] Even as a preacher he makes little account of flowery, fine speech, but both in his theory of preaching and his own pulpit practice he gives the decided preference to a plain and simple, but suitable and apt mode of expression; see chap. VI., p. 184.

words, however mocking and biting they may be, 'as spoken from a heart which could not do otherwise than break with its great sorrow.'[1] Wycliffe never said such a thing of himself. He is a man in whom the intellect predominates— pure, clear, sharp, penetrating. With Wycliffe it is as if one felt the sharp, fresh, cool breath of the morning air before sunrise; while in Luther we feel something of the kindly warmth of the morning sun himself. It was only possible to a predominantly intellectual nature to lay so great stress as Wycliffe did upon the demonstration of the Christian verities. Even in the Fathers of the Church he puts a specially high value upon the philosophical proofs which they allege in support of the doctrines of the Christian faith. Manifestly it is not merely a result of education and of the scholastic tone of his age, but in no small degree the outcome of his own individuality, that the path in which he moves with so strong a preference is that of speculation, and even of dialectical demonstration.

His genial spirit.

In Wycliffe, along with the intellectual element thus decidedly expressed, there is harmoniously combined a powerful will, equally potent in independent action and energetic in opposition —a firm and tenacious, a manly, yea, a heroic will. It is impossible to read Wycliffe's writings with an unprejudiced and susceptible mind, without being laid hold of by the strong manhood of mind which everywhere reveals itself. There is a force and fulness of character in his feeling and language which makes an overmastering impression, and keeps the mind enchained. Wycliffe sets forth his convictions, it is true, in a learned manner, with dialectical illustration and scholastic argumentativeness. And yet one sees that it is by no means a one-sided intellectual interest alone which moves him. His conviction has unmistakably a moral source. He confesses openly himself that the conviction of the truth is reached much more in a moral way than by pure intellect and science.[2]

His heroic will.

It is certain that he arrived at his own convictions more in a moral than a merely intellectual way; and hence his utterances have equally the stamp of decisive thinking, and of energetic moral earnestness. We recognise everywhere the moral pathos, the holy earnestness which wells up from the conscience and the depths of the soul. And hence the concentrated moral force which he always throws into the scale. Whether

His moral earnestness.

---

[1] *Of the Papacy in Rome* (1520), in Preface to the Jena edition of Luther's Works, 1690, I., 264.
[2] *De Dominio Divino*, I., c. 11, fol. 225, col. 2: *Credo, quod sancta conversatio, miraculorum operatio, et constans ac humilis injuriarum perpessio, foret argumentum efficacius infideli, quam disputationes scholasticae, quibus insistimus,* etc.

he is compelled to defend himself against the imputation of petty by-ends and low-minded feeling,[1] or whether he is speaking to the consciences of those who give their whole study to human traditions instead of God's Word,[2] or whether he takes occasion to address moral warnings to young men,[3] he invariably delivers his pithy words with a fulness of moral earnestness and with an arresting force. From the intensity with which he throws his whole soul into his subject springs also the warmth of feeling with which Wycliffe at one time repudiates that which he is opposing, and at other times rejoices in some conquest which he has won. Not rarely he manifests a moral indignation and horror in the very midst of a learned investigation, where one is not at all prepared for such an outburst of flaming feeling.[4] At other times, in the very middle of a disputation with opponents, he breaks out into joyful thanksgiving and praise to God that he has been set free from the sophisms by which they are still held fast.[5] The contrast between trains of scholastic reasoning and such sudden outpourings of feeling is surprising and arresting in a high degree; and this inner fire of inspiration and heart-fervour, long hidden beneath the surface, and only now and then darting forth its tongues of flame, well explains and excuses many literary faults. For whence come these frequent outbursts? and whither do they tend? In very many cases Wycliffe enters into regions of thought into which he is drawn by his heart and the innermost feeling of his soul. Often in such episodical passages have I come upon the most elevating outpourings of his moral pathos—the most precious utterances of a healthy piety. If we follow him in such places, we find no reason to regret it. The reader accompanies the author with growing veneration and love; and at the close he will not only be fain to forgive him for a digression, but in spirit he warmly presses his hand with elevated feeling and a

Intensity and pathos.

---

[1] The strongest passage of this kind which I know is one in *De Veritate Scripturae Sac.*, c. 12, fol. 34, col. 4, where he refers to the fact that he was accused of seeking by-ends of his own, and that imputations were cast upon him of falsehood and equivocation, and repels these calumnies in a high tone of earnestness and piety.

[2] *De Veritate Scripturae Sac.*, c. 20, fol. 65, col. 2. Here he presses the consciences of those who study the doctrines of men more than the Bible with one interrogation after another, in a style which makes one feel that he speaks with the authority of a theological censor, and with the spirit and power of a prophet.

[3] *Trialogus*, III., c. 22, p. 206, where he deals with the sin of Onanism with impressive earnestness.

[4] *E.g.*, *De Veritate Scripturae Sac.*, c. 12, fol. 34, cols. 3 and 4 : *Illam novitatem detestor*, etc. *De Ecclesia*, c. 8, fol. 151, cols. 1-2: *Deum contestor et numina, quod inter omnes doctrinas et consilia, quae audivi non occurrit mihi aliquod difficilius aut detestabilius. . . . Ego quidem horrerem introducere scolam istam tanquam doctor mendacii*, etc.

[5] *De Veritate Scripturae Sac.*, c. 32: *Benedictus sit Deus, qui nos liberavit ab istis argutiis!*

thankful heart. What seemed a literary fault proves, upon an unprejudiced and deeper view, to be a moral excellence.

The intense feeling and warmth of the man manifests itself ever and anon in the personal apostrophes which he addresses to an opponent,[1] as well as in the manner in which he very often speaks of himself in quite a personal way. On all occasions, indeed, he comes forward with entire straightforwardness and unreserved sincerity; never in any way concealing the changes of opinion through which he has, it may be, passed; openly confessing the fact when he has previously done homage to an error; declaring frankly what are his aims, and praying that by the help and in the fear of God he may be steadfast to the end.[2] As a preacher, in particular, Wycliffe at all times proves himself a man of perfect integrity, and at every stage of his inner development reflects it faithfully as in a mirror. At all times, whatever was highest and best in the convictions at which he had arrived he truthfully published from the pulpit; and from this perfect integrity and honour it comes to pass that his sermons furnish a standard for the state of his knowledge and manner of thinking at every stage of his career.

Absolute sincerity.

The personality of Wycliffe includes also a rich vein of wit and humour. To these he often allows a diverting play of cheerful banter, as when, in speaking of the practice of taking money in the confessional, as though penitence could prove itself to be genuine in that way, he indulges in the word-play —*revera non jurisdictio sed falsa jurisfictio;*[3] or when, in his investigations on Church property, he mentions, on the basis of an old legend, that when the Apostle Paul was on his way to Jerusalem with the money which he had collected for the Church there, his road was beset with robbers, whereas at all other times, he added, the apostle travelled in perfect safety, because

His wit and humour.

Cantabit vacuus coram latrone viator.[4]

Even in the midst of serious discussions, and in polemical pieces, he loves now and then to strike a more cheerful note. On one occasion he says:—'Fortune has no such kind intentions for me as that I should be in a position to bring forward any proof on matters

---

[1] *De Ecclesia*, c. 3, fol. 135, col. 2.
[2] Characteristic is the confession in *De Veritate Scrip. Sac.*, c. 32, fol. 117, col. 1, that he is equally on his guard against a presumptuous arrogance in the treatment of doubtful questions, as against timidity and a hypocritical faint-heartedness in defence of Scripture truth; this last, under the guidance of the Holy Ghost, he is resolved boldly to maintain.
[3] *Liber Mandatorum*, or *Decalogus*, c. 26, MS. 1339, fol. 206, col 1 : *Revera non jurisdictio sed falsa jurisfictio istud cogit*, etc.
[4] *De Civili Dominio*, I., c. 20, fol. 45, col. 2.

of Church property which could have any weight in the eyes of the doctor (a learned opponent with whom Wycliffe was at the time engaged). To every proof which I have produced, his reply has commonly been, that it is defective both in substance and form. But verily that is not the way to untie knots, for so might a magpie contradict all and every proof. I proposed the question whether the King of England is entitled to deprive the clergy who are his subjects of the temporalities, when they transgress. In reply, he slily leaves the question in this form unanswered, and introduces quite a different subject—like the woman, who, when asked, "How far is it to Lincoln?" gave for answer—"A bag full of plums." Like hers is his answer: "The King cannot take away from his clergy any of their temporalities, *brevi manu;*" *i.e.*, he cannot strip them of their property by an exercise of arbitrary power.'[1]

When certain theologians of his day by their scholastic sophistry almost made sport of the Bible, by first maintaining that, in many particulars, its language is impossible and offensive, *i.e.*, when taken according to the letter, or in the carnal verbal sense; and then, professing the deepest reverence for the Scriptures, pretended to redeem their honour by a different translation,—Wycliffe's opinion of them was, that they come in sheep's clothing, but bite with fox's teeth, and thrust out, to boot, an otter's tail. It is just what the fox does when he makes peace with the poultry and gets into the hen-roost. He is no sooner in than he falls to work and makes good use of his teeth. When they pretend that the Scriptures cannot have the apparent sense, but only the orthodox sense which they put forward, is it not, in fact, says Wycliffe, as unworthy a proceeding as to bring a false accusation against a man, though it is acknowledged immediately after that he has been lied against, or to break a man's head, though directly afterwards a healing plaster is handed to him?[2]

In such cases, indeed, his wit and humour easily pass over into mockery and sarcasm; and hence an objection sometimes made by his opponents that he had recourse to satire as a controversial weapon. In one place I find him defending himself against the accusation of having allowed himself to use irony against an opponent. 'If,' says he, 'He who sitteth in the heavens laughs at them (Psalm ii. 4), so also may all men who stand on God's side bring that school of theologians to shame with raillery, with reproaches, or with proofs, as God has given them severally the ability. Elijah, too, poured out bitter mockery and scorn upon the

His irony and sarcasm.

---

[1] *De Ecclesia*, c. 21, fol. 196, col. 2.   [2] *De Veritate Scripturae Sac.*, c. 12, fol. 31, col. 3.

priests of Baal (1 Kings xviii. 27), and Christ Himself severely reproached the Pharisees in rough and disdainful words (Matthew xxii.). When any one, from a motive of love to his neighbour, breaks out into words of reproach and scorn, in order to defend God's honour and to preserve the Church from errors, such a man, if uninfluenced by revenge and ambition, does a work worthy of praise.'[1]

The monks especially are a butt for his ridicule. In one place he has occasion to speak of the prayers of the monks, and he remarks that a principal motive which induces men to institute monastic foundations, is the delusive notion that the prayer of a monk is of more value than all temporal goods; and yet it does not at all look as if the prayer of those cloistered folks were so very powerful, unless, indeed, it be supposed that God listens to them more than to other men, on account of their red cheeks and their fat lips.[2] Wycliffe occasionally caricatures the monks in still greater detail. Of the begging friars, he goes so far as to say that 'they are like the tortoises, which quickly find their way, one close after the other, through the whole country. They are even on a footing of familiarity with noble lords and ladies, for they penetrate every house, into the most secret chambers, like the lap-dogs of women of rank.'[3] A saying of his has been preserved by the learned Carmelite, Thomas Netter of Walden, which reveals to us the tart humour of the man. Netter tells us that Wycliffe said of the Mendicant Orders, that no word of Christ can be found to justify their institution save that one—'I know you not' (Matthew xxv. 12). Many examples of Wycliffe's homely vernacular are already known from the *Trialogus*, as, *e.g.*, when he said of the Mendicants and their letters of brotherhood, that 'they sell the cat in a bag.'[4] Even in sermons he does not shun the use of such strong expressions; as when, in speaking of certain arguments which were used by the Mendicants to prove the pretended antiquity of their Orders (which was alleged, in the case of the Carmelites, to go back to the days of Elijah of Carmel, their founder), he characterises their argumentation as 'worse than the sophistry of apes.'[5]

He ridicules the monks.

Although the personality of Wycliffe comes out in his writings thus strongly, this by no means implies that he had any wish or

---

[1] *De Veritate Scripturae Sac.*, c. 22, fol. 199, col. 4; fol. 200, col. 1.
[2] *Dialogus*, or *Speculum Ecclesiae Militantis*, c. 23, MS. 1387, fol, 155, col. 2.
[3] *XXIV. Sermons*, No. IV., fol. 138, col. 3.
[4] *Trialogus*, III., c. 30, p. 352: *Videtur utique, quod fratres seminant deceptionem frivolam utrobique, et faciunt in facto magis fraudulentam commutationem, quam si venderent catum in sacco.*
[5] *Saints' Days Sermons*, No. VIII., fol. 5, col. 2: *Pejori quam simiali argutia arguunt quidam fratres*, etc.

design to put himself forward. On the contrary, he desires to place in the foreground One far higher than himself, the Lord Christ. His wish is to prepare the way for Him—as once did John the Baptist—his design is to promote God's glory and Christ's cause. In face of a reproach which one of his opponents had cast at him, that he set forth unusual views from a motive of ambition or of hostile feeling, he gives this solemn assurance in a passage already mentioned:—'Let God be my witness, that before everything I strive for God's glory and the good of the Church, from reverence of Holy Scripture, and adherence to the law of Christ.'[1] He has the consciousness, in all humility and in joyful confidence, that it is the cause of God, and of the cross and gospel of Christ, for which he fights and labours. And just because it is not with his own petty honour but with the honour of God that he has to do, he does not even hesitate in making some confessions from which otherwise a concern for his own personal credit would have held him back, *e.g.*, 'I confess that in my own case I have often, from a motive of vain ambition, departed from the doctrine of Scripture both in my reasonings and my replies, while my aim was to attain the show of fame among the people, and at the same time to strip off the pretensions of ambitious sophists.'[2] This consciousness that he was contending not for himself, but for God's honour and Christ's cause, was also the source of the joyful courage and the confident hope of final victory which filled his breast even in the menacing prospect of persecution; and, perhaps, even of an approaching death-blow to himself and his fellow-combatants. He grew holy himself with the holy aims which he pursued; his personal character was exalted by the cause which he served; and the cause which he served was never the truth as mere knowledge, but the truth as a power unto godliness. He has always and everywhere in view the moral kernel, 'the fruits;' not the leafage, but the fruit, is everything in his regard.[3] It was from glowing zeal for the cause of God, sincere love to the souls of men, upright conscientiousness before God, and heartfelt longing for the reformation of the Church of Christ, that he put forth all his energetic and indefatigable labours for the restoration of the Church to her original purity and freedom, in which she had flourished in the primitive Christian age.

Self-abnegation for Christ's sake.

---

[1] *De Veritate Scripturae Sac.*, c. 12, fol. 34, col. 4; *Testis sit mihi Deus, ego principaliter intendo honorem Dei et utilitatem ecclesiae*, etc.

[2] *Ib.*, c. 2, fol. 3, col. 1; comp. c. 5, fol. 11. col. 4; *vide* above, c. VII.

[3] Comp. *De Ecclesia*, c. 21, fol. 199, col. 2: *Ista irregularitas, qua magis attendimus ad folia quam ad fructus, creditur facere in oculis Dei sacramenta nostra vilescere.*

And what was the character of these reformation efforts of Wycliffe? This does not admit of being defined in simple and few words, and for this reason, that his reformation ideas passed through different transmutations and developments, precisely the same as those of his whole personality. Wycliffe, indeed, from the time when, in mature age, he entered upon public life and drew attention upon himself, down to the end of his career, was always inspired by the reformational spirit. That the Church as she then stood was suffering under evil conditions; that she stood in indispensable need of renovation and reform—this was and ever remained his firm conviction, and for this object he at all times continued to do what he could. But what the worst of these conditions were, and how they were to be remedied—on these points he thought differently at a later period from what he did in his earlier life. In middle life his reformational views bore an entirely ecclesiastico-political complexion; in the last six years of his course, from 1378, the political points of view retreated more into the background, and the religious motives came to the front. In the first twelve years of his public activity, the worst mischief of the Church appeared to him to be the usurpations of the Papacy upon the sovereign rights of the English Crown, the financial spoliation of the country for the benefit of the Curia in Avignon, the general secularisation of the clergy, including the monasteries and foundations, simony and the corruption of morals—all these evils were ecclesiastico-political matters; and accordingly the means and ways of remedying them which he recommended, and in part himself applied, were chiefly of an ecclesiastico-political character. State legislation and administrative measures were called for—it was the duty of Crown and Parliament, king and lords, to stem these evils, while he himself laboured to remove them by the light of knowledge, in the way of instruction, conviction, and admonition.

There was truth in all this; and yet the end aimed at was not to be reached in this way, for the weed was not plucked up by the root; with the best intentions, a wrong road was taken. Of this stage of Wycliffe's work, but only of this, what Luther said is true—that he attacked only the life of the Church, and not her doctrine. But in the last stage of his work Wycliffe undoubtedly went farther and dug deeper. The Church's doctrine as well as her life now engaged his attention, and in more than one article was emphatically assailed. His first step was to set forth with the utmost clearness, and to assert with the greatest decision, the fundamental principle that Holy Scripture alone is infallibly true and an absolute standard of truth. No one, for centuries, had so clearly recognised this truth, and established and defended it with such emphasis as Wycliffe. And not only did he learnedly and in a literary form maintain this Protestant principle, as we may well call it, but he also carried it into actual life, and practically applied it, by the institution of Biblical itinerant preaching, by the English translation of the Bible, as well as by Scripture commentaries and popular tracts. Wycliffe, however, did not stop with laying the foundation. With the Bible, as a touchstone, in his hand, he also examined several chief articles of the dominant theology of his time, found them to be untenable, and from that moment fought against them with all the fiery zeal of which he was capable: especially the doctrine of the sacraments, and in particular from the year 1381, the Romish-scholastic doctrine of the Lord's Supper, and chiefly the article touching Transubstantiation. That was an important piece of reformational criticism. But it was neither the only nor the most important piece, though it was the criticism which most forcibly arrested the attention of the world. Still weightier was the doctrine of Wycliffe touching Christ and the Church. That Christ alone is our Mediator, Saviour, and Leader, that He alone is the real and governing Head of His Church—this is what we may well call the *material principle* of the theology of Wycliffe, just as the sole authority of Holy Scripture may be called its *formal principle*. This fundamental principle of the sole mediation of Christ has an intimate connection with the evangelical doctrine of justification by faith alone; and while it is true that the setting forth of the latter doctrine by Luther was an immense advance beyond Wycliffe, a memorable deepening of insight, and a felicitous seizure of truth in the power of Divine light and guidance, to Wycliffe must still be attributed the prophetic thought—a thought of large reformational reach and bearing—of Christ alone as our Mediator and Saviour. With this harmonises his idea of the Church as the whole body of the elect. Indeed, this latter idea stands in the most profound connection with Wycliffe's fundamental view of Christ Himself. For that Augustinian conception of the Church forms with Wycliffe the conscious opposite to the clerical, hierarchical, and Popish idea of it; and it rests precisely upon the principle that the true Church is the Body of Christ. Proof enough all this, that Wycliffe examined and attacked not the life alone, but also the doctrine, of the Church of his time.

His doctrine concerning Christ.

Concerning the Church.

If we look back from Wycliffe in order to compare him with his Continental precursors, and to obtain a scale by which to measure his personal importance, the fact which first of all presents itself is, that Wycliffe exhibits in a concentrated form, in his own person, that reform movement of the preceding centuries which traced the corruption of the Church to its secularisation by means of worldly property, honour, and power; and which aimed to renew and improve its condition by leading it back to a state of apostolic poverty. *Concentrates former reforms.*

What after Gregory VII.'s time, Arnold of Brescia, and the community of the Waldenses, Francis of Assisi and the Mendicant Orders, had all in various ways aimed to effect; what St. Bernard of Clairvaux had so devoutly longed for— *His forerunners.* the return of the Church of Christ to an apostolic life and walk—the same object filled the soul of Wycliffe, in the first period of his public activity. The modern idea of the State as opposed to the hierarchical ideal, which began to dawn upon men's minds after the struggle between Boniface VIII. and Philip the Fair; which found in Marsiglio of Padua, John of Jandun, and William of Occam, its eloquent advocates and representatives, and which called forth so lively a sympathy among the English people in the middle of the 14th century—this idea was not only taken up by Wycliffe, but also utilised by him for the practical object of Church reform. In establishing and defending as a first principle the authority of Holy Scripture as the sole standard of Christian truth, and in practically labouring for Bible-reading and the spread of Biblical knowledge among the people, he was to some extent following in the footsteps of the Waldenses. But he does not appear to have been aware of this fact. There is nothing to show that he was indebted to them for any of his reforming ideas and methods; while it is certain that neither the Waldenses, nor any others before him, had asserted the authority of the Bible with a clearness, stringency, and emphasis equal to his.

In the collective history of the Church of Christ, Wycliffe marks an epoch chiefly on the ground that he was the earliest *personal embodiment* of the evangelical reformer. Before him, it is true, many ideas of reform and many efforts in the direction of it crop up here and there, which even led to conflicts of opinion and collisions of parties, and to the formation of whole reformed societies. But Wycliffe is the first important historical personage who devotes himself to the work of Church reform with the entire power of a master mind, and with the full force of will and joyful self-sacrifice of a man in Christ. To that work he devoted the labours of a life, in obedience to the earnest *The first evangelical reformer.*

pressure of conscience, and in confident trust that 'his labour was not in vain in the Lord.' He did not conceal from himself that the labours of 'evangelical men' would in the first instance be opposed and persecuted and driven back; but he consoled himself with the assurance that the ultimate issue would be a renovation of the Church upon the apostolic model. It was only after Wycliffe that other living embodiments of the spirit of Church reform, a Huss, a Savonarola, and others, appeared upon the field—a succession which issued at length in the Reformation of the sixteenth century.

THE CHAIR IN WHICH WYCLIFFE WAS CARRIED OUT OF LUTTERWORTH CHURCH WHEN STRICKEN WITH PARALYSIS, DEC. 28, 1384; STILL PRESERVED IN THE CHANCEL.

CHAPTER X.[1]

THE SUCCESSORS OF WYCLIFFE; AND SURVIVAL OF HIS INFLUENCE.

1.—The Lollards.

DURING the last years of Wycliffe's life his opponents evidently cherished the hope that his chief followers, already enfeebled and intimidated, would be hopelessly scattered after his death, and that the whole party would become extinct. Soon, however, it became plain that there was a life in the movement not at all dependent on the personality of Wycliffe. He was removed from the earthly scene; but his adherents continued his work with no appreciable diminution of energy.

It was in the year succeeding the death of Wycliffe (1385) that the name of LOLLARDS came into general use as a designation of his followers. It had its origin in the Netherlands early in the century, and seems to have been at first applied to the 'Brothers of St. Alexius,' or *fratres Cellitae*, who devoted themselves to works of love, in tending the sick and caring for the dead; but who exposed themselves to the imputation of bigotry and heresy. In England the name was occasionally heard during Wycliffe's lifetime;[2] but it was not until after his death that it became general. Its use by the hierarchy to characterise his followers is a proof to us that the 'Wycliffites' had become an independent sect, large enough to attract public attention, and formidable enough to arouse ecclesiastical animosity.[3]

The Lollard party, in the years immediately following Wycliffe's

---

[1] [Condensed from Dr. Lechler's Second Volume and Third Book, entitled *Die Nachwirkungen Wiclif's*: 'The aftereffects of Wycliffe;' with notes and additions from more recent authorities.]

[2] See ch. ix., § 5, p. 395, where the term is cited from the popish zealot Henry Crump, 1382. *Fasc. Zizan.*, p. 312: *vocavit haereticos Lollardos*.

[3] The origin of the title is obscure;

'Walter Lollard,' sometimes named as the founder of the sect, being as unhistorical a personage as 'Zadok,' the alleged founder of the Sadducees. Possibly the name comes from the Latin *lolium*, darnel or 'tares,' regarded as mingled with the pure 'wheat' of Catholic doctrine. Thus Knighton says of the Wycliffite itinerant preacher Aston, *ubique praedicans, lolium cum tritico seminavit*, col.

death, consisted, so to speak, of an inner and an outer circle. The former was composed of enthusiastic and able men, who in the first instance through the preaching of the itinerants, and subsequently through their own reading and study, had been led to the adoption of evangelical principles. Thus it seemed to them all the more necessary, after the death of their venerated, strong-souled leader, to maintain the closest bonds of alliance for mutual encouragement and a common defence against their enemies.[1]

Two classes of Lollards.

The outer and far larger circle comprised men and women, in different grades of society, who listened and read, learned and often believed. Many of these naturally passed into the inner circle, and became themselves the teachers of others. So numerous had the adherents of Wycliffe become during the period between his death and the close of the century that, according to the testimony of opponents, at least half the population had ranged themselves on the side of the Lollards.[2] 'You could scarcely meet two persons in the road, but one of them would be a disciple of Wycliffe.'

In the inner circle seven men stand pre-eminent, who formed the nucleus of the party—Nicholas of Hereford, John Aston, John Purvey, John Parker, William Swinderby, William Smith, and Richard Waytstathe. On the other hand, Philip Repyngdon, who had been allied with Wycliffe, Hereford, and Aston, at Oxford, in the proceed-

---

2659. Chaucer seems to recognise this derivation of the name, in his *Prologue to the Shipman's Tale*:

'This Loller here woll prechen us somewhat,
He woldë sow some difficultë,
Or springen cockle in oure clenë corn.'

More probably, as it seems to Dr. Lechler, the name was derived from the Old German *lollen, lullen*, 'to hum, or whine'; a satirical description of their tones. Thus Johann Hocsemius, Canon of Liège (1348) writes: *Eodem anno* (1309) *quidam hypocritae gyrovagi, qui Lollardi sive Deum laudantes vocabantur per Hannoniam et Brabantiam quasdam mulieres nobiles deceperunt. Gesta Pontificum Leodensium*, I., c. 31. If we are to follow Walsingham, this name of Lollards had been introduced into England seven years before the death of Wycliffe, as he writes of the itinerant preachers in the year 1377, *Ni vocabantur a vulgo Lollardi*. But in Riley's edition of Walsingham (*Historia Anglicana*, 1863) it is shown that this sentence is not in the original MS., but an editorial gloss in the first printed edition (Frankf., 1603). Knighton says, without assigning any date: *Sicque a vulgo Wyclyf discipuli et Wycliviani sive Lollardi vocati sunt.* The first instance of the official use of the name appears to be in a mandate of the Bishop of Worcester, 1387, which refers to five leaders and itinerant preachers of the party (Hereford, Aston, Purvey, Parker, and Swinderly) as *nomine seu ritu Lollardorum confoederati* (Wilkins, *Conc.*, III., 202). In 1389, in the records of a process instituted by the Bishop of Lincoln against certain heretics, these are spoken of as *Lollardi vulgariter nuncupati*. Hence again the phrase *lollardia sive haeretica pravitas*, 'techings that men clopith Lollards doctrin.' *Ib.*, III., 208.

[1] The mandate of the Bishop of Worcester, quoted in the preceding note, speaks of the five Wycliffites, not only as *confoederati*, but as *conspirati in collegio illicito*.

[2] See Knighton, col. 2644, *Mediam partem populi aut majorem partem sectae suae acquisiverunt;* and col. 2666, *Secta illa in maximo honore illis diebus habebatur, et in tantum multiplicata fuit, quod vix duos videres in via, quin alter eorum discipulus Wyclyffe fuerit.* So Walsingham, II., 188, under the year 1389, *Lollardi . . . in errorem suum plurimos seduxerunt.*

ings of 1382,[1] had been induced to recant, and became a persecutor of the Lollards. He was afterwards made Bishop of Lincoln (1405), and died a cardinal.

NICHOLAS OF HEREFORD, doctor of theology, Wycliffe's great helper in his Bible translation and other works, has been repeatedly mentioned in these pages.[2] After his return from Rome he is named first in a mandate of Henry Wakefield, Bishop of Worcester, against the Lollards (August 10, 1387), and is spoken of by Walsingham as chief of the party after Wycliffe's death.[3] His theological learning, as well as his indefatigable literary labours, with his zealous itinerancy, placed him for a time in the very front of the Wycliffe party.

<small>Nicholas Hereford.</small>

Next to Hereford stands JOHN ASTON, or Ashton, who, as we have already seen, had followed Philip Repyngdon in recantation; but who, unlike him, soon repented, and henceforth endeavoured by redoubled zeal to make amends for the error into which weakness and fear had betrayed him. In itinerant preaching he surpassed all others. The Bishop of Worcester, in the mandate above mentioned, couples Aston with Hereford. William Thorpe gives explicit testimony to Aston's constancy 'right perfectly unto his life's end.'

<small>John Aston.</small>

During the same period, one of the most steadfast, zealous, and distinguished of the party was JOHN PURVEY. In Wycliffe's lifetime he had been curate to the Reformer at Lutterworth, his coadjutor in the Bible translation, and in much literary work beside. On his master's death he undertook the revision of the Bible, and brought his task to a close in 1388. We must not, however, suppose that even this work absorbed his energies to the exclusion of more active labours. He too was a zealous itinerant preacher, and is included with Hereford and Aston in the mandate of Bishop Wakefield. Knighton speaks of these three, with Wycliffe himself, as the 'four arch heretics.' Purvey is depicted as a plain and homely man in person and garb, yet distinguished for mature wisdom and moral power.[4]

<small>John Purvey.</small>

After these 'first three' of Wycliffe's followers come four others,

---

[1] See above, ch. ix., § 5, pp. 390-400. Repyngdon's recantation was made Oct. 23, in the same year.

[2] See pp. 389, 393, 397, etc., and especially p. 401.

[3] *Hist. Angl.*, Riley, II., 159. *Nicolaus Hereford, Doctoris Theologiae gradum habens, sed seductoris sequens officium, quippe cui post haeresiarchum Johannem Wiclef omnes hujus sectae viri maxime adhaerebant*. On his alleged early recantation, see p. 400. He seems in the end to have relapsed, was an assessor at Brute's trial (p. 448), was made chancellor and treasurer of Hereford cathedral, and finally entered the Carthusian monastery at Coventry.

[4] The sad story of Purvey's recantation belongs to a later date. See p. 453.

also notable—PARKER and SMITH, SWINDERBY and WAYTSTATHE.

Less distinguished names. The first is to us but a name, save that he is included by the Bishop of Worcester in his letter of 1387. WILLIAM SMITH was a layman, whose picture has been drawn for us by the unfriendly hands of Knighton as that of a person uncomely and repulsive. A love-disappointment seems to have driven him to an ascetic life. Barefoot, he travelled and preached; having learned to read and write only in his maturer years. Altogether he illustrates the way in which some were drawn by irresistible force from the outer circle of adherents into the smaller class of leaders and champions of the cause.

WILLIAM SWINDERBY was a priest who had been designated by Wycliffe himself to the work of itinerancy. From his habits of life he was known as 'William the Hermit.'[1] So earnest and fearless was he in denouncing the luxuries and worldliness of the age that, as the Romish chronicler notes, even 'some honest men were well-nigh driven to despair.' When forbidden to preach in church or church-yard, 'he made a pulpit of two mill-stones in the High Street of Leicester, and there preached in defiance of the bishop.' 'There,' says Knighton, 'you might see throngs of people from every part, as well from the town as the country—double the number there used to be when they might hear him lawfully.'[2] With this 'William the Hermit' was associated 'Richard the Chaplain,' or RICHARD WAYTSTATHE, formerly attached to the Augustinian church at Leicester. These two took possession of a small chapel dedicated to John the Baptist outside the walls, where for some time they preached the Lollard doctrines.

In the outer circle of adherents the principal figures, down to the close of the reign of Richard II., were the Earl of Salisbury, Sir Thomas Latimer in Northamptonshire, Sir John Russell in Staffordshire, Sir Lewis Clifford Durham. This last it was who intervened at the Lambeth Council in 1378, by order of the Queen-mother, the Princess Joan, to protect Wycliffe from molestation.[3] To these names may be added[4] those of Sir Richard Story, Sir Reginald Hilton, of the county of Durham, and

Adherents to the Lollard cause.

---

[1] He is mentioned by Walsingham (*Hist. Angl.*, II., 53) as having preached at Leicester on Palm Sunday, 1382. *Inter quos* (Wycliffe's emissaries) *erat quidam vultum et habitum praeferens heremitae. ... Hic emissus per dictum Johannem, publice praedicavit Leycestriae, Dominica in Ramis Palmarum.*

[2] Col. 2662. 'Swinderby,' says Lechler, is to be distinguished from Robert Swinderby, mentioned in Bishop Wakefield's mandate.'

[3] See above, p. 172.

[4] See Walsingham, *Hist. Angl.*, II., 159 (year 1389). *Erant autem milites qui hanc sectam coluerunt*, etc.; also Knighton, col. 2661. *Erant enim milites—cum ducibus et comitibus ... promotores strenuissimi et propugnatores fortissimi*, etc.

Sir William Neville, third son of Lord Neville. A large number of citizens and wealthy persons also aided the Lollard cause by their influence and money. Most of their names have perished; those that remain have been preserved chiefly through the processes conducted against them by their persecutors. Among these we note Roger Dexter and his wife Alice, Nicholas Taylor, Michael Scrivener, John Harry, William Parchmener, and Roger Goldsmith, with a nun, by name Matilda, who lived as a recluse in a room in St. Peter's churchyard, Leicester.[1]

The statistics of the Lollards can hardly be accurately given; nor can we obtain more than a general view of their progress in different parts of England. Naturally, they most abounded in Wycliffe's own diocese of Lincoln, which then included Leicester and Lutterworth, and extended (until 1539) as far as Oxford.[2] *Statistics and extent of the movement.* Eight persons were apprehended in Leicester in 1389 on the charge of Lollardry, and these no doubt represented a multitude of others whose names are lost. The Leicester chronicler, Knighton, as we have seen, represents the Lollards as amounting to half the population. Eastwards the sect spread to Norwich, and in a south-easterly direction to London. To the south and west, the diocese of Salisbury contained Lollard priests, the bishop complaining in 1389 that several holding these doctrines had obtained ordination.[3] The mandate of the Bishop of Worcester against Lollard teaching has already been quoted. In the principality of Wales also, at least in the southern dioceses of St. David's and Llandaff, there were itinerant Lollard preachers in 1390.[4] From these facts we can hardly doubt that the sect had penetrated into other dioceses, and that the doctrines had widely spread throughout the land.

If we inquire concerning the inner life of the Lollard community, we learn little or nothing from Church history, but much from the incidental references of the chroniclers. They were, above all, characterised by a striving after holiness, a *Inner life of the Lollards.* zeal for the spread of Scriptural truth, for the uprooting of prevalent error, and for Church reform. Even the common people among them were men who *believed;* and they communicated, as by a sacred contagion, their convictions to those around them. Thus they became mighty.

Religious tracts had much to do with the dissemination of their doctrines. Besides Wycliffe, Hereford and others prepared many of

---

[1] Wilkins, *Concilia*, III., 208, 211.
[2] It should be noticed that it was probably during Wycliffe's incumbency of Ludgarshall (see above, p. 190) that he first sent forth his 'poor priests.' Lollards abounded in Buckinghamshire.
[3] Walsingham, *Hist. Angl.*, II., 188.
[4] Wilkins, *Concilia*, III., 215.

these short treatises, which were copied and widely distributed.[1]

Literary aids. But above all the translation of the Bible became a power. It was largely circulated not only in a complete form, but in separate books; and wherever it was known an impulse was given to the Lollard doctrines. Among the MSS. of the Wycliffe Bible that have survived the ravages of time and come into the hands of the most recent editors, no fewer than twelve are of an earlier date than 1400.[2] Some of these are very costly, showing that the precious volume was sought by the richer classes.

The Wycliffe Bible.

The Bible being thus made a comparatively familiar book, great stress was laid upon the exposition of its contents by preaching. Staff in hand, the preachers journeyed on foot from place to place,[3] and paused wherever they could obtain a hearing from gentle or simple. Knighton says: 'When an itinerant preacher arrived at the residence of some knight, the latter immediately with great willingness set about calling together the country people to some appointed place or church in order to hear the sermon; even if they did not care about going, they did not dare to stay away, or to object. For the knight was always at the preacher's side, armed with sword and shield, ready to protect him should any one dare to oppose in any way his person or his doctrine.'

Lollard preaching.

Of the character of the sermons Knighton says: 'Their teaching was at the beginning full of sweetness and devotion; but towards the end it broke out into jealousy and calumny. Nobody, they said, was upright and pleasing to God who did not hold the Word of God as they preached it; for thus in all their preaching did they hold up God's Law.'[4]

---

[1] A royal ordinance of 1388 sets forth that Master Nicholas Hereford and Master John Wycliff while he lived, *quosdam libros, libellos, schedulas* (fly-sheets) *et quaternos* (pamphlets) *diversas haereses et errores continentes, per se et fautores suos frequentius scribi, compilari, communicari et publicari fecerunt.* Wilkins, *Concilia*, p. 204. In the year 1396 several Lollards were made on their recantation to promise, 'Ne I shall her (their) books ne swych (such) books, ne hem (themselves) resceyve,' etc. *Ib.*, p. 225.

[2] See list in Forshall and Madden's *Wycliffite Versions*, vol. I., p. xxxix. These learned editors say, 'The new version was eagerly sought after, and read. Copies passed into the hands of all classes of the people. . . . The multiplication of copies must have been rapid. Nearly one hundred and fifty MSS., containing the whole or parts of Purvey's Bible, the majority of which were written within the space of forty years from its being finished, have been examined for the present edition. Others are known to have existed within the last century; and more, there can be no doubt, have escaped inquiry. How many have perished, it is impossible to calculate.' (p. xxxii.). See above, p. 221.

[3] See above, p. 197.

[4] Compare Wilkins, *Concilia*, p. 202. *Sub magnae sanctitatis velamine venenum sub labiis ore melliffuo habentes—devotionis fidelium, ecclesiae Christi et ejus ministris solitas conferri, ab iisdem subtrahere et ipsis appropriare nituntur—et haereticas propositiones, tam in ecclesiis et earum coemeteriis quam in plateis et plurimis locis profanis — non verentur et publice praedicare, et secrete in aulis, cameris, hortis et gardinis* (gardens) *Christi fideles utriusque sexus auriculari,*' etc.

The Romish historian, Lingard, alleges that these sermons were mainly controversial; but here he is confuted by the testimony of the chroniclers. Even bishops recognised some good in their sermons, baited as they were with allurements to win souls to salvation. *Lingard's error.*

The preaching, be it remembered, was in English; and the preachers were mainly of the same class as their hearers: their homely expositions of Scripture went home to the heart; they spoke, moreover, of prevailing sins and evils, as luxury and the like; they called by their right names the misdeeds of the clergy, while for themselves they sought nothing. It is no wonder that these travelling preachers stirred the land, and that the minds of men were attracted to them in a continually augmenting degree. *Effect of the preaching.*

Besides these open-air gatherings, assemblies were convened in halls and cottages, in chapels, in gardens. Here and there a little company would assemble to converse on Divine things, to build one another up in faith and knowledge.[1] At such meetings the Bible in Wycliffe's translation would be read aloud, or a tract by Wycliffe or Hereford, explaining the sacred text. Even the art of reading would be taught on such occasions. It was thus, as we have seen, that William Smith of Leicester first learned his alphabet. Many others, men and women, anxious to read the Scriptures for themselves, would follow his example. Knighton bitterly complains that the Word of God translated into English 'becomes more accessible and familiar to laymen and to women able to read than it had heretofore been to the most intelligent and learned of the clergy.' *Different services, Bible reading.*

2.—Controversies between the Lollards and their Opponents before 1399.

DURING the last fifteen years of the century the Lollards remained firm, united, and progressive. They quitted the defensive attitude, and adopted active measures for the extension and consolidation of their body. Especially did they assume the right to ordain, holding that every priest had as much power in this matter as the bishops themselves.[2]

An occurrence in London, in the year 1387, which excited considerable attention, is a significant indication of the temper of the times.

---

[1] Wilkins, *Concilia*, III., 211. *Mutuo inter se habuerunt et tenuerunt opiniones.*
[2] Walsingham, *Hist. Angl.*, II., 188. *Lollardi tantum praesumpserunt audaciam, ut eorum presbyteri more pontificum novos crearent presbyteros: practicaverunt istam perfidiam in diocesi Sarum.*

One Peter Pateshull, an Augustinian friar, having quitted the cloister and attached himself to the Lollards, began to preach against the monastic life, declaring that the life of a citizen was holier and more complete. Not only so, but in sermons at St. Christopher's Church he began to inveigh against the character of his late associates, making dark disclosures as to the conduct of the friars. This aroused bitter animosity, and a party of twelve Augustinians sallied forth from their monastery to the church, one of whom arose in the congregation and contradicted the preacher. But the Lollards, who happened to be present to the number of about a hundred, attacked the bold friar and drove him, with his brethren, from the church, chasing them to their monastery, which they would have set on fire had not one of the sheriffs of London interfered to calm their violence. The Lollards, however, induced Pateshull to write down the substance of his sermon, with an account of what he knew concerning the friars. The document laid the gravest charges against the Augustinians, including even murder. This writing was affixed to St. Paul's Cathedral, where it was read and copied by many knights and citizens who adhered to the Lollard party.[1]

In 1391, we learn from Walsingham, the Lollards preached against pilgrimages. But their boldest measure was taken in 1395, when they presented to Parliament, through Sir Thomas Latimer and Sir Richard Story, a document in which their doctrines were clearly enunciated, and the help of the legislature claimed in effecting many needed reforms. It is possible that this petition was a counter movement against the Romish party, by whom a bill had been brought in five years previously, but not passed, for the confiscation of all copies of the English Scriptures that might be found in the hands of the common people. It was John of Gaunt who, with something of his old spirit, had thwarted this measure, exclaiming, 'Let us not be the dregs of all nations, seeing that others are likewise translating the Word of God into their own language!' From this emphatic speech, and the failure of the Romish proposals, the Lollards may have anticipated a favourable reception for their plea. But they were disappointed. Their petition does not appear to have been even considered by Parliament. It was, however, fixed to the doors of St. Paul's, of Westminster Abbey, and of other churches. The bishops, dismayed by the daring of the Lollards, hastily sent a deputation to Richard II., who was then in Ireland. Thomas Arundel, Archbishop of York, and Robert Braybrook, Bishop of

---

[1] See Walsingham, *Hist. Angl.*, II., 157; followed by Foxe, *Acts and Mon.*, III., 201.

London, undertook the mission. The king immediately returned and addressed to the patrons of the Lollards, in particular to Sir Richard Story, such threatening language as for the time overawed and disheartened the party.

The conclusions which the followers of Wycliffe thus laid before Parliament and publicly displayed were briefly as follows :—[1] *The Lollard 'Conclusions.'*

1. Since the Church of England has begun to dote on temporalities after her stepmother of Rome, faith, hope, and charity have fled, and pride, with her dolorous genealogy of mortal sins, has usurped their place.

2. The customary priesthood which began in Rome, and claims more than angelic authority, is not the priesthood which Christ ordained to His apostles.

3. The priestly law of celibacy is the source of grave and shameful evils.

4. The pretended miracle of the sacrament of bread leads almost all men into idolatry. Would to God that they believed what the 'Evangelical Doctor' says in his *Trialogus*, that the bread of the altar is, 'habitualiter,'[2] the body of Christ !

5. Exorcisms and benedictions, wrought on wine, bread, water, oil, salt, wax, incense, as upon altar stones and church walls, and on robes, mitres, crosses, staves, belong to the arts of necromancy rather than to a sound theology.

6. King and bishop in one person—prelate and secular judge— pastor and worldly functionary—is a union adverse to the true interests of the kingdom. 'No man can serve two masters.'

7. The offering of special[3] prayers in our Church for the souls of the dead is a false foundation of charity.

8. Pilgrimages, prayers, and oblations made to blind crosses or 'roods,' and to deaf images of wood and stone, are nearly related to idolatry, and far from true charity.

9. Auricular confession, declared to be so necessary to a man's salvation, exalts the pride of priests and gives them opportunity of

---

[1] There are two extant MSS. of this document, one in the British Museum (Cotton, Cleopatra E. 2), the other, which seems the original, in the Bodleian Library at Oxford. The Latin text is printed by Lewis, *Hist. of John Wiclif*, p. 337, Wilkins, *Concilia*, III., p. 221, and Shirley, *Fasc. Ziz.*, p. 360. Foxe gives an English translation, *Acts and Mon.* (Pratt and Stoughton), III., p. 203. Bale says the paper was drawn up by Lord Cobham.

[2] [Others read *accidentaliter* (so Foxe). The meaning is evidently to deny the miracle of transubstantiation, while recognising 'the Lord's body' as present only in a spiritual sense. The reference is to *Trialogus* IV., c. 7, p. 267. *Ille panis est secundum habitudinem corpus Christi:* 'to be taken figuratively as the body of Christ.' Comp. p. 353 above.]

[3] The Latin MSS. read *spirituales*—an evident mistake for *speciales*.

secret conferences, leading to much evil. They say that they have the keys of heaven and hell, that they can bless or excommunicate, bind or loose at their pleasure, insomuch that for a small reward,[1] or for twelve pence, they will sell the blessing of heaven by charter and clause of warranty sealed with their common seal.

10. Manslaughter, by war or pretended law of justice for any temporal cause without a spiritual revelation, is expressly contrary to the New Testament, which is a law of grace and full of mercy. For Christ teaches to love our enemies.

11. Vows of chastity taken in our Church by women, who are by nature frail and imperfect, is the occasion of great and horrible sins.

12. The multitude of unnecessary arts practised in our kingdom nourishes much sin in waste, luxury, and showy apparel.[2] It seems to us that the trade of goldsmiths, of armourers, and all arts not necessary to men according to apostolic rule, should be suppressed for the increase of virtue.

Whatever may be thought of these several 'conclusions,' it is evident that the spirit of Wycliffe lived in his followers; while the fearlessness which could lay such a document before the Parliament and people of England attests the hold which the doctrines of the Lollards had secured upon the public mind. It was the culmination of their power. The hierarchy was now thoroughly alarmed, and the suppression of the sect was henceforth made a matter of ecclesiastical concern.

Another instructive illustration of the character of the Lollard teachings may be found in the story of Walter Brute, as related at length by Foxe.[3] The account of his pleadings before John Gilbert, Bishop of Hereford, in 1391-2, shows how fully the main doctrines of Wycliffe in regard to the supremacy of Scripture, the sole headship of Christ in the Church, and the figurative character of the Lord's Supper, were still maintained.[4] At the same time Walter Brute varies from Wycliffe in some important respects, showing the direction in which the great Reformer's doctrines would

Walter Brute.

---

[1] Lat., *bussello*.
[2] MS. *Curiositate et inter disguysyng*.
[3] *Acts and Monuments*, vol. III., pp. 131–188.
[4] Pages 136, 186, 'If any man, of what state, sect, or condition soever he be, will show me that I err in my writings or sayings, by the authority of the Sacred Scripture or by probable reason grounded on the Sacred Scripture, I will humbly and gladly receive his information.' P. 165, 'The head of the body of the Church is one, which is Christ.' P. 174, 'As Christ said, "I am very bread," not changing His essence or being into the essence or substance of bread, but was the said Christ which He was before really, and yet bread by a similitude or figurative speech, so if He would, it might be, when He said, "This is My body," but it should really have been the bread as it was before, and sacramentally or memorially to be His body. And this seemeth to me most nearly to agree to the meaning of Christ, forasmuch as He said, "Do this in remembrance of Me."'

naturally be developed. Thus we find in Brute a much clearer and sharper distinction than in Wycliffe between Law and Gospel—a decidedly nearer approach to Luther's doctrine of Justification by Faith.[1] The interpretations of the Apocalypse, which occupy so large a place in the statements of the later Confessor, are also a great advance on Wycliffe's teaching. Brute was fervid and mystical, perhaps, in part, from his Celtic nationality. 'I am,' he said, 'a Christian of the Britons, having my origin from the Britons, both by my father's and mother's side.'[2] He lays, accordingly, great stress upon the fact that the Gospel came direct from the East to Britain, not by way of Italy or Rome; 'and thus it seemeth to me the Britons, amongst other nations, have been, as it were, by the special election of God, called and converted to the faith.'

Another testimony to the thoughts and characteristic habits of the Lollards may be gathered from a poem which obtained great currency during the later years of the fourteenth century, and which was printed in 1542, in an edition of Chaucer's *Canterbury Tales*, under the title of *The Plowman's Tale*. It is certain, however, from the style and other considerations, that the poem cannot be by Chaucer. It is true that he translated and incorporated in his work *The Romance of the Rose*, in which ecclesiastical pretensions are ridiculed; but the tone and method of *The Plowman's Tale* are altogether different. It is plainly modelled upon *The Vision of Piers Plowman*,[3] written at least forty years before. The *Tale* is allegorical—a dialogue between a pelican[4]—emblem of the true Church—and a griffin, symbolising the cruelty and greed of the hierarchy.[5]

The poem relates with a kind of grim humour how the griffin, being defeated in argument, flies off, but presently returns with a flock of birds—ravens, crows, kites, hawks, and the like. The pelican is compelled to flee, but soon returns in the form of a mighty phœnix, puts the griffin and its company to flight, follows them, and dashes them without mercy to the ground. It is an almost prophetic glimpse of the apparent defeat of the Lollard movement, followed by the

The 'Plowman's Tale.'

---

[1] P. 147, 'The law of Christ is charity;' 150, 'Christ did not, by the works of the law, justify the believers in Him, but by grace justified them from their sins. And so did Christ fulfil that by grace which the law could not by justice;' 173, 'By the faith which we have in Christ, believing Him to be the true Son of God, who came down from heaven to redeem us from sin, we are justified from sin, and so do live by Him who is the true bread and meat of the soul.'

[2] P. 136, compare 142, 144.
[3] See above, ch. I., § 7, p. 70.
[4] The pelican was a favourite mediæval emblem of redemption by sacrifice; the fable being that the mother bird feeds her young with her own blood.
[5] The poem is printed in Wright's *Political Poems and Songs relating to English History* (Rolls Series), vol. I., pp. 304-346.

phœnix-like reappearance of its spirit as the animating power of the Reformation.

Piers Plowman's Creed is another popular poem of the same period, possibly by the same author; the argument of it being that *Piers Plowman's Creed* of a man seeking truth, who visits the four Mendicant Orders in succession, and, being repelled by their pride and other vices, learns at last the evangelical doctrine from a ploughman's lips.[1]

3.—Position of the Lollards at the close of the Century.

ARCHBISHOP COURTENAY, the determined opponent of Wycliffe and his followers, died in 1396, and Thomas Arundel was promoted from *Arundel Archbishop.* York to Canterbury. One of the first measures of this prelate was to convene a provincial synod (February, 1397) to deal especially with Wycliffe's doctrines as maintained in the *Trialogus.* Eighteen articles were selected for condemnation, of which the first three refer to the Eucharist, the fourth to baptism— *Synod against Wycliffe's doctrines.* especially infant baptism—the fifth to confirmation, the sixth to priestly ordination and the different grades of the hierarchy, the seventh, eighth, and ninth to matrimony, the fourteenth to extreme unction. The 'Seven Sacraments' of the Romish Church were thus treated in succession, that of penance only excepted. The remaining articles refer partly to ecclesiastical offices and possessions, partly to worldly government, as conditioned by the character of its possessors, and partly to the foundations of belief as resting on the absolute authority of the Scriptures, and to the doctrine of necessity. The opinions of Wycliffe on all these points were condemned, and the task of a formal, scientific *Woodford's Tractate.* refutation was committed to a learned Franciscan, William Woodford, an old opponent of Wycliffe. His treatise was entitled, *A Tractate against the Errors of Wycliffe in the Trialogus.*[2]

Such scholastic dissertations were but the prelude to more active proceedings. As yet the courts had taken no measures against the Wycliffites. We find, indeed, that so early as 1387 Parliament had

---

[1] Published by Pickering, London, 1856; and in the *Early English Text Society* series: Appendix to 'The Vision of Piers Plowman.'

[2] This treatise was first printed in the collection of the Jesuit Ortuin Gratius, *Fasciculus rerum*, etc., 1535, re-edited by Brown, 1690. See above, p. 4. Gratius is very emphatic in his description of the pamphlet. *Guil. Widefordi contra Johannem Wiclephum, sacrae fidei pestem et haeresiarcham, doctissimae et plane Catholicae decertationes, quibus miserum hunc hominem ita confutat, prosternit, eviscerat, ac in omnibus vincit, ut ex illis ipsis omnes ferme nostri temporis haereticos mutos effeceris!* (Index to the ed. of 1535.)

issued a mandate against the Lollards, and that in 1388 a royal ordinance was issued to the town and county of Nottingham, in which the king, assuming the position of 'defender of the Catholic faith,'[1] commanded his subjects to repress the errors of Wycliffe; but there seems to have been no result of all this until 1396, when four men from Nottingham[2] were compelled to recant the Lollard doctrines before the king's court of justice. Active measures begun against the Lollards.

But the attention of all parties was now turned to the impending revolution. In 1397 the archbishop was banished the kingdom on the charge of complicity with his brother, the Earl of Arundel, in treasonable designs; and Roger of Walden was installed at Canterbury. In 1399 Richard was deposed, and the Duke of Lancaster, the son of John of Gaunt, ascended the throne under the title of Henry the Fourth.[3] Thomas Arundel was reinstated, and the persecution of the Lollards entered upon a new phase. It was to the hierarchy that the House of Lancaster owed its elevation to the throne, and the king must repay their assistance by the unscrupulous and sanguinary repression of their foes. Deposition of Richard II.

4.—Persecution of the Lollards.

THE king and the hierarchy were now at one; and for the first time in the history of England the sword of secular authority was drawn for the suppression of religious opinion. Bloody was the persecution that followed; and the 'red rose' of Lancaster, in more senses than one, proved the appropriateness of the epithet. John of Lancaster had been Wycliffe's friend; his son, Henry of Lancaster, becomes the first and bitterest persecutor of Wycliffe's disciples.

A royal message was sent to the first Convocation summoned in the new reign (October 6, 1399), to the effect that the king would remit the exactions on ecclesiastical personages which his predecessors had been wont to make: he would always maintain the rights and freedom of the Church, and employ force, if needful, against all heresies and heretics; he only asked an interest in the prayers of the clergy. To this message Thomas Arundel, Archbishop of Canterbury, returned a grateful reply in the name of his brethren, presenting at the same time a memorial setting forth the offensive activity of the Lollards, and praying for strong measures against them. In reply, an Act was passed which gave the The king and Convocation.

[1] Wilkins, *Concilia*, III., 204.
[2] *Ib.*, p. 225.
[3] Richard II. deposed in favour of Henry of Lancaster, Sept. 30, 1399: murdered in Pontefract Castle, February 14, 1400.

bishops power to arrest all persons commonly reported to be heretics to require them to clear themselves of the charge, and, should they fail to do this, to punish them with imprisonment.

This enactment, however, was not strong enough for the emergency, and in the next year the infamous Act *de haeretico comburendo* was placed upon the statute book of England. By this law bishops were as before empowered to arrest and imprison; but authority was further given them to hand over persistent or relapsed heretics to the civil officers, 'to be by them burned on a high place before the people.'[1]

Statute for the burning of heretics.

Such was the first step in English legislation in that war to the death with so-called heresy, in which the secular and ecclesiastical authorities for many generations joined fraternal hands. Nor was the statute suffered for an instant to remain a dead letter. In the same year proceedings against two of the Lollard party were instituted before Convocation. Both were in priests' orders. One of them was the well-known John Purvey, the other was named William Sawtree.

This Sawtree had been parish priest at St. Margaret's, Lynn, where he was charged with heresy in 1399, and made a recantation before Spencer, Bishop of Norwich. He was now priest of St. Osyth in London, and was charged before Convocation with relapse. His first hearing was on February 12, 1401. He then asked time to consider his defence, which was granted. At the second meeting, February 18th, he put in a written answer on the points in dispute, in which he attempted to vindicate his position by subtle scholastic distinctions, but conceded nothing.[2] This led to a two days' discussion chiefly on the Eucharist, as the result of which the archbishop in the name of Convocation pronounced Sawtree a heretic, while on account of his former recantation he was adjudged relapsed and incorrigible. On February 24, being conducted to St. Paul's, he was solemnly degraded from office, viz., divested of his priestly robes and deprived of the tonsure; being then handed to the king's marshal. The royal mandate to the mayor and sheriffs of London commanding execution was issued on February 21, and early in March Sawtree was burned in Smithfield before a crowd of spectators. Sawtree was the first of the Lollard martyrs. A fire is always easier to kindle than to extinguish. When once the spark is kindled the flame of

Sawtree the first Lollard martyr.

---

[1] Wilkins, *Concilia*, III., 254. *Personas illas coram populo in eminenti loco comburi faciant, ut hujusmodi punitio metum incutiat mentibus aliquorum.*

[2] The document is given in Foxe, III., p. 223.

fanaticism burns high in the minds of men and seeks continually new victims.

Meantime John Purvey had escaped by recantation. The *auto da fé* of Sawtree appears to have made a terrible impression upon him, and to have shaken his resolution. On March 5, before the archbishop's commissioners, the Bishops of Bangor and Rochester, accompanied by several doctors, he recanted his opinions and submitted himself unconditionally to the archbishop and his council. On the next day, Sunday, March 6, he publicly read his recantation in English at St. Paul's Cross, enumerating seven alleged errors, which he publicly renounced.[1] It should be added as at least probable that Purvey, whose fall spread grief and consternation among the Lollards, subsequently returned to the evangelical party, as in the year 1421 he was again proceeded against by Archbishop Chichely.

<small>Purvey recants.</small>

From 1401 the work of the new Inquisition went rapidly forward. Inquiries against the Lollards were instituted in London and the neighbouring diocese of Rochester, in Oxford, Nottingham, Wigston, near Leicester, throughout the diocese of Norwich, and in the West of England as far as Bristol and its neighbourhood, as well as in Worcester. It was from this last-mentioned diocese that the next victim was taken. John Badby, tailor, of Evesham, was arraigned before the bishop in 1409 on the charge of holding heresies concerning the Lord's Supper, and on March 1, 1410, was further examined before a commission in London, Arundel again presiding. The tailor, remaining firm in the rough common-sense way in which he repudiated transubstantiation, was condemned as a persistent and incorrigible heretic, and was handed over on March 5 to the civil authorities with the hypocritical request that he might not be put to death! On the same day, however, at the king's warrant, hurriedly prepared, Badby was led out to Smithfield, and chained in a cask which was set upon a heap of wood. At that moment the Prince of Wales ('Prince Hal'), afterwards Henry the Fifth, approached the spot. Touched with compassion, he entreated the poor man to recant; but in vain. The Prior of St. Bartholomew now advanced in procession with the host, preceded by twelve torch-bearers, and offered it to the martyr's view. Badby exclaimed, 'It is consecrated bread, and not the body of God.' At a signal, the cask was overturned and the pile ignited. When Badby felt the flame he cried out, *Mercy!* (an appeal to God, and not to man!) The Prince was shocked, ordered

<small>Spread of persecution.</small>

<small>John Badby.</small>

---

[1] See Foxe, III., 286.

the fire to be extinguished and the cask to be removed. For the second time pardon was offered, with promises of money and favour on condition of recantation, but stoutly refused ; and Badby, thrust once more into the cask, endured his fate with unconquered fortitude.

When such scenes could be enacted, it was scarcely wonderful that many persons were terrified into recantation. Others languished and died in prison. But several, in many places, suffered on the funeral pile. Nor was this the case in England only: in Scotland one John Resby, a Wycliffite from England, was burned in the year 1407.[1]

Other confessors and martyrs.

Only one man need be further mentioned under this section. William Thorpe [2] had been for twenty years an itinerant preacher, partly in the North of England, partly in other districts, when in the year 1397 he was apprehended in London, but was set free on the banishment of Archbishop Arundel. In 1407 he was again seized and committed at first to prison at Shrewsbury. Afterwards the archbishop sent for him to his palace in Saltwood, Kent, to interrogate him in person. The examinations were repeated and protracted, sometimes conducted in an inquisitorial and hostile tone, sometimes in a mild and almost confidential manner. His friends visited him from time to time, and received from him written memoranda of the interviews with the archbishop, which they carefully kept. In the sixteenth century these most interesting records were published by William Tyndale, the Bible translator, and became a favourite manual with the earlier adherents of the Reformation. The book was prohibited [3] with others by royal proclamation in 1530, but has been preserved entire by John Foxe, both in Latin and English, and may be read in his *Acts and Monuments*.[4]

William Thorpe.

This work is in the highest degree attractive, not only on account of the instructive matter contained in it, but also because of the naïve simplicity of the way in which the subject is treated. The reader is amazed at the presence of mind and calmness, the clearness, warmth, and decision with which the prisoner answers the questions put to him in various tones by the archbishop ; and it is impossible to help admiring greatly the deep spiritual gladness which animated this steadfast witness for Christ. In consequence of Thorpe's obstinate refusal to submit to the authority of the Church, and his reiterated assertion

Character of Thorpe's replies.

---

[1] Hetherington, *History of the Church of Scotland* (2nd ed., 1842), p. 30.
[2] See Thorpe's testimony to Wycliffe above, p. 191.
[3] Under the title: *The Examination of William Thorpe*. Wilkins, III., 739.
[4] Pratt and Stoughton's Edition, vol. III., pp. 250–282.

that he would only follow the teaching that he found in the Word of God, the archbishop at last delivered him up. The history of his fate is unknown to us. He could hardly have been allowed to go free, and yet there is no evidence that he was burned as a persistent heretic. It is most probable that he was secretly despatched by hunger or strangling in prison. We know that he dreaded the latter as his probable fate, for in his will, which is also preserved to us, he makes this declaration: 'To witness to the truth of my convictions I am ready in humility and joy to suffer my poor body to be persecuted where God wills, and by whom, and when, and for how long a time, and to endure whatever punishment and death that He sees fit, to the honour of His name, and to the building up of the Church.' He finally requests all believers who read or listen to his testimony to pray for him—'that grace, wisdom, and knowledge may be given to me from above, so that I may end my life in the Truth for which I have witnessed, and in its cause, in true faith, steadfast hope, and perfect love.'

5.—Proceedings at Oxford, 1406-1414.

THERE has come down to us, under date October 6, 1406, a remarkable document, purporting to be the testimony of the University of Oxford concerning Wycliffe, occasioned by the report, then current in Bohemia and other European countries, that the English prelates had pronounced him a heretic, and ordered his bones to be exhumed and burned.

'The conduct of Wycliffe,' it is said in this document,[1] 'even from tender years to the time of his death, was so praiseworthy and honourable that never at any time was there any offence given by him, nor was he aspersed with any note of infamy or sinister suspicion; but in answering, reading, preaching, determining, he behaved himself laudably; and, as a valiant champion of the truth, he vanquished by proofs from Holy Scripture and according to the Catholic faith those who by wilful beggary blasphemed the religion of Christ. Never was this Doctor convicted of heretical pravity, nor was he delivered by

---

[1] The Latin original is printed in Wilkins, *Concilia*, III., p. 302. Huss and Jerome of Prague, *Historia et Monumenta*, II., p. 366; Lewis, *History of Wiclif*, p. 343; Höfler, *Concilia Pragensia* (1862), p. 53. After a preamble, the document reads, *Quia etiam sagax humanae naturae discretio hominum crudelitate pensata contra blasphemantes alternos insultus, hunc modum referendi, et hunc clypeum defensionis instituit, ut, cum vocale testimonium ubique adesse non potest, suppleat calamus per scripturam; hinc est, quod specialis benevolentiae animum ac teneritatis curam super Universitatis nostrae quondam filio Joanne Wicleff, sacrae Theologiae Professore secundum morum suorum exigentiam possidentes, corde, voce, et Scriptura suas conditiones in vita laudabiles fuisse attestamur.* Then follows the paragraph translated above.

our prelates to be burned after his burial. For God forbid that our bishops should have condemned so good and upright a man as a heretic, who in all the University had not his equal, as they believed, in his writings on logic, philosophy, theology, ethics, and the speculative sciences.'

This document was issued in the name of the chancellor and regents of the University, and sealed with the University seal, after which it was transmitted to Bohemia and other places, and seems to have been held unquestioned until the year 1411. It was then stigmatised by the Convocation of the Province of Canterbury as *literae falsitatis;* and afterwards at the Council of Constance the allegation was made that the document was a forgery by Wycliffe's friends, one Peter Payne [1] having clandestinely obtained the seal of the University. It must be observed, however, that this was not the statement of the Convocation. The phrase employed by them appears simply to mean that the *contents* of the paper were false and heretical. Had the Convocation desired to say that the seal had been abstracted and the paper forged, they would have adopted different phraseology; as when in another part of their proceedings they speak of a spurious register of ordination as *instrumentum pretensum*. The idea of forgery seems altogether an after-thought. Again, the statement of the Convocation that the principal members of the University did not take part in the affair, must be received with caution, as this might really mean only that the Romish members were outvoted by the Wycliffites. The contents of the document are certainly in favour of its genuineness;[2] for the spirit which it expresses was assuredly widely diffused in the Oxford of 1406 among influential personages of the University. Convocation itself complains of the errors prevalent among the leaders. In the year 1408 Archbishop Arundel, in a visitation of all the colleges, declares that 'this University, which once was a juicy vine, and brought forth its branches for the glory of God and the advancement of His Church, now brings forth wild grapes; and so it comes to pass that the unfruitful doctrines of the Lollards so increase in the land.' It was hereupon ordained that the heads of houses should *every month* carefully ascertain whether any of their inmates, whether graduates or undergraduates,

Side notes: Its genuineness impugned. Reasons for accepting it.

---

[1] This Payne was Vice-Principal of St. Edmund's Hall in Oxford, 1410-1415. He afterwards went to Bohemia, and in 1433 appeared at the Council of Basle as delegate of the Hussites; he died at Prague, 1455 (Foxe, vol. III., p. 814).

[2] It should in fairness be stated that Neander (*Church History*, vol. IX., p. 331, Clark's Eng. Ed.) regards the document as decidedly spurious. 'The seal of the University,' says Neander, 'was much abused in those days.' Why, then, did not the Convocation at once declare the paper to be a forgery?

had asserted or defended any tenets at variance with the doctrines of the Church. Every offender was to be first warned; if persisting, he was to be excommunicated, and to be expelled the college and University.[1] These mandates, it is true, were for a time disregarded, and in 1411 the archbishop again visited the University in person to enforce them. His determination proved at length effectual. In 1412 the principal men in the University were Papist in belief and reactionary in tone; the governing body transmitted to the archbishop and his suffragans *two hundred and sixty-seven propositions*, taken from thirteen treatises of Wycliffe, which they found erroneous and heretical. Two years later, in 1414, just after the accession of King Henry the Fifth, the University presented a memorial to His Majesty in which it was promised to use all zeal for the arrest and punishment of the Lollards. So signal was the reaction. A little while before the prelates had been compelled to put forth great endeavours to bring the University into the track of orthodoxy; now the University itself becomes the tool of the bishops for the work of inquisition! From this time Oxford appears to have repudiated the Wycliffe party, and to have become wedded to the Papal scholasticism. It was but thirty years after the death of Wycliffe. Thus one of the two sources from which the stream of Lollard doctrine had issued through the land was definitely closed.

Arundel's complaints of the University.

From this time must be dated the decline of Oxford. Culture, scientific reputation, moral influence, seem to have alike deserted the University, and the next hundred years are the most barren in all her annals.

Decline of Oxford.

6.—The Lollards in the Reign of Henry V. Lord Cobham.

HENRY V., as we have seen, was now upon the throne.[2] The year after his accession Archbishop Arundel died, and was succeeded by Henry Chichely. The prelate and the king were, if possible, more vehement against the Lollards than their predecessors had been. The 'poor priests' of Wycliffe and his immediate followers gradually disappeared; Popish itinerant preachers, like William Lindwood, went forth in increasing numbers to oppose

Henry V. and Chichely.

---

[1] Wilkins, III., 318. The fact of these strong measures being necessary attests the prevalence of the Wycliffite spirit in the University, and so far sustains the probability of such an expression of goodwill to the Reformer himself as is contained in the document of 1406. The archbishop, in these mandates, is but carrying out the spirit of his famous *Constitutions* of 1409; for which see Foxe, III., pp. 242–248.

[2] Henry V. proclaimed king, March 21, 1413; Henry Chichely installed as Archbishop of Canterbury, 1414; in which year, also, the Council of Constance held its first sittings.

the obnoxious sect, who now were compelled to meet in hidden places, in retired houses, even in holes and caves. Still they were joined by many curates and chaplains, even ordained priests; and though in a great measure compelled to discontinue their more active measures, they maintained their opinions openly, by way of protest, when challenged to the test. Wycliffe's Bible translations and tracts were largely circulated. In the esteem of the Scriptures, the deprecation of saint-worship, and the rejection of transubstantiation, these confessors remained unshaken. Scattered incidents attest their persistency, and show also the extravagances into which they were naturally carried in their resistance to prevailing beliefs.

Nor did the opposition to constituted authority confine itself to matters of belief. Disaffection to the government often openly declared itself, and was oftener suspected. The persecution of the Lollards was based as much on political as on ecclesiastical grounds. Sir John Oldcastle, 'the good Lord Cobham,'[1] as he was affectionately termed by the poor and simple, was a firm adherent of the Lollards, whose preachers he welcomed to his seat at Cowling Castle, in Kent, and refused to surrender to the command of the authorities. While Henry IV. survived the brave nobleman was let alone, but on the accession of Henry V. he was arrested and imprisoned in the Tower.[2] He escaped, however, almost immediately, and for a time was concealed in Wales. Meantime the Lollards began to gather menacingly. They mustered on a winter's night in St. Giles's Fields, then north-west of London,[3] hoping that Sir John Oldcastle would place himself at their head. The king was apprised of their designs, and ordered the city gates to be closed. The intended junction of the London with the country Lollards was thus prevented, and the design rendered abortive. Thirty-nine Lollards were apprehended, summarily condemned, and burned or hanged in St. Giles's Fields. The charge was that of traitorously devising the king's death, with that of the royal princes and many of the lords spiritual and temporal.[4] Of the sufferers four names have come down to us: Sir Roger Acton, a preacher named Beverley, one Browne, a knight, and a rich Dunstable brewer, William Murle.

A reward of a thousand marks was now offered for the apprehension of Cobham, but for a time in vain. Other interests occupied the public mind, and possibly the search may not have been very

Political grounds of persecution.

Lord Cobham.

Gathering in St. Giles's Fields.

---

[1] Sir John Oldcastle became Lord Cobham on his marriage with Lady Joan, the heiress of the title.
[2] The fact is preserved to this day by the name of 'Cobham Tower,' where he was imprisoned.
[3] January 7, 1414.
[4] Rymer, *Foedera*, IX., 89.

strict. The year 1415 was the year of Agincourt, and it was not until the king had returned a conqueror from France that the proceedings against the Lollards were energetically resumed. At length, in the autumn of 1417, Cobham was apprehended in Wales, and carried to London, where he was indicted before Parliament on the charge of being concerned in the proceedings of January, 1414. Being called on for his defence, and knowing himself prejudged by his enemies, he simply replied, 'With me it is a very small thing that I should be judged of you or of man's judgment' (1 Corinthians iv. 3). He was thereupon sentenced to be hanged as a traitor and burned as a heretic. This sentence was literally carried out; he was placed upon a sledge, as if he had been a traitor of the deepest dye, and was thus dragged through the town to St. Giles's Fields. On arriving there he was taken down from the sledge, and, immediately falling on his knees, he began to pray to God for the forgiveness of his enemies. His prayer ended, he rose, and, addressing the assembled multitude, warned them to obey God's commands written down in the Bible, and always to shun such teaching as they saw to be contrary to the life and example of Christ. He was then suspended between two gallows by chains, and the funeral pile was kindled beneath him, so that he was slowly burned. So long as life remained in him he continued to praise God and commend his soul to His divine keeping. Thus perished the most eminent man among the Wycliffites, both in social position and in moral worth and Christian courage, a martyr of blameless steadfastness and fearlessness. The accusation of high treason had not the least foundation; in fact, his execution was nothing less than a murder.

With the death of this illustrious victim, the tendency of the Lollards to become a political party seems to have come to an end. From that time forward we discern them simply as a sect, and the persecution, which still continued, was entirely religious. Inquisition into their opinions and imprisonments continued all through this reign; but in 1422 Henry died, in the prime of life and at the summit of his power. The regents for the young Henry the Sixth, John of Bedford and Humphry of Gloucester, had no desire to meddle with ecclesiastical affairs, and until 1428 persecutions seem wholly to have ceased. In that year Henry of Beaufort, Bishop of Winchester, a legitimatised son of John of Gaunt, and therefore great-uncle to the youthful king, was raised to the rank of Cardinal, and charged to lead a crusade against the Bohemian Hussites. The crusade failed, but the attention of the authorities was again directed to the Lollards; and the Pope's nuncio in England, announcing the 'oppression of the orthodox by the heretics' in Bohemia, was urgent on the English prelates to take further measures against the Lollards. It was at this time, as will be shown in a concluding section, that the sentence of the Council of Constance on Wycliffe's remains was carried out. The Archbishop of Canterbury, at a meeting of the Provincial Convocation, declared that instant measures must be taken against the heretics, who were increasing in number daily. Several Lollards were accordingly imprisoned; some died martyrs' deaths, and the persecution raged until 1431, when the reverses in France,[1] the growing weakness of the royal house, and the beginnings of the long, dreary struggle between the Houses of York and Lancaster, turned the mind of the nation away from ecclesiastical channels; and henceforth the Lollards have no history[2] save the record of earnest, obscure men, mostly poor, often illiterate, who yet prized the teachings of Holy Scripture, silently testifying against the corruptions of the professed Church of Christ, and so preparing the mind and heart of the people to welcome the Reformation of the sixteenth century.

Renewal of persecuting measures.

Maintenance of the Lollard testimony.

7.—Wycliffe, Huss, and the Council of Constance.

WE must now for a moment go back to the year 1382, and to the marriage of King Richard II. with the Princess Anne of Bohemia, a devout and godly lady, and a favourer of Lollard doctrines. She

---

[1] It was in 1431 that Joan of Arc was put to death.

[2] The *theological* ground taken by their opponents is most effectually set forth in two treatises, a knowledge of which is necessary to all who would understand the great controversy of the time. 1. Thomas Walden's *Doctrinale Antiquitatum Fidei Ecclesiae Catholicae*, about 1427. (This Walden was the compiler of the *Fasciculi Zizaniorum*, so often quoted in these pages.) He was Provincial of the Carmelites in England, and confessor of Henry V. He attended the Councils of Pisa and Constance, accompanied Henry VI. to France, and died at Rouen, 1430. 2. Pecock's *Repressor*, about 1449. 'The design of it is to defend the clergy from what he conceived to be the unjust aspersions of many of the "lay party" or "Bible-men" (Lollards), and to show that the practices for which the former were blamed admitted of a satisfactory vindication.' He vindicates six practices, or, as he calls them, 'governances,' of the clergy—'the use of images, the going on pilgrimage, the holding of landed possessions by the clergy, the retention of the various ranks of the hierarchy, the framing of ecclesiastical laws by papal and episcopal authority, and the institution of the religious orders.' Five other points are mentioned, but not discussed in this treatise: 'the invocation of the saints and priestly intercession, the costliness of ecclesiastical decorations, the ceremonies of the mass, and the sacraments generally, the taking of oaths, and the lawfulness of war and capital punishment.' Pecock's treatise—published in the Rolls Series, two vols., edited by Churchill Babington, B.D., 1860—is invaluable as showing the questions on which the Lollard controversy turned in the middle of the fifteenth century, with the arguments of the Lollards themselves, and the answers of their fairest and most candid opponents.

died in 1394. Wycliffe tells of her that she possessed the Scriptures not only in the Latin Vulgate, but in the Bohemian and German languages. Many of her countrymen became connected in various capacities with the English court, and so were conversant with the doctrines of Wycliffe. Students from the University of Prague repaired to Oxford, and took back with them copies of Wycliffe's books and tracts. Among these students Jerome of Prague became illustrious; but it is probable that others had preceded him, even so early as 1390, since Huss avowed, in his *Treatise against Stokes*, 1411, that he had known the writings of Wycliffe for twenty years. The last students known to have come from Prague to Oxford were Nicholas Faulfisch and George of Knienitz, who in 1407 revised Wycliffe's Treatise *Of the Truth of Holy Scripture*. England and Bohemia.

John Huss himself was born in 1369; he studied at the University of Prague, where he graduated as Bachelor of Arts, 1393, and Master of Arts, 1396. He afterwards became Bachelor of Divinity, but never attained the degree of Doctor. In 1398 he began to lecture, and in October, 1402, was made Rector of the University—a post which he retained until April, 1403. He seems to have lectured on text-books by masters of Prague, Paris, and Oxford; and as the copy of Wycliffe's *Five Philosophical Treatises* preserved at Stockholm is by Huss—completed in 1398—it is probable that he used these for at least his earlier lectures. The MS. is said to be arranged after the form used at that time by Bachelors in Arts and Theology. John Huss.

In the year 1402 Huss also became curate, or select preacher, of Bethlehem Chapel, in Prague, on the presentation of John of Müllheim. His duty was to preach in the Bohemian language; and in preparing himself for this work Huss was led to study the Scriptures and the theological writings of Wycliffe. These made him eager for reform; and with characteristic simplicity he sought the co-operation of his ecclesiastical superiors. A series of disputations in the University ensued with regard to Wycliffe's principles, the first being held May 28, 1403. Certain opinions of Wycliffe, including the twenty-four condemned at Blackfriars in 1382,[1] with twenty-one others, were condemned and forbidden to be propounded in future. Huss, however, persisted in lecturing, and defended these forty-five theses, when fairly interpreted. A statute was in consequence passed, forbidding bachelors to lecture at all on the *Trialogus* or *De Eucharistia*, or to discuss the doctrines and the writings of Wycliffe. His early reformation movements.

[1] See above, pp. 381–383.

The Archbishop of Prague, Sbynjek by name, who was installed in 1403, appointed Huss preacher to the Synod, which gave the bold Reformer repeated opportunity for protesting against prevalent errors and superstitions. His words were at first received with approval; in Bethlehem Chapel, where he still officiated, crowds of all classes attended his ministrations; but in 1408 the archbishop's favour was withdrawn, and Huss henceforth had to fight the battle unfriended by dignitaries in Church or State.

The ambitious king, Wenceslaus, bent on becoming Emperor, feared that Wycliffe's doctrines might stand in his way; yet neither Huss nor his friend Jerome was seized. The controversy in the University was complicated by national jealousies, the Germans and Bohemians taking opposite sides in the question between the rival popes. At length the former were outvoted, and left the University.[1] Huss was again chosen rector (1409). But the archbishop, now his declared enemy, succeeded in rousing the Pope (Alexander V.) to action. Papal bulls were issued, March 9, 1409, authorising four Doctors of Theology and four of Canonical Law to make inquiry into the alleged heresy, with a view to its suppression, demanding the surrender of Wycliffe's books, and also forbidding preaching in unconsecrated places (an attack upon the Bethlehem Chapel). Huss personally brought before this commission of inquiry what books of Wycliffe he possessed; others followed his example. Two hundred volumes, it is said, were burned (July 16, 1409), and Huss and his followers were excommunicated. Great uproar arose in consequence, Huss being still very popular. He openly defended Wycliffe in his University lectures, and continued to preach stirring sermons in Bethlehem Chapel.

German and Bohemian rivalries.

The Pope Alexander died in 1410, and no time was lost by his successor, John XXIII., in renewing proceedings against Huss. To the Papal envoys, however, who came to Prague, the king, queen, and nobles deplored Alexander's proceedings in regard to the Wycliffite teachings, as well as in the prohibition of preaching, and begged a reversal of the sentence; but the Pope and archbishop were firm. New proceedings were instituted against Huss and his coadjutors; the court and hierarchy becoming more openly divided. At this juncture the archbishop died (1411), and the proceedings were interrupted for a while.

A treatise written at this time by one Stephen, a learned Carthusian prior of Dolan, near Olmütz, entitled *The Marrow of Wheat*, or

[1] They founded the University of Leipzig as a consequence of this secession.

Anti-Wiclif,[1] describes how the doctrines of the English Reformer had spread through Bohemia and gained favour among all classes of the people. The author attacks Wycliffe personally, rather than his followers; and the work is most graphic, showing clearly how from 1408 to 1411 Wycliffism was the cause of the stirring of spirit which prevailed throughout Bohemia. *Stephen's 'Anti-Wiclif.'*

The excitement of public feeling was stimulated by the attitude of Huss in relation to a crusade now proclaimed against King Ladislaus of Naples, a partisan of the 'anti-pope,' Gregory XII. In the ground taken by the Bohemian Reformer there are many points of resemblance to the arguments by which Wycliffe opposed the crusade projected by Bishop Spencer of Norwich.[2] The people of Prague responded to the Reformer's appeal, and burned the bulls relating to crusade, as if in answer to the burning of Wycliffe's books two years before! Three young men concerned in the tumult were apprehended and put to death. The populace regarded them as martyrs; with Huss's concurrence, their bodies were interred as those of martyrs in the Bethlehem Chapel, which their enemies were reduced to calling, in ridicule, 'The Chapel of the Three Saints.' *A new crusade.*

In the meantime the theological faculty of the University declared once more against Huss, reviving the condemnation of Wycliffe's 'forty-five heresies,' and adding six of Huss's own to the number. The king's interference was petitioned to forbid the promulgation of these doctrines, and to forbid Huss to preach. To the former request Wenceslaus consented, the latter he refused. The clergy appealed to Pope John XXIII., who deputed one Peter of St. Angelo, Cardinal-deacon, to proceed against Huss. Twenty days were given to the Reformer in which to recant. In the event of refusal he was to be treated after that time as an outcast; all believers were exhorted to apprehend him, and to raze Bethlehem Chapel to the ground. His friends resisted, and in consequence were debarred from the rites of the Church. Such tumult arose that the king himself entreated Huss to retire from the scene. He consented, and in December, 1412, went into voluntary exile, *Opinions of Huss condemned.*

---

[1] *Weizenmark, oder Anti-Wikleff.* The book was printed by Bernhard Pez, (d. 1735) in his *Thesaurus Anecdotorum Novissimus*, vol. IV., part 2, pp. 150-359. The treatise is in four divisions—the first and third on the Sacrament of the Altar; the second on the constitution of the Church, especially in relation to the monastic and mendicant orders; the third on the Romish primacy and Church property.

[2] See above, p. 408. ['The declarations of Huss moved entirely within the tracks of Wiclif.' Loserth, *Wiclif and Hus*, Eng. trans., p. 140 (1884). Loserth adds that in the address delivered by Huss on the crusade, June 7, 1412, 'all the arguments, down to the details, are adopted with verbal fidelity from different tractates of Wiclif.']

after he had published a paper appealing to Christ as the Judge of all. A synod was held in Prague with a view to settle the disputes, but in vain. Meanwhile Huss in his retirement continued to preach and write with indefatigable zeal, in his Latin works making great and constant use of Wycliffe's.[1] The Pope meantime had convened a 'general council' in Rome, hoping to establish his authority against that of his rival, but in vain. The council, however, again condemned sundry writings of Wycliffe, as the *Dialogus*, *Trialogus*, and others, as containing heresies. All bishops were commanded to search out and burn these books. Any one undertaking to defend his memory was to present himself before the Pope within nine months. Nothing, however, came of these proceedings. All attention was concentrated on the approaching Council at Constance.

The Council was summoned by John XXIII., at the instance, chiefly, of Sigismund, King of Hungary and Rome. Its great object

Council of Constance.

was to consolidate the Papacy and to end the schism. For there were now *two* anti-popes, Benedict XIII., at Avignon, and Gregory XII., at Rimini. Matters of doctrine were also to be considered, and heresies to be extirpated. Early in the course of the discussions the Pope, being charged with impiety and profaneness, fled to Schaffhausen—a practical abdication, which, however, did not take effect until a year afterwards.[2] The subsequent proceedings of the council, therefore, up to the point at which our history ends, were conducted without a Pope, the council asserting its own supreme authority. King Sigismund prevailed on Huss to attend the council, on the promise of a safe conduct and of a fair and open hearing. Probably that monarch believed and expected that Huss would prove himself orthodox.

Very early in the sessions of the assembly the doctrines of Wycliffe were taken into consideration. The 'forty-five articles' were con-

Wycliffe's forty-five 'heresies.'

demned as heresies. Two hundred and sixty more had been industriously gathered from his writings,[3] but the council seems not to have had patience to hear them all. On May 4, 1415, at the eighth full session of the council, the

Sentence on Wycliffe's remains.

English Reformer himself was solemnly declared 'the leader of heresy in that age.'[4] His books were ordered to be burned, and his remains to be disinterred from their grave at Lutterworth and removed from consecrated ground, 'if

---

[1] [See the parallel passages in Loserth, *Wiclif and Hus* (Eng. trans., 1884), book II., *passim.*]

[2] John XXIII. was at length formally deposed by the council, also Benedict XIII. Gregory XII. abdicated of his own accord; Martin V. was elected in 1417.

[3] The whole 260 are given by Ortuin Gratius, *Fasc. rer. expet.* ed. 1535, p. 133.

[4] *Nostris temporibus vetus ille. . . . Nostris nova certamina suscitavit, quorum dux*

they can be distinguished from the bones of the faithful.' The reason of this proceeding was, of course, that he had died in excommunication!

Huss himself, who had in the meantime been imprisoned, was summoned to appear before the council on the 5th of June, the hearing being continued on the 7th and 8th. Thirty-nine articles were produced against him: twenty-six taken from his book *On the Church*, seven from his controversy with Dr. Palecz, and six from his reply to Stanislaus. These two were leading doctors of the Prague University, who had been commissioned in 1413 to point out the 'erroneous doctrines' of the Reformer. Huss stood his ground bravely, explaining where he had been misunderstood, and defending what he had before maintained. On his Church doctrine and the Papacy he is especially decided. 'The Church was governed infinitely better,' he said, 'in the time of the apostles than now. What can hinder Jesus Christ from governing it by His true disciples?' Referring to the absence of the Pope, he adds, 'Though, I say, the Church has no head at present, yet Jesus Christ ceaseth not to govern it.' Being required to recant these articles *en masse*, Huss implored the council, for God's sake, not to impute to him doctrines that he had never held. For never—God was his witness—had he believed or taught that the sacred elements of the Eucharist after consecration remained material bread. Opinions, he added, that he had never held he could not recant. Any errors that he had really maintained he was ready to renounce if taught better. In regard to further allegations he boldly vindicated his conduct. Charged with having publicly read the letter from the University of Oxford in favour of Wycliffe,[1] he owned that he had done so, adding that it bore the University seal. Another letter from the University was then produced by the English delegates, in which more than two hundred articles from the writings of Wycliffe were sent up to the council for condemnation. In fact, all through these proceedings the name of Wycliffe is ever on the lips of Huss's enemies.[2]

The fate of the Reformer was now sealed. In vain was the safe-conduct of Sigismund pleaded. Huss must die. On June 24th his

---

princeps exhibit quondam Johannes Wicleff pseudo-Christianus, etc. Von der Hardt, *Concil., Const.*, vol. IV., p. 99. Comp. L'Enfant's *Hist.*, vol. I., p. 231, Eng. trans.

[1] See above, p. 455.

[2] Of the 39 articles which were submitted to the council, almost all, and indeed for the great part with verbal fidelity, are to be traced back to Wycliffe; so that John Stokes was entirely in the right when he made the remark that *Huss need not boast of these doctrines as his own property, inasmuch as they belong demonstrably to Wiclif*, Loserth, p. 174.

writings were burned; on July 6th he himself was sentenced and hurried to the stake. On the showing of his very enemies, the sentence was iniquitous. Huss did not reject transubstantiation.

The two pioneers of Reformation, Wycliffe and Huss, were to each other as father and son, or rather as master and disciple. 1. Both *Wycliffe and Huss compared.* acknowledge *the Scriptures* as the standard. Wycliffe discovered this truth, Huss asserted it. On the other hand, Wycliffe refuses to hear the teaching of the Church; Huss accepts it as interpreting Scripture. 2. Both call the *Church* 'the assembly of the elect.' Wycliffe connects this idea with his views of Divine things, of the world and worldly kingdoms, of the sin-world and spirit-world. He also takes as his basis the doc- *Their doctrines.* trine of election, not, as Augustine, the fall and universal sinfulness of man. But Huss does not philosophise; he holds the doctrine simply. 3. Both believe that Christ alone is *Mediator* between God and man. Wycliffe rejects the veneration of saints and prayers to them; Huss never foregoes his trust in their intercession. 4. As to the *Sacraments,* Huss does not equal Wycliffe in sharpness of criticism. He agrees with him concerning the non-dependence of sacramental efficacy on the character of the minister, but he does not reject transubstantiation. 5. Concerning *Church Government,* Huss agrees with Wycliffe in denying the Divine right of the Pope, but only goes so far as to believe in equality among bishops, not among all priests.

Wycliffe was an original genius. Huss is to him as a planet to the sun. Wycliffe was independent; Huss yielded more deference *Their character.* to public opinion. Both were filled with zeal for God's cause; but Huss was more gentle than Wycliffe—not genial, like Luther, but sensitive and mild. Wycliffe was active and energetic; Huss was much-enduring. Wycliffe was a *man* of God; Huss a *child* of God.

A Hussite Cantionale of 1572, in the Prague University Library, contains, on page 364, a hymn in the Czech language in memory of *Wycliffe, Huss, and Luther.* Huss. The page is adorned with beautiful miniatures, on one side being three medallions; the first representing Wycliffe striking a spark, below him Huss kindling the coals, and Luther at the foot brandishing the lighted torch. Nothing could more vividly symbolize the mission of the three men than this 'triology' of medallions!

The decree of the Council of Constance in regard to Wycliffe's bones was carried out after long delay. The Bishop of Lincoln, in whose diocese was the parish of Lutterworth, was at this time Philip

Repyngdon, Wycliffe's old comrade; and he may have shrunk from being a party to the absurd indignity. As we have seen, the command to exhume the remains of the Reformer was given in May, 1415. In 1420 Repyngdon resigned, and Richard Fleming was appointed to the See. But it was still eight years before the mandate was enforced, at the peremptory bidding of Pope Clement VIII. Fleming weakly yielded, and the remains of the great Englishman were not only torn from their resting-place, but burned to ashes and cast into the little river Swift, that runs by Lutterworth on its course to the Avon. Thus, in the often quoted words of Thomas Fuller, 'the little river conveyed Wycliffe's remains into the Avon, Avon into the Severn, Severn into the narrow seas, they to the main ocean. And thus the ashes of Wycliffe are the emblem of his doctrine, which now is dispersed all the world over.'

Exhumation of Wycliffe's bones, 1428.

LUTTERWORTH: THE RIVER SWIFT.

NOTE.—The first article in the Appendix to Dr. Lechler's work is on the treatise, long attributed to Wycliffe, entitled *The Last Age of the Church*. As, however, the Wycliffe authorship of this tractate is now given up by all competent authorities, the question need not be discussed here. The author was evidently a Franciscan—belonging, says Dr. Lechler, to an inner circle of that brotherhood, 'who, with a zealous adhesion to the strictest peculiarity of their order, had been brought into a position of antagonism to the existing Church, and were attached to certain enthusiastic apocalyptical views.'

Another treatise, until recently attributed to Wycliffe, and repeatedly printed as his, is entitled *The Poor Caitiff*, and consists of a number of short pieces on the Creed, the Ten Commandments, and other religious subjects. The work is characterised by devoutness and fervour; but Shirley, Arnold, and others have satisfactorily disproved its Wycliffe authorship. Bishop Pecock attributes it to some unknown Mendicant Friar.

APPENDIX.

I.

RICHARD FITZRALPH, ARCHBISHOP OF ARMAGH.

THERE are two well-authenticated facts in the earlier life of this remarkable prelate left unmentioned by Professor Lechler, which it is desirable to bring into view. The first of these is his early connection with Balliol College, of which he was for some time a Fellow. This fact is distinctly stated in the following passage of Anthony Wood's *History and Antiquities of the Colleges and Halls in the University of Oxford.* Having stated the chief provisions of the original statutes of the college—those of the Lady Devorguilla—he goes on to say, that 'the said statutes were for divers years kept inviolable, yet not so much but that divers of the said scholars, about forty years after, having raised some doubts from them, would not content themselves to study the liberal arts—only such that were performed in the schools of arts by artists according to the aptest sense of the statutes, but also would ascend to higher faculties, though prohibited so to do by the then extrinsic masters or procurators, named Robert de Leycester, D.D., a Minorite, and Nicolas de Tingwyke, Doctor of Physic and Bachelor of Divinity. At length the matter, being controverted among them a considerable time, was in 1325 referred, with the procurators' consent, to two doctors and two masters that were formerly Fellows of this house, Drs. Richard de Kamsale and Walter de Hockstow, who then, after both parties were heard, decided this matter in the Common Hall thus: That no Fellow of this house, whether Master or Scholar, learn any Faculty, or give his mind to it, either in full term or vacation, besides the liberal arts that by artists are read and practised in the School of Arts.' The college incident here referred to occurred only about ten years before the coming of Wycliffe to Oxford and his probable admission to Balliol, and will be found in the sequel to have a bearing upon the course of study through which Wycliffe passed as a member of the University of Oxford. As Fitzralph was undoubtedly a man of enlightened views, which were considerably in advance of his age, his connection with Balliol in the first quarter of the fourteenth century, taken along with Wycliffe's in its second quarter, may serve to suggest that Balliol, then one of the youngest of the colleges of the University, was also one of the most free and liberal in its ideas; and probably, too, the remarkable impatience of divers of its scholars at being limited to the studies usually included in arts, and their eager desire to read in 'the higher faculties,' may be taken to indicate, in these young men, a more than ordinary amount of intellectual life and ardour. The archives of Balliol contain a brief Latin record of the conclusion arrived at by the four referees to whose decision the question was submitted, and a full transcript of this record is given in the report of Mr. Riley on the Balliol Papers to the Royal Commission on Historical MSS., 1874. In this document Richard Fitzralph (*Ricardus filius Radulphi*) is expressly mentioned as among the Fellows present and assenting to the decision.

The other fact in the career of Archbishop Fitzralph remaining to be mentioned is that he, as well as Bradwardine, was for some time private chaplain to the famous Richard de Bury, Bishop of Durham, who was consecrated December 19, 1333, and died April 14, 1345. This bishop was the greatest book-lover and collector of his time, and wrote a work on his favourite subject, entitled *Philobiblos*. His library was one of the choicest in England, and passed, after his death, to Durham College, in Oxford. The bishop's high appreciation of two such men as Fitzralph and Bradwardine may perhaps be taken as an indication of his own spirit and bearing on the great Church questions of the time. For the fact of their connection with him as his chaplains, see Introduction to *Registrum Palatinum Dunelmense*, edited by Sir Thomas Duffus Hardy, Deputy Keeper of the Public Records.—P. L.

II.

THE VISION OF PIERS PLOWMAN.

PROFESSOR LECHLER'S numerous quotations from Langland's Poem, only a few of which we have thought it necessary to reproduce for English readers, are all taken from the text of the two editions brought out by Thomas Wright in 1842 and 1856. But it may be useful to mention here, for the benefit of English readers who would like to look farther into this really great moral and religious allegory of the age of Wycliffe, that in 1867, 1869, and 1873, three editions of the poem, representing the three distinct forms which its text assumed successively under the author's own hand, were brought out by Rev. W. W. Skeat, in connection with the Early English Text Society. This work of Mr. Skeat is characterised by Professor Henry Morley, in his *Library of English Literature*, as singularly thorough. He publishes, with a special introduction, each of its three forms separately, as obtained from a collation of MSS., with various readings and references to the MSS. containing each form. A fourth section is assigned to the General Introduction, Notes, and Index. Besides this work on the whole Poem, Mr. Skeat has contributed to the Clarendon Press Series the first seven Passus of 'The Vision of William concerning Piers the Plowman, by William Longland, according to the version revised and enlarged by the author about A.D. 1377, with Introduction, Notes, and Glossary,' as an aid to the right study of Early English in colleges and schools, and also as a guide to the reading of the whole Poem by those to whom its English, without such help, would be obscure. Mr. Skeat's thorough study of the Poem from all points of view makes him our chief authority in any question concerning it.

Professor Morley himself has given a long and lucid analysis of the whole Poem, extending to twenty-five pages doubled-columned in the second department of his *Library of English Literature* (Cassell's), devoted to the literature of religion; and his high appreciation, both of the Poem and the Poet, may be gathered from the closing paragraph of his extremely painstaking account:—'So ends the vision, with no victory attained, a world at war, and a renewed cry for the grace of God; a new yearning to find Christ, and bring with Him the day when wrongs and hatred are no more. The fourteenth century yielded no more fervent expression of the purest Christian labour to bring man to God. Langland lays fast hold of all the words of Christ, and reads them into a Divine law of love and duty. The ideal of a Christian life shines through his poem, while it paints with homely force the evils against which it is directed. On points of theology he never disputes, but an ill life for him is an ill life, whether in Pope or peasant. He is a Church Reformer in the truest sense, seeking to strengthen the hands of the clergy by amendment of the lives and characters of those who are untrue to their holy calling.'

It is gratifying to meet with so hearty a sympathy with aims so evangelical and holy as those of 'Piers Plowman,' in a literary critic of our time of such mark as Professor Morley. Nor can we deny ourselves and our readers the pleasure of bringing up again into view, side by side with the appreciations of a German scholar and divine who has so much sympathy with Wycliffe and all his English precursors as our learned author, the noble words in which the illustrious historian of Latin Christianity has put on record his estimate of the author of Piers Plowman's vision: 'This extraordinary manifestation of the religion, of the language, of the social and political notions, of the English character, of the condition of the passions and feelings of moral and provincial England, commences, and with Chaucer and Wycliffe completes the revelation of this transition period, the reign of Edward III. Throughout its institutions, language, religious sentiment, Teutonism is now holding its first initiatory struggle with Latin Christianity. In Chaucer is heard a voice from the court, from the castle, from the city, from universal England. In Wycliffe is heard a voice from the University, from the seat of theology and scholastic philosophy, from the centre and stronghold of the hierarchy—a voice of revolt and defiance, taken up and echoed in the pulpit throughout the land against the sacerdotal domination. In the Vision of Piers Plowman is heard a voice from the wild Malvern hills, the voice, it should seem, of an humble parson, a secular priest. He has passed some years in London, but his home, his heart, is among the poor rural population of central Mercian England. . . . The visionary is no disciple, no precursor of Wycliffe in his broader religious views. The Loller of Piers Plowman is no Lollard —he applies the name as a term of reproach for a lazy, indolent vagrant. The poet is no dreamy speculative theologian—he acquiesces, seemingly with unquestioning faith, in the creed and in the usages of the Church. It is in his intense, absorbing moral feeling that he is beyond his age. With him outward observances are but hollow shows, mockeries, hypocrisies, without the inward power of religion. It is not so much in his keen, cutting satire on all matters of the Church, as his solemn installation of Reason and Conscience as the guides of the self-directed soul, that he is breaking the yoke of sacerdotal domination. In his constant appeal to the plainest, simplest scriptural truths, as in themselves the whole of religion, he is a stern Reformer. The sad, serious satirist, in his contemplation of the world around him, the wealth of the world and the woe, sees no hope but in a new order of things, in which, if the hierarchy shall subsist, it shall subsist in a form, with powers, in a spirit totally opposite to that which now rules mankind. . . . The poet who could address such opinions, though wrapt up in prudent allegory, to the popular ear, to the ear of the peasantry of England; the people who could listen with delight to such strains, were far advanced towards a revolt from Latin Christianity. Truth, true religion was not to be found with, it was not known by Pope, Cardinals, Bishops, Clergy, Monks, Friars. It was to be sought by man himself, by the individual man, by the poorest man, under the sole guidance of Reason, Conscience, and the Grace of God, vouchsafed directly, not through any intermediate human being or even sacrament, to the self-directing soul. If it yet respected all existing doctrines, it respected them not as resting on traditional or sacerdotal authority. There is a manifest appeal throughout, an unconscious installation of Scripture alone, as the ultimate judge. The test of everything is a moral and purely religious one—its agreement with holiness and charity' (Dean Milman's *History of Latin Christianity*, vi., pp. 536, 544. Ed. 1855).

III.

BALLIOL COLLEGE IN WYCLIFFE'S TIME.

1. *Illustrations of its Educational Discipline.*

By the fundamental statutes of Devorguilla, which were still in full force in Wycliffe's student days, it was provided as follows:—

'That the scholars speak Latin in common, and whoever acts anything against it, shall be rebuked by the principal. If they mend not after twice or thrice admonition, they are to be removed from common table, and eat by themselves, and be served last. If incorrigible after a week's space, to be ejected by the procurators.

'Every week a sophism to be disputed and determined in the house among the scholars by turns, so that they both *oppose* and *answer;* and if any sophister profiteth so much that he may deserve in a short time to *determine* in the schools, then shall the principal tell him that he shall first determine *at home* among his fellows. At the end of every disputation the principal shall appoint the next day of disputing; and shall moderate and correct the loquacious; and shall appoint the sophism that is next to be handled, and also the opponent, respondent, and determiner, that so they may the better provide themselves for a disputation' (*See* Wood's *History and Antiquities of the Colleges and Halls in the University of Oxford*, p. 71).

2. *Provisions of the Statutes of Sir Philip de Somerville for the study of Theology by the Fellows.*

These statutes came into operation in 1341, and assuming, as a high probability, that Wycliffe became a student of Arts and Theology at Balliol on his first coming to Oxford, these provisions throw an interesting light upon the probable course of his theological studies. The statutes empowered the Fellows, now increased from 16 to 22, to elect six of their number to hold Theological Fellowships, which they should continue to enjoy till, in due course, they obtained the usual degrees in Theology; and the curriculum of study laid out for them was a singularly liberal one. The men elected *ad intendendum sacrae theologiae* were to become *opponents* in the theological disputations in the sixth year of their studies, and were to continue to oppose for one year, or, if it seemed expedient to the society, during two years. In the ninth or tenth year they were to read the Book of Sentences; and in the twelfth or thirteenth year they should be held bound to *commence, incipere,* in the same faculty, unless hindered by legitimate and honest cause. If, as is highly probable, Wycliffe became one of these Theological Fellows of Balliol, his whole course of study in Arts and Theology must have extended, allowing four years for his Arts course, to sixteen or seventeen years, viz., from 1335 to 1351 or 1352.

The utmost care was to be taken in the election of men to these Theological Fellowships; under the sanction of a solemn oath, none were to be chosen, 'praeter honestos, castos, pacificos et humiles, ad scientiam habiles ac proficere volentes,' and none who were not already 'Regents in Arts.'

3. *Disputes among Philosophical University Sects.*

The following extract from Wood's *History of the Colleges and Halls in the University of Oxford,* under the year 1343, gives us a curious glimpse of the condition of philosophical parties in the University at the time when Wycliffe was engaged in the profound study of the philosophy and theology of his age:—

'Clashing controversies in disputations and writings among the learneder sort, especially the followers and disciples of the authors of the Nominals and Reals (Occam and Scotus), both which sects were now so fixed in every house of learning that the divisions between the northern and southern clerks were now as great, if not more, as those before. Those of the north held, as 'tis said, with Scotus, and those of the south with Occam, and in all their disputations were so violent, that the peace of the University was not thereby a little disturbed. . . . Now, forasmuch as these controversies were frequent in Oxford, causing thereby great emulation, which commonly ended in blows, the statutes for the election of the Chancellor were, without doubt, made; for whereas about these times great variance fell out in the election of that officer, some aiming to have him a northern, others a southern man, divers statutes and injunctions, chiefly reflecting upon such disorders, were, I say, this year enacted, of which was that concerning two scrutators in the elections—that is, that one should be a northern, the other a southern man, lest underhand dealing should be used, and consequently parties injured.'

Wycliffe took side with the Scotists or Realists in these subtle disputations and 'clashing controversies;' and it is curious to reflect how much this philosophical preference may have been owing to the accident of his having been born a *Borealis* instead of an *Australis*. John Duns Scotus himself was, of course, a north-countryman, and all north-countrymen in Oxford appear to have belonged to his following. The Balliol scholars in particular were the natural allies of the great Realist, for they claimed him to have been a Balliol man before he connected himself with Merton. For, as Savage dryly observes in his *Ballio-fergus*, 'There is as much contending for the breeding-place of this rare man as hath been for the birth of Homer. We conjecture him to have been of this College of Balliol, inasmuch as he was by county of Northumberland, and of Duns there, as might be seen not only in Pitsaeus, but before every volume of his works in MSS. in our library, of the gift of Bishop Gray, but torn off in the time of the late war; and for that in Northumberland was the first endowment of our College. He lived anno 1300, which was after Devorguilla's Statutes, but before those of Sir Philip Somerville, yet not after the time when it was granted by the Pope that the scholars might live in the house after they became Masters of Art; and therefore he might, for that reason, depart from this to Merton College.'

4. *Wycliffe's College Contemporaries.*

The following names of learned Fellows of Balliol College in Wycliffe's time are given by Savage in his *Ballio-fergus;* and we probably discern in them two of the partners of the Reformer's studies in philosophy and divinity:—

'William Wilton, professor in his faculty, which could be no other than divinity, by the statutes of this house made by Sir Philip de Somervyll, after which he lived here and wrote many things:—

'*Super Priora Aristotelis; Quaestiones de Anima; Super Ethica.* He was Chancellor of the University in 1373.

'Roger Whelpdale, fellow of the house, afterwards Provost of Queen's, lastly Bishop of Carlisle, a great mathematician. He wrote many books, whereof in our College library are there—

'*Summularum logicalium; De Universalibus; De Aggregatis; De Quanto et Continuo; De Compositione Continui; De Rogando Deo.* He lived in the time of Edward III., and was the first who enriched the library with MSS., besides those of uncertain donation.'—P. L.

IV.

IDENTITY OF JOHN WYCLIFFE THE REFORMER WITH JOHN WYCLIFFE THE WARDEN OF CANTERBURY HALL.

DR. LECHLER has omitted to bring forward a material argument in support of the identity of Wycliffe with the Warden of Canterbury Hall, which is supplied by one of the original chronicles of the period, an omission which may have been owing to the discredit thrown upon the authority of the chronicle by Professor Shirley in his *Note on the Two John Wiclifs*, appended to the *Fasciculi Zizaniorum*.

This Chronicle has been given to the world in the series of *Chronicles and Memorials of Great Britain and Ireland during the Middle Ages*, brought out under the direction of the Master of the Rolls, under the following title: *Chronicon Angliae, ab anno domini* 1328, *usque ad annum* 1388; *Auctore Monacho quodam Sancti Albani.* Edited by Edward Maunde Thompson, Assistant Keeper of the MSS. of the British Museum, 1874.

It is printed from a MS. of the Harleian Collection, No. 3634, written on vellum towards the close of the fourteenth century, which has hitherto escaped the notice of historians. The MS. once belonged to Archbishop Parker, and was lent by him to Foxe, the martyrologist, who several times refers to it under the title of *Chronicon Monachi D. Albani*. John Josceline, the archbishop's secretary, in his *Catalogus Historicorum*, described it thus: 'In ea multa continentur de Wicliffo, Papali Schismate et de magna Rusticorum rebellione, quae facta fuit per id tempus.' 'It contains,' says its discoverer and editor, Mr. Thompson, 'an important detailed history of the close of Edward Third's and the beginning of Richard Second's reign, which is now printed in its original shape for the first time, and which has hitherto been considered lost. The former existence of a Latin original for the translation used by John Stow in his Chronicle of England [the same translation printed in the *Archaeologia*] has been generally admitted by historians. The only writer who has thrown any doubts upon it is the late Professor Shirley, in his edition of the *Fasciculi Zizaniorum*. The translation being one of the authorities brought forward in support of a tradition that Wycliffe held the Wardenship of Canterbury Hall at Oxford, Mr. Shirley rejects its testimony on the ground of its being a compilation of the sixteenth century, while admitting, however, that the author had before him one, or perhaps two, contemporary authorities which he has indolently interwoven with his narrative, without changing one even of those expressions which most clearly reflect the image of passing events.' All this criticism is, of course, superseded by the facts that we have now before us the original Latin text of the *Chronicon Angliae* in a MS. dating from the last quarter of the fourteenth century; and that this was indisputably the work of a contemporary historian. What, then, is the testimony of this contemporary of Wycliffe, who evidently shared largely in all the ecclesiastical passions and prejudices of his time, upon the point of the Reformer's connection with Canterbury Hall? It is contained in the following passage of his *Chronicon* :—

' Dux (referring to John, Duke of Gaunt) aggregaverat sibi quendam pseudo-theologum, sive, ut melius eum nominem, verum theomachum, qui jam a multis annis in scholis, in singulis actis suis contra ecclesiam oblatraverat, *eo quod juste privatus extiterat per archiepiscopum Cantuariensem quodam beneficio, cui injuste incubuerat in Universitate Oxoniensi situato.*' The words of the translation published in the *Archaeologia* are, that 'he was justly deprived by the Archbishopp of Canterburye from a certayne benefice that he unjustly was incumbent upon within the cytye of Oxforde.'

The incident, then, in question, in the life of Wycliffe, viz., his short Wardenship of Canterbury Hall, may now be considered to be put beyond the range of reasonable doubt. Shirley admitted that 'great weight must undoubtedly be allowed to the contemporary statement of Woodford;' to which has now to be added a second contemporary statement by the Monk of St. Albans, as it now stands before us cleared of all the doubts which were thrown upon it by the acute and learned editor of the *Fasciculi Zizaniorum*.—P. L.

V.

ON THE LATE DATE AT WHICH WYCLIFFE BEGAN HIS ATTACKS UPON THE MENDICANT ORDERS.

It is one of the most valuable contributions which Dr. Lechler has made to the biography of Wycliffe that he has been able to produce from the Reformer's unpublished writings 'direct proofs' of the fact 'that Wycliffe continued to speak of the Begging Orders with all respectful recognition during the twenty years which elapsed between 1360 and 1380, and that it was in connection with the controversy opened by him on the subject of Transubstantiation, and therefore after 1381 at the earliest, that he began to oppose himself to the Mendicants, who had come forward as his antagonists on that fundamental question.'

I am happy to be able to bring forward an important testimony to the historical accuracy of this representation from the same contemporary source which was laid under contribution in the preceding section, viz., the *Chronicon Angliae* of the Monk of St. Albans. At p. 116 occurs the following remarkable passage. Describing Wycliffe, the hostile chronicler writes :—Erat utique non solum facundus, sed simulator et hypocrita solidissimus, ad unum finem intendens omnia, ut videlicet ejus fama et opinio se inter homines dilataret. Simulabatque se spernere temporalia tanquam instabilia et caduca, pro aeternorum amore ; et ideo non erat cum possessionatis ejus conversatio, sed ut magis plebis mentes deluderet, *ordinibus adhaesit mendicantium, eorum paupertatem approbans, perfectionem extollens, ut magis falleret commune vulgus.*

The distinction here taken between Wycliffe's bearing towards the *possessionati*, the 'monks possessioners,' or the old endowed orders, with whom he had little or no familiarity, and his good opinion of the Mendicant Orders, with whom he cultivated personal intercourse, agrees exactly with the view taken by Professor Lechler, and is a weighty corroboration of its historical truth. This view, however, is of so recent a date, and the opposite view, that Wycliffe had begun as early as 1360 to take up the old quarrel of *Armachanus* with the Franciscans, has been so long received, that it is not surprising that both Professor Shirley and Mr. Thompson have regarded this passage of the *Chronicon* as one which throws grave doubt on the authority or the accuracy of the compiler. Referring to the chapter on Wycliffe as it stands in the old translation of the Chronicle from which he quotes, Shirley speaks of the single sentence which I have given above in the original as enough to set aside the authority of the whole chapter (*vide* p. 523 of the *Fasc. Zizan.*). This is the more unaccountable on his part, as he had previously remarked (Introduction, p. xiv.), that the 'story which connects Wycliffe with the controversies of 1360 is implicitly contradicted by contemporary authority, and receives, to say the least, no sanction whatever from the acknowledged writings of the Reformer ;' that, in short, 'it is a part of Wycliffe's life only by courtesy and repetition.' The editor of the *Chronicon Angliae* has naturally and justly a much higher respect for the authority of its author than Professor Shirley, who had never seen it in its original text ; but he is not a little embarrassed by the very statements about Wycliffe, which, from Dr. Lechler's point of view, create no difficulty at all, but are welcome confirmations of historical truth. 'It is curious to note,' he remarks, in his *Introduction*, p. 53, 'that our Chronicler, either from ignorance, or perhaps from a natural hostility to the Mendicant Orders, has represented Wycliffe as a favourer of their views. It is, indeed, almost hopeless to account for such a glaring perversion of facts, otherwise than by an assumption of the writer's ignorance ; and yet one hardly dares to allow such ignorance in a contemporary writer. His further statement that the Duke of Lancaster appointed four friars to plead Wycliffe's cause at his trial may have some truth in it ; and it is possible that this fact led him to assume that Wycliffe was not now opposed to his former antagonists.'

The discovery of the truth of the case by Dr. Lechler puts an end at once to all these embarrassments. It vindicates the accuracy of the *Chronicon*, as to the important point now before us ; while the testimony of the *Chronicon* becomes a valuable corroboration of the biographical *datum* which Lechler has ascertained from the unpublished writings of Wycliffe.—P. L.

VI.

THE POPULARITY OF WYCLIFFE AND HIS EARLIEST DISCIPLES AS PREACHERS IN LONDON.

IF Wycliffe had confined his teaching to the schools of Oxford, it would have been only slowly and indirectly that his Reformation principles would have reached the ears and the convictions of the general public. But there is some evidence to show that he was occasionally a preacher in the pulpits of London, and that he spoke out as boldly in the crowded churches of the capital of the kingdom as he had done for many years before in the learned disputations of the University. Nor is proof wanting as to the effects which his preaching produced among the London citizens. The *Chronicon Angliae*, referred to above, is again available here, and supplies us, in particular, with some curious facts, which are new to history, touching the moral and religious influence which the Reformer's preaching began to exercise even upon the municipal administration of the city during the mayoralty of John of Northampton.

At p. 116 of the *Chronicon* we read as follows :—' Haec et his multo graviora,' referring to the new doctrines, ' cum palam non tantum Oxoniæ tractasset in scholis, sed etiam *in civitate Londoniarum publice praedicasset* . . . invenit quod diu quaesiverat, videlicet quosdam regni dominos, vel magis recte diabolos qui ejus amplecterentur deliramenta. . . . Quorum suffultus patrociniis multo audacius et animosius communicavit excommunicatam materiam, ita ut non solum dominos sed et simplices quosdam Londoniensium cives secum attraheret in erroris abysmum. Erat utique non solum facundus sed simulator, etc. . . . ut magis falleret commune vulgus. Qui profecto nullis argumentis, nulla scientia in Deo fulciebatur et floruit, ut opiniones suas probabiles demonstraret, sed sola compositione verborum quae satis eructavit. Unde intricavit minus doctorum aures audientium et ventos pavit inaniter sinê fructu. Dux tamen et dominus Henricus Percy ejus sententias collaudabant, et scientiam et probitatem coelotenus extollere satagebant. Accidit que ut eorum elatus favore, suas vanitates multo amplius dilatare non pertimesceret, sed de ecclesia in ecclesiam percurrendo auribus insereret plurimorum insanias suas falsas. Unde, licet sero, episcopi stimulati, excitarunt patrem suum archiepiscopum quasi de gravi somno, et quasi

potantem crapulatum a vino, vel potius mercenarium avaritiae inebriatum
toxico, ut ovem errantem revocaret a tam manifestae perditionis pabulo,
et curandum committeret stabulario, aut, aliud si res exigeret, uteretur
abscissionis ferro.'

Here, then, we learn for the first time what it was in Wycliffe's doings
that first stimulated the bishops to take public action against him—not so
much his quiet teaching at Oxford, nor his learned judgments given to
the King and Parliament on the points in debate between the kingdom
and the Curia, but the wide-spreading effects of his preaching in the
churches of London, *de ecclesia in ecclesiam percurrendo*. He was gaining the ears of the multitude, and was making proselytes not only among
the highest nobles of the land, but among the masses of the common
people.

Nor was it long before his preaching began to tell even upon the proceedings of the mayor and common council of the city. One of Wycliffe's
loudest complaints in the pulpit was directed against the corrupt remissness of the clergy in the exercise of the discipline of the Church against
adulterers and fornicators of both sexes. Transgressors of the seventh
commandment had been long allowed to compound for their immoralities,
and the clergy put money into their pockets by betraying the interests
both of public and domestic virtue. The Reformer's indignation passed
into the hearts of his London congregations. Many of the citizens resolved
to take steps to reform so crying a social disorder, and the Monkish
Chronicler of St. Albans has handed down to us the following long-
forgotten record of the rough-handed discipline which was brought to
bear upon a batch of the most notorious offenders.

'Londonienses isto tempore coeperunt ultra modum insolescere in per-
niciosum exemplum urbium aliarum. Revera freti *Majoris* illius anni
(1382), Johannis Northamptone auctoritate superciliosa, praesumpserant
episcopalia jura, multas dehonestationes inferentes in fornicationibus vel
adulteriis deprehensis. Captas nempe mulieres in prisona quae vocatur
Dolium apud eos primo seclusas incarcerarunt, postremo perductas ad
conspectum publicum, descissa caesarie ad modum furum quos appellatores
dicimus, circumduci fecerunt in conspectu inhabitantium civitatem, prae-
cedentibus tubicinis et fistulatoribus, ut latius innotescerent personae
earundem. Nec minus hujusmodi hominibus pepercerunt, sed eos injuriis
multis et opprobriis affecerunt. *Animati enim fuerant per Joannen
Wyclife et sequaces ejus ad hujus modi perpetrandum, in reprobationem
praelatorum.* Dicebant quoque se abominari curatorum non solum
negligentiam, sed et detestari avaritiam, qui studentes pecuniae, omissis
poenis a jure limitatis, et receptis nummis, reos fornicationis et incestus
favorabiliter in suis criminibus vivere permiserunt. Dicebant se utique
pertimescere, ne propter talia peccata in urbe perpetrata sed dissimulata,
tota civitas, quandoque, Deo ulciscente, ruinam pateretur. Quapropter
velle se purgationem facere civitatis ab hujusmodi inquinamentis, ne forte
accideret eis pestis aut gladius, vel certe absorberet eos tellus.'—*Chronicon
Angliae*, p. 349.

APPENDIX.

I add the Monk-Chronicler's portrait of the Lord Mayor of the time, John of Northampton, by whose authority these disciplinary severities had been carried out. He was evidently a follower of Wycliffe, and an admirer of his preaching; and the influence of this first Lollard Lord Mayor was, upon the Chronicler's own showing, of great account in the city.

'Erat autem Major eorum homo duri cordis et astutus, elatus propter divitias et superbus, qui nec inferioribus acquiescere, nec superiorum allegationibus sive monitis flecti, valeret, quin quod inceperat proprio ingenio, torvo proposito ad quemcumque finem perducere niteretur. *Habebat plane totius communitatis assensum ad nova molienda.*'—P. L.

VII.

WYCLIFFE'S WRITINGS.

THREE catalogues of these writings are extant, which date from the fifteenth century, and in all probability were drawn up not much later than about thirty years after Wycliffe's death. They are preserved in two MSS. of the Imperial Library of Vienna, but were only lately published. They thus remained virtually unknown to the learned world, which for centuries was obliged to have recourse to catalogues of a much later date.[1]

§ 1. *The Chief Wycliffe Catalogues.*

1. The first man who attempted to draw up a comprehensive list of the writings of Wycliffe was JOHN BALE, Bishop of Ossory (d. 1563), in his *Illustrium Majoris Britanniae Scriptorum Summarium in Quasdam Centurias Divisum*, which first appeared in 1548. At that time it included only five centuries of writers. During his exile in Germany, he enlarged the work by four additional centuries, and carried it down to A.D. 1557, in which year the enlarged edition appeared at Basel. It reckons in this form no fewer than 900 writers. In this collection, p. 451, Bale gives 242 of Wycliffe's writings, with their titles, and in 149 cases he adds their commencing words; but he does not aim at any systematic arrangement, and it is no part of his plan to indicate where the MSS. enumerated are to be found. But Bale's principal fault was the hasty way in which he picked up titles of writings of Wycliffe wherever he came upon them, and gathered them together without a trace of criticism. Hence his catalogue is entitled to very little confidence.

2. More than 150 years passed away before Bale had a successor in the same field. Wycliffe's first biographer, JOHN LEWIS, in his *Life of*

---

[1] Shirley printed in the appendix to his *Catalogue* the first two of these old lists; the third was unknown to him. See the Catalogue of the MSS. of the Imperial Library of Vienna, v. 5.

Dr. John Wiclif, 1720 (new edit., Oxford, 1820) gave a catalogue extending to 284 numbers, which, while resting upon Bale's, is in some respects an improvement upon it. Lewis's catalogue is not only richer than Bale's, but it notes also, whenever possible, the libraries where the MSS. are to be found, adding also the commencing words of the books and tracts, and sometimes also mentioning, after the title, the contents, or the occasion of each piece. But we miss in this catalogue, as much as in Bale's, any suitable classification, and even any critical sifting. Larger works and short tracts, Latin and English pieces, are all mixed miscellaneously together; many pieces enumerated by Lewis are not Wycliffe's at all, and others are entered in his list twice over.

3. The catalogue which was prefixed by H. H. BABER to his Reprint of Wycliffe's, or rather Purvey's *Translation of the New Testament*, in 1810, was drawn up on the basis of Bale's and Lewis's, but is not so complete as the latter. The only advance made by Baber was that he was the first to give a more exact account of the Wycliffe MSS. in the British Museum, as well as of the MSS. preserved in Vienna, in regard to the latter of which he made use of the catalogue of Dénis.

4. Eighteen years later, in the first edition of his *Life and Opinions of John de Wiclif*, Dr. R. VAUGHAN gave a catalogue, which was the fruit of personal investigation, carried out especially in Cambridge and Dublin, and which, besides a classification of the writings, contained a fuller account of the libraries where they are preserved, and some criticism on the genuineness of the several pieces. And in his last work on Wycliffe —*John de Wycliffe, a Monograph*, 1853—he inserted a new list which is in many respects more accurate and minute than his earlier one, although we cannot help thinking it inferior in point of comprehensiveness. In point of accuracy, too, it still leaves much to be desiderated, *e.g.*, more than one writing is twice introduced under different titles, *e.g.*, B. 544, No. 103, *De Dotatione Ecclesiae*, and 125, *Supplementum Trialogi*, which is one and the same work. Another instance is in the observations which he repeatedly makes, pp. 537 and 542, on the subject of Wycliffe's *Summa Theologica*, which are very inexact, and even confusing; for, according to these, we should have to suppose that the *Summa* is a single work, consisting of twelve chapters, whereas it is rather a comprehensive *Collection* or *Corpus*, embracing no fewer than twelve treatises, many of which would fill a goodly printed volume.

5. The most important advance in this field was made by the late Dr. WALTER WADDINGTON SHIRLEY, Professor of Church History in Oxford. As a preparatory work to a projected edition of *Select Works of Wyclif*, which he did not live to take part in, he published, in 1865, *A Catalogue of the Original Works of John Wyclif*, Oxford, at the Clarendon Press. This work, though very modest in bulk, was the fruit of considerable labour, and of correspondence and laborious collections reaching through ten or twelve years. The peculiar recommendations of this catalogue are numerous. Shirley divides the Latin and the English writings entirely from each other; he distributes the Latin works into

certain classes according to their contents; he adds testimonies and notices to aid, as far as possible, in determining the genuineness of the several writings; he endeavours to fix their several dates, at least approximately; and lastly, he indicates accurately the MSS. which contain the several works. To the catalogue of the genuine and still extant works of Wycliffe, the author adds a list both of his lost writings, and of writings which have been incorrectly attributed to him. He prints in an appendix two of the old catalogues of Wycliffe's works, mentioned above as dating from the commencement of the fifteenth century, which are found in the Vienna MSS. The little work ends with an alphabetical register of all the extant works, arranged according to their commencing words, and separated off from each other as Latin or English.

6. Last of all, THOMAS ARNOLD, in the third volume of the *Select English Works of John Wiclif*, Oxford, 1871, has given a catalogue of the English writings exclusively which are ascribed to Wycliffe, in which he places first the writings which are probably genuine, forty-one in number, and next those which are doubtful, twenty-eight in number, adding at the close a short list of others, which, in his judgment, are certainly spurious. Arnold has added to Shirley's list one English piece which he was the first to discover (*Select Works*, vol. III., pp. 130–233). It bears the title of *Lincolniensis* (Grossetête), but is nothing else than an appeal for sympathy on behalf of the persons and work of the itinerant preachers, after several of them had been tried and thrown into prison. For the rest, Arnold has directed his chief attention to the critical question of the genuineness of the several pieces, though aiming also as much as possible at the determination of their respective dates. The result reached was that he contested the genuineness of a considerable number of pieces. Of the sixty-five English works brought forward by Shirley, he pronounces decidedly against the Wycliffe authorship of eight or thereabouts, while, with respect to from fifteen to twenty others, he is unable to go further than a *non-liquet*. He has not, however, proceeded upon his own individual judgment as decisive, but has printed in his third volume, among the *Miscellaneous Works*, several of the pieces whose genuineness he does not allow.

§ 2. *Language of Wycliffe's Writings.*

To come more closely to the *Works* themselves, we have first of all to offer some remarks upon *their difference in respect of language*. Dr. Vaughan says of the English writings of Wycliffe that they are by far the more numerous. This is an error. Even looking to numbers only, Shirley's catalogue contains not fewer than ninety-six Latin works, while the English works number only sixty-five. But when we compare the two classes of pieces in respect to bulk, the Latin pieces have still more the advantage; and hence, in Arnold's judgment, the Latin works of Wycliffe 'are by far the more numerous and more copious.' In fact, the English pieces are for the most part nothing more than mere tracts of a couple of pages, and the largest of them fill at most three or four sheets; while the series of Latin works includes from ten to twelve equal to the

Trialogus in bulk, every one of which would fill a good-sized octavo volume. But the importance of their contents, too, in the case of many of the Latin works, is far superior to that of the English. Scientifically considered, it is only the Latin writings which are of value. Wycliffe's philosophical and theological position can only be learned from them with certainty and thoroughness; while his English writings are chiefly valuable in part for the history of the English language and literature, and in part for our knowledge of the influence of Wycliffe upon the English people.

And here we must not omit to mention that the genuineness of the most important of the Latin works is sufficiently attested and indeed placed beyond all doubt, partly because Wycliffe himself is accustomed to quote his own earlier works in the later, and partly because his several opponents cite different works of Wycliffe in their controversial writings. In this way a pretty copious list of his works can be gathered from the writings of William Woodford, from a mandate of Archbishop Sbynjek of Prague against Huss, from the anti-Hussite works of Friar Stephen of Dolan, but most of all from the great work of Thomas Netter, of Walden. But friends and admirers too, like Huss, mention several of his writings, and give exact quotations from them. In the Vienna MSS. his name occurs by no means unfrequently attached to his several pieces. But the case is entirely otherwise with the English writings: not one of them is mentioned in any other writing, either of Wycliffe or of his literary opponents. His popular tract on the Lord's Supper, *The Wyckett*, stands alone in being expressly mentioned as his in several of the *Acts of Process* brought against particular Lollards, but not earlier than the beginning of the sixteenth century; and in the MSS. containing these English tracts it is marvellous that his name should so rarely occur. In other words, there are almost no external testimonies in existence for the genuineness of the English writings of Wycliffe; we are thus thrown entirely upon internal grounds either for or against their Wycliffe authorship; and, as may be easily understood, the work of deciding becomes, in these circumstances, precarious and difficult.

Further, it is a very remarkable fact that of the Latin writings of Wycliffe comparatively few old MSS. are extant in England itself and in Ireland, while the whole of his English writings are to be found in English and Irish libraries. Of the ninety-six Latin works enumerated by Shirley, there are only twenty-seven of which MSS. dating from the fourteenth and fifteenth centuries are in the possession of English or Irish libraries —*i.e.*, not fully a *third*. And among those which are wanting in England itself are not a few works of the greatest importance—*e.g.*, the *Trialogus*, *De Juramento Arnoldi*, one of the earliest memorials of Wycliffe which is of high interest, etc. On the other hand, the libraries of the Continent, and chiefly the Imperial Library of Vienna, the University and Archiepiscopal Library of Prague, and even the National Library of Paris, and the Royal Library of Stockholm, are in possession of MSS. of Wycliffe's Latin works. In fact, the state of matters is this, that of the ninety-six

Latin works, including tracts, there are only six of which MSS. are extant exclusively in England or Ireland, while of the English writings not a single MS. is to be found in the Continental libraries. The latter fact finds an easy explanation in the ignorance of the English language which prevailed on the Continent, even in Bohemia, during the Hussite movement. But less easy of explanation is the fact that so few in proportion of Wycliffe's Latin writings should have been preserved in England. To impute this to the destructive inquisition of the English bishops, is forbidden by the circumstance that only two of the purely philosophical tractates enumerated by Shirley are extant in MS. in England ; and in the case of essays on logic and metaphysics such as these, it is impossible to see why the inquisition should have troubled itself about their detection and destruction.

§ 3. *Classified List.*

In now proceeding to an orderly enumeration of the several writings of Wycliffe, the object which we aim at is to present a picture of his activity as an author. With this end in view, it did not appear to me so advisable as it did to Shirley, whose object was different, to make the difference of the two languages employed in the writings the chief principle of distribution in arranging the latter. It seemed better here to subordinate the linguistic point of view, and to aim, in the first instance, at a *material* classification according to *subject* and *contents*. Shirley himself has always made a *material* division within the two chief classes of works set out by him—1, Latin works, and 2, English works. But in carrying through this material classification, we shall follow a method of our own, while rejoicing in the coincidence of his judgment with our own, as often as it occurs. In our indication of MSS. and the libraries containing them, we allow ourselves to refer simply to Shirley's admirable work ; and a Table at the end of our Catalogue shows the correspondence of Shirley's lists with our own.

We divide the works into six chief classes :
I. Scientific Works, Philosophical and Theological.
II. Sermons and practical Expositions of Scripture.
III. Practical catechetical pieces.
IV. Judgments, personal explanations, pamphlets, etc.
V. Polemical writings and pamphlets.
VI. Several letters form a species of appendix.

In the following list, the pieces that have been printed in Arnold's *Select Works* are marked * ; those in Matthew's *English Works hitherto unprinted* (Early English Text Society) † ; and those in the Wyclif Society's volumes (to 1884) ‡.

I.—SCIENTIFIC WORKS (ALL LATIN).
I. Philosophical.

1. *Logica.*
2. *Logicae Continuatio.*
3. *Quaestiones Logicae et Philosophicae.*

4. *De Ente, sive Summa Intellectualium* (includes two books, each with six tractates).
5. *De Universalibus.*
6. *Replicatio de Universalibus.*
7. *De Ente Particulari.*
8. *De Materia et Forma.*[1]
9. *De Materia.*
10. *De Compositione Hominis.*
11. *De Anima.*

II. Theological.
1. *Systematic.*

12. Here deserves to be put in the foremost place, both on account of its great extent and its inherent value, the great work of Wycliffe entitled in three catalogues of the Hussite period, *Summa Theologiae*, or *Summa in Theologia*, a name not unusual in the scholastic theology, though this name for it does not occur anywhere in his own writings, so far as I have observed. From the thirteenth century it had been customary to give this title to works of a more than ordinary comprehensive character, in which the doctrinal system of a doctor of the schools was set forth in an independent method, and not by way of commentary on the *Sentences* of Peter the Lombard; with, at the same time, a close connection and interdependence; and this even when the author had given to his work a different title. So, *e.g.*, I find that to the great work of Bradwardine, which he had entitled *De Causa Dei*, the title is given in some MSS. of *Summa de Causa Dei*. The voluminous work, too, of Richard Fitzralph, Archbishop of Armagh, *Adversus Errores Armenorum*, is constantly called *Summa*.

This *Summa* of Wycliffe comprises no fewer than fifteen books, some of them large and elaborate, *e.g.*, the 6th book, *Of the Truth of Holy Scripture*. To the main work, which is purely theological, is prefixed a more general work, of a mixed philosophico-theological character, *De Dominio*. The *Summa*, then, consists of the following series of treatises:—

(1) *De Dominio.* This appears, from the preface in several MSS., to have been the general title, with which agrees the old catalogue contained in Vienna MS. 4514.

De Dominio, Lib. I. (fragment in 19 chapters).
De Dominio Divino, Lib. II. (fragment in 6 chapters).
De Dominio Divino, Lib. III. (fragment in 6 chapters).

---

[1] As a supplement to what Shirley (*Catalogue*, p. 2) has communicated, it should be noted here that the Royal Library of Stockholm, according to Dudik's *Forschungen in Schweden für Mähren's Geschichte*, 1852, p. 198, possesses a paper MS. in 4to, probably written by Huss himself in 1398, which contains the following philosophical tracts of Wycliffe:—1. *De individuatione temporis et instantis*, in 12 chapters, pp. 1–33. 2. *De Ydeis*, pp. 34–52. 3. *De Materia et Forma*, pp. 53–76. 4. *Replicatio de Universalibus*, pp. 77–86. 5. *De veris Universalibus*, pp. 87–134. This MS. was part of the booty carried off by General Königsmark, at the taking of the Hradschin in Prague, July 26, 1648, from the 'Schatzkammer' and Library of the royal castle. See above, p. 461.

(2) *Summa Theologiae*, in 12 Books.

De Mandatis Divinis.
De Statu Innocentiae.
De Dominio Civili, Lib. I.
De Dominio Civili, Lib. II.
De Dominio Civili, Lib. III.
De Veritate Sacrae Scripturae.
De Ecclesia.
De Officio Regis.
De Potestate Papae.
De Simonia.
De Apostasia.
De Blasphemia.

13. *Trialogus.*
14. *Supplementum Trialogi, sive de Dotatione Ecclesiae;* both edited by Lechler, Oxford, 1869.
15. *De Incarnatione Verbi.*
16. *De Ecclesia et Membris.* This appears to be the correct title, and not as Shirley gives it (13) from two Vienna MS. catalogues, *De Fide Catholica.* This book is not the same with the book *De Ecclesia*, which forms the seventh part of the *Summa.*
17. *De Officio Pastorali*, edited by Lechler, Leipzig, 1863.
18. *De Eucharistia tractatus Major.*
19. *De Eucharistia et Poenitentia, sive de Confessione.*

2. *Polemical Works.*

20. *Contra Kilingham Carmelitam Determinationes.*
21. *Contra Magistrum Outredum de Ornesima* (?) *Monachum Determinatio.*
22. *Contra Wilhelmum Vynham Monachum de S. Albano Determinatione.*
23. *De Dominio Determinatio contra unum Monachum.*
24. *Responsiones ad Radulfum Strode.*
25. *Responsiones ad Argumenta cujusdam aemuli veritatis.*
26. *Responsiones ad XLIV. Quaestiones, sive ad Argutias Monachales.*
27. *Responsum ad Decem Quaestiones.*

II.—SERMONS AND PRACTICAL EXPOSITIONS OF SCRIPTURE.
I. Collections of Sermons.
1. *In Latin.*

28. *Super Evangelia Dominicalia*—Sermons on the Gospels for Sundays.
29. *Super Evangelia de Sanctis*—Sermons on the Gospels for Saints' Days.
30. *Super Epistolas*—Sermons on the Epistles for Sundays.
31. Miscellaneous Sermons—64 in number, in two series; one of 40 containing Wycliffe's earlier Sermons; the other, of 24. See p. 497, No. 7, under Vienna MS. 3928.

Single Sermons transcribed from the collections are separately mentioned in Shirley's *Catalogue, e.g., Sermo Pulcher* on Ruth ii. 4 (39), which is identical with the 24th sermon in the 24 *Miscellaneous Sermons*; and *Mulierem fortem quis inveniet?* on Proverbs xxxi. 10 (41), identical with he 5th of the 24 sermons. The *Exhortatio novi Doctoris* (38) is also a sermon, delivered at a doctoral promotion. Last of all, the tractate, *De Sex Jugis* (40), is a combination of several sermons.

2. In English.

1. *Evangelia Dominicalia*—Sermons on the Gospels for Sundays—from the First Sunday in Trinity to the close of the Church year.*
2. *Ib.*, Sermons on the Gospels for Sundays—from the First Sunday in Advent to Trinity Sunday.*
3. *Commune Sanctorum*— Sermons for Saints' Days, on Texts from the Gospels.*
4. *Proprium Sanctorum*—Sermons for Saints' Days.*
5. *Evangelia Ferialia*—Week-day Sermons on Texts from the Gospels, besides several occasional sermons.*

The whole number of these sermons on the Gospels amounts to 239.

6. *Epistolae Dominicales* — Sermons on the Epistles — fifty-five in number.*
7. The tract on the Holy Supper entitled *Wyckett*, appears as a single sermon. This has been repeatedly printed (Oxford, Vaughan, R.T.S.).

II. Practical Expositions of Scripture.
1. In Latin.

32. *Opus Evangelicum, sive de Sermone Domini in Monte*, in four parts; the last two parts also bear the title *De Antichristo*.
33. *Expositio S. Matt. c. xxiii. sive de Vae Octuplici.*
34. *Expositio S. Matt. cap. xxiv., sive de Antichristo.*
35. *In omnes Novi Testamenti Libros, praeter Apocalypsin, Commentarius.*

2. In English.

8. *Vae Octuplex*—Exposition of 23rd chapter of Matthew.*
9. Of Mynystris in the Chirche—Exposition of 24th chapter of Matthew.*

These two tracts stand in all complete collections of the English Sermons of Wycliffe. The English explanations of the Gospels of Matthew, Luke, and John, as well as the explanation of the Revelation of John, which Shirley describes, pp. 35, 36, under Nos. 6–9, were not, in all probability, written by Wycliffe; comp. Arnold in the Introduction to *Select Works*, vol. I., p. iv.

Probably, on the other hand, Wycliffe was the author of

10. The twelve pieces which occur in a collected form in several MSS., under the title *Super Cantica Sacra*,* and are published by Arnold, *Select Works*, vol. III., 5–81. The order in which they occur in the MSS. and in print is not regulated either by their dates or subjects. We enumerate them in a different order.

(1) Old Testament *Cantica*.

1. Song of Moses, Exodus xv.
2. Hymn of Moses, Deuteronomy xxxii.

3. Hannah's Song, 1 Samuel ii.
4. Israel's Song of Thanksgiving, Isaiah xii.
5. Hezekiah's Hymn of Praise, Isaiah xxxviii. 10-20.
6. Habakkuk's Prayer, iii. 2-19.

(2) Old Testament *Apocrypha*.

7. 'Song of the Three Children,' or *Benedicite*.

(3) New Testament *Hymns*.

8. The Magnificat, Luke i. 46-55.
9. Benedictus—Prayer of Zacharias, Luke i. 68-79.
10. Simeon's Hymn, Luke ii. 29-32.

(4) *Hymns* of the Ancient Church.

11. The Te Deum.
12. The 'Athanasian Creed' *Quicunque*, considered as a Psalm.

These Pieces are all arranged in one way; viz., the verses one after another are first given in Latin after the Vulgate, and then in an English translation, to which a short explanation is added.

III.—PRACTICAL CATECHETICAL PIECES.

We here use the liberty of carrying back the modern name Catechism to the Middle Age, although, as is well known, it was not then used in the sense of the present day. We also include among pieces designed for popular use a great many more classes than have been ranged under the name of Catechism since Luther's day. These works, being designed for the benefit of the people at large, are for the most part written in English. Only a few tracts belonging to this category are written in Latin.

1. *In Latin.*

36. *De septem Donis Spiritus Sancti.* ‡
37. *De Oratione Dominica.*
38. *De Salutatione Angelica.*
39. *De triplici Vinculo Amoris.* ‡
40. *Differentia inter Peccatum mortale et veniale.*

2. *In English.*

11. Of the Ten Commandments.*
12. Of the seven Works of mercy bodyly; and
13. The seven Werkys of mercy ghostly, or *Opera caritatis.**
The two pieces evidently form one whole.
14. On the seven deadly Sins. *
15. The Mirror of Christian Life. * It is to be remarked, however that according to the investigations of Arnold and Bishop Stubbs the pieces marked by Shirley 1 and 7 in this collection certainly did not belong to Wycliffe, but to a Manual of Religious Instruction drawn up by Archbishop Thoresby of York in 1357, and circulated among clergy

and laity in his diocese ; *vide* Arnold, *Select Works*, vol. III., Introd. p. vi. The remaining five pieces of this collection are printed by Arnold in vol. III., namely :—
  (2) On the Lord's Prayer.
  (3) On the *Ave Maria.*
  (4) Explanations of the Apostles' Creed.
  (5) On the Five Bodily Wits.
  (6) On the Five Spiritual Wits.

Besides the tract on the Lord's Prayer, just named, two other explanations of the Prayer by Wycliffe are found, which are to be carefully distinguished from this one, namely— .

16. The *Paternoster.*

17. *Ib.* The latter piece, which is the larger of the two, is printed in *Select Works*, vol. III., pp. 98–110.

18. On the *Ave Maria*,† to be distinguished from the tract which has been already mentioned under 15 (3).

19. Of Faith, Hope, and Charity.* Arnold's judgment on this tract is somewhat unfavourable, vol. III., Introd. p. vi.

Last of all, we think we should add here some tracts which, in Luther's phrase, form a sort of House-Table, namely :—

20. Of Wedded Men and Wifis, and of their Children also. *
21. Of Servants and Masters ; how each should keep his degree. †
22. A Short Rule of Life. *

IV.—Judgments, Personal Explanations, and the Like.

I. Judgments.

All in Latin.

41. *Ad Quaesita Regis et Concilii.* Printed in *Fasciculi Zizaniorum*, pp. 258–271.

42. *De Captivo Hispanensi.*

43. *De Juramento Arnoldi.*

II. Petitions, Personal Explanations and Defences, addressed to Public Bodies.

1. *In Latin.*

44. *Ad Parliamentum Regis.* Published first by Lewis, p. 382, and then by Shirley, *Fasciculi Zizaniorum.*

45. *Declarationes Johannis Wickliff.* Printed in Walsingham's *Historia Anglicana*, ed. Riley, vol. I., 357–363.

46. *De Condemnatione XIX. Conclusionium.* Printed in Appendix to *Fasc. Zizan.*, No. III., pp. 481–492.

47. *De Eucharistia Confessio.* Printed in Lewis, pp. 323–332 ; in Vaughan, *Life and Opinions*, vol. II., 428 ; and *Monograph*, 564, following

Lewis word for word; lastly, in an independent and critical manner in Shirley, *Fasc. Zizan.*, pp. 115-132.

48. *De Eucharistia Confessio*, shorter than the preceding.

2. *In English.*

23. Wycliffe's Petition to King and Parliament, entitled Four Articles.* Published by Dr. James, Oxford, 1608, in Two Short Treatises, etc.; but in a more correct form by Arnold, under the title: A Petition to the King and Parliament.

24. Two Confessions on the Sacrament of the Altar*—(1) 'I knowleche that the Sacrament,' etc., printed in *Select Works*, III., 499; (2) 'I beleve as Crist,' etc., III., 501.

V.—POLEMICAL WRITINGS AND PAMPHLETS.

1. *In Latin.*

These writings all relate to the Church—its worship, especially the Sacrament of the Lord's Supper; its members and ranks; its duties and rights; its needs and mischiefs; its improvement and reform. These numerous tracts are, in fact, no more than fly-sheets; and in attempting to reduce them to several chief classes, the following order may perhaps be adopted, admitting, however, in advance, that it is all the more easy to fall into errors here, that only a very small proportion of these fugitive pieces have been printed.

I. Worship.

49. *De Eucharistia Conclusiones XV.*
50. *Quaestio ad Fratres de Sacramento Altaris.*
51. *De Imaginibus.*

II. Organisation of the Church.

52. *De Ordine Christiano.*
53. *De Gradibus Cleri Ecclesiae sive de Ordinibus Ecclesiae.*
54. *De Graduationibus scholasticis.*
55. *De Praelatis contentionum.*
56. *De Clavibus Ecclesiae.*
57. *Errare in materia fidei quod potuit Ecclesia militans.*
58. *De Officio Regis Conclusio.*
59. *Speculum secularium Dominorum.*
60. *De Servitute civili et Dominio seculari.*

III. Monachism, especially the Mendicant Orders.

61. *De Religione Privata*, I.‡
62. *De Religione Privata*, II.‡
63. *De Religionibus vanis Monachorum.*‡
64. *De Perfectione statuum.*‡

65. *De nova praevaricantia mandatorum.*‡ A short fragment of this piece is *De Purgatorio*, Shirley, No. 31.

66. *De Concordantia Fratrum cum secta simplici Christi, sive De Sectis Monachorum* ‡ (*De Ordinatione Fratrum*, Wyclif Society).

67. *De Paupertate Christi, sive XXXIII. Conclusiones.*

68. *De novis Ordinibus.*‡

69. *Descriptio Fratris.*‡

70. *De mendaciis Fratrum.*‡

71. *De Fratribus ad Scholares.*

72. *De Minoribus Fratribus se extollentibus*, against the boasting of the Franciscans, in the Vienna MS., 3930 (Dénis, DCIV.), pp. 178–187. The tractate, which Shirley seems to have overlooked, begins with the words *Cum viantes et fratres.*

IV. Decay of the Church, and Church Reform.

73. *De contrarietate duorum Dominorum, suarum partium ac etiam regularum.*‡

74. *De Christo et suo adversario Antichristo.*‡

75. *De Diabolo et membris ejus.*‡

76. *De Daemonio meridiano.*‡

77. *De Solutione Satanae.*‡

78. *De detectione perfidiarum Antichristi.*‡

79. *De Citationibus frivolis et aliis versutiis Antichristi.*‡

80. *De dissensione Paparum, sive de Schismate.*‡

81. *Contra Cruciatam Papae.*‡

82. *De quatuor Sectis novellis.*‡ This tract does not refer, as Shirley gives us to understand by the place which he assigns to it under the heading of Monastic Orders, exclusively to the Monastic system, and to the four Mendicant Orders in particular, which Wycliffe, it is true, often puts together; but, according to the author's own explanation at the outset (Vienna MS. 3929, fol. 225, col. 2), and the whole course of the piece itself, he means by the four modern sects—(1) the *priests*, endowed with lands and lordships—*sacerdotes caesarei ;* (2) the landed *monastic Orders ;* (3) the *canons ;* (4) the *begging monks.*

83. *De fundatione Sectarum.*‡

84. *De quatuor Imprecationibus* ‡ (some MSS. read *interpretationibus*). This tract seems to be only a fragment of Matthew xxiv. ; *vide* p. 487, No. 34, under *Practical Expositions of Scripture in Latin.*

85. *De duobus generibus Haereticorum, i.e., Simoniaci et Apostatici.*‡

86. *De Prophetia.*

87. *De Oratione et Ecclesiae purgatione.*‡

88. *Dialogus, sive Speculum Ecclesiae militantis.*

It is a fact worthy of remark that of this book more MSS. have come down to us than of any other work of Wycliffe, with the exception of some about ten very short fly-sheets. The reason of this, no doubt, was the nature of its contents, which all relate to the reformation of the Church, and discuss this subject on more than one side. The date of the *Dialogue* may be determined with tolerable exactitude. It must be placed later than 1378, because the Papal schism is mentioned in cap. 12. Further, as Wycliffe is already attacking the doctrine of transubstantiation, cap. 18, and opposing with warmth the Mendicant Orders, cap. 32, the book cannot have been written before the year 1381.[1] On the other hand, the *Dialogus* was, without doubt, written earlier than the *Trialogus;* for, first of all, the *Dialogue* is a simpler form of colloquy than the *Trialogue;* and, secondly, the speakers introduced in the *Dialogus* are more than in the *Trialogus* abstract ideas, namely Truth (meaning Christ, as in John xiv. 6, to which there is an express reference in the Introduction) and Falsehood; whereas the speakers in the *Trialogus*, viz., Alithia, the philosopher; Pseustis, the sophistical unbeliever; and Phronesis, the ripe and deep divine, while also somewhat too abstract, still bear a much nearer likeness to living personality than Veritas or Mendacium. Last of all, the conversational form itself is kept up much more persistently in the *Trialogus* than in the *Dialogus*, whose first seven and last five chapters (1–7, 8–30) are rather monologues than dialogues; for in these Truth alone speaks, and it is only in the intervening chapters that the form of dialogue is introduced. These three differences of literary form taken together may suffice to support our conviction that the *Dialogus* is to be looked upon as Wycliffe's first attempt in this literary style, and is to be placed earlier than the *Trialogus*. But as the latter was written either in 1383 or 1384, the date of the *Dialogus* may be set down as 1382.

We have still to remark in this place that the tract *De Triplici Ecclesia*, which Shirley brings forward under No. 63, as an independent writing, is, in fact, nothing more than a fragment of the *Dialogus*, which, dropping the preface, begins with the first chapter and goes on to the seventh.

2. *In English.*

I. Doctrine of the Church.

25. *Octo in quibus seducuntur simplices Christiani.**
26. On the Sufficiency of Holy Scripture (a fly-leaf).*

II. Worship.

27. *De Confessione et Poenitentia*—against auricular confession. Here might properly be added the tract marked No. 49, in Shirley's Catalogue, Of Antecristis Song in Chirche, and also the tract Of Prayer, marked No. 50, which, however, are both only extracts from No. 63 of that catalogue, in case they belonged to Wycliffe. But Arnold, while indeed including the last-named piece, entitled On the XXV. Articles, has, at the same time, made it appear probable (p. 454) that this writing was a

---

[1] Herewith I recall and correct what I have put forth on the date of the *Dialogus* in the Prolegomena to my edition of the *Trialogus*.

reply to accusations which were brought against the Lollards by the clergy in 1388, and was therefore written, at the earliest, four years after Wycliffe's death.

III. Constitution of the Church.

28. How the office of Curatis is ordeyned of God, or *De XXXIII. Erroribus Curatorum.* †

29. For the ordre of presthod. †

30. Of Clerkis Possessioners. †

31. *De Precationibus sacris.** An exhortation to priests to pious prayer, a good life, and pure preaching of the gospel.

32. *De Stipendiis Ministrorum,* or How men schullen fynde prestis.*

33. Of Prelates. †

34. *De Obedientia Praelatorum,* or How men owen obesche (obey) to Prelates, drede curs, and kepe lawe.

35. The grete sentence of curs expounded. *

36. *De Papa.* Nos. 33–36 treat of the Hierarchy up to the Pope, of the authority of the higher clergy, and the power of the Keys. The tracts which follow occupy themselves with the monastic system, especially with the Mendicant Orders.

37. How men of privat religion shulden love more the Gospel, Goddis heste (commandment), and his Ordynance then ony new lawis, neue rulis, and ordynances of synful men.

38. Rule of St. Francis, and

39. Testament of St. Francis.

40. *Tractatus de Pseudo-freris.*†

41. Fifty Heresies and Errors of Friars.* Only that Shirley, as Lewis before him, gives to the book the less distinctive title of *Objections of Freres,* which has only the marginal note of a MS. to support it. Arnold gives the writing in *Select Works,* III., 366–401. It contains fifty chapters, and forms a comprehensive attack upon the Mendicant Orders.

42. *De Blasphemia contra Fratres.** To be carefully distinguished from the book *De Blasphemia* in Latin, which forms the last part of Wycliffe's *Summa.*

IV. Decline and Reform of the Church.

Among all these eighteen English writings last enumerated (25–42), there is not one which had not in view the disorder and corruption of the Church, and did not work for its purification and reform. But in the writings now to be named the reformation spirit and standpoint are incomparably more prominent and prevailing. I place in the front a work which equally inquires into both subjects, the Church's decline and reform.

43. The Church and her Members. * First published by Dr. Todd in Dublin, 1851, in *Three Treatises by John Wycliffe*, pp. iii.-lxxx.). Arnold's edition is after a much better MS. in the Bodleian Library.

The next following tracts occupy themselves chiefly with proving the fallen condition of the Church and opposing its corruptions.

44. *De Apostasia Cleri.** Also printed in Todd's *Three Treatises*. Let us not omit to mention here that the piece entitled 'Of Antecrist and his Meynee' (Shirley, No. 48), which Todd also published in the *Three Treatises*, was pronounced spurious by Vaughan in his *Monograph*, p. 539, and has also been referred to by Arnold (*Select Works*, I., Introduction, p. vii.) to a later date.

45. Antecrist and his Clerkis traveilen to destroie Holy Writt. †

46. How Sathanas and his Prestis casten to destroie alle good lyvynge. †

47. *Speculum de Antichristo*, or How Antecrist and his clerkis feren true Prestis fro prec hyng of Cristis Gospel bi four disceits.

48. Of feyned contemplative lif, of songe, and worldly bisynesse of Prestis, etc. †

49. How Sathanas and his Children turnen werkes of mercy ypsodown and decevyn men thereinne, etc. †

50. *De duobus generibus hereticorum* * (Simony and Apostasy).

51. *De Dominio Divino* : more correctly, Of Church lands and lordships of the Clergy. *

52. Thre thingis distroien this world, false confessoures, false men of law, and false merchauntis. †

53. *De Pontificum Romanorum Schismate.* *

The following pamphlets occupy themselves chiefly with Church reform itself, with the ways and means to be adopted to bring it about, with the defence of the persons labouring to that end, especially the itinerant preachers, and with exhortations to others to come to the help of this work.

54. Of good prechyng prestis. †

55. Why pore prestis have non benefices. †

56. *Lincolniensis,** a pamphlet hitherto unknown, which Arnold was the first to discover in a MS. of the Bodleian Library, which is of great importance for the English tracts of Wycliffe, and has been largely used by him. The short but interesting tract begins with Grossetête's description of a monk outside his cloister (hence the title *Lincolniensis*) ; but it treats chiefly of the attacks of the Begging Orders upon 'poor priests,' and calls upon knights and lords to take the persecuted men under their protection, and to join the battle for Christ's cause and the reformation of His Church.

57. For the skilles (reasons) Lordis schulden constreyne Clerkis to lyve in mekenesse, wilful povert, * etc.

58. *De Vita Sacerdotum.** The subject is the necessity of secularising the property of the Church, and reducing the priests to apostolic poverty.

VI.—LETTERS.

1. *In Latin.*

89. *Litera missa Archiepiscopo Cantuariensi.* The letter first establishes Wycliffe's principle that the clergy should possess no secular lordships, in connection with which it opposes the crusade in the cause of Pope Urban VI. The second chief subject of the letter is the doctrine of transubstantiation, which the writer desires to see brought to a decision by the Primate, agreeably to the standard of Holy Scripture. The earliest date to which the letter can be assigned is the year 1382, but possibly it might fall in the year following.

90. *Litera missa Episcopo Lincolniensi*—i.e., manifestly to Bishop John Bokyngham—is shorter than the preceding, and treats exclusively of the Lord's Supper and the doctrine of change of substance ; written either at the end of 1381, or at the beginning of 1382.

91. *Litera parva ad quendam Socium* (so in the Vienna MS. 1387, fol. 107), a short letter of commendation to some one who shared his views and his struggles.

92. *De Octo Quaestionibus propositis discipulo.* The letter noticed by Shirley in his *Catalogue*, 61 (6), under the title *De Peccato in Spiritum Sanctum*, appears to have been nothing more than an integral part of this letter, *De Octo Quaestionibus*, viz., the answer to the first question.

The letter *De Amore*, numbered (5) in Shirley, is a Latin translation of an English original (see Eng. No. 59). On the other hand, the pieces numbered (1) and (4) in Shirley, viz., *Ad Urbanum Papam* and *Ad Simplices Sacerdotes*, are both only letters by *supposition*, but not in reality. As to the latter of the two, we refer the reader to what is said upon this point above, p. 417 and note. The alleged letter to Pope Urban VI., published by Shirley in the Latin original, in *Fasc. Zizan.*, p. 341, was early translated into English in the form of a free paraphrase. This English version of it was first printed by Lewis in the appendix to his *Life and Opinions*, II., 122. In the *Select Works*, III., 504–506, Arnold has published the fragment with critical exactness upon the basis of the two original MSS. of it which are extant in England. As to its contents and form, I refer to the remarks which have been already made, chap. IX.

2. *In English.*

59. *Ad Quinque Quaestiones.** Here Wycliffe answers five questions of a friend and sympathiser on the subject of the love of God. There is no doubt that the English text is the original, and the Latin a translation (*vide* Shirley, Nos. 61, 5), for more than once the writer speaks in such a way of the Latin and the English that we must suppose that the letter was originally written in English. And as Wycliffe remarks that it is difficult to give a right answer to these questions in the English tongue, I think I may infer from this that the letter may have been written at a comparatively early date; for in his later years Wycliffe wrote so much English that in these years an expression of that kind could no longer be expected to come from him.

Note on the Vienna MSS. of Works of Wycliffe.

It may not be without interest to many readers to obtain more exact information concerning the contents of the Wycliffe MSS. preserved in the Imperial Library of Vienna, which are so frequently referred to in the above catalogue of the Reformer's works. The interest felt would be still greater if we were able to give in all cases a history of the transcripts themselves, and of all the changes of hands through which they have passed. But it is only in rare instances that we find any notices of this kind in the MSS. themselves. The following notes have been drawn up, with the help of the Catalogue of the Latin MSS. of the Imperial Library, which was published in 1864 by the Imperial Academy of Sciences. It seemed requisite, however, to add, in all cases, where possible, the numbers attached to the several volumes in the excellent catalogue of the learned Dénis.

The following list of volumes is confined to those which are of chief importance, to the exclusion of others which contain only duplicate or triplicate transcripts of the same works, and also of several volumes which contain only a small proportion of Wycliffe material, mixed up with the productions of other writers.

The numbers, which stand first in *Arabic* numerals, are those of the Catalogue now in use in the Imperial Library. The numbers in Roman numerals are those of the Dénis Catalogue.

1. No. 1294 (I. DCV.), 4to, 251, written in very small hand, in two columns, is of particular value, because the volume contains a complete copy of Book vi. of Wycliffe's *Summa*—viz., the Treatise *De Veritate Sacrae Scripturae*, pp. 1-127. At the end occurs this notice, *Correctus graviter, anno Domini* 1407, *in Vigilia Purificationis S. Mariae, Oxonii, per Nicolaum Faulfish et Georgium de Knychnitz*. This volume also contains the seventh book of the *Summa de Ecclesia*, and the work which forms the Introduction to the *Summa*, *De Dominio Divino*.

2. No. 1337 (I. CCCLXVIII.), 4to, pp. 258, contains for the most part only small tracts, all by Wycliffe, many of them extending only to a single chapter. The longest of them is the Treatise *De Trinitate*, pp. 182-243. At the end of the tract stand the initials M. F. W.

3. No. 1339 (CCCLXX.), 4to, pp. 248, contains the first portions of the *Summa*—viz., the first three books, *De Dominio Divino*, which form the Introduction to the work, but all three only in a fragmentary form, followed by the first two books of the *Summa* itself—viz., the *Liber Mandatorum*, otherwise entitled *De Mandatis Divinis*, and *De Statu Innocentiae*.

4. No. 1341 (CCCLXXII.), 4to, pp. 254, forms the continuation to No. 1339, containing the third and fourth books of the *Summa* proper—viz., the first and second books *De Civili Dominio*.

These MS. volumes 1337, 1339, 1341, and two others of less importance (one of them a duplicate of 1339), were originally the property, as appears from several notices found in them, of some one in the small town of Nimburg, which lies about ten German miles north-east of Prague. In No. 1339 occurs the date MCCCLXXXIII., which, however, it is certain, does not indicate the date of the execution of the MS. Possibly this date stood in the original copy written in England, from which this was a transcript made in Bohemia. Dénis found in the volume a business letter in the Czech language, addressed by a bootmaker to the Dean of Nimburg, from which he inferred, not without reason, that the volume was at one time in possession of this priest; it is a conjecture of my own that the Dean may have obtained it from Hussite hands, or may have confiscated it.

5. No. 1343 (CCCXCII.), 4to, pp. 230, contains the last three books of Wycliffe's *Summa;* the tenth, *De Simonia;* the eleventh, *De Apostasia;* and the twelfth, *De Blasphemia.* At the end of the eleventh book stand the words—*Explicit tractatus de Apostasia per reverendum doctorem J. W. Cujus anima per misericordiam altissimi requiescat in pace. Amen.*

6. No. 1387 (CCCLXXXIV.), fol. 215, a miscellaneous volume, containing fourteen different pieces by Wycliffe, some of them of larger size, such as the *Trialogus,* pp. 163-215, and the Treatise *De Eucharistia,* pp. 1-43; others of small bulk, *e.g.*, letters, some controversial pieces, and several commentaries on Scripture passages.

7. No. 3928 (DC.), fol. pp. 253, contains several collections of Wycliffe's sermons— 1. Sixty sermons for saints' days; 2. Twenty-four miscellaneous sermons; 3. Tractate on the Six Yokes; 4. A small tractate by a disciple of Wycliffe on the power of a prince over his clergy when sunk in mortal sin; 5. Thirty-eight sermons of Wycliffe—originally forty.

8. No. 3930, fol. pp. 359, a very miscellaneous collection, comprising several works of Wycliffe—the *Dialogus,* the *Trialogus,* etc.—mixed with pieces by Huss and several of the leading Hussites, *e.g.*, Jacob von Mies and Johann von Rokyzana.

9. No. 3932 (CCCLXXXVIII.), fol. pp. 211, bears the exact date of its transcription, 1418, while the name of the transcriber, originally inserted, has been erased. The volume begins with the *Trialogus,* which is followed by the *Dialogus,* and next by sermons and tracts.

10. No. 3933 (CCCXCI.), fol. pp. 196. This volume was once the property of a certain *Paul von Slawikowich.* It contains eleven writings of Wycliffe, all of them smaller pieces, except one entitled *De Officio Regis,* which formed the eighth book of the *Summa.* The volume closes with a *Catalogue of Wiclif's Latin Writings,* which was printed by Shirley in his *Catalogue of the Original Works of John Wyclif,* 1865.

11. No. 3934 (CCCXCVIII.), fol. pp. 151. The only writings of Wycliffe found in this volume are a collection of his Latin Sermons, pp. 1-132, extending through a whole year.

12. No. 3935 (CCCCX.), fol. pp. 343. Of this MS. only two-thirds contain writings of Wycliffe—viz., *De Dominio Divino,* the 11th and 12th books of the *Summa, De Apostasia,* and *De Blasphemia,* followed by the third book *De Statu Innocentiae,* and *De Trinitate.* The remaining third part of the MS. gives the articles of Archbishop Fitzralph against the Begging Friars, along with a sermon of his, and, in addition, several pieces relating to the disputation between Peter Payne, the zealous Wycliffite, and Johann von Pribram, which took place in Prague in 1426-1429.

13. No. 4302 (DCCCII.), 4to, pp. 274. A miscellaneous collection, written partly in the thirteenth and partly in the fifteenth centuries. It comprises three genuine works of Wycliffe—pp. 25-50, *Speculum Militantis Ecclesiae;* pp. 53-74, *Pastorale,* or *De Officio Pastorali;* and pp. 75-96, the tract *De Compositione Hominis.*

14. No. 4307 (CCCCVI.), 4to, pp. 242, contains six of Wycliffe's writings, almost all on philosophical subjects—p. 38, *De Compositione Hominis;* p. 62, *De Universalibus;* 115, *De Incarnatione;* p. 158, *De Ente in Communi;* p. 167, *De Ente Primo;* p. 190, *De Ente Particulari.* The MS. bears the name of the copyist, Peter von Czaslaw, and also the date and place of transcription, *finibus Glatovie* (Klettau), *sub anno domini,* 1433, *et eodem anno fuit Synodus Generalis Concilii cum Dominis Bohemis Basilie.*

15. No. 4343 (DLXV.), 8vo, pp. 303. A miscellaneous collection, including several small pieces of Wycliffe, *e.g.*, the *Speculum Dominorum;* also a tract by Bishop Grossetête, *De Oculo Morali,* and a defence of Wycliffe by Peter Payne.

16. No. 4483 (CCCLXII.), 4to, pp. 327, contains a sermon by Wycliffe, *De Sacramento Corporis et Sanguinis Christi,* in addition to pieces by Huss, Stanislaus, Von Znaim, and others.

17. No. 4505 (CCCCIII.), 4to, pp. 227. This MS. contains only Wycliffe pieces,

especially the following:—(1) The *Decalogus*, (2) the *Trialogus*, (3) the Supplement to the *Trialogus*. Comp. Lechler's edition of the *Trialogus*, Oxford, 1869; *Prolegomena*, p. 23.

18. 4514 (CCCXCIII.), 4to, pp. 184, contains (1) an alleged commentary of Wycliffe on the Song of Songs ; (2) the book *De Blasphemia ;* (3) an alphabetical catalogue of the writings of Wycliffe (published by Shirley, *Catalogue*, etc., 1865) ; (4) *De Officio Pastorali*.

19. No. 4515 (CCCCII.), 4to, pp. 236, contains several pieces of Wycliffe, *e.g.*, the *Dialogus*, the *De Simonia*, the *De Septem Donis Spiritus*, in addition to several writings by Huss, and against him.

20. No. 4523 (CCCXC.), 4to, p. 156. This MS. contains only writings of Wycliffe, and these exclusively on philosophical subjects, viz., the *Logica*, the *Continuatio Logicae*, the *De Universalibus*, and the *De Ideis*.

21. No. 4527 (CCCLXXXIX.), 4to, pp. 229, a volume including, among the forty-one short pieces which it brings together, letters, tracts, and controversial pieces of Wycliffe.

22. No. 4529 (CCCXCIX.), 4to, pp. 188. The largest part of this MS., pp. 1-156, contains Wycliffe's Sermons on the Gospels.

23. No. 4937, 4to, pp. 296. Among a miscellaneous collection of pieces referring for the most part to the Hussite controversies, occur, Nos. 13-15, several small pieces of Wycliffe, *e.g.*, *De Daemonio Meridiano*.

24. No. 5204, 4to, pp. 100. This MS. contains the *De Universalibus* and the *De Propositionibus Insolubilibus* of Wycliffe.

P. L.

[ON THE REFERENCES IN THIS EDITION TO WYCLIFFE'S MANUSCRIPTS.

It has not been thought necessary to repeat the numbers of the Vienna MSS. in every reference, as Dr. Lechler has been careful to do. The foregoing list will remove any difficulty. But it may be useful here to note, with regard to the works most frequently cited, that—

The *Latin Sermons* (Miscell. and Saints' Days) are quoted from MS. 3928.
De Ecclesia and *De Veritate Scripturae Sacrae* from MS. 1294.
De Dominio Divino and *Liber Mandatorum* from MS. 1339.
De Civili Dominio from MS. 1341.
De Apostasia and *De Blasphemia* from MS. 1343 or 3935.
De Eucharistia and *Dialogus* from MS. 1387.

Other works will be easily traced by reference to the foregoing list. The folio and the column of the MS., as a rule, are given.]

COMPARATIVE VIEW OF THE CATALOGUES OF WYCLIFFE'S WORKS AS GIVEN BY SHIRLEY AND LECHLER RESPECTIVELY.

I.—The Latin Works.

No. in Shirley.	No. in Lechler.	No. in Shirley.	No. in Lechler.	No in Shirley.	No. in Lechler.	No. in Shirley.	No. in Lechler.
1	1	25	87	49	39	73	76
2	2	26	51	50	44	74	80
3	3	27	36	51	45	75	81
4	7	28	40	52	46	76	74
5	10	29	75	53	20	77	52
6	8	30	77	54	21	78	64
7	9	31	65[1]	55	22	79	65
8	4	32	57	56	23	80	63
9	6	33	28	57	24	81	61
10	5	34	29	58	25	82	62
11	11	35	30	59	26	83	73
12	15	36	} 31	60	27	84	66
13	16	37		61	17	85	82
14	12 (1)	38	}	62	} 88	86	70
15	12 (2)	39	} ib.	63	}	87	68
16	13	40	}	64	67	88	70
17	14	41		65	41	89	69
18	18	42	32	66	42	90	71
19	47	43	33	67	59	91	83
20	48	44	34	68	60	92	55
21	49	45	35	69	58	93	84
22	50	46	17	70	56	94	54
23	19	47	37	71	43	95	53
24	86	48	38	72	79	96	50

[1] In part.

II.—The English Works.

No. in Shirley.	No. in Lechler.	No. in Shirley.	No. in Lechler.	No. in Shirley.	No. in Lechler.	No. in Shirley.	No. in Lechler.
1	1–5	18	30	35	57	52	42
2	6	19	28	36	20	53	58
3	7	20	29	37	54	54	24 (1)
4	8	21	32	38	35	55	Omitted.[4]
5	9	22	31	39	23	56	50
6	Omitted.[1]	23	25	40	11	57	59
7	,,	24	22	41	19	58	51
8	,,	25	52	42	12	59	53
9	,,	26	48	43	13	60	26
10	10	27	16	44	14	61	Omitted.[5]
11	15	28	18	45	43	62	36
12	34	29	49	46	44	63	Omitted.[3]
13	38	30	37	47	40	64	17
14	39	31	21	48	Omitted.[2]	65	24 (2)
15	41	32	55	49 }	,,[3]		
16	33	33	45	50 }			
17	47	34	46	51	27		

[1] See under 9.   [2] See under 44.   [3] See under 27.
[4] The alleged letter to Urban VI. See under 92.   [5] De Officio Pastorali.

WYCLIFFE CHURCH, YORKSHIRE.

INDEX.

Abbreviations.—W. signifies Wycliffe; *n.* signifies Note.

ABBOTESLEY connected with Balliol College, 99.
Abendon, Henry, 39.
'Abomination of Desolation,' 349 *n.*
Absolution, W. on, 341.
'Accident and Substance,' 346.
Acrostic, a singular, 323.
Administrators of Sacraments, question concerning their worthiness, 336, 338.
Aelfric, his Bible versions, 205.
Aevum or *aevitas*, 255.
Age, its corruption, W. on, 304.
Albigenses in England, 53.
Alfred, King, 14, 16; his Bible versions, 205.
Alliterative rhyme in Early English, 72.
Angels, W.'s doctrine of, 261.
'Anglican Church,' the, 18.
Anglo-Saxon language, 14; Bible versions, 204.
Anne of Bohemia, consort of Richard II., 460.
Anteferri, the clause, 151.
Anthropology, W.'s, 261.
Antichrist, the Papal, 317, 318, 366.
Apocalyptic views, W.'s, 326.
'Armachanus,' 54, 95, 477.
Armagh, Richard Fitzralph, Archbishop of, 54; his preferments, 55; early connexion with Balliol College, 469; chaplain to the Bishop of Durham, 470; opposition to the Mendicants, 55; sermons on evangelical poverty, 56; defends his views before the Pope, 57; compared with Grossetête and W., 61; his death, 62.
Armenian Church, the, 55.
Arnold of Brescia, 437.
Arnold, Thomas, editor of W.'s *Select English Works*, v., 11, 482; quoted *passim*.
Artes liberales, 90.
Articles, nineteen, from W.'s writings condemned, 165; his defence, 172.
Arundel, Thomas, Archbishop of Canterbury, 450; on W.'s Bible work, 219; banished and reinstated, 451; a persecutor of the Lollards, 451; on the University of Oxford, 456; death of, 457.
Assurance, Christian, W. on, 295.
Aston, John, 196, 394, 395, 396, 399, 441.
'Atomistic' view of conduct, 282.
Augustine, St., rules of interpretation, 247; affinity with W., 263 265.
Augustine, 'the apostle of the English,' 119.

Augustinians, an order of mendicant friars, 120, 323.
Aust, W. prebendary of, 156.
Australes, 88.
Authority, Positive Revelation, W. on, 234.
Avignon, the Papal court at, 49; conferences at, 141; removal from, to Rome, 163.

BABER, H. H., edition of W.'s New Testament, 221 *n.*; catalogue of W.'s writings, 481.
Bacon, Roger, acquainted with Greek, 89; his scientific greatness, 92.
Badby, John, his martyrdom, 453.
Bagster's 'English Hexapla,' edition of W.'s New Testament, 221 *n.*
Bale, John, Bishop of Ossory, 120; catalogue of W.'s writings, 480.
Ball, John, 71, 371, 373, 374.
Balliol College, Oxford, 86; connected with Richard of Armagh, 469; W. probably studied at, 87; W. master of, 98; he resigns, 101; statutes of, 99, 472; supposed poverty of, 99; W.'s contemporaries at, 474.
Banishment, W.'s alleged, 418.
Baptism, W. on, 338.
Barons, the, become truly English, 19; and the Church, 41.
Beaufort, Henry, Bishop and Cardinal, 459.
Bedeman, Laurence, 400.
Becket, Thomas, Archbishop, 17, 119, 421 *n.*
Bede, 'the Venerable,' 204.
Benedictines, the, opposed by W., 321.
Benefices declined by W.'s preachers, 195.
Berengarius of Tours, 368.
Bernard of Clairvaux, 437.
Berton, William, Chancellor of Oxford, 369.

Bethlehem Chapel, Prague, 461.
Bible. See *Scripture*.
Bible Translation, W.'s, 209; his silence respecting, 210; made from the Latin Vulgate, 215; completion and revision of, 219; MSS. multiplied (with facsimile), *ib.*, 444; circulated among the Lollards, 458; printed editions of, 220.
Bishop and Presbyter originally the same, 310.
Blackfriars, council at, 379; the condemned articles, 381.
Body of Christ, the Church, 294.
Body of Christ in the Lord's Supper, W. on, 356.
Bohemia, W.'s alleged exile to, 418; connexion with England, 461; reforming movements in, 462.
Boniface, mission to Germany, 15.
Boreales, 88.
Bracton, Henry, 40.
Bradwardine, Thomas, 64; his University career, 65; spiritual awakening, 66; lectures at Oxford, 67; royal chaplain, *ib.*; Archbishop of Canterbury, *ib.*; his death, *ib.*; compared with the Reformers, 68; his theology, 69; relations to the Church of Rome, 70; compared with W., 262, 264.
Braybrook, Bishop, 399.
Bretigny, Peace of, 134.
Britain, early evangelisation of, 14; British and Saxon Churches, 15.
Brown, Edward, editor of Ortuin Gratius, *Fasciculus*, 4.
Bruges, Conference at, on the peace, 141; on ecclesiastical questions, 142; names of the commissioners, 142; effects of W.'s visit to, 143; his part in the transactions, 312
Brute, Walter, 448.
Buckingham, John, Bishop of Lincoln, 399.

INDEX.

Buddensieg, Dr. R., ed. of W.'s *Polemical Tracts*, vii. *n*., 11.
Bulls, Papal, against W., 167.
Bury, Richard, Bishop of Durham, 470.

CAEDMON, the monk, 204.
Cain (Caym), type of the Mendicant Orders, 323.
Calixtines, the, 359.
Canon Law, W.'s studies in, 95.
Canonists, the, opposed by W., 321.
Canonisation, W. on, 300.
Canterbury Hall, Oxford, 103; W. warden of, *ib.*; his exclusion, *ib.*; attestations to the fact, 109, 475; was it legal according to the statutes? 111; the Pope's decision, *ib.*; the reasonable solution, 114; the hall now merged in Christ Church, 116.
Carmelites, an order of mendicant friars, 120, 323.
Catalogues of W.'s writings, 480, 499.
Causa Dei, Bradwardine's, 67.
Celibacy of the clergy, 309.
'Cesarean Bishops,' 312.
Chaucer, his character of a 'country priest,' 188.
Chichely, Henry, Archbishop, 457, 460.
CHRIST: Occam maintains His sole Headship of the Church, 47; the Author of Holy Scripture, 236; W.'s doctrine concerning Him, 267, 436; the Incarnation, 268; the Centre of humanity, 268; exalted views of, 270; the exclusive source of salvation, 271; threefold dignity and work of, *ib.*; Prophet, 272; Example, *ib.*, 281; Priest and Sacrifice, 273; extent of His saving work, 274; King of kings, *ib.*
Christ Church, Oxford, Canterbury Hall incorporated with, 116.

Christian life, W.'s view of the, 281.
Chronicon Angliae, on W. and Canterbury Hall, 475; on W. and the mendicants, 477; on the popularity of Wycliffite preaching in London, 478.
Church, W.'s doctrine concerning the, 287, 293, 436; constitution of, 305; moral character of the, 303; worship of the, 296; reform of the, 325; secularisation of its revenues, 327.
Citation of W. to Rome, 415.
Clergy, the, W. on, 289, 305, 308, 309; delinquent, 329.
Clifford, Sir Lewis, 172[1], 442.
Cobham, Lord, assists the Lollards, 458; apprehended and condemned, 459; his martyrdom, *ib.*
Commentaries attributed to W., 210.
Commons, the, privileges of, violated, 406.
Concordat between England and the Pope, 147.
Confession, Fitzralph on, 58.
Constance, Council of, 39, 464.
Constantine, alleged 'donation' of, 311, 325, 422 *n*.
Convocation, W. summoned before, 158, 173 *n*.
Conway, Roger, Franciscan, 63.
Councils, general power of, 46.
'Counsels of perfection,' 282.
Courtenay, William, Bishop of London, 158, 172; Archbishop of Canterbury, 378, 401; his mandate against Itinerants, 197 *n*.; his death, 450.
Courthope, Mr., on the Canterbury Hall question, 104.
Creation and Creator, the, W. on, 254.
Critical spirit of W., 425.
Crump, Henry, 395, 398.
Crown and Church, W. on, 329 *n*.
Cruciata, 411.

---
[1] Read *Lewis* for *Henry*.

Crusade for Urban VI. promoted by Bishop Spencer, 366, 408, 410, 411; its ignominious end, 414; for Gregory XII., 463.
Cup, denial of, to the laity, 350.

DANTE on the 'Donation of Constantine,' 325.
De Dominio Divino, 117.
De Haeretico Comburendo, Act, 452.
De Veritate Scripturae Sacrae, 236 *n*.
Delamere, Speaker of the Commons, 155.
Devorguilla Statutes of Balliol College, 472.
Dialectics a favourite study, 91.
Dialogus, 196.
Docetism, 353.
Doctor Evangelicus, 241, 249.
Doctor Mirabilis, 92.
Doctor Profundus, 64, 87, 262.
Doctor of Theology, duties of, 116; W. attains the degree, 117.
Dominicans (Jacobites), the, on apostolic poverty, 44; W. and the, 120, 323.
Dominium, one form of, corresponds with *Ministerium*, 259.
Donatism, alleged, of W., 337, 339.
Duns Scotus, 414.

EARNESTNESS and pathos of W., 429.
'Earthquake Council.' See *Blackfriars*.
Ecclesiastics in secular offices, 29, 136.
Edward I., 41; suggests the canonisation of Grossetête, 38, 43; contests the claims of Boniface VIII. in Scotland, 42.
Edward II., feeble reign of, 41.
Edward III. and the Pope, 49; refuses Papal tribute, 122; Jubilee of his reign, 150; troubles of his declining years, 153; his death, 167.
Edward the Black Prince, his death, 134.
Election, W.'s doctrine of, 288, 291.
Endowments, ecclesiastical, W. on, 166.
England and the Papacy, 17, 119 Church of, in the fourteenth century, 49.
English language, its growth, 14; its three periods, and Bible translations in each, 206.
English nation, its components, 13.
Episcopalianism, Gallican, 314.
Epistles, Pauline, Latin and English versions, 214.
Ethical System of W., 278.
Evangelical Reformer, W. the first, 437.
'Evangelical State,' the, 330.
Evil, W.'s doctrine of, 263, 265.
Example of Christ the standard of conduct, 281.
Excommunication, articles on, 382.
Exhumation of W.'s remains ordered by Council of Constance, 464; effected, 467.

FABER, John, Bishop of Vienna, 3.
Fable of the Owl and Feathers, 135.
Faith, saving, W. on, 276; and intellect, *ib.*; and feeling, 277; and justification, 278.
Fall, the, W.'s doctrine of, 267.
Festivals, Church, W. on, 300.
Fillingham, W. rector of, 101; excused residence, *ib. n.*
Fitzralph. See *Armagh*.
Flacius, Matthias, 4.
Fleming, Richard, Bishop of Lincoln, 467.
Foreigners in English Church livings, 148, 149, 168.
'Foreknown' and 'reprobate,' 290.
Forshall and Madden, the *Wyclifite Bible*, 10, 210, 218 *n.*, etc.

INDEX.

Foxe, John, 4; *Acts and Monuments*, quoted *passim*.
France, war with, 134.
Franciscans (Minorites), the, 44, 257; on apostolic poverty, 56; W. and the, 120, 323.
Franco-Norman ascendency in England, 13.
Francis of Assisi, 437.
Franciscan Friars, the contest with the Papacy, 44.
Frederick of Lavagna and Grossetête, 35.
French Crown, claim to, renounced by England, 134.
Fuller, Thomas, 467.

GARNIER, Arnold, Papal Nuncio, 137, 148, 151.
Gascoigne, Thomas, Chancellor of Oxford, 39.
Gerhard, anti-Romish leader, 52.
Gerson, John, 65.
Gilbert, John, Bishop of Bangor, 141; of Hereford, 147.
'Glosses,' method of study by, 94.
Goch, John of, 7.
GOD: His existence and attributes, as taught by W., 250; not the author of sin, 263.
Gospel, the, 208.
Gospels, Harmony of the, attributed to W., 212.
Gratius, Orthuinus (Ortuin), 4, 450.
Greek language, neglected in the Middle Ages, 89; W.'s ignorance of, *ib*.
Grossetête, Robert, Bishop of Lincoln, his character, 20, 40; dates of his birth and death, 21; his works, especially his *Letters*, *ib. n.*; life in Oxford, and religious awakening, 22; elected bishop, 23; reforming measures, *ib.*; journey to Lyons to the Pope, 24, etc.; firmness and conscientiousness, 25; supports the Mendicant Orders, 30; resists the nepotism of the Pope, 32, 35; his death, 38; canonisation proposed, 38, 43; known as *Lincolniensis*, 39, 95.
Guter, John, Dean of Segovia, 142.

HARDT, Von der, *Annals of the Council of Constance*, 7.
Heathen reactions in England, 14, 16.
Henry II. and Becket, 17.
Henry III., political movements in his reign, 19, 41.
Henry IV., accession of, 451; begins to persecute, 451.
Henry V. present at Badby's martyrdom, 453; accession to the throne, 457; death, 459.
Henry VI., accession to the throne, 459.
Hereford, Nicholas, helper in Bible translation, 216; sudden stoppage of his work, *ib.*; proceedings at Oxford, 389, 395, 397, 399; summoned to Rome, 400, 415; preacher among the Lollards, 401, 441; his relapse, 441 *n*.
'Heretics' in England (1150), 52; Act for the burning of (1400), 451.
Hierarchy, development of the, 311.
Historical studies, 1.
Horn, John, W.'s curate, 407; his account of W.'s death, 421.
Höfler, Constantin, his *Historians of the Hussite Movement*, 10.
Hugate, John, Master of Balliol (1366), 101.
Humour of W., 431.
Huss, John, and Luther, 2; W.'s true successor, 438, 466; birth of Huss, 461; his University work, *ib.*; proceedings against, 462; opposes crusade and retires to voluntary exile, 463; summoned before the Council at Constance,

465; condemnation and death, 466; indebtedness to W., 464.
Hussite historians, the, 10.

IDEAS, W. on, 228.
Idolatry, prevailing, 303.
Images and pictures in churches, 297.
Immorality checked by W.'s preaching, 479.
'Impanation,' 357.
Incarnation, the, W.'s doctrine of, 268; and the Eucharist, 352.
Infallibility, Papal, W. on, 313.
Investiture controversy, the, 17.
Irony and sarcasm of W., 432.
Islip, Simon, Archbishop, founder of Canterbury Hall, 103, 111.
Itinerant preachers, or 'poor priests,' sent out by W., 189; trained in Oxford (and probably Ludgarshall), 190; Lutterworth afterwards their centre, 407; relation to the parochial clergy, 192; two stages in the movement, 195; their garb and methods, 196, 444; W.'s tracts on, 199; Courtenay on, 379, 386; Lingard on, 445; their gradual disappearance, 457.

JAMES, Thomas, Bodley Librarian, *Apology for Wiclif*, 6.
Jerome, St., views on the Lord's Supper, 345; on the episcopate and presbyterate, 311.
Jerome of Prague at Oxford, 461.
Joan, Princess, mother of Richard II., 161; protects W., 172.
John, King, and the Pope, 17; political movements in his reign, 19.
John of Gaunt, Duke of Lancaster, 141, 143, 144, 153, 155, 159, 172, 375, 404.
Jubilee of Edward III., 150.
Justification by Faith, inadequacy of W.'s teachings on, 277, 283, 287.

KNIGHTON, Henry, Canon of Leicester, *De Eventibus Angliae*, 53 *n.*, 208, 443; quoted *passim*.

LAITY, W. on the, 305.
Lambeth, citation of W. to, 172.
Langham, Stephen, Archbishop, 114, 133.
Last Age of the Church, not W.'s, 63, 468.
Latimer, Lord, 154, 155, 160.
Latimer, Sir Thomas, 442, 446.
Law, the evangelical, 237, 239.
Lay preaching introduced by W., 195.
Le Bas, Life of W., 9 *n.*
Legends, Church, W. on, 426.
Leipzig University, 88, 462 *n.*
Leland, *Itinerary*, 79.
Lewis, John, *History of John Wiclif*, 6; quoted *passim; Life of Pecock*, 6; edition of the *Wiclif New Testament*, 221 *n.*; catalogue of W.'s writings, 480.
Lincoln, extent of the diocese of, 23.
Lincolniensis. See *Grossetête*.
Literary methods of W., 428.
Logical Treatises, W.'s, 226.
'Logos,' the, W. on, 253.
'Lollard,' derivation of the word, 439 *n.*
Lollards, the term applied to W.'s followers, 395, 439; their statistics, 443; their 'Conclusions,' 447; their doctrines according to Pecock, 460; their opponents, 445; martyrs, 452, 453; abortive rising in London, 458; and Hussites, 351.
London, riot in, 160; expiated, 161; citizens of, protect W., 172; outbreak of revolt in, 372; penitential procession in, 385; popularity of W.'s preaching in, 478; attempted rising of Lollards in, 458.

INDEX.

Longland, Robert, author of *Piers Plowman's Vision*, 71.
Lord's Supper, the, W. on, 339, 352.
Loserth, Dr. J., *Wiclif and Hus*, 463 *n*.
Love the centre of Christian virtues, 280.
Louis of Bavaria and the Papacy, 257.
Luard, edition of Grossetête, 21 *n*., 36 *n*.
Ludgarshall, W. rector of, 156.
Luther, 324, 350, 351, 360; on W., 2; and Huss, 466; translation of the Bible by, 215.
Lutterworth, W. rector of, 157, 187, 402, 406, 419; burning of his remains at, 467.

MADDEN, Sir Frederic, and Rev. J. Forshall, the *Wycliffite Bible*, 10, 210, 218 *n*., etc.
Magdeburg Centuries, the, 4.
Magna Charta, 18, 119.
Manuscripts of W.'s Bible, 221; of W.'s works, in Vienna, 496.
Martyrdom, W. prepared for, 331, 416.
Martyrologies, English, French, German, and Bohemian, 5.
Mass, the, W.'s early belief in, 340.
Masses for the dead, W. on, 303.
Matthew, F. D., *Wyclif's Unprinted English Works*, 11; on the spelling of W.'s name, 83 *n*.
Mayfield, a W. rector of, 104.
Mayor of London a Lollard, 480.
Meier, F. K., his *Savonarola*, 9.
Melanchthon on W., 287, 339.
'Men of the Gospel,' a name for W.'s adherents, 241.
Mendicant Friars, 320, 321, 322, 377; and Grossetête, 30; and Richard of Armagh, 56; their insidious ways, 59; their mischief in the Universities, 60; their encroachments, 62; attacked by W., 120; date of his first opposition, 121, 476.
Merit, human, W.'s doctrine concerning, 261, 283; four questions on, 284.
Merton College, Oxford, Bradwardine's, 65; question as to W.'s connexion with, 87, 97.
Metaphysical writings, W.'s, 227.
Millennium, the, W. on, 326.
Milman, Dean, on Chaucer and Longland, 471.
Mixtim Theologi, 240.
Monastic Orders, W. on, 319.
Monks ridiculed by W., 433.
More, Sir Thomas, on mediæval translations of the Bible, 202.

'NATIONS' in the mediæval Universities, 87.
Nature, the Light of, W. on, 233.
Netter, Thomas. See *Walden*.
Nicholas of Lyra, 247.
Nominalists and Realists at Oxford, 474.
Norman Bible Versions, 205.
Norman Conquest and the Papacy, 16.
Norman element in England, its decline, 18.
Normandy incorporated in France, 19.
Nottingham, Lollards at, 451.

OCCAM, William, a Franciscan, 43; a keen independent thinker, *ib.*; on apostolic poverty, 44; banished, *ib.*; protest against Papal absolutism, 46; writings and influence, 48; recognition of Scripture authority, 242.
Oldcastle, Sir John. See *Cobham*.
Ormulum, the, 206.
Otho, Cardinal Legate (1240), menaced, 19.
Oxford, in the diocese of Lincoln, 23; University, number of stu-

dents, 60; troubled by the Mendicant Friars, 59; colleges before 1350, 86; course of study, 90; length of course, 96; W.'s chief field of labour, 97; summoned by the Pope to proceed against W., 169; reception of mandate, 171; measures against W., 369, 388; tumultuous proceedings, 393; excommunications at, 397; provincial synod at, 403; testimony to W., 455; authenticity of the document challenged, 456; reaction against Wycliffite doctrines, 457; decadence of the University, *ib.*

PALACKY, Dr., on Huss, 10.
Pantheistic conceptions, narrowly escaped by W., 254.
Papal absolutism resisted by Occam, 46; claims ostensibly abandoned, 146; exactions, resistance to, 136; pretensions repelled, 42; primacy, the, 312; 'reservations,' 151; 'schism,' the, 174, 315, 362, 413.
Pardons and Indulgences, 411.
Parliament, the English, and the Papal tribute, 123; W.'s record of the debate, 125, 130; constitution of Parliament in W.'s time, 130; W. probably a member, 131; the 'Good,' 147; memorial of, to the king, 148; first of Richard II., 168; of 1382, 387; W.'s memorial to, 405.
Parliamentary debate, the first reported, 130 *n.*; rights, growth of, 41.
Parochial clergy in W.'s time, 193.
Pastoral Office, On the, by W., 193.
Pateshull, Peter, 446.
Payne, Peter, 456.
Peace of Bretigny, 134.
Peasants' Revolt, the, 371; false charges against W., 373.

Pecock, Bishop, the *Repressor,* vii., 460 *n.*
Peculiaris Regis Clericus, an office held by W., 132.
Pelagianism, 282; opposed by Bradwardine, 67.
Pelican, the, an emblem, 449 *n.*
Percy, Lord Henry, Grand Marshal, 159.
Perrers, Alice, 153, 155.
Philip IV., 'the Fair,' and the Papacy, 43, 257, 330.
Philip VI., of France, 49.
Pickards, the 3.
Pictures in churches, 297.
Piers Plowman's Creed, 450.
Piers Plowman's Vision, 70; editions of, 73 *n.*; Morley's analysis of, 471.
Pilgrimages, W. on, 301; Lollards on, 446.
Plowman's Tale, the, 449.
Pluralities, 157.
Polemical writings by W., list of, 490.
Poor Caitiff, not W.'s, 468.
'Poor Priests.' See *Itinerant.*
Pope Silvester, and Constantine, 108, 311.
—— Gregory I., 'the Great,' 15.
—— Gregory VII. (Hildebrand), 46, 293, 307, 319, 437.
—— Innocent III. and King John, 17, 122.
—— Innocent IV., 35, 56.
—— Alexander IV., 56.
—— Boniface VIII., 41, 43, 257, 437.
—— John XXII., 44, 257.
—— Clement VI., 49, 315, 363.
—— Urban V., 122, 146, 157.
—— Gregory XI., 141, 146, 152; removes from Avignon to Rome, 163; his bulls against W., 163; published in England, 167; his death, 174; a great opponent of W., 310, 321, 362.
—— Urban VI., 314, 362, 415.

Pope Benedict XIII. [('anti-pope'), 464.
—— Gregory XII. ('anti-pope'), 464.
—— John XXIII., 464.
—— Martin V., 464 *n.*
—— Clement VIII., 467.
Popes possibly unnecessary, 365.
Poverty of Jesus, 56; apostolical, 57.
Practical aims of W., 427.
'Praemunire,' statute of, 51.
Prague, University of, and W.'s teachings, 463; and Huss, *ib.*
Prayer of Bradwardine, 68 *n.*
Preachers, Dominican and Franciscan, 179; W.'s 'poor priests.' See *Itinerant.*
Preaching, W.'s views respecting, 176, 178, 183, 296; prevalent faults of, criticised by W., 180, 182; effect of W.'s, in London, 479.
Predestination, W. on, 290.
Prediction, a remarkable, 323.
Prefaces to the books in W.'s Bible, 215.
Presbyter and bishop originally one, 310, 317; and deacon, 311.
Presence, the Real, W. on, 354; threefold, 355.
Priesthood of Believers, the universal, 307.
Princes, secular, power of, in the Church, 328.
Progress in W.'s views, 223; illustrated, 224; on the Church, 294; on Papal Primacy, 312; on Monastic Orders, 320; on the Lord's Supper, 340.
'Provisions,' Papal, 49, 141, 151, 168; statute of Provisors, 51.
Psalter, the, early translations of, 207.
Pulpit, abuse of the, in W.'s time, 178.
Purgatory, W. on, 287.

Purvey, John, W. coadjutor in Bible translation, 407, 441; his revision of the work, 220; his trial, 452; recantation, 453; returns to evangelical views, *ib.*

QUADRIVIUM, 90.
Queen's College, Oxford, not W.'s *alma mater*, 86; he resided there, 101.

REALISM, W.'s, 229.
Reason and Revelation, 232, 246.
Redingate, John, nominated warden of Canterbury Hall, 114.
Reformation of the sixteenth century, 1.
Reformation-views of W., 435.
Reformers before the Reformation, 2.
'Regent Masters' at Oxford, 97.
Relics, veneration of, 301.
Repentance and conversion, W. on, 275.
Repyngdon, Philip, 390, 392, 395, 397, 399, 440, 467.
Richard II., son of the Black Prince, 154; declared heir-apparent to the crown, 154; his accession, 168, 172, 387; his deposition and murder, 451.
Richard of Armagh. See *Fitzralph*.
Richmond in Yorkshire; two places of the name, 80; 'Richmondshire,' 81.
Rigge, Robert, Chancellor of Oxford, 390, 391, 393.
Rolle, Richard, of Hampole, 207.
Roman records shed no light on W.'s history, 416 *n.*
Rome and England in the thirteenth century, 19; W. never at, 142 *n.*
Rudelbach, his *Savonarola*, 9.

SACRAMENT of the Altar, the, 360.
Sacraments, W.'s doctrine of, 333;

number of the, 334; efficacy of, 335; worthiness of administrators, 336.
Saint worship, W. on, 298.
St. Paul's, London, W. in, 159.
Saints' Days, W. on, 301.
Salvation, W.'s doctrine on, 275.
Satan, 'the loosing of,' 326, 345; his permitted power, 383; misrepresentation of W.'s views respecting, *ib.*
Savonarola, 324, 438.
Savile, Henry, editor of Bradwardine, 65.
Sawtree, John, first English Lollard martyr, 452.
Saxon element in England, its growth, 18.
Saxons, conversion of the, 15; their Church Roman, *ib.*
Sbynjek, Archbishop of Prague, 462, 483.
Schism, the Papal, 315, 363.
Schwab, Dr., on John Gerson, 9.
Science, mediæval study of, 92: W.'s knowledge of, 425.
Scotland, rival claims of Edward I. and Boniface VIII., 42; persecution extended to, 454.
Scottish Church, the, 42.
Scotus, Duns, 414.
Scripture, Holy, W. asserts its supremacy, 141; a book for all, 202, 249; 'for the people'—W.'s thought, 214; too much ignored in preaching, 180; W.'s constant appeal to, 185; and Church teaching, 243; and tradition, 234, 244; the Word of God, 236; its authority, sufficiency, and infallibility, 238; the charter of Christian liberty, 239; meaning revealed by the Holy Spirit, 245; self-interpreting, *ib.*; and the Fathers, 246; and reason, *ib.*; literal and spiritual sense of, *ib.*; W.'s great knowledge of, 241; the absolute standard of truth, 435. See Bible.
Sehnsucht und Drang, 332.
Self-denial of W., 434.
Sentences, the, of Peter the Lombard, 94, 102.
Sermons, W.'s, in two great classes, 176; Latin, 177; list of, 486; English, 187, 407; list of, 487; his topics, 184; standard of appeal, 185; method, 186; earnestness, 187.
Seventy-two Queries, Woodford's, 106, 121 *n.*
Shepherds, true and false, 308.
Shirley, Prof. W. W., on the Canterbury Hall question, 105; edition of Netter's *Fasciculi Zizaniorum* (1858),11; quoted *passim;* on the date of W.'s attack on the mendicants, 320; catalogue of W.'s writings, 481.
Sigismund, King of Hungary and Rome, and Emperor, 464.
Simony, 148.
Sincerity of W.'s character, 431.
Smith, William, 442.
Somerville, Sir P., Statutes of Balliol College, 473.
Sovereignty, Divine, W. on, 291.
Spencer, Henry, Bishop of Norwich, 408.
Spresswell, W.'s birthplace, 79.
Stages, successive, in W.'s career, 435.
Stephen, Friar of Dolan, 462, 483.
Stockholm, W.'s MSS. in, 461, 485.
Stokes, Peter, Carmelite, commissioned to Oxford, 384, 390, 391, 392, 394, 398.
Story, Sir Richard, 442, 446.
'Substance and Accident,' 346.
Sudbury, Simon, Archbishop, 141, 147, 172; murdered by rebels, 372, 378.
Summa in Theologia, W.'s great work, 256, 485; analysed, 258.

INDEX.

Summae, theological text-books, 95.
Swinderby, William, 442.
Swift, the river, 467.

TEES, valley of the, 81.
Testaments, the two, how related, 248.
Theocracy, 239.
Theology, 'queen of the sciences,' 93; as studied in the Middle Ages, 94.
Thorpe, Wm., Wycliffite preacher, 191, 194, 196, 454.
Tracts, W.'s later, 407; by W. and his successors, 443.
Tradition, 234, 240; and Scripture interpretation, 244.
Translation. See *Bible*.
Translations, episcopal, a profit to the Pope, 149.
Transubstantiation, renounced by W., 341, 343, 359; contrary to Scripture, 344; unsupported by early tradition, 345; opposed to the senses, 346; supported by false metaphysics, 346; consequences of, 347; idolatry, 348; blasphemy, 349; openly attacked by W., 367; his 'twelve theses,' 368.
Treasure, English, claimed by the Pope, W. on, 169.
Trialogus, W.'s, first printed at Basel (1525), 2; Oxford ed. by Lechler (1869), v., 11; quoted *passim*.
Tribute claimed by Rome, 313 *n.*; imposed on England, 122; refused by Parliament, 123.
Trillek, Bishop of Rochester, 131, 152.
Trinity, the, W. on, 252.
Trivium, 90.

ULLMANN, Carl, his *Reformers before the Reformation*, 9.

Unbelievers do not truly partake the Lord's Supper, 358.
Universals, reality of W.'s views on, 228.
Universities, mediæval, 85; their studies, 89.

VAUGHAN, Dr. Robert, his *Life of Wycliffe*, 8; *John Wycliffe, a Monograph, ib.*; quoted *passim*; catalogue of W.'s writings, 481.
Vienna, Wycliffe MSS. at, 483, 496.
Virgin Mary, the, W. on, 298; Assumption of, 302.
Virtue, W.'s doctrine of, 279.
Vulgate, Latin, version of Scripture, importance attached to the, 94; W.'s translation made from the, 215.

WALCH, his *Monuments of the Middle Age*, 7.
Walden, Thomas Netter of, Carmelite monk, 3; his *Fasciculi Zizaniorum*. See *Shirley*. His *Doctrinale*, 460 *n.*; on W., 337.
Waldenses, the, 53; compared with W., 243.
Walsingham, Thomas, Chronicler of St. Albans, 145, 173; on the death of W., 421, 423.
Walworth, Mayor of London, 373.
War taxes on Church property, 135.
Wars of Edward III., 49.
Wat the Tyler, 372.
Waytstathe, Richard, 442.
Wenceslaus, King of Bohemia, 462.
Wessel, John, 2, 9.
Wessenberg, Von, on the 'Reforming Councils,' 9.
Why Poor Priests have no Benefices, 193.
Wilkinson, Prebendary, on W.'s connexion with Oxford, 100 *n.*
Woodford, William, Franciscan 106, 450, 483.

Woodhall, Henry, of Canterbury Hall, 103, 111, 114.
Word of God, the, 236.
Worship, sensuousness in, 296.
Wright, Thomas, *Political Poems*, 11, 54 ; *Piers Plowman*, 73 *n*.
Writings of W., their scientific value, 424 ; drawbacks in their style, *ib.*; manysidedness of, 429; arranged in six classes, 484 (96 Latin and 65 English).
Wycclyve or Wyclyve, John, of Mayfield, 82, 98.
Wyckett, the, 249, 349 *n.*, 371, 483.
Wycliffe, a village on the Tees, 80 ; the manor-house and family, *ib.*, 82 ; the family for many generations strong Romanists, 83.

Wycliffe, family name, orthography of the, 83 *n*.
WYCLIFFE, JOHN, events of his life, topics and character of his teachings. See *Table of Contents at the beginning of this volume.*
Wycliffes, the two, 193, 475.
Wykeham, William, founds New College, 110 ; Bishop of Winchester, Lord Chancellor, 136, 394.

YORKSHIRE, character and dialect, 81.

ZWINGLI and W., 353, 360.

THE END.

UNWIN BROTHERS, THE GRESHAM PRESS, CHILWORTH AND LONDON.

FUNDERBURG LIBRARY

MANCHESTER COLLEGE

922.342
W972l